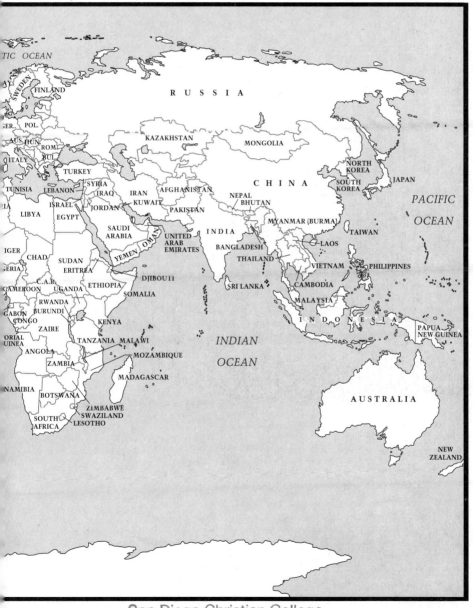

GLOBAL VOICES

Arthur W. Biddle
GENERAL EDITOR
University of Vermont

Gloria Bien
Colgate University

Miriam Cooke
Duke University

Vinay Dharwadker
University of Oklahoma

Roberto González Echevarría
Yale University

Mbulelo Mzamane
*University of Vermont
and University of Fort Hare, South Africa*

Angelita Reyes
University of Minnesota

GLOBAL VOICES

CONTEMPORARY LITERATURE
FROM THE NON-WESTERN WORLD

A BLAIR PRESS BOOK

Prentice Hall, Englewood Cliffs, NJ 07632

Library of Congress Cataloging-in-Publication Data

Global voices : contemporary literature from the non-Western world /
Arthur W. Biddle, general editor ; Gloria Bien . . . [et al.].
    p.   cm.
"A Blair Press book."
Includes bibliographical references and index.
ISBN 0–13–299793–2 (pbk.)
   1. Developing countries—Literatures. 2. Literature, Modern—20th
century. 3. Literature, Modern—20th century—Translations into
English. I. Biddle, Arthur W. II. Bien, Gloria.
PN849.U43G58 1995
808.8—dc20

94–24288
CIP

Editorial/production supervision: Julie Sullivan
Interior design: Melodie Wertelet
Cover design: Joseph Rattan Design
Cover image: Michael Garland/The Image Bank
Buyer: Robert Anderson

Printed in the United States of America

10 9 8 7 6 5 4 3 2 1

ISBN 0-13-299793-2

Acknowledgments appear on pages 833–840,
which constitute an extension of the copyright page.

Prentice-Hall International (UK) Limited, *London*
Prentice-Hall of Australia Pty. Limited, *Sydney*
Prentice-Hall Canada Inc., *Toronto*
Prentice-Hall Hispanoamericana, S.A., *Mexico*
Prentice-Hall of India Private Limited, *New Delhi*
Prentice-Hall of Japan, Inc., *Tokyo*
Simon & Schuster Asia Pte. Ltd., *Singapore*
Editora Prentice-Hall do Brasil, Ltda., *Rio de Janeiro*

No race possesses the monopoly of beauty,
of intelligence, of force and there is a place
for all at the rendezvous of victory

— AIMÉ CÉSAIRE
Martinique
Return to My Native Land

PREFACE

Global Voices exists because we want our students to experience the literature of the major regions of the non-Western world — the Caribbean, Latin America, sub-Saharan Africa, the Middle East, South Asia, and East Asia. Contemporary writers like Jamaica Kincaid, Gabriel García Márquez, Chinua Achebe, Naguib Mahfouz, Anita Desai, and Bei Dao offer a friendly bridge between our culture and theirs. The editors believe that expanding the range of literature studied beyond the traditional American, Canadian, and European canonical writers will help students better understand an increasingly interdependent world.

The Plan of the Book

The general introduction explains the rationale for this book and for the study of non-Western literature, as well as some of the differences between this literature and the more familiar Western writing. It warns of the pitfalls of ethnocentrism and raises some of the basic issues of postcolonial critical theory.

Each regional section begins with an essay outlining the major historical and social forces that dominate the region and then traces the development of contemporary literature. The main part of each section is the literary selections. We have chosen short stories, poems, and plays that represent the very best writing of the past thirty years. Headnotes provide a brief biography of the author and a helpful introduction to the piece. Footnotes gloss unfamiliar words. A regional map locates each writer's country of origin. A list of books for further reading features literary histories and critical studies as well as other works by the section's authors.

The Writers

We chose writers who we think have done interesting work. Some of them are relatively unknown beyond their native lands. Others are world famous. The following Nobel Prize laureates are featured in *Global Voices*.

1966   Shmuel Agnon   *Israel*
1967   Miguel Asturias   *Guatemala*
1968   Yasunari Kawabata   *Japan*
1971   Pablo Neruda   *Chile*
1982   Gabriel García Márquez   *Colombia*
1986   Wole Soyinka   *Nigeria*
1988   Naguib Mahfouz   *Egypt*
1990   Octavio Paz   *Mexico*
1991   Nadine Gordimer   *South Africa*
1992   Derek Walcott   *Trinidad*

The Contributing Editors

Global Voices is a collaborative project that brings together distinguished scholars who know the literature, languages, and cultures of their regions intimately.

The Caribbean — Angelita Reyes is an associate professor of Women's Studies at the University of Minnesota. She recently completed a book entitled *Crossing More Bridges: Representations of the Mother-Woman in Postcolonial Women's Writing.*

Latin America — Roberto González Echevarría is the Bass Professor of Hispanic and Comparative Literature at Yale University. His *Myth and Archive: A Theory of Latin American Narrative* (1990) received an award from the Modern Language Association.

Sub-Saharan Africa — Mbulelo Mzamane is an associate professor of English and director of African Studies at the University of Vermont. Born in South Africa, Mzamane recently published *Isimane: Women Writers in South Africa.*

The Middle East — Miriam Cooke is a professor of Arabic literature at Duke University. Her most recent book, *War's Other Voices: Women Writers on the Lebanese Civil War*, reflects her ongoing interest in issues of war and gender in Arabic literature.

South Asia — Vinay Dharwadker is an assistant professor of English at the University of Oklahoma. A native of Pune, India, he is editor of *The Oxford Anthology of Modern Indian Poetry* and the forthcoming *Columbia Book of Indian Poetry.*

East Asia — Gloria Bien is an associate professor of Chinese at Colgate University. Her research interests range from French-Chinese literary relations to multimedia computer-assisted language teaching. Bien was born in Lanzhou, China.

The General Editor — Arthur W. Biddle is a professor of English at the University of Vermont. As a Fulbright Fellow he lectured on American literature at Utkal and Patna Universities in India and at the University of Hong Kong. This is his eleventh book.

Acknowledgments

We would like to thank the many people who helped us with the making of this book. At the head of the list is our editor at Blair Press, Nancy Perry, who understood and supported our vision from the very beginning. Denise Wydra, our development editor, is surely among the very best in the business. Julie Sullivan handled production with great skill and patience. A wealth of experience and persistence marks our permissions editor, Gloria Mosesson, who phoned and faxed all over the globe.

We are also grateful to teachers and scholars from around the country who responded to the draft manuscript with valued advice: Lynne Curtis, College of Lake Country; Reed Way Dasenbrock, New Mexico State University; Susan Gardner, University of North Carolina at Charlotte; A. Wallace Hastings, Northern State University; Edward J. Martin, Columbus State Community College; Abioseh M. Porter, Drexel University; Martha Simonsen, William Rainey Harper College; Joseph Trimmer, Ball State University; and Chung-Hei Yun, Shawnee State University.

In addition, Miriam Cooke would like to thank Eric Zakim for his invaluable help with the Israeli selections. Vinay Dharwadker would like to thank the Department of English and the University of Oklahoma for their generous support with this project. And Angelita Reyes would like to thank Brenda Berrian, University of Pittsburgh, for her assistance in tracing copyright information.

My warmest thanks go also to colleagues at Utkal and Patna Universities in India who gave me inspiration and support in the planning of this book and in my teaching there. By sponsoring my visit to India, the Council for International Exchange of Scholars and the United States Educational Foundation–India allowed me to experience an ancient and rich culture at first hand and, I hope, learn a little bit from it.

Finally, I would like to thank my students at the University of Vermont who read this manuscript in its early stages of development and offered their valued comments, especially Lizabeth Bacon, Nicole Brumstead, Alex Head, Sheri Heiden, Mary Lapierre, Zakary Pelaccio, Cynthia Ruscyzk, Lucien Sonder, and Meredith Wells.

Arthur W. Biddle
North Hero, Vermont

CONTENTS

SUB-SAHARAN AFRICA

THEMATIC TABLE OF CONTENTS

LOVE AND SEXUALITY

THE INDIVIDUAL AND SOCIETY

THE CLASH OF CULTURES

COLONIZATION, POLITICS, AND POWER

ALIENATION AND EXILE

DEATH, SURVIVAL, AND EVANESCENCE

INTRODUCTION

S everal years ago I went to India to teach American literature to Indian university students who wanted to know more about William Faulkner, Emily Dickinson, Richard Wright, and Robert Frost. I'm proud to say that it wasn't *too* long before the lightbulb went on in my head. My students already knew a good deal about American authors — what did I know about Indian writers? Precious little, I had to admit. That recognition of ignorance, coupled with a determination to do something about it, was the first step on the long journey of my continuing education. One writer I encountered along the way, the Nigerian novelist Chinua Achebe, counsels, "Travelers with closed minds can tell us little except about themselves" (*Hopes and Impediments,* 16). Long ago I decided that I didn't want to be a traveler with a closed mind, whether my travels were by plane or by book. I hope you feel the same way.

When I wanted to learn about Indian literature, I asked friends in that country to recommend some books for me to read. After I returned to the United States and began work on this book, I again looked for help from people who know the literatures. These experts, who became contributing editors of *Global Voices,* have strong ties to the regions they represent. Even as I write this, our Middle Eastern editor, Miriam Cooke, is conducting research in Syria and Jordan, while Mbulelo Mzamane, editor for sub-Saharan Africa, is working to reform black higher education in the republic of South Africa. Our other editors — Gloria Bien, Vinay Dharwadker, Roberto Gonzáles Echevarría, and Angelita Reyes — also know their regions intimately, speak the languages, and study and translate the literatures. They're the best kind of guides for travelers with open minds.

MULTICULTURALISM AND THE NORTH AMERICAN READER

In the new spirit of multiculturalism, North American colleges and universities have broadened their course offerings and requirements to encourage students to learn about cultures other than their own. The editors of this book agree that expanding the range of literature studied beyond the traditional American, Canadian, and European writers that make up what is called the canon will help students better understand an increasingly interdependent world. As you read the stories, plays, and poems in this collection, you'll face some exciting intellectual and psychological challenges posed by values and ways of life that are very different from your own. Two dynamics that may run counter to your own experiences are the values placed on community and tradition.

The Power of Community

North Americans have grown accustomed to political systems and cultural practices that valorize the individual. Self-fulfillment seems such a basic right that we seldom give it much thought. Yet in many regions of the non-Western world, demands of family, village, or caste often take precedence over the individual rights and personal growth so highly prized in the West. A good example is the common practice of parents arranging a marriage between their children, who might not be left alone together until the wedding. When I asked an Indian friend about this custom, he explained it this way: "It is not just the boy and girl who marry, but their families. Attention must be paid to how the match would affect them as well as their children." Responding to the demands of the community should not be seen as pure self-sacrifice, however. Membership in a family, a clan, or a secret society bestows identity on the individual and provides a strong system of support. Seen from this perspective, fulfillment is possible only when one is in harmony with the community. You will experience the power of community in Wole Soyinka's play *The Strong Breed*, in Cheng Naishan's story "Why Parents Worry," and in Lorna Goodison's poem "For My Mother (May I Inherit Half Her Strength)," to name but three works from Nigeria, China, and Jamaica.

The Strength of Tradition

The early European settlers of North America named their new homes Nieuw Amsterdam, New England, Nova Scotia, and so on, trying to preserve ties to the old homeland. But the ties weakened over time, and life in the new country took precedence. It's still called the New World, with the emphasis on *new*. We North Americans have long prided ourselves on finding new solutions to old problems, solutions that mean breaking with the past. We are the ones who invented the skyscraper and social mobility, changing the faces of our cities and the power of class structures. As you study the literatures of the non-Western world, however, you will often find a determination to preserve the old ways that have been handed down through the generations. Sometimes these traditional values are shown to be in conflict with modern ideas and behaviors common in the West. Views on the worth of work, the nature of gender roles and marriage, the importance of material possessions and of the spiritual realm vary from culture to culture. Gabriel García Márquez's story "Balthazar's Marvelous Afternoon," Indira Sant's poem "Her Dream," and Nawal Saadawi's story "She Has No Place in Paradise" are just a few of the works that explore traditional values in Colombia, India, and Egypt.

Don't rush to judgment. It's so easy to scoff at a character's following traditional ways when they seem counter to common sense — for example, to ridicule a father's mortgaging his meager possessions to provide his daughter with a suitable dowry. Resist the impulse to compare every aspect of another culture unfavorably with your own, a practice called *ethnocentrism*. First try to understand the motivations of the character and the constraints of the situation. In other words, be an open-minded traveler.

GLOBAL VOICES

Global Voices features contemporary literatures from six major regions of the world. We focus on the contemporary because we think it provides an exciting entry point into the cultures and peoples of dozens of nations. Although each editor has defined *contemporary* slightly differently, the emphasis is on works written since 1970. Each section of the book contains an introductory essay that provides a brief historical and cultural background, then an overview of developments in literature. This essay will give you a context for reading the poems, stories, and plays. We also supply a regional map to help you orient yourself geographically and a bibliography that lists titles for further reading. The heart of each section is, of course, the literature. Selections are accompanied by headnotes, which tell a little about the author and the work, and footnotes, which define unfamiliar terms.

The Caribbean

Along with Latin America, the Caribbean is our closest neighbor. The peoples of these islands include remnants of the original inhabitants and descendants of European settlers and the slaves they brought from Africa to work their plantations. Spanish, English, French, Dutch, and Creole are all spoken at various places in the region. The Caribbean has seen an outpouring of writing in the last thirty years, much of it produced by women.

Latin America

This huge region includes the thirteen nations of South America plus Central America and part of North America — Mexico. We have added to this the Spanish-speaking islands of the Caribbean — Puerto Rico and Cuba. Since the European encounter with this part of the world beginning in 1492, the languages of the colonizing nations — Spanish and Portuguese — have become dominant. Just as important, the politics and cultures of these imperial powers have greatly influenced the development of the nations of Latin America.

Sub-Saharan Africa

Reflecting geographic, linguistic, historical, and other differences, the continent of Africa is often divided into two regions: North Africa and sub-Saharan Africa. Sub-Saharan Africa refers to those countries south of the Sahara desert, essentially all of Africa except for the tier of nations in the north — Morocco, Algeria, Tunisia, Libya, and Egypt — which we include in the Middle Eastern section of this book. During the seventeenth, eighteenth, and much of the nineteenth centuries, sub-Saharan Africa was raided for slaves for the New World. During the nineteenth and first half of the twentieth centuries, the region was colonized by European powers. Only in the last part of our century have Africans begun to determine their own destinies as they ousted colonial rulers.

The Middle East

We use this catch-all term to include the nations of North Africa and the western Asian countries from Turkey, Syria, and Israel as far east as Iran. The Arab language (although not all of these countries are Arab) and the Islamic faith (although not all of these countries are Muslim) are common denominators throughout the region. European colonialism was a factor here until recently, and many nations are trying to develop independent identities based on their traditional cultures. Memories of the Holocaust, when Germany exterminated six million European Jews in World War II, live on among Israelis. For many Arabs, the 1967 Arab-Israeli War, won by Israel, is probably the most important recent event in the region.

South Asia

Sometimes called the Indian subcontinent, this region includes Pakistan, India, Nepal, Bangladesh, and Sri Lanka. Three of the world's great religions unite and divide the area: Islam, Hinduism, and Buddhism. Ruled by Britain for nearly three hundred years, India won its independence in 1948. But British influence continues to be strong in language and literature, administration, and education. Pakistan, along with Bangladesh, split from India, and relations have been tense between these nations ever since.

East Asia

We have focused on three great nations from this part of the world: China, Japan, and Korea. Although each is proud of its distinctive heritage, these countries have had much interaction through the centuries, sharing elements of language, literature, and religion. First Japan, then Korea, and then China created great economic growth in the post–World War II era. And all face problems of modernizing their countries without westernizing them, that is, embracing developments in health care, technology, and the like while retaining their traditional values and cultures.

Bringing together the literatures from these six regions under the umbrella name "non-Western" might seem to suggest that they share great common ground. But to the reader the differences between the writings from the Caribbean and those from say, East Asia, are much greater than the similarities. One student of the subject, Aijaz Ahmad, asserts that "There is no such thing as a 'Third World Literature' which can be constructed as an internally coherent object of theoretical knowledge" (*In Theory*, 96f). Even within each region you may find common literary forms and some shared values — or you may not. A heated debate rages over whether there is such a thing as *African* literature, for instance, as opposed to literatures of Kenya, Senegal, and Nigeria.

VOICE AND IDENTITY

Nearly one hundred years ago the African American writer W. E. B. Du Bois observed that

> . . . the Negro is a sort of seventh son, born with a veil, and gifted with second sight in this American world, — a world which yields him no true self-consciousness, but only lets him see himself through the revelation of the other world. It is a peculiar sensation, this double-consciousness, this sense of always looking at one's self through the eyes of others, of measuring one's soul by the tape of a world that looks on in amused contempt and pity.
>
> — *The Souls of Black Folks*, 3

Du Bois makes two points important for our study: first, the notion of the Negro (or black or African American) as *other*, and second, the white world's practice of defining him or her. The perception of "otherness" and the question of "identity" that Du Bois alerts us to apply not only to African Americans. These are probably the dominant issues in the non-Western world today. Palestinian-born critic Edward Said echoes Du Bois in his claim that ever since the ancient Greeks, Western writers have spoken *for* the peoples of the non-Western world, denying them the right to speak on their own behalf, to have a voice of their own. Said asserts that imperial scholars and politicians, in identifying the main characteristics of a subject people, were also engaged in showing how that people were different from the Western model. Ironically, as subject peoples struggled through the process of decolonization, they accepted that identity of difference given them by the colonizers, rallied to it, and made it the core of their pride and independence movements. As an example, Said points to the negritude movement of African and Caribbean origins, the goal of which was "not to deny blackness, and not to aspire to whiteness, but to accept and celebrate blackness" ("The Politics of Knowledge," 22).

Jamaican writer Michelle Cliff relates the experience of struggling to express an identity in her own voice in her aptly titled essay "If I Could Write This in Fire, I Would Write This in Fire":

> To be colonized is to be rendered insensitive. To have those parts necessary to sustain life numbed! . . . And I think about how I need to say all this. This is who I am. I am not what you allow me to be. Whatever you decide me to be.

Here we see voice and identity coming together: "This is who I am. I am not what you allow me to be." Again and again in *Global Voices* you will find writers asserting the right to define themselves in their own words.

THE IDEA OF NATIONAL ALLEGORY

Although the thrust of this essay has been to suggest the great diversity of cultures and literatures of the world, one well-known critic insists on the similarity of non-Western narratives. Fredric Jameson believes that "third-world texts" (his term for the literature of countries that have experienced colonialism and imperialism) are necessarily allegorical. Their plots and characters represent figurative or abstract meanings. These symbolic narratives express a political stance through what Jameson calls *national allegory*. He claims that "the story of the private individual destiny is always an allegory of the embattled situation of the public third-world culture and society" ("Third-World Literature in the Era of Multinational Capitalism," 69). Note that he transforms the individual personal experience of a fictional character into something much larger. The individual, he argues, represents the collectivity, the nation.

To better understand his thesis, let's take the story of an African farmer who is forced to sell his land to repay money he borrowed from a moneylender. According to Jameson, this text is concerned with more than the plight of a single farmer. Read as a national allegory, it might suggest that the African country (like the poor farmer) must give up a priceless resource (land) in order to satisfy the greed of a capitalistic power (the moneylender). That's something of an oversimplification, but it suggests how a text might be read as national allegory. In fact, an allegorical reading would look at the narrative in all its complexity — the other characters, the uses of language and metaphor, the point of view, psychological dimensions, and so on.

A thoughtful reader might find much to quarrel about with Jameson — his insistence on a first world–third world confrontation, his insistence on the similarity and commonality rather than the multiplicity and differentiation of third-world cultures, his insistence that *all* third-world texts are national allegories. But sometimes a text does seem to call for an allegorical reading. In fact, many narratives in this collection can fruitfully be read on several levels, national allegory among them. As you engage with stories from all around the world, consider Jameson's approach. Whether you agree with everything he says, you might find that it sometimes enriches your understanding of a work.

LANGUAGE, POLITICS, AND THE MATTER OF TRANSLATION

Most readers of this book can afford the luxury of taking their language for granted. English, the native tongue of most North Americans (except for sizable numbers of Spanish speakers in the United States and French speakers in Canada), is also an international language, due to several centuries of British and American cultural, political, and military influence. Because we can take the dominance of English for granted, it can be difficult to understand the role that language plays in self-identity and national pride. In many parts of the non-Western world, however, language is problematic, especially for writers. Colonialism has often had the effect of taking the words away from the masses of the people by devaluing the indigenous tongue. Only a privileged few chosen by their colonial masters received a Western education and learned the language of the rulers — French, Dutch, German, Spanish, Portuguese, or English. Of course the rest of the population still had their native tongue, but that wouldn't advance them far in government or commerce. Nor would it provide writers with access to a sizable worldwide reading audience. How many people read Xhosa or Oriya or, perhaps more important, buy books published in those languages?

The pressure to write in the language of the colonial power has varied greatly from region to region. Even after their encounters with the West, Chinese and Japanese authors continued to write in their own languages. Because Spanish and Portuguese were introduced into Latin America five centuries ago, they have become the first languages of most people. But in sub-Saharan Africa, parts of the Middle East, India, and much of the Caribbean, the choice of language presents a dilemma. Should the Indian compose in English or Bengali? the Algerian in French or Arabic? During the 1950s and 1960s, the choice was usually English or French, the colonial language. But increasingly in the 1970s and 1980s many writers returned to their native languages in order to reconnect with their roots and to proclaim pride in their identity. It might seem ironic that it is often the writers themselves who then translate their work into English.

Most of those who write in their native tongues acknowledge that translation is necessary if they are to be widely read and admitted into the canon of world literature. The popularity of Latin American writers like García Márquez, Neruda, Vargas Llosa, and Borges in North American universities could not have happened without skillful translations into English.

Issues of power and politics aside, translation raises artistic questions. Anyone who has studied another language knows that translation is not a simple mechanical act of substituting one word for another. Because of its very nature, poetry suffers more than prose in translation. When reading a translated poem, it is arguable whether one reads the poem written by the poet or a different one by the translator. Let's look at a few lines written in French by Senegal's Leopold Sedar Senghor:

> New York! D'abord j'ai été confondu par ta beauté, ces grandes filles
>   d'or aux jambes longues.
> Si timide d'abord devant tes yeux de métal bleu, ton sourire de givre
> Si timide. Et l'angoisse au fond des rues à gratte-ciel Levant des yeux
>   de chouette parmi l'éclipse du soleil.

Collected Poetry, 369

Here is a translation of those lines by Melvin Dixon:

> New York! At first I was bewildered by your beauty,
> Those huge, long-legged, golden girls.
> So shy, at first, before your blue metallic eyes and icy smile,
> So shy. And full of despair at the end of skyscraper streets
> Raising my owl eyes at the eclipse of the sun.

Collected Poetry, 87

And another version, this one translated by John Reed and Clive Wake:

> New York! At first your beauty confused me, and your great long-
>   legged golden girls.
> I was so timid at first under your blue metallic eyes, your frosty smile
> So timid. And the disquiet in the depth of your skyscraper streets
> Lifting up owl eyes in the sun's eclipse.

Prose and Poetry, 155

As you compare the two English translations, look for differences in emphasis, tonality, voice. Do the two translations have the same meaning? If you know French, compare the original to the translations. Studying these passages should give you some idea of what is involved in translation and perhaps a greater appreciation of the translator's work.

Many of the selections included in *Global Voices* were translated from the language of original composition. We give the language of composition and the name of the translator at the end of each piece. In some cases our editors actually made the translation. For the most part, though, they have searched out the best translations available. It is only because of these translations that the voices of the world are able to speak to all of us.

Arthur W. Biddle

WORKS CITED

Achebe, Chinua. *Hopes and Impediments: Selected Essays.* New York: Doubleday Anchor, 1990.

Ahmad, Aijaz. *In Theory: Classes, Nations, Literatures.* New York: Verso, 1992.

Cliff, Michelle. "If I Could Write This in Fire, I Would Write This in Fire." In *The Land of Look Behind.* Ithaca, N.Y.: Firebrand Books, 1985.

Du Bois, W. E. B. *The Souls of Black Folks.* Chicago: McClurg, 1926.

Jameson, Fredric. "Third-World Literature in the Era of Multinational Capitalism." *Social Text* (Fall 1986): 65–88.

Said, Edward W. "The Politics of Knowledge." *Raritan* 11:1 (Summer 1991): 17–31.

Senghor, Leopold Sedar. *The Collected Poetry.* Translated by Melvin Dixon. Charlottesville: University Press of Virginia, 1991.

———. *Prose and Poetry.* Translated by John Reed and Clive Wade. London: Oxford University Press, 1965.

THE
CARIBBEAN

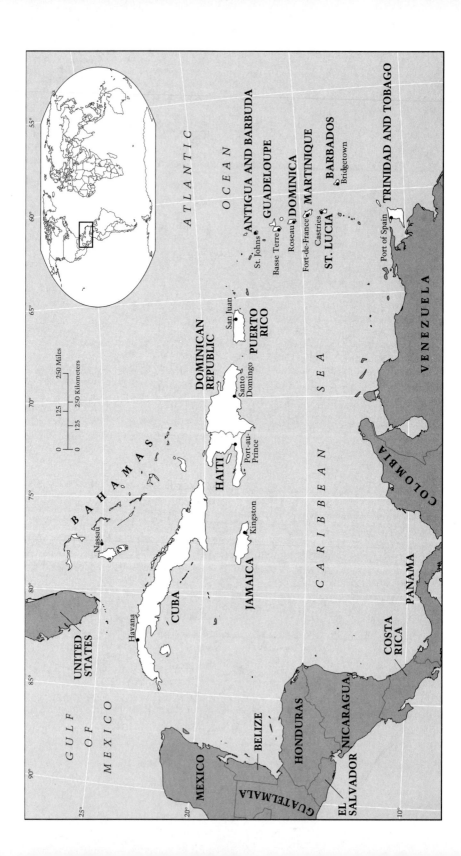

THE CARIBBEAN

In her essay "Leh We Talk See," Jamaican writer Jeannette Charles challenges the idea of "discovery" not only through her tongue-in-cheek depiction of Christopher Columbus as an interloper but also in her choice of language:

> Columbus sail de ocean blue in fourteen hundred ninety two, an when he did he discover de Caribbean. I just whan fe know how he could ah discover someplace dat already had people pon it. I does check tings out yuh know, so I pik up dis here Oxford American Dictionary, and I see dat to discover mean to be de fust to obtain site or knowledge of. When Columbus did lan', de Indian dem had don' set up a society pon de islands. So I don' see how anybody in de right min' can say dat Columbus discover de Caribbean. So leh we geh one ting straight from de beginnin', dis here Columbus wuz an interloper an not a discover as we are led to believe.

When presenting this essay at the First World Conference on Women Writers from the English Speaking Caribbean, Charles deliberately did *not* use the master language, the King's English of England. By using Jamaican patois, or Creole, Charles challenges the class hierarchy that is supported by speaking and writing in standard English. Instead, Charles's text forces the ear and eye to adjust in order to understand what is said in the Jamaican patois. By rejecting the power that is associated with standard English and presenting a new postcolonial voice for her work, Charles is "writing back" to the British Empire.

Recent events such as the liberation of Eastern Europe, the fall of the Berlin Wall, the emergence of a Palestinian nation, and the first multiracial election in South Africa have challenged the powers of those who once conquered and oppressed. These events are happening in the era of *decolonization,* a period of developing social and political consciousness and of emerging national identities. Some historians, intellectuals, and political scientists call this period the *postcolonial* era. The "post" in this word should not be understood as meaning that colonization is over. Instead, the term points to changes that are occurring as a result of colonization in its different forms: twentieth-century imperialism, nineteenth-century empire building, and eighteenth-century slavery.

It is important to understand how language often defines cultures. For example, the term *Caribbean* usually refers to the entire chain of islands in the region — regardless of cultural and linguistic differences. So Cuba is geographically a part of the Caribbean islands. Because it is Spanish-speaking, however, Cuba is usually categorized as part of Latin America, as it is here in *Global Voices*. On the other hand, the term *West Indies* usually refers to the islands colonized by England. Yet the country of Belize in Central America is English-speaking and is therefore generally described as having a West Indian culture, even though it is on the mainland.

In addition to establishing cultural identities, the languages of the colonizers historically represented power and dominance; they made those who had less power feel devalued. When writing back to the former empire, decolonized peoples must, like Jeannette Charles, write in their own languages — both literally and figuratively. They must create new languages, create new styles and new ways of seeing, out of European and African linguistic and cultural legacies. To paraphrase Jamaican writer Michelle Cliff, this process of decolonization enables people to empower themselves by claiming the identity they were taught to despise.

Many Caribbean writers use history and myth to establish this new identity. Although some, such as Derek Walcott, see the past as a potential obsession that has little light to shed on the current role of the West Indies, most others either grapple with understanding the past or use historical events as a source of empowering images and metaphors. The selections of Caribbean writing in this anthology are representative in that they demonstrate this heightened awareness of the region's historical legacy, especially the interplay of slavery, gender, race, cultural displacement, and resistance.

SLAVERY AND THE MIDDLE PASSAGE

One of the events in New World history that has most significantly shaped the meaning of colonialism in the Caribbean is slavery and the Middle Passage. The term *Middle Passage* refers to the voyage that enslaved Africans experienced before arriving in various parts of the Americas; the trip across the Atlantic Ocean on overcrowded slave ships was the middle part of this voyage. It is estimated that tens of millions of people died during this torturous journey. Toni Morrison dedicates her novel *Beloved* to the Middle Passage with the inscription "sixty million and more," the best estimation, she explains, of the number of Africans who died in captivity before reaching the New World. In postcolonial Caribbean literature, the Middle Passage has become an extended metaphor for displacement, the dispersal of people of African descent, and the foundations of slavery in the Americas. Caribbean writers repeatedly evoke slavery and the Middle Passage through references to oral traditions, folk stories, and poetry from and about Africa.

Paule Marshall, whose parents were from the island of Barbados, commented (in a 1971 interview in *Essence*) on her use of Middle Passage references throughout her novels, essays, and short stories.

> I'm trying to trace history. . . . To take, for example, the infamous triangle route of slavery and to reverse it so that we make the journey back from America to the West Indies, to Africa . . . to make that trip back. I'm not talking about in actual terms. I'm talking about a psychological and spiritual journey back in order to move forward. You have to psychologically go through chaos in order to overcome it.

Marshall finds it necessary to overcome slavery and colonialism in this manner because simple reconciliation is not enough. In the epigraph to *The Chosen Place, the Timeless People,* she comments on the persistence of historical wrongs:

> Once a great wrong has been done, it never dies. People speak the words of peace, but their hearts do not forgive. Generations perform ceremonies of reconciliation but there is no end.

Like many other Caribbean writers, Marshall is concerned with the legacy of history in general — and with slavery and the Middle Passage in particular — and desires to overcome injustices by retracing and reinterpreting them anew.

HEROIC WOMEN AND THE IMPORTANCE OF BEING MAROONED

Two particular and extreme cases are often used to evoke the experience of slavery and the response to it: that of being a woman and that of being a Maroon. Slave women had to endure particular abuse because of their gender. The sexual exploitation of African women by the Europeans was an integral part of the Atlantic crossing; the ritual rape aboard ship was referred to as *la pariade*. Many women were pregnant, had given birth, or had already killed the "unnamed" New World babies "without skin" by the time they reached the plantations.

The harrowing experience of slave women is often a focus of Caribbean writing. Not only themes of exploitation and miscegenation but also those of heroism and resistance are used to illuminate the meanings of race, class, and gender. In a talk given at the First World Conference on women writing from the English-speaking Caribbean, novelist Marlene

Nourbese Philip both describes and illustrates the resonance of this imagery in the following passage:

> [W]hen the African came to the New World she brought with her nothing but her body and all the memory and history which body could contain. The text of her history and memory was inscribed upon and within the body which would become the repository of all the tools necessary for spiritual and cultural survival. At her most unmanageable, the slave removed her body from control of the white master, either by suicide or by marronage.

Like the term *Middle Passage,* the term *Maroon* is a historical reference that has acquired deep metaphorical significance in Caribbean writing. The origin of both the term and the phenomenon of marronage is found in Jamaican history. Jamaica was controlled by the Spanish from 1494 until 1655, when the English captured it. At that time, a small band of African slaves belonging to the Spaniards fled to the mountainous interior of the island where they became the nucleus of the group of runaways known as Maroons. The word is derived from a Spanish word meaning "wild." At first it was applied only to domestic animals, but then to runaway slaves.

Many of the Maroon exploits have been handed down in folk stories and are still told today. The Maroons may have been legal slaves, but they refused to be spiritually enslaved. Their lifestyle was harsh and isolated, yet they were free from servitude. Contemporary writers such as André Schwarz-Bart in *A Woman Called Solitude,* V. S. Reid in *Nanny Town,* Michelle Cliff in *Abeng,* and Marie Chauvet in *Dance on the Volcano* use the theme of marronage to represent revolt, freedom, and independence. They also use it to reconstruct Caribbean history from the perspective of the colonized subjects and to reclaim positive self-images from even the bleakest of experiences.

Of particular interest in this context is the experience of Maroon women. Michelle Cliff uses the legendary story of a heroic Maroon woman named Nanny in her latest novel, *Free Enterprise.* During the First Maroon War in Jamaica (c. 1729–1739), a woman known as Nanny inspired and led the Windward Maroons of Jamaica in their successful resistance against slavery. According to tradition, Nanny practiced *obeah* (African-Caribbean magico-religion) and knew the medicinal properties of local plants and herbs. She was called a "woman of science" — a religious woman and a technician of the unseen. Historians speculate that Nanny was an Ashanti who probably experienced the Atlantic slave crossing. Her name (Akan: Nanna/Ni), which was modified in the New World, refers to the venerated characteristics of the earth-woman as ancestor, healer, spiritual leader, and politician. In this anthology, Lorna Goodison attests to the courage and spiritual survival of West Indian women in her poem dedicated to "Nanny."

CREOLIZATION AND COLORISM

One of the most obvious legacies of slavery in contemporary Caribbean society is the mix of distinct cultures and races and the ambivalence that this creates. Mulattos are people with one black parent and one white; the term *Creole* originally referred to any white person born in the colonies but has come to mean the blending of races and cultures. *Colorism,* or prejudicial preference for lighter-skinned complexions, has its origins in the early years of slavery and colonial racism. One study cites one hundred and eight possible categories of skin complexions that were part of the Code Noire in Haiti before 1804. Light-skinned mulattos and light-skinned Creoles were also referred to as "chappés" from the French word *échapper* (to escape) — they had escaped the misfortune of being black.

The ambivalent attitudes toward Creolization and the persistence of colorism are illustrated in the life and work of the writer Jean Rhys. Rhys was a white West Indian and the great-granddaughter of a slave owner; she left Dominica at seventeen and made Europe her permanent home. Rhys grappled with but apparently never fully resolved the dilemma posed by her Creole heritage and her European literary sensibility. For example, throughout the first section of her unfinished autobiography, Rhys refers to the ambivalent relationships she had during her childhood with "coloured" and black relatives and neighbors in Dominica. In this respect, Rhys was a distinct product of her New World cultural landscape.

In fiction as in life Rhys had a fascination with the issues of colorism. Certainly these poignant themes are all manifested in the short story included here, "The Day They Burned the Books." In this story the subject of being "white" and therefore having a supposedly superior European heritage involves two playmates. The narrator relates that "whenever the subject was brought up — people's relations and whether they had a drop of coloured blood or whether they hadn't — my father would grow impatient and interrupt. 'Who's white?' he would say. 'Damned few.'" In her life's writing, Rhys attempted to reclaim her own sense of life through ambivalent characters who ask the questions "Who am I?" and "Where am I to be?"

IDENTITY CRISIS AND ROOTLESSNESS

Historical factors other than Creolization have contributed to the sense of cultural displacement that pervades Caribbean writing. Populations such as the descendants of indentured servants brought by the English from India — or "the East Indies" — also experience a feeling of rootlessness from being cut off from the country and culture that originally gave them an identity. East Indians in the West Indies have been able to preserve much of their culture. Yet there is often the sense that this ploy for cultural survival has its drawbacks as well, since nostalgia for an idealized past can prevent people from facing the reality of the present.

The Trinidadian writer V. S. Naipaul is a good example of an East Indian in the West Indies who has wrestled with this sense of cultural displacement through his life and work. In his youth, Naipaul vowed to leave Trinidad as a rejection of his society. He emigrated to England where he attended Oxford University, and England has remained his home.

Naipaul's early views of colonial people and situations are often harsh. Naipaul's early novels such as *The Mystic Masseur* (1957) and *Miguel Street* (1959) satirize and even ridicule West Indians — of both African and East Indian descent — and the culture that has made them the way they are. In *The Middle Passage,* he describes East Indians in the West Indies rather unsympathetically:

> A peasant-minded, money-minded community, spiritually static because cut off from roots, its religion reduced to rites without philosophy, set in a materialist colonial society: a combination of historical accidents and national temperament has turned the Trinidadian Indian into the complete colonial, even more philistine than the white.

Other authors may depict the ironies and eccentricities of Caribbean culture, but Naipaul laughs *at* his characters rather than with them.

Such portrayals have led other writers to see Naipaul as lacking in compassion. But his harsh views can be seen as the result of disillusionment. Naipaul's Hindu characters are mocked most ruthlessly when they cling through material artifacts and religious rituals to an India they have never known. Naipaul himself knows that this nostalgia is both unwarranted and unproductive; when he traveled to India himself for the first time, he was severely disappointed to find the country did not live up to the India that had been glorified by the East Indians in Trinidad. His works *An Area of Darkness* (1964) — which recounts his voyage to India — and *The Mimic Men* (1967) explore the East Indians' relationship to a mythicized India and reveal the depths of Naipaul's disillusionment.

RESISTANCE AND NEGRITUDE

Resistance to ongoing oppression has often been accomplished by usurping the very power to create cultural value. Caribbean writers achieve this by rediscovering and glorifying whatever in their cultures and histories had previously been hidden and devalued. In *The Pleasures of Exile* (1960), George Lamming describes Caribbean writers' strategy of recovering previously "shameful" models of existence:

> Unlike the previous governments and departments of education, unlike the businessman importing commodities, the West Indian novelist did not look out across the sea to another source. He looked in and down at what had traditionally been ignored. For the first time, the West Indian peasant becomes other than a cheap source of labour. He became through the novelists' eye a living existence, living in silence and joy and fear, involved in riot and carnival. It is the West Indian novel that has restored the West Indian peasant to his true and original status of personality.

This strategy of resistance and rebellion is demonstrated in Paule Marshall's novel *The Chosen Place, the Timeless People*. In this book the peasants are an anathema to the upper class elite of Bournehills Island because they refuse to "develop." They insist on performing the same masque at Carnival every year, celebrating Cuffee Ned, a slave who led a briefly successful slave rebellion on the island in the nineteenth century. As the character Merle Kinbona in the novel explains, the peasants hold on to and celebrate the past because it is still meaningful to them:

> "You know," she began after a moment, "sometimes strangers to Bournehills wonder why we go on about Cuffee Ned and Pyre Hill when all that happened donkeys' years ago and should have been done with and forgotten. But we're an odd, half-mad people, I guess. We don't ever forget anything, and yesterday comes like today to us."

The upper class despises these reminders of what they consider to be an embarrassing past, but the peasants — and Marshall — have transformed Carnival and the Cuffee Ned masque into a political performance of resistance.

Earl Lovelace makes similar use of the carnivalesque in his classic novel *The Dragon Can't Dance*. Lovelace shows the Caribbean as a culture still marred by exploitation where few of the indigenous individuals are able to move up to the ruling class. The central character, Aldrick, understands this but initially rejects overt political rebellion because he is afraid this would mean giving up his culture. Yet Aldrick's smoldering sense of injustice eventually finds a means of expression *within* his culture, when he becomes the Dragon Man in the Trinidad Carnival. Aldrick transforms this cultural practice into a dance of rebellion and liberation, dancing the dance for all those he has seen oppressed.

Another form of resistance in Caribbean literature that seeks to elevate that which had been devalued is the idea of *negritude*. A direct rebellion against colorism and the presumed superiority of French culture, negritude began as a literary movement. Its political significance was soon apparent, however, as it proclaimed the essential importance and value of "being black in the world." In 1934, three students attending university in Paris launched negritude as a literary movement with the founding of *The Black Student*. The three students were Aimé Césaire (from Martinique), Leopold Senghor (from Senegal), and Léon Damas (from French Guyana), all of whom later became famous as political figures and writers. The most famous literary statement of negritude is Aimé Césaire's passionate *Return to My Native Land* (1938), a long poem in which he reflects on and responds to the exploitation of black people during colonization:

> *Hurray for those who never invented anything*
> *for those who never explored anything*
> *for those who never conquered anything*
> *hurray for joy*
> *hurray for love*
> *hurray for the pain of incarnate tears!* . . .
> *My négritude is no leaf stone that reflects the noise of the day*
> *My négritude is no spot on the dead eye of the earth*
> *My négritude is no tower and no cathedral*
> *It dives into the red flesh of the soil*
> *It dives into the flowing flesh of the sky*
> *Piercing the weight of oppression with its erect patience.* . . .

Thus negritude would come to mean an affirmation of African consciousness in both Europe and in the New World.

WRITING BACK

Cultural displacement, a crisis of identity, devaluation, and overt oppression are part of the Caribbean legacy, as they are part of the legacy of colonized peoples around the globe. To write back to the empire, Caribbean writers have needed to find their own voice, whether by forging their own languages or by reinterpreting history from their own perspectives. The writers included in the following pages write from a variety of positions and have tried diverse solutions, but they are all to some extent attempting to discover and shape their own destinies by writing in new styles and with positive identities.

Angelita Reyes

FOR FURTHER READING

Primary Works

Brathwaite, Edward Kamau. *History of the Voice: The Development of the Nation Language in Anglophone Caribbean Poetry.* London: New Beacon Books, 1984.

——. *Middle Passages.* Newcastle on Tyne, England: Bloodaxe Books, 1992.

——. *Third World Poems.* Harlow Essex, England: Longman, 1983.

Césaire, Aimé. *Aimé Césaire: The Collected Poetry, 1939–1976.* Translated by Clayton Eshleman and Annette Smith. Berkeley: University of California Press, 1983.

——. *Lost Body.* Translated by Clayton Eshleman and Annette Smith. New York: G. Brazilier, 1986.

——. *Lyric and Dramatic Poetry, 1946–82.* Translated by Clayton Eshleman and Annette Smith. Charlottesville: University Press of Virginia, 1990.

——. *Return to My Native Land.* Translated by John Berger and Anna Bostock. Baltimore: Penguin Books, 1970.

Cliff, Michelle. *Abeng.* Trumansburg, New York: The Crossing Press, 1984.

——. *Bodies of Water.* New York: Dutton, 1990

——. *Claiming an Identity They Taught Me to Despise.* Watertown, Mass.: Persephone Press, 1980.

——. *No Telephone to Heaven.* New York: Vintage Books, 1989.

Goodison, Lorna. *Baby Mother and the King of Swords.* London: Longman, 1990.

——. *Heartease.* London: New Beacon Books, 1988.

——. *I Am Becoming My Mother.* London: New Beacon Books, 1986.

——. *Selected Poems.* Ann Arbor: University of Michigan Press, 1992.

Kincaid, Jamaica. *A Small Place.* New York: Farrar Straus Giroux, 1988.

——. *Annie John.* New York: Farrar Straus Giroux, 1985.

——. *Lucy.* New York: Farrar Straus Giroux, 1990.

Lamming, George. *Natives of My Person.* New York: Holt, Rinehart and Winston, 1972.

——. *The Pleasures of Exile.* London: M. Joseph, 1960.

——. *Season of Adventure.* London: Allison and Busby, 1979.

——. *Water with Berries.* New York: Holt, Rinehart and Winston, 1972.

Lovelace, Earl. *A Brief Conversion and Other Stories.* Portsmouth, N.H.: Heinemann, 1988.

——. *Jestina's Calypso and Other Plays.* London: Heinemann, 1984.

——. *The Dragon Can't Dance.* Washington, D.C.: Three Continents Press, 1981.

——. *The Wine of Astonishment.* London: Heinemann, 1983.

Marshall, Paule. *Daughters.* New York: Atheneum, 1991.

——. *Reena and Other Stories.* Old Westbury, New York: Feminist Press, 1983.

——. *Soul, Clap Hands and Sing.* Washington, D.C.: Howard University Press, 1988.

——. *The Chosen Place, The Timeless People.* New York: Vintage Books, 1984.

Naipaul, V. S. *A Way in the World.* London: Heinemann, 1994.

——— . *India: A Million Mutinies Now.* London: Heinemann, 1990.

——— . *The Enigma of Arrival.* New York: Knopf, 1987.

——— . *Finding the Center.* New York: Knopf, 1984.

——— . *Miguel Street.* London: Penguin Books, 1959.

Nichols, Grace. *Lazy Thoughts of a Lazy Woman, and Other Poems.* London: Virago, 1989.

——— . *The Fat Black Woman's Poems.* London: Virago, 1984.

——— . *Whole of a Morning Sky.* London: Virago, 1986.

Rhys, Jean. *The Collected Short Stories.* Edited by Diana Athill. New York: Norton, 1987.

——— . *Smile, Please: An Unfinished Autobiography.* London: Deutsch, 1979.

——— . *Tales of the Wide Caribbean.* Edited by Kenneth Ramchand. London: Heinemann Educational Books, 1985.

——— . *Wide Sargasso Sea.* New York: W. W. Norton & Co., 1982.

Schwarz-Bart, Simone. *Between Two Worlds.* Translated by Barbara Bray. Portsmouth, N.H.: Heinemann, 1992.

——— . *The Bridge of Beyond.* Translated by Barbara Bray. London: Heinemann Educational Books, 1982.

Walcott, Derek. *Collected Poems 1948–1984.* New York: Farrar, Straus, & Giroux, 1986.

——— . *The Antilles: Fragments of Epic Memory.* New York: Farrar Straus Giroux, 1993.

——— . *Omeros.* New York: Farrar Straus Giroux, 1990.

——— . *The Arkansas Testament.* New York: Farrar Straus Giroux, 1987.

Zobel, Joseph. *Black Shack Alley.* Translated by Keith Q. Warner. Washington, D.C.: Three Continents Press, 1980.

Secondary Works

Boyce Davies, Carole, and Elaine Savory Fido, eds. *Out of the Kumbla: Caribbean Women and Literature.* Trenton, N.J.: Africa World Press, 1990.

Coombs, Orde, ed. *Is Massa Day Dead? Black Moods in the Caribbean.* New York: Doubleday, 1974.

Cudjoe, Selwyn. *Resistance and Caribbean Literature.* Columbus: Ohio University Press, 1980.

Horowitz, Michael M., ed. *Peoples and Cultures of the Caribbean.* New York: The Natural History Press, 1971.

Ramshand, Kenneth. *The West Indian Novel and Its Background.* London: Faber and Faber, 1970.

Warner-Lewis, Maureen. *Guinea's Other Suns: The African Dynamic in Trinidad Culture.* Dover, Mass.: The Majority Press, 1991.

ANTIGUA

JAMAICA KINCAID

Born in St. Johns, Antigua, Jamaica Kincaid (1949–) spent her early childhood in the Caribbean but emigrated to the United States to continue her education. Her stories and essays have appeared in Ms., The New Yorker, Rolling Stone, *and* The Paris Review. *In 1984 she won the Morton Dauwen Zabel Award of the American Academy and Institute of Arts and Letters for her first collection of short stories,* At the Bottom of the River *(1983). Her second book,* Annie John *(1985) is an autobiographical novel, which explores a girl's "coming of age" in the Caribbean. Kincaid's most recent novel is* Lucy *(1991).*

Much of Kincaid's writing deals with the dynamics of the mother-daughter relationship. In "Girl," Kincaid evokes folk expressions and the ubiquitous voice of the mother, who is adamant on instructing her daughter about life and survival as the mother sees it.

Girl

Wash the white clothes on Monday and put them on the stone heap; wash the color clothes on Tuesday and put them on the clothesline to dry; don't walk barehead in the hot sun; cook pumpkin fritters in very hot sweet oil; soak your little cloths right after you take them off; when buying cotton to make yourself a nice blouse, be sure that it doesn't have gum on it, because that way it won't holdup well after a wash; soak salt fish overnight before you cook it; is it true that you sing benna° in Sunday school?; always eat your food in such a way that it won't turn someone else's stomach; on Sundays try to walk like a lady and not like the slut you are so bent on becoming; don't sing benna in Sunday school; you mustn't speak to warf-rat boys, not even to give directions; don't eat fruits on the street — flies will follow you; *but I don't sing benna on Sundays at all and never in Sunday school;* this is how to sew on a button; this is how to make a buttonhole for the button you have just sewed on; this is how to hem a dress when you see the hem coming down and so to prevent yourself from looking like the slut I know you are so bent

benna: calypso-like popular music

on becoming; this is how you iron your father's khaki shirt so that it doesn't have a crease; this is how you iron your father's khaki pants so that they don't have a crease; this is how you grow okra — far from the house, because okra tree harbors red ants; when you are growing dasheen,° make sure it gets plenty of water or else it makes your throat itch when you are eating it; this is how you sweep a corner; this is how you sweep a whole house; this is how you sweep a yard; this is how you smile to someone you don't like too much; this is how you smile to someone you don't like at all; this is how you smile to someone you like completely; this is how you set a table for tea; this is how you set a table for dinner; this is how you set a table for dinner with an important guest; this is how you set a table for lunch; this is how you set a table for breakfast; this is how to behave in the presence of men who don't know you very well, and this way they won't recognize immediately the slut I have warned you against becoming; be sure to wash every day, even if it is with your own spit; don't squat down to play marbles — you are not a boy, you know; don't pick people's flowers — you might catch something; don't throw stones at blackbirds, because it might not be a blackbird at all; this is how to make a bread pudding; this is how to make doukona;° this is how to make pepper pot; this is how to make a good medicine for a cold; this is how to make a good medicine to throw away a child before it even becomes a child; this is how to catch a fish; this is how to throw back a fish you don't like; and that way something bad won't fall on you; this is how to bully a man; this is how a man bullies you; this is how to love a man, and if this doesn't work there are other ways, and if they don't work don't feel too bad about giving up; this is how to spit up in the air if you feel like it, and this is how to move quick so that it doesn't fall on you; this is how to make ends meet; always squeeze bread to make sure it's fresh; *but what if the baker won't let me feel the bread?*; you mean to say that after all you are really going to be the kind of woman who the baker won't let near the bread?

dasheen: a starchy vegetable similar to a large white potato
doukona: cornmeal

BARBADOS

GEORGE LAMMING

George Lamming (1927–) is among the early generation of modern West Indian writers. His major autobiographical novel, In the Castle of My Skin, *is a coming-of-age story set in his island home of Barbados. Like many of his contemporaries, Lamming also celebrates the peasants — their closeness to the earth and their exploited existence. At the same time his writing reflects an awareness of outside influences, such as "black consciousness," that his characters know are beneficial to their self-esteem. Lamming has lived in England for many years; hence, his writing brings into focus not only the Caribbean experience, but also that ethos as it is experienced in England — once the "mother country." His short stories are also set in England, and his engaging humor informs his classic story, "A Wedding in Spring," which celebrates the joys, sorrows, and triumphs of West Indian immigrants struggling with life in a foreign environment.*

A Wedding in Spring

London was their first lesson in cities. The solitude and hugeness of the place had joined their lives more closely than ever; but it was the force of similar childhoods which now threatened to separate them: three men and a woman, island people from the Caribbean, who waited in separate rooms of the same basement, sharing the nervousness of the night.

The wedding was only a day away.

Snooker thought he could hear the sweat spilling out of his pores. Talking to himself, old-woman-like in trouble, he started: "Is downright, absolute stupid to make me harness myself in dis mornin' costume. . . . I ain't no Prince Philip or ever want to be. . . ."

A pause drew his attention to the morning suit he had rented. The top hat sat on its crown, almost imitating itself. It provoked Snooker. He watched it, swore at it, then stooped as though he was going to sit on it.

"Now what you think you doin'?"

Snooker was alerted. He heard the closing creak of the door and the blurred chuckle of Knickerbocker's voice redeeming the status of the top hat.

Snooker was silent. He watched Knickerbocker hold the top hat out like some extraordinary fruit in his hand.

"Is what Beresford think it is at all?" he said, turning his back on the suit to face Knickerbocker. "My body, not to mention my face, ain't shape for dis kind o' get-up."

"Even de beggar can be king," said Knickerbocker, "an' dis is de kind o' headpiece kings does wear." He cuddled the top hat to his chest. "An' tomorrow," he added, lifting his head towards Snooker, "I goin' to play king."

"You goin' to play jackass," Snooker said sharply.

"So what?" Knickerbocker smiled. "Christ did ride on one."

"Is ride these clothes goin' ride you tomorrow," said Snooker, "'cause you ain't got no practice in wearin' them."

"You goin' see who ride what," said Knickerbocker, "I sittin' in de back o' dat limousine jus' so, watch me, Snooker." He was determined to prove his passion for formal dress. He had lowered his body onto the chair, fitting the top hat on his head at precisely the angle his imagination had shaped. He crossed his legs, and plucked at the imaginary seams of his morning trousers. The chair leaned with him while he felt the air for the leather rest which would hold his hand.

Snooker refused to look. But Knickerbocker had already entered the fantasy which the wedding would make real. His head was loud with bells and his eyes turned wild round the crowd, hilarious with praise, as they acknowledged his white gloved welcome. Even the police had removed their helmets in homage to the splendour which he had brought to a drab and enfeebled London. He was teaching the English their own tune. So he didn't hear Snooker's warning until the leather rest refused his hand and the crowd vanished into the shadows which filled the room. The chair had collapsed like a pack of cards under Knickerbocker's body. He looked like a cripple on his back.

Now he was afraid, and he really frightened Snooker too, the way he probed his hands with fearful certainty under and across his thighs. His guess was right. There was a split the size of a sword running down the leg and through the crutch of the only pair of trousers he owned.

"You break up my bes' chair," Snooker said sadly, carrying the top hat like wet crockery across the room. It had fallen into the sink.

The crisis had begun. Knickerbocker crouched on all fours, his buttocks cocked at the mirror, to measure the damage he had done. The basement was still: Knickerbocker considering his black exposure while Snooker collected the wreckage in both hands, wondering how he could fit his chair together again. They didn't speak, but they could hear, behind the door, a quiet tumble of furniture, and after an interval of silence, the sullen ticking of the clock in Flo's room.

She was alone, twisting her hair into knotty plaits that rose like spikes out of her skull. She did not only disapprove of her brother's wedding but she also thought it a conspiracy against all they had learnt. Preoccupied and disdainful, she saw the Vaseline melt and slip like frying lard over her hands. The last plait done, she stuck the comb like a plough into the low shrub of hair at the back of her neck. She scrubbed her ears with her thumb; stretched the under lid of each eye to tell her health; and finally gave her bottom a belligerent slap with both hands. She was in a fighting mood.

"As if he ain't done born poor," she said, caught in that whispering self-talk which filled the basement night. "Borrowin' an' hockin' every piece o' possession to make a fool o' himself, an' worse still dat he should go sell Snooker his bicycle to rent mornin' suit an' limousine. Gran Gran. . . . Gawd res' her in de grave, would go wild if she know what Beresford doin' . . . an' for what . . . for who he bringin' his own downfall."

It was probably too late to make Beresford change his mind: what with all those West Indians he had asked to drop in after the ceremony for a drink: the Jamaican with the macaw face who arrived by chance every Sunday at supper time, and Caruso, the calypsonian, who made his living by turning every rumour into a song that could scandalise your name for life. She was afraid of Caruso, with his malicious tongue, and his sly, secretive, slanderous manner. Moreover, Caruso never travelled without his gang: Slip Disk, Toodles and Square Dick; then there were Lice-Preserver, Gunner, Crim, Clarke Gable Number Two, and the young Sir Winston. They were all from "back home," idle, godless, and greedy. Then she reflected that they were not really idle. They worked with Beresford in the same tyre factory.

"But idle or no idle," she frowned, "I ain't want Beresford marry no white woman. If there goin' be any disgrace, let me disgrace him first."

She was plotting against the wedding. She wanted to bribe Snooker and Knickerbocker into a sudden disagreement with her brother. Knickerbocker's disapproval would have been particularly damaging since it was he who had introduced the English girl to Beresford. And there was something else about Knickerbocker that Flo knew.

The door opened on Snooker who was waiting in the passage for Knickerbocker. Flo watched him in the dark and counted three before leaning her hand on his head. Her anger had given way to a superb display of weakness: a woman outraged, defenceless, and innocent of words which could tell her feeling.

"Snooker."

"What happen now?"

"I want all you two speak to Beresford," she said. Her voice was a whimper appropriate with grief.

"Let the man make his own bed," said Snooker, "is he got to lie down in it."

"But is this Englan' turn his head an' make him lose his senses." Flo crouched lower, tightening her hand against Snooker's neck.

"He keep his head all right," said Snooker, "but is the way he harken what his mother say, like he walkin' in infancy all life long."

"Ma wasn't ever goin' encourage him in trouble like this," Flo said.

"Is too late to change anything," said Snooker, "except these kiss-me-tail mornin' clothes. Is like playin' ju-ju warrior with all that silk cravat° an' fish-shape' frock they call a coat. I ain't wearin' it."

"Forget 'bout that," said Flo, "is the whole thing we got to stop complete."

Knickerbocker was slipping through the shadows, silent and massive as a wall which now rose behind Flo. The light made a white mask over his face. Flo seemed to feel her failure, sudden and complete. Knickerbocker had brought a different kind of trouble. He was fingering the safety-pins which closed the gap in his trousers. He trusted Flo's opinion in these details. He stooped forward and turned to let her judge whether he had done a good job.

"Move your tail out of my face," she shouted, "what the hell you take me for."

Knickerbocker looked hurt. He raised his body to full height, bringing his hands shamefully over the safety-pins. He couldn't understand Flo's fury: the angry and unwarranted rebuke, the petulant slam of the door in his face. And Snooker wouldn't talk. They stood in the dark like dogs shut out.

Beresford was waiting in the end room. He looked tipsy and a little vacant under the light; but he had heard Flo's voice echoing down the passage, and he knew the others were near. It was his wish that they should join him for a drink. He watched the bottle making splinters with the light, sugar brown and green, over the three glasses and a cup. The label had lost its lettering; so he turned to the broken envelope on his stomach and went on talking to himself.

All night that voice had made dialogue with itself about his bride. His mood was reflective, nostalgic. He needed comfort, and he turned to read his mother's letter again.

> . . . concernin the lady in question you must choose like i would have you in respect to caracter an so forth. i excuse and forgive your long silence since courtship i know takes time. pay my wellmeanin and prayerful respects to the lady in question. give flo my love and my remembrance to snooker and knick. . . .

The light was swimming under his eyes; the words seemed to harden and slip off the page. He thought of Flo and wished she would try to share his mother's approval.

---

cravat: a necktie

. . . if the weddin come to pass, see that you dress proper. i mean real proper, like the folks in that land would have you. hope you keepin the bike in good condition. . . .

The page had fallen from his hand in a moment of distraction. He was beginning to regret that he had sold the bicycle to Snooker. But his mood didn't last. He heard a knock on the door and saw Knickerbocker's head emerge through the light.

"Help yuhself, Knick."

Beresford squeezed the letter into his pocket while he watched Knickerbocker close in on the table.

"I go take one," Knickerbocker said, "just one."

"Get a next glass if the cup don't suit you."

"Any vessel will do," Knickerbocker said.

Knickerbocker poured rum like water as though his arm could not understand the size of a drink. They touched cup and glass, making twisted faces when the rum started its course down their throats.

"Where Snooker?"

"Puttin' up the bike," Knickerbocker said. "But Flo in a rage."

"She'll come round all right," said Beresford. "Is just that she in two minds, one for me an' one 'gainst the wedding."

"You fix up for the limousine?"

"Flo self do it this mornin'," said Beresford, "they comin' for half pas' four."

"Who goin' partner me if Flo don't come to the church?"

"Flo goin' go all right," said Beresford.

"But you never can know with Flo."

Beresford looked doubtful, but he had to postpone his misgivings.

Knickerbocker poured more rum to avoid further talk, and Beresford held out his glass. They understood the pause. Now they were quiet, rehearsing the day that was so near. The room in half light and liquor was preparing them for melancholy: two men of similar tastes temporarily spared the intrusion of female company. They were a club whose rules were part of their instinct.

"Snooker ask me to swap places with him," Knickerbocker said.

"He don't want to be my best man?" Beresford asked.

"He ain't feel friendly with the morning suit," Knickerbocker said.

"But what is proper is proper."

"Is what I say too," Knickerbocker agreed. "If you doin' a thing, you mus' do it as the done thing is doed."

Beresford considered this change. He was open to any suggestion.

"Snooker or you, it ain't make no difference," he said.

"Then I goin' course wid you to de altar," Knickerbocker said.

Was it the rum or the intimacy of their talk which had dulled their senses? They hadn't heard the door open and they couldn't guess how long Flo had been standing there, rigid as wire, with hands akimbo, and her head, bull shaped, feeding on some scheme that would undo their plans.

"Get yuhself a glass, Flo," Beresford offered.

"Not me, Berry, thanks all the same."

"What you put your face in mournin' like that for?" Knickerbocker said. He was trying to relieve the tension with his banter. "Those whom God join together . . ."

"What you callin' God in this for?" Flo charged. "It ain't God join my brother wid any hawk-nose English woman. Is his stupid excitement."

"There ain't nothin' wrong wid the chick," Knickerbocker parried.

"Chick, my eye!" Flo was advancing towards them. "He let a little piece o' left-over white tail put him in heat."

"Flo!"

Beresford's glass had fallen to the floor. He was standing, erect, wilful, his hands nervous and eager for action. Knickerbocker thought he would hit her.

"Don't you threaten me wid any look you lookin'," Flo challenged him. "Knickerbocker, here, know what I sayin' is true. Look him good in his face an' ask him why he ain't marry her."

"Take it easy, Flo, take it easy," Knickerbocker cautioned. "Beresford marryin' 'cause he don't want to roam wild like a bush beast in this London jungle."

"An' she, you know where she been roamin' all this time?" Flo answered. Knickerbocker fumbled for the cup.

"Is jus' what Seven Foot Walker tell you back in Port-o'-Spain," Beresford threw in.

Whatever the English girl's past, Beresford felt he had to defend his woman's honour. His hands were now steady as stone watching Flo wince as she waited to hear him through.

"That man take you for a long ride, Flo, an' then he drop you like a latch key that won't fit no more. You been in mournin' ever since that mornin' he turn tail an' lef' you waitin'. An' is why you set yuh scorpion tongue on my English woman."

"Me an' Seven Foot Walker . . ."

"Yes, you an' Seven Foot Walker!"

"Take it easy," Knickerbocker begged them. "Take it easy . . ."

"I goin' to tell you, Berry, I goin' to tell you . . ."

"Take it easy," Knickerbocker pleaded, "take it easy . . ."

Flo was equipped for this kind of war. Her eyes were points of flame and her tongue was tight and her memory like an ally demanding vengeance was ready with malice. She was going to murder them with her knowledge of what had happened between Knickerbocker and the English girl. Time, place, and circumstance: they were weapons which now loitered in her memory waiting for release. She was bursting with passion and spite.

Knickerbocker felt his loyalty waver. He was worried. But Flo's words never came. The door opened and Snooker walked in casual as a bird, making music on his old guitar. He was humming: "Nobody knows the trouble I've seen." And his indifference was like a reprieve.

"The limousine man outside to see you," he said. "Somebody got to make some kind o' down payment."

The crisis had been postponed.

London had never seen anything like it before. The Spring was decisive, a hard, clear sky and the huge sun naked as a skull eating through the shadows of the afternoon. High up on the balcony of a fifth-floor flat an elderly man with a distressful paunch was feeding birdseed to a flock of pigeons. He hated foreigners and noise, but the day had done something to his temper. He was feeling fine. The pigeons soon flew away, cruising in circles above the enormous crowd which kept watch outside the church; then closed their ranks and settled one by one over the familiar steeple.

The weather was right; but the crowd, irreverent and forgetful in their fun, had misjudged the meaning of the day. The legend of English reticence was stone-cold dead. An old-age pensioner with no teeth at all couldn't stop laughing to the chorus, a thousand times chuckled: "Cor bli'me, look at my lads." He would say, "'Ere comes a next in 'is tails, smashers the lot o' them," and then: "Cor bli'me, look at my lads." A contingent of Cypriots on their way to the Colonial Office had folded their banners to pause for a moment that turned to hours outside the church. The Irish were irrepressible with welcome. Someone burst a balloon, and two small boys, swift and effortless as a breeze, opened their fists and watched the firecrackers join in the gradual hysteria of the day.

Snooker wished the crowd away; yet he was beyond anger. Sullen and reluctant as he seemed he had remained loyal to Beresford's wish. His mind alternated between worrying and wondering why the order of events had changed. It was half an hour since he had arrived with the bride. Her parents had refused at the last moment to have anything to do with the wedding, and Snooker accepted to take her father's place. He saw himself transferred from one role to another; but the second seemed more urgent. It was the intimacy of their childhood, his and Beresford's, which had coaxed him into wearing the morning suit. He had to make sure that the bride would keep her promise. But Beresford had not arrived; nor Knickerbocker, nor Flo.

Snooker remembered fragments of the argument in the basement room the night before; and he tried to avoid any thought of Flo. He looked round the church and the boys from "back home" looked at him and he knew they, too, were puzzled. They were all there: Caruso, Slip Disk, Lice-Preserver, and an incredibly fat woman whom they called Tiny. Behind him, two rows away, he could hear Toodles and Square Dick rehearsing in whispers what they had witnessed outside. There had been some altercation at the door when the verger° asked Caruso to surrender his guitar. Tiny and Slip Disk had gone ahead, and the verger was about to show his firmness when he noticed Lice-Preserver who was wearing full evening dress and a sword. The verger suddenly changed his mind and indicated a pew, staring in terror at the sword that hung like a frozen tail down Lice-Preserver's side. Snooker closed his eyes and tried to pray.

But trouble was brewing outside. The West Indians had refused to share in this impromptu picnic. They had journeyed from Brixton and Camden Town, the whole borough of Paddington and the Holloway Road, to keep faith with the boys from "back home." One of the Irishmen had a momentary lapse into prejudice and said something shocking about the missing bridegroom. The West Indians bristled and waited for an argument. But a dog intervened, an energetic, white poodle which kicked its hind legs up and shook its ears in frenzy at them. The poodle frisked and howled as though the air and the organ music had turned its head. Another firecracker went off, and the Irishman tried to sing his way out of a fight. But the West Indians were showing signs of a different agitation. They had become curious, attentive. They narrowed the circle to whisper their secret.

"Ain't it his sister standin' over yonder?"

They were slow to believe their own recognition.

"Is Flo, all right," a voice answered, "but she not dress for the wedding."

"Seems she not goin'," a man said as though he wanted to disbelieve his suspicion.

"An' they wus so close," the other added, "close, close, she an' that brother."

Flo was nervous. She stood away from the crowd, half hearing the rumour of her brother's delay. She tried to avoid the faces she knew, wondering what Beresford had decided to do. Half an hour before she left the house she had cancelled the limousine and hidden his morning suit. Now she regretted her action. She didn't want the wedding to take place, but she couldn't bear the thought of humiliating her brother before this crowd. The spectacle of the crowd was like a rebuke to her own stubbornness.

She was retreating further away. Would Beresford find the morning suit? And the limousine? He had set his heart on arriving with Knickerbocker in the limousine. She knew how fixed he was in his convictions, like his grandfather whose wedding could not proceed; had, indeed, to be postponed because he would not repeat the words: *All my worldly goods I thee endow.* He had sworn never to part with his cow. He had a thing about his cow, like Beresford and the morning suit. Puzzled, indecisive, Flo looked round at the faces, eager as they for some sign of an arrival; but it seemed she had lost her memory of the London streets.

verger: an attendant responsible for the care of a church's interior

The basement rooms were nearly half a mile from the nearest tube station; and the bus strike was on. Beresford looked defeated. He had found the morning suit, but there was no way of arranging for another limousine. Each second followed like a whole season of waiting. The two men stood in front of the house, hailing cabs, pleading for lifts.

"Is to get there," Beresford said, "is to get there 'fore my girl leave the church."

"I goin' deal wid Flo," Knickerbocker swore. "Tomorrow or a year from tomorrow I goin' deal wid Flo."

"How long you think they will wait?"

Beresford had dashed forward again, hailing an empty cab. The driver saw them, slowed down, and suddenly changed his mind. Knickerbocker swore again. Then: a moment of revelation.

"Tell you what," Knickerbocker said. He looked as though he had surprised himself.

"What, what!" Beresford insisted.

"Wait here," Knickerbocker said, rushing back to the basement room. "I don't give a goddam. We goin' make it."

The crowd waited outside the church, but they looked a little bored. A clock struck the half-hour. The vicar came out to the steps and looked up at the sky. The man in the fifth floor flat was eating pork sausages and drinking tea. The pigeons were dozing. The sun leaned away and the trees sprang shadows through the early evening.

Someone said: "It's getting on."

It seemed that the entire crowd had agreed on an interval of silence. It was then the woman with the frisky white poodle held her breast and gasped. She had seen them: Beresford and Knickerbocker. They were arriving. It was an odd and unpredictable appearance. Head down, his shoulders arched and harnessed in the morning coat, Knickerbocker was frantically pedalling Snooker's bicycle towards the crowd. Beresford sat on the bar, clutching both top hats to his stomach. The silk cravats sailed like flags round their necks. The crowd tried to find their reaction. At first: astonishment. Later: a state of utter incomprehension.

They made a gap through which the bicycle free-wheeled towards the church. And suddenly there was applause, loud and spontaneous as thunder. The Irishman burst into song. The whole rhythm of the day had changed. A firecracker dripped flames over the church steeple and the pigeons dispersed. But crisis was always near. Knickerbocker was trying to dismount when one tail of the coat got stuck between the spokes. The other tail dangled like a bone on a string, and the impatient white poodle charged upon them. She was barking and snapping at Knickerbocker's coat tails. Beresford fell from the bar on to his knees, and the poodle caught the end of his silk cravat. It turned to threads between her teeth.

The crowd could not determine their response. They were hysterical, sympathetic. One tail of Knickerbocker's coat had been taken. He was aiming a kick at the poodle; and immediately the crowd took sides. They didn't want harm to come to the animal. The poodle stiffened her tail and stood still. She was enjoying this exercise until she saw the woman moving in behind her. There was murder in the woman's eyes. The poodle lost heart. But the top hats were her last temptation. Stiff with fright, she leapt to one side seizing them between her teeth like loaves. And she was off. The small boys shouted: "Come back, Satire, come back!" But the poodle hadn't got very far. Her stub of tail had been safely caught between Flo's hand. The poodle was howling for release. Flo lifted the animal by the collar and shook its head like a box of bones.

Knickerbocker was clawing his rump for the missing tail of the morning coat. Beresford hung his head, swinging the silk cravat like a kitchen rag down his side. Neither could move. Flo's rage had paralysed their speech. She had captured the top hats, and it was clear that the wedding had now lost its importance for her. It was a trifle compared with her brother's disgrace.

The vicar° had come out to the steps, and all the boys from "back home" stood round him: Toodles, Caruso, and Square Dick, Slip Disk, Clarke Gable Number Two, and the young Sir Winston. Lice-Preserver was carrying the sword in his right hand. But the poodle had disappeared.

Flo stood behind her brother, dripping with tears as she fixed the top hat on his head. Neither spoke. They were too weak to resist her. She was leading them up the steps into the church. The vicar went scarlet.

"Which is the man?" he shouted. But Flo was indifferent to his fury.

"It don't matter," she said. "You ju' go marry my brother."

And she walked between Knickerbocker and her brother with the vicar and the congregation of boys from "back home" following like a funeral procession to the altar.

Outside, the crowd were quiet. In a far corner of sunlight and leaves, the poodle sat under a tree licking her paws, while the fat man from the fifth-floor flat kept repeating like an idiot to himself: "But how, how, how extraordinary!"

PAULE MARSHALL

Paule Marshall (1929–) was born in New York City of Barbadian parents who had emigrated to the United States. Her major fiction includes Brown Girl, Brownstones *(1959),* The Chosen Place, The Timeless People *(1969),* Praisesong for the Widow *(1983), and* Daughters

---

vicar: a member of the clergy appointed by a bishop to officiate in the church

(1991). She is the recipient of numerous awards, fellowships, and literary citations. Recognized as one of the foremost African American writers, Marshall is also hailed by Caribbean writers and critics as a product of the Caribbean. Such an embracing of two cultures is fitting for Marshall, whose creative writing and nonfiction essays attest to the interconnectedness of West Indian and African American cultures. Marshall writes about women who are touchstones in their communities and who must struggle to move beyond mere survival and endurance.

The following is an excerpt from her novel The Chosen Place, The Timeless People, *which is set on the fictitious island of Bournehills in the Caribbean. Merle Kinbona, the protagonist, is British-educated and a descendant of a slave owner and slave woman. She has returned to the island of her childhood after being in England for fifteen years. Her identity, however, is framed within a cultural kinship to the poor people of the island. Saul Amron and his wife Harriet are Americans who have recently arrived on the island. Saul is the director of an American development project that aims to transform the rural economy and he sincerely wants to achieve a rapport with the Bournehills peasants. Social and economic class distinctions are evident, as each group knows its place in this society.*

from The Chosen Place, The Timeless People

"Saul, do you think it might help if you wrote a letter to the editor pointing out how your comments were misconstrued and explaining the project in the right terms?" It was Harriet speaking in a voice that like the hand she had extended to him before sought to restrain him.

"I don't know if that'll do any good," he said. "The damage has been done. Besides, that unprincipled bastard might not even publish the letter."

"Our best bet, Saul, might be to hold a meeting in the village," Allen said. "Maybe we could straighten it out that way."

"Yes," he said, pausing. "I was thinking of that."

"Wait." Merle spoke up. "I know it's none of my business but I'll tell you what. I'm thinking of giving a party in a day or two—oh, nothing elaborate, just what we call a little fete—to welcome back Vere and Allen and because, for the first time in a long time, I feel like a party for some reason—and if you like you could explain about the article then. Most of Bournehills will be here. I always invite everybody, you know, the great and the small. Throw the whole lot in together, I say. And they all usually come, even though, of course, each group keeps to itself. You'll see. Class! It's a curse upon us. But you'll have a chance to meet everybody one time; and since there's always some speechmaking at a fete in Bournehills—we all love to hold forth; I'm not the only offender—you could have your say then. How's that?"

He thought for a time, frowning down at the floorboards, his hands deep in his pockets. "Yes," he said, "that might be a way to do it. We'll see."

As Merle had said, most of Bournehills came to the party she held two nights later. And this included not only a large cross section of the population of Spiretown, the only genuine village in the district, but also people from the tiny settlements — sometimes no more than three or four houses — scattered over the outlying hills. The guests — the more important ones — filled the shabby drawing room, whose tall doors stood open to the night. The rest were gathered in somewhat tense but noisy groups around to the front of the guesthouse under the shorn cassia tree which had been hung with a tilly lamp, and in the side yard, where Allen had his garden not far from Carrington's kitchen door. They sat on the precipitous steps leading down the south wall of the house to the beach and spilled over onto the beach itself, where they stood in great faceless numbers under the far-reaching shadow of the veranda, while behind them, down the stretch of shingle, the breakers pounded and clawed at the land. The torn spume, soaring up into the darkness each time a wave struck, was a brief, brilliant pyrotechnic display in the light from the house.

But surprisingly, although the guesthouse was crowded both inside and out, the long veranda stood empty — this, in spite of the fact that Carrington's two helpers had set out a table with rum and beer, and the strong kerosene gas lamps glowed a welcome from the overhang to the roof. And it was to remain empty — like some no man's land no one dared cross, until almost the end of the party, even though Merle kept urging those outside, especially the ones on the darkened beach below, to come up. Periodically, she would lean over the railing and plead with them to come upstairs. But to no avail. Each time she called down they would look off, making it appear that she was speaking to someone other than they, gently ignoring her. As the evening progressed and they still held their ground, her voice took on an increasingly exasperated note: "But, oh, crime," she cried angrily at one point, "why won't you come upstairs, yes, and stop acting as though you weren't invited to the damn fete, too?"

Inside the drawing room and separated from the guests outside by the empty veranda, Saul, with Harriet at one side and Merle, who was introducing them, at the other, met "the great people" of Bournehills as they were referred to — the postmaster, the magistrate and clerk of the small district court atop Westminster, the managers of the various Kingsley-owned estates dotting the hills who were, by tradition, mostly white; the parochial officer, the matron of the almshouse, all of them far less affluent and impressive versions of the people at Lyle Hutson's reception.

The headmaster of the grammar school, a tall, black, elaborately correct man, bowed with old-world courtliness over Harriet's hand and invited them both to come and see the rosebushes the Queen had planted in the schoolyard on her last visit to the island. And the manager of the sugar mill at Cane Vale, a large harried-looking man named Erskine Vaughan, with sandy hair and freckles sprinkled over his tan face (he was a third cousin of Merle's), gave Saul permission, when he asked, to visit the factory.

The men were at one side of the long rectangular room, their wives at the other, the women seated in stiff, almost painful decorum. Their hands, as they held them up to Saul and Harriet, felt boneless.

The magistrate's wife detained Harriet; and Merle, wearing one of her bright-figured dresses with a matching stole, her hair straightened and drawn back from her face, led Saul over to the rector of the parish church, a bland, weary-eyed Anglican father with olive-tinted skin and a vast sloping front under his white full-skirted cassock which was soiled at the hem. He held the small glass of rum he was nursing between his hands as if it were the eucharistic wine.

Slipping her arm through his, she said, "Meet my father-confessor, Dr. Amron. He's been after my soul for years, even though I keep telling him it's no use and he's wasting his time, that God doesn't want me."

"Neither does the devil, I'm beginning to fear, dear Merle," the rector said.

She laughed, impenitent, her head back, and her earrings, the ones with the saints which she wore all the time, performed their jig. "Purgatory then, is that it?" she cried. "Is that what's ahead for me? One long endless limbo between heaven and hell? Well, I'm ready. I've been in training for it these eight years I've been back." With that she held her face up to him for the kiss she demanded from everyone as her due.

"The church and the rumshop!" she said in a scathing aside to Saul as they left the drawing room. "They're one and the same, you know. Both a damn conspiracy to keep us pacified and in ignorance. Just you wait, though, come the revolution we're going to ban them both!"

Outside the house, under the lighted cassia tree in front as well as in the yards to the side, Saul met those guests who had not entered the drawing room although the doors stood open to them, and who even refused, until much later in the evening when the speechmaking began, to venture onto the veranda. Almost everyone he met there, men and women alike, "worked in the canes" as it was put in Bournehills, in the fields set high on the slopes or at the mill. And most, he learned, also cultivated their own tiny plots, sometimes no more than a quarter of an acre adjoining their houses or lying on the stony lands north of Spiretown, which they either owned outright or rented from Kingsley and Sons.

They had brought with them the strong, fecund, raw-sugar smell of those fields, and this had become part of their own body smell and heat. And the evidence of their labors out under the sun was to be seen in the faces of even the youngest as they stood about the yard, the men talking in small groups while tossing down the little glasses of rum, the women and children standing quietly aside draped like nuns against the night chill in old shawls and lengths of cloth covering their heads.

Saul saw several of the men from the rumshop, and he chatted for some time with the cane cutter, Stinger, whose billhook had stung the air repeatedly that first night. Sitting beside him on the steps leading down to the beach, he listened as Stinger, in answer to a question of his, spoke of the way in which the crop was harvested. He felt himself drawn to the man by the easy, quietly authoritative way he spoke of his work and his sober, introspective air; and above all, by something he sensed behind the eyes half-hidden under the cap he wore, an obscure sadness, an undefined remorse which was like a reflection of the same emotion in himself. He asked if he might come and watch him work sometime. Stinger looked up at him for a moment, his eyes touched by the dull glint from his bill-hook lying across his knees. (He was seldom without the knife, Saul was to discover.) Then, slowly, cryptically, he smiled, more to himself than to Saul. "Yes," he said, "you must come sometime, 'cause in the manner of speaking maybe that's what the old place is here for, for people like your-self to come and see what another man's life is like."

Minutes later, standing talking to Allen and the young man Vere, for whom the party was also being held, he spied Stinger's opponent from the rumshop, the tall lean man, Ferguson. He was at the center of a group of men arguing passionately out on the potholed road behind the guest-house. Ferguson, his thick glasses flashing in the light from the lamp in the cassia tree nearby, was holding forth as usual about Cuffee Ned,° his long attenuated body weaving and darting and thrusting like a fencer's as he harangued the others. The curses flew like spittle from his lips.

". . . What the fuckarse you all mean I don't know what I'm talking," he was shouting — and again it was almost impossible to make out the words. "He's goin' come again I tell you. What the shite you all know? Cuffee's goin' come. Ain't any of you ignoramuses ever heard of the sec-ond coming? Well, who the bloody hell you think they was talking about if not Cuffee? You think just because they cut off his head and put it on a pike on Westminster Road that that was the end of him? You think maybe 'cause he's been gone a little time that you'll never see him again? 'Oh, ye of little faith!' Matthew one, verse three. Disbelievers all. They couldn't kill off somebody like Cuffee just like so, don't you jackasses re-alize that? He said as much himself. 'Cording to the book in the big li-brary in town, he laughed when he saw them coming with the ax. He knew there wasn't no doing away with him for good. He's goin' come

---

Cuffee Ned: according to Bournehills history, Cuffee Ned was a nineteenth-century slave who led the briefly enjoyed Pyre Hill slave revolt on the island. The Bourne-hills peasants continue to celebrate the Pyre Hill rebellion and see Cuffee Ned as a hero, to the embarrassment of the island's educated elite.

again I say — or he's goin' send somebody just like him, mark my words. You think he was making any rasshole sport . . . ?"

With Ferguson's voice soaring like that of an Old Testament prophet through the yard, Saul moved on, making his way toward the beach on the other side of the house and the guests there whom he had yet to meet. And he was wondering vaguely as he slowly crossed to the stone steps leading down, stopping to introduce himself along the way, how it was that with all the people he had spoken with so far not one of them had referred, even indirectly, to the newspaper article on the project, not even the man Stinger with whom he had talked at length. They might not have seen it.

Merle, who had disappeared, returned, bringing Harriet, whom she had rescued from the drawing room, with her. "Ah, so you want to meet that bunch down on the beach," she said when she learned where he was headed. "Good. Maybe you can get them to stop their nonsense and come upstairs. But first say hello to these ladies over here."

She led them over to a group of old women standing off by themselves near the steps. Leesy was among them, looking frail and insubstantial except for her tough, workswollen hands. She was wearing an oversized jacket that had belonged to her late husband. A stained fedora,° his also, sat at a rakish angle atop the spotless white cloth she had wound about her head, and her face — what little of it that could be seen beneath the hat — was as expressionless as always, aloof, inaccessible, her rheumy eyes fey and critical. The other women, swathed like her against the chill, were silent also. But they gave the impression of being on the verge of uttering some word, some dark pronouncement which they would intone in prophetic Delphic voices. Under the hats their ancient eyes appeared disdainful of everything around them, of the fete, of the laughter and animated talk filling the yard, of the small glasses of rum they held in their hands, of the house, the night, the sea, everything, including Saul's and Harriet's hands as they held them out.

"Don't mind how harmless these ladies look," Merle said laughingly, embracing each of them in turn. "They don't have a kind word to say about anybody or anything."

"Did you see the headline the other day?" one of them said as soon as the three had left. The woman who spoke was so old the irises of her eyes were slowly being eaten away around the edges. She had been humming an atonal hymn under her breath all along, and it continued even as she spoke, underscoring the words. "Did you see the headline, I ask." She addressed no one in particular.

"You think you's the only body can read a newspaper, Mary Griggs?" Leesy said in her flat, spare way, staring straight ahead.

"I guess it means Bournehills is going to come like Trinidad soon or one of them other big places . . ." the old woman said, still humming.

---

fedora: a soft hat, generally made of felt, with the crown creased lengthwise

"Trinidad what! New York, you mean," another woman said.

". . . with plenty money and thing sharing 'bout the place . . ." Mary Griggs continued.

"Ha!" It was Leesy again, and her scathing laugh went beyond cynicism even.

". . . and plenty work stirring."

"Ha!"

They fell silent once again.

It was damp and chilly down on the beach, the heavy night dew that had fallen adding to the salt drift off the sea, and the guests there were even more bundled than those above. It was almost as though they were in hiding under the lengths of ragged cloth and bleached flour sacks with which they had all, even the men, cloaked themselves. They stood in scattered groups over the wide strand, looking, as Merle had accused them, as if they hadn't been invited to the party but, strolling along the beach and seeing the house afloat like some brightly lighted pleasure boat on the sea of darkness, had paused to look on. Something in the set, still poses they maintained, a tableau-like quality, even suggested that they had simply appeared out of the darkness; one moment the beach below the guesthouse was empty, the next there they were, a human still life against the night sea.

Saul had difficulty making out their faces as he and Harriet, with Merle leading the way and talking steadily, moved from one to another of the static groupings. He had a fleeting impression of the harsh high bones that structured their faces and of their deep-set eyes which seemed to be regarding him from the other end of a long dimly lit corridor, whose distance was measurable both in space and time, and down which he was certain he would have to travel if he were ever to know them or they to know him. Moreover, as he occasionally, with Merle watching, leaned in close to repeat his name over the loud crash of a wave, he had the odd feeling that the youngest among them, including even the babies asleep on their mothers' breasts, were in some way unimaginably old.

Offering his hand, saying simply that he was glad to meet them, he sought, in the brief moments he spent with each, to penetrate the tunnel of their eyes, to get at what lay there. And under cover of the darkness he felt them assessing him: his outer self first — his large, somewhat soft white body that had never known real physical labor, the eyes that had gone numb after his first wife's death, the coarse hair that had begun to recede at the temples. They saw even farther, he sensed; their gaze discovering the badly flawed man within and all the things about him which he would gladly have kept hidden: his deep and abiding dissatisfaction with himself, for one, his large capacity for failing those closest to him, his arrogance, born of that defensive superiority which had been his heritage as a Jew, his selfishness — for in everything he did, no matter how selfless it might appear, he was always after raising his own stock. . . .

And they did the same with Harriet. Turning to where she stood at his side, her hair drawing down the light from the veranda above, they bent on her the same veiled, even gaze from under the cloths covering their heads. And it, too, plumbed deep, reaching behind that unruffled surface of hers which made it seem none of this was strange, and behind the smile that deferred to them. The masked smiles they gave her in return held a profound recognition.

"Pleased to have your acquaintanceship," they said with Elizabethan formality, and extended their hands in the same slow eloquent manner as they raised them to wave along the roads, that salute which seemed to make of them witnesses after some fact.

Their faces, what little of them he had been able to see, remained with Saul long after he and Harriet had returned upstairs. All during the rest of the evening, part of his mind, his thoughts, dwelt on them. He found himself wanting to return to the beach and speak further with them. If he could have done it without appearing impolite, he would have liked to probe deeper into those eyes, to understand the meaning of the expression there.

The shopkeeper, Delbert, had arrived meanwhile. They had brought him on his palanquin° bed over to the guesthouse in the back of the ramshackle pickup truck he used for hauling supplies from town, and had placed him, still on the bed, out under the cassia. He lay in his loud shirt and chewed Panama hat, the broken leg in its cast. He had been given a water glass half-filled with rum and he drank slowly from this while listening like some gentle, unobtrusive arbiter to the talk around him. And from time to time, for no apparent reason, he would loose the startling laugh that wrenched him like a pain, laughing at the colossal joke that would forever remain private. Behind him, the tall steepled spur of Westminster looming above the house took up the sound and repeated it endlessly.

"I see you was in the paper the other day," he said as Saul, still puzzling over those on the beach, came over to greet him. Delbert was smiling, the smile rearranging the wrinkles that were scored like tribal markings into his flesh; but the stained eyes under the hatbrim were watchful.

"Yes, I know," he began carefully, noting to himself that Delbert was the first to mention the article. It was as though only he had the authority to bring it up. "But I'm afraid the way they wrote about us gives the wrong impression altogether. It makes it look as if we've come thinking we can work miracles, and that we've got the money to do it, which just isn't true, I've been very disturbed about the whole thing and I've asked Mrs. Kinbona if I might say a few words later to try and set the record straight."

"Well," Delbert said, the laugh beginning to rumble like a hunger pang, "you're going to have to speak loud and clear if you want the folks over on that side to hear — " the hand with the pink underbelly waved in the direction of the beach. A look passed swiftly between them and was gone.

palanquin: a portable couch or bed for one person

The party had grown more lively by now, due mostly to the rum, but also to Merle who, her voice bearing her along, flitted from one group to another, imparting to each something of her special ambience. The speechmaking began shortly thereafter, with a long procession of speakers drawn from every part of the house and yard taking their place on the veranda which was crowded now at both ends with those from outside.

Merle spoke first, and standing there with the stole draped across her shoulders and her eyes giving off their warm light, she looked happy, young. The damaged portrait of the handsome young woman her face called to mind might have been restored. "Well," she began in her abrupt way, her smile taking them all in, "as you see I've got a few guests in the place for a change. Things are looking up. . . ." Then, as to be expected, she went on at length.

The headmaster of the grammar school followed with an equally long speech welcoming "the strangers from America who have taken up their abode in our humble village." His talk was interspersed with literary allusions and Latin quotations, each of which was greeted with a loud "Hear! Hear!" Afterward, a respectful hush fell even among the elite gathered in the drawing room doorway as Delbert, speaking from his litter, recalled those who had gone away from Bournehills for what had seemed forever only to return. He cited among these Vere, Allen, Merle, himself. (He had worked for many years as a young man on the Panama Canal.) "It's like there're some of us the old place just won't let go," he said.

Several speakers later Ferguson gave a slightly drunken but moving account of life in the district during the reign of his hero, speaking of it with a nostalgia that made it seem he had been alive at the time. ". . . Cuffee had us planting the fields together, I tell you," he cried. "Reaping our crops together, sharing whatsomever we had with each other. We was a people then, man; and it was beautiful to see!" Behind his glasses his oversized eyes were filled with the memory.

Vere spoke. Dressed in the blue suit, the rare light flooding his face when he smiled, he told briefly of his experiences while away. But he had often, he said, longed for home, and the floor of the veranda shuddered as the guests stamped their feet in approval. Finally, a flushed and ebullient Allen (he had been drinking beer), his happiness at being back evident in his wide grin, introduced Saul.

As the latter took his place at the railing midway along the veranda he turned so part of him was to the silent crowd on the beach. It was to them, perhaps more than any other group present, to whom he spoke — the holdouts who, in spite of Merle's pleading, cajoling, and bullying continued to stand like so many ghosts washed up by the sea under the great shadow of the house. His face inclined toward their indistinct forms; pitting his voice against the sea's so they might hear him, he spoke to them.

He dealt first with the newspaper article, saying he was sure many of them were probably wondering just how much of it was true. Part of it was true, he said. They had come to Bournehills with the hope in mind of helping to improve life in the district. Unfortunately, he said, the article had overstated matters.

"First of all, we don't have millions of dollars as was stated," he declared. "We have some money, yes, enough to cover our work for the next few months, and we should be receiving more once we have more definite plans. But it's unlikely that it will ever be in the millions of dollars. Nor have we come, Dr. Fuso and myself, believing we can 'revolutionize' life in Bournehills or 'transform' it in a short time. We wouldn't be so foolish. Nor are we 'Americans to the Rescue' as the headline put it. I mention all this because we're very concerned that you not get the wrong idea either about us or how much we can do. Perhaps," he said, "if I tell you in my own words why we've come to Bournehills and what we hope to accomplish while here it might help to clear up any confusion the article might have caused."

Leaning against the railing, part of him to the faceless crowd below, he spoke then of the project, confining himself, as he had done at Lyle Hutson's, to the first phase of the work. And as he talked, pausing occasionally to search for the right word or when a wave broke with a thunderous detonation on the reefs, drowning out his voice, he sensed that everyone was paying only scant attention to what he was saying. They were more interested in him at this point, it was clear, in the kind of man he was. This, rather than the project which they had probably already dismissed as just another vague scheme destined to fail like all the others, was the basis on which he was being judged, and would be judged in the months to come. He wondered how he would fare. His faults, it had always seemed to him, were so glaring. Those on the beach had already, in a moment's glance, seen through to them. But what to do? His faults, his many shortcomings had become like old friends over the years. He would be a stranger to himself without them. All he could hope for at this late stage was that he might prove acceptable despite them. And understanding all this, he felt suddenly uncertain (for he might well fail), and presumptuous: for who was he to be talking about transforming their lives? And painfully conscious suddenly of his white skin and the meaning it held for people like themselves, he very much wanted their acceptance, especially that of the stubborn guests below, whose faces had eluded him even when he stood up close shaking their hands.

". . . We've come to learn," he was saying. "In fact you might say that the next six months to a year will be mainly a period of learning and getting acquainted on both our parts. It will give you a chance to get to know us and decide whether we're the kind of people you'd care to have work along with you in solving some of the district's problems, and it'll give us the opportunity to get acquainted with you and learn about life here. There's a great deal we need to know which you can teach us. We're interested, for instance, in understanding about the crops and would like to spend some time out in the fields and over at the mill seeing for ourselves how the canes are reaped and the sugar made. We want, in other words, to find out firsthand how you go about your day-to-day life in Bournehills. Also, we'd like to hear directly from you what you feel are the main things wrong in the district and what in your opinion most needs to be done.

"Much of our time, then, these first few months will be pretty much spent walking around observing and occasionally asking some questions. We won't, I warn you, look as if we're doing very much, and some of you will probably start asking when are we going to get around to doing something concrete. But we'll be hard at work all the same, even though it won't look like it.

"So," he said, rising, "you should be seeing quite a lot of us in the coming weeks. I hope you won't mind — " his smile reached out tentatively. "As for my wife and I, and I know I also speak for Dr. Fuso, we're very much looking forward to living in Bournehills. I hear you have the best sea air in the world, that it's known to cure whatever ails someone, so I expect to leave here a new man."

Merle was the first to come over when the applause — the light pounding of the right foot on the shaky floorboards which was their way — had ceased. "Well," she said, "you did all right for yourself." Her face raised to his, she was openly reappraising him. Her smile had little of its usual edge, but was speculative and strangely mild. Then, abruptly, she said, "You know one thing, I'm sorry now about the way I got on at Sugar's the other night . . ."

"That's all right," he said with a laugh. "I considered it part of the initiation rites. They're standard in my profession." But he spoke absently, because his attention was once again directed to the crowd below the veranda. They had not joined in the applause, and peering down through the darkness he saw that the beach was completely deserted. They had quietly — every man, woman and child — slipped away as soon as he had finished speaking, disappearing so swiftly and soundlessly up the beach it was as if they had simply merged with the night or returned to the sea. It made him wonder for a moment whether they had even been there.

"But I wonder why these people from Away can't learn, yes," Leesy said, taking off the fedora and then slowly unwinding her headcloth before the mirror in her tiny bedroom. The glass was as dim and mottled as her eyes. "Every time you look here comes another set of them with a big plan. They're goin' to do this, they're goin' do the other, and they end up not doing a blast. And they always got to come during crop when people are busy trying to get their few canes out the ground and over to Cane Vale, always walking about and looking, the lot of them, like they never seen poor people before. I tell you they's some confused and troubled souls you see them there. . . ."

She draped a dark cloth over the mirror so that the ghosts of the family dead would not come to look at themselves while she slept, and then slowly and painfully, wearing a long nightgown that resembled a shroud, she climbed the short stepladder to the high bed in which she had been born, and in which she could die when she felt it was time. She lay like a figure carved upon a catafalque° on the hard mattress of cus-cus grass, an effigy of someone already dead, utterly still, more self-contained and certain in her way than Harriet even.

"And it's not that the gentleman tonight doesn't look like he means well," she said, addressing the shadows which had also arranged themselves for sleep around the room. In the flickering light of the kerosene lamp she kept burning at a low all night they appeared to nod in agreement. "He talks direct. He's a man, you can see, don't put on no lot of airs like some them who come here calling themselves trying to help. And he's the first one ever said he wanted to go out in a cane field and see for himself how we have to work. You can tell he's a decent somebody. But what's the use? He'll never get to know this place. He'll never understand it. Bournehills! Change Bournehills! Improve conditions! Ha!" Her laugh was full of a secret knowing. "The only way you could maybe change things around here would be to take one of Bryce-Parker's bulldozers from the conservation scheme and lay the whole place flat flat flat and then start fresh."

After a long silence broken only by the sound of her tangled breathing (it seemed about to fail at any moment), she said, "Multi-millions!" and sucking her teeth, slept.

EDWARD KAMAU BRATHWAITE

The writings of Edward Kamau Brathwaite (1930–) range through poetry, literary criticism, and historical essays. A "Bajan" writer — from Barbados — he currently teaches in the department of comparative literature at New York University. His poetry collections include The Arrivants *(1981),* Masks *(1981),* Middle Passages *(1992),* Mother Poem *(1977), and* Sun Poem *(1982). Similar to many contemporary Caribbean poets, Brathwaite is conscious of the historical African presence and that relationship to the Middle Passage. Xango, or Chango, is an African deity whose concept and image was brought to the New World by the African slaves. Many of the allusions and metaphors in his poetry are from an African Caribbean folk culture and the celebration of the folk. Brathwaite intersects the use of Creole — "nation language" — and standard English. He creates new spellings, grammatical sequences, and onomatopoeia in his poetry, which is meant to echo the spoken word.*

catafalque: an ornamental structure sometimes used in funerals to hold the body

Red Rising

I

When the earth was made
when the wheels of the sky were being fashioned
when my songs were first heard in the voice of the coot of the
    owl
hillaby soufriere and kilimanjaro were standing towards me with
    water with fire

at the centre of the air   5

there
in the keel of the blue
the son of my song, father-giver, the sun/sum°
walks the four corners of the magnet, caught in the wind, blind

in the eye of ihs own hurricane   10

and the trees on the mountain become mine: living eye of my branches
of bone; flute
where is my hope hope where is my psalter

my children wear masks dancing towards me the mews of their
    origen earth   15

so that this place which is called mine
which will never know that cold scalpel of skull, hill of dearth

brain corals ignite and ignore it

and that this place which is called now
which will never again glow: coal balloon anthracite:° into cross-   20

roads of hollows

black spot of my life: *jah*
blue spot of my life: *love*
yellow spot of my life: *iises°*
red spot of my dream that still flowers flowers flowers   25

let us give thanks

when the earth was made
when the sky first spoke with the voice of the rain/bow

sun/sum: soul, or the origin of spiritual life
anthracite: a clean-burning, lustrous coal
iises: praises

when the wind gave milk to its music
when the suns of my morning walked out of their shallow thrill/
    dren   30

2

So that for centuries now have i fought against these opposites
how i am sucked from water into air
how the air surrounds me blue all the way

      from ocean to the other shore
      from halleluja to the black hole of hell   35

      from this white furnace where i burn
      to those green sandy ant-hills where you grow your yam

you would think that i would hate eclipses
   my power powdered over as it were

      but it's hallucination my fine friend   40
      a fan a feather; some

      one else's breath of shadow
      the moon's cool or some plan/et's

      but can you ever guess how i
      who have wracked   45

      you wrong
      long too to be black

      be
      come part of that hool that shrinks us all to stars

      how i   50
      with all these loco

      motives in me

      would like to straighten
      strangle eye/self out

      grow a beard wear dark glasses   55
      driving the pack straight far

      ward into indigo and vi
      olet and on into ice like a miss

      ile

rather than this surrendered curve   60
this habit forming bicycle of rains and seasons
weathers when i tear my hair

i will never i now know make it over the atlantic of that nebula

but that you may live my fond retreating future
i will accept i will accept the bonds that blind me   65
turning my face down/wards to my approaching past these
    morning chill/dren

Xango°

I

Hail

there is new breath here

huh

there is a victory of sparrows

erzulie° with green wings

    feathers sheen of sperm   5

hah

there is a west wind
sails open eyes the conch shell sings hallelujahs

i take you love at last my love
my night my dream my horse my gold/en horn my africa   10

softly of cheek now
sweet of pillow

cry
of thorn

pasture   15
to my fire

we word with salt this moisture vision
we make from vision

black and bone and riddim

hah   20

there is a gourd tree here
a boy with knotted snakes and coffle wires

Xango, erzulie: African Caribbean deities evoked in ritual ceremonies

a child
with water courses valleys clotted blood

these tendrils knitted to the cold 25
un

pearl and wail
the earth on which he steps breaks furl

in rain

bow 30

tears

the
tiger clue

is his

the bamboo 35
clumps the bougainvillea

bells

his syllables
taste of wood of cedar lignum vitae phlox

these gutterals 40
are his own mon general mon frere

his childhood of a stone
is rolled away he rings from rebells of the bone his liberated day

2

over the prairies now
comanche horsemen halt 45

it is the buff the brown the rose
that brings them closer

the thousand tangled wilful heads
bull yellow tossing

the stretch the itch the musk 50
the mollusc in the nostril

the flare of drum
feet plundering the night from mud to arizona

the bison plunge into the thunders river
hammering the red trail blazing west to chattanooga 55

destroying de soto francisco coronado°

un
hooking the waggons john

ford and his fearless cow
boy crews j   60

p morgan° is dead
coca cola is drowned

the statue of liberty's never been born
manhattan is an island where cows cruise on flowers

3

and all this while he smiles carved terra cotta   65
high life/ing in abomey
he has learned to live with rebellions

book and bribe
bomb
blast and the wrecked village   70

he is earning his place on the corner
phantom jet flight of angels
computer conjur man

he embraces them all

for there is green at the root of his bullet   75
michelangelo working away at the roof of his murderous rocket

he anointeth the sun with oil
star.tick.star.tick.crick.et.clock.tick

and his blues will inherit the world

4

he comes inward from the desert   80
with the sheriffs

he flows out of the rivers out of the water
toilets with shrimp and the moon's monthly oysters

he comes up over the hill/slide with grave
diggers he walks he walks   85

de soto, francisco, coronado: European explorers of the Americas
jp morgan: American financier

in the street with moonlight with whistles with police kleghorns
with the whores pisstle

5

after so many twists
after so many journeys
after so many changes   90

bop hard bop soul bop funk
new thing marley soul rock skank
bunk johnson is ridin again

after so many turns
after so many failures pain   95
the salt the dread the acid

greet

him
he speaks
so softly near   100

you

hear
him
he teaches

face   105
and faith
and how to use your seed and soul and lissom

touch
him
he will heal   110

you

word
and balm
and water

flow   115

embrace
him
he will shatter outwards to your light and calm and history

your thunder has come home

DOMINICA

JEAN RHYS

*Jean Rhys (1890–1979), much acclaimed by American feminist critics
as a British writer who was ahead of her times and paid for it, now has
been rightfully recognized as a British West Indian writer. Rhys was
born of Welsh parentage on the island of Dominica. She left Dominica
for England in 1910. When Europe became her home, the West Indies
remained a part of her literary consciousness.*

*Rhys represents for Western readers the complex paradigm of a
Caribbean writer. Rhys wrote in response to her sense of differentness
in European society, a feeling she sought to subvert. Her literary characters' lack of hope reflects how powerless members of society are
often relegated to this self-negating otherness. Although written forty
years after she left Dominica, her most famous novel,* Wide Sargasso
Sea *(1966), attests to the celebration and rootedness of her Caribbean
consciousness. It enabled her to make a final attempt at coming to
terms with her complex West Indian sensibility during the last years of
her life.* Wide Sargasso Sea *won the W. H. Smith Literary Prize for 1967
and brought Rhys late fame at the age of seventy-six.*

*"The Day They Burned the Books" is one of Rhys's seminal short
stories. As in most of her writing, the sense of place, parent-child relationships, the repercussions of colonialism and slavery, inform the pre-
occupations of the narrative theme. The story also evokes both the
beauty and the colonial legacies of Dominica.*

The Day They Burned the Books

My friend Eddie was a small, thin boy. You could see the blue veins in
his wrists and temples. People said that he had consumption and wasn't
long for this world. I loved, but sometimes despised him.

His father, Mr Sawyer, was a strange man. Nobody could make out
what he was doing in our part of the world at all. He was not a planter or
a doctor or a lawyer or a banker. He didn't keep a store. He wasn't a
schoolmaster or a government official. He wasn't — that was the point —
a gentleman. We had several resident romantics who had fallen in love
with the moon on the Caribees — they were all gentlemen and quite unlike Mr Sawyer who hadn't an 'h' in his composition. Besides, he detested

the moon and everything else about the Caribbean and he didn't mind telling you so.

He was agent for a small steamship line which in those days linked up Venezuela and Trinidad with the smaller islands, but he couldn't make much out of that. He must have a private income, people decided, but they never decided why he had chosen to settle in a place he didn't like and to marry a coloured woman. Though a decent, respectable, nicely educated coloured woman, mind you.

Mrs Sawyer must have been very pretty once but, what with one thing and another, that was in days gone by.

When Mr Sawyer was drunk — this often happened — he used to be very rude to her. She never answered him.

'Look at the nigger showing off,' he would say; and she would smile as if she knew she ought to see the joke but couldn't. 'You damned, long-eyed gloomy half-caste, you don't smell right,' he would say; and she never answered, not even to whisper, 'You don't smell right to me, either.'

The story went that once they had ventured to give a dinner party and that when the servant, Mildred, was bringing in coffee, he had pulled Mrs Sawyer's hair. 'Not a wig, you see,' he bawled. Even then, if you can believe it, Mrs Sawyer had laughed and tried to pretend that it was all part of the joke, this mysterious, obscure, sacred English joke.

But Mildred told the other servants in the town that her eyes had gone wicked, like a soucriant's° eyes, and that afterwards she had picked up some of the hair he pulled out and put it in an envelope, and that Mr Sawyer ought to look out (hair is obeah° as well as hands).

Of course, Mrs Sawyer had her compensations. They lived in a very pleasant house in Hill Street. The garden was large and they had a fine mango tree, which bore prolifically. The fruit was small, round, very sweet and juicy — a lovely, red-and-yellow colour when it was ripe. Perhaps it was one of the compensations, I used to think.

Mr Sawyer built a room onto the back of this house. It was unpainted inside and the wood smelt very sweet. Bookshelves lined the walls. Every time the Royal Mail steamer came in it brought a package for him, and gradually the empty shelves filled.

Once I went there with Eddie to borrow *The Arabian Nights*. That was on a Saturday afternoon, one of those hot, still afternoons when you felt that everything had gone to sleep, even the water in the gutters. But Mrs Sawyer was not asleep. She put her head in at the door and looked at us, and I knew that she hated the room and hated the books.

It was Eddie with the pale blue eyes and straw-coloured hair — the living image of his father, though often as silent as his mother — who first

soucriant: a mythical witch who divests herself of human form and flies about at night, sucking the blood of humans and animals
obeah: African Caribbean magico-religion

infected me with doubts about 'home', meaning England. He would be so quiet when others who had never seen it — none of us had ever seen it — were talking about its delights, gesticulating freely as we talked — London, the beautiful, rosy-cheeked ladies, the theatres, the shops, the fog, the blazing coal fires in winter, the exotic food (whitebait eaten to the sound of violins), strawberries and cream — the word 'strawberries' always spoken with a guttural and throaty sound which we imagined to be the proper English pronunciation.

'I don't like strawberries,' Eddie said on one occasion.

'You *don't like* strawberries?'

'No, and I don't like daffodils either. Dad's always going on about them. He says they lick the flowers here into a cocked hat and I bet that's a lie.'

We were all too shocked to say, 'You don't know a thing about it.' We were so shocked that nobody spoke to him for the rest of the day. But I for one admired him. I also was tired of learning and reciting poems in praise of daffodils, and my relations with the few 'real' English boys and girls I had met were awkward. I had discovered that if I called myself English they would snub me haughtily: 'You're not English; you're a horrid colonial.' 'Well, I don't much want to be English,' I would say. 'It's much more fun to be French or Spanish or something like that — and, as a matter of fact, I am a bit.' Then I was too killingly funny, quite ridiculous. Not only a horrid colonial, but also ridiculous. Heads I win, tails you lose — that was the English. I had thought about all this, and thought hard, but I had never dared to tell anybody what I thought and I realized that Eddie had been very bold.

But he was bold, and stronger than you would think. For one thing, he never felt the heat; some coldness in his fair skin resisted it. He didn't burn red or brown, he didn't freckle much.

Hot days seemed to make him feel especially energetic. 'Now we'll run twice round the lawn and then you can pretend you're dying of thirst in the desert and that I'm an Arab chieftain bringing you water.'

'You must drink slowly,' he would say, 'for if you're very thirsty and you drink quickly you die.'

So I learnt the voluptuousness of drinking slowly when you are very thirsty — small mouthful by small mouthful, until the glass of pink, iced Coca-Cola was empty.

Just after my twelfth birthday Mr Sawyer died suddenly, and as Eddie's special friend I went to the funeral, wearing a new white dress. My straight hair was damped with sugar and water the night before and plaited into tight little plaits, so that it should be fluffy for the occasion.

When it was all over everybody said how nice Mrs Sawyer had looked, walking like a queen behind the coffin and crying her eyeballs out at the right moment, and wasn't Eddie a funny boy? He hadn't cried at all.

After this Eddie and I took possession of the room with the books. No one else ever entered it, except Mildred to sweep and dust in the mornings, and gradually the ghost of Mr Sawyer pulling Mrs Sawyer's hair faded though this took a little time. The blinds were always half-way down and going in out of the sun was like stepping into a pool of brown-green water. It was empty except for the bookshelves, a desk with a green baize top and a wicker rocking-chair.

'My room,' Eddie called it. 'My books,' he would say, 'my books.'

I don't know how long this lasted. I don't know whether it was weeks after Mr Sawyer's death or months after, that I see myself and Eddie in the room. But there we are and there, unexpectedly, are Mrs Sawyer and Mildred. Mrs Sawyer's mouth tight, her eyes pleased. She is pulling all the books out of the shelves and piling them into two heaps. The big, fat glossy ones — the good-looking ones, Mildred explains in a whisper — lie in one heap. The *Encyclopaedia Britannica, British Flowers, Birds and Beasts*, various histories, books with maps, Froude's *English in the West Indies* and so on — they are going to be sold. The unimportant books, with paper covers or damaged covers or torn pages, lie in another heap. They are going to be burnt — yes, burnt.

Mildred's expression was extraordinary as she said that — half hugely delighted, half-shocked, even frightened. And as for Mrs Sawyer — well, I knew bad temper (I had often seen it), I knew rage, but this was hate. I recognized the difference at once and stared at her curiously. I edged closer to her so that I could see the titles of the books she was handling.

It was the poetry shelf. *Poems*, Lord Byron, *Poetical Works*, Milton, and so on. Vlung, vlung, vlung — all thrown into the heap that were to be sold. But a book by Christina Rossetti, though also bound in leather, went into the heap that was to be burnt, and by a flicker in Mrs Sawyer's eyes I knew that worse than men who wrote books were women who wrote books — infinitely worse. Men could be mercifully shot; women must be tortured.

Mrs Sawyer did not seem to notice that we were there, but she was breathing free and easy and her hands had got the rhythm of tearing and pitching. She looked beautiful, too — beautiful as the sky outside which was a very dark blue, or the mango tree, long sprays of brown and gold.

When Eddie said 'No', she did not even glance at him.

'No,' he said again in a high voice. 'Not that one. I was reading that one.'

She laughed and he rushed at her, his eyes starting out of his head, shrieking, 'Now I've got to hate you too. Now I hate you too.'

He snatched the book out of her hand and gave her a violent push. She fell into the rocking-chair.

Well, I wasn't going to be left out of all this, so I grabbed a book from the condemned pile and dived under Mildred's outstretched arm.

Then we were both in the garden. We ran along the path, bordered with crotons.° We pelted down the path, though they did not follow us and we could hear Mildred laughing — kyah, kyah, kyah, kyah. As I ran I

crotons: shrubs

put the book I had taken into the loose front of my brown holland dress. It felt warm and alive.

When we got into the street we walked sedately, for we feared the black children's ridicule. I felt very happy, because I had saved this book and it was my book and I would read it from the beginning to the triumphant words 'The End'. But I was uneasy when I thought of Mrs Sawyer.

'What will she do?' I said.

'Nothing,' Eddie said. 'Not to me.'

He was white as a ghost in his sailor suit, a blue-white even in the setting sun, and his father's sneer was clamped on his face.

'But she'll tell your mother all sorts of lies about you,' he said. 'She's an awful liar. She can't make up a story to save her life, but she makes up lies about people all right.'

'My mother won't take any notice of her,' I said. Though I was not at all sure.

'Why not? Because she's . . . because she isn't white?'

Well, I knew the answer to that one. Whenever the subject was brought up — people's relations and whether they had a drop of coloured blood or whether they hadn't — my father would grow impatient and interrupt. 'Who's white?' he would say. 'Damned few.'

So *I* said, 'Who's white? Damned few.'

'You can go to the devil,' Eddie said. 'She's prettier than your mother. When she's asleep her mouth smiles and she has curling eyelashes and quantities and quantities and *quantities* of hair.'

'Yes,' I said truthfully. 'She's prettier than my mother.'

It was a red sunset that evening, a huge, sad, frightening sunset.

'Look, let's go back,' I said. 'If you're sure she won't be vexed with you, let's go back. It'll be dark soon.'

At his gate he asked me not to go. 'Don't go yet, don't go yet.'

We sat under the mango tree and I was holding his hand when he began to cry. Drops fell on my hand like the water from the dripstone in the filter in our yard. Then I began to cry too and when I felt my own tears on my hand I thought, 'Now perhaps we're married.'

'Yes, certainly, now we're married,' I thought. But I didn't say anything. I didn't say a thing until I was sure he had stopped. Then I asked, 'What's your book?'

'It's *Kim*,' he said. 'But it got torn. It starts at page twenty now. What's the one you took?'

'I don't know; it's too dark to see,' I said.

When I got home I rushed into my bedroom and locked the door because I knew that this book was the most important thing that had ever happened to me and I did not want anybody to be there when I looked at it.

But I was very disappointed, because it was in French and seemed dull. *Fort Comme La Mort,*° it was called. . . .

Fort Comme La Mort: literally, "strong as death" (French)

GUADELOUPE

SIMONE SCHWARZ-BART

In much of her writing, Simone Schwarz-Bart (1938–) presents themes of lineage and history, celebrating the Guadeloupan peasant. Born in Guadeloupe, which is French-speaking, Schwarz-Bart incorporates journey motifs and Caribbean folklore, myths, and religion in her writing. Her work in English translation includes The Bridge of Beyond *(1974),* Between Two Worlds *(1981), and* Your Handsome Captain *(1989). She also has literary collaborations with her spouse, the well-known author André Schwarz-Bart.*

Her first novel, The Bridge of Beyond, *narrates the lives of three generations of women who live in an isolated hamlet in Guadeloupe. The story concentrates on the lives and struggles of the main character, Télumée Miracle, and the important women in her life. The novel incorporates themes such as the legacies of slavery in the New World and depicts the lives of the peasants who are the descendants of the once-enslaved Africans. Schwarz-Bart's writing is poetic as she evokes and celebrates the sentiments of Guadeloupan peasant culture.*

from **The Bridge of Beyond**

A man's country may be cramped or vast according to the size of his heart. I've never found my country too small, though that isn't to say my heart is great. And if I could choose it's here in Guadeloupe that I'd be born again, suffer and die. Yet not long back my ancestors were slaves on this volcanic, hurricane-swept, mosquito-ridden, nasty-minded island. But I didn't come into the world to weigh the world's woe. I prefer to dream, on and on, standing in my garden, just like any other old woman of my age, till death comes and takes me as I dream, me and all my joy.

When I was a child my mother, Victory, often talked to me about my grandmother Toussine. She spoke of her with fervor and veneration: Toussine, she'd say, was a woman who helped you hold your head up, and people with this gift are rare. My mother's reverence for Toussine was such I came to regard her as some mythical being not of this world, so that for me she was legendary even while still alive.

I got into the habit of calling her, as men called her, Queen Without a Name. But her maiden name had been Toussine Lougandor.

Her mother was Minerva, a fortunate woman freed by the abolition of slavery from a master notorious for cruelty and caprice. After the abolition Minerva wandered in search of a refuge far from the plantation and its vagaries, and she came to rest at L'Abandonnée. Some runaway slaves came there afterwards, and a village grew up. The wanderers seeking refuge were countless, and many would not settle anywhere permanently for fear the old days might return. One Negro from Dominica vanished as soon as he learned he had sired a child, and those in L'Abandonnée whom Minerva had scorned now laughed at her swollen belly. But when dark-skinned Xango took on the shame of my great-grandmother Minerva, the laughter stopped dead, and those who had been amusing themselves at others' misfortunes choked on their own bile. Little Toussine came into the world, and Xango loved her as if she were his own. As the child grew, shooting up as gracefully as a sugar cane, she became the light of his eyes, the blood in his veins, the air in his lungs. Thus through the love and respect lavished on her by Xango, Minerva, now long dead, could walk without shame along the main street of the hamlet, head high, back arched, arms akimbo, and foul breath turned from her to blow over better pastures. And so life began for young Toussine, as delicately as dawn on a clear day.

They lived in a hamlet swept alternately by winds from the land and winds from the sea. A steep road ran along by cliffs and wastelands, leading, it seemed, to nothing human. And that was why it was called the deserted village, L'Abandonnée. At certain times everyone there would be filled with dread, like travelers lost in a strange land. Still young and strong, always dressed in a worker's overall, Minerva had a glossy, light mahogany skin and black eyes brimming over with kindness. She had an unshakable faith in life. When things went wrong she would say that nothing, no one, would ever wear out the soul God had chosen out for her and put in her body. All the year round she fertilized vanilla, picked coffee, hoed the banana groves, and weeded the rows of sweet potatoes. And her daughter Toussine was no more given to dreaming than she. Almost as soon as she woke the child would make herself useful sweeping, gathering fruit, peeling vegetables. In the afternoon she would go to the forest to collect leaves for the rabbits, and sometimes the whim would take her to kneel in the shade of the mahoganies and look for the flat brightly colored seeds that are made into necklaces. When she came back with a huge pile of greenstuff on her head, Xango delighted to see her with leaves hanging down over her face, and would fling both arms in the air and shout: "Hate me, so long as you love Toussine. Pinch me till you draw blood, but don't touch so much as the hem of her robe." And he would laugh and cry just to look at the radiant, frank-faced child whose features were said to be like those of the Negro from Dominica, whom he would have liked to meet once, just to see. But as yet she was not in full bloom. It was when she was fifteen that she stood out from all the other girls with the unexpected grace of a red canna growing on a mountain, so that the old folk said she in herself was the youth of L'Abandonnée.

There was also in L'Abandonnée at that time a young fisherman called Jeremiah who filled one's soul with the same radiance. But he paid no attention to girls, to whom his friends used to say, laughing, "When Jeremiah falls in love it will be with a mermaid." But this didn't make him any less handsome, and the girls' hearts shriveled up with vexation. He was nineteen and already the best fisherman in Caret cove. Where on earth did he get those hauls of vivaneaux, tazars, and blue balarous?° Nowhere but from beneath his boat, the *Headwind*, in which he used to go off forever, from morn till night and night till morn; all he lived for was hearing the sound of the waves in his ears and feeling the tradewinds caressing his face. Such was Jeremiah when Toussine was for everyone a red canna growing on a high mountain.

On windless days when the sea was dead calm Jeremiah would go into the forest to cut the lianas° he made into lobster pots. One afternoon when he left the beach for this purpose, Toussine appeared in his path, right in the middle of a wood. She was wearing one of her mother's old dresses that came down to her ankles, and with her heap of greenstuff coming down over her eyes and hiding her face, she looked as if she didn't know where she was going. The young man asked her, "Is this L'Abandonnée's latest fashion in donkeys?" She threw down her burden, looked at him, and said in surprise, almost in tears: "A girl just goes to collect greenstuff from the forest, and here I am, insulted." With that, she burst out laughing and scampered off into the shadow. It was then Jeremiah was caught in the finest lobster pot he ever saw. When he got back from his excursion his friends noticed he looked absentminded, but they did not ask any questions. Real fishermen, those who have taken the sea for their native country, often have that lost look. So his friends just thought dry land didn't agree with Jeremiah, and that his natural element was the water. But they sang a different tune in the days that followed, when they saw Jeremiah neglecting the *Headwind*, deserting her and leaving her high and dry on the beach. Consulting among themselves, they came to the conclusion he must be under the spell of the Guiablesse, the most wicked of spirits, the woman with the cloven hoof who feeds exclusively on your desire to live, and whose charms drive you sooner or later to suicide. They asked him if he hadn't met someone that ill-fated day when he went up into the forest. Eventually Jeremiah confessed: "The only Guiablesse I met that day," he said, "is called Toussine — Xango's Toussine." Then they said, chuckling, "Oh, so that's it! Now we see. But it's not such a problem as you might think; if you want our

vivaneaux, tazars, blue balarous: fish of the Caribbean Sea
lianas: the name given to various climbing and twining plants that abound in the tropics

opinion there are no prince's daughters in L'Abandonnée that we know of. Fortunately we're only a pack of Negroes all in the same boat, without any fathers and mothers before God. Here everyone is everyone's else's equal, and none of our women can boast of having three eyes or two tourmalines sleeping in the hollow of her thighs. True, you'll say *she* isn't like all the others, the women you see everywhere, like lizards, protected by the very insipidity of their flesh. We answer: Jeremiah, you say well, as usual. For we too have eyes, and when Toussine brushes against our pupils our sight is refreshed. All these words to say just one thing, friend: Beautiful as she is, the girl is like you, and when you appear with her in the street you will be a good match for her. One more thing. When you go to tell her parents of your intentions, remember we don't have any cannibals here, and Xango and Minerva won't eat you."

Then they left Jeremiah to himself, so that he could make his decision like a man.

Thank God for my friends, thought Jeremiah the day he went to see Toussine's parents, dressed as usual and carrying a fine catch of pink crabs. As soon as they opened the door he told them he loved Toussine, and they asked him right in, without even consulting the young lady. Their behavior gave the impression they knew all about Jeremiah, what he did in life on land and sea, and that he was in a position to take a wife, have children, and bring up a family. It was the beginning of one of those warm Guadeloupe afternoons, lit up at the end by the arrival of Toussine with a tray spread with an embroidered cloth, with vermouth for the men and sapodilla syrup° for the weaker sex. When Jeremiah left, Minerva told him the door of the cottage would be open to him day and night from now on, and he knew he could consider the vermouth and the invitation as marking definite victory: for in the case of such a choice morsel as Toussine it isn't usual for people to fall on someone's neck the first time of asking, as if they were trying to get rid of a beast that had something wrong with it. That evening, to celebrate this triumph, Jeremiah and his friends decided to go night fishing, and they brought back so much fish their expedition was long remembered in L'Abandonnée. But they had enjoyed catching those coulirous too much to sell them on the beach, so they gave them away, and that too remained in everyone's memory. At noon that day the men, with glasses of rum in their hands, threw out their chests with satisfaction, tapped them three times, and exulted: "In spite of all, the race of men is not dead." The women shook their heads and whispered, "What one does a thousand undo." "But in the meanwhile," said one of them, as if reluctantly, "it does spread a little hope." And the sated tongues went full tilt, while inside Jeremiah's head the sound of the waves had started up again.

sapodilla syrup: a syrup made from an edible-fruit tree indigenous to tropical America

Jeremiah came every afternoon. He was treated not as a suitor but rather as if he were Toussine's brother, the son Minerva and Xango had never had. No acid had eaten into the young man's soul, and my poor great-grandmother couldn't take her eyes off him. Gay by temperament, she was doubly gay to see this scrap of her own country, the man sent by St. Anthony in person especially for her daughter. In the overflowing of her joy she would sometimes tease her. "I hope you're fond of fish, Miss Toussine. Come along you lucky girl, and I'll teach you to make a court-bouillon that'll make Jeremiah lick the fingers of both hands, polite as he is."

Then she would hold out her wide yellow skirt and sing to her daughter:

I want a fisherman for a husband
To catch me fine sea bream

I don't know if you know
But I want a fisherman

O oar before, he pleases me
O oar behind, I die.

But Toussine scarcely listened. Since Jeremiah had taken to spending his afternoons with her his image danced continually in her mind's eye, and she spent the whole day admiring the one she loved, unsuspected, as she thought, by all the world. She looked at his figure and saw it was slim and supple. She looked at his fingers and saw they were nimble and slender, like coconut leaves in the wind. She gazed into his eyes, and her body was filled with a great peace. But what she liked best of all about the man St. Anthony had sent her was the satiny, iridescent skin like the juicy flesh of certain mauve coco plums, so delicious under one's teeth. Minerva with her song about the fisherman knew very well how her daughter passed her time, but she still sang and danced just for the pleasure of seeing Toussine go on dreaming.

Here, as everywhere else, reality was not made up entirely of laughing and singing, dancing and dreaming: for one ray of sun on one cottage there was a whole village still in the shade. All through the preparations for the wedding, L'Abandonnée remained full of the same surliness, the same typical human desire to bring the level of the world down a peg, the same heavy malice weighing down on the chambers of the heart. The breeze blowing over Minerva's cottage embittered the women, made them more unaccountable than ever, fierce, fanciful, always ready with some new shrewishness. "What I say is, Toussine's more for ornament than for use. Beauty's got no market value. The main thing is not getting married, but sticking together year in year out," said one. "They're laughing now, but after laughter come tears, and three months from now Minerva's happy band will find itself with six eyes to cry with," said another. The most savage of all were those living with a man on a temporary basis. They grudged in advance the scrap of gold that was going to gleam on her finger, they wondered if she really possessed some unique and exceptional quality, some virtue or merit so great it elicited marriage. And to console themselves and soothe a deep-seated resentment, they would come right up to Minerva's cottage at dusk and mutter, with a kind of savage frenzy, incantations like:

Married today
Divorced tomorrow
But Mrs. just the same.

Minerva knew these women had nothing in their lives but a few planks balanced on four stones and a procession of men over their bellies. For these lost Negresses, marriage was the greatest and perhaps the only dignity. But when she couldn't stand hearing them any longer, Minerva would plant her hands on her hips and shout: "I'm not the only one with a daughter, my fine windbags, and I wish yours the same you wish my Toussine. For, under the sun, the saying has never gone unfulfilled. All they that take the sword shall perish with the sword." Then she would go inside and shut the doors and let the mad bitches yelp.

On the day of the wedding all the village paths were swept and decorated as for the local feast day. Xango and Minerva's cottage was surrounded by huts of woven coconut palm. The one reserved for the bridal couple was a great bouquet of hibiscus, mignonette, and orange blossom — the scent was intoxicating. Rows of tables stretched as far as the eye could see, and you were offered whatever drink you were thirsty for, whatever meat would tickle your palate. There was meat of pig, sheep, and cattle, and even poultry served in the liquor it was cooked in. Blood pudding rose up in shining coils; tiered cakes were weighed down with lacy frosting; every kind of water ice melted before your eyes — custard-apple, water-lemon, coconut. But for the Negroes of L'Abandonnée all this was nothing without some music, and when they saw the three bands, one for quadrilles and mazurkas, one for the fashionable beguine, and the traditional combination of drum, wind instruments, and horn, then they knew they'd really have something worth talking about at least once in their lives. And this assuaged the hearts swollen with jealousy. For three days everyone left behind hills and plateaus, troubles and indignities of every kind, to relax, dance, and salute the bridal couple, going to and fro before them in the flower-decked tent, congratulating Toussine on her luck and Jeremiah on his best of luck. It was impossible to count how many mouths uttered the word luck, for that was the theme they decided to adopt for telling their descendants, in later years, of the wedding of Toussine and Jeremiah.

The years flowed over it all, and Toussine was still the same dragonfly with shimmering blue wings, Jeremiah still the same glossy-coated sea dog. He continued to go out alone, never bringing back an empty boat, however niggardly the sea. Scandalmongers said he used witchcraft and had a spirit go out fishing in his stead when no one else was about. But in fact his only secret was his enormous patience. When the fish would not bite at all, he dived for lambis. If there were no lambis, he put out long rods with hooks or live crabs to tempt the octopi. He knew the sea as the hunter knows the forest. When the wind had gone and the boat was hauled up on the shore, he would make for his little cottage, pour the money he'd earned into his wife's lap, and have a snack as he waited for the sun to abate. Then the two of them would go to tend their garden. While he dug, she would mark out the rows; while be burned weeds, she would sow. And the sudden dusk of the islands would come down over them, and Jeremiah would take advantage of the deepening dark to have a little hors d'oeuvre of his wife's body, there on the ground, murmuring all sorts of foolishness to her, as on the very first day. "I still don't know what it is I like best about you — one day it's your eyes, the next your woodland laugh, another your hair, and the day after the lightness of your step; another, the beauty spot on your temple, and then the day after that the grains of rice I glimpse when you smile at me." And to this air on the mandolin, Toussine, trembling with delight, would reply with a cool, rough little air on the flute: "My dear, anyone just seeing you in the street would give you the host without asking you to go to confession, but you're a dangerous man, and you'd have buried me long ago if people ever died of happiness." Then they would go indoors and Jeremiah would address the evening, casting a last look over the fields: "How can one help loving a garden?"

Their prosperity began with a grass path shaded by coconut palms and kept up as beautifully as if it led to a castle. In fact it led to a little wooden house with two rooms, a thatched roof, and a floor supported on four large cornerstones. There was a hut for cooking in, three blackened stones for a hearth, and a covered tank so that Toussine could do her washing without having to go and gossip with the neighbors by the river. As the women did their washing they would pick quarrels to give zest to the work, comparing their respective fates and filling their hearts with bitterness and rancor. Meanwhile Toussine's linen would be boiling away in a pan in the back yard, and she took advantage of every minute to make her house more attractive. Right in front of the door she'd planted a huge bed of Indian poppies, which flowered all year round. To the right there was an orange tree with hummingbirds and to the left clumps of Congo cane from which she used to cut pieces to give to her daughters, Eloisine and Meranee, for their tea. She would go to and fro amid all this in a sort of permanent joy and richness, as if Indian poppies, Congo canes, hummingbirds, and orange trees were enough to fill a woman's heart with complete satisfaction. And because of the richness and joy she felt in return for so little, people envied and hated her. She could withdraw at will into the recesses of her own soul, but she was reserved, not disillusioned. And because she bloomed like that, in solitude, she was also accused of being an aristocrat stuck-up. Late every Sunday evening she would walk through the village on Jeremiah's arm to look at the place and the people and the animals just before they disappeared in the darkness. She was happy, herself part of all that spectacle, that close and familiar universe. She came to be the thorn in some people's flesh, the delight of others, and because she had a distant manner they thought she put on aristocratic airs.

After the grass path came a veranda, which surrounded the little house, giving constant cool and shade if you moved the bench according to the time of day. Then there were the two windows back and front, real windows with slatted shutters, so that you could close the door and shut yourself safely away from spirits and still breathe in the scents of evening. But the true sign of their prosperity was the bed they inherited from Minerva and Xango. It was a vast thing of locust wood with tall head posts and three mattresses, which took up the entire bedroom. Toussine used to put vetiver roots under the mattresses, and citronella leaves, so that whenever anyone lay down there were all sorts of delicious scents: the children said it was a magic bed. It was a great object of curiosity in that poor village, where everyone else still slept on old clothes laid down on the floor at night, carefully folded up in the morning, and spread in the sun to get rid of the fleas. People would come and weigh up the grass path, the real windows with slatted shutters, the bed with its oval-paneled headboard lording it beyond the open door, and the red-bordered counterpane, which seemed an additional insult. And some of the women would say with a touch of bitterness, "Who do they take themselves for, these wealthy Negroes? Toussine and Jeremiah, with their two-roomed house, their wooden veranda, their slatted shutters, and their bed with three mattresses and red borders — do they think all these things make them white?"

Later on Toussine also had a satin scarf, a broad necklace of gold and silver alloy, garnet earrings, and high-vamped slippers she wore twice a year, on Ash Wednesday and Christmas Day. And as the wave showed no sign of flagging, the time came when the other Negroes were no longer surprised, and talked about other things, other people, other pains and other wonders. They had got used to the prosperity as they had got used to their own poverty. The subject of Toussine and wealthy Negroes was a thing of the past; it had all become quite ordinary.

Translated from the French by Barbara Bray

GUYANA

GRACE NICHOLS

Grace Nichols (1950–), born in Guyana, is a novelist, children's writer, and poet. She is best known for her collections of poetry; i is a long-memoried woman (1983), The Fat Black Women Poems (1984), and Lazy Thoughts of a Lazy Woman (1989). Similar to other contemporary Caribbean writers, Nichols focuses on images of individuals against the backdrop of New World history and colonization. To convey images of history and culture, she uses Creole language as a way to present indigenous West Indian identities. Her images are also those of the cultural exile — the West Indian who emigrates to the "mother" country (which would be England for the English-speaking islands) and who has to endure being the perpetual outsider yearning for home. As she writes in one of her poems, "I get accustom to de English life/But I still miss back-home side."

Wherever I Hang

I leave me people, me land, me home
For reasons, I not too sure
I forsake de sun
And de humming-bird splendor
Had big rats in de floorboard   5
So I pick up me new-world-self
And come, to this place call England
At first I feeling like I in a dream —
De misty grayness
I touching de walls to see if they real   10
They solid to de seam
And de people pouring from de underground system
Like beans
And when I look up to de sky
I see Lord Nelson° high — too high to lie   15

Lord Nelson: British admiral (1758–1805) whose statue stands near one of the stations in London's subway (underground) system

And is so I sending home photos of myself
Among de pigeons and de snow
And is so I warding off de cold
And is so, little by little
I begin to change my calypso ways 20
Never visiting nobody
Before giving them clear warning
And waiting me turn in queue
Now, after all this time
I get accustom to de English life 25
But I still miss back-home side
To tell you de truth
I don't know really where I belaang

    Yes, divided to de ocean
    Divided to de bone 30

Wherever I hang me knickers° — that's my home.

Tropical Death

The fat black woman want
a brilliant tropical death
not a cold sojourn
in some North Europe far/forlorn

The fat black woman want 5
some heat/hibiscus at her feet
blue sea dress
to wrap her neat

The fat black woman want
some bawl 10
no quiet jerk tear wiping
a polite hearse withdrawal

The fat black woman want
all her dead rights
first night 15
third night
nine night°
all the sleepless droning
red-eyed wake nights

knickers: underwear
first night, third night, nine night: reference to a "set'n up" or ritual funeral wake that
   is held for nine nights to show respect for a deceased person

In the heart   20
of her mother's sweetbreast
In the shade
of the sun leaf's cool bless
In the bloom
of her people's bloodrest   25

the fat black woman want
a brilliant tropical death yes

JAMAICA

MICHELLE CLIFF

Michelle Cliff (1946–) was born in Jamaica and educated in the United States and Europe. She is among the leading international post-colonial novelists and essayists writing about the intersections of race, class, and gender. She has received numerous awards and fellowships for her essays, articles, and lectures. Cliff's writing concerns the inter-connections of history and the creative imagination. Her first novel, Abeng, *celebrates the heroic resistance of a Maroon woman in Jamaica and her legacies. Similarly, Cliff's most recent novel,* Free Enterprise, *is about an African American woman, Mary Ellen Pleasant, whose resis-tance to bondage and slavery was gender-oriented.*

Similar to Jean Rhys, Cliff is, in the Jamaican sense, a white Creole. But unlike Rhys, Cliff has come to a clear reconciliation regarding her European and African heritage. Much of her writing is about the process of "claiming an identity they taught me to despise" — the need to affirm all of her ancestry, as a product of a colonized society. For Cliff, the process is one of "spiritual integrity."

If I Could Write This in Fire, I Would Write This in Fire

I

We were standing under the waterfall at the top of Orange River. Our chests were just beginning to mound — slight hills on either side. In the center of each were our nipples, which were losing their sideways look and rounding into perceptible buttons of dark flesh. Too fast it seemed. We touched each other, then, quickly and almost simultaneously, raised our arms to examine the hairs growing underneath. Another sign. Mine was wispy and light-brown. My friend Zoe had dark hair curled up tight. In each little patch the riverwater caught the sun so we glistened.

The waterfall had come about when my uncles dammed up the river to bring power to the sugar mill. Usually, when I say "sugar mill" to anyone not familiar with the Jamaican countryside or for that matter my family,

I can tell their minds cast an image of tall smokestacks, enormous copper cauldrons, a man in a broad-brimmed hat with a whip, and several dozens of slaves — that is, if they have any idea of how large sugar mills once operated. It's a grandiose expression — like plantation, verandah, outbuilding. (Try substituting farm, porch, outside toilet.) To some people it even sounds romantic.

Our sugar mill was little more than a round-roofed shed, which contained a wheel and woodfire. We paid an old man to run it, tend the fire, and then either bartered or gave the sugar away, after my grandmother had taken what she needed. Our canefield was about two acres of flat land next to the river. My grandmother had six acres in all — one donkey, a mule, two cows, some chickens, a few pigs, and stray dogs and cats who had taken up residence in the yard.

Her house had four rooms, no electricity, no running water. The kitchen was a shed in the back with a small pot-bellied stove. Across from the stove was a mahogany counter, which had a white enamel basin set into it. The only light source was a window, a small space covered partly by a wooden shutter. We washed our faces and hands in enamel bowls with cold water carried in kerosene tins from the river and poured from enamel pitchers. Our chamber pots were enamel also, and in the morning we carefully placed them on the steps at the side of the house where my grandmother collected them and disposed of their contents. The outhouse was about thirty yards from the back door — a "closet" as we called it — infested with lizards capable of changing color. When the door was shut it was totally dark, and the lizards made their presence known by the noise of their scurrying through the torn newspaper, or the soft shudder when they dropped from the walls. I remember most clearly the stench of the toilet, which seemed to hang in the air in that climate.

But because every little piece of reality exists in relation to another little piece, our situation was not that simple. It was to our yard that people came with news first. It was in my grandmother's parlor that the Disciples of Christ held their meetings. Zoe lived with her mother and sister on borrowed ground in a place called Breezy Hill. She and I saw each other almost every day on our school vacations over a period of three years. Each morning early — as I sat on the cement porch with my coffee cut with condensed milk — she appeared: in her straw hat, school tunic faded from blue to gray, white blouse, sneakers hanging around her neck. We had coffee together, and a piece of hard-dough bread with butter and cheese, waited a bit and headed for the river. At first we were shy with each other. We did not start from the same place.

There was land. My grandparents' farm. And there was color.

(My family was called *red*. A term which signified a degree of whiteness. "We's just a flock of red people," a cousin of mine said once.) In the hierarchy of shades I was considered among the lightest. The countrywomen who visited by grandmother commented on my "tall" hair — meaning long. Wavy, not curly.

I had spent the years from three to ten in New York and spoke — at first — like an American. I wore American clothes: shorts, slacks, bathing suit. Because of my American past I was looked upon as the creator of games. Cowboys and Indians. Cops and Robbers. Peter Pan.

(While the primary colonial identification for Jamaicans was English, American colonialism was a strong force in my childhood — and of course continues today. We were sent American movies and American music. American aluminum companies had already discovered bauxite on the island and were shipping the ore to their mainland. United Fruit bought our bananas. White Americans came to Montego Bay, Ocho Rios, and Kingston for their vacations and their cruise ships docked in Port Antonio and other places. In some ways America was seen as a better place than England by many Jamaicans. The farm laborers sent to work in American agribusiness came home with dollars and gifts and new clothes; there were few who mentioned American racism. Many of the middle class who emigrated to Brooklyn or Staten Island or Manhattan were able to pass into the white American world — saving their blackness for other Jamaicans or for trips home; in some cases, forgetting it altogether. Those middle-class Jamaicans who could not pass for white managed differently — not unlike the Bajans in Paule Marshall's *Brown Girl, Brownstones* — saving, working, investing, buying property. Completely separate in most cases from Black Americans.)

I was someone who had experience with the place that sent us triple features of B-grade westerns and gangster movies. And I had tall hair and light skin. And I was the granddaughter of my grandmother. So I had power. I was the cowboy, Zoe was my sidekick, the boys we knew were Indians. I was the detective, Zoe was my "girl," the boys were the robbers. I was Peter Pan, Zoe was Wendy Darling, the boys were the lost boys. And the terrain around the river — jungled and dark green — was Tombstone, or Chicago, or Never-Never Land.

This place and my friendship with Zoe never touched my life in Kingston. We did not correspond with each other when I left my grandmother's home.

I never visited Zoe's home the entire time I knew her. It was a given: never suggested, never raised.

Zoe went to a state school held in a country church in Red Hills. It had been my mother's school. I went to a private all-girls school where I was taught by white Englishwomen and pale Jamaicans. In her school the students were caned as punishment. In mine the harshest punishment I remember was being sent to sit under the *lignum vitae* to "commune with nature." Some of the girls were out-and-out white (English and American), the rest of us were colored — only a few were dark. Our uniforms were blood-red gabardine, heavy and hot. Classes were held in buildings meant to recreate England: damp with stone floors, facing onto a cloister, or quad as they called it. We began each day with the headmistress leading us in English hymns. The entire school stood for an hour in the zinc-roofed gymnasium.

Occasionally a girl fainted, or threw up. Once, a girl had a grand mal seizure. To any such disturbance the response was always "keep singing." While she flailed on the stone floor, I wondered what the mistresses would do. We sang "Faith of Our Fathers," and watched our classmate as her eyes rolled back in her head. I thought of people swallowing their tongues. This student was dark — here on a scholarship — and the only woman who came forward to help her was the gamesmistress, the only dark teacher. She kneeled beside the girl and slid the white web belt from her tennis shorts, clamping it between the girl's teeth. When the seizure was over, she carried the girl to a tumbling mat in a corner of the gym and covered her so she wouldn't get chilled.

Were the other women unable to touch this girl because of her darkness? I think that now. Her darkness and her scholarship. She lived on Windward Road with her grandmother; her mother was a maid. But darkness is usually enough for women like those to hold back. Then, we usually excused that kind of behavior by saying they were "ladies." (We were constantly being told we should be ladies also. One teacher went so far as to tell us many people thought Jamaicans lived in trees and we had to show these people they were mistaken.) In short, we felt insufficient to judge the behavior of these women. The English ones (who had the corner on power in the school) had come all this way to teach us. Shouldn't we treat them as the missionaries they were certain they were? The creole Jamaicans had a different role: they were passing on to those of us who were light-skinned the creole heritage of collaboration, assimilation, loyalty to our betters. We were expected to be willing subjects in this outpost of civilization.

The girl left school that day and never returned.

After prayers we filed into our classrooms. After classes we had games: tennis, field hockey, rounders (what the English call baseball), netball (what the English call basketball). For games we were divided into "houses" — groups named for Joan of Arc, Edith Cavell, Florence Nightingale, Jane Austen. Four white heroines. Two martyrs. One saint. Two nurses. (None of us knew then that there were Black women with Nightingale at Scutari.) One novelist. Three involved in white men's wars. Two dead in white men's wars. *Pride and Prejudice.*

Those of us in Cavell wore red badges and recited her last words before a firing squad in W. W. I: "Patriotism is not enough. I must have no hatred or bitterness toward anyone."

Sorry to say I grew up to have exactly that.

Looking back: To try and see when the background changed places with the foreground. To try and locate the vanishing point: where the lines of perspective converge and disappear. Lines of color and class. Lines of history and social context. Lines of denial and rejection. When did *we* (the light-skinned middle-class Jamaicans) take over for *them* as oppressors? I need to see when and how this happened. When what should have been reality was overtaken by what was surely unreality. When the house nigger became master.

"What's the matter with you? You think you're white or something?"
"Child, what you want to know 'bout Garvey for? The man was nothing but a damn fool."
"They not our kind of people."
Why did we wear wide-brimmed hats and try to get into Oxford? Why did we not return?

Great Expectations: a novel about origins and denial. about the futility and tragedy of that denial. about attempting assimilation. We learned this novel from a light-skinned Jamaican woman — she concentrated on what she called the "love affair" between Pip and Estella.

Looking back: Through the last page of *Sula.* "And the loss pressed down on her chest and came up into her throat. 'We was girls together,' she said as though explaining something." It was Zoe, and Zoe alone, I thought of. She snapped into my mind and I remembered no one else. Through the greens and blues of the riverbank. The flame of red hibiscus in front of my grandmother's house. The cracked grave of a former landowner. The fruit of the ackee which poisons those who don't know how to prepare it.

"What is to become of us?"
We borrowed a baby from a woman and used her as our dolly. Dressed and undressed her. Dipped her in the riverwater. Fed her with the milk her mother had left with us: and giggled because we knew where the milk had come from.

A letter: "I am desperate. I need to get away. I beg you one fifty-dollar."

I send the money because this is what she asks for. I visit her on a trip back home. Her front teeth are gone. Her husband beats her and she suffers blackouts. I sit on her chair. She is given birth control pills which aggravate her "condition." We boil up sorrel and ginger. She is being taught by Peace Corps volunteers to embroider linen mats with little lambs on them and gives me one as a keepsake. We cool off the sorrel with a block of ice brought from the shop nearby. The shopkeeper immediately recognizes me as my grandmother's granddaughter and refuses to sell me cigarettes. (I am twenty-seven.) We sit in the doorway of her house, pushing back the colored plastic strands which form a curtain, and talk about Babylon and Dred. About Manley and what he's doing for Jamaica. About how hard it is. We walk along the railway tracks — no longer used — to Crooked River and the post office. Her little daughter walks beside us and we recite a poem for her: "Mornin' buddy/Me no buddy fe wunna/ Who den, den I saw?" and on and on.

I can come and go. And I leave. To complete my education in London.

2

Their goddam kings and their goddam queens. Grandmotherly Victoria spreading herself thin across the globe. Elizabeth II on our TV screens. We stop what we are doing. We quiet down. We pay our respects.

1981: In Massachusetts I get up at 5 a.m. to watch the royal wedding. I tell myself maybe the IRA will intervene. It's got to be better than starving themselves to death. Better to be a kamikaze in St. Paul's Cathedral than a hostage in Ulster. And last week Black and white people smashed storefronts all over the United Kingdom. But I really don't believe we'll see royal blood on TV. I watch because they once ruled us. In the back of the cathedral a Maori woman sings an aria from Handel, and I notice that she is surrounded by the colored subjects.

To those of us in the commonwealth the royal family was the perfect symbol of hegemony. To those of us who were dark in the dark nations, the prime minister, the parliament barely existed. We believed in royalty — we were convinced in this belief. Maybe it played on some ancestral memories of West Africa — where other kings and queens had been. Altars and castles and magic.

The faces of our new rulers were everywhere in my childhood. Calendars, newsreels, magazines. Their presences were often among us. Attending test matches between the West Indians and South Africans. They were our landlords. Not always absentee. And no matter what Black leader we might elect — were we to choose independence — we would be losing something almost holy in our impudence.

WE ARE HERE BECAUSE YOU WERE THERE
BLACK PEOPLE AGAINST STATE BRUTALITY
BLACK WOMEN WILL NOT BE INTIMIDATED
WELCOME TO BRITAIN . . . WELCOME TO SECOND-CLASS CITIZENSHIP
(slogans of the Black movement in Britain)

Indian women cleaning the toilets in Heathrow airport. This is the first thing I notice. Dark women in saris trudging buckets back and forth as other dark women in saris — some covered by loosefitting winter coats — form a line to have their passports stamped.

The triangle trade: molasses/rum/slaves. Robinson Crusoe was on a slave-trading journey. Robert Browning was a mulatto. Holding pens. Jamaica was a seasoning station. Split tongues. Sliced ears. Whipped bodies. The constant pretense of civility against rape. Still. Iron collars. Tinplate masks. The latter a precaution: to stop the slaves from eating the sugar cane.

A pregnant woman is to be whipped — they dig a hole to accommodate her belly and place her face down on the ground. Many of us became light-skinned very fast. Traced ourselves through bastard lines to reach the duke of Devonshire. The earl of Cornwall. The lord of this and the lord of that. Our mothers' rapes were the things unspoken.

You say: But Britain freed her slaves in 1833. Yes.

Tea plantations in India and Ceylon. Mines in Africa. The Cape-to-Cairo Railroad. Rhodes scholars. Suez Crisis. The white man's bloody burden. Boer War. Bantustans. Sitting in a theatre in London in the seventies. A play called *West of Suez*. A lousy play about British colonials. The finale comes when several well-known white actors are machine-gunned by several lesser-known Black actors. (As Nina Simone says: "This is a show tune but the show hasn't been written for it yet.")

The red empire of geography classes. "The sun never sets on the British empire and you can't trust it in the dark." Or with the dark peoples. "Because of the Industrial Revolution European countries went in search of markets and raw materials." Another geography (or was it a history) lesson.

Their bloody kings and their bloody queens. Their bloody peers. Their bloody generals. Admirals. Explorers. Livingstone. Hillary. Kitchener. All the bwanas° And all their beaters, porters, sherpas. Who found the source

bwana: master, boss

of the Nile. Victoria Falls. The tops of mountains. Their so-called discoveries reek of untruth. How many dark people died so they could misname the physical features in their blasted gazetteer. A statistic we shall never know. Dr. Livingstone, I presume you are here to rape our land and enslave our people.

There are statues of these dead white men all over London.

An interesting fact: The swear word "bloody" is a contraction of "by my lady" — a reference to the Virgin Mary. They do tend to use their ladies. Name ages for them. Places for them. Use them as screens, inspirations, symbols. And many of the ladies comply. While the national martyr Edith Cavell was being executed by the Germans in 1915 in Belgium (called "poor little Belgium" by the allies in the war), the Belgians were engaged in the exploitation of the land and peoples of the Congo.

And will we ever know how many dark peoples were "imported" to fight in white men's wars. Probably not. Just as we will never know how many hearts were cut from African people so that the Christian doctor might be a success — i.e., extend a white man's life. Our Sister Killjoy observes this from her black-eyed squint.

Dr. Schweitzer — humanitarian, authority on Bach, winner of the Nobel Peace Prize — on the people of Africa: "The Negro is a child, and with children nothing can be done without the use of authority. We must, therefore, so arrange the circumstances of our daily life that my authority can find expression. With regard to Negroes, then, I have coined the formula: 'I am your brother, it is true, but your elder brother.'" (*On the Edge of the Primeval Forest*, 1961)

They like to pretend we didn't fight back. We did: with obeah,° poison, revolution. It simply was not enough.

"Colonies . . . these places where 'niggers' are cheap and the earth is rich." (W.E.B. DuBois, "The Souls of White Folk")

A cousin is visiting me from Cal Tech where he is getting a degree in engineering. I am learning about the Italian Renaissance. My cousin is recognizably Black and speaks with an accent. I am not and do not — unless I am back home, where the "twang" comes upon me. We sit for some time in a bar in his hotel and are not served. A light-skinned Jamaican comes over to our table. He is an older man — a professor at the University of London. "Don't bother with it, you hear. They don't serve us in

obeah: African Caribbean magico-religion

this bar." A run-of-the-mill incident for all recognizably Black people in this city. But for me it is not.

Henry's eyes fill up, but he refuses to believe our informant. "No, man, the girl is just busy." (The girl is a fifty-year-old white woman, who may just be following orders. But I do not mention this. I have chosen sides.) All I can manage to say is, "Jesus Christ, I hate the fucking English." Henry looks at me. (In the family I am known as the "lady cousin." It has to do with how I look. And the fact that I am twenty-seven and unmarried — for all they know, unattached. They do not know that I am really the lesbian cousin.) Our informant says — gently, but with a distinct tone of disappointment — "My dear, is that what you're studying at the university?"

You see — the whole business is very complicated.

Henry and I leave without drinks and go to meet some of his white colleagues at a restaurant I know near Covent Garden Opera House. The restaurant caters to theatre types and so I hope there won't be a repeat of the bar scene — at least they know how to pretend. Besides, I tell myself, the owners are Italian *and* gay; they *must* be halfway decent. Henry and his colleagues work for an American company which is paying their way through Cal Tech. They mine bauxite from the hills in the middle of the island and send it to the United States. A turnaround occurs at dinner: Henry joins the white men in a sustained mockery of the waiters: their accents and the way they walk. He whispers to me: "Why you want to bring us to a battyman's den, lady?" (*Battyman = faggot* in Jamaican.) I keep quiet.

We put the white men in a taxi and Henry walks me to the underground station. He asks me to sleep with him. (It wouldn't be incest. His mother was a maid in the house of an uncle and Henry has not seen her since his birth. He was taken into the family. She was let go.) I say that I can't. I plead exams. I can't say that I don't want to. Because I remember what happened in the bar. But I can't say that I'm a lesbian either — even though I want to believe his alliance with the white men at dinner was forced: not really him. He doesn't buy my excuse. "Come on, lady, let's do it. What's the matter, you 'fraid?" I pretend I am back home and start patois° to show him somehow I am not afraid, not English, not white. I tell him he's a married man and he tells me he's a ram goat. I take the train to where I am staying and try to forget the whole thing. But I don't. I remember our different skins and our different experiences within them. And I have a hard time realizing that I am angry with Henry. That to him — no use in pretending — a queer is a queer.

patois: Jamaican dialect

1981: I hear on the radio that Bob Marley is dead and I drive over the Mohawk Trail listening to a program of his music and I cry and cry and cry. Someone says: "It wasn't the ganja° that killed him, it was poverty and working in a steel foundry when he was young."

I flash back to my childhood and a young man who worked for an aunt I lived with once. He taught me to smoke ganja behind the house. And to peel an orange with the tip of a machete without cutting through the skin — "Love" it was called: a necklace of orange rind the result. I think about him because I heard he had become a Rastaman. And then I think about Rastas.

We are sitting on the porch of an uncle's house in Kingston — the family and I — and a Rastaman comes to the gate. We have guns but they are locked behind a false closet. We have dogs but they are tied up. We are Jamaicans and know that Rastas mean no harm. We let him in and he sits on the side of the porch and shows us his brooms and brushes. We buy some to take back to New York. "Peace, missis."

There were many Rastas in my childhood. Walking the roadside with their goods. Sitting outside their shacks in the mountains. The outsides painted bright — sometimes with words. Gathering at Palisadoes Airport to greet the Conquering Lion of Judah. They were considered figures of fun by most middle-class Jamaicans. Harmless — like Marcus Garvey.

Later: white American hippies trying to create the effect of dred° in their straight white hair. The ganja joint held between their straight white teeth. "Man, the grass is good." Hanging out by the Sheraton pool. Light-skinned Jamaicans also dred-locked, also assuming the ganja. Both groups moving to the music but not the words. Harmless. "Peace, brother."

3

My grandmother: "Let us thank God for a fruitful place."
My grandfather: "Let us rescue the perishing world."

This evening on the road in western Massachusetts there are pockets of fog. Then clear spaces. Across from a pond a dog staggers in front of my headlights. I look closer and see that his mouth is foaming. He stumbles to the side of the road — I go to call the police.

I drive back to the house, radio playing "difficult" piano pieces. And I think about how I need to say all this. This is who I am. I am not what

ganja: marijuana
dred: a natural lock of hair traditionally worn by Rastafarians

you allow me to be. Whatever you decide me to be. In a bookstore in London I show the woman at the counter my book and she stares at me for a minute, then says: "You're a Jamaican." "Yes." "You're not at all like our Jamaicans."

Encountering the void is nothing more nor less than understanding invisibility. Of being fogbound.

> *Then:* It was never a question of passing. It was a question of hiding. Behind Black and white perceptions of who we were — who they thought we were. Tropics. Plantations. Calypso. Cricket. We were the people with the musical voices and the coronation mugs on our parlor tables. I would be whatever figure these foreign imaginations cared for me to be. It would be so simple to let others fill in for me. So easy to startle them with a flash of anger when their visions got out of hand — but never to sustain the anger for myself.
>
> It could become a life lived within myself. A life cut off. I know who I am but you will never know who I am. I may in fact lose touch with who I am.
>
> I hid from my real sources. But my real sources were also hidden from me.

> *Now:* It is not a question of relinquishing privilege. It is a question of grasping more of myself. I have found that in the real sources are concealed my survival. My speech. My voice. To be colonized is to be rendered insensitive. To have those parts necessary to sustain life numbed. And this is in some cases — in my case — perceived as privilege. The test of a colonized person is to walk through a shantytown in Kingston and not bat an eye. This I cannot do. Because part of me lives there — and as I grasp more of this part I realize what needs to be done with the rest of my life.

Sometimes I used to think we were like the Marranos — the Sephardic Jews forced to pretend they were Christians. The name was given to them by the Christians, and meant "pigs." But once out of Spain and Portugal, they became Jews openly again. Some settled in Jamaica. They knew who the enemy was and acted for their own survival. But they remained Jews always.

We also knew who the enemy was — I remember jokes about the English. Saying they stank. saying they were stingy. that they drank too much and couldn't hold their liquor. that they had bad teeth. were dirty and dishonest. were limey bastards. and horse-faced bitches. We said the men only wanted to sleep with Jamaican women. And that the women made pigs of themselves with Jamaican men.

But of course this was seen by us — the light-skinned middle class — with a double vision. We learned to cherish that part of us that was them — and to deny the part that was not. Believing in some cases that the latter part had ceased to exist.

None of this is as simple as it may sound. We were colorists and we aspired to oppressor status. (Of course, almost any aspiration instilled by Western civilization is to oppressor status: success, for example.) Color was the symbol of our potential: color taking in hair "quality," skin tone, freckles, nose-width, eyes. We did not see that color symbolism was a method of keeping us apart: in the society, in the family, between friends. Those of us who were light-skinned, straight-haired, etc., were given to believe that we could actually attain whiteness — or at least those qualities of the colonizer which made him superior. We were convinced of white supremacy. If we failed, we were not really responsible for our failures: we had all the advantages — but it was that one persistent drop of blood, that single rogue gene that made us unable to conceptualize abstract ideas, made us love darkness rather than despise it, which was to be blamed for our failure. Our dark part had taken over: an inherited imbalance in which the doom of the creole was sealed.

I am trying to write this as clearly as possible, but as I write I realize that what I say may sound fabulous, or even mythic. It is. It is insane.

Under this system of colorism — the system which prevailed in my childhood in Jamaica, and which has carried over to the present — rarely will dark and light people co-mingle. Rarely will they achieve between themselves an intimacy informed with identity. (I should say here that I am using the categories light and dark both literally and symbolically. There are dark Jamaicans who have achieved lightness and the "advantages" which go with it by their successful pursuit of oppressor status.)

Under this system light and dark people will meet in those ways in which the light-skinned person imitates the oppressor. But imitation goes only so far: the light-skinned person becomes an oppressor in fact. He/she will have a dark chauffeur, a dark nanny, a dark maid, and a dark gardener. These employees will be paid badly. Because of the slave past, because of their dark skin, the servants of the middle class have been used according to the traditions of the slavocracy. They are not seen as workers for their own sake, but for the sake of the family who has employed them. It was not until Michael Manley became prime minister that a minimum wage for houseworkers was enacted — and the indignation of the middle class was profound.

During Manley's leadership the middle class began to abandon the island in droves. Toronto. Miami. New York. Leaving their houses and businesses behind and sewing cash into the tops of suitcases. Today — with a new regime — they are returning: "Come back to the way things used to be" the tourist advertisement on American TV says. "Make it Jamaica again. Make it your own."

But let me return to the situation of houseservants as I remember it: They will be paid badly, but they will be "given" room and board. However, the key to the larder will be kept by the mistress in her dresser drawer. They will spend Christmas with the family of their employers and be given a length of English wool for trousers or a few yards of cotton for dresses. They will see their children on their days off: their extended family will care for the children the rest of the time. When the employers visit their relations in the country, the servants may be asked along — oftentimes the servants of the middle class come from the same part of the countryside their employers have come from. But they will be expected to work while they are there. Back in town, there are parts of the house they are allowed to move freely around; other parts they are not allowed to enter. When the family watches the TV the servant is allowed to watch also, but only while standing in a doorway. The servant may have a radio in his/her room, also a dresser and a cot. Perhaps a mirror. There will usually be one ceiling light. And one small square louvered window.

A true story: One middle-class Jamaican woman ordered a Persian rug from Harrod's in London. The day it arrived so did her new maid. She was going downtown to have her hair touched up, and told the maid to vacuum the rug. She told the maid she would find the vacuum cleaner in the same shed as the power mower. And when she returned she found that the fine nap of her new rug had been removed.

The reaction of the mistress was to tell her friends that the "girl" was backward. She did not fire her until she found that the maid had scrubbed the Teflon from her new set of pots, saying she thought they were coated with "nastiness."

The houseworker/mistress relationship in which one Black woman is the oppressor of another Black woman is a cornerstone of the experience of many Jamaican women.

I remember another true story: In a middle-class family's home one Christmas, a relation was visiting from New York. This woman had brought gifts for everybody, including the housemaid. The maid had been released from a mental institution recently, where they had "treated" her for depression. This visiting light-skinned woman had brought the dark woman a bright red rayon blouse and presented it to her in the garden one afternoon, while the family was having tea. The maid thanked her softly, and the other woman moved toward her as if to embrace her. Then she stopped, her face suddenly covered with tears, and ran into the house, saying, "My God, I can't, I can't."

We are women who come from a place almost incredible in its beauty. It is a beauty which can mask a great deal and which has been used in that way. But that the beauty is there is a fact. I remember what I thought the freedom of my childhood, in which the fruitful place was something I took for granted. Just as I took for granted Zoe's appearance every morning on my school vacations — in the sense that I knew she would be there. That she would always be the one to visit me. The perishing world of my grandfather's graces at the table, if I ever seriously thought about it, was somewhere else.

Our souls were affected by the beauty of Jamaica, as much as they were affected by our fears of darkness.

There is no ending to this piece of writing. There is no way to end it. As I read back over it, I see that we/they/I may become confused in the mind of the reader: but these pronouns have always co-existed in my mind. The Rastas talk of the "I and I" — a pronoun in which they combine themselves with Jah. Jah is a contraction of Jahweh and Jehova, but to me always sounds like the beginning of Jamaica. I and Jamaica is who I am. No matter how far I travel — how deep the ambivalence I feel about ever returning. And Jamaica is a place in which we/they/I connect and disconnect — change place.

LORNA GOODISON

Lorna Goodison (1947–) is one of the leading poets of Jamaica who has become internationally known. Goodison's poetry employs Jamaica-island folk rhythms. Her poetry is a provoking mixture of sensuality and history. Much of her performance poetry reflects an unabashed love for the folk voice of Jamaica — Creole, or Jamaica patois. She won the prestigious Commonwealth Prize for Poetry in 1986 and has been a fellow at the University of Iowa International Writing Program. In her collections, I Am Becoming My Mother *and* Tamarind Season, *Goodison characterizes the tensions of race, class, and gender through her command of language, incantations, and Creole imagery. Her poetry depicts the "redemptive joy of life" even as she writes about colonization and what the colonizers left behind in Jamaica and the larger Caribbean.*

Her poetry reflects a range of sentiments and observations, from the historical imagery of a Maroon warrior woman, Nanny, to honoring a literary persona, Jean Rhys, to the personal celebration of mothers and daughters in "For My Mother." Goodison's poetry is performance — her words and rhythms are meant to be heard, to be "talked," to be felt from within.

The Mulatta° and the Minotaur

And shall I tell you what the minotaur° said to me
as we dined by the Nile on almond eyes and tea?
No, I shall not reveal that yet.
Here, I'll record just how we met.
We faced each other and a bystander said,   5
'Shield your eyes, he's wearing God's head'
but it was already turbulent and deeply stained
with the merciless indigo of hell's rain.
And I, delaying my dying, hung my innocence high
and it glowed pale and waterwash against the sky.   10
And we met, but he was on his way
So he marked my left breast with this stain
which is indelible till we meet again.
And our lives rocketed through separate centuries
and we gave life to sons in sevens   15
and I was suckled of a great love or two
split not all the way asunder
and stuck together with glue.
And he wed the faultless wind
and wrestled with phantasms   20
and fantastic djinn°
and came through the other side whole and alone
with a countenance clear as wind-worried bones
and the seal of a serpent engorged by a dove
imprinted on marching orders for love.   25

mulatta: biracial woman
minotaur: in Greek mythology, the monster who has the body of a man and the head of a bull. He was contained in the Cretan labyrinth and fed human flesh, and was slain by Theseus.
djinn: a genie or spirit

And I was suckled of a great love or two
split not all the way asunder
and stuck together with glue.
For the Queen of Sheba had willed me
her bloodstone ring,   30
a flight of phoenix feathers
and her looser black things.
So,
Minotaur;
God's-head wearer   35
Galileo
Conqueror-of-Paris
Someone I don't know
There will be a next time
Centuries ago.   40

Lullaby for Jean Rhys

SLEEP IT OFF LADY
the night nurse is here
dressed in rain forest colours
used stars in her hair.
Drink this final dark potion   5
and straighten your night-dress
wear your transparent slippers
you must look your best
for you just might go dancing
atop hard-headed trees   10
with a man who is virile
and anxious to please.

Sleep now Miss Rhys.

Nanny

My womb was sealed
with molten wax
of killer bees
for nothing should enter
nothing should leave   5
the state of perpetual siege
the condition of the warrior.

From then my whole body would quicken
at the birth of everyone of my people's children.
I was schooled in the green-giving ways   10
of the roots and vines
made accomplice to the healing acts
of Chainey root, fever grass & vervain.°

My breasts flattened
settled unmoving against my chest   15
my movements ran equal
to the rhythms of the forest.

I could sense and sift
the footfall of men
from the animals   20
and smell danger
death's odour
in the wind's shift.

When my eyes rendered
light from the dark   25
my battle song opened
into a solitaire's moan
I became most knowing
and forever alone.

When my training was over   30
they circled my waist with pumpkin seeds
and dried okra, a traveller's jigida
and sold me to the traders
all my weapons within me.
I was sent, tell that to history.   35

When your sorrow obscures the skies
other women like me will rise.

For My Mother (May I Inherit Half Her Strength)

My mother loved my father
I write this as an absolute
in this my thirtieth year
the year to discard absolutes

Chainey root, fever grass, vervain: medicinal herbs

he appeared, her fate disguised,   5
as a sunday player in a cricket match,
he had ridden from a country
one hundred miles south of hers.

She tells me he dressed the part,
visiting dandy, maroon blazer   10
cream serge pants, seam like razor,
and the beret and the two-tone shoes.

My father stopped to speak to her sister,
till he looked and saw her by the oleander,
sure in the kingdom of my blue-eyed grandmother.   15
He never played the cricket match that day.

He wooed her with words and he won her.
He had nothing but words to woo her.
On a visit to distant Kingston he wrote,

'I stood on the corner of King Street and looked,   20
and not one woman in that town was lovely as you'.

My mother was a child of the petite bourgeoisie
studying to be a teacher, she oiled her hands
to hold pens.
My father barely knew his father, his mother died young, 25
he was a boy who grew with his granny.

My mother's trousseau came by steamer through the snows
of Montreal
where her sisters Albertha of the cheekbones and the
perennial Rose, combed Jewlit backstreets with French-   30
turned names for Doris' wedding things.

Such a wedding Harvey River, Hanover, had never seen
Who anywhere had seen a veil fifteen chantilly yards long?
and a crepe de chine dress with inlets of silk godettes
and a neck-line clasped with jewelled pins!   35

And on her wedding day she wept. For it was a brazen bride in
      those days
who smiled.
and her bouquet looked for the world like a sheaf of wheat
against the unknown of her belly,
a sheaf of wheat backed by maidenhair fern, representing Harvey
      River   40
her face washed by something other than river water.

My father made one assertive move, he took the imported cherub
 down
from the heights of the cake and dropped it in the soft territory
between her breasts . . . and she cried.

When I came to know my mother many years later, I knew her
 as the figure   45
who sat at the first thing I learned to read: 'SINGER', and she
 breast-fed
my brother while she sewed; and she taught us to read while she
 sewed and
she sat in judgement over all our disputes as she sewed.

She could work miracles, she would make a garment from a
 square of cloth
in a span that defied time. Or feed twenty people on a stew made
 from   50
fallen-from-the-head cabbage leaves and a carrot and a cho-cho°
 and a palmful
of meat.
And she rose early and sent us clean into the world and she went
 to bed in
the dark, for my father came in always last.

There is a place somewhere where my mother never took the
 younger ones   55
a country where my father with the always smile
my father whom all women loved, who had the perpetual quality
 of wonder
given only to a child . . . hurt his bride.

Even at his death there was this 'Friend' who stood by her side,
but my mother is adamant that that has no place in the memory
 of   60
my father.

When he died, she sewed dark dresses for the women amongst us
and she summoned that walk, straight-backed, that she gave
 to us
and buried him dry-eyed.

Just that morning, weeks after   65
she stood delivering bananas from their skin
singing in that flat hill country voice

cho-cho: a wholesome fruit cultivated in the Caribbean, known as *chayotes* in Europe
 and *christophine* in the French Caribbean

she fell down a note to the realization that she did
not have to be brave, just this once
and she cried.   70

For her hands grown coarse with raising nine children
for her body for twenty years permanently fat
for the time she pawned her machine for my sister's
Senior Cambridge fees
and for the pain she bore with the eyes of a queen   75

and she cried also because she loved him.

MARTINIQUE

AIMÉ CÉSAIRE

Aimé Césaire (1913–) was born in Basse-Point, Martinique. He was an excellent student during his elementary education in Martinique and went on to further his education in France. There, in France before World War II, he met other Caribbean, West African, and African American students at the university who were also later to become famous as poets and statesmen. Foremost, he met Leopold Senghor, the famous writer from Senegal, West Africa, with whom be became involved in the poetics and politics of black culture.

The following excerpt is from his famous poem, Return to My Native Land. *The poem celebrates black culture as the poet laments about the process of colonization. Powerful images of poverty and exploitation of colonized peoples are juxtaposed with the poet's celebration of the ancestral homelands of Africa and the Caribbean as he speaks of "ancestral Bambaras." Césaire celebrates negritude as observer and participant. Césaire is also a playwright, essayist, teacher, and local politician in Martinique. He is considered one of the most significant and widely read authors from the French-speaking Caribbean.*

from Return to My Native Land

my negritude is not a stone
nor deafness flung out against the clamor of the day
my negritude is not a white speck of dead water
on the dead eye of the earth
my negritude is neither tower nor cathedral   5

it plunges into the red flesh of the soil
it plunges into the blaxing flesh of the sky
my negritude riddles with holes
the dense affliction of its worthy patience.

Heia for the royal Kailcedrate!°   10
Heia for those who have never invented anything

Kailcedrate: a type of tree

those who never explored anything
those who never tamed anything

those who give themselves up to the essence of all things
ignorant of surfaces but struck by the movement of all things   15
free of the desire to tame but familiar with the play of the world

*   *   *

And also my racial geography: the map of the world
made for my use, colored not with the arbitrary colors
of schoolmen but with the geometry of my spilt blood
I accept
and the definition of my biology, no longer miserably   5
confined to a facial angle, to a type of hair, to a
nose sufficiently flattened, to a pigmentation sufficiently
melanose, negritude is no longer a cephalic index or a
plasma or a soma;
we are measured with the compasses of suffering   10

and the Negro every day lower, more cowardly, more
sterile, less profound, more spent beyond himself, more
separate from himself, more cunning with himself, less
straight to himself,
I accept, I accept it all   15
and far from the palatial sea which breaks under a weeping
        syzygy° of blebs°
the body of my country marvelously recumbent in my despairing
        hands
its bones shaken, and in its veins blood pausing like
the drop of vegetable milk hesitant at the wound of the bulb . . .

And now suddenly strength and life attack me like a   20
bull the wave of life streams over the nipple of the
Morne, veins and veinlets throng with new blood, the
enormous lung of cyclones breathing, the fire hoarded
in volcanoes, and the gigantic seismic pulse beats the
measure of a living body within my blaze.   25

Upright now, my country and I, hair in the wind, my
hand small in its enormous fist and our strength not
inside us but above in a voice that bores through the
night and its listeners like the sting of an apocalyptic
wasp. And the voice declares that for centuries Europe   30

syzygy: a conjuction of two heavenly bodies
blebs: bubbles

has stuffed us with lies and crammed us with plague,
for it is not true that:
the work of man is finished
we have nothing to do in the world
we are the parasites of the world   35
our job is to keep in step with the world.
The work of man is only just beginning
It remains for him to conquer
at the four corners of his fervor
every rigid prohibition.   40
No race holds a monopoly of beauty, intelligence and strength
there is room for all at the meeting-place of conquest
we know now
that the sun revolves round our earth illuminating the plot
which we alone have selected   45
that every star falls at our command from the sky to the earth
without limit or cease.

Now I see what the ordeal means: my country is the
"spear of the night" of my ancestral Bambaras. It shrinks
and its desparate blade retracts if it is offered checken-   50
blodd, its temper wants the blood of man, the fat of
man, the liver of man, the heart of man and not the
blood of chickens

Translated from the French by
John Berger and Anna Bostock

JOSEPH ZOBEL

Joseph Zobel (1915–) was born in Martinique. He first began his writing career in journalism with a local newspaper. Like many French-speaking writers, he left his island home for France where he attended the Institute of Ethnology of the Sorbonne. He also studied drama. His most well-known novel is Black Shack Alley, *which is a coming-of-age novel.* Black Shack Alley *has been made into an acclaimed film. Zobel began writing in the 1950s about the positive qualities of rural life in Martinique when it was not fashionable to do so. Many of his short stories and novels feature the proud peasant communities of Martinique. In his story, "The Gift," he evokes images of childhood innocence, social class distinctions, and the awe of myth and magic. Zobel currently lives and writes in Senegal, West Africa.*

The Gift

Of course there were sorcerers. Real ones. So many things happened which the old women and the old men blamed on sorcery, and not just to scare the children! But I didn't know any. Perhaps I didn't know where to look. In any case, I had never come across any proof that a particular person was endowed with supernatural powers. No matter how often people reminded me that, by day, sorcerers seemed like anyone else, that their evil activities blossomed forth only by night or in secret hideaways, I was still not convinced. I saw no one whose appearance or behavior seemed to fit the image I had formed from fables we children heard during the vigil for the dead or from the many ghost stories passed from person to person throughout the countryside and in which we loved to steep our imaginations.

No one, that is to say, until I discovered Monsieur Atis. Perhaps "discovered" is not the right word. Monsieur Atis was someone I had known as long as I can remember, who was there as soon as I began exploring the world around me and recognizing what I saw: grown-ups, things, trees; Monsieur Walter who made the bread, Madame Walter who ran the bakery shop; Mademoiselle Choutte who made coconut macaroons on Saturday night and Sunday afternoon; the wheelwright and his apprentice who, both armed with long tongs, placed a huge, red-hot hoop of iron around a wooden wheel, not quite so large, and then splashed it with cold water so that it tightened fast about the wood, and the whole thing became a beautiful wagon wheel, which I would have liked to roll about until the carter came to fetch it. And the carpenter who seemed to enjoy making corkscrew shavings, blonde or mahogany, like the hair on little girls in books. And the mango trees! Those on town property whose fruit we could gather from the ground or even pick whenever we liked, and those which belonged to Monsieur Tertulien or Madame Zizine, whose fruit had to be gathered on the run when it was ripe enough to be blown down by the wind. And then there were the animals, the insects, and also the plants, those which were sweet to chew on, and those which were poison. And the tasty wild fruit.

All those things, all those rules of living, all that knowledge which we acquired so effortlessly, day by day.

It was just this way that I came to know Monsieur Atis. His trade was the most solitary of all. Even more solitary than that of the shoemaker, who, while beating the leather on the bottom of an old clothes iron laid on his knee, or while tugging on the greased thread, liked to laugh and chat with those who came to sit in his shop.

But Monsieur Atis could neither talk nor even look up from his task. In addition, he had one eye riveted, so to speak, to his work by means of a strange black device with a glass lens, which he wore like a monocle.

With delicate tweezers, leaning over a stand covered with small instruments, he adjusted the dainty spoked wheels of the clocks which no longer ticked until he had brought them back to life. No one else in town had this power, this magic skill, but there was no need for him to hide, to live under cover of darkness. He worked in broad daylight, in sight of passersby, of anyone, or all alone. That was what delighted me about him. To me, Monsieur Atis himself did not seem to belong to exactly the same race as the others in town — and yet he had been born here like anyone else, like the trees which grew here, and had never been away.

He did not have fancy clothes, but was always clean-shaven. (One could even watch him shave every morning in front of a little mirror, the kind the Syrian peddlers sell, hooked onto his half-open door.) He fixed his woolly hair by applying a great deal of vaseline and parting it down the middle with determined brush strokes. He always wore a clean shirt and hemp sandals on his feet.

He certainly wasn't rich; his wife brought bread, gasoline, rice, lard, and salt cod on credit, like all the "unfortunates" of the town; and though the house he lived in belonged to him, it was actually no more than a wooden shack, like all the others that clustered humbly at the bottom of the village and whose courtyards lay next to the cane fields which dominated our lives.

So he was not rich, but he enjoyed as much prestige as those who had two-story houses at the top of the town: Monsieur Aristide, for instance, a mulatto who owned a huge estate at Morne Régal and ran a café right opposite the church where the plantation managers came to play pool, along with the tax collector, my schoolmaster, and the foremen at the factory. Even the white plantation owners brought Monsieur Atis their watches to repair.

No, certainly not rich, but the watches of every size, of every description, which adorned the wall behind his workbench, and the alarm clocks lined up on the shelves above created a marvelous world in which he was master, and into which I had managed to penetrate.

Since then, I have lived in constant awe of Monsieur Atis. His craft seemed to me a calm, honest, and unpretentious form of magic of the most authentic and convincing sort. And because I have never been able to love anything whatever without showing it, he became aware of my devotion and, in return, considered me one of the most polite, helpful, and perhaps most intelligent children in town.

I was the only one whom he entrusted occasionally with a watch, nicely packed in a small box, to deliver to a client who had forgotten to fetch it Saturday night or Sunday after Mass.

"Make sure he sees the bill right on top, and wait."

Sometimes I collected money, but more often I was told, "Thank Monsieur Atis for me and say that I'll be around tomorrow to settle up with him."

Then I would suffer the humiliating sensation of having failed in my mission.

When I began, he would remind me again and again, "Whatever you do, don't drop it."

After hearing this so often, I soon understood that a watch is like a fresh egg, with one difference: if it falls, the case may not break, but everything inside will die quietly, instead of splashing dramatically over the ground like the yolk and white of an egg.

I could feel the watch ticking in my hand, through its wrappings, like the heart of a frightened little bird captured or rescued on a windy day. I had learned to make my own heart beat fall into rhythm with it. In the end, Monsieur Atis' apprehensions subsided, and when he gave me a watch to deliver, he reminded me instead to persuade the client that he was badly in need of money.

Eventually, too, my admiration for Monsieur Atis led to a taste, a passion, for watches. A classic passion, nourished by the pain of never possessing the desired object.

But how was it that given the special brand of ethics, defiant of all morality and resistant to spankings, by which we children never hesitated to appropriate anything that seemed necessary to our games, our fancy — and that we dared not ask from the grown-ups for fear of being rebuffed — how was it that I never felt tempted to steal even a small watch from Monsieur Atis? Whether it was the purity of my feelings for him, or a result of the magic powers which I had conferred upon Monsieur Atis, the idea never crossed my mind.

I think, on the contrary, that if by some miracle I had acquired a watch, I would have entrusted it to him.

My greatest delight at that time was the catalogue he had given me.

This catalogue had become for me a kind of imaginary world. An enchanted world which I felt as though I had created myself. I knew it by heart; I could describe every watch illustrated in it. There were also alarm clocks, chimes, mantelpiece ornaments, and barometers, but it was only the watches, pocket watches, wrist-watches, and chronometers that interested me. To enter this enchanged world, all I had to do was open the catalogue. It was even more intriguing to me than Monsieur Atis' workshop. I could recite the contents with my eyes closed, pointing out that such and such a model was in stainless steel, with ten rubies, a phosphorescent face, and a five-year guarantee, and that another was wafer thin, with twelve rubies, and waterproof.

Of course I had my favorites.

I could have chosen a gold one, with a ten-year guarantee and a case. Three or four of these were scattered through the catalogue, but I had grouped them together into a kind of glittering constellation which did not tempt me the least bit. The one I had chosen, and which to me was worth the whole catalogue, was a little silver watch with a guilloche pattern (I did not know what this meant, but felt it must be pretty) with a gold emblem, thirty-five millimeters in diameter, twelve rubies, a five-year guarantee, and a silver chain. That was the one I intended to buy when I grew up, and never had I desired anything so ardently, or with such conviction.

The picture of it in the catalogue so dominated my mind that the watch somehow reserved a place in the inevitable chain of events which the future held in store for me.

It was Monsieur Atis himself who put an end to this ambition — but in the most extraordinary way. The more I knew him, in fact, the more reasons I had for considering him a magician.

One day, for no particular reason — it was neither my birthday, nor Christmas, nor New Year's Day — Monsieur Atis gave me a watch.

"Here, this is for you. Do you like it?"

If at that very moment he had waved his hand and turned a toad to marble, I wouldn't have been more surprised.

I was seized with panic. With the watch clutched tightly in my fist, I ran off as though I had just committed a theft, or were being pursued by an evil spirit, and did not stop until I reached my mother's hut, where I quickly hid it in the rag stuffing of my mattress.

All day I kept the secret to myself, but that evening I went to meet my mother on her way home from work, far outside the town. As soon as I saw her with her big bamboo basket on her head, I ran up shouting, "I have a watch! Monsieur Atis gave me a watch!" I was out of breath and could say no more.

"What's the matter?" asked my mother, who hadn't understood any of my shouting.

"A watch! I have a watch! Monsieur Atis gave it to me."

My mother seemed to find my excitement extremely childish. At first she thought I had some kind of bad news.

But when I showed it to her, back in our hut, and she realized it was a beautiful watch, ticking away energetically and insistently, she exclaimed, "But it's a man's watch! It's a good one. And you want me to believe Monsieur Atis gave it to you?"

I couldn't possibly convince her. Without another word, she took the watch, grabbed me by the hand and marched off to Monsieur Atis' shop.

"Oh, yes," Monsieur Atis assured her, "I gave it to him. How else, after all. . . . The child is so well behaved, so honest and thoughtful! It's a very old watch."

"Just what I thought," said my mother. "When he told me you gave it to him, I realized it must be an old watch that doesn't work any more."

"Oh, no! It works very well," said Monsieur Atis. "I gave him the key to wind it up. But you should buy him a chain for it. Just a little silver chain. . . . The works are excellent, you know. Better than watches nowadays. Why, I don't expect to see the day it stops working!"

My mother seemed dumbfounded, both with surprise and delight. Monsieur Atis began to laugh.

"It works, don't worry, otherwise I would never have given it to him. It will go on working as long as I go on living."

To show her gratitude, my mother promised, "I'll hide it away. He won't have it until he's grown up. A watch like that isn't a toy!"

I was delighted that my mother shared my joy. I was grateful to her for appropriating the watch and hiding it for me. She did not even talk about it, for fear of arousing jealousy.

My catalogue immediately lost its magic; the photographs of watches lost their haunting effect upon me. Even the little silver watch with the guilloche pattern now left me cold. I no longer spent hours perusing the pictures.

Instead, my watch, hidden away where I could not find it, became an obsession with me, all the more powerful in that I had hardly looked at it or handled it when Monsieur Atis had given it to me. In my mind it was like a place or a person I had once known and would like to see again.

So one day, I started looking. It shouldn't be hard to find; our bare, cramped hut had few corners in which to hide things: the angles of the beams, the heap of crates and planks used as a frame for the bed, the army of little tin cans gathered here and there. The search was soon over.

Only the big basket was left, the wicker hamper which served both as a trunk and a strongbox, for linen, Sunday clothes, jewels, everything that must be cared for and treasured. The watch was there, simply tucked away beneath a lace petticoat which my mother wore with her mauve sateen dress for Mass on New Year's Day, for the funerals of local dignitaries, and (this had happened once) when she had to hold a friend's baby at its baptism.

It was in a cardboard box — a flat box which had once held medicine — its key tied on with a crude bit of string, among the religious medals, the offering card for the church, and a necklace of garnet-colored glass with a gilt fastener, no doubt my mother's most precious belongings. It was as though I saw it for the first time, and yet I recognized it. It was not very shiny, silver probably, worn to a smooth patina, with a locomotive engraved on the back, and on the front, its fascinating white enamel face with handsome blue numerals each set apart from the next by a gold dot. My first move was to take the key, open the case, and wind the movement, as I had seen Monsieur Atis do so many times. And the watch began to palpitate with a powerful, discreet rhythm, like a pulse which began in the very bowels of the earth. I handled it with a thousand loving gestures — a kind of adoration, of improvised worship. But at last I had to bring myself to put it away, exactly as I had found it, so as not to leave any traces of my intrusion.

The watch was no longer mentioned. Neither by Monsieur Atis, nor my mother. Nor by me, of course. But two or three times a week, I would slip into the hut, open the hamper, take out the watch, wind it, listen to it, put it in my pocket, look at the time. I would put it on the table and stare at the hands until they marked a new hour. I would have liked to polish it with lemon juice and ashes, as I had seen people do with rings, chains, and silver medals. Or better still, if only I had been able to obtain some of the liquid which Monsieur Atis used on a flannel rag! But it was better to avoid anything which might betray me.

After a while, I lost my scruples; the watch belonged to me, I was only looking at it, handling it gently, all alone, putting it carefully back in place, every time. I was doing no harm.

I would be lying, however, if I pretended that I never once wanted to take it out with me, to show it off. But I knew very well that to yield to the temptation was to give away my secret, to expose myself to a dreadful spanking, and to risk not seeing the watch again for a long time, since it would be hidden away more carefully than ever.

Soon the first Sunday of the local festival was at hand. For the occasion, my mother gave me two pennies. I was to pay my second annual visit to my godfather (the first took place on New Year's Day) and this would mean as much as ten pennies for me. In one way or another, and without asking — for I really was a well-brought-up child who did not ask grown-ups for anything, certainly not for money — in one way or another, I managed to collect about a franc to treat myself to a few of the amusements that were not free, especially a few rides on the merry-go-round.

This first Sunday of the festival was the occasion I had waited for. Just this once — still unbeknown to my mother — I would take my watch out with me. The truth was, this time the temptation had been so great that my scruples and fears gave way; I could not resist.

That Sunday I waited until my mother had returned from Mass and had put the scarf which she had worn that morning back in the hamper. I was then almost certain that she would not open the hamper again until the following Sunday. As soon as she had left to go to market, I pulled out the watch, wound it up, and put it in my pocket.

But disobedient children never get away with anything; they haven't a chance!

In the crowd near the merry-go-round, where the horses flashed by to the roar of drums and the clarinet, I took out my watch to look at the time, rather proud but pretending to be casual. Someone passing behind me jostled my elbow; the watch flew out of my hands and fell on the pavement. I picked it up so quickly that it might not have fallen at all. But it had stopped ticking. I shook it, pressed it again to my ear, looking at it as though it were a person who has lost consciousness but will revive at any moment. I moved away from the crowds, taking the watch off by itself the way one would isolate someone who suddenly felt faint; I opened it, wound it; the key turned and turned, but the watch remained still. What could I do?

I thought of putting it back where it came from. My mother would never notice. At least not for a long time. Yes, of course, but it was sadness much more than the fear of being discovered that hung over me now. There was only one solution: to take the watch to Monsieur Atis, to tell him that it had stopped working for no particular reason. Perhaps because it hadn't been used for a long time, one never knew. Then he would repair it; I would put it back in its hiding place and not touch it again. Since my mother never went to Monsieur Atis' shop, there was every chance that she would never find out.

Heartened by this thought, I set out resolutely to see Monsieur Atis.

In spite of my preoccupied state of mind, as soon as I came into town I noticed a certain commotion in the streets. People ahead of me were running. I even thought I heard shouts.

There was a crowd milling in front of Monsieur Atis' house. It was Madame Atis who was shouting. Neighbors were rushing into the house, clutching bouquets of those leaves whose odor is used to revive women when they succumb to heat prostration on Good Friday, following the Way of the Cross. Others brought vials of medicine. They came out of the house wearing the expressions of passengers who arrive at a bus stop just as the bus has left. Madame Atis' lamentations kept bringing more people to the scene.

Monsieur Atis was dead.

"His heart," said someone.

"All of a sudden," said someone else, "at about four o'clock."

I took out my watch.

Just as I thought: it had stopped at exactly four o'clock.

Translated from the French
by Merloyd Lawrence

ST. LUCIA

DEREK WALCOTT

Derek Walcott (1930–) was born in St. Lucia (Hewanora is its Amerindian name) — the Caribbean island which is often called the "Helen of the Antilles" because it was colonized and fought over many times by England and France. Walcott as poet, dramatist, and essayist is the recipient of the 1992 Nobel Prize for literature. Although the Nobel prize expanded Walcott's position in literary circles, he was already one of the most internationally known and accomplished poets of the Caribbean. He has published three collections of plays and more than a dozen books of poems, most recently, Derek Walcott: Poems 1965–1980 *(1992). He currently teaches creative writing at Boston University.*

From a European critical perspective Walcott is considered a classical poet. In much of his writing, however, Walcott transforms the style of the classical epic to celebrate West Indian peasant cultures and to denounce the tragedy involved in the historical making of the West Indies. Despite his commanding knowledge and usage of the European canon, Walcott equally celebrates the folk ethos and sentiments of the common island people.

Sea Grapes

That sail which leans on light,
tired of islands,
a schooner beating up the Caribbean

for home, could be Odysseus,°
home-bound on the Aegean;   5
that father and husband's

longing, under gnarled sour grapes, is
like the adulterer hearing Nausicaa's° name
in every gull's outcry.

Odysseus: the hero of the famous epic poem of ancient Greece (the *Odyssey*), attributed to Homer, in which is described the ten years' journey of Odysseus (Ulysses) on his way home to Ithaca after the fall of Troy
Nausicaa: a major character in the *Odyssey*, with whom Odysseus had a love affair

This brings nobody peace. The ancient war   10
between obsession and responsibility
will never finish and has been the same

for the sea-wanderer or the one on shore
now wriggling on his sandals to walk home,
since Troy sighed its last flame,   15

and the blind giant's boulder heaved the trough
from whose groundswell the great hexameters come
to the conclusions of exhausted surf.

The classics can console. But not enough.

The Swamp

Gnawing the highway's edges, its black mouth
Hums quietly: 'Home, come home . . . '

Behind its viscous breath the very word 'growth'
Grows fungi, rot;
White mottling its root.   5

More dreaded
Than canebrake,° quarry, or sun-shocked gully-bed
Its horrors held Hemingway's hero rooted
To sure, clear shallows.

It begins nothing. Limbo of cracker convicts, Negroes.   10
Its black mood
Each sunset takes a smear of your life's blood.

Fearful, original sinuosities! Each mangrove sapling
Serpentlike, its roots obscene
As a six-fingered hand,   15

Conceals within its clutch the mossbacked toad,
Toadstools, the potent ginger-lily,
Petals of blood,

The speckled vulva of the tiger-orchid;
Outlandish phalloi   20
Haunting the travellers of its one road.

Deep, deeper than sleep
Like death,
Too rich in its decrescence, too close of breath,

canebrake: an access road in the cane field

In the fast-filling night, note   25
How the last bird drinks darkness with its throat,
How the wild saplings slip

Backward to darkness, go black
With widening amnesia, take the edge
Of nothing to them slowly, merge   30

Limb, tongue and sinew into a knot
Like chaos, like the road
Ahead.

The Castaway

The starved eye devours the seascape for the morsel
Of a sail.

The horizon threads it infinitely.

Action breeds frenzy. I lie,
Sailing the ribbed shadow of a palm,   5
Afraid lest my own footprints multiply.

Blowing sand, thin as smoke,
Bored, shifts its dunes.
The surf tires of its castles like a child.

The salt green vine with yellow trumpet-flower,   10
A net, inches across nothing.
Nothing: the rage with which the sandfly's head is filled.

Pleasures of an old man:
Morning: contemplative evacuation, considering
The dried leaf, nature's plan.   15

In the sun, the dog's faeces
Crusts, whitens like coral.
We end in earth, from earth began.
In our own entrails, genesis.

If I listen I can hear the polyp build,   20
The silence thwanged by two waves of the sea.
Cracking a sea-louse, I make thunder split.

Godlike, annihilating godhead, art
And self, I abandon
Dead metaphors: the almond's leaf-like heart,   25

The ripe brain rotting like a yellow nut
Hatching
Its babel of sea-lice, sandfly and maggot,

That green wine bottle's gospel choked with sand,
Labelled, a wrecked ship,   30
Clenched seawood nailed and white as a man's hand.

TRINIDAD

V. S. NAIPAUL

V. S. Naipaul (1932–) was born in Trinidad of a Brahman family whose grandparents came from India. Naipaul developed journalistic and literary talents at an early age. Disenchanted with life and cultures in Trinidad, he emigrated to England where he attended Oxford University. Naipaul's extensive travels in India, Africa, South America, the United States, and the Caribbean have been incorporated into much of his writing. Naipaul is one of the most successful contemporary writers; his short stories, novels, and nonfiction books and articles are too numerous to list. However, among his major novels are A House for Mr. Biswas *(1961),* Mr. Stone and the Knight Companion *(1963), and* The Mimic Men *(1967). Naipaul's early writing consisted of satire and humor.*

The selection here is from Naipaul's first published novel, The Mystic Masseur. *A satire about aspects of East Indian life in Trinidad,* The Mystic Masseur *centers on the success of Ganesh Ramsumair and his becoming a masseur who is known throughout the island for his 'mysticism' and for being all things to all men. Naipaul's satire about 'mystic masseurs' and the Trinidadian educational system is obvious throughout the novel. Naipaul is critical of Ganesh and his need to be validated by English culture.*

from **The Mystic Masseur**

The Quarrel with Ramlogan

'I suppose,' Ganesh wrote in *The Years of Guilt*, 'I had always, from the first day I stepped into Shri Ramlogan's shop, considered it as settled that I was going to marry his daughter. I never questioned it. It all seemed preordained.'

What happened was this.

One day when Ganesh called Ramlogan was wearing a clean shirt. Also, he looked freshly washed, his hair looked freshly oiled; and his movements were silent and deliberate, as though he were doing a *puja.*°

puja: a Hindu prayer ceremony

He dragged up the small bench from the corner and placed it near the table; then sat on it and watched Ganesh eat, all without saying a word. First he looked at Ganesh's face, then at Ganesh's plate, and there his gaze rested until Ganesh had eaten the last handful of rice.

'Your belly full, sahib?'°

'Yes, my belly full.' Ganesh wiped his plate clean with an extended index finger.

'It must be hard for you, sahib, now that your father dead.'

Ganesh licked his finger. 'I don't really miss him, you know.'

'No, sahib, don't tell me. I *know* is hard for you. Supposing, just supposing — I just putting this up to you as a superstition, sahib — but just supposing you did want to get married, it have nobody at all to fix up things for you.'

'I don't even know if I want to get married.' Ganesh rose from the table, rubbing his belly until he belched his appreciation of Ramlogan's food.

Ramlogan rearranged the roses in the vase. 'Still, you is a educated man, and you could take care of yourself. Not like me, sahib. Since I was five I been working, with nobody looking after me. Still, all that do something for me. Guess what it do for me, sahib.'

'Can't guess. Tell me what it do.'

'It give me cha'acter and sensa values, sahib. That's what it give me. Cha'acter and sensa values.'

Ganesh took the brass jar of water from the table and went to the Demerara window to wash his hands and gargle.

Ramlogan was smoothing out the oilcloth with both hands and dusting away some crumbs, mere specks. 'I know,' he said apologetically, 'that for a man like you, educated and reading books night and day, shopkeeping is a low thing. But I don't care what people think. You, sahib, answer me this as a educated man: you does let other people worry you?'

Ganesh, gargling, thought at once of Miller and the row at the school in Port of Spain, but when he spat out the water into the yard he said, 'Nah. I don't care what people say.'

Ramlogan pounded across the floor and took the brass jar from Ganesh. 'I go put this away, sahib. You sit down in the hammock. Ooops! Let me dust it for you first.'

When he had seated Ganesh, Ramlogan started to walk up and down in front of the hammock.

'People can't harm me,' he said, holding his hands at his back. 'All right, people don't like me. All right, they stop coming to my shop. That harm me? That change my cha'acter? I just go to San Fernando and open a little stall in the market. No, don't stop me, sahib. Is exactly what I would do. Take a stall in the market. And what happen? Tell me, what happen?'

sahib: a title of respect, similar to *sir* or *mister*

Ganesh belched again, softly.

'What happen?' Ramlogan gave a short crooked laugh. 'Bam! In five years I have a whole chain of grocery shop. Who laughing then? Then you go see them coming round and begging, "Mr Ramlogan" — that's what it go be then, you know: *Mister* Ramlogan — "Mr Ramlogan, gimme this, gimme that, Mr Ramlogan." Begging me to go up for elections and a hundred and one stupid things.'

Ganesh said, 'You ain't have to start opening stall in San Fernando market now, thank God.'

'That is it, sahib. Just just as you say. Is all God work. Count my property now. Is true I is illiterate, but you just sit down in that hammock and count my property.'

Ramlogan was walking and talking with such unusual energy that the sweat broke and shone on his forehead. Suddenly he halted and stood directly in front of Ganesh. He took away his hands from behind his back and started to count off his fingers. 'Two acres near Chaguanas. Good land, too. Ten acres in Penal. You never know when I could scrape together enough to make the drillers put a oil-well there. A house in Fuente Grove. Not much, but is something. Two three houses in Siparia. Add up all that and you find you looking at a man worth about twelve thousand dollars, cool cool.'

Ramlogan passed his hand over his forehead and behind his neck. 'I know is hard to believe, sahib. But is the gospel truth. I think is a good idea, sahib, for you to married Leela.'

'All right,' Ganesh said.

He never saw Leela again until the night of their wedding, and both he and Ramlogan pretended he had never seen her at all, because they were both good Hindus and knew it was wrong for a man to see his wife before marriage.

He still had to go to Ramlogan's, to make arrangements for the wedding, but he remained in the shop itself and never went to the back room.

'You is not like Soomintra damn fool of a husband,' Ramlogan told him. 'You is a modern man and you must have a modern wedding.'

So he didn't send the messenger around to give the saffron-dyed rice to friends and relations and announce the wedding. 'That old-fashion,' he said. He wanted printed invitations on scalloped and gilt-edged cards. 'And we must have nice wordings, sahib.'

'But you can't have nice wordings on a thing like a invitation.'

'You is the educated man, sahib. You could think of some.'

'R.S.V.P.?'

'What that mean?'

'It don't mean nothing, but it nice to have it.'

'Let we have it then, man, sahib! You is a modern man, and too besides, it sound as pretty wordings.'

Ganesh himself went to San Fernando to get the cards printed. The printer's shop was, at first sight, a little disappointing. It looked black and bleak and seemed to be manned only by a thin youth in ragged khaki shorts who whistled as he operated the hand-press. But when Ganesh saw the cards go in blank and come out with his prose miraculously transformed into all the authority of type, he was struck with something like awe. He stayed to watch the boy set up a cinema hand-bill. The boy, whistling without intermission, ignored Ganesh altogether.

'Is on this sort of machine they does print books?' Ganesh asked.

'What else you think it make for?'

'You print any good books lately?'

The boy dabbed some ink on the roller. 'You ever hear of Trinidad people writing books?'

'*I* writing a book.'

The boy spat into a bin full of ink-stained paper. 'This must be a funny sort of shop, you know. The number of people who come in here and ask me to print the books they writing in invisible ink, man!'

'What you name?'

'Basdeo.'

'All right, Basdeo, boy. The day go come when I go send you a book to print.'

'Sure, man. Sure. You write it and I print it.'

Ganesh didn't think he liked Basdeo's Hollywood manner, and he instantly regretted what he had said. But so far as this business of writing books was concerned, he seemed to have no will: it was the second time he had committed himself. It all seemed pre-ordained.

'Yes, they is pretty invitation cards,' Ramlogan said, but there was no joy in his voice.

'But what happen now to make your face long long as mango?'

'Education, sahib, is one hell of a thing. When you is a poor illiterate man like me, all sort of people does want to take advantage on you.'

Ramlogan began to cry. 'Right now, right right now, as you sitting down on that bench there and I sitting down on this stool behind my shop counter, looking at these pretty pretty cards, you wouldn't believe what people trying to do to me. Right now it have a man in Siparia trying to rob my two house there, all because I can't read, and the people in Penal behaving in a funny way.'

'What they doing so?'

'Ah, sahib. That is just like you. I know you want to help me, but is too late now. All sort of paper with fine fine writing they did make me sign and everything, and now — now everything lost.'

Ganesh had not seen Ramlogan cry so much since the funeral. He said, 'Well, look. If is the dowry you worried about, you could stop. I don't want a big dowry.'

'Is the shame, sahib, that eating me up. You know how with these Hindu weddings everybody does know how much the boy get from the girl father. When, the morning after the wedding the boy sit down and they give him a plate of kedgeree,° with the girl father having to give money and keep on giving until the boy eat the kedgeree, everybody go see what I give you, and they go say, "Look, Ramlogan marrying off his second and best daughter to a boy with a college education, and this is all the man giving." Is that what eating me up, sahib. I know that for you, educated and reading books night and day, it wouldn't mean much, but for me, sahib, what about my cha'acter and sensa values?'

'You must stop crying and listen. When it come to eating the kedgeree, I go eat quick, not to shame you. Not too quick, because that would make people think you poor as a church-rat. But I wouldn't take much from you.'

Ramlogan smiled through his tears. 'Is just like you, sahib, just what I did expect from you. I wish Leela did see you and then she woulda know what sort of man I choose for she husband.'

'I wish I did see Leela too.'

'Smatterer fact, sahib, I know it have some modern people nowadays who don't even like waiting for money before they eat the kedgeree.'

'But is the custom, man.'

'Yes, sahib, the custom. But still I think is a disgrace in these modern times. Now, if it was *I* was getting married, I wouldn't want any dowry and I woulda say, "To hell with the kedgeree, man."'

As soon as the invitations were out Ganesh had to stop visiting Ramlogan altogether, but he wasn't alone in his house for long. Dozens of women descended on him with their children. He had no idea who most of them were; sometimes he recognized a face and found it hard to believe that the woman with the children hanging about her was the same cousin who was only a child herself when he first went to Port of Spain.

The children treated Ganesh with contempt.

A small boy with a running nose said to him one day, 'They tell me is you who getting married.'

'Yes, is me.'

The boy said, 'Ahaha!' and ran away laughing and jeering.

The boy's mother said, 'Is something we have to face these days. The children getting modern.'

Then one day Ganesh discovered his aunt among the women, she who had been one of the principal mourners at his father's funeral. He learnt that she had not only arranged everything then, but had also paid for it all. When Ganesh offered to pay back the money she became annoyed and told him not to be stupid.

kedgeree: an Asian Indian dish of rice, peas, onions, and condiments

'This life is a funny thing, eh,' she said. 'One day somebody dead and you cry. Two days later somebody married, and then you laugh. Oh, Ganeshwa boy, at a time like this you want your own family around you, but what family you have? Your father, he dead; your mother, she dead too.'

She was so moved she couldn't cry; and for the first time Ganesh realized what a big thing his marriage was.

Ganesh thought it almost a miracle that so many people could live happily in one small house without any sort of organization. They had left him the bedroom, but they swarmed over the rest of the house and managed as best they could. First they had made it into an extended picnic site; then they had made it into a cramped camping site. But they looked happy enough and Ganesh presently discovered that the anarchy was only apparent. Of the dozens of women who wandered freely about the house there was one, tall and silent, whom he had learnt to call King George. It might have been her real name for all he knew: he had never seen her before. King George ruled the house.

'King George got a hand,' his aunt said.

'A hand?'

'She got a hand for sharing things out. Give King George a little penny cake and give she twelve children to share it out to, and you could bet your bottom dollar that King George share it fair and square.'

'You know she, then?'

'Know she! Is I who take up King George. Mark you, I think I was very lucky coming across she. Now I take she everywhere with me.'

'She related to us?'

'You could say so. Phulbassia is a sort of cousin to King George and you is a sort of cousin to Phulbassia.'

The aunt belched, not the polite after-dinner belch, but a long, stuttering thing. 'Is the wind,' she explained without apology. 'It have a long time now — since your father dead, come to think of it — I suffering from this wind.'

'You see a doctor?'

'Doctor? They does only make up things. One of them tell me — you know what? — that I have a lazy liver. Is something I asking myself a long time now: how a liver could be lazy, eh?'

She belched again, said, 'You see?' and rubbed her hands over her breasts.

Ganesh thought of this aunt as Lady Belcher and then as The Great Belcher. In a few days she had a devastating effect on the other women in the house. They all began belching and rubbing their breasts and complaining about the wind. All except King George.

Ganesh was glad when the time came for him to be anointed with saffron. For those days he was confined to his room, where his father's body had lain that night, and where now The Great Belcher, King George, and a few other anonymous women gathered to rub him down. When they left the room they sang Hindi wedding songs of a most pessimistic nature, and Ganesh wondered how Leela was putting up with her own seclusion and anointing.

All day long he remained in his room, consoling himself with *The Science of Thought Review*. He read through all the numbers Mr Stewart had given him, some of them many times over. All day he heard the children romping, squealing, and being beaten; the mothers beating, shouting, and thumping about on the floor.

On the day before the wedding, when the women had come in to rub him down for the last time, he asked The Great Belcher, 'I never think about it before, but what those people outside eating? Who paying for it?'

'You.'

He almost sat up in bed, but King George's strong arm kept him down.

'Ramlogan did say that we mustn't get you worried about that,' The Great Belcher said. 'He say your head hot with enough worries already. But King George looking after everything. She got a account with Ramlogan. He go settle with you after the wedding.'

'Oh God! I ain't even married the man daughter yet, and already he start!'

Fourways was nearly as excited at the wedding as it had been at the funeral. Hundreds of people, from Fourways and elsewhere, were fed at Ramlogan's. There were dancers, drummers, and singers, for those who were not interested in the details of the night-long ceremony. The yard behind Ramlogan's shop was beautifully illuminated with all sorts of lights, except electric ones; and the decorations — mainly fruit hanging from coconut-palm arches — were pleasing. All this for Ganesh, and Ganesh felt it and was pleased. The thought of marriage had at first embarrassed him, then, when he spoke with his aunt, awed him; now he was simply thrilled.

All through the ceremony he had to pretend, with everyone else, that he had never seen Leela. She sat at his side veiled from head to toe, until the blanket was thrown over them and he unveiled her face. In the mellow light under the pink blanket she was as a stranger. She was no longer the giggling girl simpering behind the lace curtains. Already she looked chastened and impassive, a good Hindu wife.

Shortly afterwards it was over, and they were man and wife. Leela was taken away and Ganesh was left alone to face the kedgeree-eating ceremony the next morning.

Still in all his bridegroom's regalia, satin robes, and tasselled crown, he sat down on some blankets in the yard, before the plate of kedgeree. It looked white and unpalatable, and he knew it would be easy to resist any temptation to touch it.

Ramlogan was the first to offer money to induce Ganesh to eat. He was a little haggard after staying awake all night, but he looked pleased and happy enough when he placed five twenty-dollar bills in the brass plate next to the kedgeree. He stepped back, folded his arms, looked from the money to Ganesh to the small group standing by, and smiled.

He stood smiling for nearly two minutes; but Ganesh didn't even look at the kedgeree.

'Give the boy money, man,' Ramlogan cried to the people around. 'Give him money, man. Come on, don't act as if you is all poor poor as church-rat.' He moved among them, laughing, and rallying them. Some put down small amounts in the brass plate.

Still Ganesh sat, serene and aloof, like an over-dressed Buddha.

A little crowd began to gather.

'The boy have sense, man.' Anxiety broke into Ramlogan's voice. 'When you think a college education is these days?'

He put down another hundred dollars. 'Eat, boy, eat it up. I don't want you to starve. Not yet, anyway.' He laughed, but no one laughed with him.

Ganesh didn't eat.

He heard a man saying, 'Well, this thing was bound to happen some day.'

People said, 'Come on, Ramlogan. Give the boy money, man. What you think he sitting down there for? To take out his photo?'

Ramlogan gave a short, forced laugh, and lost his temper. 'If he think he going to get any more money from me he damn well mistaken. Let him don't eat. Think I care if he starve? Think I care?'

He walked away.

The crowd grew bigger; the laughter grew louder.

Ramlogan came back and the crowd cheered him.

He put down two hundred dollars on the brass plate and, before he rose, whispered to Ganesh, 'Remember your promise, sahib. Eat, boy; eat, son; eat, sahib; eat, pundit sahib. I beg you, eat.'

A man shouted, 'No! I not going to eat!'

Ramlogan stood up and turned around. 'You, haul your tail away from here quick, quick, before I break it up for you. Don't meddle in what don't concern you.'

The crowd roared.

Ramlogan bent down again to whisper. 'You see, sahib, how you making me shame.' This time his whisper promised tears. 'You see, sahib, what you doing to my cha'acter and sensa values.'

Ganesh didn't move.

The crowd was beginning to treat him like a hero.

In the end Ganesh got from Ramlogan: a cow and a heifer, fifteen hundred dollars in cash, and a house in Fuente Grove. Ramlogan also cancelled the bill for the food he had sent to Ganesh's house.

The ceremony ended at about nine in the morning; but Ramlogan was sweating long before then.

'The boy and I was only having a joke,' he said again and again at the end. 'He done know long time now what I was going to give him. We was only making joke, you know.'

Ganesh returned home after the wedding. It would be three days before Leela could come to live with him and in that time The Great Belcher tried to restore order to the house. Most of the guests had left as suddenly as they had arrived; though from time to time Ganesh still saw a straggler who wandered about the house and ate.

'King George gone to Arima yesterday,' The Great Belcher told him. 'Somebody dead there yesterday. I going tomorrow myself, but I send King George ahead to arrange everything.'

Then she decided to give Ganesh the facts of life.

'These modern girls is hell self,' she said. 'And from what I see and hear, this Leela is a modern girl. Anyway, you got to make the best of what is yours.'

She paused to belch. 'All she want to make she straight as a arrow is a little blows every now and then.'

Ganesh said, 'You know, I think Ramlogan really vex with me now after the kedgeree business.'

'Wasn't a nice thing to do, but it serve Ramlogan right. When a man start taking over woman job, match-making, he deserve all he get.'

'But I go have to leave here now. You know Fuente Grove? It have a house there Ramlogan give me.'

'But what you want in a small outa the way place like that? All the work it have doing there is work in the canefield.'

'It ain't that I want to do.' Ganesh paused, and added hesitantly, 'I thinking of taking up massaging people.'

She laughed so much she belched. 'This wind, man, and then you — you want to kill me or what, boy? Massaging people! What you know about massaging people?'

'Pa was a good massager and I know all he did know.'

'But you must have a hand for that sort of thing. Think what go happen if any- and everybody start running round saying, "I thinking of taking up massaging people." It go have so much massagers in Trinidad they go have to start massaging one another.'

'I feel I have a hand for it. Just like King George.'

'She have her own sort of hand. She born that way.'

Ganesh told her about Leela's foot.

She twisted her mouth. 'It sound good. But a man like you should be doing something else. Bookwork, man.'

'I going to do that too.' And then it came out again. 'I thinking of writing some books.'

'Good thing. It have money in books, you know. I suppose the man who write the *Macdonald Farmer's Almanac* just peeling money. Why you don't try your hand at something like the *Napoleon Book of Fate*? I just *feel* you could do that sort of thing good.'

'People go want to buy that sort of book?'

'Is exactly what Trinidad want, boy. Take all the Indians in the towns. They ain't have any pundit or anything near them, you know. How they go know what to do and what not to do, when and not when? They just have to guess.'

Ganesh was thoughtful. 'Yes, is that self I go do. A little bit of massaging and a little bit of writing.'

'I know a boy who could make anything you write sell as hot cakes all over Trinidad. Let we say, you selling the book at two shillings, forty-eight cents. You give the boy six cents a book. Let we say now, you print four five thousand — '

'It make about two thousand dollars, but — wait, man! I ain't even write the book yet.'

'I know you, boy. Once you put your mind to it, you go write nice nice books.'

She belched.

As soon as Leela had come to live with Ganesh and the last guest had left the village, Ramlogan declared war on Ganesh and that very evening ran through Fourways crying out, chanting, his declaration. 'See how he rob me. Me with my wife dead, me now without children, me a poor widow. See how he forget everything I do for him. He forget all that I give him, he forget how I help burn his father, he forget all the help I give him. See how he rob me. See how he shame me. Watch me here now, so help me God, if I don't here and now do for the son of a bitch.'

Ganesh ordered Leela to bolt the doors and windows and put out the lights. He took one of his father's old walking-sticks and remained in the middle of the front room.

Leela began to cry. 'The man is my own father and here you is taking up big stick to beat him.'

Ganesh heard Ramlogan shouting from the road, 'Ganesh, you damn little piss-in-tail boy, you want property, eh? You know the only place you could take my property? You going to take it away on your chest, six foot of it.'

Ganesh said, 'Leela, in the bedroom it have a little copy-book. Go bring it. And it have a pencil in the table drawer. Bring that too.'

She brought the book and pencil and Ganesh wrote, *Carry away his property on my chest.* Below he wrote the date. He had no particular reason for doing this except that he was afraid and felt he had to do something.

Leela cried. 'You working magic on my own father!'

Ganesh said, 'Leela, why you getting 'fraid? We not staying in this place long. In a few days we moving to Fuente Grove. Nothing to 'fraid.'

Leela continued to cry and Ganesh loosened his leather belt and beat her.

She cried out, 'Oh God! Oh God! He go kill me today self!'

It was their first beating, a formal affair done without anger on Ganesh's part or resentment on Leela's; and although it formed no part of the marriage ceremony itself, it meant much to both of them. It meant that they had grown up and become independent. Ganesh had become a man; Leela a wife as privileged as any other big woman. Now she too would have tales to tell of her husband's beatings; and when she went home she would be able to look sad and sullen as every woman should.

The moment was precious.

Leela cried for a bit and said, 'Man, I really getting worried about Pa.'

This was another first: she had called him 'man.' There could be no doubt about it now: they were adults. Three days before Ganesh was hardly better than a boy, anxious and diffident. Now he had suddenly lost these qualities and he thought, 'My father was right. I shoulda get married long before now.'

Leela said, 'Man, I getting really worried about Pa. Tonight he not going to do you anything. He just go shout a lot and go away, but he won't forget you. I see him horsewhip a man in Penal really bad one time.'

They heard Ramlogan shouting from the road, 'Ganesh, this is the last time I warning you.'

Leela said, 'Man, you must do something to make Pa feel nice. Otherwise I don't know.'

Ramlogan's shout sounded hoarse now. 'Ganesh, tonight self I sharpening up a cutlass for you. I make up my mind to send you to hospital and go to jail for you. Look out, I warning you.'

And then, as Leela had said, Ramlogan went away.

The next morning, after Ganesh had done his *puja* and eaten the first meal that Leela had cooked for him, he said, 'Leela, you got any pictures of your father?'

She was sitting at the kitchen table, cleaning rice for the midday meal. 'Why you want it for?' she asked with alarm.

'You forgetting yourself, girl. Somebody make you a policeman now to ask me question? Is a old picture?'

Leela wept over the rice. 'Not so old, man. Two three years now Pa did go to San Fernando and Chong take out a photo of Pa by hisself and another one with Pa and Soomintra and me. Just before Soomintra did get married. They was pretty photos. Paintings behind and plants in front.'

'I just want a picture of your father. What I don't want is your tears.'

He followed her to the bedroom, and while he put on his town clothes — khaki trousers, blue shirt, brown hat, brown shoes — Leela pulled out her suitcase, an Anchor Cigarettes coupons-gift, from under the bed and looked for the photograph.

'Gimme,' he said, when she found it, and snatched it away. 'This go settle your father.'

She ran after him to the steps. 'Where you going, man?'

'Leela, you know, for a girl who ain't married three days yet you too damn fast.'

He had to pass Ramlogan's shop. He took care to swing his father's walking stick, and behaved as though the shop didn't exist.

And sure enough, he heard Ramlogan calling out, 'Ganesh, you playing man this morning, eh? Swinging walking-stick as if you is some master-stickman. But, boy, when I get after you, you not going to run fast enough.'

Ganesh walked past without a word.

Leela confessed later that she had gone to the shop that morning to warn Ramlogan. She found him mounted on his stool and miserable.

'Pa, I have something to tell you.'

'I have nothing to do with you or your husband. I only want you to take a message to him. Tell him for me that Ramlogan say the only way he going to get my property is to take it away on his chest.'

'He write that down last night in a copy-book. And then, Pa, this morning he ask me for a photo of you and he have it now.'

Ramlogan slid, practically fell, off his stool. 'Oh God! Oh God! I didn't know he was that sort of man. He look so quiet.' He stamped up and down behind the counter. 'Oh God! What I do to your husband to make him prosecute me in this way? What he going to do with the picture?'

Leela was sobbing.

Ramlogan looked at the glass case on the counter. 'All that I do for him. Leela, I didn't want any glass case in my shop.'

'No, Pa, you didn't want any glass case in the shop.'

'It for he I get the glass case. Oh God! Leela, is only one thing he going to do with the picture. Work magic and *obeah*,° Leela.'

In his agitation Ramlogan was clutching at his hair, slapping his chest and belly, and beating on the counter. 'And then he go want more property.' Ramlogan's voice palpitated with true anguish.

Leela shrieked. 'What you going to do to my husband, Pa? Is only three days now I married him.'

'Soomintra, poor little Soomintra, she did tell me when we was going to take out the photos. "Pa, I don't think we should take out any photos." God, oh God! Leela, why I didn't listen to poor little Soomintra?'

Ramlogan passed a grubby hand over the brown-paper patch on the glass case, and shook away his tears.

'And last night, Pa, he beat me.'

'Come, Leela, come, daughter.' He leaned over the counter and put his

obeah: African Caribbean magico-religion

hands on her shoulder. 'Is your fate, Leela. Is my fate too. We can't fight it, Leela.'

'Pa,' Leela wailed, 'what you going to do to him? He is my husband, you know.'

Ramlogan withdrew his hands and wiped his eyes. He beat on the counter until the glass case rattled. 'That is what they call education these days. They teaching a new subject. Pickpocketing.'

Leela gave another shriek. 'The man is my husband, Pa.'

When, later that afternoon, Ganesh came back to Fourways, he was surprised to hear Ramlogan shouting, 'Oh, sahib! Sahib! What happen that you passing without saying anything? People go think we vex.'

Ganesh saw Ramlogan smiling broadly behind the counter. 'What you want me to say when you have a sharpen cutlass underneath the counter, eh?'

'Cutlass? Sharpen cutlass? You making joke, sahib. Come in, man, sahib, and sit down. Yes, sit down, and let we have a chat. Eh, but is just like old times, eh, sahib?'

'Things change now.'

'Ah, sahib. Don't say you vex with me.'

'I ain't vex with you.'

'Is for stupid illiterate people like me to get vex. And when illiterate people get vex they does start thinking about working magic against people and all that sort of thing. Educated people don't do that sort of thing.'

'You go be surprised.'

Ramlogan tried to draw Ganesh's attention to the glass case. 'Is a nice modern thing, ain't so, sahib? Nice, pretty, little modern thing.' A drowsy fly was buzzing on the outside, anxious to join its fellows inside. Ramlogan brought down his hand quickly on the glass and killed the fly. He threw it out of the side window and wiped his hands on his trousers. 'These flies *is* a botheration, sahib. What is a good way of getting rid of these botherations, sahib?'

'I ain't know anything about flies, man.'

Ramlogan smiled and tried again. 'How you like being a married man, sahib?'

'These modern girls is hell self. They does keep forgetting their place.'

'Sahib, I have to hand it to you. Only three days you married and you find that out already. Is the valua education. You want some salmon, sahib? Is just as good as any salmon in San Fernando.'

'Don't like San Fernando people.'

'How business there for you, sahib?'

'Tomorrow, please God, we go see what happen.'

'Oh God! Sahib, I didn't mean anything bad last night. Was only a little drunk I was, sahib. A old man like me can't hold his liquor, sahib. I don't mind how much you want from me. I is a good good Hindu, sahib.

Take away everything from me and it don't make no difference, once you leave me with my cha'acter.'

'You is a damn funny sort of man, you know.'

Ramlogan slapped at another fly and missed. 'What go happen tomorrow, sahib?'

Ganesh rose from the bench and dusted the seat of his trousers. 'Oh, tomorrow is one big secret.'

Ramlogan rubbed his hands along the edge of the counter.

'Why you crying?'

'Oh, sahib, I is a poor man. You *must* feel sorry for me.'

'Leela go be all right with me. You mustn't cry for she.'

He found Leela in the kitchen, squatting before the low *chulha* fire, stirring boiling rice in a blue enamel pot.

'Leela, I have a good mind to take off my belt and give you a good dose of blows before I even wash my hand or do anything else.'

She adjusted the veil over her head before turning to him. 'What happen now, man?'

'Girl, how you let all your father bad blood run in your veins, eh? How you playing you don't know what happen, when you know that you run around telling Tom, Dick, and Harry my business?'

She faced the *chulha*° again and stirred the pot. 'Man, if we start quarrelling now, the rice go boil too soft and you know you don't like it like that.'

'All right, but I go want you answer me later on.'

After the meal she confessed and he surprised her by not beating her.

So she was emboldened to ask, 'Man, what you do with Pa photo?'

'I think I settle your father. Tomorrow it wouldn't have one man in Trinidad who wouldn't know about him. Look, Leela, if you start this crying again, I go make you taste my hand again. Start packing. Tomorrow self we moving to Fuente Grove.'

And the next morning the *Trinidad Sentinel* carried this story on page five:

BENEFACTOR ENDOWS CULTURAL INSTITUTE

Shri Ramlogan, merchant, of Fourways, near Debe, has donated a considerable sum of money with the view of founding a Cultural Institute at Fuente Grove. The aim of the proposed Institute, which has yet to be named, will be the furthering of Hindu Cultural and Science of Thought in Trinidad.

The President of the Institute, it is learnt, will be Ganesh Ramsumair, B.A.

chulha: an earthen fireplace for cooking

And there was, in a prominent place, a photograph of a formally attired and slimmer Ramlogan, a potted plant at his side, standing against a background of Greek ruins.

The counter of Ramlogan's shop was covered with copies of the *Trinidad Sentinel* and the *Port of Spain Herald*. Ramlogan didn't look up when Ganesh came into the shop. He was gazing intently at the photograph and trying to frown.

'Don't bother with the *Herald*,' Ganesh said. 'I didn't give them the story.'

Ramlogan didn't look up. He frowned more severely and said, 'Hmmh!' He turned the page over and read a brief item about the danger of tubercular cows. 'They pay you anything?'

'The man wanted *me* to pay.'

'Son of a bitch.'

Ganesh made an approving noise.

'So, sahib.' Ramlogan looked up at last. 'Was really this you wanted the money for?'

'Really really.'

'And you really going to write books at Fuente Grove and everything?'

'Really going to write books.'

'Yes, man. Been reading it here, sahib. Is a great thing, and you is a great man, sahib.'

'Since when you start reading?'

'I learning all all the time, sahib. I does read only a little tiny little bit. Smatterer fact, it have a hundred and one words I just can't make head or tail outa. Tell you what, sahib. Why you don't read it out to me? When you read I could just shut my eyes and listen.'

'You does behave funny afterwards. Why you just don't look at the photo, eh?'

'Is a nice photo, sahib.'

'You look at it. I got to go now.'

Ganesh and Leela moved to Fuente Grove that afternoon; but just before they left Fourways a letter arrived. It contained the oil royalties for the quarter; and the information that his oil had been exhausted and he was to receive no more royalties.

Ramlogan's dowry seemed providential. It was another remarkable co-incidence that gave Ganesh fresh evidence that big things were ahead of him.

'Great things going to happen in Fuente Grove,' Ganesh told Leela. 'Really great things.'

EARL LOVELACE

Earl Lovelace (1935–) was born in Trinidad and spent some time studying at Howard University in the United States. Lovelace's writing of poetry, short stories, and novels reflects his concern for the "little fellers" of the Caribbean — the underclass and the economically dispossessed. Caribbean history has been the story of one group of people exploiting another. In much of his writing Lovelace shows how the Caribbean is still a history of exploitation, where a few individuals are able to move up to the ruling class to become neo-metropolitanites.

The Dragon Can't Dance is a novel about a people remembering their past as they attempt to cope with the present. For them, history must not be forgotten. Lovelace often pursues how the "little fellers" use their history to empower themselves to change the present. Lovelace's novel exemplifies Carnival as a form of resistance through which characters reactualize their past to understand and change their present circumstance. While he celebrates the cultural intersections in the West Indies, he also recognizes the violence that patterned the development of Caribbean history.

from The Dragon Can't Dance

Prologue

The Hill

This is the hill tall above the city where Taffy, a man who say he is Christ, put himself up on a cross one burning midday and say to his followers: 'Crucify me! Let me die for my people. Stone me with stones as you stone Jesus, I will love you still.' And when they start to stone him in truth he get vex and start to cuss: 'Get me down! Get me down!' he say. 'Let every sinnerman bear his own blasted burden; who is I to die for people who ain't have sense enough to know that they can't pelt a man with big stones when so much little pebbles lying on the ground.'

This is the hill, Calvary Hill, where the sun set on starvation and rise on potholed roads, thrones for stray dogs that you could play banjo on their rib bones, holding garbage piled high like a cathedral spire, sparkling with flies buzzing like torpedoes; and if you want to pass from your yard to the road you have to be a high-jumper to jump over the gutter full up with dirty water, and hold your nose. Is noise whole day. Laughter is not laughter; it is a groan coming from the bosom of these houses — no — not houses, shacks that leap out of the red dirt and stone, thin like smoke, fragile like kite paper, balancing on their rickety pillars as broomsticks on the edge of a juggler's nose.

This is the hill, swelling and curling like a machauel snake° from Observatory Street to the mango fields in the back of Morvant, its guts stretched to bursting with a thousand narrow streets and alleys and lanes and traces and holes, holding the people who come on the edge of this city to make it home.

This hill is it; and in it; in Alice Street, named for Princess Alice, the Queen's aunt — Alice — soft word on the lips, is a yard before which grows a governor plum tree that has battled its way up through the tough red dirt and stands now, its roots spread out like claws, gripping the earth, its leaves rust red and green, a bouquet in this desert place: a tree bearing fruit that never ripens for Miss Olive's seven, and the area's other children, lean and hard like whips, their wise yellowed eyes filled with malnutrition and too early knowing — innocence was in the womb — children imitating the grown-up laughter and the big-man pose of their elders, who survive here, holding their poverty as a possession, tending it stubbornly as Miss Cleothilda tends her flower garden, clasping it to their bosom as a pass-key whose function they only half-remembered now, and, grown rusty, they wore as jewellery, a charm, a charmed medallion whose magic invested them with a mysterious purity, made them the blue-bloods of a resistance lived by their ancestors all through slavery, carried on in their unceasing escape — as Maroons,° as Runways, as Bush Negroes, as Rebels: and when they could not perform in space that escape that would take them away from the scene of their brutalization they took a stand in the very guts of the slave plantation, among tobacco and coffee and cotton and canes, asserting their humanness in the most wonderful acts of sabotage they could imagine and perform, making a religion of laziness and neglect and stupidity and waste: singing hosannahs for flood and hurricane and earthquake, praying for damage and pestilence: continuing it still after Emancipation, that emancipated them to a more profound idleness and waste when, refusing to be grist for the mill of the colonial machinery that kept on grinding in its belly people to spit out sugar and cocoa and copra,° they turned up this hill to pitch camp here on the eyebrow of the enemy, to cultivate again with no less fervor the religion with its Trinity of Idleness, Laziness and Waste, so that now, one hundred and twenty-five years after Emancipation, Aldrick Prospect, an aristocrat in this tradition, not knowing where his next meal was coming from, would get up at midday from sleep, yawn, stretch, then start to think of where he might get something to eat, his brain working in the

machauel snake: a large snake that swallows its prey whole (similar to a boa constrictor)
Maroon: a runaway slave
copra: the dried kernel of the coconut

same smooth unhurried nonchalance with which he moved his feet, a slow, cruising crawl which he quickened only at Carnival.

Carnival

Carnival it is that springs this hill alive. Right after Christmas young men get off street corners where they had watched and waited, rubber-tipped sticks peeping out of their back pockets, killing time in dice games, watching the area high-school girls ripening, holding over them the promise of violence and the threat of abuse to keep them respectful, to discourage them from passing them by with that wonderful show of contempt such schoolgirls seem to be required to master to lift them above these slums and these 'hooligans', their brethren, standing at street corners, watching the road grow richer with traffic, the drains float down their filth, holding their backs pressed against the sides of shop buildings from dawn until the scream of police jeeps drive them sullenly on the run, to bring into their waiting a sense of dangerousness and adventure they are happy to embrace, since in these daily police raids they see as much an acknowledgement of their presence as an effort to wrench from them sovereignty of these streets. This moves them to strain all the harder to hold their poses on the walls, to keep alive their visibility and aliveness. And these walls to which they return as soon as the police have driven off, their ritual harassment complete, become more their territory, these walls on which they have scrawled their own names and that of their gangs, Marabuntas, Apple-Jackers, Brimstone, Shane — hard names derived from the movies which on some nights they slip off the walls to see, Western movies of the gun talk and the quick draw and the slow crawl, smooth grand gestures which they imitate so exquisitely as though those gestures were their own borrowed to the movie stars for them to later reclaim as proper to their person, that person that leans against the wall, one foot drawn up to touch the thigh, the hat brim turned down, the eyelid half closed, the body held in that relaxed aliveness, like a deer, watching the world from under the street lamp whose bulb they dutifully shatter as soon as it is changed: that person savouring his rebellion as a ripe starch mango, a matchstick fixed between his teeth at an angle that he alone could measure, and no one imitate.

With Carnival now, they troop off street corners, desert their battlefield and territory, and turn up the hill to the steelband tent to assemble before steel drums cut to various lengths and tuned and fashioned to give out the different tones — bass, alto, cello — instruments that had their beginnings in kerosene tins, biscuit drums, anything that could sound a note, anything that could ring; metal drums looted from roadsides, emptied of their garbage and pressed into service to celebrate the great war's end, and to accompany the calypsonian's instant song: It's your moustache we want, Hitler.

Now, the steelband tent will become a cathedral, and these young men priests. They will draw from back pockets those rubber-tipped sticks, which they had carried around all year, as the one link to the music that is their life, their soul, and touch them to the cracked faces of the drums. Hours, hours; days, days; for weeks they beat these drums, beat these drums, hammering out from them a cry, the cry, the sound, stroking them more gently than they will ever caress a woman; and then they have it. At last, they have it. They have the tune that will sing their person and their pose, that will soar over the hill, ring over the valley of shacks, and laugh the hard tears of their living when, for Carnival, they enter Port of Spain.

Calypso

Up on the hill with Carnival coming, radios go on full blast, trembling these shacks, booming out calypsos, the songs that announce in this season the new rhythms for people to walk in, rhythms that climb over the red dirt and stone, break-away rhythms that laugh through the groans of these sights, these smells, that swim through the bones of these enduring people so that they shout: Life! They cry: Hurrah! They drink a rum and say: Fuck it! They walk with a tall hot beauty between the garbage and dog shit, proclaiming life, exulting in the bare bones of their person and their skin.

Up on the hill with Carnival coming and calypso tunes swimming in the hair of these shacks, piercing their nostrils, everybody catches the spirit and these women with baskets and with their heads tied, these women winding daily down this hill on which no buses run, tramping down this asphalt lane slashed across this mountain's face, on their way, to Port of Spain city, to market, to work as a domestic, or to any other menial task they inherit because of their beauty; these women, in this season, bounce with that tall delicious softness of bosom and hip, their movements a dance, as if they were earth priestesses heralding a new spring.

The children dance too, coming home from school in the hot afternoon when the sun has cooked the castles of dog shit well, so that its fumes rise like incense proper to these streets. They dance, skipping along, singing calypsos whose words they know by heart already, swishing their skirt tails, moving their waists, laughing, their laughter scattering like shells into the hard flesh of the hill. Dance! There is dancing in the calypso. Dance! If the words mourn the death of a neighbour, the music insists that you dance; if it tells the troubles of a brother, the music says dance. Dance to the hurt! Dance! If you catching hell, dance, and the government don't care, dance! Your woman take your money and run away with another man, dance. Dance! Dance! Dance! It is in dancing that you ward off evil. Dancing is a chant that cuts off the power from the devil. Dance! Dance! Dance! Carnival brings this dancing to every crevice on this hill.

The Dragon

With the door of his little shack half open, Aldrick worked solemnly on his dragon costume, saying nothing to Basil, the little boy of ten who came from somewhere in the neighbourhood of Alice Street, appeared just so a year before, in the ragged khaki pants and sleeveless merino that was his uniform all that year, and stood at the door and gazed in at the dragon costume Aldrick was then making, looking from the costume to Aldrick with a fullness of wonderment and fascination and awe, leaving, only when dark fell, to return next day and the next all through the making of the dragon costume, maintaining that attitude of reverence throughout, as if he were in the presence of holiness, until one day Aldrick asked him to run to Miss Cleothilda's parlour and buy him a pack of cigarettes; and cemented in that act the boy's apprenticeship to dragon making. So the boy was here again this year. And, working now, he seemed to divine exactly which tool or piece of material Aldrick needed for his work, and he handed it to him with a ceremonial solemnity as if he, the boy, were an acolyte, and Aldrick the priest.

In truth, it was in a spirit of priesthood that Aldrick addressed his work; for, the making of his dragon costume was to him always a new miracle, a new test not only of his skill but of his faith: for though he knew exactly what he had to do, it was only by faith that he could bring alive from these scraps of cloth and tin that dragon, its mouth breathing fire, its tail threshing the ground, its nine chains rattling, that would contain the beauty and threat and terror that was the message he took each year to Port of Spain.° It was in this message that he asserted before the world his self. It was through it that he demanded that others *see* him, recognize his personhood, be warned of his dangerousness.

Aldrick worked slowly, deliberately; and every thread he sewed, every scale he put on the body of the dragon, was a thought, a gesture, an adventure, a name that celebrated some part of his journey to and his surviving upon this hill. He worked, as it were, in a flood of memories, not trying to assemble them, to link them to get a linear meaning, but letting them soak him through and through; and his life grew before him, in the texture of his paint and the angles of his dragon's scales, as he worked. And, working now, he sewed scales for his grandfather, who he remembered from the far distance of his boyhood on that browning green hill between the giant immortelle trees° above the cocoa and dying bananas, a short man, stiff as the varnished straight-backed chair on which he sat in the front room, alone, tall before the table set with his breakfast of eggs and goat's milk and his grandmother's home-made bread and avocado, alone as if the rest of the family, his own wife and daughters and grand-

---

Port of Spain: the capital city of Trinidad
immortelle trees: a name for various flowers of papery texture

children, were not fit companions when he broke bread; alone in the front room, the altar of the house, the clean polished room with framed and passe-partouted photographs of members of the family on the walls, and a big one of his brother George who was in America, and one of God Bless This House, with its green cherries and red leaves, hanging near the hat rack with the mirror in it, above the varnished chairs, around the little centre table of cedar upon the polished floor upon which only visitors trod — and not many of them either, certainly, none from the village itself — except for Christmas Day when the whole family came into that room smelling now of Christmas, smelling now of new curtains and fresh varnish and balloons.

He knitted into his dragon this old man, stern and stiff and unbending, the last pillar of a falling building, whose slightest shift would collapse the entire structure, puzzling over him, this man, his mother's father, remembering him still holding on then to the five acres of mountain and stone that had exhausted its substance, if it ever had any, years before he bought it, holding on with a passion so fierce that it blinded him to the dwindling size of the fruit the tired brown trees tugged out of the earth, as if the land, that mountain and stone land, held some promise that he alone knew of, that was never revealed to his wife or to his children, and that would be already lost to Aldrick by the time he was old enough to understand; remained with the old man, kept as the photograph of a long departed lover from an affair itself lived, lost, gone — no, rather as the letter from that lover who never came, who had written fifty years before promising that she was coming, and who after fifty years he still kept waiting for, no longer really expecting her to turn up, but continuing to wait in that kind of active martyred hopelessness that seems a hope, reproaching her with his very patience and waiting for every minute of the fifty years, so that if she ever came he could say: I kept my part of the bargain; and if she never came his waiting would be a monument to his faith. For that reason, in the cause of his martyrdom and faith that was not really faith at all but a wicked reproach to the promise of the land, to the promise for which he could only have held God responsible, the waiting man refusing to listen to anyone who suggests that the lover is not coming, he refused to hear anything against the promise of the land. And towards the end, for all the toil and time he had put in on the land with his wife and children and grandchildren, he expected as return not produce, not cocoa or coffee or bananas or oranges, but that he could say to God, who must have been the one to make him the promise: I kept my part of the bargain. You told me to cutlass and hoe and weed and sow; well, I have done all of it. I have kept my part of the bargain.

Immersed in this perverse mission, he ceased to be any kind of flesh and blood man, had become the symbol of an unyielding and triumphant martyrdom, intent on inflicting on his family the land and its promise which he had waited on for fifty years, in vain, so that even when his daughters, the two youngest, were twenty-five and twenty-two, and the avocados were the smallest they had ever been, growing smaller from year to year, and the cocoa field, riddled with witches broom and black pod, was so diseased that no amount of pruning or cutlassing or mulching could rehabilitate: even after all those years of seeing what must have been withering and dying all around him, and the disappearing meaning in the promise that he might have honestly believed in once, even then he would resist their going as the pillar resists the falling of the building it is holding up from toppling.

'The children big now, Cyrus,' his grandmother had said, speaking to him in that moaning tone that had known years of silence, years of being hurled back by the old man's stubborn unyielding faith. 'And the land old and things ain't bearing right, and is all right for we who old, who accustomed to this nothing, who ain't looking for no future from this world . . . I want them to go where they could get a chance to be somebody. Their chance, Cyrus. Their own chance.'

'What?' he asked, irritated as a man just waked from sleep. 'What?' Then he said, 'No'.

'You going to say no, Cyrus, without thinking. You going to say no? What they going to do here in Manzanilla? Catch fish in the sea?'

'They have land. They have a house here.'

'And for how many is this mansion?'

'What?' For she had never talked so to him before, never raised her voice above a supplicating meekness. 'Rose!'

'I ain't no rose again, Cyrus. I ain't no rose. Look at me! This skin and bones ain't no rose. Let the children go.'

'Go! And didn't Lorna go? Didn't Lorna go?'

'Yes, Lorna went, and married and have children.'

'Married? You call that skufflin' little fella a husband? Driftin' around, can't settle down, can't mind his children. That is the married that Lorna married?'

'Is Lorna life. You can't make life for people; they have to live it for theyself. And she is not the first — '

'And she won't be the last of your children to throw away their life if your foolishness prevail.'

'They going, Cyrus. They going. I going to tell them to go. Do what you want. You live your life already, and I live it here with you. Okay. But I telling them to go. They can't breathe in this place.'

'They will breathe well in Port of Spain. You better go with them: you will breathe well too.'

He worked it all into the latticework of this dragon, into the scales and the threads, the exodus then of his grandmother and his two unmarried aunts from Manzanilla, leaving the tall immortelle and the dying bananas and the cocoa trees with pods small as grains of pigeon peas, and the old road and the old man (and he, thinking: Who will varnish the tables?

Who will polish the floor?), unyielding to the last, as if he knew that whatever route they took their fate would be worse than to keep faith with a promise that he could not, if he were sane, expect still to be honoured. He worked it all in: they, his grandmother and young aunts, leaving for a house in St. James; he, back to his mother rocking the last baby to sleep and waiting for his father, Sam Prospect, the miracle man, who she was crazy enough to go with when he left the cocoa estate in Manzanilla to go to Port of Spain, without money or schooling or trade, filled with that sense of escape and that idea of his manness which had no chance to flower under the foreman, among labourers and cocoa and immortelle, and which would not find it easier in the city where he went from job to job, giving one up for another after a month or two, or maybe it was fired, working longest as a barman in a rum shop, fathering five children and ever so often disappearing, leaving the children and their mother waiting: she, sending little notes by Aldrick to his aunts and grandmother: 'Send a little money, send a little sugar, until Sam come home,' and when Sam did not come home, leaving the eldest boy to take care of the smaller ones, going out to work, washing and cleaning, a maid in white people kitchen; then at last Sam suddenly reappearing with long hurried strides as if he had just stepped out to the corner and was returning to go out again, hollow-eyed from nights gambling, coming home with a big brown paper bag with groceries and presents for the children; and his mother, who had prayed so often and long for his returning, going down on her knees on the floor of hardened mud in the Spiritual Baptist church up on Laventille where God came down every Wednesday night if the police didn't get there before Him, now that he had come, saying not a word, not even crying. He would hear them in the kitchen, his father pleading, saying, Hush, Lorna, hush; and his mother not saying a word, and he, Sam, promising again to get a good job and settle down and see about her and the children; and then his mother finally saying, between the cracking of the paper as she took the groceries out the bag, in a voice that threatened to rise from its whispering into a scream: Don't, Sam. Don't promise anything. Just go as you going. Don't promise anything. And his father saying, softly, with tears in his voice, Hush, hush, hush — he must have been holding her in his arms and rocking her like a baby, saying, hush, hush, hush: for the paper would be no longer crackling.

Oh, the miracle of their surviving: the miracle of his mother bringing up five children and waiting, waiting, for Sam, the miracle man, always moving with that busy speed, always on the look out for a better break, a better job, a chance, trying to the very end of his days to be the man he had left Manzanilla to become, so that when the crane fell on his back and broke it, down on the wharves where he had been working off and on for two weeks, they had to take his hands out his pockets.

Maybe that was his gift to his children, this sense of miracle and manness, this surviving on nothing and standing up still on your own two feet to be counted as somebody in a world where people were people, were human, by the amount of their property. Or, maybe it was not something acquired by him (Sam Prospect) but an ancestral gift handed down to generations of Prospects and later inherited by Aldrick; for when his mother died not too long after, and Aldrick and the rest of the children scattered across the face of the country, each one taken in by one relative or another, he would encounter this same sense of miracle and manness in his father's brother, Freddie, Uncle Freddie into whose care he was entrusted; Uncle Freddie from whom he learnt to make dragon; Uncle Freddie cooler than water and smoother, having the run of the city in a way his brother Sam never did, knowing at his age that it was wasteful to hurry, not wasting a gesture, saying to Aldrick the only words that he, Aldrick, could remember even now as his most often, no, his only lecture: 'Take it easy!' Take it easy: the words with which he answered every salutation and made every promise and consoled everyone. Take it easy, worked now into his dragon and its growing story of lives of miracle and manness and faith.

Working there now, thoughts of Sylvia kept nagging at his brain. Suddenly, since the night he had surprised her going to meet Guy, she had refused to leave his mind; and now, every time he turned he would see her flitting by or standing in that long soft sullen pose, her eyes and spirit and provoking limbs piercing and surrounding and entangling him like Shango drums that he was already fated to dance to; and he tried to puzzle out in his mind: how come he had managed to escape her before. Then, yesterday evening as he worked on his dragon costume, she had appeared before his open door, with high heeled shoes a size too big on, and one of those dresses that used to be fashionable seven years before, a white dress with no band at the waist, a bow at the back, three-quarter length sleeves, and long down to just below her knees, an ancient, almost bridal dress that someone, some aunt or cousin had handed over to her mother who had passed it on to her. She had appeared at the doorway of his little room in this outlandish costume, with red lipstick on her mouth, and her hair combed back and brushed up to a point at the back of her head and held together by a length of white ribbon, and stood there looking at him sew scales into the cloth of the dragon, stood there with a warm virginal softness and trembling about her, as if she had come both to give herself and to resist his taking her.

'You see I ain't have no space even to invite you in,' he had said, with a little half nervous laugh that was kinda new for him, indicating with a sweep of one hand the cluttered room with scattered pieces of cloth and tins of paint and scraps of tin, all the time aware of her white dress and red lipstick and high heeled shoes slack around her feet.

She had grinned back, softly too, half frightened, it seemed, waiting with that warm waiting that suggested the reaffirmation of an intimacy that she felt that their meeting a few nights before had created between them, waiting as if she expected from him a question to which she already had the answer, holding herself at arm's length away, watching as he worked the needle through the cloth of his costume.

'You like how it coming?' He lifted his head to say that, holding up for her gaze the section of the costume he was sewing.

'I ain't get my costume yet,' she said, as if she could wait no longer for the question she had stood there expecting.

He heard the words. He wanted to look at her; instead, he watched his needle and sewed, his mind tumbling, wanting to ask her the questions that were already tumbling in his head: You mean . . . ? You didn't? Guy didn't?

'I ain't get my costume yet,' she said again, her voice firmer now, containing neither triumph nor pride nor the joy that might have bubbled in it if his question had come first.

What he heard was the challenge and promise in her remark, the same challenge and promise that had resided in her person all these last years, that he had tried so hard to ignore, that he had successfully managed to ignore until she brought it to his door a few nights before; and she was bringing it again, hurling it at him now, with all the fragile softness and youth and warmth of her womanness, announced and emphasized and shouted out in the pathos and beauty and ridiculousness of the handed down dress and the oversized shoes and the lipstick and the ribbon in her hair.

He would not escape her this time. He was doomed: this came to his mind after she left — and she had waited the eternity at his door for some word from him, some sign that he understood, at least acknowledged what her words were saying. She had waited the eternity during which he continued to sew scales onto the costume, refusing even to think of her meaning, far more comment on it, thinking to try to smile, to make some joke, thinking to find some hole to escape through, knowing that for his manness' sake the smile nor the joke wouldn't do. He couldn't let this girl come and stand before his door and be more woman than he was man. He couldn't let her come with that virginal and bridal and lady-like dignity and hope, that not only concerned him — indeed, went beyond being a challenge to him, was a statement of her promise to living, to her own hopes — and make a joke of it.

You is a princess, girl. You don't need those clothes and that lipstick, you is a princess just as you is everyday: the words came to his lips to say, but to say even that now, as hollow as it might have sounded, would not be a compliment; it would be a proposal. He couldn't do that. And he knew that it was not just the matter of buying her a costume either — not that he had the money even for that — but to make even that offer now was to begin to contradict the very guts and fibre of his own living: Aldrick was a dragon. He was a hustler, working nowhere; and the only responsibility he was prepared to bear now was to his dragon, that presentation on Carnival day of the self that he had lived the whole year. He had his life.

'Sylvia . . . ' And as he raised his head he could see her alive eyes, eager, burning, shielding that invitation and promise, that woman-softness that was more prophecy than warning that she had the power to draw him into that world of ordinary living and caring that he had avoided all his life. 'Sylvia . . .' He knew he had to say something now. What, he didn't know even as he was preparing to say it. Then, mercifully, he heard Philo calling out his name. He turned to the sound. 'Haii!' he cried to the approaching Philo, 'Haii!'

She did not blink. Even as Philo approached she had stood there, her eyes fastened on Aldrick, as if she still had enough patience and strength and faith to wait on him, the stubborn wilfulness and truth to not be the one to surrender or default, enduring in the fifteen or twenty seconds it took Philo to cross the yard to Aldrick's place, the silence that was not of her making — she had said her piece — waiting still for Aldrick to complete whatever it was he had begun when he said her name; and she would not move even when Philo come up and turned to her, feigning surprise: 'Haii! That is you, Sylvia? No, that is not you.' Not even when he stepped up to her an arm's length away and let his muscled eyes rove over her in inspection from head to toe. Even when he reached out to put his hand on her in that friendly sensual way some men try to touch a beauty which they cannot otherwise embrace, she did not move: as she felt his touch, she slapped his face. It was only then that she turned and walked away.

'Sylvia!' Aldrick cried; and maybe the word might have died in his brain, or maybe he had suddenly gone deaf; he didn't hear a sound. He watched her walking away with that tall chaste insolent and disdaining tread, her head in the air, dragging her feet a little to keep the shoes from slipping off her feet.

'What wrong with her?' Philo had asked.

'You asking *me*!' But even as he said so he was thinking that Philo's coming had not rescued him at all. It had merely postponed the questions he had to face from not so much Sylvia as from himself; so that long after Philo left — and he had remained only a short time, holding his face where she had slapped him, and asking over and over again: 'What wrong with her?' — he was still thinking: I ain't get my costume yet, the words, which he had earlier failed to acknowledge, bouncing and flipping in his brain, turning him to their promise, to their challenge, causing in him a feeling of guilt, a sensation that he was alarmed and surprised that he could still feel.

'Haii! But what the hell I here worrying myself about?' he cried, when he came to himself and found himself seated at the edge of his bed, darkness gathering, the lamp not yet lit, and the boy still there. 'I ain't responsible for her. All I do is just see this girl going one night to meet a man;

that is all. I don't even know if she went and meet him. I don't even know what under her dress. Haii!' He laughed aloud. 'Aldrick, you growing old, boy. You getting soft . . . And you.' He turned to the boy. 'It nearly dark, you ain't going home?' even then searching for a match to light the lamp, not looking at the boy.

'I leaving home,' the boy said.

He laughed, his back still turned to the boy. 'Don't make that kinda joke with me. Not today. You leaving home? What you leaving home for?' He turned now from the lamp he had lighted and saw the boy's face, and his own tone changed. He said softly, 'What you leaving home for?'

'He beat me again. Everytime he get drunk he beat me. He beat everybody in the house.' The boy was crying.

'Who . . . ?' And now to his surprise, Aldrick realized that after two Carnivals, two years of the boy coming to his place and working with him, all he knew of him was his first name. He sat down on his bed, and his voice came squeaking out his belly: 'Who? Who is that beating you and everybody? Your father?'

'He ain't my father. He living with my mother. Fisheye.'

'Fisheye is your step-father?'

'You know him?'

Aldrick did know Fisheye. This knowledge made him cautious. 'Well, maybe you do something wrong. Maybe you don't learn your lessons or something. I used to get licks for that too, and I never leave home.'

'You don't know him when he drunk. My big brother Leroy: he beat Leroy so bad he break Leroy hand, and when they was carrying Leroy to hospital he tell my mother to tell the doctor that Leroy fall down from a tree, else he going to break her hand too.'

'He really don't make fun,' Aldrick said. 'But I . . . I not going to encourage you to run away. Where you will go? You have anybody near by where you could stay? 'cause I . . . you can't stay here, you know. You see how small this place is.'

Aldrick saw the boy's eyes filling again.

'Is not that I don't want you here, man; but, look at the size of this place.' And all the time thinking: two years, and I don't know the boy full name or where he living or who his mother is or anything. Look at that, eh! And, *I ain't get my costume yet* flashed across his brain. 'Look, this ain't my business, you know,' he said, with a kind of softness and aggravation. 'This is between you and you step-father. I serious. I mean, this is family business. I don't know anything about it. I mean, I don't know what it is between you and your mother and Fisheye. You understand?'

The boy said nothing, and Aldrick fell silent, waiting for the boy to understand and to leave, and when he saw that the boy was not going to leave without his urging, he said: 'Okay, wipe your face and go. I can't do nothing. This is family business. You have to understand that.'

The boy left then, backing out of the door, dragging his feet, his eyes overflowing.

'Fisheye is a hell of a man,' Aldrick said aloud. Then he lit a cigarette and went to the door. 'Wha — !' The boy was still there. Aldrick began to tell him again that it was family business, that his own place was too small, and so on, when he remembered that the boy had heard all that before.

'Okay,' Aldrick said, 'Okay. Come, let's go. I going to carry you home. Come. It ain't my business, you know, but I going to have a talk with him anyway.'

Aldrick went inside and slipped on his shoes. He didn't know where this softness was coming from. Maybe he was getting old in truth. 'Come,' he said to the boy when he was ready, strengthening his resolve; for, on Calvary Hill Fisheye was a man whose business even the police were reluctant to meddle in.

LATIN
AMERICA

LATIN AMERICA

Latin American literature is the fictional, poetic, dramatic, and essayistic work produced by authors writing within the traditions established in countries below the Rio Grande, reaching all the way down to the southern tip of Argentina, and including the major Antilles. Since these countries were once a part of the Spanish or Portuguese empires, the predominant languages are Spanish and Portuguese. Brazil, where Portuguese is spoken, is a huge country with a powerful literary tradition of its own, related in some ways but independent from the rest of Latin American letters. Hence, though it will be included in this anthology under the rubric of Latin American literature, its independence from Spanish American literature must always be kept in mind.

LANGUAGE AND IDENTITY

Because there are still large populations of what once were thriving native civilizations, many languages other than Spanish and Portuguese are still spoken in the region, each with its distinctive and rich lore, poetry, and sometimes drama. The dominant Spanish or Portuguese literatures have often attempted to incorporate these traditions, with varying degrees of success. But since they are oral, native poetry and narrative have played an ancillary role in the constitution of Latin American literature, which is essentially part of the modern literature of the West — although one of its most powerful and recurrent tendencies is to deny it. Latin American literature's own status and the legitimacy of its links to the European tradition are among the main concerns of Latin American literature.

A measure of the poignancy of this issue may be gleaned from the debates surrounding the very name by which the area is known. Since all of the nations in the region emerged from the empires created by the two countries that occupy the Iberian Peninsula, some decided to call the area Iberoamérica. But others objected, arguing that the entire continent was peopled before the arrival of the Europeans and wished to call the continent Indoamérica. However, this did not sit well with people from areas such as the Caribbean, where the predominant non-European groups are of African origin. Besides, why must the continent's natives continue to be named after India, perpetuating the Europeans' original error? Others argued in favor of using Spanish America for all countries, except Brazil, while yet others favored Hispanic America. The debate assumes, of course, that a name can accurately reflect the continent's ethnic, cultural, and historical diversity — a dubious proposition. Usage eventually prevails, and Latin America is the term most commonly accepted and the one that will be used here to refer to the region.

Latin America is at once like the rest of the postcolonial world and very different from it. The presence of large masses of non-European peoples not assimilated to the economy — or victimized by it — and unable to retreat to their original ways of life gives Latin American society the same instability and internal tension found in other regions of the world now emerging from the debacle of European imperialism. The difference lies in the sheer length of time — five centuries of history — that is involved in the case of Latin America.

One of the burdens of Latin America is a Western culture that reaches back to the Middle Ages, when the ideological foundations of the Iberian empires in the New World were set. As already discussed, Latin American writers sometimes still seek legitimacy by focusing on their role as heirs of a European tradition. This demonstrates the degree of assimilation to the West that five centuries have brought about.

On the other hand, the struggles, too, are centuries old and have developed facets that other regions may not yet have experienced. Because most of the countries in Latin America became independent in the first half of the nineteenth century, there has been time to develop partial solutions or myths of national unity to try to cover the rifts and contradictions of the social fabric. There has also been time for these solutions to deteriorate — their precariousness becomes evident periodically. For example, Mexico is a country where a major, bloody revolution in the early decades of this century brought to power a party dedicated to enfranchising economically and politically its vast and impoverished Indian population. If there is a country where official rhetoric vaunts the incorporation of its non-European masses, it is Mexico. Yet as this book goes to press, Mexico is coping with Indian uprisings in the state of Chiapas. The wounds of the Spanish conquest have never really healed.

There are many misconceptions regarding Latin America, particularly in the United States. For instance, some believe that the language, say of Puerto Rico, is not Spanish but a dialect different from the Castilian spoken in Madrid. But it is the same language: Castilian is merely another name for Spanish. In fact, Spanish is more uniform today than English, and Mexicans, Spaniards, Paraguayans, and Puerto Ricans speak and write the same language with insignificant variations. As with other languages, it becomes even more "standard" as one moves up in social class, making the literatures of the various countries (including Spain, of course) not only intelligible throughout, but one large literary tradition encompassing them all. This uniformity is due to two main factors. First, Spanish underwent its last telling linguistic transformations during the sixteenth century. Spanish was not brought from Spain to the New World: it developed and set in Spain and the New World at almost the same time. Second, the deliberate policy of the Spanish Crown in the sixteenth century recognized that to govern and convert to Christianity such a huge and widely scattered population, a uniform language was needed. The differences between the Portuguese spoken and written today in Brazil and that of the mother country are, on the other hand, more significant, but not to the point where either can be considered a dialect of the other or where cultural exchange between them can be truly affected.

EARLY WRITING

Although Latin American literature as a self-conscious activity began in the early nineteenth century, after the wars of independence, it recognized the voluminous literary production in the Spanish viceroyalties as a precursor. Hence, one could argue that there has been a Latin American literature since the sixteenth and seventeenth centuries. Two major figures from this period continue to have an influence. Garcilaso de la Vega, el Inca (1539–1616) was the son of a Spanish conquistador of aristocratic background and an Incan noblewoman. His monumental history of Peru, *Royal Commentaries of the Incas* (1609/1917), was written to correct Spanish histories of the conquest. It was also a defense of his mother's peoples and a detailed evocation of their culture. Written in a Spanish whose elegance is comparable to that of his contemporary Miguel de Cervantes, *The Royal Commentaries* may well be the first great work of the literature of the Americas. Sor Juana Inés de la Cruz (1651/1695), a Mexican nun, was the last great baroque poet, and the first great figure of Latin American letters, recognized as a famous writer in her own lifetime. She wrote poetry in various meters, several plays, and a defense of her right as a woman to dedicate herself to intellectual pursuits. This *Respuesta a Sor Filotea*, the first feminist manifesto in the Americas, along with several of Sor Juana's poems and plays, are considered classics of Latin American literature.

But it was during the first half of the nineteenth century that literary activity among Latin Americans became self-conscious, meaning that writers, critics, and historians wrote with the idea that Latin American literature could exist as a distinct entity. These founders of Latin American literature included the Argentine Juan María Gutiérrez, who published in 1846 an anthology called *América poética*, featuring poets from across the continent; the Chilean José Domingo Cortés, who published poetic anthologies of various countries; and the Venezuela-born Domingo del Monte, who in the 1830s gathered in his house in Havana the first group of self-defined Cuban writers. Many of these founders of Latin American literature came to know each other in Paris, where they were diplomats or political exiles. In the French capital, which has been since then a kind of Latin American intellectual capital, these writers formed groups, published journals, and acquired a pan–Latin American consciousness and sense of mission.

By the end of the nineteenth century, Latin American literature could boast several major writers. First and foremost there is Joaquim María Machado de Assis (1839–1908), a Brazilian novelist who was the first great modern writer from Latin America. In Spanish, there was Cuban romantic poet José María de Heredia (1803–1839), Argentine prose writer and statesman, Domingo Faustino Sarmiento (1811–1888), and Cuban poet and patriot José Martí (1853–1895). Sarmiento's *Facundo* (1845), a penetrating analysis of the Argentine hinterlands written as a biography of *gaucho* Facundo Quiroga, is perhaps the classic of Spanish-language literature in nineteenth-century Latin America.

The sustained contacts among Latin American writers, particularly poets, throughout the nineteenth century finally produced, in the 1890s, a literary movement called *modernismo*. *Modernista* poets were highly sophisticated and French oriented, rejecting the literary traditions of Spain. But their refined prosody and their extremely elegant use of the language were also a turn back to the colonial Baroque and poets like Sor Juana. *Modernistas* had a collective sense of belonging to a modern world that was at once American and artificial — art as the product of craft, not nature, was of the essence. *Modernismo* appears superficial, but it was anything but that in the poetry of Rubén Darío (1867–1916), a Nicaraguan, the foremost poet of the movement. Darío became the first Latin American literary celebrity. He was as famous in Argentina as he was in Cuba, and his style changed the course of Spanish poetry. It was the first time that a literary school created in Latin America had a telling impact on the mother country.

TWENTIETH-CENTURY AVANT-GARDE

Contemporary Latin American literature, as represented in this anthology, is heir to a more recent artistic movement, which could be broadly called the avant-garde. In the 1920s, in the aftermath of World War I, when all the promises of the nineteenth century seemed to have been broken, a series of rebellious artistic movements arose in Europe and the Americas. Traditional forms were shattered in painting, music, and architecture. In literature, surrealism, partly inspired by the discoveries of psychoanalysis, experimented with automatic writing. The surreal was the reality behind or beneath the surface of things, a level not ruled by common sense and ordinary perception. The rules of versification and even for the printing of poems were thrown out the window.

In Latin America, with its anxiety to be modern and new, the avant-garde had enormous impact. Magazines such as *Revista de Avance* (Havana) and *Proa* (Buenos Aires) were founded to disseminate the new styles. In São Paolo, in 1922, a whole week devoted to the new art was celebrated. An outrageous group of Brazilian artists declared themselves "antropophagists," that is, in favor of cannibalism, a transgression they gleefully accepted as the literal and metaphorical condition of being Americans. Art and artists would rather be irreverent, even abominable, than commonplace and predictable.

The avant-garde movement in the arts coincided with political unrest. Mexico took the lead, beginning its already mentioned revolution in 1910. At issue was the incorporation of Indians in the body politic. Poverty, corruption, and a widening gap between the poor and rich, and between the modern cities and the backward and exploited hinterlands, made for a very volatile situation. A continentwide movement of university reform began in Córdoba, Argentina, also in 1922. It politicized students all over Latin America. Communist and other radical parties were founded. Dictators such as the Cuban Gerardo Machado were toppled, whereas others, like Anastasio Somoza in Nicaragua and Rafael Leónidas Trujillo in the Dominican Republic, came to power with the support of the United States and local elites. Thus, the tenor of contemporary Latin American politics was set in the 1920s, pitting the military and the rich, aided directly or indirectly by the United States, against the poor (both peasants and urban dwellers) and students, intellectuals, and artists. Most of the older writers included in this anthology (Carpentier, Guillén, Neruda) entered the political and artistic arenas simultaneously in the 1920s.

The feeling of historical crisis that colors most Latin American literature coincided with the avant-garde's penchant for breaks and fresh beginnings. It was clearly a fortunate and perhaps fortuitous marriage. This is evident in Neruda's poetry, including *Canto General,* from which "The Heights of Macchu Picchu" is taken. Neruda writes inspired by the ruins of the Incan city, which mark the historical chasm upon which Latin America was erected. The new and the old are conjoined by Neruda's poetic imagination and voice. Such harmony, involving nature, the silent stones of the ruins, and the creative consciousness of the poet, is a romantic ideal that is still at the core of Latin American literature, though its political realization may appear distant.

Neruda's poetic appropriation of the Incan past reveals another trait of Latin American literature since the avant-garde: the desire to incorporate into art the non-European cultures in the area. This tendency, which coincides and sometimes becomes a part of political movements, is part of the overall synthesis to which Neruda's poem aspires. Whole movements such as the Afro-Antillian or Indigenista movements have invested enormous efforts to bring this about. Alejo Carpentier and Nicolás Guillén, both Cuban, were part of the Afro-Antillian movement. Carpentier became an expert on Afro-Cuban music and wrote a novel, ¡Ecué-Yamba-O! (1933) that incorporates techniques of the avant-garde and various patterns of Afro-Cuban music. But many other authors, not necessarily associated directly with any of these movements, saw in these cultures within Latin America, but not part of mainstream literary culture, alluring alternatives to the commonplaces of Western art. Octavio Paz, for instance, uses Aztec calendar patterns in his powerful poem *Sunstone* (1958).

REGIONAL NARRATIVE

By the 1940s, the experiments of the avant-garde, together with the incorporation of native elements, had yielded a distinctive Latin American strain of modern narrative. In the novel, the works of Mariano Azuela (Mexico, 1873–1952), Ricardo Güiraldes (Argentina, 1886–1927), José Eustasio Rivera (Colombia, 1889–1928), and Rómulo Gallegos (Venezuela, 1889–1969) had become known throughout the continent and Spain. These so-called *novelas de la tierra,* or regionalist novels, described in a detailed and critical manner the life of rural Latin America. Azuela's focus in *Los de abajo* (*The Underdogs,* 1915) is the Mexican Revolution and its overwhelming tide of violence. Güiraldes, in *Don Segundo Sombra* (1926), Rivera, in *La vorágine* (*The Vortex,* 1924), and Gallegos, in *Doña Bárbara* (1929), paint broad canvases and tell archetypal stories that border on myth. In Brazil, a parallel movement developed in the novel of the northeast, which documents with pitiless precision the exploitation of peasants. Graziliano Ramos's *Vidas secas* (*Barren Lives,* 1938) is among the best known among these. The main theme of *novelas de la tierra* is the uneasy coexistence of the modern and the premodern in Latin America, such as the struggle between land tenure systems that hark back to medieval Spain and progressive ideas about agrarian reform derived from the Enlightenment.

MAGICAL REALISM

As the 1940s arrived, and with them many Latin American artists and intellectuals fleeing the fall of the Spanish Republic, the rising tide of fascism in Europe, and eventually the outbreak of World War II, these novels gave way to more experimental forms of fiction. It was in the 1940s that Carpentier and others put forth the theory of "magical realism," or "American marvelous reality," to define Latin American art, particularly the narrative. In the broadest sense, these terms referred to an art that was the product of avant-garde techniques, particularly surrealism, nineteenth-century realism, and an appeal to the beliefs of Latin Americans of non-European origin. In his well-known story "Journey Back to the Source," for instance, Carpentier tells the life of his protagonist backwards, after a black sorcerer, with a movement of his magic wand, reverses the flow of time. What magical realism attempts to capture is the unresolved combination of modern and prehistoric cultures in Latin America, the clash between beliefs molded by post-Enlightenment societies that have experienced the industrial and the postindustrial eras, and doctrines and customs shaped by forms of thought whose origin is religious and prescientific. The magic element is portrayed as fantastic in magical realist stories from the perspective of some characters, and perfectly normal from that of others. The legacy of magical realism reaches into the present in the works of prominent writers such as Gabriel García Márquez.

Although not connected in a direct way, the work of João Guimarães Rosa in Brazil shares traits with that of Carpentier, Asturias, and other Spanish-language writers associated with magical realism. But Guimarães Rosa is at once more folkloric and more metaphysical. His stories are derived from those he heard in the Brazilian plains (the *sertão*), where he worked for some years as a doctor. His masterpiece, *Grande sertão, varedas* (The Devil to Pay in the Backlands, 1956), combines many of these tales around a nucleus whose main theme is evil and the workings of the devil. Guimarães Rosa, however, owes as much to Goethe and to Joyce as he does to folktales.

But Brazil is a country where magical realism has had to coexist with the avant-garde, which seems to have had a much longer life here than elsewhere in Latin America. A case in point is the emergence of a strong "concrete poetry" movement led by Augusto and Haroldo de Campos. Concrete poetry attempted to exploit the visual component of language, playing with its relationship with meaning. Poems were printed in recognizable shapes that were somehow linked to their verbal meaning. This ploy has a history that reaches back to the Greeks and has had several recurrences throughout history, but only the Brazilians were bold enough to turn it into a whole poetic movement.

NEW FICTION

Until the early 1960s one would have said that, in spite of the considerable production and quality of Latin American fiction writers, poetry was the predominant literary expression of the region. Peruvian César Vallejo; Cubans Nicolás Guillén and José Lezama Lima; Chileans Gabriela Mistral, Nicanor Parra, and Pablo Neruda; Puerto Rican Luis Palés Matos; Uruguayan Juana de Ibarbouru; and more recently Octavio Paz constitute quite a constellation of poets. In fact, the first Latin American to receive the Nobel Prize in literature was the poet Gabriela Mistral.

But in the middle 1960s there appeared a number of short story writers and novelists of such quality and worldwide appeal that the whole character of Latin American literature seemed to have changed. These writers, whose sudden fame and dissemination came to be known as the "Boom of the Latin American novel," made Latin American literature the only literature truly known in the entire world. The new writers were Julio Cortázar, an Argentine like Borges; Carlos Fuentes, a Mexican whose ideas owed much to Octavio Paz at the start; Mario Vargas Llosa, from Peru; and Colombian Gabriel García Márquez. The latter's *One Hundred Years of Solitude,* published in 1967, reached unprecedented sales throughout Latin America and Spain. It was subsequently translated into all major languages and became a best-seller throughout the world. Eventually, García Márquez, who is also a first-rate short story writer and the author of many other superb novels, was awarded the Nobel Prize for literature. In the meantime Borges came to be considered a modern classic, and Cortázar, Fuentes, and Vargas Llosa continued to produce original work and to be read, celebrated, and honored everywhere.

But the Boom was not only the result of the (perhaps) fortuitous emergence of a few writers of undeniable quality. It also had political roots. After coming to power in 1959, the Cuban Revolution gained international attention. With its youthful leaders and irreverent and combative policies, particularly with regard to the United States, it seemed to be the long-awaited redemption of the poor and the downtrodden in Latin America. Backed by the Soviets, who provided the funds as well as the model, Cuban cultural organizations began to promote the Latin American arts by the awarding of prizes, the organization of symposia, and the publication of journals and books. With the exception of Borges and very few others, most Latin American writers backed the revolution by participating in all of these activities. By the 1970s, as the revolution became increasingly repressive and dependent on the whims of Fidel Castro, who was transformed from rebel to Latin American dictator in the traditional way, many writers broke ranks. But the euphoric sense of power and the feeling of being at center stage in world affairs, with which the Revolution infused Latin American writers and intellectuals at first, had a lasting and profound effect on the evolution of Latin American literature.

A measure of the impact Latin American literature has had on a worldwide scale is the fact that four of the writers in this anthology have received the Nobel Prize (adding Mistral makes five for the region). The four are Asturias, Neruda, García Márquez, and Paz. Many believed that at least two others, Borges and Carpentier, should have also received the award. The Cervantes Prize, which has become the most coveted in Spanish (it is given by the King of Spain) has been won by many Latin Americans, including, of course, Borges, Carpentier, and Fuentes. This recognition, needless to say, also reveals to what degree the Latin

American literary tradition is part and parcel of the cultural values of the West, no matter how many clamor that it should be aligned with non-Western literatures.

CONTINUITY AND CHANGE

If one were to isolate the most salient characteristic of Latin American literature, it would be a paradoxical sense of a historical break as well as continuity, a feeling that it emerges in the midst of a crisis of cosmic dimensions, like the discovery and conquest of the New World. Much derision was heaped, and rightly so, upon the vacuous celebrations of the 1492 quincentenary. But retrospective rage cannot diminish the momentousness of the discovery. Before the fifteenth century, Europeans believed themselves to be the center of a relatively small world around which the universe revolved. After 1492 the sense of a shared planet, the feeling that Europe was not the center of the universe, shook the foundations of thought and recast the very justifications for conquest. The Spanish Empire was established with much self-doubt and in the midst of bitter polemics about its own legality. These struggles are evident in the myriad laws issued by the Spanish Crown to govern its vast and variegated empire. Latin America and its literature have retained not only the sense of crisis, but also the polemical tendency that grew around it. As Mexican novelist Carlos Fuentes has written: "The Roman legalistic tradition is one of the strongest components in Latin American culture: from Cortés to Zapata, we only believe in what is written down and codified."

Octavio Paz said that Latin American literature is a "literature of foundations." What Paz means is that Latin American writing is forever questioning its own legitimacy, its own principles and beginnings, as well as the very reality and existence of Latin America. It is expressed in Neruda's poetic self, which feels a personal and historical emptiness before the ruins of Macchu Picchu, and in the opening lines of *One Hundred Years of Solitude,* which describe an Edenic world in which things even lack names. It is the vertigo of the man in Borges's "Circular Ruins," who suddenly suspects that he is but another person's dream.

If there is a difference between Latin American literature and that of the modern West, it lies in this foundational quality. I would add that this element allows Latin American literature to be concerned in a rather impudent way with what I would call universal issues. The literature of the West, even the most modern, or postmodern, assumes that the major questions have been solved or are too cumbersome to introduce without embarrassment. Only in the most ironic or indirect way would a French, English, or North American novelist deal with themes such as the very foundation of the history and culture of those societies. But

Latin American writers feel that their literature emerged with and at the major historical break in the West since the birth of Christ: the discovery and conquest of America. This is why Carpentier can make Columbus and Queen Isabella, engaged in a love affair, the protagonists of one of his last novels, *The Harp and the Shadow* (1979), and García Márquez make Simón Bolivar the protagonist of *The General in the Labyrinth* (1989).

There is a certain naïveté in this stance, as well as an homage to the romantic roots of all modern literature. Carpentier was open in recognizing his debt to William Blake and maintained that all modern Latin American literature was essentially romantic. It was his view that the task of Latin American writers was to name things for the first time, like Blake's Adam, and like Columbus. This burning proximity to the origins of the modern tradition is another distinguishing trait of Latin American literature.

The exuberance of the Latin American muse, then, is due to its lack of measure, its lack of a sense of proportion. This is why no classicism has ever prospered in Latin America. Latin Americans' sense of place in world history does not allow for discretion nor for acquiescent imitation. Latin American history figures so prominently in Latin American literature — both poetry and fiction — not necessarily because of the writer's political commitment but because Latin American history is mythical in its conception. Latin America's world is ruled by heroes and antiheroes of incommensurable proportions: drug kingpins like Pablo Escobar, whose net worth was larger than his country's national budget; military goons in Argentina and Chile who can make thousands "disappear"; and dictators like Fidel Castro, whose reign has lasted thirty-five years (still counting). Time itself is hyperbolic in Latin America. The present, as we can see in the Chiapas revolt in Mexico, has a density of five hundred years and still includes the soldiers, friars, and natives who first met in the sixteenth century.

Roberto González Echevarría

FOR FURTHER READING

Primary Works

Arenas, Reinaldo. *The Ill-Fated Peregrinations of Fray Servando.* Translated by Andrew Hurley. New York: Avon Books, 1987.

Asturias, Miguel Angel. *El señor presidente.* Translated by Frances Partridge. 1963. Reprint, New York: Atheneum, 1972.

Borges, Jorge Luis. *Ficciones.* Translated by Anthony Kerrigan et al. New York: Grove Press, 1962.

Campos, Haroldo de. *Galaxias.* São Paolo: Editora Ex Libris, 1984.

Carpentier, Alejo. *War of Time*. Translated by Frances Partridge. New York: Knopf, 1970.

Cortázar, Julio. *Blow-up and Other Stories*. Translated by Paul Blackburn. New York: Random House, 1967.

Ferré, Rosario. *The Youngest Doll*. Translated by Rosario Ferré and Diana Vélez. Lincoln: The University of Nebraska Press, 1991.

Fuentes, Carlos. *The Death of Artemio Cruz*. Translated by Sam Hileman. New York: Farrar, Straus and Giroux, 1964.

García Márquez, Gabriel. *Love in the Time of Cholera*. Translated by Edith Grossman. New York: Knopf, 1988.

Guillén, Nicolás. *Man Making Words: Selected Poems of Nicolás Guillén*. Translated by Robert Márquez and David Arthur McMurray. Amherst: University of Massachusetts Press, 1972.

Lezama Lima, José. *Paradiso*. Translated by Gregory Rabassa. New York: Farrar, Straus and Giroux, 1974.

Lispector, Clarice. *The Hour of the Star*. Translated by Giovanni Pontiero. Manchester, England: Caracaanet, 1986.

Rosa, João Guimarães. *The Devil to Pay in the Backlands*. Translated by James L. Taylor and Harriet de Onís. New York: Knopf 1963.

Secondary Works

Alazraki, Jaime, and Ivar Ivask, eds. *The Final Island: The Fiction of Julio Cortázar*. Norman, Ok.: The University of Oklahoma Press, 1978.

Bloom, Harold, ed. *Gabriel García Márquez*. New York: Chelsea House, 1989.

Bloom, Harold, ed. *Jorge Luis Borges*. New York: Chelsea House, 1986.

Bloom, Harold, ed. *Pablo Neruda*. New York: Chelsea House, 1989.

Faria Coutinho, Eduardo de. *The Synthesis Novel in Latin America: A Study of Guimarães Rosa's Grande sertão, veredas*. Chapel Hill: University of North Carolina, 1991.

Faris, Wendy B. *Carlos Fuentes*. New York: Frederick Ungar, 1983.

Fitz, Earl E. *Clarice Lispector*. Boston: Twayne, 1985.

Franchetti, Paulo. *Alguns aspectos da teoria da poesia concreta*. São Paolo: Editora da UNICAMP, 1989.

González Echevarría, Roberto. *Alejo Carpentier: The Pilgrim at Home*. Ithaca: Cornell University Press, 1977.

———. "An Outcast of the Island." *The New York Times Book Review*, 24 October 1993.

González Echevarría, Roberto, and Enrique Pupo-Walker. *The Cambridge History of Latin American Literature*. 3 vols. Cambridge: Cambridge University Press, 1995.

Grossman, Edith. *The Antipoetry of Nicanor Parra*. New York: New York University Press, 1975.

Ivask, Ivar, ed. *The Perpetual Present: The Poetry and Prose of Octavio Paz*. Norman, Ok.: The University of Oklahoma Press, 1973.

Kutzinski, Vera M. *Against the American Grain: Myth and History in William*

Carlos Williams, Jay Wright and Nicolás Guillén. Baltimore: The Johns Hopkins University Press, 1987.

Leal, Luis. *Juan Rulfo*. Boston: Twayne, 1983.

Magnarelli, Sharon. "Luisa Valenzuela: From *Hay que sonreír* to *Cambio de armas.*" *World Literature Today* 58 (1984): 9–13.

Neruda, Pablo. *Canto General*. Translated by Jack Schmitt. Introduction by Roberto González Echevarría. Berkeley: University of California Press, 1991.

Parra, Nicanor. *Antipoems*. New York: New Directions, 1985.

Paz, Octavio. *The Collected Poems of Octavio Paz*. Translated by Eliot Weinberger. New York: New Directions, 1987.

Prieto, René. *Miguel Angel Asturias's Archeology of Return*. Cambridge: Cambridge University Press, 1993.

Rodríguez Monegal, Emir, ed. *The Borzoi Anthology of Latin American Literature*. New York: Knopf, 1977.

Rulfo, Juan. *The Burning Plain and Other Stories*. Translated by George D. Schade. Austin: University of Texas Press, 1967.

Solé, Carlos A., ed. *Latin American Writers*. 3 vols. New York: Scribners, 1989.

Souza, Raymond D. *The Poetic Fiction of José Lezama Lima*. Columbia, Mo.: University of Missouri Press, 1983.

Valenzuela, Luisa. *Black Novel with Argentines*. Translated by Toby Talbot. New York: Simon and Schuster, 1992.

Vargas Llosa, Mario. *Aunt Julia and the Scriptwriter*. Translated by Helen Lane. New York: Avon Books, 1983.

Williams, Raymond Leslie. *Mario Vargas Llosa*. New York: Ungar, 1986.

ARGENTINA ☼

JORGE LUIS BORGES

Perhaps the best known Latin American writer of all time, Jorge Luis Borges (1899–1986) was a self-effacing and bookish man; paradoxically, he was nearly blind for most of his adult life. He had an extensive education in his native Buenos Aires and Switzerland, and in his youth he traveled through Europe and spent some time in Spain. Borges knew many languages and was particularly fond of English and German writers, whom he read in the original languages. He began writing as a poet, singing the praises of his native city in Fervor of Buenos Aires *(1923), and continued to write verse throughout his life. Although many consider him a major poet, it was as a short story writer that Borges became well known. His first collection,* The Universal History of Infamy *(1935), told tales of deceit and adventure. The stories themselves are deceptive in their simplicity, containing already some of the traits that would make Borges's fiction famous. Borges's most important book was* Ficciones *(1944), which had a wide impact on the next two or three generations of Latin American writers; the 1962 English translation also had enormous influence in the United States and England. Borges's stories are paradoxical, metaphysical, and sometimes fraught with violence. He liked to mix history and fiction and make readers doubt even their own existence. This is the theme of "The Circular Ruins," which might lead readers to believe that they too are in another's dream.*

The Circular Ruins

And if he left off dreaming about you. . . .

— *Through the Looking-Glass,* IV

Nobody saw him come ashore in the encompassing night, nobody saw the bamboo craft run aground in the sacred mud, but within a few days everyone knew that the quiet man had come from the south and that his home was among the numberless villages upstream on the steep slopes of the mountain, where the Zend° language is barely tainted by Greek and

Zend language: The language of the Zoroastrians, in ancient Persia, in which their scriptures, or *Avesta*, were written

where lepers are rare. The fact is that the gray man pressed his lips to the mud, scrambled up the bank without parting (perhaps without feeling) the brushy thorns that tore his flesh, and dragged himself, faint and bleeding, to the circular opening watched over by a stone tiger, or horse, which once was the color of fire and is now the color of ash. This opening is a temple which was destroyed ages ago by flames, which the swampy wilderness later desecrated, and whose god no longer receives the reverence of men. The stranger laid himself down at the foot of the image.

Wakened by the sun high overhead, he noticed — somehow without amazement — that his wounds had healed. He shut his pale eyes and slept again, not because of weariness but because he willed it. He knew that this temple was the place he needed for his unswerving purpose; he knew that downstream the encroaching trees had also failed to choke the ruins of another auspicious temple with its own fire-ravaged, dead gods; he knew that his first duty was to sleep. Along about midnight, he was awakened by the forlorn call of a bird. Footprints, some figs, and a water jug told him that men who lived nearby had looked on his sleep with a kind of awe and either sought his protection or else were in dread of his witchcraft. He felt the chill of fear and searched the crumbling walls for a burial niche, where he covered himself over with leaves he had never seen before.

His guiding purpose, though it was supernatural, was not impossible. He wanted to dream a man; he wanted to dream him down to the last detail and project him into the world of reality. This mystical aim had taxed the whole range of his mind. Had anyone asked him his own name or anything about his life before then, he would not have known what to answer. This forsaken, broken temple suited him because it held few visible things, and also because the neighboring villagers would look after his frugal needs. The rice and fruit of their offerings were nourishment enough for his body, whose one task was to sleep and to dream.

At the outset, his dreams were chaotic; later on, they were of a dialectic nature. The stranger dreamed himself at the center of a circular amphitheater which in some way was also the burnt-out temple. Crowds of silent disciples exhausted the tiers of seats; the faces of the farthest of them hung centuries away from him and at a height of the stars, but their features were clear and exact. The man lectured on anatomy, cosmography, and witchcraft. The faces listened, bright and eager, and did their best to answer sensibly, as if they felt the importance of his questions, which would raise one of them out of an existence as a shadow and place him in the real world. Whether asleep or awake, the man pondered the answers of his phantoms and, not letting himself be misled by imposters, divined in certain of their quandaries a growing intelligence. He was in search of a soul worthy of taking a place in the world.

After nine or ten nights he realized, feeling bitter over it, that nothing could be expected from those pupils who passively accepted his teaching, but that he might, however, hold hopes for those who from time to time hazarded reasonable doubts about what he taught. The former, although they deserved love and affection, could never become real; the latter, in their dim way, were already real. One evening (now his evenings were also given over to sleeping, now he was only awake for an hour or two at dawn) he dismissed his vast dream-school forever and kept a single disciple. He was a quiet, sallow, and at times rebellious young man with sharp features akin to those of his dreamer. The sudden disappearance of his fellow pupils did not disturb him for very long, and his progress, at the end of a few private lessons, amazed his teacher. Nonetheless, a catastrophe intervened. One morning, the man emerged from his sleep as from a sticky wasteland, glanced up at the faint evening light, which at first he confused with the dawn, and realized that he had not been dreaming. All that night and the next day, the hideous lucidity of insomnia weighed down on him. To tire himself out he tried to explore the surrounding forest, but all he managed, there in a thicket of hemlocks, were some snatches of broken sleep, fleetingly tinged with visions of a crude and worthless nature. He tried to reassemble his school, and barely had he uttered a few brief words of counsel when the whole class went awry and vanished. In his almost endless wakefulness, tears of anger stung his old eyes.

He realized that, though he may penetrate all the riddles of the higher and lower orders, the task of shaping the senseless and dizzying stuff of dreams is the hardest that a man can attempt — much harder than weaving a rope of sand or of coining the faceless wind. He realized that an initial failure was to be expected. He then swore he would forget the populous vision which in the beginning had led him astray, and he sought another method. Before attempting it, he spent a month rebuilding the strength his fever had consumed. He gave up all thoughts of dreaming and almost at once managed to sleep a reasonable part of the day. The few times he dreamed during this period he did not dwell on his dreams. Before taking up his task again, he waited until the moon was a perfect circle. Then, in the evening, he cleansed himself in the waters of the river, worshiped the gods of the planets, uttered the prescribed syllables of an all-powerful name, and slept. Almost at once, he had a dream of a beating heart.

He dreamed it throbbing, warm, secret. It was the size of a closed fist, a darkish red in the dimness of a human body still without a face or sex. With anxious love he dreamed it for fourteen lucid nights. Each night he perceived it more clearly. He did not touch it, but limited himself to witnessing it, to observing it, to correcting it now and then with a look. He felt it, he lived it from different distances and from many angles. On the fourteenth night he touched the pulmonary artery with a finger and then the whole heart, inside and out. The examination satisfied him. For one night he deliberately did not dream; after that he went back to the heart again, invoked the name of a planet, and set out to envision another of the principal organs. Before a year was over he came to the skeleton, the eyelids. The countless strands of hair were perhaps the hardest task of all. He dreamed a whole man, a young man, but the young man could not stand up or speak, nor could he open his eyes. Night after night, the man dreamed him asleep.

In the cosmogonies° of the Gnostics,° the demiurges mold a red Adam who is unable to stand on his feet; as clumsy and crude and elementary as that Adam of dust was the Adam of dreams wrought by the nights of the magician. One evening the man was at the point of destroying all his handiwork (it would have been better for him had he done so), but in the end he restrained himself. Having exhausted his prayers to the gods of the earth and river, he threw himself down at the feet of the stone image that may have been a tiger or a stallion, and asked for its blind aid. That same evening he dreamed of the image. He dreamed it alive, quivering; it was no unnatural cross between tiger and stallion but at one and the same time both these violent creatures and also a bull, a rose, a thunderstorm. This manifold god revealed to him that its earthly name was Fire, that there in the circular temple (and in others like it) sacrifices had once been made to it, that it had been worshiped, and that through its magic the phantom of the man's dreams would be wakened to life in such a way that — except for Fire itself and the dreamer — every being in the world would accept him as a man of flesh and blood. The god ordered that, once instructed in the rites, the disciple should be sent downstream to the other ruined temple, whose pyramids still survived, so that in that abandoned place some human voice might exalt him. In the dreamer's dream, the dreamed one awoke.

The magician carried out these orders. He devoted a period of time (which finally spanned two years) to initiating his disciple into the riddles of the universe and the worship of Fire. Deep inside, it pained him to say good-bye to his creature. Under the pretext of teaching him more fully, each day he drew out the hours set aside for sleep. Also, he reshaped the somewhat faulty right shoulder. From time to time, he was troubled by the feeling that all this had already happened, but for the most part his days were happy. On closing his eyes he would think, "Now I will be with my son." Or, less frequently, "The son I have begotten awaits me and he will not exist if I do not go to him."

Little by little, he was training the young man for reality. On one occasion he commanded him to set up a flag on a distant peak. The next day, there on the peak, a fiery pennant shone. He tried other, similar exercises, each bolder than the one before. He realized with a certain bitterness that his son was ready — and perhaps impatient — to be born. That night he kissed him for the first time and sent him down the river to the

cosmogonies: stories about the creation or origin of the world
Gnostics: members of an early Christian sect whose beliefs combined Christianity with Greek and Asian philosophies

other temple, whose whitened ruins were still to be glimpsed over miles and miles of impenetrable forest and swamp. At the very end (so that the boy would never know he was a phantom, so that he would think himself a man like all men), the magician imbued his disciple with total oblivion of his long years of apprenticeship.

His triumph and his peace were blemished by a touch of weariness. In the morning and evening dusk, he prostrated himself before the stone idol, perhaps imagining that his unreal son was performing the same rites farther down the river in other circular ruins. At night he no longer dreamed, or else he dreamed the way all men dream. He now perceived with a certain vagueness the sounds and shapes of the world, for his absent son was taking nourishment from the magician's decreasing consciousness. His life's purpose was fulfilled; the man lived on in a kind of ecstasy. After a length of time that certain tellers of the story count in years and others in half-decades, he was awakened one midnight by two rowers. He could not see their faces, but they spoke to him about a magic man in a temple up north who walked on fire without being burned. The magician suddenly remembered the god's words. He remembered that of all the creatures in the world, Fire was the only one who knew his son was a phantom. This recollection, comforting at first, ended by tormenting him. He feared that his son might wonder at this strange privilege and in some way discover his condition as a mere appearance. Not to be a man but to be the projection of another man's dreams — what an unparalleled humiliation, how bewildering! Every father cares for the child he has begotten — he has allowed — in some moment of confusion or happiness. It is understandable, then, that the magician should fear for the future of a son thought out organ by organ and feature by feature over the course of a thousand and one secret nights.

The end of these anxieties came suddenly, but certain signs foretold it. First (after a long drought), a far-off cloud on a hilltop, as light as a bird; next, toward the south, the sky, which took on the rosy hue of a leopard's gums; then, the pillars of smoke that turned the metal of the nights to rust; finally, the headlong panic of the forest animals. For what had happened many centuries ago was happening again. The ruins of the fire god's shrine were destroyed by fire. In a birdless dawn the magician saw the circling sheets of flame closing in on him. For a moment, he thought of taking refuge in the river, but then he realized that death was coming to crown his years and to release him from his labors. He walked into the leaping pennants of flame. They did not bite into his flesh, but caressed him and flooded him without heat or burning. In relief, in humiliation, in terror, he understood that he, too, was an appearance, that someone else was dreaming him.

Translated from the Spanish by
Norman Thomas di Giovanni

JULIO CORTÁZAR

Julio Cortázar (1914–1984) lived in Paris from 1952 until his death, working mostly as a translator for UNESCO. In 1963 his novel Hopscotch made him an international celebrity: it was the first strong sign of life in the soon-to-be revitalized Latin American novel. A playful, complicated text whose chapters could be read in at least two sequences suggested by an opening "instruction table," it told the tale of Argentines and other Latin American intellectuals and artists in Paris. The huge novel faithfully reflected its author, a giant of a man (six feet six inches tall), full of kindness and a certain childish naïveté but quite cultured, particularly in the area of modern, avant-garde art.

By 1963 Cortázar had already published three collections of short stories. He went on to publish several others. One of Cortázar's stories became internationally famous when it was used as the basis for Antonioni's film Blow-Up. Cortázar was particularly interested in alterations of everyday reality that compete with the reality we think we live in. In one story the character dreams that he is an Aztec warrior killed in battle, but he has just died in a motorcycle crash (or is the Aztec warrior dreaming that he is in the crash?). In "Continuity of Parks" a man confronts yet a different alternative reality.

Continuity of Parks

He had begun to read the novel a few days before. He had put it down because of some urgent business conferences, opened it again on his way back to the estate by train; he permitted himself a slowly growing interest in the plot, in the characterizations. That afternoon, after writing a letter giving his power of attorney and discussing a matter of joint ownership with the manager of his estate, he returned to the book in the tranquility of his study which looked out upon the park with its oaks. Sprawled in his favorite armchair, its back toward the door — even the possibility of an intrusion would have irritated him, had he thought of it — he let his left hand caress repeatedly the green velvet upholstery and set to reading the final chapters. He remembered effortlessly the names and his mental image of the characters; the novel spread its glamour over him almost at once. He tasted the almost perverse pleasure of disengaging himself line by line from the things around him, and at the same time feeling his head rest comfortably on the green velvet of the chair with its high back, sensing that the cigarettes rested within reach of his hand, that beyond the great windows the air of afternoon danced under the oak trees in the park. Word by word, licked up by the sordid dilemma of the hero and heroine, letting himself be absorbed to the point where the images settled down and took on color and movement, he was witness to the final encounter in the mountain cabin. The woman arrived first, apprehensive; now the lover came in, his face cut by the backlash of a branch. Admirably, she stanched the blood with her kisses, but he rebuffed her caresses; he had not come to perform again the ceremonies of a secret passion, protected by a world of dry leaves and furtive paths through the forest. The dagger warmed itself against his chest, and underneath liberty pounded, hidden close. A lustful, panting dialogue raced down the pages like a rivulet of snakes, and one felt it had all been decided from eternity. Even to those caresses which writhed about the lover's body, as though wishing to keep him there, to dissuade him from it; they sketched abominably the frame of that other body it was necessary to destroy. Nothing had been forgotten: alibis, unforeseen hazards, possible mistakes. From this hour on, each instant had its use minutely assigned. The cold-blooded, twice-gone-over reexamination of the details was barely broken off so that a hand could caress a cheek. It was beginning to get dark.

Not looking at one another now, rigidly fixed upon the task which awaited them, they separated at the cabin door. She was to follow the trail that led north. On the path leading in the opposite direction, he turned for a moment to watch her running, her hair loosened and flying. He ran in turn, crouching among the trees and hedges until, in the yellowish fog of dusk, he could distinguish the avenue of trees which led up to the house. The dogs were not supposed to bark, they did not bark. The estate manager would not be there at this hour, and he was not there. He went up the three porch steps and entered. The woman's words reached him over the thudding of blood in his ears: first a blue chamber, then a hall, then a carpeted stairway. At the top, two doors. No one in the first room, no one in the second. The door of the salon, and then, the knife in hand, the light from the great windows, the high back of an armchair covered in green velvet, the head of the man in the chair reading a novel.

*Translated from The Spanish
by Paul Blackburn*

LUISA VALENZUELA

Luisa Valenzuela (1938–) has become one of the most read and discussed women writers from Latin America. She has managed to acquire a voice of her own through her social satire and biting irony. She is very much in the tradition of Jorge Luis Borges and (above all) Julio

Cortázar in her pitiless critique of political figures and institutions. But her reach is wider, for she is profoundly interested in popular culture and in sexism, not just machismo. In Valenzuela's fiction, sexual roles are fluid; she debunks, often through raucous mockery, the belief that sexual roles are fixed in the essential nature of gender. She has published a handful of novels and collections of stories, but is known in English mostly for The Lizard's Tail *(1983). The following selection, with obvious echoes of Franz Kafka and Julio Cortázar, is a ruthless satire of censorship, a common phenomenon in Latin America during dictatorships.*

The Censors

Poor Juan! One day they caught him with his guard down before he could even realize that what he had taken to be a stroke of luck was really one of fate's dirty tricks. These things happen the minute you're careless, as one often is. Juancito let happiness — a feeling you can't trust — get the better of him when he received from a confidential source Mariana's new address in Paris and knew that she hadn't forgotten him. Without thinking twice, he sat down at his table and wrote her a letter. *The* letter. The same one that now keeps his mind off his job during the day and won't let him sleep at night (what had he scrawled, what had he put on that sheet of paper he sent to Mariana?).

Juan knows there won't be a problem with the letter's contents, that it's irreproachable, harmless. But what about the rest? He knows that they examine, sniff, feel, and read between the lines of each and every letter, and check its tiniest comma and most accidental stain. He knows that all letters pass from hand to hand and go through all sorts of tests in the huge censorship offices and that, in the end, very few continue on their way. Usually it takes months, even years, if there aren't any snags; all this time the freedom, maybe even the life, of both sender and receiver is in jeopardy. And that's why Juan's so troubled: thinking that something might happen to Mariana because of his letter. Of all people, Mariana, who must finally feel safe there where she always dreamt about living. But he knows that the *Censor's Secret Command* operates all over the world and cashes in on the discount in air fares; there's nothing to stop them from going as far as that obscure Paris neighborhood, kidnapping Mariana, and returning to their cozy homes, certain of having fulfilled their noble mission.

Well, you've got to beat them to the punch, do what every one tries to do: sabotage the machinery, throw sand in its gears, that is to say get to the bottom of the problem to try to stop it.

This was Juan's sound plan when he, along with many others, applied for a censor's job — not because he had a calling like others or needed a job: no, he applied simply to intercept his own letter, an idea none too original but comforting. He was hired immediately, for each day more and more censors are needed and no one would bother to check on his references.

Ulterior motives couldn't be overlooked by the *Censorship Division*, but they needn't be too strict with those who applied. They knew how hard it would be for the poor guys to find the letter they wanted and even if they did, what's a letter or two compared to all the others that the new censor would snap up? That's how Juan managed to join the *Post Office's Censorship Division*, with a certain goal in mind.

The building had a festive air on the outside that contrasted with its inner staidness. Little by little, Juan was absorbed by his job, and he felt at peace since he was doing everything he could to retrieve his letter to Mariana. He didn't even worry when, in his first month, he was sent to *Section K* where envelopes are very carefully screened for explosives.

It's true that on the third day a fellow worker had his right hand blown off by a letter, but the division chief claimed it was sheer negligence on the victim's part. Juan and the other employees were allowed to go back to their work, though feeling less secure. After work, one of them tried to organize a strike to demand higher wages for unhealthy work, but Juan didn't join in; after thinking it over, he reported the man to his superiors and thus he got promoted.

You don't form a habit by doing something once, he told himself as he left his boss's office. And when he was transferred to *Section J*, where letters are carefully checked for poison dust, he felt he had climbed a rung in the ladder.

By working hard, he quickly reached *Section E* where the job became more interesting, for he could now read and analyze the letters' contents. Here he could even hope to get hold of his letter to Marianna, which, judging by the time that had elapsed, would have gone through the other sections and was probably floating around in this one.

Soon his work became so absorbing that his noble mission blurred in his mind. Day after day he crossed out whole paragraphs in red ink, pitilessly chucking many letters into the censored basket. These were horrible days when he was shocked by the subtle and conniving ways employed by people to pass on subversive messages; his instincts were so sharp that he found behind a simple "the weather's unsettled" or "prices continue to soar" the wavering hand of someone secretly scheming to overthrow the Government.

His zeal brought him swift promotion. We don't know if this made him happy. Very few letters reached him in *Section B* — only a handful passed the other hurdles — so he read them over and over again, passed them under a magnifying glass, searched for microdots with an electron microscope, and tuned his sense of smell so that he was beat by the time he made it home. He'd barely manage to warm up his soup, eat some fruit, and fall into bed, satisfied with having done his duty. Only his darling mother worried, but she couldn't get him back on the right track. She'd say, though it wasn't always true: Lola called, she's at the bar with the girls, they miss you, they're waiting for you. Or else she'd leave a bottle of red wine on the table. But Juan wouldn't indulge: any distraction could make him lose his edge and the perfect censor had to be alert, keen, attentive, and sharp to nab cheats. He had a truly patriotic task, both self-sacrificing and uplifting.

His basket for censored letters became the best fed as well as the most cunning in the whole *Censorship Division*. He was about to congratulate himself for having finally discovered his true mission, when his letter to Mariana reached his hands. Naturally, he censored it without regret. And just as naturally, he couldn't stop them from executing him the following morning, one more victim of his devotion to his work.

Translated from the Spanish by David Unger

BRAZIL

JOÃO GUIMARÃES ROSA

A medical doctor and diplomat, João Guimarães Rosa (1908–1967) successfully blends the regionalist tendencies of the northeastern Brazilian novel and the avant-garde slant of groups centered in São Paolo. He was in Brazil's diplomatic corps for many years, including a stint in Nazi Germany, where he was interned in a camp, accused of helping Jews flee the country. As a young doctor, Rosa would ask his impoverished patients to pay him by telling him stories. Some of these he wove together in his complex novel The Devil to Pay in the Backlands *(1956), set in the Brazilian plains. Some, like the late critic Emir Rodríguez Monegal, consider it the best Latin American novel ever. Rosa was also a master of the short story, publishing several collections in his lifetime; others were collected posthumously. "The Third Bank of the River," perhaps his finest story, begins with a deliberate effort to highlight the conventional, even boring, character of the father, who then embarks on a weird adventure that takes on allegorical dimensions.*

The Third Bank of the River

Father was a reliable, law-abiding, practical man, and had been ever since he was a boy, as various people of good sense testified when I asked them about him. I don't remember that he seemed any crazier or even any moodier than anyone else we knew. He just didn't talk much. It was our mother who gave the orders and scolded us every day — my sister, my brother, and me. Then one day my father ordered a canoe for himself.

He took the matter very seriously. He had the canoe made to his specifications of fine *vinhático*° wood; a small one, with a narrow board in the stern as though to leave only enough room for the oarsman. Every bit of it was hand-hewn of special strong wood carefully shaped, fit to last in the water for twenty or thirty years. Mother railed at the idea. How could a man who had never fiddled away his time on such tricks propose to go fishing and hunting now, at his time of life? Father said nothing. Our

---

vinhático: a kind of Brazilian hardwood

house was closer to the river then than it is now, less than a quarter of a league away: there rolled the river, great, deep, and silent, always silent. It was so wide that you could hardly see the bank on the other side. I can never forget the day the canoe was ready.

Neither happy nor excited nor downcast, Father pulled his hat well down on his head and said one firm goodbye. He spoke not another word, took neither food nor other supplies, gave no parting advice. We thought Mother would have a fit, but she only blanched white, bit her lip, and said bitterly, "Go or stay, but if you go, don't you ever come back!"

Father left his answer in suspense. He gave me a mild look and motioned me to go aside with him a few steps. I was afraid of Mother's anger, but I obeyed anyway, that time. The turn things had taken gave me the courage to ask, "Father, will you take me with you in that canoe?" But he just gave me a long look in return: gave me his blessing and motioned me to go back. I pretended to go, but instead turned off into a deep woodsy hollow to watch. Father stepped into the canoe, untied it, and began to paddle off. The canoe slipped away, a straight, even shadow like an alligator, slithery, long.

Our father never came back. He hadn't gone anywhere. He stuck to that stretch of the river, staying halfway across, always in the canoe, never to spring out of it, ever again. The strangeness of that truth was enough to dismay us all. What had never been before, was. Our relatives, the neighbors, and all our acquaintances met and took counsel together.

Mother, though, behaved very reasonably, with the result that everybody believed what no one wanted to put into words about our father: that he was mad. Only a few of them thought he might be keeping a vow, or — who could tell? — maybe he was sick with some hideous disease like leprosy, and that was what had made him desert us to live out another life, close to his family and yet far enough away. The news spread by word of mouth, carried by people like travelers and those who lived along the banks of the river, who said of Father that he never landed at spit or cove, by day or by night, but always stuck to the river, lonely and outside human society. Finally, Mother and our relatives realized that the provisions he had hidden in the canoe must be getting low and thought that he would have to either land somewhere and go away from us for good — that seemed the most likely — or repent once and for all and come back home.

But they were wrong. I had made myself responsible for stealing a bit of food for him every day, an idea that had come to me the very first night, when the family had lighted bonfires on the riverbank and in their glare prayed and called out to Father. Every day from then on I went back to the river with a lump of hard brown sugar, some corn bread, or a bunch of bananas. Once, at the end of an hour of waiting that had dragged on and on, I caught sight of Father; he was way off, sitting in the bottom of the canoe as if suspended in the mirror smoothness of the river. He saw me, but he did not paddle over or make any sign. I held up the things to eat and then laid them in a hollowed-out rock in the river bluff, safe from any animals who might nose around and where they would be kept dry in rain or dew. Time after time, day after day, I did the same thing. Much later I had a surprise: Mother knew about my mission but, saying nothing and pretending she didn't, made it easier for me by putting out leftovers where I was sure to find them. Mother almost never showed what she was thinking.

Finally she sent for an uncle of ours, her brother, to help with the farm and with money matters, and she got a tutor for us children. She also arranged for the priest to come in his vestments to the river edge to exorcise Father and call upon him to desist from his sad obsession. Another time, she tried to scare Father by getting two soldiers to come. But none of it was any use. Father passed by at a distance, discernible only dimly through the river haze, going by in the canoe without ever letting anyone go close enough to touch him or even talk to him. The reporters who went out in a launch and tried to take his picture not long ago failed just like everybody else; Father crossed over to the other bank and steered the canoe into the thick swamp that goes on for miles, part reeds and part brush. Only he knew every hand's breadth of its blackness.

We just had to try to get used to it. But it was hard, and we never really managed. I'm judging by myself, of course. Whether I wanted to or not, my thoughts kept circling back and I found myself thinking of Father. The hard nub of it was that I couldn't begin to understand how he could hold out. Day and night, in bright sunshine or in rainstorms, in muggy heat or in the terrible cold spells in the middle of the year, without shelter or any protection but the old hat on his head, all through the weeks, and months, and years — he marked in no way the passing of his life. Father never landed, never put in at either shore or stopped at any of the river islands or sandbars; and he never again stepped onto grass or solid earth. It was true that in order to catch a little sleep he may have tied up the canoe at some concealed islet spit. But he never lighted a fire on shore, had no lamp or candle, never struck a match again. He did no more than taste food; even the morsels he took from what we left for him along the roots of the fig tree or in the hollow stone at the foot of the cliff could not have been enough to keep him alive. Wasn't he ever sick? And what constant strength he must have had in his arms to maintain himself and the canoe ready for the piling up of the floodwaters where danger rolls on the great current, sweeping the bodies of dead animals and tree trunks downstream — frightening, threatening, crashing into him. And he never spoke another word to a living soul. We never talked about him, either. We only thought of him. Father could never be forgotten; and if, for short periods of time, we pretended to ourselves that we had forgotten, it was only to find ourselves roused suddenly by his memory, startled by it again and again.

My sister married; but Mother would have no festivities. He came into our minds whenever we ate something especially tasty, and when we were wrapped up snugly at night we thought of those bare unsheltered nights of cold, heavy rain, and Father with only his hand and maybe a calabash° to bail the storm water out of the canoe. Every so often someone who knew us would remark that I was getting to look more and more like my father. But I knew that now he must be bushy-haired and bearded, his nails long, his body cadaverous and gaunt, burnt black by the sun, hairy as a beast and almost as naked, even with the pieces of clothing we left for him at intervals.

He never felt the need to know anything about us; had he no family affection? But out of love, love and respect, whenever I was praised for something good I had done, I would say, "It was Father who taught me how to do it that way." It wasn't true, exactly, but it was a truthful kind of lie. If he didn't remember us any more and didn't want to know how we were, why didn't he go farther up the river or down it, away to landing places where he would never be found? Only he knew. When my sister had a baby boy, she got it into her head that she must show Father his grandson. All of us went and stood on the bluff. The day was fine and my sister was wearing the white dress she had worn at her wedding. She lifted the baby up in her arms and her husband held a parasol over the two of them. We called and we waited. Our father didn't come. My sister wept; we all cried and hugged one another as we stood there.

After that my sister moved far away with her husband, and my brother decided to go live in the city. Times changed, with the slow swiftness of time. Mother went away too in the end, to live with my sister because she was growing old. I stayed on here, the only one of the family who was left. I could never think of marriage. I stayed where I was, burdened down with all life's cumbrous baggage. I knew Father needed me, as he wandered up and down on the river in the wilderness, even though he never gave a reason for what he had done. When at last I made up my mind that I had to know and finally made a firm attempt to find out, people told me rumor had it that Father might have given some explanation to the man who made the canoe for him. But now the builder was dead; and no one really knew or could recollect any more except that there had been some silly talk in the beginning, when the river was first swollen by such endless torrents of rain that everyone was afraid the world was coming to an end; then they had said that Father might have received a warning, like Noah, and so prepared the canoe ahead of time. I could half-recall the story. I could not even blame my father. And a few first white hairs began to appear on my head.

I was a man whose words were all sorrowful. Why did I feel so guilty,

calabash: a hollowed out, hard-crusted fruit, like a gourd

so guilty? Was it because of my father, who made his absence felt always, and because of the river-river-river, the river — flowing forever? I was suffering the onset of old age — this life of mine only postponed the inevitable. I had bed spells, pains in the belly, dizziness, twinges of rheumatism. And he? Why, oh why must he do what he did? He must suffer terribly. Old as he was, was he not bound to weaken in vigor sooner or later and let the canoe overturn or, when the river rose, let it drift unguided for hours downstream, until it finally went over the brink of the loud rushing fall of the cataract, with its wild boiling and death? My heart shrank. He was out there, with none of my easy security. I was guilty of I knew not what, filled with boundless sorrow in the deepest part of me. If I only knew — if only things were otherwise. And then, little by little, the idea came to me.

I could not even wait until next day. Was I crazy? No. In our house, the word *crazy* was not spoken, had never been spoken again in all those years; no one was condemned as crazy. Either no one is crazy, or everyone is. I just went, taking along a sheet to wave with. I was very much in my right mind. I waited. After a long time he appeared; his indistinct bulk took form. He was there, sitting in the stern. He was there, a shout away. I called out several times. And I said the words which were making me say them, the sworn promise, the declaration. I had to force my voice to say, "Father, you're getting old, you've done your part. . . . You can come back now, you don't have to stay any longer. . . . You come back now, and I'll do it, right now or whenever you want me to; it's what we both want. I'll take your place in the canoe!" And as I said it my heart beat to the rhythm of what was truest and best in me.

He heard me. He got to his feet. He dipped the paddle in the water, the bow pointed toward me; he had agreed. And suddenly I shuddered deeply, because he had lifted his arm and gestured a greeting — the first, after so many years. And I could not. . . . Panic-stricken, my hair standing on end, I ran, I fled, I left the place behind me in a mad headlong rush. For he seemed to be coming from the hereafter. And I am pleading, pleading, pleading for forgiveness.

I was struck by the solemn ice of fear, and I fell ill. I knew that no one ever heard of him again. Can I be a man, after having thus failed him? I am what never was — the unspeakable. I know it is too late for salvation now, but I am afraid to cut life short in the shallows of the world. At least, when death comes to the body, let them take me and put me in a wretched little canoe, and on the water that flows forever past its unending banks, let me go — down the river, away from the river, into the river — the river.

*Translated from the Portuguese
by Barbara Shelby*

CLARICE LISPECTOR

Born in the Ukraine a few months before her parents emigrated to Brazil, Clarice Lispector (1925–1977) is one of the most original Latin American writers of the twentieth century. Her first novel, Close to the Savage Heart, *appeared before she was twenty and created a stir. Like the rest of her novels, it is an intimate, self-reflective text that lays bare her tortured inner self. At the time of its publication, Brazilian novels depicting the northeast dominated the scene, with regional themes and socio-political criticism. Lispector's personal focus was seen by some as narcissistic and self-absorbed, not to mention her experimentation with syntax and usage of standard Portuguese. But she eventually became admired and imitated for precisely those traits, and portions of her later novels were sung by popular singers and rock groups.*

Lispector was also an accomplished short story writer (often with animals as characters), and she wrote children's books and essays. "The Crime of the Mathematics Professor" is taken from her collection Family Ties *(1960). The story establishes an ironic counterpoint between the modest, private ritual performed by the professor and the organized ritual taking place in a church.*

The Crime of the Mathematics Professor

When the man reached the top of the highest hill, bells were tolling in the city below him. Nothing could be clearly distinguished but the irregular roofs of the houses. The man stood there, near the only tree on the hilltop. He was holding a heavy bag.

He looked down myopically at the tiny Catholics slowly entering the church and tried to hear the voices of the children scattered about the square. The morning was clear, yet the sounds barely reached the hilltop. He looked down also at the river, which seemed motionless, and he thought: it is Sunday. He could see in the distance the high mountain with its arid cliffs. Although the air was not cold, he turned up his collar. Finally, he placed the bag carefully on the ground. Then he took off his glasses, apparently to breathe more freely, for with the glasses in his hand he inhaled deeply. The bright light hit the lenses, glancing off in sharp signals. Without the glasses the man's eyes twinkled and looked younger. He put the glasses on, returning to middle age, and picked up the bag.

"It is heavy as stone," he thought.

He strained his eyes to see the flow of the river; he inclined his head to hear better: the river remained motionless and only the shrillest voice succeeded, momentarily, in reaching the height. Yes, he was quite alone. The cool air seemed inhospitable, for he had lived in the greater warmth of the city. He stood looking at the lone tree, whose branches were swaying. After a time, he decided there was no reason to put it off any longer.

Nevertheless, he continued to procrastinate. Obviously his glasses bothered him, for he took them off again, breathed deeply, and put them in his pocket.

Then he opened the bag, inserted a thin hand, and pulled out the dead dog. His whole being was concentrated on that hand, and he kept his eyes tightly shut. When he opened them, the air was even clearer and the merry bells were calling the faithful to the comfort of punishment.

The unknown dog lay in full view.

The man began working methodically. He picked up the dog, black and stiff, and placed him in a little declivity of the earth. But, as though he had already accomplished a great deal, he put on his glasses, sat down beside the dog, and looked about.

He contemplated the empty hilltop with a certain futility. Seated as he was, he could no longer see the little city below. He breathed deeply again. He reached into the bag and pulled out a shovel. He thought about the choice of a place. It could be right there under the tree. This idea disturbed him. If it had been the other, the real dog, he would have buried him where he himself would have liked to be buried — in the very center of the hilltop, facing the sun with empty eyes. The unknown dog was a substitute and, in order to perfect the act, he wanted to give him exactly the same treatment the other would have received. There was no confusion in the man's mind. He understood himself coldly, consistently.

He tried scrupulously to ascertain the exact center of the hilltop. This was not easy, for the lone tree stood to one side, setting itself up as a false center and dividing the area asymmetrically.

"I really don't have to bury him in the center," the man conceded, "for I might well have buried the other anywhere, perhaps at the spot where I am now standing."

He wanted to give the act the fatality of mere chance, the stamp of a plain and external event, in the same category as the children in the square or the Catholics entering the church. It all had to be utterly visible, right there on the surface of the earth under the sky. The act and he himself had to be freed from the remoteness and impunity of a thought.

The mere idea of burying the dog at the spot where he was standing caused the man to jump backward with an agility unsuited to his small but singularly heavy body. For he seemed to see the dog's grave beneath his feet.

He began digging rhythmically. Sometimes he stopped to take off his glasses and put them on again. He perspired profusely. The grave was shallow, not because he wanted to spare himself but because the thought occurred to him:

"If it were for the real dog, it would not be deep. I would bury him as near the surface as possible."

He believed that the dog, with very little earth above him, would not lose the power of sensation.

Finally he put the shovel down, gently picked up the unknown dog, and placed him in the grave.

What a strange face the dog had! When, with a shock, he had come upon the dog, dead on a street corner, the idea of burying him had so astonished and weighed upon his heart that he had not even noticed this hard nose and dried drivel. It was an alien and objective dog.

The body was slightly bigger than the hole. The grave would be a barely perceptible protuberance on the hilltop. That was the way he wanted it. He covered the dog with earth and smoothed the surface with his hands, pleasurably feeling the dog's shape in his palms as though he were caressing the animal. The dog was now part of the terrain. The man rose, shook the earth from his hands, and looked away from the grave. He thought, with a certain pleasure:

"I have done it."

He sighed. An innocent smile of liberation appeared on his face. Yes, he had done everything. His crime had been punished and he was free.

Now at last he could think of the real dog without constraint. The real dog who right now must be wandering, puzzled, sniffing through the streets of the other city, where he had no owner.

He concentrated his thoughts on the real dog as if on his own life. His bittersweet affection for the animal helped to overcome the handicap of distance.

"While I was making you in my image, you were making me in yours," he thought. "I called you Joseph so that your name could serve you also as a soul. And you — how can I ever know the name you gave me with your great love, greater, I'm afraid, than my love for you.

"We understood each other too well, you with the human name I gave you, I with the name you told me only by your insistent look." The man smiled affectionately, free now to recollect at will.

"I remember when you were small and weak. How funny you were then! You would wag your tail and look at me, while I was discovering in you a new way of knowing my soul. Yet even then, day by day, you were growing into a dog that could be utterly forsaken. Meanwhile, our games were becoming dangerous because of our excess of mutual understanding." The man recalled this with satisfaction. "They always ended with you biting me and grumbling and with me throwing a book at you and laughing. But my laughter was forced. And who can say what it may already have meant. You were a dog that could be forsaken at any time.

"How you used to sniff the streets!" thought the man, with a faint smile. "Really, not a single stone escaped your investigation. . . . This was your childish side. Or was it just your obligation as a dog? And, for the rest, were you merely playing at being mine? For you were uncon-querable. Wagging your tail calmly, you seemed silently to reject the name I had given you. Oh, yes, you were unconquerable. I did not want you to eat meat lest it make you ferocious. But one day you jumped on the table and, amidst the happy shrills of the children, snapped up the roast. With a fierceness that does not come from what is eaten, you glared at me mute and unyielding, with the meat in your mouth. For, al-though mine, you never relinquished, even a little, your past or your na-ture. And, apprehensive, I began to understand that I did not have to re-linquish any part of my own self for you to love me, and this was beginning to trouble me. You expected us to reach a mutual understand-ing on the basis of the resistant reality of our two natures. Neither my fe-rocity nor yours should be changed into gentleness: this is what you were gradually teaching me and it was becoming burdensome. Without asking for anything, you asked for too much. From you I demanded your being a dog, from me you demanded that I be a man. And I pretended as well as I could. Sometimes, sitting before me, how you stared at my face! I would look at the ceiling, cough, examine my fingernails. But you would not take your eyes off me. Whom might you tell what you discovered? I would say to myself: 'Pretend quickly that you are someone else, deceive him, pat him, throw him a bone.' But nothing would divert your atten-tion: you kept staring at me. I was a fool. I trembled with horror, while you were the innocent one. What if I had turned suddenly and shown you my real face? I know what you would have done. You would have got up and gone to the door, bristling, deeply hurt. Oh, you were a dog that could be forsaken at any time. I could choose. Yet you wagged your tail with self-assurance.

"Sometimes, in retaliation, I perceived your own anguish. Not the an-guish of being a dog, for this was your only possible form, but the anguish of existing in so perfect a way that it became an unbearable happiness. Then you would jump on my lap and lick my face with a completely sur-rendered love and with a dangerous element of hate, as though it had been I, through my friendship, who had found you out. I can see clearly now that it was not I who had a dog: it was you who had a person.

"But you had a person powerful enough to choose, and he chose to desert you. He deserted you and felt relief. Yes, relief, for you demanded, with the simple, calm incomprehension of a heroic dog, that I be a man. I deserted you with an excuse approved by everyone in the household: how could I move from one city to another with my family and all my belong-ings and take a dog along, too! With all the problems of adapting to a new school and a new city, why should I burden myself with a dog! 'Which will only be in the way,' said Martha sensibly. 'Which will annoy the pas-sengers,' said my mother-in-law, unintentionally helping me to justify myself. The children cried but I turned away from them. Nor did I look at you, Joseph. Only the two of us know why I deserted you: because you represented the constant possibility of the crime I never committed. The possibility of my sinning, which, in my eyes, was already a sin. So I sinned immediately in order to be immediately guilty. And this crime took the place of the greater one that I lacked the courage to commit." So thought the man, with ever increasing clarity.

"There are so many ways of being guilty and damning yourself forever, of betraying yourself, of evading yourself," he continued. "I chose to hurt a dog. For I knew that this crime was considered petty. I knew that no one would be consigned to hell for deserting a dog who had trusted him. I knew my crime was unpunishable."

As the man sat there on the hilltop, his mathematical mind was cold and rational. Now at last, its icy plenitude enabled him to see clearly that what he had done to the dog would be eternally impune. For no one has ever devised a punishment for the great crimes in disguise and for the deep treasons.

A man could still manage to outsmart the Final Judgment. No one would accuse him of this crime. Not even the Church.

"They are all accessories, Joseph. If I knocked on every door and begged them to convict me, to punish me, they would scowl and slam the doors in my face. No one condemns me for my crime. Not even you, Joseph. For if this powerful person that I am chose to call you back, you would jump up and lick my face with joy and forgiveness. I would turn the other cheek for you to kiss."

The man took off his glasses, breathed deeply, and put them on again.

He looked at the covered grave. There he had buried an unknown dog as a tribute to the forsaken one, trying in this way to pay the debt with which, alarmingly, no one would charge him. Trying to punish himself with an act of kindness and thus free himself of his crime. As a man drops a dime in a hat so that he may feel free to eat his cake, although the cake is the cause of the beggar's lack of bread.

But as if Joseph were demanding of him much more than a lie; as if the dog were demanding that, by a last desperate effort, he be a man and assume full responsibility for his crime, he stared at the grave where he had buried his own weakness.

And now, more mathematical than ever, he looked for a way to erase his redemption. He would not be solaced. He bent over and solemnly, calmly, with simple movements, uncovered the dog. It looked unfamiliar with earth on its lashes and with its open, glazed eyes. Thus, the mathematics professor renewed his crime eternally. He looked to the sky and to the earth around him, asking them to witness what he had just done. Then he started down the hill toward the little city below.

Translated from the Portuguese
by William L. Grossman

HAROLDO DE CAMPOS

A lawyer by training, Haroldo de Campos (1929–) has been one of the leading literary figures in modern Brazil. He is known primarily for founding, with his brother Augusto, the concrete poetry movement in 1952 in São Paolo, a city that has been the center of the Brazilian avant-garde since the twenties. Campos has also been a cultural promoter, critic, and a translator of German and Spanish texts — including some by Octavio Paz — into Portuguese. Campos's recent criticism deals with the origins of Brazilian literature.

The following poems are examples of Campos's work with concrete poetry. Poetry in various graphic forms has been practiced since the time of the ancient Greeks. Meaning in these poems is suggested not only by the words themselves, but also by their arrangement on the page.

Two Concrete Poems

```
speech
silver
        silence
        gold
                heads                               5
                silver
                    tails
                    gold
                        speech
                        silence                     10
                    stop
        silver              golden
        silence             speech
                                clarity
```

```
if
to be born
to die        to be born
to die        to be born    to die
                    to be reborn    to die again   to be reborn   5
                                    to die again   to be reborn
                                                   to die again
                                                        again
```

```
                                    again
                            not be born                    10
          not to be dead   not to be born
not to be dead   not to be born   not to be dead
                                to be born to die to
                                    be born
                                to die to be born
                                to die                     15
                                if
```

*Translated from the Portuguese by
Mary Ellen Solt and Marco Guimarães*

CHILE

PABLO NERUDA

*Born Neftalí Eliecer Ricardo Reyes Basoalto, Pablo Neruda (1904–
1973) changed his name in 1920, apparently in homage to Paul Valéry.
He was to become one of the greatest poets of the century and was
awarded the Novel Prize in 1971 in recognition for his achievements.
Neruda wrote more than fifty books of poetry of great variety, including his immensely popular* Twenty Love Poems and a Song of Despair
*(1924). These are among the most widely known and recited love poems
in the Spanish language.* Residence on Earth *(1933), an ambitious book
of surrealist imagery detailing an apocalyptic world full of menace and
fear, changed Spanish-language poetry. But Neruda's grandest project
was his* Canto general *(1950), which includes "The Heights of Macchu
Picchu." It is an epic covering the sweep of American history, from its
geological beginnings to the present. It is also a hymn to those who
have fought oppression and a lament for the betrayals that the common people have had to endure. Neruda is a cosmic poet who was inspired by the ruins of the Inca citadel he visited in the 1940s, particularly by their nearly extraterrestrial quality. Neruda aspires to become
the voice of the dead who once peopled the city. "The Heights of Macchu Picchu" is a poem about conversion, about an experience so powerful that it profoundly changed the person experiencing it.*

The Heights of Macchu Picchu°

I

From air to air, like an
empty net
I went between the streets and atmosphere, arriving and
    departing,
in the advent of autumn the outstretched coin
of the leaves, and between springtime and the ears of corn,   5

Macchu Picchu: An Inca citadel in the heart of the Andes whose ruins were discovered
  in 1911 by American archaeologist Hiram Bingham

all that the greatest love, as within a falling
glove, hands us like a long moon.

(Days of vivid splendor in the inclemency
of corpses: steel transformed
into acid silence: 10
nights frayed to the last flour:
beleaguered stamens of the nuptial land.)
Someone awaiting me among the violins
discovered a world like an entombed tower
spiraling down beneath all   15
the harsh sulphur-colored leaves:
father down, in the gold of geology,
like a sword enveloped in meteors,
I plunged my turbulent and tender hand
into the genital matrix of the earth.   20

I put my brow amid the deep waves,
descended like a drop amid the sulphurous peace,
and, like a blind man, returned to the jasmine
of the spent human springtime.

        2

If the lofty germ is carried from flower to flower   25
and the rock preserves its flower disseminated
in its hammered suit of diamond and sand,
man crumples the petal of light which he gathers
in determinate deep-sea springs
and drills the quivering metal in his hands.   30
And all along, amid clothing and mist, upon the sunken table,
like a jumbled quantity, lies the soul:
quartz and vigilance, tears in the ocean
like pools of cold: yet he still
torments it under the habitual rug, rips it   35
in the hostile vestments of wire.

No: in corridors, air, sea or on roads,
who guards (like red poppies) his blood
without a dagger? Rage has extenuated
the sad trade of the merchant of souls,   40
and, while at the top of the plum tree, the dew
has left for a thousand years its transparent letter
upon the same branch that awaits it, O heart, O brow crushed
between the autumn cavities.

How many times in the wintry streets of a city or in   45
a bus or a boat at dusk, or in the deepest
loneliness, a night of revelry beneath the sound
of shadows and bells, in the very grotto of human pleasure
I've tried to stop and seek the eternal unfathomable lode
that I touched before on stone or in the lightning unleashed by
    a kiss.   50

(Whatever in grain like a yellow tale
of swollen little breasts keep repeating a number
perpetually tender in the germinal layers,
and which, always identical, is stripped to ivory,
and whatever in water is a transparent land, a bell   55
from the distant snows down to the bloody waves.)

I could grasp nothing but a clump of faces or precipitous
masks, like rings of empty gold,
like scattered clothes, offspring of an enraged autumn
that would have made the miserable tree of the frightened races
    shake.   60
I had no place to rest my hand,
which, fluid like the water of an impounded spring
or firm as a chunk of anthracite or crystal,
would have returned the warmth or cold of my outstretched
    hand.
What was man? In what part of his conversation begun   65
amid shops and whistles, in which of his metallic movements
lived the indestructible, the imperishable, life?

3

Like corn man was husked in the bottomless
granary of forgotten deeds, the miserable course of
events, from one to seven, to eight,   70
and not one death but many deaths came to each:
every day a little death, dust, maggot, a lamp
quenched in the mire of the slums, a little thick-winged death
entered each man like a short lance,
and man was driven by bread or by knife: 75
herdsman, child of the seaports, dark captain of the plow,
or rodent of the teeming streets:

all were consumed awaiting their death, their daily ration of
    death:
and the ominous adversity of each day was like
a black glass from which they drank trembling.   80

4

Mighty death invited me many times:
it was like the invisible salt in the waves,
and what its invisible taste disseminated
was like halves of sinking and rising
or vast structures of wind and glacier.   85
I came to the cutting edge, to the narrows
of the air, to the shroud of agriculture and stone,
to the stellar void of the final steps
and the vertiginous spiraling road:
but, wide sea, O death! you do not come in waves   90
but in a galloping nocturnal clarity
or like the total numbers of the night.
You never rummaged around in pockets, your visit
was not possible without red vestments:
without an auroral carpet of enclosed silence: 95
without towering entombed patrimonies of tears.

I could not love in each being a tree
with a little autumn on its back (the death of a thousand leaves),
all the false deaths and resurrections
without land, without abyss: 100
I've tried to swim in the most expansive lives,
in the most free-flowing estuaries,
and when man went on denying me
and kept blocking path and door so that
my headspring hands could not touch his wounded inexistence,   105
then I went from street to street and river to river,
city to city and bed to bed,
my brackish mask traversed the desert,
and in the last humiliated homes, without light or fire,
without bread, without stone, without silence, alone,   110
I rolled on dying of my own death.

5

It was not you, solemn death, iron-plumed bird,
that the poor heir of these rooms
carried, between rushed meals, under his empty skin:
rather a poor petal with its cord exterminated: 115
an atom from the breast that did not come to combat
or the harsh dew that did not fall on his brow.

It was what could not be revived, a bit
of the little death without peace or territory:
a bone, a bell that died within him.   120
I raised the bandages dressed in iodine, sank my hands
into the pitiful sorrows killed by death,
and in the wound I found nothing but a chilling gust
that entered through the vague interstices of the soul.

6

And so I scaled the ladder of the earth   125
amid the atrocious maze of lost jungles
up to you, Macchu Picchu.
High citadel of terraced stones,
at long last the dwelling of him whom the earth
did not conceal in its slumbering vestments.   130
In you, as in two parallel lines,
the cradle of lightning and man
was rocked in a wind of thorns.

Mother of stone, sea spray of the condors.

Towering reef of the human dawn.   135

Spade lost in the primal sand.

This was the dwelling, this is the site:
here the full kernels of corn rose
and fell again like red hailstones.

Here the golden fiber emerged from the vicuña°   140
to clothe love, tombs, mothers,
the king, prayers, warriors.

Here man's feet rested at night
beside the eagle's feet, in the high gory
retreats, and at dawn   145
they trod the rarefied mist with feet of thunder
and touched lands and stones
until they recognized them in the night or in death.

I behold vestments and hands,
the vestige of water in the sonorous void,
the wall tempered by the touch of a face   150
that beheld with my eyes the earthen lamps,
that oiled with my hands the vanished

vicuña: a South American wild mammal of the camel family

wood: because everything — clothing, skin, vessels,
words, wine, bread —   155
is gone, fallen to earth.

And the air flowed with orange-blossom
fingers over all the sleeping:
a thousand years of air, months, weeks of air,
of blue wind, of iron cordillera,°   160
like gentle hurricanes of footsteps
polishing the solitary precinct of stone.

        7

O remains of a single abyss, shadows of one gorge —
the deep one — the real, most searing death
attained the scale   165
of your magnitude,
and from the quarried stones,
from the spires,
from the terraced aqueducts
you tumbled as in autumn   170
to a single death.
Today the empty air no longer weeps,
no longer knows your feet of clay,
has now forgotten your pitchers that filtered the sky
when the lightning's knives emptied it,   175
and the powerful tree was eaten away
by the mist and felled by the wind.
It sustained a hand that fell suddenly
from the heights to the end of time.
You are no more, spider hands, fragile   180
filaments, spun web:
all that you were has fallen: customs, frayed
syllables, masks of dazzling light.

But a permanence of stone and word:
the citadel was raised like a chalice in the hands   185
of all, the living, the dead, the silent, sustained
by so much death, a wall, from so much life a stroke
of stone petals: the permanent rose, the dwelling:
this Andean reef of glacial colonies.

When the clay-colored hand   190
turned to clay, when the little eyelids closed,
filled with rough walls, brimming with castles,

cordillera: a mountain range

and when the entire man was trapped in his hole,
exactitude remained hoisted aloft:
this high site of the human dawn: 195
the highest vessel that has contained silence:
a life of stone after so many lives.

8

Rise up with me, American love.

Kiss the secret stones with me.
The torrential silver of the Urubamba°   200
makes the pollen fly to its yellow cup.
It spans the void of the grapevine,
the petrous° plant, the hard wreath
upon the silence of the highland casket.
Come, minuscule life, between the wings   205
of the earth, while — crystal and cold, pounded air
extracting assailed emeralds —
O, wild water, you run down from the snow.

Love, love, even the abrupt night,
from the sonorous Andean flint   210
to the dawn's red knees,
contemplates the snow's blind child.

O, sonorous threaded Wilkamayu,°
when you beat your lineal thunder
to a white froth, like wounded snow,   215
when your precipitous storm
sings and batters, awakening the sky,
what language do you bring to the ear recently
wrenched from your Andean froth?

Who seized the cold's lightning   220
and left it shackled in the heights,
dispersed in its glacial tears,
smitten in its swift swords,
hammering its embattled stamens,
borne on its warrior's bed,   225
startled in its rocky end?

What are your tormented sparks saying?
Did your secret insurgent lightning

Urubamba: a river in the Andes (Peru)
petrous: stony
Wilkamayu: a river in the Andes

once journey charged with words?
Who keeps on shattering frozen syllables, 230
black languages, golden banners,
deep mouths, muffled cries,
in your slender arterial waters?

Who keeps on cutting floral eyelids
that come to gaze from the earth? 235
Who hurls down the dead clusters
that fell in your cascade hands
to strip the night stripped
in the coal of geology?

Who flings the branch down from its bonds? 240
Who once again entombs farewells?

Love, love, never touch the brink
or worship the sunken head:
let time attain its stature
in its salon of shattered headsprings, 245
and, between the swift water and the walls,
gather the air from the gorge,
the parallel sheets of the wind,
the cordilleras' blind canal,
the harsh greeting of the dew, 250
and, rise up, flower by flower, through the dense growth,
treading the hurtling serpent.

In the steep zone — forest and stone,
mist of green stars, radiant jungle —
Mantur explodes like a blinding lake 255
or a new layer of silence.

Come to my very heart, to my dawn,
up to the crowned solitudes.
The dead kingdom is still alive.

And over the Sundial the sanguinary shadow 260
of the condor crosses like a black ship.

9

Sidereal eagle, vineyard of mist.
Lost bastion, blind scimitar.
Spangled waistband, solemn bread.
Torrential stairway, immense eyelid. 265
Triangular tunic, stone pollen.
Granite lamp, stone bread.

Mineral serpent, stone rose.
Entombed ship, stone headspring.
Moonhorse, stone light.   270
Equinoctial square, stone vapor.
Ultimate geometry, stone book.
Tympanum fashioned amid the squalls.
Madrepore° of sunken time.
Rampart tempered by fingers.   275
Ceiling assailed by feathers.
Mirror bouquets, stormy foundations.
Thrones toppled by the vine.
Regime of the enraged claw.
Hurricane sustained on the slopes.   280
Immobile cataract of turquoise.
Patriarchal bell of the sleeping.
Hitching ring of the tamed snows.
Iron recumbent upon its statues.
Inaccessible dark tempest.   285
Puma° hands, bloodstained rock.
Towering sombrero, snowy dispute.
Night raised on fingers and roots.
Window of the mists, hardened dove.
Nocturnal plant, statue of thunder.   290
Essential cordillera, searoof.
Architecture of lost eagles.
Skyrope, heavenly bee.
Bloody level, man-made star.
Mineral bubble, quartz moon.   295
Andean serpent, brow of amaranth.°
Cupola of silence, pure land.
Seabride, tree of cathedrals.
Cluster of salt, black-winged cherry tree.
Snow-capped teeth, cold thunderbolt.   300
Scored moon, menacing stone.
Headdresses of the cold, action of the air.
Volcano of hands, obscure cataract.
Silver wave, pointer of time.

10

Stone upon stone, and man, where was he?   305
Air upon air, and man, where was he?

madrepore: a form of coral
puma: a mountain lion
amaranth: a plant with colorful leaves

Time upon time, and man, where was he?
Were you too a broken shard
of inconclusive man, of empty raptor,
who on the streets today, on the trails,   310
on the dead autumn leaves, keeps
tearing away at the heart right up to the grave?
Poor hand, foot, poor life . . .
Did the days of light
unraveled in you, like raindrops   315
on the banners of a feast day,
give petal by petal of their dark food
to the empty mouth?
                          Hunger, coral of mankind,
hunger, secret plant, woodcutters' stump,   320
hunger, did the edge of your reef rise up
to these high suspended towers?

I want to know, salt of the roads,
show me the spoon — architecture, let me
scratch at the stamens of stone with a little stick,   325
ascend the rungs of the air up to the void,
scrape the innards until I touch mankind.

Macchu Picchu, did you put
stone upon stone and, at the base, tatters?
Coal upon coal and, at the bottom, tears?   330
Fire in gold and, within it, the trembling
drop of red blood?
Bring me back the slave that you buried!
Shake from the earth the hard bread
of the poor wretch, show me   335
the slave's clothing and his window.
Tell me how he slept when he lived.
Tell me if his sleep was
harsh, gaping, like a black chasm
worn by fatigue upon the wall.   340
The wall, the wall! If upon his sleep
each layer of stone weighed down, and if he fell beneath it
as beneath a moon, with his dream!
Ancient America, sunken bride,
your fingers too,   345
on leaving the jungle for the high void of the gods,
beneath the nuptial standards of light and decorum,
mingling with the thunder of drums and spears,
your fingers, your fingers too,
which the abstract rose, the cold line, and   350

the crimson breast of the new grain transferred
to the fabric of radiant substance, to the hard cavities —
did you, entombed America, did you too store in the depths
of your bitter intestine, like an eagle, hunger?

II

Through the hazy splendor,   355
through the stone night, let me plunge my hand,
and let the aged heart of the forsaken beat in me
like a bird captive for a thousand years!
Let me forget, today, this joy, which is greater than the sea,
because man is greater than the sea and its islands,   360
and we must fall into him as into a well to emerge from the
     bottom
with a bouquet of secret water and sunken truths.
Let me forget, great stone, the powerful proportion,
the transcendent measure, the honeycombed stones,
and from the square let me today run   365
my hand over the hypotenuse of rough blood and sackcloth.
When, like a horseshoe of red elytra, the frenzied condor
beats my temples in the order of its flight,
and the hurricane of cruel feathers sweeps the somber dust
from the diagonal steps, I do not see the swift brute,   370
I do not see the blind cycle of its claws,
I see the man of old, the servant, asleep in the fields,
I see a body, a thousand bodies, a man, a thousand women,
black with rain and night, beneath the black squall,   375
with the heavy stone of the statue:
Juan Stonecutter, son of Wiracocha,°
Juan Coldeater, son of a green star,
Juan Barefoot, grandson of turquoise,
rise up to be born with me, my brother.

12

Rise up to be born with me, my brother.   380

Give me your hand from the deep
zone of your disseminated sorrow.
You'll not return from the bottom of the rocks.
You'll not return from subterranean time.
Your stiff voice will not return.   385
Your drilled eyes will not return.

Wiracocha: an Incan god

Behold me from the depths of the earth,
laborer, weaver, silent herdsman:
tamer of the tutelary guanacos:°
mason of the defied scaffold: 390
bearer of the Andean tears:
jeweler with your fingers crushed:
tiller trembling in the seed:
potter spilt in your clay:
bring to the cup of this new life, brothers,   395
all your timeless buried sorrows.
Show me your blood and your furrow,
tell me: I was punished here,
because the jewel did not shine or the earth
did not surrender the gemstone or kernel on time: 400
show me the stone on which you fell
and the wood on which you were crucified,
strike the old flintstones,
the old lamps, the whips sticking
throughout the centuries to your wounds   405
and the war clubs glistening red.
I've come to speak through your dead mouths.
Throughout the earth join all
the silent scattered lips
and from the depths speak to me all night long,   410
as if I were anchored with you,
tell me everything, chain by chain,
link by link, and step by step,
sharpen the knives that you've kept,
put them in my breast and in my hand,   415
like a river of yellow lightning,
like a river of buried jaguars,
and let me weep hours, days, years,
blind ages, stellar centuries.

Give me silence, water, hope.   420

Give me struggle, iron, volcanoes.

Cling to my body like magnets.

Hasten to my veins and to my mouth.

Speak through my words and my blood.

Translated from the Spanish by Jack Schmitt

guanaco: a wild South American mammal of the camel family

NICANOR PARRA

A professor of theoretical physics at the University of Chile, Nicanor Parra (1914–) is one of the most original Latin American poets. He is, in fact, a self-styled antipoet: he is against lyricism and rejects the tropes and tone of conventional poetry. Parra's most famous and influential book is Poems and Antipoems *(1954). He is irreverent, prosaic, humorous, and eager to denounce all the pretensions of the bourgeoisie. But he goes, in fact, further: he mocks the human condition in general and presents himself as a hapless spokesperson for the common individual, caught in a world without meaning.*

The poems included here are among the most representative. In "Litany of the Little Bourgeois" Parra describes the predicament of modern men and women, attempting to get by in a society made of falsehoods. Though it is evident that Parra has learned a good deal from T. S. Eliot, the modern master who comes to mind when reading Parra is really Charlie Chaplin. In many ways Parra, as a poet, is the complete opposite of his countryman and contemporary Pablo Neruda.

Litany of the Little Bourgeois°

If you want to get to the heaven
Of the little bourgeois, you must go
By the road of Art for Art's sake°
And swallow a lot of saliva:
The apprenticeship is almost interminable.   5

A list of what you must learn how to do:

Tie your necktie artistically
Slip your card to the right people
Polish shoes that are already shined
Consult the Venetian mirror   10
(Head-on and in profile)
Toss down a shot of brandy
Tell a viola from a violin
Receive guests in your pajamas   15
Keep your hair from falling
And swallow a lot of saliva.

Best to have everything in your kit.
If the wife falls for somebody else

little bourgeois: a conventional, middle-class person
Art for Art's sake: the belief that art must be independent of social issues

We recommend the following:
Shave with razor blades   20
Admire the Beauties of Nature
Crumple a sheet of paper
Have a long talk on the phone
Shoot darts with a popgun
Clean your nails with your teeth   25
And swallow a lot of saliva.

If he wants to shine at social gatherings
The little bourgeois
Must know how to walk on all fours
How to smile and sneeze at the same time   30
Waltz on the edge of the abyss
Deify the organs of sex
Undress in front of a mirror
Rape a rose with a pencil
And swallow tons of saliva.   35

And after all that we might well ask:
Was Jesus Christ a little bourgeois?

As we have seen, if you want to reach
The heaven of the little bourgeois,
You must be an accomplished acrobat: 40
To be able to get to heaven,
You must be a wonderful acrobat.

And how right the authentic artist is
To amuse himself killing bedbugs!

To escape from the vicious circle   45
We suggest the *acte gratuite:*°

Appear and disappear
Walk in a cataleptic trance
Waltz on a pile of debris
Rock an old man in your arms   50
With your eyes fixed on his
Ask a dying man what time it is
Spit in the palm of your hand
Go to fires in a morning coat
Break into a funeral procession   55
Go beyond the female sex
Lift the top from that tomb to see

acte gratuite: practiced by avant-garde artists, an action or deed totally disconnected
   from its context and with no discernible purpose

If they're growing trees in there
And cross from one sidewalk to the other
Without regard for when or why   60
... For the sake of the word alone ...
... With his movie-star mustache ...
... With the speed of thought ...

Translated from the Spanish
by James Laughlin

Mummies

One mummy walks on snow
Another mummy walks on ice
Another mummy walks on sand.

A mummy walks through the meadow
A second mummy goes with her.   5

One mummy talks on the phone
Another mummy views herself in the mirror.
One mummy fires her revolver.

All the mummies change places
Almost all the mummies withdraw.   10

A few mummies sit down at the table
Some mummies offer cigarettes
One mummy seems to be dancing.

One mummy older than the others
Puts her baby to her breast.   15

Translated from the Spanish
by Miller Williams

Test

What is an antipoet
Someone who deals in coffins and urns?
A general who's not sure of himself?
A priest who believes in nothing?
A drifter who finds everything funny   5
Even old age and death?

A speaker you can't trust?
A dancer at the edge of a cliff?
A narcissist who loves everyone?
A joker who goes for the jugular   10
And is mean just for the hell of it?
A poet who sleeps in a chair?
A modern-day alchemist?
An armchair revolutionary?
A petit-bourgeois?   15
A fake?
     a god?
          a naive person?
A peasant from Santiago, Chile?
Underline the right answer.   20

What is antipoetry
A tempest in a teapot?
A spot of snow on a rock?
A tray piled high with human shit
As Father Salvatierra° believes?   25
A mirror that doesn't lie?
A slap in the face
Of the president of the Writers' Society?°
(God save his soul)
A warning to young poets?   30
A jet-propelled coffin?
A coffin in centrifugal orbit?
A coffin run on kerosene?
A funeral parlor without a corpse?
Put an X   35
Next to the right answer.

Translated from the Spanish by David Unger

I Take Back Everything I've Said

Before I go
I'm supposed to get a last wish:
Generous reader
         burn this book

Father Salvatierra: a Chilean priest, whose name means savior of the world
Writer's Society: a fictional organization used to satirize such writing groups

It's not at all what I wanted to say   5
Though it was written in blood
It's not what I wanted to say.

No lot could be sadder than mine
I was defeated by my own shadow:
My words took vengeance on me.   10

Forgive me, reader, good reader
If I cannot leave you
With a warm embrace. I leave you
With a forced and sad smile.

Maybe that's all I am
But listen to my last word:
I take back everything I've said.
With the greatest bitterness in the world
I take back everything I've said.

Translated from the Spanish
by Miller Williams

COLOMBIA ☼

GABRIEL GARCÍA MÁRQUEZ

*Awarded the Nobel Prize in 1982, Gabriel García Márquez (1928–) se-
cured his reputation with the publication of his masterpiece,* One Hundred Years of Solitude *(1967). However, many consider* Love in the
Time of Cholera *(1985) his most enduring book. García Márquez's fictions are intricate, well-wrought, and steeped in literary tradition
going back to Greek tragedy. They also portray in minute and convincing detail, with a touch of nostalgia, the rural and small-town world of
provincial Colombia.*

*García Márquez is a "magical realist," simultaneously presenting a
world of archaic values and practices that has remained largely intact
in Latin America since colonial times, and the modern world. García
Márquez learned from Alejo Carpentier to work with concurrent historical epochs. But he is also indebted to two American masters,
William Faulkner and Ernest Hemingway, as he has acknowledged
many times. "Balthazar's Marvelous Afternoon" contains all of these
influences.*

Balthazar's Marvelous Afternoon

The cage was finished. Balthazar hung it under the eave, from force of
habit, and when he finished lunch everyone was already saying that it
was the most beautiful cage in the world. So many people came to see
it that a crowd formed in front of the house, and Balthazar had to take it
down and close the shop.

"You have to shave," Ursula, his wife, told him. "You look like a Capuchin."°

"It's bad to shave after lunch," said Balthazar.

He had two weeks' growth, short, hard, and bristly hair like the mane
of a mule, and the general expression of a frightened boy. But it was a
false expression. In February he was thirty; he had been living with Ursula for four years, without marrying her and without having children,
and life had given him many reasons to be on guard but none to be fright-

---

Capuchin: a monk of a certain Franciscan order

ened. He did not even know that for some people the cage he had just made was the most beautiful one in the world. For him, accustomed to making cages since childhood, it had been hardly any more difficult than the others.

"Then rest for a while," said the woman. "With that beard you can't show yourself anywhere."

While he was resting, he had to get out of his hammock several times to show the cage to the neighbors. Ursula had paid little attention to it until then. She was annoyed because her husband had neglected the work of his carpenter's shop to devote himself entirely to the cage, and for two weeks had slept poorly, turning over and muttering incoherencies, and he hadn't thought of shaving. But her annoyance dissolved in the face of the finished cage. When Balthazar woke up from his nap, she had ironed his pants and a shirt; she had put them on a chair near the hammock and had carried the cage to the dining table. She regarded it in silence.

"How much will you charge?" she asked.

"I don't know," Balthazar answered. "I'm going to ask for thirty pesos to see if they'll give me twenty."

"Ask for fifty," said Ursula. "You've lost a lot of sleep in these two weeks. Furthermore, it's rather large. I think it's the biggest cage I've ever seen in my life."

Balthazar began to shave.

"Do you think they'll give me fifty pesos?"

"That's nothing for Mr. Chepe Montiel, and the cage is worth it," said Ursula. "You should ask for sixty."

The house lay in the stifling shadow. It was the first week of April and the heat seemed less bearable because of the chirping of the cicadas. When he finished dressing, Balthazar opened the door to the patio to cool off the house, and a group of children entered the dining room.

The news had spread. Dr. Octavio Giraldo, an old physician, happy with life but tired of his profession, thought about Balthazar's cage while he was eating lunch with his invalid wife. On the inside terrace, where they put the table on hot days, there were many flowerpots and two cages with canaries. His wife liked birds, and she liked them so much that she hated cats because they could eat them up. Thinking about her, Dr. Giraldo went to see a patient that afternoon, and when he returned he went by Balthazar's house to inspect the cage.

There were a lot of people in the dining room. The cage was on display on the table: with its enormous dome of wire, three stories inside, with passageways and compartments especially for eating and sleeping and swings in the space set aside for the birds' recreation, it seemed like a small-scale model of a gigantic ice factory. The doctor inspected it carefully, without touching it, thinking that in effect the cage was better than its reputation, and much more beautiful than any he had ever dreamed of for his wife.

"This is a flight of the imagination," he said. He sought out Balthazar among the group of people and, fixing his maternal eyes on him, added, "You would have been an extraordinary architect."

Balthazar blushed.

"Thank you," he said.

"It's true," said the doctor. He was smoothly and delicately fat, like a woman who had been beautiful in her youth, and he had delicate hands. His voice seemed like that of a priest speaking Latin. "You wouldn't even need to put birds in it," he said, making the cage turn in front of the audience's eyes as if he were auctioning it off. "It would be enough to hang it in the trees so it could sing by itself." He put it back on the table, thought a moment, looking at the cage, and said:

"Fine, then I'll take it."

"It's sold," said Ursula.

"It belongs to the son of Mr. Chepe Montiel," said Balthazar. "He ordered it specially."

The doctor adopted a respectful attitude.

"Did he give you the design?"

"No," said Balthazar. "He said he wanted a large cage, like this one, for a pair of troupials."°

The doctor looked at the cage.

"But this isn't for troupials."

"Of course it is, Doctor," said Balthazar, approaching the table. The children surrounded him. "The measurements are carefully calculated," he said, pointing to the different compartments with his forefinger. Then he struck the dome with his knuckles, and the cage filled with resonant chords.

"It's the strongest wire you can find, and each joint is soldered outside and in," he said.

"It's even big enough for a parrot," interrupted one of the children.

"That it is," said Balthazar.

The doctor turned his head.

"Fine, but he didn't give you the design," he said. "He gave you no exact specifications, aside from making it a cage big enough for troupials. Isn't that right?"

"That's right," said Balthazar.

"Then there's no problem," said the doctor. "One thing is a cage big enough for troupials, and another is this cage. There's no proof that this one is the one you were asked to make."

"It's this very one," said Balthazar, confused. "That's why I made it."

The doctor made an impatient gesture.

"You could make another one," said Ursula, looking at her husband. And then, to the doctor: "You're not in any hurry."

troupial: a South American bird

"I promised it to my wife for this afternoon," said the doctor.

"I'm very sorry, Doctor," said Balthazar, "but I can't sell you something that's sold already."

The doctor shrugged his shoulder. Drying the sweat from his neck with a handkerchief, he contemplated the cage silently with the fixed, unfocused gaze of one who looks at a ship which is sailing away.

"How much did they pay you for it?"

Balthazar sought out Ursula's eyes without replying.

"Sixty pesos," she said.

The doctor kept looking at the cage. "It's very pretty." He sighed. "Extremely pretty." Then, moving toward the door, he began to fan himself energetically, smiling, and the trace of that episode disappeared forever from his memory.

"Montiel is very rich," he said.

In truth, José Montiel was not as rich as he seemed, but he would have been capable of doing anything to become so. A few blocks from there, in a house crammed with equipment, where no one had ever smelled a smell that couldn't be sold, he remained indifferent to the news of the cage. His wife, tortured by an obsession with death, closed the doors and windows after lunch and lay for two hours with her eyes opened to the shadow of the room, while José Montiel took his siesta.° The clamor of many voices surprised her there. Then she opened the door to the living room and found a crowd in front of the house, and Balthazar with the cage in the middle of the crowd, dressed in white, freshly shaved, with that expression of decorous candor with which the poor approach the houses of the wealthy.

"What a marvelous thing!" José Montiel's wife exclaimed, with a radiant expression, leading Balthazar inside. "I've never seen anything like it in my life," she said, and added, annoyed by the crowd which piled up at the door:

"But bring it inside before they turn the living room into a grandstand."

Balthazar was no stranger to José Montiel's house. On different occasions, because of his skill and forthright way of dealing, he had been called in to do minor carpentry jobs. But he never felt at ease among the rich. He used to think about them, about their ugly and argumentative wives, about their tremendous surgical operations, and he always experienced a feeling of pity. When he entered their houses, he couldn't move without dragging his feet.

"Is Pepe home?" he asked.

He had put the cage on the dining-room table.

"He's at school," said José Montiel's wife. "But he shouldn't be long," and she added, "Montiel is taking a bath."

---

siesta: approximately noontime, when the heat of the day is at its highest and it is customary to rest in some countries

In reality, José Montiel had not had time to bathe. He was giving himself an urgent alcohol rub, in order to come out and see what was going on. He was such a cautious man that he slept without an electric fan so he could watch over the noises of the house while he slept.

"Adelaide!" he shouted. "What's going on?"

"Come and see what a marvelous thing!" his wife shouted.

José Montiel, obese and hairy, his towel draped around his neck, appeared at the bedroom window.

"What is that?"

"Pepe's cage," said Balthazar.

His wife looked at him perplexedly.

"Whose?"

"Pepe's," replied Balthazar. And then, turning toward José Montiel, "Pepe ordered it."

Nothing happened at that instant, but Balthazar felt as if someone had just opened the bathroom door on him. José Montiel came out of the bedroom in his underwear.

"Pepe!" he shouted.

"He's not back," whispered his wife, motionless.

Pepe appeared in the doorway. He was about twelve, and had the same curved eyelashes and was as quietly pathetic as his mother.

"Come here," José Montiel said to him. "Did you order this?"

The child lowered his head. Grabbing him by the hair, José Montiel forced Pepe to look him in the eye.

"Answer me."

The child bit his lip without replying.

"Montiel," whispered his wife.

José Montiel let the child go and turned toward Balthazar in a fury. "I'm very sorry, Balthazar," he said. "But you should have consulted me before going on. Only to you would it occur to contract with a minor." As he spoke, his face recovered its serenity. He lifted the cage without looking at it and gave it to Balthazar.

"Take it away at once, and try to sell it to whomever you can," he said. "Above all, I beg you not to argue with me." He patted him on the back and explained, "The doctor has forbidden me to get angry."

The child had remained motionless, without blinking, until Balthazar looked at him uncertainly with the cage in his hand. Then he emitted a guttural sound, like a dog's growl, and threw himself on the floor screaming.

José Montiel looked at him, unmoved, while the mother tried to pacify him. "Don't even pick him up," he said. "Let him break his head on the floor, and then put salt and lemon on it so he can rage to his heart's content." The child was shrieking tearlessly while his mother held him by the wrists.

"Leave him alone," José Montiel insisted.

Balthazar observed the child as he would have observed the death throes of a rabid animal. It was almost four o'clock. At that hour, at his house, Ursula was singing a very old song and cutting slices of onion.

"Pepe," said Balthazar.

He approached the child, smiling, and held the cage out to him. The child jumped up, embraced the cage which was almost as big as he was, and stood looking at Balthazar through the wirework without knowing what to say. He hadn't shed one tear.

"Balthazar," said José Montiel softly. "I told you already to take it away."

"Give it back," the woman ordered the child.

"Keep it," said Balthazar. And then, to José Montiel: "After all, that's what I made it for."

José Montiel followed him into the living room.

"Don't be foolish, Balthazar," he was saying, blocking his path. "Take your piece of furniture home and don't be silly. I have no intention of paying you a cent."

"It doesn't matter," said Balthazar. "I made it expressly as a gift for Pepe. I didn't expect to charge anything for it."

As Balthazar made his way through the spectators who were blocking the door, José Montiel was shouting in the middle of the living room. He was very pale and his eyes were beginning to get red.

"Idiot!" he was shouting. "Take your trinket out of here. The last thing we need is for some nobody to give orders in my house. Son of a bitch!"

In the pool hall, Balthazar was received with an ovation. Until that moment, he thought that he had made a better cage than ever before, that he'd had to give it to the son of José Montiel so he wouldn't keep crying, and that none of these things was particularly important. But then he realized that all of this had a certain importance for many people, and he felt a little excited.

"So they gave you fifty pesos for the cage."

"Sixty," said Balthazar.

"Score one for you," someone said. "You're the only one who has managed to get such a pile of money out of Mr. Chepe Montiel. We have to celebrate."

They bought him a beer, and Balthazar responded with a round for everybody. Since it was the first time he had ever been out drinking, by dusk he was completely drunk, and he was talking about a fabulous project of a thousand cages, at sixty pesos each, and then of a million cages, till he had sixty million pesos. "We have to make a lot of things to sell to the rich before they die," he was saying, blind drunk. "All of them are sick, and they're going to die. They're so screwed up they can't even get angry any more." For two hours he was paying for the jukebox, which played without interruption. Everybody toasted Balthazar's health, good luck, and fortune, and the death of the rich, but at mealtime they left him alone in the pool hall.

Ursula had waited for him until eight, with a dish of fried meat covered with slices of onion. Someone told her that her husband was in the pool hall, delirious with happiness, buying beers for everyone, but she didn't believe it, because Balthazar had never got drunk. When she went to bed, almost at midnight, Balthazar was in a lighted room where there were little tables, each with four chairs, and an outdoor dance floor, where the plovers were walking around. His face was smeared with rouge, and since he couldn't take one more step, he thought he wanted to lie down with two women in the same bed. He had spent so much that he had had to leave his watch in pawn, with the promise to pay the next day. A moment later, spread-eagled in the street, he realized that his shoes were being taken off, but he didn't want to abandon the happiest dream of his life. The women who passed on their way to five-o'clock Mass didn't dare look at him, thinking he was dead.

Translated from the Spanish by
Gregory Rabassa and J. S. Bernstein

CUBA

NICOLÁS GUILLÉN

A mulatto, Nicolás Guillén (1902–1989) wrote his first book of poems,
Son Motifs in 1930. It became the most influential collection of verse
on Afro-Antillean themes of the century. Guillén was, with Alejo Car-
pentier and others, part of the Afro-Cuban movement, which celebrated
the island's African heritage. He was able to imitate the rhythm of Afro-
Cuban music in his poems, which drew heavily from popular pieces.

Guillén's poems decry discrimination by white Cubans and self-
hatred by blacks. He was an avant-garde poet who had much in com-
mon with Spanish poets such as Federico García Lorca, who visited
Cuba in 1930. Guillén himself was in Spain at the start of the Spanish
civil war in 1936. His poetry took on an increasingly political tone dur-
ing this period. Guillén joined the communist party in the 1930s and
spent some time in jail and exile as a result. With the triumph of the
Cuban Revolution he became president of the Writers' Union and was
declared Cuba's national poet. "Ballad of the Two Grandfathers" ex-
presses the anguish of the mulatto, whose ancestry is divided by vio-
lence; "The Grandfather" reveals the true heritage of a woman who is
trying to pass as white.

Ballad of the Two Grandfathers

Shadows I alone can see,
my two grandfathers go with me.

Skin drum of wood,
bone-pointed spear:
my black grandfather.   5
Broad neck with ruff,
gray battle gear:
my white grandfather.

Torso rockhard, and feet are bare,
those of the black;   10
antarctic glass from pupils stare,
those of the white.

Africa of the humid forests
and the great, stilled gongs . . .
"I'm dying!"   15
(says my black grandfather.)
Waters dark with alligators,
mornings green with coco-palms . . .
"I'm tiring!"
(says my white grandfather.)   20
Oh bitter wind that fills the sails,
oh galleon burning gold . . .
"I'm dying!"
(says my black grandfather.)
Oh glass beads hung in deceit   25
'round necks of virgin coasts . . .
"I'm tiring!"
(says my white grandfather.)
Oh pure metal-hammered sun
imprisoned in the tropics' ring;   30
oh round, clear moon
above the monkeys' dream!

So many ships, so many ships!
So many Blacks, so many Blacks!
Such vast glow of sugarcane!   35
Such a whip has the slaver!
Rock of grieving and of blood,
and half-opened veins and eyes,
and empty dawns,
and sugarmill dusks,   40
and a great voice, strong voice,
shattering the silence.
So many ships, so many ships,
so many Blacks!

Shadows I alone can see,   45
my two grandfathers go with me.

Don Federico° shouting,
and Taita Facundo° hushed;
both dreaming in the night,
they walk, they walk.   50
I unite them.

Don Federico and **Taita Facundo:** invented, archetypical names of the Spanish and
    African grandfathers

<pre>
                — Federico!
Facundo! The two embrace.
The two of them sigh.
Two strong heads raised,   55
both the same size,
beneath stars on high;
both the same size,
black anguish, white anguish,
both the same size,   60
they shout, they dream, they cry, they sing.
They dream, cry, sing.
They sing!
</pre>

Translated from the Spanish
by Jill Netchinsky

The Grandfather

This angelic lady with eyes from the North,
who follows the beat of her European blood,
knows not that in this rhythm's thorough flood
a black man beats dark drums that are hoarse.

Beneath the straight course of her small, Nordic nose   5
her mouth traverses a thin, delicate line;
no crow flies to stain the solitary snows,
of her skin with its tremulous, naked shine.

Ah, my lady! behold the mysteries below,
ride the live waters that deep inside you flow,   10
and watch lilies, lotuses, and roses as you go;

and on the fresh shore, restless, you will then see
the sweet dark shadow of the grandfather flee,
he who curled your yellow head indelibly.

Translated from the Spanish
by Vera M. Kutzinski

ALEJO CARPENTIER

One of the foremost Latin American novelists, Alejo Carpentier (1904–1980) was also a journalist, musicologist, and diplomat. He was involved in the avant-garde movements of the 1920s, particularly surrealism, and was among the founders of the Afro-Cuban movement. This artistic and political group focused on the African component of Cuban culture, and attempted to incorporate it into its art.

Carpentier's research into Afro-Cuban culture led him to write ¡Ecué-Yamba-O! (Praise Be Thou Lord), a novel about the lives of blacks on the island, and a history of Cuban music. But Carpentier is known above all for novels such as The Kingdom of this World *(1949), about the Haitian Revolution, and* The Lost Steps *(1953), which tells of a journey into the South American jungle by a musicologist. Carpentier's chief contributions to Latin American fiction were showing how New World history could be incorporated into fiction and his theory of magical realism. His impact on younger novelists like Gabriel García Márquez has been vast.*

This story, written in the 1940s, demonstrates Carpentier's penchant for playing with time in the form of various historical epochs, which are shuffled almost imperceptibly. This soldier, about to participate in an invasion, is first a Greek in Homeric times and finally an Allied soldier on the eve of D-Day in World War II.

Like the Night

I

Though the headlands still lay in shadow, the sea between them was beginning to turn green when the lookout blew his conch to announce that the fifty black ships sent us by King Agamemnon° had arrived. Hearing the signal, those who had been waiting for so many days on the dung-covered threshing floors began carrying the wheat towards the shore, where rollers were already being made ready so that the vessels could be brought right up to the walls of the fortress. When the keels touched the sand there was a certain amount of wrangling with the steersmen, because the Mycenaeans° had so often been told about our complete ignorance of nautical matters that they tried to keep us at a distance with their poles. Moreover, the beach was now crowded with children, who got between the soldiers' legs, hindered their movements and scrambled

---

Agamemnon: in Greek legend, the leader of the Greek armies in the Trojan War
Mycenaeans: Greeks from the city of Mycenae

up the sides of the ships to steal nuts from under the oarsmen's benches. The transparent waves of dawn were breaking amidst cries, insults, tussles and blows, and our leading citizens could not make their speeches of welcome in the middle of this pandemonium. I had been expecting something more solemn, more ceremonious, from our meeting with these men who had come to fetch us to fight for them, and I walked off, feeling somewhat disillusioned, towards the fig-tree on whose thickest branch I often sat astride, gripping the wood with my knees, because it reminded me somewhat of a woman's body.

As the ships were drawn out of the water, and the tops of the mountains behind began to catch the sun, my first bad impression gradually faded; it had clearly been the result of a sleepless night of waiting, and also of my having drunk too heavily the day before, with the young men recently arrived on the coast from inland, who were to embark with us soon after dawn. As I watched the procession of men carrying jars, black wine-skins and baskets, moving towards the ships, a warm pride swelled within me, and a sense of my superiority as a soldier. That oil, that resinated wine,° and above all that wheat from which biscuits would be cooked under the cinders at nights while we slept under the shelter of the wet prows in some mysterious and unknown bay on the way to the Great City of Ships — the same grain that I had helped to winnow with my shovel — all these things were being put on board for me; nor need I tire my long muscular limbs, and arms designed for handling an ashwood pike, with tasks only fit for men who knew nothing but the smell of the soil — men who looked at the earth over the sweating backs of their animals, or spent their lives crouched over it, weeding, uprooting and raking, almost in the same attitudes as their own browsing cattle. These men would never pass under the clouds that at this time of day darken the distant green islands, whence the acrid-scented silphium° was brought. They would never know the wide streets of the Trojans' city,° the city we were now going to surround, attack and destroy. For days and days, the messengers sent us by the Mycenaean King had been telling us about Priam's° insolence, and the sufferings that threatened our people through the arrogant behavior of his subjects. They had been jeering at our manly way of life; and, trembling with rage, we had heard of the challenges hurled at us long-haired Achaeans° by the men of Ilium, although our courage is unmatched by any other race. Cries of rage were heard, fists were clenched and shaken, oaths sworn with the hands palm up-

resinated wine: Greek wine fermented in vats caulked with resin, from which it acquires some flavor
silphium: a resinous plant
Trojans' city: Troy, in present-day Turkey, against which the Greeks fought the Trojan War
Priam: Trojan king
Achaeans: people of ancient Greece

wards, and shields thrown against the walls, when we heard of the rape of Helen of Sparta.° In loud voices the emissaries told us of her marvelous beauty, her noble bearing and adorable way of walking, and described the cruelties she had endured in her miserable captivity, while wine flowed from skins into helmets. That same evening, when the whole town was seething with indignation, we were told that the fifty black ships were being sent. Fires were lit in the bronze foundries, while old women brought wood from the mountains. And now, several days later, here I was gazing at the vessels drawn up at my feet, with their powerful keels and their masts at rest between the bulwarks like a man's virility between his thighs; I felt as if in some sense I was the owner of these timbers, transformed by some portentous carpentry unknown to our people into race-horses of the ocean, ready to carry us where the greatest adventure of all time was now unfolding like an epic. And I, son of a harness-maker and grandson of a castrator of bulls, was to have the good fortune to go where these deeds were being done whose luster reached us in sailors' stories; I was to have the honor of seeing the walls of Troy, of following noble leaders, and contributing my energy and strength to the cause of rescuing Helen of Sparta — a manly undertaking and the supreme triumph of a war that would give us prosperity, happiness and pride in ourselves for ever. I took a deep breath of the breeze blowing from the olive-covered hillside, and thought how splendid it would be to die in such a just conflict, for the cause of Reason itself. But the idea of being pierced by an enemy lance made me think of my mother's grief and also of another, perhaps even profounder grief, though in this case the news would have to be heard with dry eyes — because the hearer was head of the family. I walked slowly down to the town by the shepherds' path. Three kids were gamboling in the thyme-scented air. Down on the beach the loading of wheat was still going on.

2

The impending departure of the ships was being celebrated on all sides with thrumming of guitars and clashing of cymbals. The sailors from *La Gallarda*° were dancing the zarambeque° with enfranchised negresses, and singing familiar coplas° — like the song of the *Moza del Retoño*, wherein groping hands supplied the blanks left in the words. Meanwhile the shipment of wine, oil and grain was still going on, with the help of the overseer's Indian servants, who were impatient to return to their na-

Helen of Sparta: woman who became known as Helen of Troy
La Gallarda: name of the Spanish ship, which means something like "The Proud One"
zarambeque: a dance of African origin that was danced in Spanish American ports and in Spain during the sixteenth century
coplas: a Spanish poem usually sung to the guitar, often, as in the one mentioned here, full of off-color jokes and allusions

tive land. Our future chaplain was on his way to the harbor, driving be-fore him two mules loaded with the bellows and pipes of a wooden organ. Whenever I met any of the men from the ships, there were noisy em-braces, exaggerated gestures, and enough laughter and boasting to bring the women to their windows. We seemed to be men of a different race, expressly created to carry out exploits beyond the ken of the baker, the wool-carder and the merchant who hawked holland shirts,° embroidered by parties of nuns in their patios. In the middle of the square, their brass instruments flashing in the sun, the Captain's six trumpeters were play-ing popular airs, while the Burgundian° drummers were thundering on their instruments, and a sackbut° with a mouthpiece like a dragon was bellowing as if it wanted to bite.

In his shop, smelling of calfskin and Cordoban leather, my father was driving his awl into a stirrup-strap with the half-heartedness of someone whose mind is elsewhere. When he saw me, he took me in his arms with serene sadness, perhaps remembering the horrible death of Cristobalillo, the companion of my youthful escapades, whom the Indians of the Dragon's Mouth° had pierced with their arrows. But he knew that every-one was wild to embark for the Indies these days — although most men in possession of their senses were already realizing that it was the "mad-ness of many for the gain of a few." He spoke in praise of good craftsman-ship, and told me that a man could gain as much respect by carrying the harness-maker's standard in the Corpus Christi° procession as he got from dangerous exploits. He pointed out the advantages of a well-provided table, a full coffer and a peaceful old age. But, probably having realized that the excitement in the town was steadily increasing, and that my mood was not attuned to such sensible reasoning, he gently led me to the door of my mother's room. This was the moment I had most dreaded, and I could hardly restrain my own tears when I saw hers, for we had put off telling her of my departure until everyone knew that my name had been entered in the books of the Casa de la Contratación.° I thanked her for the vows she had made to the Virgin of Navigators° in exchange for my speedy return, and promised her everything she asked of me, such as to have no sinful dealings with the women of those far-off countries, whom the Devil kept in a state of paradisial nakedness, in order to confuse and

holland shirts: shirts made of linen from Holland (then part of the Spanish empire) and reputed to be especially white
Burgundian: from Burgundy, a region of eastern France
sackbut: a wind musical instrument
Dragon's Mouth: the name given to the mouth of the Orinoco River
Corpus Christi: "body of Christ" (Latin); the Catholic feast celebrating the institution of the Eucharist, or communion
Casa de la Contratación: institution in Seville that regulated the commerce of Spain with its American colonies
Virgin of Navigators: presumably the Virgin that looks after sailors

mislead unwary Christians, even if they were not actually corrupted by the sight of such a careless display of flesh. Then, realizing that it was useless to make demands of someone who was already dreaming of what lay beyond the horizon, my mother began asking me anxiously about the safety of the ships and the skill of their pilots. I exaggerated the solidity and seaworthiness of *La Gallarda,* declaring that her pilot was a veteran of the Indies and a comrade of Nuño Garcia.° And to distract her from her fears I told her about the wonders of the New World, where all diseases could be cured by the Claw of the Great Beast and Bezoar stones;° I told her, too, that in the country of the Omeguas° there was a city built entirely of gold, so large that it would take a good walker a night and two days to cross it, and that we should surely go there unless we found our fortune in some as yet undiscovered regions, inhabited by rich tribes for us to conquer. Gently shaking her head, my mother then said that travelers returned from the Indies told lying, boastful stories, and spoke of Amazons and anthropophagi,° of terrible Bermudan tempests, and poisoned spears that transformed anyone they pierced into a statue. Seeing that she confronted all my hopeful remarks with unpleasant facts, I talked to her of our high-minded aims, and tried to make her see the plight of all the poor idol-worshippers who did not even know the sign of the cross. We should win over thousands of souls to our holy religion, and carry out Christ's commandments to the Apostles.° We were soldiers of God as well as soldiers of the king, and by baptising the Indians and freeing them from their barbarous superstitions, our nation would win imperishable glory, and greater happiness, prosperity, and power than all the kingdoms of Europe. Soothed by my remarks, my mother hung a scapulary° round my neck and gave me various ointments against the bites of poisonous creatures, at the same time making me promise that I would never go to sleep without wearing some woollen socks she had made for me herself. And as the cathedral bells began pealing, she went to look for an embroidered shawl that she only wore on very important occasions. On the way to church I noticed that, in spite of everything, my parents had as it were grown in stature because of their pride in having a son in the Captain's fleet, and that they greeted people more often and more demonstratively than usual. It is always gratifying to have a brave son, on his way to fight for a splendid and just cause. I looked towards the harbor. Grain was still being carried onto the ships.

Nuño García: veteran Spanish navigator
Claw of the Great Beast and Bezoar Stone: objects that, according to European medieval lore, had curative qualities
Omeguas: imaginary kingdom
Amazons and anthropophagi: mythological warlike women and cannibals
Apostles: twelve disciples of Christ
scapulary: two small pieces of cloth joined by strings, worn around the neck and under the clothes by some Catholics

3

I used to call her my sweetheart, although no one yet knew that we were in love. When I saw her father near the ships I realized that she would be alone, so I followed the dreary jetty battered by the winds, splashed with green water and edged with chains and rings green with slime, until I reached the last house, with green shutters that were always closed. Hardly had I sounded the tarnished knocker than the door opened, and I entered the house along with a gust of wind full of sea-spray. The lamps had already been lit because of the mist. My sweetheart sat down beside me in a deep armchair covered in old brocade, and rested her head on my shoulder with such a sad air of resignation that I did not dare question those beloved eyes, because they seemed to be gazing at nothing with an air of amazement. The strange objects that filled the room now took on a new significance for me. Some link bound me to the astrolabe, the compass and the windrose;° as well as to the sawfish° hanging from the beams of the ceiling and the charts by Mercator and Ortellius° spread out on either side of the fireplace amongst maps of the heavens populated by Bears, Dogs and Archers.° Above the whistling of the wind as it crept under the doors, I heard the voice of my sweetheart asking how our preparations were going. Reassured to find that it was possible to talk of something other than ourselves, I told her about the Sulpicians and Recollects° who were to embark with us, and praised the piety of the gentlemen and farmers chosen by the man who would take possession of these far-off countries in the name of the king of France. I told her what I knew of the great river Colbert,° bordered with ancient trees draped in silvery moss, its red waters flowing majestically beneath a sky white with herons. We were taking provisions for six months. The lowest decks of the *Belle* and the *Aimable* were full of corn. We were undertaking the important task of civilizing the vast areas of forest lying between the burning Gulf of Mexico and Chicagúa, and we would teach new skills to the inhabitants. Just when I thought my sweetheart was listening most attentively to what I was saying, she suddenly sat up, and said with unexpected vehemence that there was nothing glorious about the enterprise that had set all the town bells ringing since dawn. Last night, with her eyes inflamed with weeping, her anxiety to know something about the

astrolabe, compass, and windrose: instruments of navigation
sawfish: fish related to the sharks and rays that can attain a length of twelve to eighteen feet
Mercator and Ortellius: the first a Flemish mathematician and cartographer (1512–1594), the second a Flemish cartographer (1527–1598) who was named geographer of the realm by Philip II of Spain in 1575
Bears Dogs and Archers: constellations
Sulpicians and Recollects: religious orders
the great river Colbert: the name originally given the Mississippi by the French

world across the sea to which I was going had driven her to pick up Montaigne's Essays,° and read everything to do with America in the chapter on Coaches. There she had learned about the treachery of the Spaniards, and how they had succeeded in passing themselves off as gods, with their horses and bombards. Aflame with virginal indignation, my sweetheart showed me the passage where the skeptical Bordelais° says of the Indians that "we have made use of their ignorance and inexperience to draw them more easily unto fraud, luxury, avarice and all manner of inhumanity and cruelty by the example of our life and pattern of our customs." Blinded by her distress at such perfidy, this devout young woman who always wore a gold cross on her bosom actually approved of a writer who could impiously declare that the savages of the New World had no reason to exchange their religion for ours, since their own had served them very well for a long time. I realized that these errors only came from the resentment of a girl in love — and a very charming girl — against the man who was forcing her to wait for him for so long, merely because he wanted to make his fortune quickly in a much advertised undertaking. But although I understood this, I felt deeply wounded by her scorn for my courage, and lack of interest in an adventure that would make my name famous; for the news of some exploit of mine, or of some region I had pacified, might well lead to the King's conferring a title on me — even though it might involve a few Indians dying by my hand. No great deed is achieved without a struggle, and as for our holy faith, the Word must be imposed with blood. But it was jealousy that made my sweetheart paint such an ugly picture of the island of Santo Domingo,° where we were to make a landing, describing it in adorably unsuitable words as "a paradise of wicked women." It was obvious that in spite of her chastity, she knew what sort of women they were who often embarked for Cap Français from a jetty nearby, under the supervision of the police and amid shouts of laughter and coarse jokes from the sailors. Someone, perhaps one of the servants, may have told her that a certain sort of abstinence is not healthy for a man, and she was imagining me beset by greater perils than the floods, storms and waterdragons that abound in American rivers, in some Eden of nudity and demoralizing heat. In the end I began to be annoyed that we should be having this wrangle instead of the tender farewells I had expected at such a moment. I started abusing the cowardice of women, their incapacity for heroism, the way their philosophy was bounded by baby-linen and workboxes, when a loud knocking an-

Montaigne essays: essays written by Michel de Montaigne (1533–1592), who questioned, among many other things, the need to convert American native peoples to Christianity, hence undermining the justification Spain used to conquer the New World
Bordelais: from Bordeaux, in France, a city of which Montaigne was once mayor
Santo Domingo: the island originally called Hispaniola by the Spaniards (containing today the Dominican Republic and Haiti)

nounced the untimely return of her father. I jumped out of a back window, unnoticed by anyone in the marketplace, for passersby, fishermen and drunkards — already numerous even so early in the evening — had gathered round a table on which a man stood shouting. I took him at first for a hawker trying to sell Orvieto elixir,° but he turned out to be a hermit demanding the liberation of the holy places. I shrugged my shoulders and went on my way. Some time ago I had been on the point of enlisting in Foulke de Neuilly's° crusade. A malignant fever — cured thanks to God and my sainted mother's ointments — most opportunely kept me shivering in bed on the day of departure: that adventure ended, as everyone knows, in a war between Christians and Christians. The crusades had fallen into disrepute. Besides, I had other things to think about.

4

The wind had died down. Still annoyed by my stupid quarrel with my betrothed, I went off to the harbor to look at the ships. They were all moored to the jetty, side by side, with hatches open, receiving thousands of sacks of wheaten flour between their brightly camouflaged sides. The infantry regiments were going slowly up the gangways, amid the shouts of stevedores, blasts from the boatswain's whistle, and signals tearing through the mist to set the cranes in motion. On the decks, shapeless objects and menacing machines were being heaped together under tarpaulins. From time to time an aluminum wing revolved slowly above the bulwarks before disappearing into the darkness of the hold. The generals' horses, suspended from webbing bands, traveled over the roofs of the shops like the horses of the Valkyrie.° I was standing on a high iron gangway watching the final preparations, when suddenly I became agonizingly aware that there were only a few hours left — hardly thirteen — before I too should have to board one of those ships now being loaded with weapons for my use. Then I thought of women; of the days of abstinence lying ahead; of the sadness of dying without having once more taken my pleasure from another warm body. Full of impatience, and still angry because I had not even got a kiss from my sweetheart, I strode off towards the house where the dancers lived. Christopher, very drunk, was already shut into his girl's room. My girl embraced me, laughing and crying, saying that she was proud of me, that I looked very handsome in my uniform, and that a fortuneteller had read the cards and told her that no

---

Orvieto elixir: a potion from the Italian town of Orvieto that was thought during the Middle Ages to possess medicinal qualities

Foulke de Neuilly: twelfth-century preacher and organizer of the fourth crusade, who was originally in the parish of Neuilly-sur-Marne, in France

Valkyrie: Germanic mythological women who appear in battle on horseback to choose those who will die

harm would come to me during the Great Landing.° She more than once called me a "hero," as if she knew how cruelly her flattery contrasted with my sweetheart's unjust remarks. I went out on to the roof. The lights were going up in the town, outlining the gigantic geometry of the buildings in luminous points. Below, in the streets, was a confused swarm of heads and hats.

At this distance it was impossible to tell women from men in the evening mist. Yet it was in order that this crowd of unknown human beings should go on existing that I was due to make my way to the ships soon after dawn. I should plough the stormy ocean during the winter months, and land on a remote shore under attack from steel and fire, in defense of my countrymen's principles. It was the last time a sword would be brandished over the maps of the West. This time we should finish off the new Teutonic Order° for good and all, and advance as victors into that longed-for future when man would be reconciled with man. My mistress laid her trembling hand on my head, perhaps guessing at the nobility of my thoughts. She was naked under the half-open flaps of her dressing-gown.

5

I returned home a few hours before dawn, walking unsteadily from the wine with which I had tried to cheat the fatigue of a body surfeited with enjoyment of another body. I was hungry and sleepy, and at the same time deeply disturbed by the thought of my approaching departure. I laid my weapons and belt on a stool and threw myself on my bed. Then I realized, with a start of surprise, that there was someone lying under the thick woollen blanket; and I was just stretching out my hand for my knife when I found myself embraced by two burning hot arms, which clasped me round the neck like the arms of a drowning man, while two inexpressibly smooth legs twined themselves between mine. I was struck dumb with astonishment when I saw that the person who had slipped into my bed was my sweetheart. Between her sobs, she told me how she had escaped in the darkness, run away in terror from barking dogs and crept furtively through my father's garden to the window of my room. Here she had waited for me in terror and impatience. After our stupid quarrel that afternoon, she had thought of the dangers and sufferings lying in wait for me, with that sense of impotent longing to lighten a soldier's hazardous lot which women so often express by offering their own bodies — as if this sacrifice of their jealously guarded virginity, at the moment of departure and without hope of enjoyment, this reckless abandon-

the Great Landing: D-Day invasion of Normandy by the Allies near the end of World War II, in June of 1944
Teutonic Order: the Nazi Party

ment to another's pleasure, could have the propitiatory power of ritual ablution. There is a unique and special freshness in an encounter with a chaste body never touched by a lover's hands, a felicitous clumsiness of response, an intuitive candor that, through some obscure promptings, divines and adopts the attitudes that favor the closest possible physical union. As I lay in my sweetheart's arms, and felt the little fleece that timidly brushed against one of my thighs, I grew more and more angry at having exhausted my strength in all too familiar coupling, in the absurd belief that I was ensuring my future serenity by means of present excesses. And now that I was being offered this so desirable compliance, I lay almost insensible beneath my sweetheart's tremulous and impatient body. I would not say that my youth was incapable of catching fire once again that night, under the stimulus of this new pleasure. But the idea that it was a virgin who was offering herself to me, and that her closed and intact flesh would require a slow and sustained effort on my part, filled me with an obsessive fear of failure. I pushed my sweetheart to one side, kissing her gently on the shoulders, and began telling her with assumed sincerity what a mistake it would be for our nuptial joys to be marred by the hurry of departure; how ashamed she would be if she became pregnant, and how sad it was for children to grow up with no father to teach them how to get green honey out of hollow tree trunks and look for cuttlefish under stones. She listened, with her large bright eyes burning in the darkness, and I was aware that she was in the grip of a resentment drawn from the underworld of the instincts, and felt nothing but scorn for a man who, when offered such an opportunity, invoked reason and prudence, instead of taking her by force, leaving her bleeding on the bed like a trophy of the chase, defiled, with breasts bitten, but having become a woman in her hour of defeat. Just then we heard the lowing of cattle going to be sacrificed on the shore, and the watchmen blowing their conches. With scorn written all over her face, my sweetheart got quickly out of bed without letting me touch her, and with a gesture not so much of modesty as of someone taking back what they were on the point of selling too cheap, she covered those charms which had suddenly begun to enflame my desire. Before I could stop her she had jumped out of the window. I saw her running away as fast as she could among the olives and I realized in that instant that it would be easier for me to enter the city of Troy without a scratch than to regain what I had lost.

When I went down to the ships with my parents, my soldier's pride had been replaced by an intolerable sense of disgust, of inner emptiness and self-depreciation. And when the steersmen pushed the ships away from the shore with their strong poles, and the masts stood erect between the rows of oarsmen, I realized that the display, excesses and feasting which precede the departure of soldiers to the battlefield were now over. There was no time now for garlands, laurel-wreaths, wine-drinking in every house, envious glances from weaklings and favors from women. Instead our lot would consist in bugle calls, mud, rain-soaked bread, the arrogance of our leaders, blood spilt in error, the sickly tainted smell of gangrene. I already felt less confident that my courage would contribute to the power and happiness of the long-haired Achaeans. A veteran soldier, going to war because it was his profession and with no more enthusiasm than a sheep-shearer on his way to the pen, was telling anyone prepared to listen that Helen of Sparta was very happy to be in Troy, and that when she disported herself in Paris's° bed, her hoarse cries of enjoyment brought blushes to the cheeks of the virgins who lived in Priam's palace. It was said that the whole story of the unhappy captivity of Leda's daughter,° and of the insults and humiliations the Trojans had subjected her to, was simply war propaganda, inspired by Agamemnon with the consent of Menelaus.° In fact, behind this enterprise and the noble ideals it had set up as a screen, a great many aims were concealed that would not benefit the combatants in the very least: above all — so said the old soldier — to sell more pottery, more cloth, more vases decorated with scenes from chariot races, and to open new ways of access to Asia, whose peoples had a passion for barter, and so put an end once and for all to Trojan competition. Too heavily loaded with flour and men, the ship responded slowly to the oars. I gazed for a long time at the sunlit houses of my native town. I was nearly in tears. I took off my helmet and hid my eyes behind its crest; I had taken great trouble to make it round and smooth — like the magnificent crests of the men who could order their accoutrements of war from the most highly skilled craftsmen, and who had voyaged on the swiftest and longest ship ever known.

Translated from the Spanish
by Frances Partridge

JOSÉ LEZAMA LIMA

Considered today a major modern writer on a par with Borges, Neruda, and Paz, José Lezama Lima (1910–1976) was known only to a small though influential group of admirers until 1966. In that year, his novel Paradiso *created a scandal, both for its explicit depiction of the characters' sexual lives and for its baroque language. But Lezama had been*

Paris: in Greek legend, the Trojan prince who eloped with Helen of Troy and caused the Trojan War
Leda's daughter: Helen, daughter of Leda and Zeus, who visited Leda in the form of a swan
Menelaus: in Greek mythology, the husband of Helen and king of Sparta

publishing poetry and essays since he was twenty-one and had coedited a major literary journal, Orígenes, *between 1944 and 1956.* Orígenes *was both a journal and a school of modern poetics, an esoteric form of Catholicism and nationalism blended in obscure but compelling texts.*

Lezama had a comprehensive poetic system, drawn from often obscure sources both ancient and modern, which included theories of history and the image. Paradiso, *an autobiographical novel of education, is a summa of this system. The protagonist José Cemí, like Lezama, has lost his father (the colonel) and is raised by the oracular Rialta, his mother. In the first text we see Lezama's penchant for numerology and symbolism, as the widowed Rialta joins in her children's game of jacks. The second is a story told to Cemí by one of his friends, Fronesis, and shows Lezama's fascination with sin as well as with sexuality.*

from Paradiso

When the house regained its atmosphere of harmony, Rialta had great rings under her eyes from weeping. She and Baldovina came out of the farthest room, where they had been hiding from the tumult of the scene between Doña Augusta and Uncle Alberto. During their confrontation, Rialta wept and sobbed. It had been the first disturbance in her life since the death of her husband. The state in which she might find Augusta filled her with real terror.

In the courtyard Rialta's three children were playing jacks. A thread seemed to join her sobs to the solemn bounce of the duck-tripe ball,° to the tinkle of the jacks as they yielded to the pressure of the open hand that picked them up with a quick movement synchronized with the rise and fall of the sticky white ball. Violante, the eldest child, played with assurance, and as the game progressed, she was the one who spread out the cluster of jacks with the most precision. At first she scattered them, then she brought them together and fitted them into her cupped palm. The three children were so absorbed that the rising of the ball became crystallized like a fountain, and their staring eyes made the jacks ecstatic as they scattered, like contemplating the constellations during lingering intervals in the night. They had reached that point of choral ecstasy that children achieve so easily. Their time, the time of those around them, and the time of the external situation all coincided in a kind of temporal abandonment, where camphor or poppy seeds, in a silent and nocturnal vegetal growth, prepare an oval and crystalline identity, and where the

duck-tripe ball: tightly wound duck tripe was used to make balls for games such as jacks isolation of a group provokes a communication that is like a universal mirror.

Rialta did not wish to break the circle formed by her children, completely absorbed in their game. She sat on the floor beside them, penetrating the silence that was intent on the rising and the falling of the ball. The square formed by Rialta and her three children changed into a circle. The children shifted slightly to let their mother in. She was anxious to reach their island that was held up by a circle with flickering edges and a vertical line determined by the moving points of the ball propelled toward a small imaginary sky, falling momentarily down to the tiles that seemed to be liquid plates as the fixed looks that were the sum of the square transformed them into waves traveling toward infinity.

Violante had reached seven as she picked up the jacks, Eloísa three, and José Cemí, sweating copiously, five. Rialta began to throw the ball and her earlier concern helped the rise of the ball coincide with the semi-circle of her hand as it picked up the jacks. The looks of the four absorbed people came together at the center of the circle. The total concentration of will on the rhythm of the ball bouncing on the tiles had the effect of isolating the tiles, of giving them a liquid reflection, as if they were contracting to capture an image. A rapid animism was transmuting the tiles, and their inorganic world was being transfused into the receptive cosmos of the image. For a moment they seemed on guard, like a cocked ear or a deer's start when he catches the hint of a cloaked sound, the threshold of a delicate feeling that hurries to discover whether it is a visit, an enemy, or a conspiracy.

To the four jacks players, the tiles were an oscillating crystal that broke up silently after coming together silently, never losing its tremor, making way for fragments of military cloth, feeling harsh hobnails, freshly polished buttons. The fragments disappeared, reappearing at once, joined to new and larger pieces, the buttons falling into their sequence. The collar of the tunic was precisely starched, waiting for the face that would complete it. Rialta, peacefully hallucinated, went on playing jacks, getting close to twelve, the way one climbs up a staircase half-asleep, carrying a glass of water with such assurance that the water in it does not move. The rim of the circle was hardening until it began to look like incandescent metal. Suddenly, in a flash, the cloud broke up to make way for a new vision. On the tiles imprisoned by the circle the full tunic of the Colonel appeared, a darkish yellow that grew lighter, the buttons on the four pockets brighter than copper. Above the stiff collar, the absent face, smiling from a distance, happy perhaps, partaking in some undecipherable contentment that could not be shared, while he watched his wife and children inside that circle that united them in a space and time under his gaze. Penetrating that vision, seemingly released by the flash that preceded it, the four inside the illuminated circle experienced a sensation that was cut short as it opened up inside for an instant, and then the fragments and the totality coincided in the blink of a vision cut by a sword.

Rialta nestled her head in her arms and let go the anguish that had accumulated that day; she wept until she was sated. The three children abandoned the game and ran out into the courtyard. There, without looking at each other, they slipped between the areca tree° and the steps that led to the kitchen. Then Cemí went out to the entranceway, stopped at the main door, and looked out at the Prado,° where the passing of a cloud made a cool roof for two skaters sucking strawberry ices. . . .

When Dr. Santurce's family said goodbye to Ricardo Fronesis, they expressed insistent but false desires to have him stay for dinner. Fronesis begged off, pleading a morning exam, but just as he was leaving, he turned to Cemí and, in a prelude to an enjoyable friendship, said that tomorrow after five he would call to take him to a provincial café where they might talk.

The next day Fronesis did not come by for him, but at a quarter to five he rang up to say that he was waiting at the Café Semiramis, next to the hotel with the colonial façade, of which it was a pompous prolongation.

For the first time Cemí, in his adolescence, realized that he had been summoned and led over to a corner to talk. He felt the word "friendship" taking on flesh. He felt the birth of friendship. That meeting was the fullness of his adolescence. He felt sought after by someone outside his own family. And Fronesis always showed, along with the good cheer that burst forth from his spiritual health, a stoical dignity, which seemed to withdraw from things, paradoxically, in order to achieve his ineffable charm.

Fronesis told Cemí at the beginning of their conversation that he had preferred ringing him up to stopping by for him, because he would have had to play the role of visitor, repeating with slight variations the visit to Tres Suertes.° He also preferred talking to him alone; since they were both in their last year of preparatory school, there was a lot of magic thread to be cut. Fronesis rescued the dry cliché by inserting the word "magic," transforming a commonplace into a fey night in Baghdad.

Fronesis told Cemí that he spent every weekend in Cárdenas° sculling. Cemí noticed the sharp angularity under his sleeves; the cloth hid a musculature exercised in swimming and competent in boating. These well-spaced exercises did not bring his muscles together in shameful clusters; instead, they sent blind energy pouring through his distributive channels.

The manly green of Fronesis's eyes became fixed on a point in the dis-

areca tree: a small, decorative palm
the Prado: a central boulevard in Havana, lined by trees
Tres Suertes: Three Fortunes, name of a sugar-mill town
Cárdenas: port town east of Havana

tance, and suddenly he exclaimed: "Here comes Godofredo the Devil again." Cemí glanced around and saw the redheaded, one-eyed man approaching. He was whistling a tune that scattered like the fragments of a gilded serpent.

"Godofredo the Devil," Fronesis began, "takes a strange pleasure in passing in front of people he thinks know his story. He won't look them in the face, a sign of his indifferent hatred, which he can show only by turning his face. My father, being a provincial lawyer at the center of almost every bit of gossip that passes around town, knows his terrible story. As Godofredo knows he knows, he imagines my father must have told me too, and so he supposes that any moment now I'm going to start telling you the story that ends up with his blind eye. He can't hold himself back whenever he sees me, and he tries to come close, but he always keeps his head turned like that, afraid that if I stare at him, he might lose the eye he has left.

"When he was fifteen, Godofredo the Devil had hallucinations about Pablo's wife. Pablo was the head machinist at Tres Suertes and, at the age of thirty-four, was seventeen years older than his wife, and this, combined with his Saturday-night drinking bouts, lent a certain irregularity to the nighttime hours they had together. On some summer nights Fileba, which is what she was called, could not liquefy the density of Pablo's sleep, thickened as it was by the load of spirits and his hoarse, rummy breath. To get away from her flirting, Pablo would pull a pillow over his head, and this stopped the pounding of Fileba's little hands from waking him up. Finally, fatigued, she would drop off with an ill-humored stiffness, dreaming about monsters carrying her away naked to the hilltops. She would wake up and Pablo would still have the pillow over his head. It was raining and the dampness kept her sleeping until the first singing of dawn.

"One Saturday, Godofredo took Pablo home and helped put him to bed. Pablo was so drunk that he almost had to carry him on his back. He noticed Fileba's paleness more carefully, her eyes enlarged by the mortification of so many nights. And he began to hang around the house like a wolf cub who knows that the girl of the house has tied the dove to the kitchen table by its leg.°

"Thinking himself master of a secret, Godofredo began to court her. She refused to have trysts or to play the game of the precocious evil one. Another Saturday when he again brought Pablo home on his back, Fileba left Pablo at the door as he was about to take a step into the house. Pablo stumbled, fell head first onto the floor of the living room, so she put down a mat for him and brought him the usual pillow. While she was preparing a strong brew, she went out to take a look at the Saturday

wolf cub who knows . . . : a phrase meaning "the prey can be easily had"

drunkard and noticed Godofredo making his Luciferine rounds, and that time she closed the windows and called in some neighbors to keep her company.

"That was when Father Eufrasio arrived at Tres Suertes, taking a disoriented priest's vacation. Too much study of concupiscence in St. Paul° and copulation without pleasure had sucked the marrow out of him, putting his reason out of kilter. How to keep the other body at a distance in an amorous encounter and still attain the leap of supreme energy in the moan of pain was plaguing him like a turnstile spinning in a space ringed by great vultures. He went on vacation under the pretext of visiting a younger brother, the one in charge of the cane-cutting gangs, for a few days. The disorientation he was experiencing was not known to the denizens of Tres Suertes, so that his prolonged, immutable looks and his glassy silences were indecipherable to everybody around him, out there where the lowing of cows drives away all theological subtleties about the reproductive sensorium.°

"With the priest's arrival, to pretend that at Tres Suertes they followed the same customs as townspeople, some girls began to call on him. Naturally they knew nothing about his derangement, or about his strange problem of concupiscence. Fileba's gentleness brought her along and Father Eufrasio was getting to hear all about the midnight pillows of Pablo the machinist. Whispered confidences demonstrated that she was supplicating carnal closeness, while Pablo was trying to put off the terrible attacks of her flesh, which he had to alienate to keep his vital reserves untouched. At the approach of the concupiscent act, he deflated at his virile tip, languishing hopelessly.

"Thus the nights that Pablo dedicated to the sabbat° came to be used by Eufrasio and Fileba, and when Pablo the machinist got home, he could fall asleep without having to cover his head with a pillow like a shield. Meanwhile, Godofredo the Devil discovered that the couple disappeared every Saturday into a little nest owned by the priest's younger brother, who was unaware of the priest's novel methods for curing his concupiscent complexes.

"One day Godofredo went to get Pablo in the village bar before he downed his fourth glass. On the way back to Tres Suertes he was playing out the long thread of Fileba's betrayal. He told Pablo that if he had doubts, he might lurk nearby and actually watch the couple go into the house of sin. Pablo hid behind a mulberry tree, and Godofredo along the wall near the door, to prove, in the dim light, that the couple decidedly

St. Paul: a Jew who converted to Christianity and became one of the early fathers of the Church
sensorium: the sexual organs
sabbat: a day of demonological orgies

did enter the house of sin. Around ten o'clock, in the exaggerated smile of the crescent moon, not from the tamped-down path to the door of the house but from a short cut, the couple appeared, lightened by the lunar whiteness, which gave them the pallor of sin.

"When Pablo the machinist, behind the mulberry tree, had proof of the truth, which sucked at him like an octopus, he went back to the bar, totaled up a staggering number of fourth glasses of straight cognac, and started shouting so loud that some country police arrived. Seeing it was Pablo, they covered him with their capes to keep the heavy dew off and took care of him till they were certain that the key that had been describing grand circles in the air finally came to rest in the keyhole. With a scintilla of clarity he fell on the living-room sofa where he and Fileba had posed for their newlywed pictures, a piece of furniture which had been bought secondhand for their wedding but which held firm on the tragic occasion of Pablo the machinist's collapse as he placed his demon in the service of his fate."

At that point in the tale, Cemí realized that Fronesis was making an effort to go on, but certain hesitations showed that he was entering the real whirlwind a little fearfully.

"Meanwhile, Godofredo the Devil felt around the walls and windows with his nails for a peephole to be able to watch the couple. At last he stationed himself at the window and peered through the lower corner. Like a marine apparition contemplated through the tube of a telescope, a strange combination of figures rose to view. Fileba, naked, lay on the bed weeping, showing the fullness of her body. But it was hardly suffused with pleasure; rather, she seemed indifferent, frigid. Eufrasio, his pants off, was still wearing his shirt and undershirt. A string was tied to one end of the bed and stretched to wrap around his testicles, purple from the gradual strangulation, as Eufrasio drew back with an almost liturgical slowness. His phallus, in the culmination of its erection, looked like a great votive candle that had been lit for a very sinful soul. His scorched, rigid cheeks were receiving infernal slaps. When the seminal reason of Augustine° finally came out, the testicular strangulation was as much as the string could stand, and a sweaty moan struggling for silence trembled through the disoriented man's body. Fileba was crying, covering her mouth to keep from making noise, but her eyes shot out cold flashes, the congealed rays of a copper mine on an endless Siberian steppe, a glance like a halcyon's,° dead in the stormy coldness, drifting into eternity wide-eyed. Thus she watched Eufrasio dress and leave the room without glanc-

Augustine: Saint Augustine, a church father who wrote much about the temptations of the flesh in his *Confessions*
halcyon: in ancient legend, a bird whose eye was supposed to have a calming influence on the sea

ing at her. The distance of his body and the painful orgasm, which the deranged priest considered the fulfillment of unbreakable Pauline laws,° had been attained to perfection.

"She ran home as fast as she could, shaking. Pablo was lying down with the light out and the pillow over his face. She tried to sleep, for endless hours pretended to sleep, but then she noticed that Pablo's hands weren't crossed over the pillow shield on his face, as usual in his Saturday-night exhaustion. She nervously presumed an unexpected ending; then she saw the flaccid hands of the one who accompanied her on a last night. She turned on the light. She saw in a shock that the pillow was soaked with blood, his shirt still wet. The machete on the floor near the slit throat had begun to oxidize with the coagulation of the blood. Pablo, before lying down to recuperate, had washed his face with the cool water of night. Fileba tugged at the pillow on the floor, but like a gorgon° soaked in somber purple, it began to cast off threads and spurts of blood. She quickly turned on all the lights and opened up the living-room window. Her shouts are still remembered by some of the people at Tres Suertes who were awakened at midnight.

"Around dawn, Godofredo the Devil slipped past Pablo's house. The whole neighborhood had crowded into the street, still alarmed by Fileba's shouts. He overheard the gossip and perplexities that were being woven about the machinist's suicide. He hastened off along the main road, and as he got farther from the plantation, he was being wrapped in an implacable army of vines. The trees and bushes cut off his path. Around his waist he wore a machete for his work as a cane cutter. He shouted and kicked at the trees, and flung himself on the vines, and they drew back from his slashes, coiling like rearing serpents. The vines around his waist, as he beat them, whistled like a hurricane wind. One among all those vines took its vengeance on him, and drawing back, it drove forward and engraved a cross on his right eye, the canon eye.°

"That was how Godofredo the Devil lost his right eye and also lost his reason. His walks describe immense, implacable circles, with the radii zigzagging like bolts of lightning. When the rains of April come, he throws himself into ditches, his body stops trembling, and the humus puts his fever to sleep. The incessant rain also softens the flames of the red hair of Godofredo the Devil, the malignant flower of the crossroads."

Translated from the Spanish
by Gregory Rabassa

Pauline laws: laws presumably governing priestly abstinence
gorgon: in Greek mythology, three sisters with snakes on their hair, of terrifying appearance
canon eye: the right eye, through which understanding presumably entered

REINALDO ARENAS

Reinaldo Arenas (1943–1990), a peasant from eastern Cuba, was fifteen when the revolution came to power. He had a haphazard education and upbringing, complicated by his homosexuality and the taboos of Cuban society. Arenas learned much from stories he heard from his grandmother, and he read voraciously. He soon became a prolific and highly original writer, though persecuted for his sexuality and refusal to conform. His first novel, Singing from the Well, *won him a second prize in the 1965 competition sponsored by the Cuban Writers' Union. It was published in 1967 in Cuba, the only one of his books to be published in his country. His second novel,* Hallucinations, *appeared in 1969, in Mexico City.*

Arenas became a celebrity abroad but continued to be hounded by the Cuban authorities, who confiscated his manuscripts and eventually jailed him. Arenas's short stories are among the best from Latin America. Like some of his novels, they tell of his sexual and artistic awakening. In "The Wounded," for instance, we soon discover that the dying young man is a double of the narrator, called Reinaldo, who is planning to write a book. In 1980, Arenas fled to the United States. Suffering from AIDS, he committed suicide in 1990.

The Wounded

This morning, before rising, his sorrows were lilac. Then he lifted his head a little higher and they were blue, but he leaned further, almost sitting up in bed, and then the sorrows clothed themselves in a violent yellow. Finally, he sat up. At once he opened the tricolored glass of the window and the sorrows revealed their natural pigmentation: the street a shabby grey; the pines, always indecisive, displaying a blackened green; the buildings wounding him with their new-born red; and the sky with its facade a stubborn blue.

After a half hour he walked to the bathroom.

And he brushed his teeth.

A little later and he was dressed. Then he went and shut the window. Watching through the lowest triangle in the glass, he saw a purple woman cross the sidewalk carrying a purple child in her arms, although she hardly stood out against the purple facades of the buildings.

After exactly one hour of standing next to the window he went to the only chair in the room.

And he sat down.

"The days pass like thin dogs with nowhere to go," he said aloud, and he thought to note it down for the book he had been planning to write. But he didn't bother.

Actually, since the day that he locked himself in his room and refused to answer when his mother called him to dinner, and told her later, shouting, that he preferred to starve to death than ever to return to work *because I just can't put up with this. Because now there's nobody who can stand this hell, because every day they squeeze me more. And even after you're asphyxiated they're going to keep squeezing to see what they can get out of you, because now they go so far as to expect me to join the militia, and do guard duty, and work a thousand hours, and enlist in a productive work brigade, and become a packhorse. And burst. Because I . . .* since then he had decided to write a book. And now it was a month ago that he had stopped going to work and the pages were still blank, and the typewriter, with the cover still on, was lying in the corner of the room like a dog in the sun.

At the end of his first week of isolation, when his mother's terrible threats were reduced to an innocuous whining, Reinaldo came down from his room and stopped at the kitchen door, staring at the papaya growing next to the patio wall. His mother wasted no time; with a striking dexterity she spread the contents of the refrigerator and her pots on the table. And she said to him, "Eat." And she cried.

He sat down at the table. He tried the soup, and although it burned his tongue, he continued to eat. And he decided that as soon as he finished the meal he would lock himself up in his room and begin to work on the book. And while he did in fact finish the meal and lock himself in his room, he didn't write anything.

But from then on he came downstairs to the kitchen three times a day when his mother called him. And then three days ago, when he woke up, he stayed in bed for only three hours before sitting up and looking at his sorrows through the colored glass, and then going to the bathroom to brush his teeth. And the day before yesterday he lay awake for only two hours, and he contemplated his sorrows for an hour, and even opened the window. Yesterday he stayed in bed for only one hour after waking up, and he stared at his sorrows for no more than a half-hour, and afterwards he brushed his teeth and even took a warm bath; in the afternoon he went to the street and walked to the beach.

Reinaldo stood facing the sea the whole afternoon, watching the waves roll in like great, dead gulls that dissolved on the beach. Finally, he spent a long time contemplating the sun that was beginning to sink into the sea. Thus night fell upon him.

"Solitude pullulates in the smallest twigs of the eucalyptus," he said aloud. And he thought that the sentence was worth noting down for the book he was planning to write. But he had neither pencil nor paper on him, and he decided to write it down when he got home.

When the shadows were almost palpable and the sea was no more than a blackened and echoing void, he began to walk. But he didn't go home. He walked through the dimly lit streets; he took a bus *where women armed with pocketbooks of incredible dimensions trampled on me unendingly,* and he got off in front of the Amadeo Roldán Theater,° where a group of Czechoslovakian singers were giving a recital.

Since he still had almost his whole monthly salary, he bought a ticket in the orchestra. And he entered the hall as they were turning down the lights. Guiding himself by the two blue bulbs flickering at the back of the theater, he found a seat and sat down.

Suddenly, a little while after the show had begun and one of the Czech women dressed in a dazzling costume was singing a popular Spanish song, he felt, as one who discovers an unsuspected pain, that it was entirely out of the question for him to go on living. *No, I didn't feel that exactly, it was even more; while that fat Czech, wrapped in her lamé suit was sliding around the stage like a shiny whale, gripping the microphone like the most destructive of weapons, bathed in sweat, which, unfortunately, was not blood, and repeating, "Don Quixote, Don Quixote," in an endless bleating, I felt not that I could not go on living, but rather that I must die in that instant, but in that very instant, without a moment's grace, without hoping for explanations or consolation. That is what I felt, and it was as if I had suddenly discovered that my arms were falling off and I didn't even feel any pain. . . .* But he remained seated, enjoying the show, and only at the end did he get up without applauding and leave.

And now he was sitting in his chair with his feet lying on the bed, calmly reviewing what had happened without trying to find an explanation. Then he stopped thinking, reclined further in the seat, and closed his eyes. And since nothing important happened to him for the rest of the day, night fell immediately. And in a moment, the first fanfares of the dawn were sounding.

It was then that he seemed to hear someone knocking insistently on the door of the house. He held his breath and listened: there was no doubt, someone was calling urgently. He jumped to his feet. He ran down the stairs — silently — crossed the living room in a flash (for in that moment the knocking grew more insistent, although it didn't seem to be produced by a hand, but by something heavier and softer), and he opened the door. In that instant the wounded man collapsed and fell at his feet.

It was not without an effort that he managed to bring him into the living room. Then he shut the door. Supporting him on his shoulders, he got

Amadeo Roldán Theater: a theater in Havana named after a great Cuban composer

him up the steps and put him in his room. And he laid him in the bed very carefully. Then he turned on the lights and looked him over: the wounds did not come from any firearm, neither were they inflicted by a knife; it seemed as though someone had scratched him deeply with enormous fingernails.

His whole face was furrowed by those deep scratches, and the blood, dripping from the corners of his mouth, was spilling onto the sheets. He opened his shirt carefully and he could see on the side of his chest, more or less where he thought the heart was, that the wound (or the rip) became deeper and the blood almost bubbled out.

"You're not going to die," Reinaldo said aloud and to himself.

And he began to take off his clothes. Then he brought water from the bathroom and he washed the wounds as well as his inexperience permitted. And he tried to stop the bleeding with all of his clean handkerchiefs and underwear. When it seemed that the blood was hardly oozing, he went downstairs for gauze and alcohol; he also brought a bottle, almost empty, of hydrogen peroxide. He removed the wet handkerchiefs and underwear, threw them in the sink and emptied the peroxide on the wounds, which began to foam instantly as though they were boiling. And he bound all the wounds. Exhausted he remained motionless before the bed and contemplated the wounded man for a few moments: he was almost a boy. Then he drew the sheet up to his shoulders. He went down to the living room at once and mopped up the spots of blood on the floor and the staircase. In a few minutes he was once again at the side of the wounded man, who was moaning weakly. He went for some water and moistened his lips. As he put the glass on the floor he discovered the wounded man's clothing next to his feet. With a certain apprehension he began to go through the pockets: in the first he found a wad of money, "Seventy-seven pesos," and he returned them to their place (actually there were eighty); in the second pocket he only found a pack of *Populares* cigarettes and a comb — "No matches," he said, and he put back the cigarettes and the comb; when his fingers were going through the last pocket they hit upon a plastic card. He understood almost without looking that it must be an ID card of some trade union. Raising it to eye-level, he began to read: the wounded man was named Reinaldo. When he finished reading he put the card back in its place, put the clothing away, and, pulling the chair close to the bed where the wounded man was breathing painfully, he sat down. With a gesture of appreciable tenderness, he laid his hand upon his face.

"We are also the same age," he said with an insuperable tranquility.

In the morning he was still sitting next to the wounded man, who was now struggling in very short moans that were hardly more than frustrated breaths. Then he heard someone knocking at the door (knocking and trying to open at the same time).

"What do you want?" he said, since he was sure it must be his mother.

"Open up," she answered, still trying to open it herself, "I have to get your dirty clothes."

"I'll bring them down to you in a minute," Reinaldo answered.

"Open up," his mother said, and tried to open the door with greater insistence.

"Stop bugging me!" her son shouted (those were the words he used when he wanted to end a battle with his mother), and he went to the bathroom to get water for the wounded man.

His mother went downstairs muttering.

In a moment Reinaldo picked up the dirty clothing and went downstairs to eat his breakfast; but first he locked his room.

"Here are the clothes," he said to his mother. And he sat down at the table.

His mother served him breakfast and looked at him for a while "with the eyes of a tired cow," he thought, and then she went off to the kitchen. Reinaldo then stuffed the bread in his pocket and poured the coffee into a bottle, and, making sure that his mother wouldn't see him, he went up to his room. He tried there, with considerable patience, to make the wounded man eat some breakfast, but the light coffee had hardly reached his throat when it rose to his lips and spilled onto the pillow. Reinaldo kept insisting and for a moment he was convinced that the wounded man had swallowed a few mouthfuls. He spent the rest of the day next to him, and there was an instant in which the wounded man opened his eyes and smiled at him. Reinaldo tried to speak to him but the wounded man was already lowering his eyelids.

The afternoon was coming to an end and the brilliance of the sun, shattering against the window panes, bathed the two Reinaldos with its halo of blue, violet, and shocking yellow.

With the first waves of the night his mother's pounding was heard on the bedroom door.

"I'm sleeping," Reinaldo responded with thinly veiled fury.

His mother went downstairs cursing.

But at midnight, when Reinaldo was almost dozing off in front of the wounded man, his mother began to insist again; now she was trying to open the door with the key to her room. Reinaldo didn't answer, but he realized with a mixture of rage and anguish that it was necessary to move the wounded man.

"But I'm not going to let you die," he said.

The following morning he went downstairs to eat breakfast. While he was eating his bread and butter he sensed that his mother was going to assail him with some complaint, so he grunted loudly in a way that made the bread crumbs shoot out of his mouth and scatter all over the table. His mother went to the refrigerator and brought him a glass of water, then she disappeared. Reinaldo accomplished the same operation with the bread and coffee as the day before. And he got up and headed toward his room. His mother was there, struggling with the lock.

"Have you lost some treasure?" he said to her with furious irony.

"I have to clean that room," his mother answered.

"Don't worry about that," he said, "I know how to clean it."

He opened the door deftly, entered, and closed it in his mother's face, and she let out a bellow. But he didn't allow his ears to listen to it. He began to give the coffee to the wounded man, and he observed happily that the glass was emptying. Then he sat down next to him and waited for the night.

It was the third day that he hadn't slept, and his face had turned so pale that it stood out in the darkness like a floating handkerchief. At midnight he sat shaking his head, trying to overcome his fatigue, then he washed his face and began to walk from one corner of the room to the other.

"I'm not going to sleep," he said aloud.

But at dawn, when a remnant of cold wind which had slipped in between the bathroom shutters grazed his neck, Reinaldo carefully moved the wounded man to one side of the mattress and got into bed next to him.

They lay wrapped in the same sheet.

It wasn't morning yet when Reinaldo heard something knocking on the window pane. He rose quickly, and, walking to the window, peered out through the glass; he almost felt resigned on discovering the source of the sound: it was his mother placing a ladder against the high window of the room and beginning to ascend with the motion of an unbalanced tortoise. Reinaldo opened the window and contemplated his mother for a moment as she panted wearily in search of the support of a rung.

"This really takes it!" Reinaldo said with terrifying tranquility.

His mother, in the distressing predicament of a lizard halfway up a wall, lifted her eyes and remained momentarily disconcerted, but then she immediately climbed back down, and sitting on the first rung of the ladder, began to sob. She mixed in some very loud moans with the sobs, as if they were beating her, and she let loose a curse. The moan was always the same, but the curse varied, replaced each time by another of higher caliber, as if it were chosen with great care from an infinite repertoire.

Reinaldo closed the window and sat next to the wounded man.

"Now I really do have to take you out of this room," he said out loud while he laid a hand on his neck. And in that moment he noticed that his hand was warm. The wounded man was developing a very high fever.

As the day advanced, so likewise the fever advanced. Towards evening the wounded man was hardly breathing and seemed to dissolve in sweat and tiny moans.

Reinaldo paced from one side of the room to the other, watching the window, touching the wounded man, obliging him to drink some water in which he had dissolved all the pills he had at hand. He was waiting for the opportunity to move him to a place where his mother would not discover him. Meanwhile, he discovered with ever-renewed terror that the wounded man was getting worse.

As it got dark, his mother knocked at the bedroom door.

"Aren't you going to eat!" she screeched.

"Bring me all the pills you can find in the medicine chest," Reinaldo said, "I'm really sick."

"Oh my God!" his mother cried out, but she didn't add anything more. And she went downstairs.

In a few seconds she was knocking at the door again.

"Here are the pills," she said.

"Bring them here," her son said, opening the door, taking the bottle of pills, and locking it again with incredible dexterity.

"And what do you have?" he heard his mother saying, still stationed at the door.

"Nothing," he answered.

He threw all the pills in a glass of water and he raised it to the lips of the wounded man who seemed to be dozing. Then he sat next to him on the bed and remained there, contemplating him until midnight.

Then he began to wrap him in the sheets with special care.

When the wounded man was completely bundled up, Reinaldo carried him in his arms down to the living room. Everything was silent. Reinaldo laid the wounded man on the floor. He opened the kitchen door and went out to the patio with him. There he placed that long white bundle on the dew-soaked grass; he took the wooden ladder (the one his mother had used for her climb), steadying one end against the eaves, and he began to scale the house with the wounded man in his arms, managing an unbelievable balancing act. In the darkness, Reinaldo's silhouette climbing up the ladder with that large, white bundle which almost seemed to float amidst the shadows, looked like an illustration from a book of fantastic tales. Finally, he reached the roof. With the wounded man in his arms he went sliding across the tiles that creaked and shattered; he arrived thus at one side of the house where the roof sank to form a gutter in which all the leaves that had fallen onto the tiles had accumulated. Reinaldo laid the wounded man on those leaves and began to camouflage him with them. In a short time only a bed of leaves could be seen, as always, next to an incredibly thin boy who seemed to push them about indifferently.

In the morning, when his mother knocked at the door, Reinaldo shouted, "Open up," from his bed. His mother entered with a disturbed face and excited gestures, and when he said to her with infinite calm, "What do you want?" she felt disconcerted and even answered, "Nothing," and, bewildered, walked into the bathroom. But there she found something her laments and complaints could latch onto: "How horrible!" she said, and now she held up in one hand the blood-stained underwear and handkerchiefs which he had forgotten to hide. "How horrible!" she said again, now with a gesture of compassion as she was leaving the room. Reinaldo thought that the best thing to do was to strangle her. But when he was alone he opened the colored pane, and, getting on top of the window, he grabbed onto the edge of the eaves and climbed onto the roof. He spent the rest of the day climbing up and down, carrying (with difficulty) a great many liters of milk and dishes of food, notable quantities of bandages, bottles of syrups and pills, and other medicines. At midnight he lay down next to that exaggerated pile of dampening leaves, and he fell asleep looking at the sky. But at daybreak, the blows, already incessant, of a downpour made him open his eyes; still half-asleep, he looked above as if he wished to say, "This can't be," and he ran to his room, entering through the window. Equipping himself with all his sheets and blankets, he got back up on the roof. He began at once to cover the wounded man with the bedclothes. And he stayed at his side and let himself be drenched by the rain.

"You're safer this way," he said. "It's bound to clear up any minute."

But the downpour not only continued, it kept growing stronger until it transformed itself into a gigantic stream that filled the whole vault of the heavens. Reinaldo fought with the water, turning the gutters and even trying to construct some sort of dam with the broken tiles in order to keep the wounded man from getting soaked, but the current was carrying off the leaves, the pieces of tile, the sheets, and was now sliding, like an angry brook, in the direction of the wounded man. So Reinaldo lay himself down, pressing his body against the gutters, taking the place of a dike. But the downpour kept growing and the current began to flow over his body. Reinaldo took the wounded man in his arms and lifted him up high. He supported him that way, panting, until the last droplets were dissolving in the air.

It was morning. Reinaldo tenderly laid the body of the wounded man on the damp tiles and began to uncover him. The wounded man's mouth was terribly yellow, almost green, and it was so cold that Reinaldo nervously placed his ear to it to listen for signs of life.

"You're not going to die," he said.

And he ran across the glistening tiles, balancing himself precariously; he jumped to the bedroom window and went down to the kitchen. Before his mother's astonished eyes, he began to prepare a complicated concoction with leaves grabbed at random from all the plants on the patio and the pills that remained in the medicine chest; he also threw in two eggs that were in the refrigerator, a little iodine and milk. As soon as that boiled, giving off a bluish smoke and an indescribable odor, he went off with the potion, headed for the bedroom. His mother's astonishment exploded then in a small shriek which he didn't listen to anyway. With the potion in a jar that burnt his fingers, he launched himself toward the roof and managed to grab onto the tiles, but the container jumped from his hands and rolling down the roof, fell to the ground. Reinaldo saw it fall on the creeping grass of the patio while its contents dispersed into the air. He ran immediately to the wounded man and he observed him for a moment: the boy was in his death throes.

Reinaldo ran down to the kitchen and, to his mother's amazement, which exploded now as soon as he arrived, he prepared another and more complicated potion. And he scaled the wall to the roof more successfully. Panting hard, he reached the wounded man, who had turned completely purple. "Drink," he said, as he lifted the thick liquid to his lips. But the wounded man did not drink; he remained very still with his lips contracted and the bluish potion spilling out of them. "Drink," Reinaldo repeated. Then he put the pitcher down on the tiles and with a gesture of annoyance, he lowered his ear to the chest of the wounded man. Reinaldo heard the trill of two hummingbirds that had been bustling about the upper branches of the pines for a little while. The wounded man was dead.

At midnight Reinaldo came down from the roof and went out to the street. He walked to the park and sat down on a bench beneath tall trees inhabited by whispers and music (there were loudspeakers on most of the trunks); people were strolling in the distance near the lower branches and the flower-beds. Then he walked to the sea wall and listened to the roar of the sea for a while. At dawn he headed home.

He began to climb carefully to the roof; once above, he walked to the wounded man and remained standing for a time, looking at him. Then he crouched next to him and laid his face next to the other, frozen face. At once he sat down and placing his hands on his knees, he looked up above. The sky advanced like a sharpened knife, and a wet frog jumped past his face. The trees were shedding their first leaves after the downpour; they were scattered on the tiles, rolling then to the gutters with the brief crackle of scorched paper. An enormous moon cut a timeless path across the sky. Then the chill of dawn began to invade him like an invisible mist.

"Oh Reinaldo, now you've got no escape," Reinaldo said. And it was impossible to say which of the two he was referring to.

Tears began to flow warmly, like the first drops that roll through the gutters on a burning hot day.

On the third day after his death, the wounded man's body began to lose its stiffness; the flesh became soft and a thick water, like curdled milk, came out of his ears. And towards evening some knowing buzzards that had been circling in the sky descended swiftly and alighted upon the roof tiles of the house. Reinaldo saw them descend from the window of his room, and in a flash he got up on the roof and tried to scare them away with threatening gestures and pieces of roof tile that he threw at them. The buzzards lifted up in a short flight and returned at once to sit next to the wounded man. Reinaldo ran to his room, took the newspapers that were under his bed, and returning, covered the wounded man with them; then, to keep the wind from uncovering him, he placed some tiles on the wrapping. He spent the rest of the day in a vigil next to the wounded man, and when the more daring buzzards glided close to his head, he hurled imprecations and shook his fist. And he even managed to hit one of those big, ugly birds, which fell stunned, spinning down to the patio where his mother was doing the wash.

Reinaldo stayed at it for a week, playing out his role of guardian with a real passion. He had provided himself with a great quantity of canned foods and preserves that he kept beneath the roof tiles, and only at night would he come down to his room, where he would sleep until a little before dawn.

On the seventh day of his vigil the rainstorm began again, but he didn't try to cover himself; he sat down next to the wounded man and began to observe the rain that seemed to be in no hurry. The wounded man had started to rot and the odor that rose from his body became so awful that Reinaldo thought it might reach his mother and, continuing to spread, would flood the whole neighborhood. Finally, the rain began to let up and by midnight it had stopped.

Reinaldo went down to his room. He was more weary than ever; he was panting like a dog and his lips were completely blue. He walked to the mirror and contemplated his face. Without taking his eyes off himself, he began to try out various kinds of smiles. In the end, he crossed the room and got into bed without taking off his drenched clothing. He felt as if he were sinking in a very still and bottomless river. Thus, he fell off to sleep.

When he woke up the tricolor brilliance of the sun was bathing his room. It was almost getting dark. Suddenly he sat up in bed with a jerk. He opened the window. And he jumped up to the roof.

A great band of buzzards cawed on the roof tiles, devouring the wounded man with alarming speed. Reinaldo went up to the pack and hurled himself against them, but they kept gulping indifferently, and even when he kicked them, they continued devouring. They seemed like debauched creatures that vehemently refused to abandon an orgy. Finally, he began to throw pieces of roof tile, to shout, and to grab them by the claws and slam them against the roof. But they kept devouring. The more prudent flew off provided with a bone or a long piece of gut that came unfurled in the air like a serpent. Although Reinaldo continued threatening, shouting, kicking them, it was useless; as darkness fell, three of those ugly, obstinate birds flew off with the last of the wounded man's bones tightly clutched in their claws. They vanished into the red sky. Reinaldo saw them disappear and remained standing on the roof for a moment; his head stood out against the radiance of the sunset. A fine rain began to drum upon the highest leaves. Reinaldo walked to the edge of the eaves and jumped down to his room.

Leaning his face against the window pane, he now saw the rain of colors falling on the street.

"It's raining as if the sky had opened all of its gargoyles. It's raining as if it were crying, as if all of the creatures on high were dissolving into tears. It's raining, and the tumult of the rain makes such an incredible sob that even I myself in this moment could not surpass it."

He said all of this aloud, and he thought it would be good to note it down for the book he had planned to write.

Translated from the
Spanish by Andrew Bush

GUATEMALA ☀

MIGUEL ANGEL ASTURIAS

In 1967, Miguel Angel Asturias (1899–1974) became the first Latin American novelist to be awarded the Nobel Prize. Of Mayan and Spanish ancestry, his youth coincided with the brutal dictatorship of Manuel Estrada Cabrera (1898–1920), which forced his family to move from the capital to the countryside. There he came into contact with indigenous cultures. But it was not until his studies of anthropology in Paris that Asturias came to know Mayan culture well. He translated (from a French translation) the Popol Vuh, *the sacred book of the Mayas, and published* Legends of Guatemala *(1930) to great acclaim. In Paris he was also involved with the surrealists. Surrealism and ethnography, in addition to a deep political commitment, are the most telling influences in his work.*

His best-known book, El señor presidente *(Mr. President, 1946), from which this excerpt is drawn, is basically the story of Estrada Cabrera's dictatorship, told in a poetic, often grotesque tone that betrays the author's surrealist past. In "Angel Face" Asturias introduces a central character in his novel: a diabolical figure endowed with both beauty and perversity. The slovenly, grotesque setting is typical of Asturias's landscapes. With experiments such as this, Austurias paved the way for the new Latin American novel and showed how to write politically committed novels that were not strictly realistic or mere propaganda.*

Angel Face

Covered in bits of paper, leather and rags, skeleton umbrellas, brims of straw hats, saucepans with holes in them, broken china, cardboard boxes, pulped books, pieces of glass, shoes curled up by the sun, collars, egg-shells, scraps of cotton and food — the Zany went on dreaming. Now he saw himself in a large patio surrounded by masks; soon he realised that they were the faces of people watching a cock-fight. The fight blazed up like paper in a flame. One of the combatants expired without pain before the spectators' eyes, which were glazed with pleasure to see the curved spurs drawn out smothered in blood. A smell of brandy. Tobacco-stained spittle. Entrails. Savage exhaustion. Somnolence. Weakness. Tropical noon. Someone was tiptoeing through his dream so as not to wake him . . .

It was the Zany's mother. The mistress of a cock-breeder who played the guitar with flinty fingernails, she had been the victim of his jealousy and his vices. The story of her troubles was endless: at the mercy of this worthless man and a martyr to the child born to her under the "direct" influence of a changing moon, so the midwives said, in her agony she had connected her baby's disproportionately large head — a round head with a double crown like the moon — with the bony faces of all the other patients in the hospital, and the expressions of fear and disgust, the hiccups, gloom and vomiting of the drunken cock-breeder.

The Zany became aware of the rustle of starched petticoats — wind and leaves — and ran after her with tears in his eyes.

He found relief in her motherly bosom. The entrails of the woman who had given birth to him absorbed the pain of his wounds like blotting-paper. What a deep and imperturbable refuge. What abundance of love! My pretty little lily! My fine big lily! How I love you! How I love you!

The cock-breeder was singing softly into the hollow of his ear:

Why not,
Why not,
Why not, my sugar-plum lollypop,
For I am a cock lollypop
And when I raise my foot lollypop
I drag my wing lollypop!

The Zany raised his head and without speaking said:
"I'm sorry, Mamma, I'm sorry!"
And the apparition stroked his face tenderly and replied:
"I'm sorry, my son, I'm sorry!"
From a long way off he heard his father's voice, emerging from a glass of brandy:

I was hooked
I was hooked
I was hooked by a white woman,
And when the yucca grows well
Only the leaves are torn up!

The Zany murmured:
"I'm sick to my soul, Mamma!"
And the apparition stroked his face tenderly and replied:
"I'm sick to my soul, my son!"
Happiness does not taste of flesh. Close beside them the shadow of a

pine tree by kissing the earth, as cool as a river. And in the pine tree a bird was singing, a bird that was also a little gold bell.

"I am the Rose-Apple of the Bird of Paradise, I am life, half my body is a lie, the other half is truth; I am a rose and I am an apple, I give to everyone one glass eye and one real eye; those who see with my glass eye see because they dream, those who see with my real eye see because they are looking! I am life, the Rose-Apple of the Bird of Paradise; I am the lie in every truth, and the truth in every fabrication!"

Suddenly the idiot left his mother's lap and ran to watch the circus go by: horses with long manes like weeping-willows ridden by women dressed in spangles; carriages decorated with flowers and paper streamers reeled along the paved streets as unsteadily as drunkards. A troupe of squalid street musicians, trumpeters, fiddle-scrapers and drum-beaters. Floury-faced clowns were distributing bright-colored programs announcing a gala performance in honor of the President of the Republic, the Benefactor of his Country, Head of the Great Liberal Party and Protector of Studious Youth.°

The idiot's gaze wandered round the high vaulted roof. The circus performers left him alone in a building standing above a bottomless abyss the color of verdigris. The seats were hanging from the curtains like suspension bridges. The confessionals went up and down between the earth and sky like lifts carrying souls, operated by the Angel of the Golden Ball and the Devil with Eleven Thousand Horns.° The Virgin of Carmel° came out from her shrine through the wall of glass enclosing her, just as light passes through a window, and asked what he wanted and whom he was looking for. And he was delighted to stop and talk to her, to the owner of the house, the sweetest of the angels, the reason for the existence of the saints and the poor people's pastrycook. This great lady was less than three feet tall, but when she spoke she gave the impression of understanding everything like a full-grown person. The Zany explained by signs how much he enjoyed chewing wax; and half-smiling, half-serious, she told him to take one of the lighted tapers from the altar. Then, gathering up her too-long silver cloak, she led him by the hand to a basin full of colored fish and gave him the rainbow to suck like barley-sugar. Perfect bliss! He felt happy from the tip of his tongue to the tip of his toes. It was something he had never had in his life: a piece of wax to chew like copal,° peppermint-flavored barley-sugar, a basin full of colored fish, and a mother who sang as she massaged his injured leg: "Get well, get well,

President of the Republic . . . : a series of vacuous titles describing the dictator in election propaganda
Angel of the Golden Ball and the Devil with Eleven Thousand Horns: the first would lead the soul to heaven, and the second to hell
Virgin of Carmel: the idiot takes the woman who comes out to meet him to be a religious image of the virgin greeting him
copal: a hard resin obtained from several tropical trees

my little frog's bottom, seven little farts for you and your mamma!" All this was his as he slept on the garbage.

But happiness lasts no longer than a shower in the sunshine . . . Down the path of beaten earth the color of milk leading to the rubbish-dump came a wood-cutter followed by his dog; he carried a faggot of sticks on his back, his coat folded over it and his machete in his arms like a baby. The gulley was not deep, but the falling dusk had plunged it in shadows and shrouded the rubbish piled up in its depths. The wood-cutter turned and looked back. He could have sworn he was being followed. Further on, he stopped again. He sensed the presence of some hidden person. The dog howled, with its hair standing on end as if it saw the devil. An eddy of wind lifted some dirty bits of paper, stained as with women's blood or beetroot juice. The sky looked very far away, very blue, decorated like the vault of a very high tomb with sleepily circling turkey-buzzards. Suddenly the dog raced off to the place where the Zany was lying. The wood-cutter trembled with fear. He followed the dog cautiously, step by step, to see who the dead man was. He was in danger of cutting his feet on broken glass, bottle-ends and sardine-tins, and had to jump over foul-smelling excrement and nameless patches of darkness. The hollows were full of water, like harbors among the garbage.

Without putting down his load — his fear was a heavier burden — he caught hold of one of the supposed corpse's feet, and was astonished to find a living man, whose panting breath combined with his cries and the dog's barking to make a graph of his distress, like wind when it is laced with rain. The footsteps of someone walking through a little wood of pines and ancient guava trees° nearby agitated the wood-cutter even more. Suppose it was a policeman! Oh well, really, that would be the last straw!

"Quiet!" he said to the dog. And as it went on barking he gave it a kick. "Shut up, you brute, be quiet!"

Should he run for it? But flight would be a confession of guilt. Worse still, if it were a policeman. And turning to the injured man:

"Here quick, I'll help you get up! My God, they've half killed you! Quick, don't be scared, don't shout; I'm not hurting you! I was just coming along, and saw you lying there . . . "

"I saw you digging him out," interrupted a voice behind him, "and I turned back in case it was someone I knew; let's get him out of here."

The wood-cutter turned his head to reply, and nearly fainted with fear. He gave a gasp, and would have made off except that he was supporting a man who could barely stand. The man who had spoken was an angel: a complexion of golden marble, fair hair, a small mouth and an almost feminine appearance, in strong contrast with the manly expression of his black eyes. He was wearing grey. In the fading light he seemed to be

guava trees: trees of tropical America that bear pear-shaped fruit dressed in a cloud. In his slender hands he held a thin cane and a broad-brimmed hat which looked like a dove.

"An angel!" The wood-cutter couldn't take his eyes from him. "An angel," he repeated, "an angel!"

"It's obvious from his clothes that he's very poor," said the newcomer. "What a sad thing it is to be poor!"

"That depends; everything in this world depends on something else. Look at me; I'm very poor; but I've got my work, my wife and my hut, and I don't think I'm to be pitied," stammered the wood-cutter like a man talking in his sleep, hoping to ingratiate himself with this angel, who might recompense his Christian resignation by changing him from a wood-cutter to a king, if he so wished. And for a second he saw himself dressed in gold, with a red cloak, a crown on his head and a scepter set with jewels in his hand. The rubbish dump seemed far away . . .

"Strange!" remarked the new arrival, raising his voice above the Zany's groans.

"Why strange? After all, we poor men are more resigned than other people. And what can we do, anyway? It's true that with the schools and all that, anyone who learns to read gets ideas into his head. Even my wife gets sad sometimes and says she'd like to have wings on Sundays."

The injured man fainted two or three times as they descended the steeper part of the slope. The trees rose and sank before his moribund eyes like the fingers of Chinese dancers.° The remarks of the men who were now almost carrying him zigzagged in his ears like drunk men on a slippery floor. There was a great black patch before his eyes. Sudden cold shivers blew through his body, setting ablaze the ashes of his burning fancies.

"So your wife wants wings on Sundays?" said the stranger. "Wings! And if she had them they'd be no use to her."

"That's right; she says she wants them to go out with, and when she's fed up with me she asks the wind for them."

The wood-cutter stopped to wipe the sweat from his forehead with his sleeve, and exclaimed:

"He's no light weight!"

The new arrival said:

"Her legs are quite good enough for that; even if she had wings she wouldn't go."

"Not she; nor yet out of good nature neither, but because women are birds who can't live without their cage, and because I carry home too few bits of wood to go breaking them on her back" — he remembered at this point that he was talking to an angel and hastily gilded the pill — "for her own good, of course."

The stranger was silent.

fingers of Chinese dancers: up-and-down hand gestures of dancers

"Who can have beaten up this poor chap?" went on the wood-cutter, changing the subject out of embarrassment at what he had just said.

"There are plenty . . . "

"It's true, some people'll do anything, but this chap looks as if — as if they'd had no mercy on him. A jab in the mouth with a knife and off with him to the rubbish dump!"

"He's probably got other wounds."

"Looks to me as if the one in his lip was done with a razor, and they chucked him away here so that the crime shouldn't be found out, eh?"

"But what a place!"

"Just what I was going to say."

The trees were covered with turkey-buzzards making ready to leave the gully. The Zany's fear was stronger even than his pain, and kept him mute; he curled himself up like a hedgehog in a deathly silence.

The wind ran lightly over the plain, blowing from the town into the country, delicate, gentle, familiar . . .

The stranger looked at his watch, and after putting some money in the wounded man's pocket and bidding the wood-cutter a friendly goodbye, he walked quickly away.

The sky was cloudless and resplendent. The outermost houses of the town looked out at the countryside with their electric lights burning like matches in a darkened theater. Sinuous groves of trees were beginning to appear out of the darkness near the first houses: mud huts smelling of straw, wooden cabins smelling of ladino,° big houses with sordid front yards stinking like stables, and inns where it was usual to find fodder for sale, a servant girl with a lover in the barracks, and a group of muleteers sitting in the darkness.

When he reached the first houses the wood-cutter abandoned the injured man, after telling him how to get to the hospital. The Zany half-opened his eyes in search of help, or something to cure his hiccups; but it was on shut doors in a deserted street that his moribund gaze fastened itself like a sharp thorn. Far off bugles could be heard, testifying to the submission of a nomad race, and bells tremulously tolling thrice for the souls of dead Christians: Mer — cy! Mer — cy! Mer — cy!

He was terrified by a turkey-buzzard dragging itself through the shadows. The creature had a broken wing and its angry complaints sounded to him like a threat. Slowly he moved away, step by step, leaning against the walls, against the motionless trembling of the walls, giving moan after moan, not knowing where he was going, with the wind in his face, the wind which had bitten ice before it blew at night. He was shaken by hiccups . . .

The wood-cutter dropped his bundle of wood in the courtyard of his hut as usual. His dog had got home before him and received him effu-

ladino: a mestizo; a person of mixed blood

sively. He pushed it aside, and without taking off his hat opened his coat so that it hung on his shoulders like a bat's wings; then he went up to the fire in the corner of the room, where his wife was cooking pancakes, and told her what had happened.

"I met an angel on the rubbish dump."

The light from the flames flickered on the bamboo walls and the straw roof, like the wings of other angels.

From the hut there emerged a tremulous stream of white, vegetal smoke.

Translated from the Spanish
by Frances Partridge

MEXICO

OCTAVIO PAZ

*Mexico's leading intellectual and artistic figure, Octavio Paz (1914–)
was awarded the Nobel Prize in 1991. He is, with Pablo Neruda and
César Vallejo, one of several Latin American poets whose work has
had wide international acclaim and impact. His central theme has
been Mexico's culture. Paz's* The Labyrinth of Solitude *(1950), a book-
length essay on Mexican history from a psycho-mythic perspective, has
had enormous influence on other Mexican writers, particularly Carlos
Fuentes. Paz's poetry, attuned to European and North American trends,
has shown the same concern with Mexico. In* Sunstone *(1957), for instance, he incorporates the complex numerology of the Aztec calendar
into the structure of the poem. Love, particularly carnal love, is the
moving force in Paz's poetry, both to bring opposites together and to
generate violence.*

*Paz, like Fuentes, is very aware of the continued presence of the past
in Mexico. In "San Ildefonso Nocturne" the past lives on as a colonial
building in Mexico City, originally the College of San Ildefonso, but
used for other purposes through the years. The reincarnations of the
building throughout Mexican history highlight the presence of the past,
durable as stone. The visual arrangement of the poem reflects the tangible nature of the building and its permanence.*

San Ildefonso Nocturne°

I

In my window night
                    invents another night,
another space:
                    carnival convulsed
in a square yard of blackness.   5
                    Momentary

San Ildefonso Nocturne: a nocturne, in music, is a romantic or dreamy composition,
appropriate for night; hence, the poem is a night meditation before the San Ildefonso
building.

confederations of fire,
                    nomadic geometries,
errant numbers.
                    From yellow to green to red,   10
the spiral unwinds.
                    Window:
magnetic plate of calls and answers,
high-voltage calligraphy,
false heaven/hell of industry   15
on the changing skin of the moment.

Sign-seeds:
                    the night shoots them off,
they rise,
                    bursting above,   20
                              fall
still burning
                    in a cone of shadow,
                                        reappear,
rambling sparks,   25
                    syllable-clusters,
spinning flames
                    that scatter,
                              smithereens once more.
The city invents and erases them.   30

I am at the entrance to a tunnel.
These phrases drill through time.
Perhaps I am that which waits at the end of the tunnel.
I speak with eyes closed.
                              Someone   35
has planted
                    a forest of magnetic needles
in my eyelids,
                    someone
guides the thread of these words.   40
                              The page
has become an ants' nest.
                              The void
has settled at the pit of my stomach.
                              I fall   45
endlessly through that void.
                              I fall without falling.
My hands are cold,
                    my feet cold —

but the alphabets are burning, burning.   50
                              Space
makes and unmakes itself.
                              The night insists,
the night touches my forehead,
                              touches my thoughts.   55
What does it want?

  2

Empty streets, squinting lights.
                              On a corner,
the ghost of a dog
                  searches the garbage   60
for a spectral bone.
                      Uproar in a nearby patio:
cacophonous cockpit.
                      Mexico, circa 1931.
Loitering sparrows,   65
                      a flock of children
builds a nest
              of unsold newspapers.
In the desolation
                  the streetlights invent   70
unreal pools of yellowish light.
                              Apparitions:
time splits open:
                  a lugubrious, lascivious clatter of heels,
beneath *a sky of soot*   75
                  the flash of a skirt.
C'est la mort — ou la morte . . . °
                              The indifferent wind
rips posters from the walls.

At this hour,   80
                  the red walls of San Ildefonso
are black, and they breathe:
                              sun turned to time,
time turned to stone,
                  stone turned to body.   85
These streets were once canals.
                              In the sun,
the houses were silver:
                  city of mortar and stone,

C'est la mort . . . : "it is death" (French)

moon fallen in the lake.   90
                    Over the filled canals
and the buried idols
                    the *criollos*° erected
another city
                    — not white, but red and gold —   95
idea turned to space, tangible number.
                              They placed it
at the crossroads of eight directions,
                              its doors
open to the invisible: 100
                    heaven and hell.

Sleeping district.
                    We walk through galleries of echoes,
past broken images:
                    our history.   105
Hushed nation of stones.
                    Churches,
dome-growths,
                    their facades
petrified gardens of symbols.   110
                    Shipwrecked
in the spiteful proliferation of dwarf houses:
humiliated palaces,
                    fountains without water,
affronted frontispieces.   115
                    Cumuli,°
insubstantial madrepore,°
                    accumulate
over the ponderous bulks,
                    conquered   120
not by the weight of the years
but by the infamy of the present.

                    Zócalo Plaza,°

vast as the earth:
                    diaphanous space,   125
court of echoes.
                    There,

criollos: the Spanish who settled in Spanish America
cumuli: clouds
madrepore: coral; thus, the clouds are thin and lacking substance, shaped like
    madrepores shrouding the building
Zócalo Plaza: a central square in Mexico City

with Alyosha K and Julien S,°
                    we devised bolts of lightning
against the century and its cliques.   130
                                   The wind of thought
carried us away,
                the verbal wind,
the wind that plays with mirrors,
                           master of reflections,   135
builder of cities of air,
                      geometries
hung from the thread of reason.

Shut down for the night,
                     the yellow trolleys,   140
giant worms.
               S's and Z's:
a crazed auto, insect with malicious eyes.
                                 Ideas,
fruits within an arm's reach,   145
                like stars,
                        burning.
The girandola° is burning,
                    the adolescent dialogue,
the scorched hasty frame.   150
                 The bronze fist
of the towers beats
            12 times.
               Night
bursts into pieces,   155
             gathers them by itself,
and becomes one, intact.
               We disperse,
not there in the plaza with its dead trains,
                         but here,   160
on this page: petrified letters.

    3

The boy who walks through this poem,
between San Ildefonso and the Zócalo,
is the man who writes it:
                this page too   165

Alyosha K and Julian S: characters from novels by Dostoyevsky and Stendhal, respectively

girandola: a firework rotating while burning

is a ramble through the night.
                              Here the friendly ghosts
become flesh,
                    ideas dissolve.

Good, we wanted good: 170
                         to set the world right.
We didn't lack integrity:
                         we lacked humility.
What we wanted was not innocently wanted.
Precepts and concepts,   175
                         the arrogance of theologians,
to beat with a cross,
                         to institute with blood,
to build the house with bricks of crime,
to declare obligatory communion.   180
                              Some
became secretaries to the secretary
to the General Secretary of the Inferno.
                              Rage
became philosophy,   185
                    its drivel has covered the planet.
Reason came down to earth,
took the form of a gallows
                    — and is worshiped by millions.
Circular plot: 190
               we have all been,
in the Grand Theater of Filth,
judge, executioner, victim, witness,
                         we have all
given false testimony   195
                    against the others
and against ourselves.
                    And the most vile: we
were the public that applauded or yawned in its seats.
The guilt that knows no guilt,   200
                         innocence
was the greatest guilt.
                    Each year was a mountain of bones.

Conversions, retractions, excommunications,
reconciliations, apostasies, recantations,   205
the zigzag of the demonolatries and the androlatries,°

demonolatries and androlatries: the worship of devils

bewitchments and aberrations:
my history.
                    Are they the histories of an error?
History is the error.   210
                    Beyond dates,
before names,
                    truth is that
which history scorns:
                                the everyday   215
— everyone's anonymous heartbeat,
                                    the unique
beat of every one —
                    the unrepeatable
everyday, identical to all days.   220
                                Truth
is the base of a time without history.
                                    The weight
of the weightless moment:
                            a few stones in the sun   225
seen long ago,
                    today return,
stones of time that are also stone
beneath this sun of time,
sun that comes from a dateless day,   230
                                sun
that lights up these words,
                            sun of words
that burns out when they are named.
                                Suns, words, stones,   235
burn and burn out:
                    the moment burns them
without burning.
                    Hidden, unmoving, untouchable,
the present — not its presences — is always.   240

Between seeing and making,
                            contemplation or action,
I chose the act of words:
                            to make them, to inhabit them,
to give eyes to the language.   245
                            Poetry is not truth:
it is the resurrection of presences,
                            history
transfigured in the truth of undated time.

Poetry,   250
     like history, is made;
               poetry,
like truth, is seen.
          Poetry:
             incarnation   255
of the-sun-on-the-stones in a name,
                dissolution
of the name in a beyond of stones.
Poetry,
     suspension bridge between history and truth,   260
is not a path toward this or that:
              it is to see
the stillness in motion,
         change
in stillness.   265
      History is the path:
it goes nowhere,
       we all walk it,
truth is to walk it.
        We neither go nor come: 270
we are in the hands of time.
         Truth:
to know ourselves,
      from the beginning,
           hung.   275
Brotherhood over the void.

   4

Ideas scatter,
     the ghosts remain:
truth of the lived and suffered.
An almost empty taste remains: 280
         time
— shared fury —
      time
— shared oblivion —
       in the end transfigured   285
in memory and its incarnations.
        What remains is
time as portioned body: language.

In the window,
     travesties of battle: 290

the commercial sky of advertisements
                              flares up, goes out.
Behind,
        barely visible,
                        the true constellations.   295
Among the water towers, antennas, rooftops,
a liquid column,
                    more mental than corporeal,
a waterfall of silence:
                        the moon.   300
                        Neither phantom nor idea:
once a goddess,
                today an errant clarity.

My wife sleeps.
                    She too is a moon,   305
a clarity that travels
                    not between the reefs of the clouds,
but between the rocks and wracks of dreams:
she too is a soul.
                    She flows below her closed eyes,   310
a silent torrent
                rushing down
from her forehead to her feet,
                            she tumbles within,
bursts out from within,   315
                        her heartbeats sculpt her,
traveling through herself
                        she invents herself,
inventing herself
                    she copies it,   320
she is an arm of the sea
                        between the islands of her breasts,
her belly a lagoon
                    where darkness and its foliage
grow pale,   325
            she flows through her shape,
rises,
        falls,
            scatters in herself,
                            ties   330
herself to her flowing,
                    disperses in her form:
she too is a body.
                Truth

is the swell of a breath
and the visions closed eyes see:
the palpable mystery of the person.

335

The night is at the point of running over.
                                   It grows light.
The horizon has become aquatic.

340

                         To rush down
from the heights of this hour:
                    will dying
be a falling or a rising,
                 a sensation or a cessation?

345

I close my eyes,
              I hear in my skull
the footsteps of my blood,
                    I hear
time pass through my temples.

350

                     I am still alive.
The room is covered with moon.
                         Woman:
fountain in the night.
                 I am bound to her quiet flowing.

355

Translated from the Spanish
by Eliot Weinberger

JUAN RULFO

Juan Rulfo (1918–1986) holds a central place in modern Latin American fiction that was earned with only two brief books: a collection of short stories, The Burning Plain *(1953), and a novel,* Pedro Páramo *(1955). Both deal with the violence — physical, moral, and psychological — of rural Mexico in the wake of the revolution (1910–1917). Rulfo's plots are intricate, though the stories appear simple, and his characters seem motivated by primal passions like lust, a craving for power, and mostly revenge. His prose style is understated, and the characters' utterances are laconic and brief.*

Tightly wrought, Pedro Páramo *is one of the models for Gabriel García Márquez's* One Hundred Years of Solitude. *In "Tell Them Not to Kill Me," revenge is meted out by a son who comes back many years after a crime; he is now invested with military powers. As the con-*

demned man pleads to his own son to intervene on his behalf, we learn of the deed he committed many years ago during a drought. The arid plain is an important presence in the tragedy.

Tell Them Not to Kill Me!

"Tell them not to kill me, Justino! Go on and tell them that. For God's sake! Tell them. Tell them please for God's sake."

"I can't. There's a sergeant there who doesn't want to hear anything about you."

"Make him listen to you. Use your wits and tell him that scaring me has been enough. Tell him please for God's sake."

"But it's not just to scare you. It seems they really mean to kill you. And I don't want to go back there."

"Go on once more. Just once, to see what you can do."

"No. I don't feel like going. Because if I do they'll know I'm your son. If I keep bothering them they'll end up knowing who I am and will decide to shoot me too. Better leave things the way they are now."

"Go on, Justino. Tell them to take a little pity on me. Just tell them that."

Justino clenched his teeth and shook his head saying no.

And he kept on shaking his head for some time.

"Tell the sergeant to let you see the colonel. And tell him how old I am — How little I'm worth. What will he get out of killing me? Nothing. After all he must have a soul. Tell him to do it for the blessed salvation of his soul."

Justino got up from the pile of stones which he was sitting on and walked to the gate of the corral. Then he turned around to say, "All right, I'll go. But if they decide to shoot me too, who'll take care of my wife and kids?"

"Providence will take care of them, Justino. You go there now and see what you can do for me. That's what matters."

They'd brought him in at dawn. The morning was well along now and he was still there, tied to a post, waiting. He couldn't keep still. He'd tried to sleep for a while to calm down, but he couldn't. He wasn't hungry either. All he wanted was to live. Now that he knew they were really going to kill him, all he could feel was his great desire to stay alive, like a recently resuscitated man.

Who would've thought that old business that happened so long ago and that was buried the way he thought it was would turn up? That business when he had to kill Don Lupe. Not for nothing either, as the Alimas° tried to make out, but because he had his reasons. He remembered: Don Lupe Terreros, the owner of the Puerta de Piedra° — and besides that, his compadre° — was the one he, Juvencio Nava, had to kill, because he'd refused to let him pasture his animals, when he was the owner of the Puerta de Piedra and his compadre too.

At first he didn't do anything because he felt compromised. But later, when the drouth came, when he saw how his animals were dying off one by one, plagued by hunger, and how his compadre Lupe continued to refuse to let him use his pastures, then was when he began breaking through the fence and driving his herd of skinny animals to the pasture where they could get their fill of grass. And Don Lupe didn't like it and ordered the fence mended, so that he, Juvencio Nava, had to cut open the hole again. So, during the day the hole was stopped up and at night it was opened again, while the stock stayed there right next to the fence, always waiting — his stock that before had lived just smelling the grass without being able to taste it.

And he and Don Lupe argued again and again without coming to any agreement.

Until one day Don Lupe said to him, "Look here, Juvencio, if you let another animal in my pasture, I'll kill it."

And he answered him, "Look here, Don Lupe, it's not my fault that the animals look out for themselves. They're innocent. You'll have to pay for it, if you kill them."

And he killed one of my yearlings.

This happened thirty-five years ago in March, because in April I was already up in the mountains, running away from the summons. The ten cows I gave the judge didn't do me any good, or the lien on my house either, to pay for getting me out of jail. Still later they used up what was left to pay so they wouldn't keep after me, but they kept after me just the same. That's why I came to live with my son on this other piece of land of mine which is called Palo de Venado.° And my son grew up and got married to my daughter-in-law Ignacia and has had eight children now. So it happened a long time ago and ought to be forgotten by now. But I guess it's not.

I figured then that with about a hundred pesos everything could be fixed up. The dead Don Lupe left just his wife and two little kids still crawling. And his widow died soon afterward too — they say from grief. They took the kids far off to some relatives. So there was nothing to fear from them.

the Alimas: people from the town of Alima
Puerta de Piedra: the name of the farm
compadre: someone for whose son or daughter one has stood as grandfather; literally, "cofather"
Palo de Venado: name of a town or hacienda

But the rest of the people took the position that I was still summoned to be tried just to scare me so they could keep on robbing me. Every time someone came to the village they told me, "There are some strangers in town, Juvencio."

And I would take off to the mountains, hiding among the madrone thickets and passing the days with nothing to eat but herbs. Sometimes I had to go out at midnight, as though the dogs were after me. It's been that way my whole life. Not just a year or two. My whole life.

And now they've come for him when he no longer expected anyone, confident that people had forgotten all about it, believing that he'd spend at least his last days peacefully. "At least," he thought, "I'll have some peace in my old age. They'll leave me alone."

He'd clung to this hope with all his heart. That's why it was hard for him to imagine that he'd die like this, suddenly, at this time of life, after having fought so much to ward off death, after having spent his best years running from one place to another because of the alarms, now when his body had become all dried up and leathery from the bad days when he had to be in hiding from everybody.

Hadn't he even let his wife go off and leave him? The day when he learned his wife had left him, the idea of going out in search of her didn't even cross his mind. He let her go without trying to find out at all who she went with or where, so he wouldn't have to go down to the village. He let her go as he'd let everything else go, without putting up a fight. All he had left to take care of was his life, and he'd do that, if nothing else. He couldn't let them kill him. He couldn't. Much less now.

But that's why they brought him from there, from Palo de Venado. They didn't need to tie him so he'd follow them. He walked alone, tied by his fear. They realized he couldn't run with his old body, with those skinny legs of his like dry bark, cramped up with the fear of dying. Because that's where he was headed. For death. They told him so.

That's when he knew. He began to feel that stinging in his stomach that always came on suddenly when he saw death nearby, making his eyes big with fear and his mouth swell up with those mouthfuls of sour water he had to swallow unwillingly. And that thing that made his feet heavy while his head felt soft and his heart pounded with all its force against his ribs. No, he couldn't get used to the idea that they were going to kill him.

There must be some hope. Somewhere there must still be some hope left. Maybe they'd made a mistake. Perhaps they were looking for another Juvencio Nava and not him.

He walked along in silence between those men, with his arms fallen at his sides. The early morning hour was dark, starless. The wind blew slowly, whipping the dry earth back and forth, which was filled with that odor like urine that dusty roads have.

His eyes, that had become squinty with the years, were looking down at the ground, here under his feet, in spite of the darkness. There in the earth was his whole life. Sixty years of living on it, of holding it tight in his hands, of tasting it like one tastes the flavor of meat. For a long time he'd been crumbling it with his eyes, savoring each piece as if it were the last one, almost knowing it would be the last.

Then, as if wanting to say something, he looked at the men who were marching along next to him. He was going to tell them to let him loose, to let him go; "I haven't hurt anybody, boys," he was going to say to them, but he kept silent. "A little further on I'll tell them," he thought. And he just looked at them. He could even imagine they were his friends, but he didn't want to. They weren't. He didn't know who they were. He watched them moving at his side and bending down from time to time to see where the road continued.

He'd seen them for the first time at nightfall, that dusky hour when everything seems scorched. They'd crossed the furrows trodding on the tender corn. And he'd gone down on account of that — to tell them that the corn was beginning to grow there. But that didn't stop them.

He'd seen them in time. He'd always had the luck to see everything in time. He could've hidden, gone up in the mountains for a few hours until they left and then come down again. Already it was time for the rains to have come, but the rains didn't come and the corn was beginning to wither. Soon it'd be all dried up.

So it hadn't even been worthwhile, his coming down and placing himself among those men like in a hole, never to get out again.

And now he continued beside them, holding back how he wanted to tell them to let him go. He didn't see their faces, he only saw their bodies, which swung toward him and then away from him. So when he started talking he didn't know if they'd heard him. He said, "I've never hurt anybody." That's what he said. But nothing changed. Not one of the bodies seemed to pay attention. The faces didn't turn to look at him. They kept right on, as if they were walking in their sleep.

Then he thought that there was nothing else he could say, that he would have to look for hope somewhere else. He let his arms fall again to his sides and went by the first houses of the village, among those four men, darkened by the black color of the night.

"Colonel, here is the man."

They'd stopped in front of the narrow doorway. He stood with his hat in his hand, respectfully, waiting to see someone come out. But only the voice came out, "Which man?"

"From Palo de Venado, colonel. The one you ordered us to bring in."

"Ask him if he ever lived in Alima," came the voice from inside again.

"Hey, you. Ever lived in Alima?" the sergeant facing him repeated the question.

"Yes. Tell the colonel that's where I'm from. And that I lived there till not long ago."

"Ask him if he knew Guadalupe Terreros."

"He says did you know Guadalupe Terreros?"

"Don Lupe? Yes. Tell him that I knew him. He's dead."

Then the voice inside changed tone: "I know he died," it said. And the voice continued talking, as if it was conversing with someone there on the other side of the reed wall.

"Guadalupe Terreros was my father. When I grew up and looked for him they told me he was dead. It's hard to grow up knowing that the thing we have to hang on to to take roots from is dead. That's what happened to us.

"Later on I learned that he was killed by being hacked first with a machete and then an ox goad stuck in his belly. They told me he lasted more than two days and that when they found him, lying in an arroyo,° he was still in agony and begging that his family be taken care of.

"As time goes by you seem to forget this. You try to forget it. What you can't forget is finding out that the one who did it is still alive, feeding his rotten soul with the illusion of eternal life. I couldn't forgive that man, even though I don't know him; but the fact that I know where he is makes me want to finish him off. I can't forgive his still living. He should never have been born."

From here, from outside, all he said was clearly heard. Then he ordered, "Take him and tie him up awhile, so he'll suffer, and then shoot him!"

"Look at me, colonel!" he begged. "I'm not worth anything now. It won't be long before I die all by myself, crippled by old age. Don't kill me!"

"Take him away!" repeated the voice from inside.

"I've already paid, colonel. I've paid many times over. They took everything away from me. They punished me in many ways. I've spent about forty years hiding like a leper, always with the fear they'd kill me at any moment. I don't deserve to die like this, colonel. Let the Lord pardon me, at least. Don't kill me! Tell them not to kill me!"

There he was, as if they'd beaten him, waving his hat against the ground. Shouting.

Immediately the voice from inside said, "Tie him up and give him something to drink until he gets drunk so the shots won't hurt him."

Finally, now, he'd been quieted. There he was, slumped down at the foot of the post. His son Justino had come and his son Justino had gone and had returned and now was coming again.

He slung him on top of the burro. He cinched him up tight against the saddle so he wouldn't fall off on the road. He put his head in a sack so it wouldn't give such a bad impression. And then he made the burro giddap, and away they went in a hurry to reach Palo de Venado in time to arrange the wake for the dead man.

arroyo: a brook

"Your daughter-in-law and grandchildren will miss you," he was saying to him. "They'll look at your face and won't believe it's you. They'll
think the coyote has been eating on you when they see your face full of
holes from all those bullets they shot at you."

Translated from the Spanish
by George D. Schade

CARLOS FUENTES

The son of a diplomat, Carlos Fuentes (1928–) spent a great deal of his
childhood abroad, mostly in Washington, D.C., where he learned Eng-
lish. He studied international law later in Geneva and also learned
French. Fuentes is one of the most cultured writers in the world today,
at home in several cultures and in many literatures. He was one of the
writers (with Mario Vargas Llosa, Julio Cortázar and Gabriel García
Márquez) who revitalized the Latin American novel. Active in politics,
Fuentes has also served his government as a diplomat (he was ambas-
sador to France) and has been a constant and probing commentator on
current events.

The core of his fiction is concerned with Mexico's identity. Fuentes
is particularly obsessed with the currency of the past in Mexican his-
tory and the continued presence of warring forces (Aztec, Spanish) that
make up the nation and account for its penchant for violence. "The
Doll Queen" shows Fuentes's linking of past and present through the
childhood memories of the narrator-protagonist and how these memo-
ries suddenly become a part of the present. Just as the violence of the
Conquest of Mexico is reenacted in the Mexican Revolution, an indi-
vidual's past is never dead in Fuentes's stories.

The Doll Queen

To María Pilar and José Donoso

I

I went because that card — such a strange card — reminded me of her existence. I found it in a forgotten book whose pages had revived the
specter of a childish calligraphy. For the first time in a long while I was
rearranging my books. I met surprise after surprise, since some, placed on

the highest shelves, had not been read for a long time. So long a time that the edges of the leaves were grainy, and a mixture of gold dust and grayish scale fell on my open palm, reminiscent of the lacquer covering certain bodies glimpsed first in dreams and later in the deceptive reality of the first ballet performance to which we're taken. It was a book from my childhood — perhaps from the childhood of many children — that related a series of more or less truculent exemplary tales which had the virtue of precipitating us onto our elders' knees to ask them, over and over again: Why? Children who are ungrateful to their parents, maidens kidnapped by splendid horsemen and returned home in shame — as well as those who happily abandon hearth and home; old men who in exchange for an overdue mortgage demand the hand of the sweetest, most long-suffering daughter of the threatened family . . . Why? I do not recall their answers. I only know that from among the stained pages came fluttering a white card in Amilamia's atrocious hand: *Amilamia wil not forget her good friend — com see me here wher I draw it.*

And on the other side was that sketch of a path starting from an X that indicated, doubtlessly, the park bench where I, an adolescent rebelling against prescribed and tedious education, forgot my classroom schedule to spend some hours reading books which, if not in fact written by me, seemed to be: who could doubt that only from my imagination could spring all those corsairs, those couriers of the tsar, those boys slightly younger than I who floated all day down a great American river on a raft. Clutching the side of the park bench as if it were the bow of a magic saddle, at first I didn't hear the sound of the light steps that stopped behind me after running down the graveled garden path. It was Amilamia, and I don't know how long the child would have kept me company in silence had not her mischievous spirit one afternoon chosen to tickle my ear with down from a dandelion she blew toward me, her lips puffed out and her brow furrowed in a frown.

She asked my name, and after considering it very seriously, she told me hers with a smile which, if not candid, was not too rehearsed. Quickly I realized that Amilamia had discovered, if discovered is the word, a form of expression midway between the ingenuousness of her years and the forms of adult mimicry that well-brought-up children have to know, particularly for the solemn moments of introduction and of leave-taking. Amilamia's seriousness was, rather, a gift of nature, whereas her moments of spontaneity, by contrast, seemed artificial. I like to remember her, afternoon after afternoon, in a succession of images that in their totality sum up the complete Amilamia. And it never ceases to surprise me that I cannot think of her as she really was, or remember how she actually moved — light, questioning, constantly looking around her. I must remember her fixed forever in time, as in a photograph album. Amilamia in the distance, a point at the spot where the hill began its descent from a lake of clover toward the flat meadow where I, sitting on the bench, used to read: a point of fluctuating shadow and sunshine and a hand that waved to me from high on the hill. Amilamia frozen in her flight down the hill, her white skirt ballooning, the flowered panties gathered on her legs with elastic, her mouth open and eyes half closed against the streaming air, the child crying with pleasure. Amilamia sitting beneath the eucalyptus trees, pretending to cry so that I would go over to her. Amilamia lying on her stomach with a flower in her hand: the petals of a flower which I discovered later didn't grow in this garden but somewhere else, perhaps in the garden of Amilamia's house, since the pocket of her blue-checked apron was often filled with those white blossoms. Amilamia watching me read, holding with both hands to the slats of the green bench, asking questions with her gray eyes: I recall that she never asked me what I was reading, as if she could divine in my eyes the images born of the pages. Amilamia laughing with pleasure when I lifted her by the waist and whirled her around my head; she seemed to discover a new perspective on the world in that slow flight. Amilamia turning her back to me and waving goodbye, her arm held high, the fingers moving excitedly. And Amilamia in the thousand postures she affected around my bench, hanging upside down, her bloomers billowing; sitting on the gravel with her legs crossed and her chin resting on her fist; lying on the grass, baring her belly button to the sun; weaving tree branches, drawing animals in the mud with a twig, licking the slats of the bench, hiding under the seat, breaking off the loose bark from the ancient tree trunks, staring at the horizon beyond the hill, humming with her eyes closed, imitating the voices of birds, dogs, cats, hens, horses. All for me, and yet nothing. It was her way of being with me, all these things I remember, but also her way of being alone in the park. Yes, perhaps my memory of her is fragmentary because reading alternated with my contemplation of the chubby-cheeked child with smooth hair that changed in the reflection of the light: now wheat-colored, now burnt chestnut. And it is only today that I think how Amilamia in that moment established the other point of support for my life, the one that created the tension between my own irresolute childhood and the wide world, the promised land that was beginning to be mine through my reading.

Not then. Then I dreamed about the women in my books, about the quintessential female — the word disturbed me — who assumed the disguise of Queen to buy the necklace in secret, about the imagined beings of mythology — half recognizable, half white-breasted, damp-bellied salamanders — who awaited monarchs in their beds. And thus, imperceptibly, I moved from indifference toward my childish companion to an acceptance of the child's grace and seriousness and from there to an unexpected rejection of a presence that became useless to me. She irritated me, finally. I who was fourteen was irritated by that child of seven who was not yet memory or nostalgia, but rather the past and its reality. I had let myself be dragged along by weakness. We had run together, holding hands, across the meadow. Together we had shaken the pines and picked up the cones that Amilamia guarded jealously in her apron pocket. Together we had constructed paper boats and followed them, happy and gay, to the edge of the drain. And that afternoon, amid shouts of glee, when we tumbled together down the hill and rolled to a stop at its foot, Amilamia was on my chest, her hair between my lips; but when I felt her panting breath in my ear and her little arms sticky from sweets around my neck, I angrily pushed away her arms and let her fall. Amilamia cried, rubbing her wounded elbow and knee, and I returned to my bench. Then Amilamia went away and the following day she returned, handed me the card without a word, and disappeared, humming, into the woods. I hesitated whether to tear up the card or keep it in the pages of the book: *Afternoons on the Farm.* Even my reading had become infantile because of Amilamia. She did not return to the park. After a few days I left on my vacation, and when I returned it was to the duties of the first year of prep school. I never saw her again.

2

And now, almost rejecting the image that is unfamiliar without being fantastic, but is all the more painful for being so real, I return to that forgotten park and stopping before the grove of pines and eucalyptus I recognize the smallness of the bosky° enclosure that my memory has insisted on drawing with an amplitude that allows sufficient space for the vast swell of my imagination. After all, Michel Strogoff and Huckleberry Finn, Milady de Winter and Geneviève de Brabant° were born, lived, and died here: in a little garden surrounded by mossy iron railings, sparsely planted with old, neglected trees, scarcely adorned by a concrete bench painted to look like wood which forces me to think that my beautiful wrought-iron green bench never existed, or was part of my ordered, retrospective delirium. And the hill . . . How believe the promontory Amilamia ascended and descended in her daily coming and going, that steep slope we rolled down together, was *this.* A barely elevated patch of dark stubble with no more height and depth than what my memory had created.

Com see me here wher I draw it. So I would have to cross the garden, leave the woods behind, descend the hill in three loping steps, cut through that narrow grove of chestnuts — it was here, surely, where the child gathered the white petals — open the squeaking park gate and instantly recall . . . know . . . find oneself in the street, realize that every afternoon of one's adolescence, as if by a miracle, one had succeeded in suspending the beat of the surrounding city, annulling that flood tide of

bosky: forestlike
Michel Strogoff . . . Geneviève de Brabant: literary characters

whistles, bells, voices, sobs, engines, radios, imprecations. Which was the true magnet, the silent garden or the feverish city?

I wait for the light to change, and cross to the other side, my eyes never leaving the red iris detaining the traffic. I consult Amilamia's card. After all, that rudimentary map is the true magnet of the moment I am living, and just thinking about it disturbs me. I was obliged, after the lost afternoons of my fourteenth year, to follow the channels of discipline; now I find myself, at twenty-nine, duly certified with a diploma, owner of an office, assured of a moderate income, a bachelor still, with no family to maintain, slightly bored with sleeping with secretaries, scarcely excited by an occasional outing to the country or to the beach, feeling the lack of a central attraction such as my books, my park, and Amilamia once afforded me. I walk down the street of this gray suburb. The one-story houses, doorways peeling paint, succeed each other monotonously. Faint neighborhood sounds barely interrupt the general uniformity: the squeal of a knife sharpener here, the hammering of a shoe repairman there. The neighborhood children are playing in the dead-end streets. The music of an organ grinder reaches my ears, mingled with the voices of children's rounds. I stop a moment to watch them, with the sensation, as fleeting, that Amilamia must be among these groups of children, immodestly exhibiting her flowered panties, hanging by her knees from some balcony, still fond of acrobatic excesses, her apron pocket filled with white petals. I smile, and for the first time I am able to imagine the young lady of twenty-two who, even if she still lives at this address, will laugh at my memories, or who perhaps will have forgotten the afternoons spent in the garden.

The house is identical to all the rest. The heavy entry door, two grilled windows with closed shutters. A one-story house, topped by a false neoclassic balustrade that probably conceals the practicalities of the roof terrace: clothes hanging on a line, tubs of water, servants' quarters, a chicken coop. Before I ring the bell, I want to rid myself of any illusion. Amilamia no longer lives here. Why would she stay fifteen years in the same house? Besides, in spite of her precocious independence and aloneness, she seemed to be a well-brought-up, well-behaved child, and this neighborhood is no longer elegant; Amilamia's parents, without doubt, have moved. But perhaps the new tenants will know where.

I press the bell and wait. I ring again. Here is another contingency: no one is home. And will I feel the need to look again for my childhood friend? No. Because it will not happen a second time that I open a book from my adolescence and find Amilamia's card. I'll return to my routine, I'll forget the moment whose importance lay in its fleeting surprise.

I ring once more. I press my ear to the door and am startled: I can hear harsh, irregular breathing on the other side; the sound of labored breathing, accompanied by the disagreeable odor of stale tobacco, filters through the cracks in the door.

"Good afternoon. Could you tell me . . . ?"

When he hears my voice, the person moves away with heavy and unsure steps. I press the bell again, shouting this time: "Hey! Open up! What's the matter? Don't you hear me?"

No response. I continue to ring, with no result. I move back from the door, still staring at the tiny cracks, as if distance might give me perspective, or even penetration. With my attention fixed on that damned door, I cross the street, walking backward. A piercing scream, followed by a prolonged and ferocious blast of a whistle, saves me in time. Dazed, I seek the person whose voice has just saved me. I see only the automobile moving down the street and I hang on to a lamppost, a hold that more than security offers me support as icy blood rushes through my burning, sweaty skin. I look toward the house that had been, that was, that must be, Amilamia's. There, behind the balustrade, as I had known there would be, are fluttering clothes hung out to dry. I don't know what else is hanging there — skirts, pajamas, blouses — I don't know. All I see is that starched little blue-checked apron, clamped by clothespins to the long cord swinging between an iron bar and a nail in the white wall of the terrace.

3

In the Bureau of Records I have been told that the property is in the name of a Señor R. Valdivia, who rents the house. To whom? That they don't know. Who is Valdivia? He is down as a businessman. Where does he live? Who are *you?* the young woman asked me with haughty curiosity. I haven't been able to show myself calm and assured. Sleep has not relieved my nervous fatigue. Valdivia. As I leave the Bureau, the sun offends me. I associated the aversion provoked by the hazy sun sifting through the clouds — thus all the more intense — with a desire to return to the humid, shaded park. No. It is only a desire to know if Amilamia lives in that house and why they won't let me enter. But what I must reject is the absurd idea that kept me awake all night. Having seen the apron drying on the flat roof, the apron in which she kept the flowers, I had begun to believe that in that house lived a seven-year-old girl I had known fourteen or fifteen years before . . . She must have a little girl! Yes. Amilamia, at twenty-two, is the mother of a girl who perhaps dresses the same, looks the same, repeats the same games, and — who knows — maybe even goes to the same park. And deep in thought, I arrive once more at the door of the house. I ring the bell and wait for the labored breathing on the other side of the door. I am mistaken. The door is opened by a woman who can't be more than fifty. But wrapped in a shawl, dressed in black and in flat black shoes, with no makeup and her salt-and-pepper hair pulled into a knot, she seems to have abandoned all illusion or pretense of youth. She observes me with eyes so indifferent they seem almost cruel.

"You want something?"

"Señor Valdivia sent me." I cough and run my hand over my hair. I should have picked up my briefcase at the office. I realize that without it I cannot play my role very well.

"Valdivia?" the woman asks without alarm, without interest.

"Yes. The owner of this house."

One thing is clear. The woman will reveal nothing by her face. She looks at me, impassive.

"Oh, yes. The owner of the house."

"May I come in?"

In bad comedies, I think, the traveling salesman sticks a foot in the door so they can't close the door in his face. I do the same, but the woman steps back and with a gesture of her hand invites me to come into what must have been a garage. On one side there is a glass-paneled door, its paint faded. I walk toward the door over the yellow tiles of the entry-way and ask again, turning toward the woman, who follows me with tiny steps: "This way?"

I notice for the first time that in her pale hands she carries a chaplet,° which she toys with ceaselessly. I haven't seen one of those old-fashioned rosaries since my childhood and I want to say something about it, but the brusque, decisive manner with which the woman opens the door pre-cludes any gratuitous conversation. We enter a long, narrow room. The woman quickly opens the shutters. But because of four large perennials growing in glass-encrusted porcelain pots the room remains in shadow. The only other objects in the room are an old high-backed cane sofa and a rocking chair. But it is neither the plants nor the sparseness of the furni-ture that holds my attention.

The woman asks me to sit on the sofa before she sits down in the rocking chair. Beside me, on the cane arm of the sofa, there is an open magazine.

"Señor Valdivia sends his apologies for not having come himself."

The woman rocks, unblinking. I peer at the comic book out of the cor-ner of my eye.

"He sends greetings and . . ."

I stop, waiting for a reaction from the woman. She continues to rock. The magazine is covered with red scribbles.

". . . and asks me to inform you that he must disturb you for a few days . . ."

My eyes search the room rapidly.

". . . A reassessment of the house must be made for tax purposes. It seems it hasn't been done for . . . You have been living here since . . . ?"

Yes. That is a stubby lipstick lying under the chair. If the woman smiles, it is while the slow-moving hands caress the chaplet. I sense, for

chaplet: a string of prayer beads

an instant, a swift flash of ridicule that does not quite disturb her features. She still does not answer.

". . . for at least fifteen years, isn't that so?"

She does not agree. She does not disagree. And on the pale thin lips there is not the least trace of lipstick . . .

". . . you, your husband, and . . . ?"

She stares at me, never changing expression, almost daring me to continue. We sit a moment in silence, she playing with the rosary, I leaning forward, my hands on my knees. I rise.

"Well then, I'll be back this afternoon with the papers . . ."

The woman nods and in silence picks up the lipstick and the comic book and hides them in the folds of her shawl.

4

The scene has not changed. This afternoon, as I write sham figures in my notebook and feign interest in determining the value of the dull floor-boards and the length of the living room, the woman rocks, the three decades of the chaplet whispering through her fingers. I sigh as I finish the supposed inventory of the living room and ask for permission to see the rest of the house. The woman rises, bracing her long black-clad arms on the seat of the rocking chair and adjusting the shawl on her narrow, bony shoulders.

She opens the frosted-glass door and we enter a dining room with very little additional furniture. But the aluminum-legged table and the four aluminum-and-plastic chairs lack even the hint of distinction of the living-room furniture. The other window, with wrought-iron grill and closed shutters, must sometime illuminate this bare-walled dining room, devoid of either shelves or sideboards. The only object on the table is a plastic fruit dish with a cluster of black grapes, two peaches, and a buzzing corona of flies. The woman, her arms crossed, her face expressionless, stops behind me. I take the risk of breaking the order of things: clearly, these rooms will not tell me anything I really want to know.

"Couldn't we go up to the roof?" I ask. "That might be the best way to measure the total area."

The woman's eyes light up as she looks at me, or perhaps it is only the contrast with the shadows of the dining room.

"What for?" she says at last. "Señor . . . Valdivia . . . knows the dimensions very well."

And those pauses, before and after the owner's name, are the first indication that something has at last begun to trouble the woman, forcing her, in self-defense, to resort to a kind of irony.

"I don't know." I make an effort to smile. "Perhaps I prefer to go from top to bottom and not" — my false smile drains away — "from bottom to top."

"You will go the way I show you," the woman says, her arms crossed over her chest, a silver crucifix dangling over her dark belly.

Before smiling weakly, I force myself to realize that in these shadows my gestures are of no use, aren't even symbolic. I open the notebook with a creak of the cardboard cover and continue making notes with the greatest possible speed, never glancing up, taking down numbers and estimates for a job whose fiction — the light flush in my cheeks and the perceptible dryness of my tongue tell me — is deceiving no one. And as I cover the graph paper with absurd signs, with square roots and algebraic formulas, I ask myself what is keeping me from getting to the point, from asking about Amilamia and getting out of here with a satisfactory answer. Nothing. And yet I am certain, even if I obtained a response, I would not have the truth. My slim, silent companion is a person I wouldn't look at twice in the street, but in this almost uninhabited house with the coarse furniture, she ceases to be an anonymous face in the crowd and is converted into a stock character of mystery. Such is the paradox, and if memories of Amilamia have once again aroused my appetite for the imaginary, I shall follow the rules of the game, I shall exhaust appearances, and not rest until I have the answer — perhaps simple and clear-cut, immediate and obvious — that lies beyond the veils the señora of the rosary unexpectedly places in my path. Do I bestow a gratuitous strangeness on my reluctant hostess? If so, I'll only take greater pleasure in the labyrinths of my own invention. And the flies are still buzzing around the fruit dish, occasionally pausing on the damaged end of the peach, a nibbled bite — I lean closer, using the pretext of my notes — where little teeth have left their mark in the velvety skin and ocher flesh of the fruit. I do not look toward the señora. I pretend I am taking notes. The fruit seems to be bitten but not touched. I crouch down to see better, rest my hands on the table, move my lips closer as if wishing to repeat the act of biting without touching. I look down and see another sign near my feet: the track of two tires that seem to be bicycle tires, the print of two rubber tires that come as far as the edge of the table and then lead away, growing fainter, the length of the room, toward the señora . . .

I close my notebook.

"Let us go on, señora."

When I turn toward her, I find her standing with her hands resting on the back of a chair. Seated before her, coughing from the smoke of his black cigarette, is a man with heavy shoulders and hidden eyes: those eyes, scarcely visible behind swollen, wrinkled lids as thick and drooped as the neck of an ancient turtle, seem nevertheless to follow my every movement. The half-shaven cheeks, crisscrossed by a thousand gray furrows, sag from protruding cheekbones, and his greenish hands are folded under his arms. He is wearing a coarse blue shirt, and his rumpled hair is so curly it looks like the bottom of a barnacle-covered ship. He does not move, and the only sign of his existence is that difficult whistling breathing (as if every breath must breach a floodgate of phlegm, irritation, and abuse) I had already heard through the chinks of the door.

Ridiculously, he murmurs: "Good afternoon . . ." and I am disposed to forget everything: the mystery, Amilamia, the assessment, the bicycle tracks. The apparition of this asthmatic old bear justifies a prompt retreat. I repeat "Good afternoon," this time with an inflection of farewell. The turtle's mask dissolves into an atrocious smile: every pore of that flesh seems fabricated of brittle rubber, of painted, peeling oilcloth. The arm reaches out and detains me.

"Valdivia died four years ago," says the man in a distant, choking voice that issues from his belly instead of his larynx: a weak, high-pitched voice.

In the grip of that strong, almost painful, claw, I tell myself it is useless to pretend. But the waxen, rubber faces observing me say nothing, and so I am able, in spite of everything, to pretend one more time, to pretend I am speaking to myself when I say: "Amilamia . . ."

Yes: no one will have to pretend any longer. The fist that clutches my arm affirms its strength for only an instant, immediately its grip loosens, then it falls, weak and trembling, before lifting to take the waxen hand touching his shoulder: the señora, perplexed for the first time, looks at me with the eyes of a violated bird and sobs with a dry moan that does not disturb the rigid astonishment of her features. Suddenly the ogres of my imagination are two solitary, abandoned, wounded old people, scarcely able to console themselves in this shuddering clasp of hands that fills me with shame. My fantasy has brought me to this stark dining room to violate the intimacy and the secret of two human beings exiled from life by something I no longer have the right to share. I have never despised myself more. Never have words failed me so clumsily. Any gesture of mine would be in vain: shall I come closer, shall I touch them, shall I caress the woman's head, shall I ask them to excuse my intrusion? I return the notebook to my jacket pocket. I toss into oblivion all the clues in my detective story: the comic book, the lipstick, the nibbled fruit, the bicycle tracks, the blue-checked apron . . . I decide to leave the house without saying anything more. The old man, from behind his thick eyelids, must have noticed.

The high breathy voice says: "Did you know her?"

The past, so natural, used by them every day, finally shatters my illusions. There is the answer. Did you know her? How long? How long must the world have lived without Amilamia, assassinated first by my forgetfulness, and then revived, scarcely yesterday, by a sad impotent memory? When did those serious gray eyes cease to be astonished by the delight of an always solitary garden? When did those lips cease to pout or press together thinly in that ceremonious seriousness with which, I now realize, Amilamia must have discovered and consecrated the objects and events of a life that, she perhaps knew intuitively, was fleeting?

"Yes, we played together in the park. A long time ago."

"How old was she?" says the old man, his voice even more muffled.

"She must have been about seven. No, older than that."

The woman's voice rises, as she lifts her arms, seemingly to implore: "What was she like, señor? Tell us what she was like, please."

I close my eyes. "Amilamia is a memory for me, too. I can only picture her through the things she touched, the things she brought, what she discovered in the park. Yes. Now I see her, coming down the hill. No. It isn't true that it was a scarcely elevated patch of stubble. It was a hill, with grass, and Amilamia's comings and goings had traced a path, and she waved to me from the top before she started down, accompanied by the music, yes, the music I saw, the painting I smelled, the tastes I heard, the odors I touched . . . my hallucination . . . " Do they hear me? "She came waving, dressed in white, in a blue-checked apron . . . the one you have hanging on the roof terrace . . ."

They take my arm and still I do not open my eyes.

"What was she like, señor?"

"Her eyes were gray and the color of her hair changed in the reflection of the sun and the shadow of the trees . . ."

They lead me gently, the two of them. I hear the man's labored breathing, the crucifix on the rosary hitting against the woman's body.

"Tell us, please . . ."

"The air brought tears to her eyes when she ran; when she reached my bench her cheeks were silvered with happy tears . . ."

I do not open my eyes. Now we are going upstairs. Two, five, eight, nine, twelve steps. Four hands guide my body.

"What was she like, what was she like?"

"She sat beneath the eucalyptus and wove garlands from the branches and pretended to cry so I would stop reading and go over to her . . ."

Hinges creak. The odor overpowers everything else: it routs the other senses, it takes its seat like a yellow Mongol° upon the throne of my hallucination; heavy as a coffin, insinuating as the slither of draped silk, ornamented as a Turkish scepter, opaque as a deep, lost vein of ore, brilliant as a dead star. The hands no longer hold me. More than the sobbing, it is the trembling of the old people that envelops me. Slowly, I open my eyes: first through the dizzying liquid of my corneas, then through the web of my eyelashes, the room suffocated in that gigantic battle of perfumes is disclosed, effluvia and frosty, almost fleshlike petals: the presence of the flowers is so strong here they seem to take on the quality of living flesh — the sweetness of the jasmine, the nausea of the lilies, the tomb of the tuberose, the temple of the gardenia. Illuminated through the incandescent wax lips of heavy, sputtering candles, the small windowless bedroom with its aura of wax and humid flowers assaults the very center

Mongol: a native of Mongolia

of my plexus,° and from there, only there at the solar center of life, am I able to come to, and perceive beyond the candles, amid the scattered flowers, the plethora of used toys: the colored hoops and wrinkled balloons, cherries dried to transparency, wooden horses with scraggly manes, the scooter, blind hairless dolls, bears spilling their sawdust, punctured oilcloth ducks, moth-eaten dogs, frayed jumping ropes, glass jars of dried candy, worn-out shoes, the tricycle (three wheels? no, two, and not a bicycle's — two parallel wheels below), little wool and leather shoes; and, facing me, within reach of my hand, the small coffin supported on blue crates decorated with paper flowers, flowers of life this time, carnations and sunflowers, poppies and tulips, but like the others, the ones of death, all part of a compilation created by the atmosphere of this funeral hothouse in which reposes, inside the silvered coffin, between the black silk sheets, on the pillow of white satin, that motionless and serene face framed in lace, highlighted with rose-colored tints, eyebrows traced by the lightest pencil, closed lids, real eyelashes, thick, that cast a tenuous shadow on cheeks as healthy as in the park days. Serious red lips, set almost in the angry pout that Amilamia feigned so I would come to play. Hands joined over her breast. A chaplet, identical to the mother's, strangling that waxen neck. Small white shroud on the clean, prepubescent, docile body.

The old people, sobbing, or kneeling.

I reach out my hand and run my fingers over the porcelain face of my little friend. I feel the coldness of those painted features, of the doll queen who presides over the pomp of this royal chamber of death. Porcelain, wax, cotton. *Amilamia wil not forget her good friend — com see me here wher I draw it.*

I withdraw my fingers from the sham cadaver. Traces of my fingerprints remain where I touched the skin of the doll.

And nausea crawls in my stomach where the candle smoke and the sweet stench of the lilies in the enclosed room have settled. I turn my back on Amilamia's sepulcher. The woman's hand touches my arm. Her wildly staring eyes bear no relation to the quiet, steady voice.

"Don't come back, señor. If you truly loved her, don't come back again."

I touch the hand of Amilamia's mother. I see through nauseous eyes the old man's head buried between his knees, and I go out of the room and to the stairway, to the living room, to the patio, to the street.

5

If not a year, nine or ten months have passed. The memory of that idolatry no longer frightens me. I have forgotten the odor of the flowers and the image of the petrified doll. The real Amilamia has returned to my

---

plexus: a network of nerves and vessels in the abdomen

memory and I have felt, if not content, sane again: the park, the living child, my hours of adolescent reading, have triumphed over the specters of a sick cult. The image of life is the more powerful. I tell myself that I shall live forever with my real Amilamia, the conqueror of the caricature of death. And one day I dare look again at that notebook with graph paper in which I wrote down the data of the spurious assessment. And from its pages, once again, Amilamia's card falls out, with its terrible childish scrawl and its map for getting from the park to her house. I smile as I pick it up. I bite one of the edges, thinking that, in spite of everything, the poor old people might accept this gift.

Whistling, I put on my jacket and straighten my tie. Why not go see them and offer them this card with the child's own writing?

I am almost running as I approach the one-story house. Rain is beginning to fall in large isolated drops, bringing out of the earth with magical immediacy the odor of dewy benediction that stirs the humus and quickens all that lives with its roots in the dust.

I ring the bell. The rain gets heavier and I become insistent. A shrill voice shouts: "I'm coming!" and I wait for the mother with her eternal rosary to open the door for me. I turn up the collar of my jacket. My clothes, my body, too, smell different in the rain. The door opens.

"What do you want? How wonderful you've come!"

The misshapen girl sitting in the wheelchair places one hand on the doorknob and smiles at me with an indecipherable, wry grin. The hump on her chest makes the dress into a curtain over her body, a piece of white cloth that nonetheless lends an air of coquetry to the bluechecked apron. The little woman extracts a pack of cigarettes from her apron pocket and quickly lights a cigarette, staining the end with orange-painted lips. The smoke causes the beautiful gray eyes to squint. She fixes her coppery, wheat-colored, permanent-waved hair, all the time staring at me with a desolate, inquisitive, hopeful — but at the same time fearful — expression.

"No, Carlos. Go away. Don't come back."

And from the house, at the same moment, I hear the high labored breathing of the old man, coming closer.

"Where are you? Don't you know you're not supposed to answer the door? Get back! Devil's spawn! Do I have to beat you again?"

And the rain trickles down my forehead, over my cheeks, and into my mouth, and the little frightened hands drop the comic book onto the wet paving stones.

Translated from the Spanish
by Margaret Sayers Peden

PERU ☼

MARIO VARGAS LLOSA

Peru's leading intellectual figure, Mario Vargas Llosa (1936–) ran un-
successfully for the presidency of his country in the early 1990s. He is a
prolific novelist, playwright, short story writer, and essayist. With Julio
Cortázar, Carlos Fuentes and Gabriel García Márquez, Vargas Llosa
was at the center of the revitalization of the Latin American novel. Of
the four, he is the most realistic and conventional. Vargas Llosa came
to prominence in 1963 with The Time of the Hero, *a novel about life in*
a military school.

This excerpt is taken from The War of the End of the World *(1981).*
During the nineteenth century, in the interior of Brazil a religious fa-
natic known as Conselheiro (Counselor) is followed by a huge band of
disciples drawn from the dregs of society. The army of the Republic is
sent to crush them but suffers several humiliating defeats before it can
wipe out the ragtag army of outlaws. The republican army represents
the modern world of coastal Brazil, anxious to be in synchrony with
Europe; Conselheiro's army stands for the backward, uncivilized inte-
rior. Vargas Llosa is chiefly interested in how men organize violence in
society, whether in institutions like the army or in improvised groups
of outlaws.

from The War of the End of the World

Big João was born near the sea, on a sugarcane plantation in Recôncavo,
the owner of which, Sir Adalberto de Gumúcio, was a great lover of
horses. He boasted of possessing the most spirited sorrels and the mares
with the most finely turned ankles in all of Bahia° and of having produced these specimens of first-rate horseflesh without any need of English studs, thanks to astute matings which he himself supervised. He
prided himself less (in public) on having achieved the same happy result
with the blacks of his slave quarters, so as not to further stir the troubled
waters of the quarrels that this had aroused with the Baron de Canabrava
and with the Church, but the truth of the matter was that he dealt with

Bahia: a state in eastern Brazil whose capital is Salvador

his slaves in exactly the same way that he had dealt with his horses. His method was ruled by his eye and by his inspiration. It consisted of selecting the most lively and most shapely young black girls and giving them as concubines to the males that he regarded as the purest because of their harmonious features and even-colored skins. The best couples were given special food and work privileges so as to produce as many offspring as possible. The chaplain, the missionaries, and the hierarchy of Salvador had repeatedly reproved him for throwing blacks together in this fashion, "making them live together like animals," but instead of putting an end to such practices, these reprimands resulted only in his engaging in them more discreetly.

Big João was the result of one of these combinations arranged by this great landowner with the inclinations of a perfectionist. In João's case the product born of the mating was undeniably magnificent. The boy had very bright, sparkling eyes and teeth that when he laughed filled his round blue-black face with light. He was plump, vivacious, playful, and his mother — a beautiful woman who gave birth every nine months — suspected that he would have an exceptional future. She was not mistaken. Sir Adalberto de Gumúcio became fond of him when he was still a baby crawling on all fours and took him out of the slave quarters to the manor house — a rectangular building, with a hip roof,° Tuscan columns,° and balconies with wooden railings that overlooked the cane fields, the neoclassic° chapel, the sugar mill, the distillery, and an avenue of royal palms — thinking that he could be a servant boy for his daughters and later on a butler or a coachman. He did not want him to be ruined at an early age, as frequently happened with children sent out into the fields to clear land and harvest sugarcane.

But the one who claimed Big João for herself was Miss Adelinha Isabel de Gumúcio, Master Adalberto's unmarried sister, who lived with him. She was slender and small-boned, with a little turned-up nose that seemed to be continually sniffing the world's bad odors, and she spent her time weaving coifs and shawls, embroidering tablecloths, bedspreads, blouses, or preparing desserts, tasks at which she excelled. But most of the time she did not even taste the cream puffs, the almond tortes, the meringues with chocolate filling, the almond sponge cakes that were the delight of her nieces and nephews, her sister-in-law and her brother. Miss Adelinha took a great liking to Big João from the day she saw him climbing the water tank. Terrified at seeing, some seven feet or so off the ground, a little boy scarcely old enough to toddle, she ordered him to climb down, but João went on up the little ladder. By the time Miss Adelinha called a servant, the little boy had already reached the edge of

---

hip roof, Tuscan columns, neoclassic: the house has the outward appearance of a Greek temple — with tall columns and square angles — which contrast with the remoteness of the region.

the tank and fallen into the water. They fished him out, vomiting and wide-eyed with fear. Miss Adelinha undressed him, bundled him up, and held him in her arms till he fell asleep.

Shortly thereafter, Master Adalberto's sister installed João in her bedroom, in one of the cradles that her nieces had slept in. She had it placed right next to her bed, and he slept all night at her side, the way other ladies have their favorite little maidservants and their little lap dogs sleep next to them. From that moment on, João enjoyed special privileges. Miss Adelinha always dressed him in one-piece romper suits, navy blue or bright red or golden yellow, which she made for him herself. He went with her every day to the promontory from which there was a panoramic view of the islands and the late-afternoon sun, setting them on fire, and accompanied her when she made visits and trips to neighboring villages to distribute alms. On Sundays he went to church with her, carrying her prie-dieu.° Miss Adelinha taught him how to hold skeins of wool so that she could comb them, to change the spools of the loom, to mix colors for the dye, and to thread needles, as well as how to serve as her kitchen boy. To measure how long things should cook, they recited together the Credos and Our Fathers° that the recipe called for. She personally prepared him for his First Communion, took Communion with him, and made him marvelous chocolate to celebrate the occasion.

But, contrary to what should have happened in the case of a child who had grown up amid walls covered with wallpaper, jacaranda° furniture upholstered in damask and silks, and sideboards full of crystalware, spending his days engaged in feminine pursuits in the shadow of a delicate-natured woman, Big João did not turn into a gentle, tame creature, as almost always happened to house slaves. From earliest childhood on, he was unusually strong, so that despite the fact that he was the same age as Little João, the cook's son, he appeared to be several years older. At play he was brutal, and Miss Adelinha used to say sadly: "He's not made for civilized life. He yearns to be out in the open." Because the boy was constantly on the lookout for the slightest chance to go out for a ramble in the countryside. One time, as they were walking through the cane fields, on seeing him look longingly at the blacks naked to the waist hacking away with machetes amid the green leaves, the senhorita remarked to him: "You look as though you envied them." "Yes, mistress, I envy them," he replied. A little after that, Master Adalberto had him put on a black armband and sent him to the slave quarters of the plantation to attend his mother's funeral. João did not feel any great emotion, for he had seen very little of her. He was vaguely ill at ease all during the ceremony, sitting underneath a bower of straw, and in the cortege to the cemetery,

prie-dieu: a small, low reading desk, for kneeling at prayer
Credos and Our Fathers: Catholic prayers
jacaranda: a kind of Brazilian wood

surrounded by blacks who stared at him without trying to conceal their envy or their scorn for his knickers, his striped blouse, and his shoes that were such a sharp contrast to their coarse cotton shirts and bare feet. He had never been affectionate with his mistress, thereby causing the Gumúcio family to think that perhaps he was one of those churls with no feelings, capable of spitting on the hand that fed them. But not even this portent would ever have led them to suspect that Big João would be capable of doing what he did.

It happened during Miss Adelinha's trip to the Convent of the Incarnation, where she went on retreat every year. Little João drove the coach drawn by two horses and Big João sat next to him on the coach box. The trip took around eight hours; they left the plantation at dawn so as to arrive at the convent by mid-afternoon. But two days later the nuns sent a messenger to ask why Senhorita Adelinha hadn't arrived on the date that had been set. Master Adalberto directed the searches by the police from Bahia and the servants on the plantation who scoured the region for an entire month, questioning any number of people. Every inch of the road between the convent and the plantation was gone over with a fine-tooth comb, yet not the slightest trace of the coach, its occupants, or the horses was found. As in the fantastic stories recounted by the wandering *cantadores,*° they seemed to have vanished in thin air.

The truth began to come to light months later, when a magistrate of the Orphans' Court in Salvador discovered the monogram of the Gumúcio family, covered over with paint, on the secondhand coach that he had bought from a dealer in the upper town. The dealer confessed that he had acquired the coach in a village inhabited by *cafuzos* — Negro-Indian halfbreeds — knowing that it was stolen, but without the thought ever crossing his mind that the thieves might also be murderers. The Baron de Canabrava offered a very high price for the heads of Big João and Little João, while Gumúcio implored that they be captured alive. A gang of outlaws that was operating in the backlands turned Little João in to the police for the reward. The cook's son was so dirty and disheveled that he was unrecognizable when they subjected him to torture to make him talk.

He swore that the whole thing had not been planned by him but by the devil that had possessed his companion since childhood. He had been driving the coach, whistling through his teeth, thinking of the sweets awaiting him at the Convent of the Incarnation, when all of a sudden Big João had ordered him to rein in the horses. When Miss Adelinha asked why they were stopping, Little João saw his companion hit her in the face so hard she fainted, grab the reins from him, and spur the horses on to the promontory that their mistress was in the habit of climbing up to in order to contemplate the view of the islands. There, with a determination

cantadores: singers, minstrels

such that Little João, terror-stricken, had not dared to cross him, Big João had subjected Miss Adelinha to a thousand evil acts. He had stripped her naked and laughed at her as she covered her breasts with one trembling hand and her privates with the other, and had made her run all about, trying to dodge the stones he threw at her as he heaped upon her the most abominable insults that the younger boy had ever heard. Then he suddenly plunged a dagger into her belly and once she was dead vent his fury on her by lopping off her breasts and her head. Then, panting, drenched with sweat, he fell asleep alongside the bloody corpse. Little João was so terrified that his legs buckled beneath him when he tried to run away.

When Big João woke up a while later, he was calm. He gazed indifferently at the carnage all about them. Then he ordered the Kid to help him dig a grave, and they buried the pieces of Miss Adelinha it it. They had waited until it got dark to make their escape and gradually put distance between themselves and the scene of the crime; in the daytime they hid the coach in a cave or a thicket or a ravine and at night galloped on; the one clear idea in their minds was that they ought to head away from the sea. When they managed to sell the coach and the horses, they bought provisions to take with them as they went into the *sertão*,° with the hope of joining one or another of the bands of fugitive slaves who, as many stories had it, were everywhere in the scrublands of the interior. They lived on the run, avoiding the towns and getting food to eat by begging or by petty thefts. Only once did João the Kid try to get Big João to talk about what had happened. They were lying underneath a tree, smoking cigars, and in a sudden fit of boldness he asked him point-blank: "Why did you kill the mistress?" "Because I've got the Dog in me," Big João answered immediately. "Don't talk to me about that any more." The Kid thought that his companion had told him the truth.

He was growing more and more afraid of this companion of his since childhood, for after the murder of their mistress, Big João became less and less like his former self. He scarcely said a word to him, and, on the other hand, he continually surprised him by talking to himself in a low voice, his eyes bloodshot. One night he heard him call the Devil "Father" and ask him to come to his aid. "Haven't I done enough already, Father?" he stammered, his body writhing. "What more do you want me to do?" The Kid became convinced that Big João had made a pact with the Evil One and feared that, in order to continue accumulating merit, he would sacrifice him as he had their mistress. He decided to beat him to it. He planned everything, but the night that he crawled over to him, all set to plunge his knife into him, he was trembling so violently that Big João opened his eyes before he could do the deed. Big João saw him leaning over him with the blade quivering in his hand. His intention was unmistakable, but Big João didn't turn a hair. "Kill me, Kid," he heard him say.

sertão: the vast Brazilian plains

He ran off as fast as his legs could carry him, feeling that devils were pursuing him.

The Kid was hanged in the prison in Salvador and Senhorita Adelinha's remains were transferred to the neoclassic chapel of the plantation, but her murderer was not found, despite the fact that the Gumúcio family periodically raised the reward for his capture. And yet, after the Kid had run off, Big João had made no attempt to hide himself. A towering giant, half naked, miserable, eating what fell into the animal traps he set or the fruit he plucked from trees, he roamed the byways like a ghost. He went through the towns in broad daylight, asking for food, and the suffering in his face so moved people that they would usually toss him a few scraps.

One day, at a crossroads on the outskirts of Pombal,° he came upon a handful of people who were listening to the words of a gaunt man, enveloped in a deep-purple tunic, whose hair came down to his shoulders and whose eyes looked like burning coals. As it happened, he was speaking at that very moment of the Devil, whom he called Lucifer, the Dog, Can, and Beelzebub, of the catastrophes and crimes that he caused in the world, and of what men who wanted to be saved must do. His voice was persuasive; it reached a person's soul without passing by way of his head, and even to a being as addlebrained as Big João, it seemed like a balm that healed old and terrible wounds. João stood there listening to him, rooted to the spot, not even blinking, moved to his very bones by what he was hearing and by the music of the voice uttering those words. The figure of the saint was blurred at times by the tears that welled up in João's eyes. When the man went on his way, he began to follow him at a distance, like a timid animal.

Translated from the Spanish
by Helen R. Lane

***

Pombal: a Brazilian town

PUERTO RICO

ROSARIO FERRÉ

A professor, critic, and writer, Rosario Ferré (1938–) comes from one of the most prominent and wealthiest families in Puerto Rico. Her father was governor of the island. Ferré received an excellent education, graduating from Wellesley College in Massachusetts. After a divorce, she studied literature at the University of Puerto Rico. Ferré has written on the works of Sor Juana Inés de la Cruz, Mexican nun and great poet of the seventeenth century. In the 1970s, Ferré and other young Puerto Rican writers and critics published a successful avant-garde journal, Zona de carga y descarga. *Her stories show clear influences of writers like Horacio Quiroga and Julio Cortázar. Ferré has also authored essays on feminist topics.*

In fiction, her most important collection of stories is Pandora's Papers *from which "The Youngest Doll" is taken. The combination of illness and the exchange of young women gives this story a mythic air. Ferré also recreates the atmosphere of well-to-do, provincial Puerto Rican families.*

The Youngest Doll

Early in the morning the maiden aunt had taken her rocking chair out onto the porch facing the canefields, as she always did whenever she woke up with the urge to make a doll. As a young woman, she had often bathed in the river, but one day when the heavy rains had fed the dragontail current, she had a soft feeling of melting snow in the marrow of her bones. With her head nestled among the black rock's reverberations she could hear the slamming of salty foam on the beach mingled with the sound of the waves, and she suddenly thought that her hair had poured out to sea at last. At that very moment, she felt a sharp bite in her calf. Screaming, she was pulled out of the water, and, writhing in pain, was taken home in a stretcher.

The doctor who examined her assured her it was nothing, that she had probably been bitten by an angry river prawn.° But the days passed and

river prawn: a kind of crayfish

the scab would not heal. A month later, the doctor concluded that the prawn had worked its way into the soft flesh of her calf and had nestled there to grow. He prescribed a mustard plaster so that the heat would force it out. The aunt spent a whole week with her leg covered with mustard from thigh to ankle, but when the treatment was over, they found that the ulcer had grown even larger and that it was covered with a slimy, stonelike substance that couldn't be removed without endangering the whole leg. She then resigned herself to living with the prawn permanently curled up in her calf.

She had been very beautiful, but the prawn hidden under the long, gauzy folds of her skirt stripped her of all vanity. She locked herself up in her house, refusing to see any suitors. At first she devoted herself entirely to bringing up her sister's children, dragging her monstrous leg around the house quite nimbly. In those days, the family was nearly ruined; they lived surrounded by a past that was breaking up around them with the same impassive musicality with which the crystal chandelier crumbled on the frayed embroidered linen cloth of the dining-room table. Her nieces adored her. She would comb their hair, bathe and feed them, and when she read them stories, they would sit around her and furtively lift the starched ruffle of her skirt so as to sniff the aroma of ripe sweetsop° that oozed from her leg when it was at rest.

As the girls grew up, the aunt devoted herself to making dolls for them to play with. At first they were just plain dolls, with cottony stuffing from the gourd tree in the garden and stray buttons sewn on for eyes. As time passed, though, she began to refine her craft more and more, thus earning the respect and admiration of the whole family. The birth of a new doll was always cause for a ritual celebration, which explains why it never occurred to the aunt to sell them for a profit, even when the girls had grown up and the family was beginning to fall into need. The aunt continued to increase the size of the dolls so that their height and other measurements conformed to those of each of the girls. There were nine of them, and the aunt would make one doll for each per year, so it became necessary to set aside a room for the dolls alone in the house. When the eldest girl turned eighteen, there were one hundred and twenty-six dolls of all ages in the room. Opening the door gave you the impression of entering a dovecote, or the ballroom in the czarina's palace, or a warehouse in which someone had spread out a row of tobacco leaves to dry. But the aunt didn't enter the room for any of these pleasures. Instead, she would unlatch the door and gently pick up each doll, murmuring a lullaby as she rocked it: "This is how you were when you were a year old, this is you at two, and like this at three," measuring out each year of their lives against the hollow they had left in her arms.

The day the eldest turned ten, the aunt sat down in her rocking chair

sweetsop: an evergreen shrub of tropical America

facing the canefields and hardly ever got up again. She would rock away entire days on the porch, watching the patterns of rain shift like watercolor over the canefields, and coming out of her stupor only when the doctor would pay her a visit, or she awoke with the desire to make a doll. Then she would call out so that everyone in the house would come and help her. On that day, one could see the hired help making repeated trips to town like cheerful Inca messengers,° bringing wax, porcelain clay, needles, spools of thread of every shade and color. While these preparations were taking place, the aunt would call the niece she had dreamt about the night before into her bedroom and take her measurements. Then she would make a wax mask of the child's face, covering it with plaster on both sides, like a living face sheathed in two dead ones. Then she would draw out an endless flaxen thread of melted wax through a pinpoint on her chin. The porcelain of the hands and face was always translucent; it had an ivory tint to it that formed a great contrast with the curdled whiteness of the bisque faces. For the body, the aunt would always send out to the garden for twenty glossy gourds. She would hold them in one hand and, with an expert twist of her knife, would slice them up and lean them against the railing of the balcony, so that the sun and wind would dry the cottony guano° brains out. After a few days, she would scrape off the dried fluff with a teaspoon and, with infinite patience, feed it into the doll's mouth.

The only items the aunt would agree to use in the birth of a doll that were not made by her with whatever materials came to her from the land, were the glass eyeballs. They were mailed to her directly from Europe in all colors, but the aunt considered them useless until she had left them submerged at the bottom of the stream for a few days, so that they would learn to recognize the slightest stirring of the prawn's antennae. Only then would she carefully rinse them in ammonia water and place them, glossy as gems and nestled in a bed of cotton, at the bottom of one of her Dutch cookie tins. The dolls were always outfitted in the same way, even though the girls were growing up. She would dress the younger ones in Swiss embroidery and the older ones in silk guipure,° and on each of their heads she would tie the same bow, wide and white and trembling like the breast of a dove.

The girls began to marry and leave home. On their wedding day, the aunt would give each of them their last doll, kissing them on the forehead and telling them with a smile, "Here is your Easter Sunday." She would reassure the grooms by explaining to them that the doll was merely

Inca messengers: the great Inca civilization, which was thriving in the area of present-day Peru at the time of the Spanish conquest, used very fast foot-messengers, or *chasquis,* for communications.
guano: straw
guipure: a kind of embroidery

a sentimental ornament, of the kind that people used to place on the lid of grand pianos in the old days. From the porch, the aunt would watch the girls walk down the fanlike staircase for the last time. They would carry a modest checkered cardboard suitcase in one hand, the other hand slipped around the waist of the exuberant doll made in their image and likeness, still wearing the same old-fashioned kid slippers and gloves, and with Valenciennes° bloomers barely showing under their snowy, embroidered skirts. But the hands and faces of these new dolls looked less transparent than those of the old: they had the consistency of skim milk. This difference concealed a more subtle one: the wedding doll was never stuffed with cotton but was filled with honey.

All the girls had married, and only the youngest niece was left at home when the doctor paid his monthly visit to the aunt, bringing his son along this time, who had just returned from studying medicine up north. The young man lifted the starched ruffle of the aunt's skirt and looked intently at the huge ulcer which oozed a perfumed sperm from the tip of its greenish scales. He pulled out his stethoscope and listened to it carefully. The aunt thought he was listening for the prawn's breathing, to see if it was still alive, and so she fondly lifted his hand and placed it on the spot where he could feel the constant movement of the creature's antennae. The young man released the ruffle and looked fixedly at his father. "You could have cured this from the start," he told him. "That's true," his father answered, "but I just wanted you to come and see the prawn that has been paying for your education these twenty years."

From then on it was the young doctor who visited the old aunt every month. His interest in the youngest niece was evident from the start, so that the aunt was able to begin her last doll in plenty of time. He would always show up for the visit wearing a pair of brightly polished shoes, a starched collar, and an ostentatious tiepin of extravagant poor taste. After examining the aunt he would sit in the parlor, leaning his paper silhouette against the oval frame of the chair, and each time would hand the youngest an identical bouquet of purple forget-me-nots. She would offer him ginger cookies and would hold the bouquet with the tip of her fingers, as if she were holding a purple sea urchin turned inside out. She made up her mind to marry him because she was intrigued by his drowsy profile, and also because she was deathly curious to find out what dolphin flesh was like.

On her wedding day, as she was about to leave the house, the youngest was surprised to find that the doll the aunt had given her as a wedding present was warm. As she slipped her arm around her waist, she examined her attentively, but quickly forgot about it, so amazed was she at the excellence of the craft. The doll's face and hands were made of the

Valenciennes: a frilly undergarment

most delicate Mikado porcelain,° and in her half-open and slightly sad smile she recognized her full set of baby teeth. There was also another notable detail: the aunt had embedded her diamond eardrops in the doll's pupils.

The young doctor took off to live in town, in a square house that made one think of a cement block. Each day he made his wife sit out on the balcony, so that passersby would be sure to see that he had married into society. Motionless inside her cubicle of heat, the youngest began to suspect that it wasn't just her husband's silhouette that was made of paper, but his soul as well. Her suspicions were soon confirmed. One day he pried out the doll's eyes with the tip of his scalpel and pawned them for a fancy gold pocket watch with a long, embossed chain. From then on the doll remained seated as always on the lid of the grand piano, but with her gaze modestly lowered.

A few months later the doctor noticed the doll was missing from her usual place and asked the youngest what she'd done with it. A sisterhood of pious ladies had offered him a healthy sum for the porcelain hands and face, which they thought would be perfect for the image of the Veronica° in the next Lenten procession. The youngest answered him that the ants had at last discovered the doll was filled with honey and, streaming over the piano, had devoured it in a single night. "Since the hands and face were made of Mikado porcelain and were as delicate as sugar," she said, "the ants have probably taken them to some underground burrow and at this very moment are probably wearing down their teeth, gnawing furiously at fingers and eyelids to no avail." That night the doctor dug up all the ground around the house, but could not find the doll.

As the years passed the doctor became a millionaire. He had slowly acquired the whole town as his clientele, people who didn't mind paying exorbitant fees in order to see a genuine member of the extinct sugarcane aristocracy up close. The youngest went on sitting in her chair out on the balcony, motionless in her muslin and lace, and always with lowered eyelids. Whenever her husband's patients, draped in necklaces and feathers and carrying elaborate handbags and canes, would sit beside her, perhaps coughing or sneezing, or shaking their doleful rolls of flesh with a jingling of coins, they would notice a strange scent that would involuntarily make them think of a slowly oozing sweetsop. They would then feel an uncontrollable urge to rub their hands together as if they were paws.

There was only one thing missing from the doctor's otherwise-perfect happiness. He noticed that, although he was aging naturally, the youngest still kept the same firm, porcelained skin she had had, when he had called on her at the big house on the plantation. One night he decided to

Mikado porcelain: Japanese porcelain
the Veronica: the image of the woman who wiped Jesus' face while he was carrying the cross

go into her bedroom, to watch her as she slept. He noticed that her chest wasn't moving. He gently placed his stethoscope over her heart and heard a distant swish of water. Then the doll lifted up her eyelids, and out of the empty sockets of her eyes came the frenzied antennae of all those prawns.

Translated from the Spanish by
Rosario Ferré and Diana Vélez

SUB-SAHARAN AFRICA

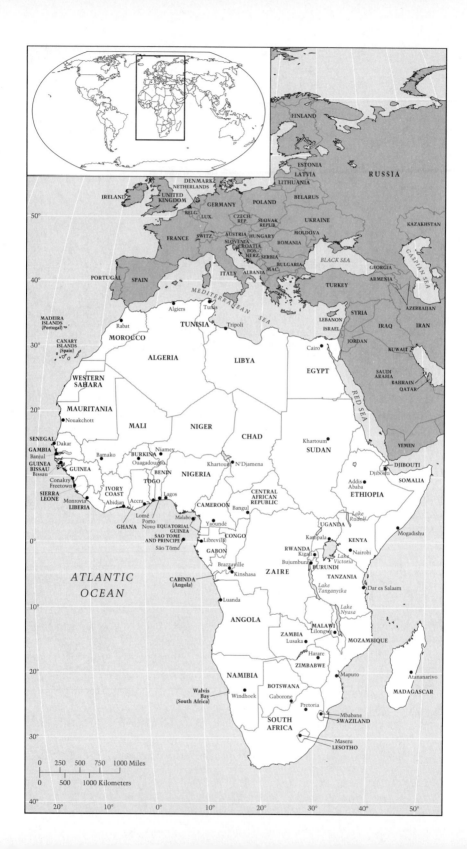

SUB-SAHARAN AFRICA

There is no African literature in the sense of a composite whole. Africa is not a country. It is the most complex continent we have, with over a thousand different language groups, each with its specific culture. The literature of sub-Saharan Africa comes in hundreds of languages indigenous to Africa; it also comes in Arabic as well as in several European languages, including English, French, and Portuguese.

There are, however, some useful approaches we can adopt to infuse some coherence into the study of writings from various African countries. The first approach is to look at the history of the continent as the whole, focusing on the historical phases through which all of Africa has passed. The second approach is to refine this broad-brushed portrait by attending to the specific and individual histories of various regions.

Any introduction to African history, culture, or literature must combat the twin obstacles of ethnocentrism and cultural imperialism. *Ethnocentrism* means putting one's own culture at the center and judging other cultures according to the standards of one's own; *cultural imperialism* is the insistence by members of a more powerful society that their ways of doing things are superior. Such attitudes toward Africa may be dispelled by cultivating *cultural relativism,* that is, by judging other cultures according to their own standards.

PRECONQUEST

Too often, the teaching of the history of Africa in our schools, like the teaching of American history, begins with conquest. The earlier phase is relegated to prehistory. Ethnocentrism and cultural imperialism are reinforced by beginning the study of colonized cultures with their conquest. Cultural relativism is best served in this case by studying life on the continent in its preconquest phase, largely through its oral traditions, or *orature.*

Orature is a feature of preliterate peoples and societies that have recently acquired literacy. It informs the "popular" — which is not always synonymous with the "unsophisticated" — imagination. A culture's orature expresses its complex thought patterns: its cosmological, ontological, and theological views; its ethical, aesthetic, and other social values;

as well as its history and culture. It is dynamic and capable of incorporating new forms of social consciousness. It is an ever-present store of knowledge that is added upon and modified but never eradicated by encounter with novelty. An unbroken line links the *griot* from West Africa and the *imbongi* from South Africa to the singer of the Negro spirituals; the blues singer to the performer of high life and *juju* music, as well as to the *mbaganga*, reggae, and rap artists.

Africa's preconquest phase saw the rise and fall of vast empire states — ancient Egypt, Kush, Meroe, Nubia, Carthage, Ghana, Mali, Songhai, Zimbabwe, KwaZulu — which existed alongside decentralized states that had forms of social organization and civilizations no less impressive. The orature of these societies persists — to varying degrees and in various forms — throughout history and down to the present day. Because of this strong oral tradition, the cultures of preconquest Africa were never completely eradicated, even in the phases of encroachment and colonialism. They have always informed and shaped the consciousness of African writers and continue to do so today.

ENCROACHMENT

The sources of encroachment lay outside the continent. Encroachment started with the Islamization, or Arabization, that began earlier than the tenth century in some areas and continued in the Europeanization, or Christianization, that occurred between the seventeenth and nineteenth centuries. There were two distinct forces of disruption at work, the external — mainly from the Arabian Peninsula and Europe — and the internal — such as decaying social structures, decadent practices, and customs that were laudable in themselves but easy for outsiders to exploit. Two of the contemporary writers represented in this anthology — Chinua Achebe (Nigeria) and Sembeue Ousmane (Senegal) — often examine the dynamics of encroachment, specifically, the effects of external pressures exerted on structures ready to collapse in on themselves.

East Africa has long been influenced by the Middle East and other parts of Asia, as has the literature from the region, particularly in Arabic. Somalia, Djibouti, and Sudan have been the most heavily influenced by Islamic culture as a result of their proximity to the Arab world. Mogadishu, Somalia's capital, was founded as an Islamic trading post in the tenth century.

Farther south, along the coast, Arabs and Africans combined, as early as the ninth century, to form the culture and the language called KiSwahili, which developed into a regional *linqua Africana* with a rich literature. The Amharic language in Ethiopia produced the other early literature in the region.

COLONIALISM

Although Islamic encroachment persisted over several centuries, the process generated less hostility and resistance than Christian encroachment. Islamic messengers were willing to adapt themselves and their message to local conditions. European Christians, on the other hand, sought to impose not only their religion but also their culture, including industrial technology and a heightened sense of racism. This difference, combined with the very real economic subservience of Africans and their agricultural resources, distinguishes full-blown European colonialism from earlier Islamic (and even early Christian) encroachment. Eventually the bitter scarification caused by this colonialism resulted in the rejection of the overbearing messengers of European culture.

West Africa

With the exception of Liberia, originally established to resettle ex-slaves from the United States, all the contemporary states of West Africa (including Central Africa) were the creation of competing European colonial powers — France, Britain, Germany, Portugal, Belgium — who divided the area among themselves. The current borders were traced at the Berlin Conferences of 1884–1885. The principal European powers partitioned Africa and carved it into spheres of influence — usually making arbitrary divisions, but sometimes carrying out the classical colonial ploy of divide-and-rule. People who belonged together — such as the Lund of Zambia, Zaire, and Angola, and the Yoruba of Nigeria and Benin — were thus separated into different "nations," and peoples known to harbor animosity for one another were brought together within the same national boundaries. France and Britain emerged as the dominant political powers in West Africa.

The French sought to impose their will through the agency of local people who derived their power from the French. These were turned into a buffer caste of new elites, trained to do their masters' bidding and alienated from the local communities or countries from which they were sprung. The French educational system was the main instrument for their socialization, a simultaneous process of assimilation and alienation, resulting in the creation of black French men.

Thus the French policy of assimilation was designed to absorb selected Africans into French culture, French government, the French civil service, and the French colonial system, by imparting French values to them. The French policy of assimilation meant psychological, political, and even cultural estrangement to the affected blacks. Literature from francophone Africa in its beginnings had little or no bearing upon traditional values. It merely sang the splendors of France and exhibited symptoms of an alienated elite. It was detribalized literature.

Like the French, the British sought the most cost-effective ways of running their colonies, conserving British lives in the malaria-infested zone of West Africa while exploiting the human and material resources of their colonies to the limit. Unlike the French, however, the British had no desire to absorb Africans into their ranks or to wipe out tradition even among educated Africans, who were introduced to British ways but without being removed altogether from their own customs.

The British manipulated traditional cultures and structures, which they employed in the service of colonialism. They used traditional rulers to do their bidding by making it manifestly clear that they had the power to depose errant chiefs. They replaced any rulers who opposed them with malleable puppets. In a few instances, as among the Ibo, they created chieftaincies where none had ever existed — the subject of Achebe's novel *Arrow of God*.

East Africa

European interest in the Horn of Africa resulted from its strategic location as an easterly projection into the Indian Ocean. Britain and France became interested in the region because the Red Sea was the link with the markets of Asia. This was especially true after the construction of the Suez Canal in 1869.

South of the Horn, Kenya and Uganda were taken by the British toward the close of the nineteenth century. Tanzania, originally a German colony, fell into British hands after World War I. The European settler populations in Tanzania and Uganda were smaller. As a result, a system of indirect rule, as in British West Africa, evolved. Ugandan and Tanzanian literature thus share a common trait of rootedness.

In Kenya, which enjoys a mild climate, the British encouraged the growth of a settler community. Although constituting about 1 percent of the population, the settlers took the best agricultural land in the highlands around Nairobi. Settler colonialism in Kenya led to the Mau Mau uprising in the 1950s. A great deal of the literature deals with the Mau Mau revolt and its consequences.

Southern Africa

European settlements in Southern Africa began in the sixteenth century with small numbers of Portuguese along the coast of Angola and Mozambique, where they established stations for the transatlantic export trade in slaves. In 1652, the Dutch established a settlement that they called the Cape of Good Hope. They seized the land of the Khoisan and reduced them to servitude. In addition, they imported slaves from Asia and other parts of Africa. In the process, a new society of free European settlers and subordinated people of mixed European, African, and Asian descent evolved at the Cape, which, like the antebellum American South, became racially stratified. Dutch settlers were reinforced in 1688 by the

French Huguenots and subsequently by settlers from Germany. The descendants of these early settlers came to regard themselves as Afrikaners, or Boers.

The British took over the Cape Colony during the Napoleonic wars, and by 1820 significant numbers of English-speaking people occupied the Eastern Cape. Anglo-Boer relations were exacerbated by the abolition of slavery and the extension of limited rights to other population groups in the colony. In response, a large number of Afrikaners in the 1830s moved into the interior, where they deprived Africans of their land and coerced them into supplying corvée (unpaid) labor for the Afrikaners' farms and public works.

The discovery of diamonds in the 1860s and gold in 1886 brought more European settlers into the interior of Southern Africa. In the 1890s, the British occupied present-day Zambia and Zimbabwe. More British traders, missionaries, and settlers invaded Malawi. At about the same time that the Portuguese expanded inland from their coastal enclaves, the Germans seized Namibia, later entrusted to South Africa as a mandated territory.

ANTICOLONIALISM AND INDEPENDENCE

Colonialism and its literature framed blacks as victims. Pain, suffering, and resignation were indeed widespread. However, people also experienced celebration, stoicism, and heroism. A culture of fear that was sometimes paralyzing coexisted with a culture of resistance that was imbued with qualities of transcendence. Anticolonial literature focused on this culture of resistance, sometimes creating it in the process. More than anything, it marked a shift in Africans' understanding of the part they were to play in their own fates.

These positive qualities ensured the ultimate triumph of the downtrodden over their oppressors. People came out on top precisely because they had been creative fighters. Africans were active agents of their own emancipation, not passive spectators — and they knew this to be so. The era of independence in the 1960s was marked by a great deal of euphoria and optimism. The literature of the period is "honeymoon" literature, which rarely addressed problems. It is the literature of an emerging Africa announcing itself and whom it would serve.

West Africa

In due course the intellectual arrogance implicit in the French policy of assimilation, with its Francocentric assumptions, sparked a revolt of the mind that found expression in negritude, a counterhegemonic cultural movement. For Africans like Leopold Sedar Senghor, it became a metaphoric return to the self after a brief sojourn in Europe. Negritude was an affirmation of the sum total of the cultural values of the Negro world.

Negritude was thus an expression of the collective consciousness of Africans as racially oppressed people. The literary preoccupation of the movement was cultural imperialism. It represented the resistance of people of African origin universally as a symbolic progression from subordination to independence and alienation, through revolt, to self-affirmation.

The literature of anglophone West Africa exhibited strong traits of ethnic consciousness from the beginning. Writers such as Chinua Achebe and Wole Soyinka, with one foot in each culture, could write without sentimentality about both tradition and modernity because their African identity had not been subverted in their absorption of European influences. Because of this integrated sense of identity, they had little use for the stridency of negritude. "A tiger does not proclaim its tigritude; it pounces," Soyinka pronounced.

The year 1958 was an important landmark in the literary history of anglophone West Africa with the publication of Achebe's *Things Fall Apart*, the classic novel of preconquest times and the period of encroachment. Achebe's work, and that of writers such as Gabriel Okara who soon followed him, was part of the cultural nationalism that paralleled political independence.

Soyinka came to prominence in the 1960s and became Africa's leading playwright. His dramaturgy was based on ancient Yoruba traditions and cosmogony, which he bent to accommodate an essentially modern aesthetic sensibility. Soyinka as poet, novelist, and playwright absorbed the techniques of modernism and simultaneously brought the resources of orature into English literature.

East Africa

Creative writing in English in East Africa began later than it did in West Africa. Its hostile attitude toward European settler colonialism brought it closer to the tradition of protest literature in Southern Africa than to the anglophone West African writers' preoccupation with tradition and contact with the West. Kenyan literature, in particular, is preoccupied with land — the dominant "character" in the fiction of Ngugi wa Thiong'o, East Africa's major author. The early Ngugi subscribed to the view that Africa's cultural traditions, including the circumcision of women, may be objectionable to "foreigners" but nonetheless must be preserved to bind African society. His later work shows a keener awareness of the dynamics of social change and has a didactic contemporary political purpose.

Okot p'Bitek, from Uganda, emerged after Ngugi as the most significant poet in East Africa. The publication of the English version of p'Bitek's *Song of Lawino* (1966) pointed at the direction African literature was taking in its use of the techniques of orature and in its satiric treatment of Africans who have lost their cultural heritage and become carbon copies of Europeans.

Southern Africa

A new phase of regrouping among the dispossessed Africans culminated in the formation in 1912 of the African National Congress (ANC), the first pan-African organization on the continent. Mild forms of protest, mainly petitions and delegations, characterized the first four decades of the ANC's existence. With the coming to power of the apartheid regime in 1948, however, more militant measures were adopted. During the 1950s, passive resistance, first introduced in South Africa in the early 1900s by the Indian leader Mohandas K. Gandhi, was adopted on a massive scale.

The political situation continued to deteriorate, though, and in 1960 the police killed sixty-nine anti-apartheid demonstrators in Sharpeville. Thereafter, the government banned the ANC and the PAC, a splinter group from the ANC, and arrested most of its leaders, such as Nelson Mandela. Political and literary figures who were not in prison, had not been placed under banning orders, or had not been banished to remote areas went into exile.

From 1969, resistance resurfaced, spurred by the teachings of Steve Biko and Black Consciousness, a movement that utilized the resources of culture and literature to foment revolution. The high-water mark of Black Consciousness was the eruption in 1976 of student demonstrations against the forced use in schools of the Afrikaans language, identified by the rebellious youth as the language of the oppressor. During the crackdown that followed, many youths left South Africa and joined the exiled organizations, thus helping to invigorate then.

By the 1980s extraparliamentary opposition to apartheid had grown to such an extent that hundreds of grassroots organizations, including cultural and literary groups, sprouted all over the country and led to the eventual collapse of apartheid. Following the release of political prisoners and the unbanning of the ANC and the PAC in 1990, the first nonracial elections in South Africa, held in April 1994, brought an ANC-led government to power, with Mandela as the first president ever elected on universal suffrage in the country.

The rigidity of segregation and apartheid has given rise to various cultural configurations and literary traditions in South Africa, of which the most important are

- the liberal school of literature written mainly in English by authors of European descent for predominantly white readers and appealing for the infusion of liberal humanist ideals in race relations;
- the protest tradition, written mainly in English by authors who are

black (indigenous Africans, South Africans of mixed race, Asian Africans), addressed to white sympathizers and occasionally to readers from the oppressed groups for the purpose of denouncing racism;
- writing in the indigenous languages mainly for young adults of school-age; and
- Afrikaans literature intended primarily for the *volk* (Afrikaners), whose virtues it extols while putting down the "natives," with the emergence occasionally of dissident writers opposed to apartheid.

Nadine Gordimer's work, especially from the 1950s, constantly probes the limits of liberalism in the context of South Africa. Her work exposes liberalism as bold at the verbal level but impotent to effect meaningful change. In her post-Sharpeville work she veers increasingly toward liberation literature, and her recent work promises to look just as critically at South Africa's new masters. Njabulo Simakahle Ndebele, on the other hand, is one of the best African short story writers to emerge from South Africa. His work brings together the finest threads in the tradition, with its emphasis on allowing protest (though it is not totally absent from his writing), to take a backseat. With Ndebele, we move from protest literature's spectacular and surface meaning to a literature of interiority and introspection.

In Zimbabwe, independent since 1980 after a protracted war of liberation, Stanlake Samkange, a historian who wrote on the wars of dispossession, became that country's first novelist in English. Charles Mungoshi has been the most sustained voice in Zimbabwean literature, followed by Chenjerai Hove and Dambudzo Marechera. Zimbabwe's other literary languages are Shona and Ndebele.

David Rubadiri was the first writer of note to emerge from Malawi. His poetry was preoccupied with colonial occupation and the demise of ancient African kingdoms. The oppression that followed the attainment of "flag independence" (independence in name only) in Malawi produced censorship as rigid as that of apartheid in South Africa. The political climate lent itself to poetry: the writers steered from the explicit medium of prose to the implicit language of poetry. The work of Jack Mapanje employs images and motifs from orature to make incisive criticism of the oppressive regime and the neocolonial state in Malawi. Other Malawian poets of note include Felix Mnthali, Steve Chimombe, and Frank Chipasula.

Lusophone (Portuguese-speaking) Africa, whose independence came only after a 1974 military coup in Portugal, saw the harshest form of oppression in Southern Africa, a combination of blatant exploitation and gross neglect. The armed struggle was particularly fierce in Angola and Mozambique. Poets of the stature of José Craveirinho worked, as did other celebrated writers, in concert with the Movement for the Liberation of Mozambique — better known by its Portuguese acronym FRELIMO. Agostinho Neto, Angola's first African president, was also the leader of the People's Movement for the Liberation of Angola — the MPLA. These writers reflect the collective aspirations of the African people in their respective countries.

NEOCOLONIALISM AND POSTCOLONIALISM

The literature of celebration that came with independence was short-lived; it gave way to the literature of disillusionment. What had gone wrong? At the onset of independence, governments came to power that sought to create a new sense of nationhood from the myriad ethnic groups that characterize nearly every African "nation." There seemed to be a general consensus that, left to chart its own course, the continent would fragment into a multitude of tribal factions. Tribalism was thus identified as an enemy to unity, and therefore an obstacle to progress.

The emergence of one-party states in Africa was justified in the name of nationhood. Slogans such as "One Zambia, One Nation" expressed the sentiments of the day. The objectives seemed, indeed, noble. Development would come about only if the people of each nation worked in communal fashion for the economic well-being of all.

For many of the new states, the enemy to progress that soon emerged was not tribalism but corruption, which could not be resolved by simply adopting a one-party state after the fashion of Eastern Europe. Arguments were advanced advocating government by decree. African nations were in need of benevolent dictators, it was said. The spate of coups that swept across the continent was welcomed by some as the solution to the problem of corruption. Soon it became manifestly clear, however, that the military regimes were themselves not immune to corruption. If anything, they dipped their long fingers into the national tills with brazen impunity. What was definitely missing was accountability.

It became evident, too, that yesterday's heroes of the liberation struggle had become today's oppressors. The new leaders, whether civilian or military, had stepped into the shoes and donned the uniforms of the retiring colonial officers. Something else had become obvious: the colonialists had walked out through the front door and crept back through the side entrance.

Africa had simply acquired flag independence. President Kwame Nkrumah, who had led Ghana to independence, had been wrong in pronouncing to his people: "Seek ye first the political kingdom and all else will be given unto you." Leopold Sedar Senghor, Senegal's first president, had been equally wrong in proposing that cultural affirmation would be the driving force to liberation. There was a new force in the land, neatly camouflaged but just as devastating: neocolonialism. Africa's new rulers had become a buffer caste in the service of Western corporate interests. Flag independence, African countries came to realize, was not synonymous with economic independence.

Literary responses to neocolonialism, like the political battles fought since independence, reflect the second generation of struggles for self-determination upon which the citizens of most African states have embarked. Their goal is to resolve the crisis of legitimacy that plagues Africa between the people and the mechanisms and power of the state, a crisis largely inherited from the colonial period and exacerbated by graft from the independence era.

As we approach the twenty-first century, Africa faces grave problems. Though it emerged fairly recently from colonialism in the 1960s, almost everywhere in Africa the dreams of independence belong to a fast fading past. Wars, drought, famine, corruption, demagoguery, and every conceivable social, political, and economic disaster have ravaged the continent. For many, the euphoria of yesterday has given way to despair.

Postcolonialism in African society, as in most formerly colonized areas, remains an ideal, like democracy and socialism. It is a process and not a finished product; it is utopian even and remains in a formative phase. For now in Africa it is proving as elusive as nationhood itself.

Studying the quest for postcolonialism in African society, however, brings to mind the task ahead for all humanity in our post–cold war era: to create the foundation for a global village with social and economic justice, international law, and a sustainable environment for the twenty-first century — in short, the only world order that makes sense.

African writers reflect this challenge and join in the quest for solutions. As Africans from the Portuguese-speaking countries say: *a luta continua* — the struggle continues.

Mbulelo Mzamane

FOR FURTHER READING

Primary Works

Achebe, Chinua. *Things Fall Apart*. New York: Fawcett, 1959.

———. *No Longer at Ease*. New York: Fawcett, 1960.

———. *Anthills of the Savannah*. New York: Anchor, 1987.

———. *Hopes and Impediments*. New York: Doubleday, 1989.

Aidoo, Ama Ata. *No Sweetness Here*. Garden City, NY: Doubleday, 1972.

———. *Changes: A Love Story*. New York: Feminist Press, 1993.

Gordimer, Nadine. *Selected Stories*. New York: Viking, 1976.

———. *A Sport of Nature*. New York, Knopf, 1987.

———. *My Son's Story*. New York: Farrar Strauss Giroux, 1990.

Head, Bessie. *The Collector of Treasures.* London: Heinemann, 1977.

———. *Tales of Tenderness.* London: Heinemann, 1989.

———. *A Woman Alone.* London: Heinemann, 1990.

Mapanje, Jack. *Of Chameleons and Gods.* London: Heinemann, 1981.

———. *The Chattering Wagtails of Mikuyu Prison.* London: Heinemann, 1994.

Ndebele, Njabulo Simakahle. *Fools and Other Stories.* London: Readers International, 1986.

Ngugi wa Thiong'o. *Weep Not Child.* New York: Collier Books, 1969.

———. *Decolonising the Mind: The Politics of Language in African Literature.* Portsmouth, N.H.: Heinemann, 1986.

———. *Matigari.* Portsmouth, N.H.: Heinemann, 1987.

Ousmane, Sembene. *God's Bits of Wood.* Garden City, NY: Anchor, 1970.

———. *Tribal Scars.* Portsmouth, N.H.: Heinemann, 1987.

Okara, Gabriel. *The Voice.* London: Heinemann, 1964.

———. *The Fisherman's Invocation.* London: Heinemann.

p'Bitek, Okot. *Song of Lawino and Song of Okol.* Portsmouth, N.H.: Heinemann, 1984.

Senghor, Leopold Sedar. *Collected Poetry.* Charlottesville: University Press of Virginia, 1991.

Soyinka, Wole. *The Interpreters.* Portsmouth, N.H.: Heinemann, 1970.

———. *Death and the King's Horseman.* New York: Norton, 1975.

———. *Myth, Literature and the African Worldview.* New York: Cambridge University Press, 1976.

Secondary Works

Moore, Geraldo. *Twelve African Writers.* London: Fabver, 1974.

Nkosi, Lewis. *Tasks and Masks: Themes and Styles in African Literature.* London: Heinemann, 1981.

Gikandi, Simon. *Reading the African Novel.* Portsmouth, N.H.: Heinemann, 1987.

Mortimer, Mildred. *Journeys Through the French African Novel.* Portsmouth, N.H.: Heinemann, 1990.

Ngara, Emmanuel. *Ideology and Form in African Poetry.* Portsmouth, N.H.: Heinemann, 1990.

AGOSTINHO NETO

Agostinho Neto (1922–1979) was born in Angola and studied medicine in Portugal. A militant worker for independence, he served several terms of imprisonment under the Portuguese colonial regime. As president of the People's Movement for the Liberation of Angola, he led his country to independence and became its first president in 1975. He remained president until his death in 1979.

Neto wrote about the plight of the peasants and workers in Angola. His poetry shows them in a state of deprivation, cut off from the simple joys of life and relegated to a destitute world of servitude by the bearers of "Western Civilization." The recurrence of concepts such as dream *and* will *in his work, however, suggests the promise of a richer life and identifies the action necessary to counteract defeatism and escapism and to overcome oppression.*

Night

I live
in the dark quarters of the world
without light, nor life.

Anxious to live,
I walk in the streets   5
feeling my way
leaning into my shapeless dreams,
stumbling into servitude.
        — Dark quarters
        worlds of wretchedness   10
where the will is watered down
and men
are confused with things.
I walk, lurching,
through the unlit   15
unknown streets crowded
with mystery and terror,

I, arm in arm with ghosts,
And the night too is dark.

Translated from the Portuguese
by Marga Holness

Kinaxixi°

I was glad to sit down
On a bench in Kinaxixi
at six o'clock of a hot evening
and just sit there. . . .

Someone would come   5
maybe
to sit beside me

And I would see the black faces
of the people going uptown
in no hurry   10
expressing absence in the
jumbled Kimbundu° they conversed in.

I would see the tired footsteps
of the servants whose fathers also are servants
looking for love here, glory there, wanting   15
something more than drunkenness in every
alcohol

Neither happiness nor hate

After the sun had set
lights would be turned on and I   20
would wander off
thinking that our life after all is simple
too simple
for anyone who is tired and still has to walk.

Translated from the Portuguese
by Marga Holness

Kinaxixi: a working-class residential area in Angola
Kimbundu: a widely spoken language in Angola

African Poetry

Out on the horizon
there are fires
and the dark silhouettes of the beaters
with arms outstretched,
in the air, the green smell of burning palms   5

African poetry

In the street

a line of Bailundu° bearers
tremble under the weight of their load
in the room   10
a mulatto° girl with meek eyes
colors her face with rice powder and rouge
a woman wriggles her hips under a garish cloth
on the bed

a man, sleepless, dreams   15
of buying knives and forks so he can eat at table
in the sky the glow
of fires

and the silhouette of black men dancing
with arms outstretched   20
in the air, the hot music of marimbas

African poetry

and in the street the bearers
in the room the mulatto girl
on the bed the man, sleepless   25

the burnings consume
consume
the hot earth with horizons afire.

Translated from the Portuguese
by Marga Holness

Bailundu: an ethnic group in Angola who speak Kimbundu
mulatto: a person having mixed white and black ancestry

Western Civilizations

Sheets of tin nailed to posts
driven in the ground
make up the house.

Some rags complete
the intimate landscape.   5

The sun slanting through cracks
welcomes the owner.

After twelve hours of slave
labor

breaking rock   10
shifting rock
breaking rock
shifting rock
fair weather
wet weather   15
breaking rock
shifting rock

Old age comes early
a mat on dark nights
is enough when he dies   20
gratefully
of hunger.

Translated from the Portuguese
by Marga Holness

BOTSWANA

BESSIE HEAD

Bessie Head (1937–1986) was born in Pietermaritzburg, South Africa, of a white mother who was placed in a mental asylum soon after, and a black father. She was raised in an orphanage and educated through money that her mother left her. Trained as a teacher, she worked for a short while as a journalist before leaving South Africa permanently in 1963 to live in Serowe, Botswana. She became a naturalized citizen of Botswana.

The opening of the story — "The long-term central state prison in the south . . ." — suggests South Africa, although the setting of "The Collector of Treasures" and of most of Head's work is Botswana. She deals with women's creativity and their marginalized position in society. Botswana's independence may have benefited many men, but it has failed to improve the lot of most women. The magnitude of the problem calls for drastic measures — some may feel that the measures adopted in the story are too drastic. Certainly, the story shows that a "second generation" of struggles, led by women, is under way.

The Collector of Treasures

The long-term central state prison in the south was a whole day's journey away from the villages of the northern part of the country. They had left the village of Puleng° at about nine that morning and all day long the police truck droned as it sped southwards on the wide, dusty cross-country track-road. The everyday world of ploughed fields, grazing cattle, and vast expanses of bush and forest seemed indifferent to the hungry eyes of the prisoner who gazed out at them through the wire mesh grating at the back of the police truck. At some point during the journey, the prisoner seemed to strike at some ultimate source of pain and loneliness within her being and, overcome by it, she slowly crumpled forward in a wasted heap, oblivious to everything but her pain. Sunset swept by, then dusk, then dark and still the truck droned on, impersonally, uncaring.

At first, faintly on the horizon, the orange glow of the city lights of the

---

Puleng: a village in Botswana

new independence town of Gaborone,° appeared like an astonishing phantom in the overwhelming darkness of the bush, until the truck struck tarred roads, neon lights, shops and cinemas, and made the bush a phantom amidst a blaze of light. All this passed untimed, unwatched by the crumpled prisoner; she did not stir as the truck finally droned to a halt outside the prison gates. The torchlight struck the side of her face like an agonising blow. Thinking she was asleep, the policeman called out briskly:

'You must awaken now. We have arrived.'

He struggled with the lock in the dark and pulled open the grating. She crawled painfully forward, in silence.

Together, they walked up a short flight of stairs and waited awhile as the man tapped lightly, several times, on the heavy iron prison door. The night-duty attendant opened the door a crack, peered out and then opened the door a little wider for them to enter. He quietly and casually led the way to a small office, looked at his colleague and asked: 'What do we have here?'

'It's the husband murder case from Puleng village,' the other replied, handing over a file.

The attendant took the file and sat down at a table on which lay open a large record book. In a big, bold scrawl he recorded the details: Dikeledi Mokopi. Charge: Man-slaughter. Sentence: Life. A night-duty wardress appeared and led the prisoner away to a side cubicle, where she was asked to undress.

'Have you any money on you?' the wardress queried, handing her a plain, green cotton dress which was the prison uniform. The prisoner silently shook her head.

'So, you have killed your husband, have you?' the wardress remarked, with a flicker of humour. 'You'll be in good company. We have four other women here for the same crime. It's becoming the fashion these days. Come with me,' and she led the way along a corridor, turned left and stopped at an iron gate which she opened with a key, waited for the prisoner to walk in ahead of her and then locked it with the key again. They entered a small, immensely high-walled courtyard. On one side were toilets, showers, and a cupboard. On the other, an empty concrete quadrangle. The wardress walked to the cupboard, unlocked it and took out a thick roll of clean-smelling blankets which she handed to the prisoner. At the lower end of the walled courtyard was a heavy iron door which led to the cell. The wardress walked up to this door, banged on it loudly and called out: 'I say, will you women in there light your candle?'

A voice within called out: 'All right,' and they could hear the scratch-scratch of a match. The wardress again inserted a key, opened the door and watched for a while as the prisoner spread out her blankets on the

Gaborone: the capital of Botswana

floor. The four women prisoners already confined in the cell sat up briefly, and stared silently at their new companion. As the door was locked, they all greeted her quietly and one of the women asked: 'Where do you come from?'

'Puleng', the newcomer replied, and seemingly satisfied with that, the light was blown out and the women lay down to continue their interrupted sleep. And as though she had reached the end of her destination, the new prisoner too fell into a deep sleep as soon as she had pulled her blankets about her.

The breakfast gong sounded at six the next morning. The women stirred themselves for their daily routine. They stood up, shook out their blankets and rolled them up into neat bundles. The day-duty wardress rattled the key in the lock and let them out into the small concrete courtyard so that they could perform their morning toilet. Then, with a loud clatter of pails and plates, two male prisoners appeared at the gate with breakfast. The men handed each woman a plate of porridge and a mug of black tea and they settled themselves on the concrete floor to eat. They turned and looked at their new companion and one of the women, a spokesman for the group said kindly:

'You should take care. The tea has no sugar in it. What we usually do is scoop the sugar off the porridge and put it into the tea.'

The woman, Dikeledi, looked up and smiled. She had experienced such terror during the awaiting-trial period that she looked more like a skeleton than a human being. The skin creaked tautly over her cheeks. The other woman smiled, but after her own fashion. Her face permanently wore a look of cynical, whimsical humour. She had a full, plump figure. She introduced herself and her companions: 'My name is Kebonye. Then that's Otsetswe, Galeboe, and Monwana. What may your name be?'

'Dikeledi Mokopi.'

'How is it that you have such a tragic name,' Kebonye observed. 'Why did your parents have to name you *tears*?'

'My father passed away at that time and it is my mother's tears that I am named after,' Dikeledi said, then added: 'She herself passed away six years later and I was brought up by my uncle.'

Kebonye shook her head sympathetically, slowly raising a spoonful of porridge to her mouth. That swallowed, she asked next:

'And what may your crime be?'

'I have killed my husband.'

'We are all here for the same crime,' Kebonye said, then with her cynical smile asked: 'Do you feel any sorrow about the crime?'

'Not really,' the other woman replied.

'How did you kill him?'

'I cut off all his special parts with a knife,' Dikeledi said.

'I did it with a razor,' Kebonye said. She sighed and added: 'I have had a troubled life.'

A little silence followed while they all busied themselves with their food, they Kebonye continued musingly:

'Our men do not think that we need tenderness and care. You know, my husband used to kick me between the legs when he wanted that. I once aborted with a child, due to this treatment. I could see that there was no way to appeal to him if I felt ill, so I once said to him that if he liked he could keep some other woman as well because I couldn't manage to satisfy all his needs. Well, he was an education-officer and each year he used to suspend about seventeen male teachers for making school girls pregnant, but he used to do the same. The last time it happened the parents of the girl were very angry and came to report the matter to me. I told them: "You leave it to me. I have seen enough." And so I killed him.'

They sat in silence and completed their meal, then they took their plates and cups to rinse them in the wash-room. The wardress produced some pails and a broom. Their sleeping quarters had to be flushed out with water; there was not a speck of dirt anywhere, but that was prison routine. All that was left was an inspection by the director of the prison. Here again Kebonye turned to the newcomer and warned:

'You must be careful when the chief comes to inspect. He is mad about one thing — attention! Stand up straight! Hands at your sides! If this is not done you should see how he stands here and curses. He does not mind anything but that. He is mad about that.'

Inspection over, the women were taken through a number of gates to an open, sunny yard, fenced in by high, barbed-wire where they did their daily work. The prison was a rehabilitation centre where the prisoners produced goods which were sold in the prison store; the women produced garments of cloth and wool; the men did carpentry, shoe-making, brick-making, and vegetable production.

Dikeledi had a number of skills — she could knit, sew, and weave baskets. All the women at present were busy knitting woollen garments; some were learners and did their work slowly and painstakingly. They looked at Dikeledi with interest as she took a ball of wool and a pair of knitting needles and rapidly cast on stitches. She had soft, caressing, almost boneless hands of strange power — work of a beautiful design grew from those hands. By mid-morning she had completed the front part of a jersey and they all stopped to admire the pattern she had invented in her own head.

'You are a gifted person,' Kebonye remarked, admiringly.

'All my friends say so,' Dikeledi replied smiling. 'You know, I am the woman whose thatch does not leak. Whenever my friends wanted to thatch their huts, I was there. They would never do it without me. I was always busy and employed because it was with these hands that I fed and reared my children. My husband left me after four years of marriage but I managed well enough to feed those mouths. If people did not pay me in money for my work, they paid me with gifts of food.'

'It's not so bad here,' Kebonye said. 'We get a little money saved for us out of the sale of our work, and if you work like that you can still produce money for your children. How many children do you have?'

'I have three sons.'

'Are they in good care?'

'Yes.'

'I like lunch,' Kebonye said, oddly turning the conversation. 'It is the best meal of the day. We get samp° and meat and vegetables.'

So the day passed pleasantly enough with chatter and work and at sunset the women were once more taken back to the cell for lock-up time. They unrolled their blankets and prepared their beds, and with the candle lit continued to talk a while longer. Just as they were about to retire for the night, Dikeledi nodded to her new-found friend, Kebonye:

'Thank you for all your kindness to me' she said, softly.

'We must help each other,' Kebonye replied, with her amused, cynical smile. 'This is a terrible world. There is only misery here.'

And so the woman Dikeledi began phase three of a life that had been ashen in its loneliness and unhappiness. And yet she had always found gold amidst the ash, deep loves that had joined her heart to the hearts of others. She smiled tenderly at Kebonye because she knew already that she had found another such love. She was the collector of such treasures.

There were really only two kinds of men in the society. The one kind created such misery and chaos that he could be broadly damned as evil. If one watched the village dogs chasing a bitch on heat, they usually moved around in packs of four or five. As the mating progressed one dog would attempt to gain dominance over the festivities and oust all the others from the bitch's vulva. The rest of the hapless dogs would stand around yapping and snapping in its face while the top dog indulged in a continuous spurt of orgasms, day and night until he was exhausted. No doubt, during that Herculean feat, the dog imagined he was the only penis in the world and that there had to be a scramble for it. That kind of man lived near the animal level and behaved just the same. Like the dogs and bulls and donkeys, he also accepted no responsibility for the young he procreated and like the dogs and bulls and donkeys, he also made females abort. Since that kind of man was in the majority in the society, he needed a little analysing as he was responsible for the complete breakdown of family life. He could be analysed over three time-spans. In the old days, before the colonial invasion of Africa, he was a man who lived by the traditions and taboos outlined for all the people by the forefathers of the tribe. He had little individual freedom to assess whether these traditions were compassionate or not — they demanded that he comply and obey the rules, without thought. But when the laws of the ancestors are examined,

samp: coarse, hulled corn; a Southern African staple dish

they appear on the whole to have been vast, external disciplines for the good of the society as a whole, with little attention given to individual preferences and needs. The ancestors made so many errors and one of the most bitter-making things was that they relegated to men a superior position in the tribe, while women were regarded, in a congenital sense, as being an inferior form of human life. To this day, women still suffered from all the calamities that befall an inferior form of human life. The colonial era and the period of migratory mining labour to South Africa was a further affliction visited on this man. It broke the hold of the ancestors. It broke the old, traditional form of family life and for long periods a man was separated from his wife and children while he worked for a pittance in another land in order to raise the money to pay his British Colonial poll-tax.° British Colonialism scarcely enriched his life. He then became 'the boy' of the white man and a machine-tool of the South African mines. African independence seemed merely one more affliction on top of the afflictions that had visited this man's life. Independence° suddenly and dramatically changed the pattern of colonial subservience. More jobs became available under the new government's localization programme and salaries sky-rocketed at the same time. It provided the first occasion for family life of a new order, above the childlike discipline of custom, the degradation of colonialism. Men and women, in order to survive, had to turn inwards to their own resources. It was the man who arrived at this turning point, a broken wreck with no inner resources at all. It was as though he was hideous to himself and in an effort to flee his own inner emptiness, he spun away from himself in a dizzy kind of death dance of wild destruction and dissipation.

One such man was Garesego Mokopi, the husband of Dikeledi. For four years prior to independence, he had worked as a clerk in the district administration service, at a steady salary of R50.00° a month. Soon after independence his salary shot up to R200.00 per month. Even during his lean days he had had a taste for womanising and drink; now he had the resources for a real spree. He was not seen at home again and lived and slept around the village, from woman to woman. He left his wife and three sons — Banabothe, the eldest, aged four; Inalame, aged three; and the youngest, Motsomi, aged one — to their own resources. Perhaps he did so because she was the boring, semi-literate traditional sort, and there were a lot of exciting new women around. Independence produced marvels indeed.

There was another kind of man in the society with the power to create himself anew. He turned all his resources, both emotional and material,

British colonial poll-tax: a tax charged per head of family in British colonies
independence: from British colonial rule in 1966
R50.00: Fifty rand, South African currency, also used in Botswana until the introduction of the country's own currency

towards his family life and he went on and on with his own quiet rhythm, like a river. He was a poem of tenderness.

One such man was Paul Thebolo and he and his wife, Kenalepe, and their three children, came to live in the village of Puleng in 1966, the year of independence. Paul Thebolo had been offered the principalship of a primary school in the village. They were allocated an empty field beside the yard of Dikeledi Mokopi, for their new home.

Neighbours are the centre of the universe to each other. They help each other at all times and mutually loan each other's goods. Dikeledi Mokopi kept an interested eye on the yard of her new neighbours. At first, only the man appeared with some workmen to erect the fence, which was set up with incredible speed and efficiency. The man impressed her immediately when she went around to introduce herself and find out a little about the newcomers. He was tall, large-boned, slow-moving. He was so peaceful as a person that the sunlight and shadow played all kinds of tricks with his eyes, making it difficult to determine their exact colour. When he stood still and looked reflective, the sunlight liked to creep into his eyes and nestle there; so sometimes his eyes were the colour of shade, and sometimes light brown.

He turned and smiled at her in a friendly way when she introduced herself and explained that he and his wife were on transfer from the village of Bobonong. His wife and children were living with relatives in the village until the yard was prepared. He was in a hurry to settle down as the school term would start in a month's time. They were, he said, going to erect two mud huts first and later he intended setting up a small house of bricks. His wife would be coming around in a few days with some women to erect the mud walls of the huts.

'I would like to offer my help too,' Dikeledi said. 'If work always starts early in the morning and there are about six of us, we can get both walls erected in a week. If you want one of the huts done in woman's thatch, all my friends know that I am the woman whose thatch does not leak.'

The man smilingly replied that he would impart all this information to his wife, then he added charmingly that he thought she would like his wife when they met. His wife was a very friendly person; everyone liked her.

Dikeledi walked back to her own yard with a high heart. She had few callers. None of her relatives called for fear that since her husband had left her she would become dependent on them for many things. The people who called did business with her; they wanted her to make dresses for their children or knit jerseys for the winter time and at times when she had no orders at all, she made baskets which she sold. In these ways she supported herself and the three children but she was lonely for true friends.

All turned out as the husband had said — he had a lovely wife. She was fairly tall and thin with a bright, vivacious manner. She made no effort to conceal that normally, and every day, she was a very happy person. And all turned out as Dikeledi had said. The work-party of six women erected the mud walls of the huts in one week; two weeks later, the thatch was complete. The Thebolo family moved into their new abode and Dikeledi Mokopi moved into one of the most prosperous and happy periods of her life. Her life took a big, wide upward curve. Her relationship with the Thebolo family was more than the usual friendly exchange of neighbours. It was rich and creative.

It was not long before the two women had going one of those deep, affectionate, sharing-everything kind of friendships that only women know how to have. It seemed that Kenalepe wanted endless amounts of dresses made for herself and her three little girls. Since Dikeledi would not accept cash for these services — she protested about the many benefits she received from her good neighbours — Paul Thebolo arranged that she be paid in household goods for these services so that for some years Dikeledi was always assured of her basic household needs — the full bag of corn, sugar, tea, powdered milk, and cooking oil. Kenalepe was also the kind of woman who made the whole world spin around her; her attractive personality attracted a whole range of women to her yard and also a whole range of customers for her dressmaking friend, Dikeledi. Eventually, Dikeledi became swamped with work, was forced to buy a second sewing-machine and employ a helper. The two women did everything together — they were forever together at weddings, funerals, and parties in the village. In their leisure hours they freely discussed all their intimate affairs with each other, so that each knew thoroughly the details of the other's life.

'You are a lucky someone,' Dikeledi remarked one day, wistfully. 'Not everyone has the gift of a husband like Paul.'

'Oh yes,' Kenalepe said happily. 'He is an honest somebody.' She knew a little of Dikeledi's list of woes and queried: 'But why did you marry a man like Garesego? I looked carefully at him when you pointed him out to me near the shops the other day and I could see at one glance that he is a butterfly.'

'I think I mostly wanted to get out of my uncle's yard,' Dikeledi replied. 'I never liked my uncle. Rich as he was, he was a hard man and very selfish. I was only a servant there and pushed about. I went there when I was six years old when my mother died, and it was not a happy life. All his children despised me because I was their servant. Uncle paid for my education for six years, then he said I must leave school. I longed for more because as you know, education opens up the world for one. Garesego was a friend of my uncle and he was the only man who proposed for me. They discussed it between themselves and then my uncle said: "You'd better marry Garesego because you're just hanging around here like a chain on my neck." I agreed, just to get away from that terrible man. Garesego said at that time that he'd rather be married to my sort than the educated kind because those women were stubborn and wanted to lay down the rules for men. Really, I did not ever protest when he started running about. You know what the other women do. They chase after the man from one hut to another and beat up the girlfriends. The man just runs into another hut, that's all. So you don't really win. I wasn't going to do anything like that. I am satisfied I have children. They are a blessing to me.'

'Oh, it isn't enough,' her friend said, shaking her head in deep sympathy. 'I am amazed at how life imparts its gifts. Some people get too much. Others get nothing at all. I have always been lucky in life. One day my parents will visit — they live in the south — and you'll see the fuss they make over me. Paul is just the same. He takes care of everything so that I never have a day of worry . . .'

The man Paul, attracted as wide a range of male friends as his wife. They had guests every evening; illiterate men who wanted him to fill tax forms or write letters for them, or his own colleagues who wanted to debate the political issues of the day — there was always something new happening every day now that the country had independence. The two women sat on the edge of these debates and listened with fascinated ears, but they never participated. The following day they would chew over the debates with wise, earnest expressions.

'Men's minds travel widely and boldly,' Kenalepe would comment. 'It makes me shiver the way they freely criticise our new government. Did you hear what Petros said last night? He said he knew all those bastards and they were just a lot of crooks who would pull a lot of dirty tricks. Oh dear! I shivered so much when he said that. The way they talk about the government makes you feel in your bones that this is not a safe world to be in, not like the old days when we didn't have governments. And Lentswe said that ten per cent of the population in England really control all the wealth of the country, while the rest live at starvation level. And he said communism would sort all this out. I gathered from the way they discussed this matter that our government is not in favour of communism. I trembled so much when this became clear to me . . .' She paused and laughed proudly. 'I've heard Paul say this several times: "The British only ruled us for eighty years." I wonder why Paul is so fond of saying that?'

And so a completely new world opened up for Dikeledi. It was so impossibly rich and happy that, as the days went by, she immersed herself more deeply in it and quite overlooked the barrenness of her own life. But it hung there like a nagging ache in the mind of her friend, Kenalepe.

'You ought to find another man,' she urged one day, when they had one of their personal discussions. 'It's not good for a woman to live alone.'

'And who would that be?' Dikeledi asked, disillusioned. 'I'd only be bringing trouble into my life whereas now it is all in order. I have my eldest son at school and I can manage to pay the school fees. That's all I really care about.'

'I mean,' said Kenalepe, 'we are also here to make love and enjoy it.'

'Oh I never really cared for it,' the other replied. 'When you experience the worst of it, it just puts you off altogether.'

'What do you mean by that?' Kenalepe asked, wide-eyed.

'I mean it was just jump on and jump off and I used to wonder what it was all about. I developed a dislike for it.'

'You mean Garesego was like that!' Kenalepe said, flabbergasted. 'Why, that's just like a cock hopping from hen to hen. I wonder what he is doing with all those women. I'm sure they are just after his money and so they flatter him . . . ' She paused and then added earnestly: 'That's really all the more reason you should find another man. Oh, if you knew what it was really like, you would long for it, I can tell you! I sometimes think I enjoy that side of life far too much. Paul knows a lot about all that. And he always has some new trick with which to surprise me. He has a certain way of smiling when he has thought up something new and I shiver a little and say to myself: "Ha, what is Paul going to do tonight!"'

Kenalepe paused and smiled at her friend, slyly.

'I can loan Paul to you if you like,' she said, then raised one hand to block the protest on her friend's face. 'I would do it because I have never had a friend like you in my life before whom I trust so much. Paul had other girls you know, before he married me, so it's not such an uncommon thing to him. Besides, we used to make love long before we got married and I never got pregnant. He takes care of that side too. I wouldn't mind loaning him because I am expecting another child and I don't feel so well these days . . . '

Dikeledi stared at the ground for a long moment, then she looked up at her friend with tears in her eyes.

'I cannot accept such a gift from you,' she said, deeply moved. 'But if you are ill I will wash for you and cook for you.'

Not put off by her friend's refusal of her generous offer, Kenalepe mentioned the discussion to her husband that very night. He was so taken off-guard by the unexpectedness of the subject that at first he looked slightly astonished, and burst out into loud laughter and for such a lengthy time that he seemed unable to stop.

'Why are you laughing like that?' Kenalepe asked, surprised.

He laughed a bit more, then suddenly turned very serious and thoughtful and was lost in his own thoughts for some time. When she asked him what he was thinking he merely replied: 'I don't want to tell you everything. I want to keep some of my secrets to myself.'

The next day Kenalepe reported this to her friend.

'Now whatever does he mean by that? I want to keep some of my secrets to myself?'

'I think,' Dikeledi said smiling, 'I think he has a conceit about being a good man. Also, when someone loves someone too much, it hurts them to say so. They'd rather keep silent.'

Shortly after this Kenalepe had a miscarriage and had to be admitted to hospital for a minor operation. Dikeledi kept her promise 'to wash and cook' for her friend. She ran both their homes, fed the children and kept everything in order. Also, people complained about the poorness of the hospital diet and each day she scoured the village for eggs and chicken, cooked them, and took them to Kenalepe every day at the lunch-hour.

One evening Dikeledi ran into a snag with her routine. She had just dished up supper for the Thebolo children when a customer came around with an urgent request for an alteration on a wedding dress. The wedding was to take place the next day. She left the children seated around the fire eating and returned to her own home. An hour later, her own children asleep and settled, she thought she would check the Thebolo yard to see if all was well there. She entered the children's hut and noted that they had put themselves to bed and were fast asleep. Their supper plates lay scattered and unwashed around the fire. The hut which Paul and Kenalepe shared was in darkness. It meant that Paul had not yet returned from his usual evening visit to his wife. Dikeledi collected the plates and washed them, then poured the dirty dishwater on the still-glowing embers of the outdoor fire. She piled the plates one on top of the other and carried them to the third additional hut which was used as a kitchen. Just then Paul Thebolo entered the yard, noted the lamp and movement in the kitchen hut and walked over to it. He paused at the open door.

'What are you doing now, Mma-Banabothe?'° he asked, addressing her affectionately in the customary way by the name of her eldest son, Banabothe.

'I know quite well what I am doing,' Dikeledi replied happily. She turned around to say that it was not a good thing to leave dirty dishes standing overnight but her mouth flew open with surprise. Two soft pools of cool liquid light were in his eyes and something infinitely sweet passed between them; it was too beautiful to be love.

'You are a very good woman, Mma-Banabothe,' he said softly.

It was the truth and the gift was offered like a nugget of gold. Only men like Paul Thebolo could offer such gifts. She took it and stored another treasure in her heart. She bowed her knee in the traditional curtsey and walked quietly away to her own home.

Eight years passed for Dikeledi in a quiet rhythm of work and friendship with the Thebolo's. The crisis came with the eldest son, Banabothe. He had to take his primary school leaving examination at the end of the year. This serious event sobered him up considerably as like all boys he

Mma-Banabothe: mother of Banabothe

was very fond of playtime. He brought his books home and told his mother that he would like to study in the evenings. He would like to pass with a 'Grade A' to please her. With a flushed and proud face Dikeledi mentioned this to her friend, Kenalepe.

'Banabothe is studying every night now,' she said. 'He never really cared for studies. I am so pleased about this that I bought him a spare lamp and removed him from the children's hut to my own hut where things will be peaceful for him. We both sit up late at night now. I sew on buttons and fix hems and he does his studies . . .'

She also opened a savings account at the post office in order to have some standby money to pay the fees for his secondary education. They were rather high — R85.oo. But in spite of all her hoarding of odd cents, towards the end of the year, she was short on R2o.oo to cover the fees. Midway during the Christmas school holidays the results were announced. Banabothe passed with a 'Grade A'. His mother was almost hysterical in her joy at his achievement. But what to do? The two youngest sons had already started primary school and she would never manage to cover all their fees from her resources. She decided to remind Garesego Mokopi that he was the father of the children. She had not seen him in eight years except as a passer-by in the village. Sometimes he waved but he had never talked to her or enquired about her life or that of the children. It did not matter. She was a lower form of human life. Then this unpleasant something turned up at his office one day, just as he was about to leave for lunch. She had heard from village gossip, that he had eventually settled down with a married woman who had a brood of children of her own. He had ousted her husband, in a typical village sensation of brawls, curses, and abuse. Most probably the husband did not care because there were always arms outstretched towards a man, as long as he looked like a man. The attraction of this particular woman for Garesego Mokopi, so her former lovers said with a snicker, was that she went in for heady forms of love-making like biting and scratching.

Garesego Mokopi walked out of his office and looked irritably at the ghost from his past, his wife. She obviously wanted to talk to him and he walked towards her, looking at his watch all the while. Like all the new 'success men', he had developed a paunch, his eyes were blood-shot, his face was bloated, and the odour of the beer and sex from the previous night clung faintly around him. He indicated with his eyes that they should move around to the back of the office block where they could talk in privacy.

'You must hurry with whatever you want to say,' he said impatiently. 'The lunch-hour is very short and I have to be back at the office by two.'

Not to him could she talk of the pride she felt in Banabothe's achievement, so she said simply and quietly: 'Garesego, I beg you to help me pay Banabothe's fees for secondary school. He has passed with a "Grade A" and as you know, the school fees must be produced on the first day of school or else he will be turned away. I have struggled to save money the whole year but I am short by R20.00.'

She handed him her post office savings book, which he took, glanced at and handed back to her. Then he smiled, a smirky know-all smile, and thought he was delivering her a blow in the face.

'Why don't you ask Paul Thebolo for the money?' he said. 'Everyone knows he's keeping two homes and that you are his spare. Everyone knows about that full bag of corn he delivers to your home every six months so why can't he pay the school fees as well?'

She neither denied this, nor confirmed it. The blow glanced off her face which she raised slightly, in pride. Then she walked away.

As was their habit, the two women got together that afternoon and Dikeledi reported this conversation with her husband to Kenalepe who tossed back her head in anger and said fiercely: 'The filthy pig himself! He thinks every man is like him, does he? I shall report this matter to Paul, then he'll see something.'

And indeed Garesego did see something but it was just up his alley. He was a female prostitute in his innermost being and like all professional prostitutes, he enjoyed publicity and sensation — it promoted his cause. He smiled genially and expansively when a madly angry Paul Thebolo came up to the door of his house where he lived with *his* concubine. Garesego had been through a lot of these dramas over those eight years and he almost knew by rote the dialogue that would follow.

'You bastard!' Paul Thebolo spat out. 'Your wife isn't my concubine, do you hear?'

'Then why are you keeping her in food?' Garesego drawled. 'Men only do that for women they fuck! They never do it for nothing.'

Paul Thebolo rested one hand against the wall, half dizzy with anger, and he said tensely: 'You defile life, Garesego Mokopi. There's nothing else in your world but defilement. Mma-Banabothe makes clothes for my wife and children and she will never accept money from me so how else must I pay her?'

'It only proves the story both ways,' the other replied, vilely. 'Women do that for men who fuck them.'

Paul Thebolo shot out the other hand, punched him soundly in one grinning eye and walked away. Who could hide a livid, swollen eye? To every surprised enquiry, he replied with an injured air:

'It was done by my wife's lover, Paul Thebolo.'

It certainly brought the attention of the whole village upon him, which was all he really wanted. Those kinds of men were the bottom rung of government. They secretly hungered to be the President with all eyes on them. He worked up the sensation a little further. He announced that he would pay the school fees of the child of his concubine, who was also to enter secondary school, but not the school fees of his own child, Banabothe. People half liked the smear on Paul Thebolo; he was too good to be true. They delighted in making him a part of the general dirt of the village, so they turned on Garesego and scolded: 'Your wife might be getting things from Paul Thebolo but it's beyond the purse of any man to pay the school fees of his own children as well as the school fees of another man's children. Banabothe wouldn't be there had you not procreated him, Garesego, so it is your duty to care for him. Besides, it's your fault if your wife takes another man. You left her alone all these years.'

So that story was lived with for two weeks, mostly because people wanted to say that Paul Thebolo was a part of life too and as uncertain of his morals as they were. But the story took such a dramatic turn that it made all the men shudder with horror. It was some weeks before they could find the courage to go to bed with women; they preferred to do something else.

Garesego's obscene thought processes were his own undoing. He really believed that another man had a stake in his hen-pen and like any cock, his hair was up about it. He thought he'd walk in and re-establish his own claim to it and so, after two weeks, once the swelling in his eye had died down, he espied Banabothe in the village and asked him to take a note to his mother. He said the child should bring a reply. The note read: 'Dear Mother, I am coming home again so that we may settle our differences. Will you prepare a meal for me and some hot water that I might take a bath. Gare.'

Dikeledi took the note, read it and shook with rage. All its overtones were clear to her. He was coming home for some sex. They had had no differences. They had not even talked to each other.

'Banabothe,' she said. 'Will you play nearby? I want to think a bit then I will send you to your father with the reply.'

Her thought processes were not very clear to her. There was something she could not immediately touch upon. Her life had become holy to her during all those years she had struggled to maintain herself and the children. She had filled her life with treasures of kindness and love she had gathered from others and it was all this that she wanted to protect from defilement by an evil man. Her first panic-stricken thought was to gather up the children and flee the village. But where to go? Garesego did not want a divorce, she had left him to approach her about the matter, she had desisted from taking any other man. She turned her thoughts this way and that and could find no way out except to face him. If she wrote back, don't you dare put foot in the yard I don't want to see you, he would ignore it. Black women didn't have that kind of power. A thoughtful, brooding look came over her face. At last, at peace with herself, she went into her hut and wrote a reply: 'Sir, I shall prepare everything as you have said. Dikeledi.'

It was about midday when Banabothe sped back with the reply to his father. All afternoon Dikeledi busied herself making preparations for the appearance of her husband at sunset. At one point Kenalepe approached the yard and looked around in amazement at the massive preparations, the large iron water pot full of water with a fire burning under it, the extra cooking pots on the fire. Only later Kenalepe brought the knife into focus. But it was only a vague blur, a large kitchen knife used to cut meat and Dikeledi knelt at a grinding-stone and sharpened it slowly and methodically. What was in focus then was the final and tragic expression on the upturned face of her friend. It threw her into confusion and blocked their usual free and easy feminine chatter. When Dikeledi said: 'I am making some preparations for Garesego. He is coming home tonight,' Kenalepe beat a hasty retreat to her own home terrified. They knew they were involved because when she mentioned this to Paul he was distracted and uneasy for the rest of the day. He kept on doing upside-down sorts of things, not replying to questions, absent-mindedly leaving a cup of tea until it got quite cold, and every now and again he stood up and paced about, lost in his own thoughts. So deep was their sense of disturbance that towards evening they no longer made a pretence of talking. They just sat in silence in their hut. Then, at about nine o'clock, they heard those wild and agonized bellows. They both rushed out together to the yard of Dikeledi Mokopi.

He came home at sunset and found everything ready for him as he had requested, and he settled himself down to enjoy a man's life. He had brought a pack of beer along and sat outdoors slowly savouring it while every now and then his eye swept over the Thebolo yard. Only the woman and children moved about the yard. The man was out of sight. Garesego smiled to himself, pleased that he could crow as loud as he liked with no answering challenge.

A basin of warm water was placed before him to wash his hands and then Dikeledi served him his meal. At a separate distance she also served the children and then instructed them to wash and prepare for bed. She noted that Garesego displayed no interest in the children whatsoever. He was entirely wrapped up in himself and thought only of himself and his own comfort. Any tenderness he offered the children might have broken her and swerved her mind away from the deed she had carefully planned all that afternoon. She was beneath his regard and notice too for when she eventually brought her own plate of food and sat near him, he never once glanced at her face. He drank his beer and cast his glance every now and again at the Thebolo yard. Not once did the man of the yard appear until it became too dark to distinguish anything any more. He was completely satisfied with that. He could repeat the performance every day until he broke the mettle of the other cock again and forced him into angry abuse. He liked that sort of thing.

'Garesego, do you think you could help me with Banabothe's school fees?' Dikeledi asked at one point.

'Oh, I'll think about it,' he replied casually.

She stood up and carried buckets of water into the hut, which she poured into a large tin bath that he might bathe himself, then while he took his bath she busied herself tidying up and completing the last of the household chores. Those done, she entered the children's hut. They played hard during the day and they had already fallen asleep with exhaustion. She knelt down near their sleeping mats and stared at them for a long while, with an extremely tender expression. Then she blew out their lamp and walked to her own hut. Garesego lay sprawled across the bed in such a manner that indicated he only thought of himself and did not intend sharing the bed with anyone else. Satiated with food and drink, he had fallen into a deep, heavy sleep the moment his head touched the pillow. His concubine had no doubt taught him that the correct way for a man to go to bed, was naked. So he lay, unguarded and defenceless, sprawled across the bed on his back.

The bath made a loud clatter as Dikeledi removed it from the room, but still he slept on, lost to the world. She re-entered the hut and closed the door. Then she bent down and reached for the knife under the bed which she had merely concealed with a cloth. With the precision and skill of her hard-working hands, she grasped hold of his genitals and cut them off with one stroke. In doing so, she slit the main artery which ran on the inside of the groin. A massive spurt of blood arched its way across the bed. And Garesego bellowed. He bellowed his anguish. Then all was silent. She stood and watched his death anguish with an intent and brooding look, missing not one detail of it. A knock on the door stirred her out of her reverie. It was the boy, Banabothe. She opened the door and stared at him, speechless. He was trembling violently.

'Mother,' he said, in a terrified whisper. 'Didn't I hear father cry?'

'I have killed him,' she said, waving her hand in the air with a gesture that said — well, that's that. Then she added sharply: 'Banabothe, go and call the police.'

He turned and fled into the night. A second pair of footsteps followed hard on his heels. It was Kenalepe running back to her own yard, half out of her mind with fear. Out of the dark Paul Thebolo stepped towards the hut and entered it. He took in every detail and then he turned and looked at Dikeledi with such a tortured expression that for a time words failed him. At last he said: 'You don't have to worry about the children, Mma-Banabothe. I'll take them as my own and give them all a secondary school education.'

GHANA ◈

AMA ATA AIDOO

Ama Ata Aidoo (1940–), feminist author and activist, was born in the central region of Ghana. Educated in Ghana and the United States, she taught at universities in Africa and North America. She was formerly an education minister in Ghana. Her work falls into various genres: fiction, drama, and poetry. It deals with social change in Ghana as a result of contact with the West and celebrates the resilience of her culture, especially as embodied in her female characters.

Her story deals with women's subordination in society and their betrayal by men, including sons and lovers. Aidoo does more than lament women's plight, however. In "Something to Talk About on the Way to the Funeral," Aunt Araba is economically self-empowered, and when her strength fails her, a younger woman whom she has trained carries on her legacy. Aidoo's work often employs the techniques of oral storytelling.

Something to Talk About on the Way to the Funeral

. . . Adwoa my sister, when did you come back?

'Last night.'

Did you come specially for Auntie Araba?

'What else, my sister? I just rushed into my room to pick up my *akatado*° when I heard the news. How could I remain another hour in Tarkwa° after getting such news? I arrived in the night.'

And your husband?

'He could not come. You know government-work. You must give notice several days ahead if you want to go away for half of one day. O, and so many other problems. But he will see to all that before next *Akwanbo*.° Then we may both be present for the festival and the libation ceremony if her family plans it for a day around that time.'

---

akatado: an item of clothing
Tarkwa: a place name in Ghana
Akwanbo: a festival

Did you hear the Bosoë dance group, practising the bread song?

'Yes. I hear they are going to make it the chief song at the funeral this afternoon. It is most fitting that they should do that. After all, when the group was formed, Auntie Araba's bread song was the first one they turned into a Bosoë song and danced to.'

Yes, it was a familiar song in those days. Indeed it had been heard around here for over twenty years. First in Auntie Araba's own voice with its delicate thin sweetness that clung like asawa berry on the tongue: which later, much later, had roughened a little. Then all of a sudden, it changed again, completely. Yes, it still was a woman's voice. But it was deeper and this time, like good honey, was rough and heavy, its sweetness within itself.

'Are you talking of when Mansa took over the hawking of the bread?'

Yes. That is how, in fact, that whole little quarter came to be known as *Bosohwe*. Very often, Auntie Araba did not have to carry the bread. The moment the aroma burst out of the oven, children began tugging at their parents' clothes for pennies and threepences. Certainly, the first batch was nearly always in those penny rows. Dozens of them. Of course, the children always caught the aroma before their mothers did.

'Were we not among them?'

We were, my sister. We remember that on market days and other holidays, Auntie Araba's ovenside became a little market-place all by itself. And then there was Auntie Araba herself. She always was a beautiful woman. Even three months ago when they were saying that all her life was gone, I thought she looked better than some of us who claim to be in our prime. If she was a young woman at this time when they are selling beauty to our big men in the towns, she would have made something for herself.

'Though it is a crying shame that young girls should be doing that. As for our big men! Hmm, let me shut my trouble-seeking mouth up. But our big men are something else too. You know, indeed, these our educated big men have never been up to much good.'

Like you know, my sister. After all, was it not a lawyer-or-a-doctor-or-something-like-that who was at the bottom of all Auntie Araba's troubles?

I did not know that, my sister.

Yes, my sister. One speaks of it only in whispers. Let me turn my head and look behind me. . . . And don't go standing in the river telling people. Or if you do, you better not say that you heard it from me.

'How could I do that? Am I a baby?'

Yes, Auntie Araba was always a beauty. My mother says she really was a come-and-have-a-look type, when she was a girl. Her plaits hung at the back of her neck like the branches of a giant tree, while the skin of her arms shone like charcoal from good wood. And since her family is one of these families with always some members abroad, when Auntie

Araba was just about getting ready for her puberty, they sent her to go and stay at A — with some lady relative. That's where she learnt to mess around with flour so well. But after less than four years, they found she was in trouble.

'Eh-eh!'

Eh-eh, my sister. And now bring your ear nearer.

. . . .

'That lawyer-or-doctor-or-something-like-that who was the lady's husband?'

Yes.

'And what did they do about it?'

They did not want to spoil their marriage so they hushed up everything and sent her home quietly. Very quietly. That girl was our own Auntie Araba. And that child is Ato, the big scholar we hear of.

'*Ei*, there are plenty of things in the world's old box to pick up and talk about, my sister.'

You have said it. But be quiet and listen. I have not finished the story. If anything like that had happened to me, my life would have been ruined. Not that there is much to it now. But when Auntie Araba returned home to her mother, she was looking like a ram from the north. Big, beautiful and strong. And her mother did not behave as childishly as some would in a case like this. No, she did not tear herself apart as if the world had fallen down. . . .

'Look at how Mother Kuma treated her daughter. Rained insults on her head daily, refused to give her food and then drove her out of their house. Ah, and look at what the father of Mansa did to her too. . . . '

But isn't this what I am coming to? This is what I am coming to.

'Ah-h-h . . . '

Anyway, Auntie Araba's mother took her daughter in and treated her like an egg until the baby was born. And then did Auntie Araba tighten her girdle and get ready to work? Lord, there is no type of dough of flour they say she has not mixed and fried or baked. *Epitsi! Tatare! Atwemo! Bofrot! Boodo! Boodoo-ngo! Sweetbad° Hei*, she went there and dashed here. But they say that somehow, she was not getting much from these efforts. Some people even say that they landed her in debts.

'But I think someone should have told her that these things are good to eat but they suit more the tastes of the town-dwellers. I myself cannot see any man or woman who spends his living days on the farm, wasting

epitsi: a cake made from plantain, a banana-like plant, that is edible when cooked
tatare: a pancake made from plantain
boodo: a sweet, unleavened corn bread
atwemo: a plain, sugared pastry drawn out in strips and fried in hot oil
boodoo-ngo: a bread made from unleavened cornmeal mixed with palm oil and baked
bofrot: doughnuts
sweetbad: a hard, coconut pastry, baked or fried

his pennies on any of these sweeties which only satisfy the tongue but do not fill the stomach. Our people in the villages might buy *tatare* and *epitsi*, yes, but not the others.'

Like you know, my sister. This is what Auntie Araba discovered, but only after some time. I don't know who advised her to drop all those fancy foods. But she did, and finally started baking bread, ordinary bread. That turned out better for her.

'And how did she come to marry Egya Nyaako?'

They say that she grew in beauty and in strength after her baby was weaned. Good men and rich from all the villages of the state wanted to marry her.

'*Ei*, so soon? Were they prepared to take her with her baby?'

Yes.

'Hmm, a good woman does not rot.'

That is what our fathers said.

'And she chose Egya Nyaako?'

Yes. But then, we should remember that he was a good man himself.

'Yes, he was. I used to be one of those he hired regularly during the cocoa harvests. He never insisted that we press down the cocoa as most of these farmers do. No, he never tried to cheat us out of our fair pay.'

Which is not what I can say of his heir!

'Not from what we've heard about him. A real mean one they say he is.'

So Auntie agreed to marry Egya Nyaako and she and her son came to live here. The boy, this big scholar we now know of, went with the other youngsters to the school the first day they started it here. In the old Wesleyan chapel.° They say she used to say that if she never could sleep her fill, it was because she wanted to give her son a good education.

'*Poo*, pity. And that must have been true. She mixed and rolled her dough far into the night, and with the first cock-crow, got up from bed to light her fires. Except on Sundays.'

She certainly went to church twice every Sunday. She was a good Christian. And yet, look at how the boy turned out and what he did to her.

'Yes? You know I have been away much of the time. And I have never heard much of him to respect. Besides, I only know very little.'

That is the story I am telling you. I am taking you to bird-town so I can't understand why you insist on searching for eggs from the suburb!

'I will not interrupt you again, my sister.'

Maybe, it was because she never had any more children and therefore, Ato became an only child. They say she spoilt him. Though I am not sure I would not have done the same if I had been in her position. But they say that before he was six years old, he was fighting her. And he continued to

---

Wesleyan chapel: a Methodist church, named for its founder, John Wesley

fight her until he became a big scholar. And then his father came to acknowledge him as his son, and it seems that ruined him completely.

'Do you mean that lawyer-or-doctor-or-something-like-that man?'

Himself. They say he and his lady wife never had a male child so when he was finishing Stan' 7° or so, he came to father him.

'*Poo*, scholars!'

It is a shame, my sister. Just when all the big troubles were over.

'If I had been Auntie Araba, eh, I would have charged him about a thousand pounds for neglect.'

But Auntie Araba was not you. They say she was very happy that at last the boy was going to know his real father. She even hoped that that would settle his wild spirits. No, she did not want to make trouble. So this big man from the city came one day with his friends or relatives and met Auntie Araba and her relatives. It was one Sunday afternoon. In two big cars. They say some of her sisters and relatives had sharpened their mouths ready to give him what he deserved. But when they saw all the big men and their big cars, they kept quiet. They murmured among themselves, and that was all. He told them, I mean this new father, that he was going to send Ato to college.

'And did he?'

Yes he did. And he spoilt him even more than his mother had done. He gave him lots of money. I don't know what college he sent him to since I don't know about colleges. But he used to come here to spend some of his holidays. And every time, he left his mother with big debts to pay from his high living. Though I must add that she did not seem to mind.

'You know how mothers are, even when they have got several children.'

But, my sister, she really had a big blow when he put Mansa into trouble. Mansa's father nearly killed her.

'I hear Mansa's father is a proud man who believes that there is nothing which any man from his age group can do which he cannot do better.'

So you know. When school education came here, all his children were too old to go to school except Mansa. And he used to boast that he was only going to feel he had done his best by her when she reached the biggest college in the white man's land.

'And did he have the money?'

Don't ask me. As if I was in his pocket! Whether he had the money or not, he was certainly saying these things. But then people also knew him to add on these occasions, 'let us say it will be good, so it shall be good'. Don't laugh, my sister. Now, you can imagine how he felt when Ato did this to his daughter Mansa. I remember they reported him as saying that

Stan' 7: Standard 7, or seventh grade

he was going to sue Ato for heavy damages. But luckily, Ato just stopped coming here in the holidays. But of course, his mother Auntie Araba was here. And she got something from Mansa's father. And under his very nose was Mansa's own mother. He used to go up and down ranting about some women who had no sense to advise their sons to keep their manhoods between their thighs, until they could afford the consequences of letting them loose, and other mothers who had not the courage to tie their daughters to their mats.

'O Lord.'

Yes, my sister.

'Hmm, I never knew any of these things.'

This is because you have been away in *the Mines* all the time. But me, I have been here. I am one of those who sit in that village waiting for the travellers. But also in connection with this story, I have had the chance to know so much because my husband's family house is in that quarter. I say, Mansa's father never let anyone sleep. And so about the sixth month of Mansa's pregnancy, her mother and Auntie Araba decided to do something about the situation. Auntie Araba would take Mansa in, see her through until the baby was born and then later, they would think about what to do. So Mansa went to live with her. And from that moment, people did not even know how to describe the relationship between the two. Some people said they were like mother and daughter. Others that they were like sisters. Still more others even said they were like friends. When the baby was born, Auntie Araba took one or two of her relatives with her to Mansa's parents. Their purpose was simple. Mansa had returned from the battlefield safe. The baby looked strong and sound. If Mansa's father wanted her to go back to school . . .

'Yes, some girls do this.'

But Mansa's father had lost interest in Mansa's education.

'I can understand him.'

I too. So Auntie Araba said that in that case, there was no problem. Mansa was a good girl. Not like one of these *yetse-yetse* things who think putting a toe in a classroom turns them into goddesses. The child and mother should go on living with her until Ato finished his education. Then they could marry properly.

'Our Auntie Araba is going to heaven.'

If there is any heaven and God is not like man, my sister.

'What did Mansa's parents say?'

What else could they say? Her mother was very happy. She knew that if Mansa came back to live with them she would always remind her father of everything and then there would never be peace for anybody in the house. They say that from that time, the baking business grew and grew and grew. Mansa's hands pulled in money like a good hunter's gun does with game. Auntie Araba herself became young again. She used to say that if all mothers knew they would get daughters-in-law like Mansa, birth pains would be easier to bear. When her husband Egya Nyaako died, would she not have gone mad if Mansa was not with her? She was afraid of the time when her son would finish college, come and marry Mansa properly and take her away. Three years later, Ato finished college. He is a teacher, as you know, my sister. The government was sending him to teach somewhere far away from here. Then about two weeks or so before Christmas, they got a letter from him that he was coming home.

'Ah, I am sure Mansa was very glad.'

Don't say it loudly, my sister. The news spread very fast. We teased her. 'These days some women go round with a smile playing round their lips all the time. Maybe there is a bird on the neem tree behind their back door which is giving them special good news,' we said. Auntie Araba told her friends that her day of doom was coming upon her. What was she going to do on her own? But her friends knew that she was also very glad. So far, she had looked after her charges very well. But if you boil anything for too long, it burns. Her real glory would come only when her son came to take away his bride and his child.

'And the boy-child was a very handsome somebody too.'

And clever, my sister. Before he was two, he was delighting us all by imitating his grandmother and his mother singing the bread-hawking song. A week before the Saturday Ato was expected, Mansa moved back to her parents' house.

'That was a good thing to do.'

She could not have been better advised. That Saturday, people saw her at her bath quite early. My little girl had caught a fever and I myself had not gone to the farm. When eleven o'clock struck, I met Mansa in the market-place, looking like a festive dish. I asked her if what we had heard was true, that our lord and master was coming on the market-day lorry that afternoon. She said I had heard right.

'Maybe she was very eager to see him and could not wait in the house.'

Could you have waited quietly if you had been her?

'Oh, women. We are to be pitied.'

Tell me, my sister. I had wanted to put a stick under the story and clear it all for you. But we are already in town.

'Yes, look at that crowd. Is Auntie Araba's family house near the mouth of this road?'

Oh yes. Until the town grew to the big thing it is, the Twidan Abusia house was right on the road but now it is behind about four or so other houses. Why?

'I think I can hear singing.'

Yes, you are right.

'She is going to get a good funeral.'

That, my sister, is an answer to a question no one will ask.

'So finish me the story.'

Hmm, kinsman, when the market lorry arrived, there was no Scholar-Teacher-Ato on it.

'No?'

No.

'What did Auntie Araba and Mansa do?'

What could they do? Everyone said that the road always has stories to tell. Perhaps he had only missed the lorry. Perhaps he had fallen ill just on that day or a day or so before. They would wait for a while. Perhaps he would arrive that evening if he thought he could get another lorry, it being a market day. But he did not come any time that Saturday or the next morning. And no one saw him on Monday or Tuesday.

'Ohhh . . . '

They don't say, ohhh. . . . We heard about the middle of the next week — I have forgotten now whether it was the Wednesday or Thursday — that he had come.

'Eheh?'

Nyo. But he brought some news with him. He could not marry Mansa.

'Oh, why? After spoiling her . . . '

If you don't shut up, I will stop.

'Forgive me and go on, my sister.'

Let us stand in this alley here — that is the funeral parlour over there. I don't want anyone to overhear us.

'You are right.'

Chicha Ato said he could not marry Mansa because he had got another girl into trouble.

'Whopei!'°

She had been in the college too. Her mother is a big lady and her father is a big man. They said if he did not marry their daughter, they would finish him. . . .

'Whopei!'

His lawyer-father thought it advisable for him to wed that girl soon because they were afraid of what the girl's father would do.

'Whopei!'

So he could not marry our Mansa.

'Whopei!'

They don't say, Whopei, my sister.

'So what did they do?'

Who?

'Everybody. Mansa? Auntie Araba?'

What could they do?

'Whopei!'

That was just before you came back to have your third baby, I think.

'About three years ago?'

Whopei!: an exclamation of shock

Yes.

'It was my fourth. I had the third in Aboso but it died.'

Then it was your fourth. Yes, it was just before you came.

'I thought Auntie Araba was not looking like herself. But I had enough troubles of my own and had no eyes to go prying into other people's affairs. . . . So that was that. . . . '

Yes. From then on, Auntie Araba was just lost.

'And Mansa-ah?'

She really is like Auntie herself. She has all of her character. She too is a good woman. If she had stayed here, I am sure someone else would have married her. But she left.

'And the child?'

She left him with her mother. Haven't you seen him since you came?

'No. Because it will not occur to anybody to point him out to me until I ask. And I cannot recognise him from my mind. I do not know him at all.'

He is around, with the other schoolchildren.

'So what does Mansa do?'

When she left, everyone said she would become a whore in the city.

'Whopei. People are bad.'

Yes. But perhaps they would have been right if Mansa had not been the Mansa we all know. We hear Auntie Araba sent her to a friend and she found her a job with some people. They bake hundreds of loaves of bread an hour with machines.

'A good person does not rot.'

No. She sent money and other things home.

'May God bless her. And Auntie Araba herself?'

As I was telling you. After this affair, she never became herself again. She stopped baking. Immediately. She told her friends that she felt old age was coming on her. Then a few months later, they say she started getting some very bad stomach aches. She tried here, she tried there. Hospitals first, then our own doctors and their herbs. Nothing did any good.

'O our end! Couldn't the hospital doctors cut her up and find out?'

My sister, they say they don't work like that. They have to find out what is wrong before they cut people up.

'And they could not find out what was wrong with Auntie Araba?'

No. She spent whatever she had on this stomach. Egya Nyaako, as you know, had already died. So, about three months ago, she packed up all she had and came here, to squat by her ancestral hearth.

'And yesterday afternoon she died?'

Yes, and yesterday afternoon she died.

'Her spirit was gone.'

Certainly it was her son who drove it away. And then Mansa left with her soul.

'Have you ever seen Chicha Ato's lady-wife?'

No. We hear they had a church wedding. But Auntie Araba did not put her feet there. And he never brought her to Ofuntumase.°

'Maybe the two of them may come here today?'

I don't see how he can fail to come. But she, I don't know. Some of these ladies will not set foot in a place like this for fear of getting dirty.

'Hmmm . . . it is their own cassava!° But do you think Mansa will come and wail for Auntie Araba?'

My sister, if you have come, do you think Mansa will not?

Ofuntumase: an area in Ghana
cassava: tropical plant cultivated for its edible roots

NGUGI WA THIONG'O

Ngugi wa Thiong'o (1938 –) was born in Limuru, Kenya, and educated in East Africa and England. He has taught in Africa and the United States. Imprisoned for a year for his relentless criticism of one-party dictatorship in Kenya, he left after his release. He advocates writing in African languages and now writes in Kikuyu. His work has changed from portraying the colonial era to reflecting the world of barroom politicians and the people who argue about, or exploit, present-day Kenya.

The story "Minutes of Glory" is about the lives of exploited barmaids, who are particularly harassed by the nouveaux riches who have emerged since independence. Many of the women, uprooted from their villages by economic necessity, are doomed to work as prostitutes. The destitute members of society also include many former guerrillas who fought in the Mau Mau war of liberation. Betrayal and destitution thus go hand in hand for Ngugi, in whose work race, class, and gender intersect.

Minutes of Glory

Her name was Wanjiru. But she liked better her Christian one, Beatrice. It sounded more pure and more beautiful. Not that she was ugly; but she could not be called beautiful either. Her body, dark and full fleshed, had the form, yes, but it was as if it waited to be filled by the spirit. She worked in beer halls where sons of women came to drown their inner lives in beer cans and froth. Nobody seemed to notice her. Except, perhaps, when a proprietor or an impatient customer called out her name, Beatrice; then other customers would raise their heads briefly, a few seconds, as if to behold the bearer of such a beautiful name, but not finding anybody there, they would resume their drinking, their ribald jokes, their laughter and play with the other serving girls. She was like a wounded bird in flight: a forced landing now and then but nevertheless wobbling from place to place so that she would variously be found in Alaska, Paradise, The Modern, Thome and other beer-halls all over Limuru.° Some-

Limuru: a town in Kenya

times it was because an irate proprietor found she was not attracting enough customers; he would sack her without notice and without a salary. She would wobble to the next bar. But sometimes she was simply tired of nesting in one place, a daily witness of familiar scenes; girls even more decidedly ugly than she were fought over by numerous claimants at closing hours. What do they have that I don't have? She would ask herself, depressed. She longed for a bar-kingdom where she would be at least one of the rulers, where petitioners would bring their gifts of beer, frustrated smiles and often curses that hid more lust and love than hate.

She left Limuru town proper and tried the mushrooming townlets around. She worked at Ngarariga, Kamiritho, Rironi and even Tiekunu° and everywhere the story was the same. Oh, yes, occasionally she would get a client; but none cared for her as she would have liked, none really wanted her enough to fight over her. She was always a hard-up customer's last resort. No make-believe even, not for her that sweet pretence that men indulged in after their fifth bottle of Tusker.° The following night or during a pay-day, the same client would pretend not to know her; he would be trying his money-power over girls who already had more than a fair share of admirers.

She resented this. She saw in every girl a rival and adopted a sullen attitude. Nyagūthiī especially was the thorn that always pricked her wounded flesh. Nyagūthiī, arrogant and aloof, but men always in her courtyard; Nyagūthiī, fighting with men, and to her they would bring propitiating gifts which she accepted as of right. Nyagūthiī could look bored, impatient, or downright contemptuous and still men would cling to her as if they enjoyed being whipped with biting words, curled lips and the indifferent eyes of a free woman. Nyagūthiī was also a bird in flight, never really able to settle in one place, but in her case it was because she hungered for change and excitement: new faces and new territories for her conquest. Beatrice resented her very shadow. She saw in her the girl she would have liked to be, a girl who was both totally immersed in and yet completely above the underworld of bar violence and sex. Wherever Beatrice went the long shadow of Nyagūthiī would sooner or later follow her.

She fled Limuru for Ilmorog in Chiri District.° Ilmorog had once been a ghost village, but had been resurrected to life by that legendary woman, Nyang'endo,° to whom every pop group had paid their tribute. It was of her that the young dancing Muthuu and Muchun g' wa° sang:

Ngarariga, Kamiritho, Rironi . . . Tiekuna: small Kenyan towns
Tusker: popular beer in East Africa
Ilmorog in Chiri District: an area in Kenya
Nyang'endo: a woman's name, obviously some village celebrity
Muthuu and Muchu n'gwa: personal names in Kikuyu

When I left Nairobi for Ilmorog
Never did I know
I would bear this wonder-child mine
Nyang'endo.

As a result, Ilmorog was always seen as a town of hope where the weary and down-trodden would find their rest and fresh water. But again Nyagūthiī followed her.

She found that Ilmorog, despite the legend, despite the songs and dances, was not different from Limuru. She tried various tricks. Clothes? But even here she never earned enough to buy herself glittering robes. What was seventy-five shillings° a month without house allowance, *posho*,° without salaried boy-friends? By that time, Ambi had reached Ilmorog, and Beatrice thought that this would be the answer. Had she not, in Limuru, seen girls blacker than herself transformed overnight from ugly sins into white stars by a touch of skin-lightening creams? And men would ogle them, would even talk with exaggerated pride of their new-born girl friends. Men were strange creatures, Beatrice thought in moments of searching analysis. They talked heatedly against Ambi, Butone, Firesnow, Moonsnow,° wigs, straightened hair; but they always went for a girl with an Ambi-lightened skin and head covered with a wig made in imitation of European or Indian hair. Beatrice never tried to find the root cause of this black self-hatred, she simply accepted the contradiction and applied herself to Ambi with a vengeance. She had to rub out her black shame. But even Ambi she could not afford in abundance; she could only apply it to her face and to her arms so that her legs and her neck retained their blackness. Besides there were parts of her face she could not readily reach — behind the ears and above the eyelashes, for instance — and these were a constant source of shame and irritation to her Ambi-self.

She would always remember this Ambi period as one of her deepest humiliation before her later minutes of glory. She worked in Ilmorog Starlight Bar and Lodging. Nyagūthiī, with her bangled hands, her huge earrings, served behind the counter. The owner was a good Christian soul who regularly went to church and paid all his dues to *Harambee*° projects. Pot-belly. Grey hairs. Soft-spoken. A respectable family man, well known in Ilmorog. Hardworking even, for he would not leave the bar until the closing hours, or more precisely, until Nyagūthiī left. He had no eyes for any other girl; he hung around her, and surreptitiously brought her gifts of clothes without receiving gratitude in kind. Only the promise. Only the hope for tomorrow. Other girls he gave eighty shillings a month.

shillings: East African currency, inherited from the British
posho: cornmeal
Ambi, Butone, Firesnow, Moonsnow: skin-lightening creams
Harambee: a popular Kenyan slogan in Swahili meaning "let's pull together in one direction"

Nyagūthiī had a room to herself. Nyagūthiī woke up whenever she liked to take the stock. But Beatrice and the other girls had to wake up at five or so, make tea for the lodgers, clean up the bar and wash dishes and glasses. Then they would hang around the bar in shifts until two o'clock when they would go for a small break. At five o'clock, they had to be in again, ready for customers whom they would now serve with frothy beers and smiles until twelve o'clock or for as long as there were customers thirsty for more Tuskers and Pilsners.° What often galled Beatrice, although in her case it did not matter one way or another, was the owner's insistence that the girls should sleep in Starlight. They would otherwise be late for work, he said. But what he really wanted was for the girls to use their bodies to attract more lodgers in Starlight. Most of the girls, led by Nyagūthiī, defied the rule and bribed the watchman to let them out and in. They wanted to meet their regular or one-night boy-friends in places where they would be free and where they would be treated as not just barmaids. Beatrice always slept in. Her occasional one-night patrons wanted to spend the minimum. Came a night when the owner, refused by Nyagūthiī, approached her. He started by finding fault with her work; he called her names, then as suddenly he started praising her, although in a grudging almost contemptuous manner. He grabbed her, struggled with her, pot-belly, grey hairs, and everything. Beatrice felt an unusual revulsion for the man. She could not, she would not bring herself to accept that which had so recently been cast aside by Nyagūthiī. My God, she wept inside, what does Nyagūthiī have that I don't have? The man now humiliated himself before her. He implored. He promised her gifts. But she would not yield. That night she too defied the rule. She jumped through a window; she sought a bed in another bar and only came back at six. The proprietor called her in front of all the others and dismissed her. But Beatrice was rather surprised at herself.

She stayed a month without a job. She lived from room to room at the capricious mercy of the other girls. She did not have the heart to leave Ilmorog and start all over again in a new town. The wound hurt. She was tired of wandering. She stopped using Ambi. No money. She looked at herself in the mirror. She had so aged, hardly a year after she had fallen from grace. Why then was she scrupulous, she would ask herself. But somehow she had a horror of soliciting lovers or directly bartering her body for hard cash. What she wanted was decent work and a man or several men who cared for her. Perhaps she took that need for a man, for a home and for a child with her to bed. Perhaps it was this genuine need that scared off men who wanted other things from barmaids. She wept late at nights and remembered home. At such moments, her mother's village in Nyeri seemed the sweetest place on God's earth. She would invest the life of her peasant mother and father with romantic illusions of im-

Pilsner: an imported beer popular in Kenya

measurable peace and harmony. She longed to go back home to see them. But how could she go back with empty hands? In any case the place was now a distant landscape in the memory. Her life was here in the bar among this crowd of lost strangers. Fallen from grace, fallen from grace. She was part of a generation which would never again be one with the soil, the crops, the wind and the moon. Not for them that whispering in dark hedges, not for her that dance and love-making under the glare of the moon, with the hills of TumuTumu rising to touch the sky. She remembered that girl from her home village who, despite a life of apparent glamour being the kept mistress of one rich man after another in Limuru, had gassed herself to death. This generation was not awed by the mystery of death, just as it was callous to the mystery of life; for how many unmarried mothers had thrown their babies into latrines rather than lose that glamour? The girl's death became the subject of jokes. She had gone metric° — without pains, they said. Thereafter, for a week, Beatrice thought of going metric. But she could not bring herself to do it.

She wanted love; she wanted life.

A new bar was opened in Ilmorog. Treetop Bar, Lodging and Restaurant. Why Treetop, Beatrice could not understand unless because it was a storied building: tea-shop on the ground floor and beer-shop in a room at the top. The rest were rooms for five-minute or one-night lodgers. The owner was a retired civil servant but one who still played at politics. He was enormously wealthy with business sites and enterprises in every major town in Kenya. Big shots from all over the country came to his bar. Big men in Mercedes. Big men in their Bentleys. Big men in their Jaguars and Daimlers. Big men with uniformed chauffeurs drowsing with boredom in cars waiting outside. There were others not so big who came to pay respects to the great. They talked politics mostly. And about their work. Gossip was rife. Didn't you know? Indeed so and so has been promoted. Really? And so and so has been sacked. Embezzlement of public funds. So foolish you know. Not clever about it at all. They argued, they quarrelled, sometimes they fought it out with fists, especially during the elections campaign. The only point on which they were all agreed was that the Luo° community was the root cause of all the trouble in Kenya; that intellectuals and University students were living in an ivory tower of privilege and arrogance; that Kiambu had more than a lion's share of developments; that men from Nyeri and Muranga° had acquired all the big business in Nairobi° and were even encroaching on Chiri District; that African workers, especially those on the farms, where lazy and jealous of 'us' who had sweated ourselves to sudden prosperity. Otherwise

gone metric: become modern (like switching from the old system of measurement to the metric system)
Luo: a major ethnic group in East Africa
Kiambu, Nyeri, Muranga: cities or districts in Kenya
Nairobi: capital and largest city in Kenya

each would hymn his own praises or return compliments. Occasionally in moments of drunken ebullience and self-praise, one would order two rounds of beer for each man present in the bar. Even the poor from Ilmorog would come to Treetop to dine at the gates of the *nouveaux riches.*°

Here Beatrice got a job as a sweeper and bedmaker. Here for a few weeks she felt closer to greatness. Now she made beds for men she had previously known as names. She watched how even the poor tried to drink and act big in front of the big. But soon fate caught up with her. Girls flocked to Treetop from other bars. Girls she had known at Limuru, girls she had known at Ilmorog. And most had attached themselves to one or several big men, often playing a hide-and-not-to-be-found game with their numerous lovers. And Nyagūthiī was there behind the counter, with the eyes of the rich and the poor fixed on her. And she, with her big eyes, bangled hands and earrings maintained the same air of bored indifference. Beatrice as a sweeper and bedmaker became even more invisible. Girls who had fallen into good fortune looked down upon her.

She fought life with dreams. In between putting clean sheets on beds that had just witnessed a five-minute struggle that ended in a half-strangled cry and a pool, she would stand by the window and watch the cars and the chauffeurs, so that soon she knew all the owners by the number plates of their cars and the uniforms of their chauffeurs. She dreamt of lovers who would come for her in sleek Mercedes sports cars made for two. She saw herself linking hands with such a lover, walking in the streets of Nairobi and Mombasa,° tapping the ground with high heels, quick, quick short steps. And suddenly she would stop in front of a display glass window, exclaiming at the same time; Oh darling, won't you buy me those . . . ? Those what, he would ask, affecting anger. Those stockings, darling. It was as an owner of several stockings, ladderless and holeless, that she thought of her well-being. Never again would she mend torn things. Never, never, never. Do you understand? Never. She was next the proud owner of different coloured wigs, blonde wigs, brunette wigs, redhead wigs, Afro wigs, wigs, wigs, all the wigs in the world. Only then would the whole earth sing hallelujah to the one Beatrice. At such moments, she would feel exalted, lifted out of her murky self, no longer a floor sweeper and bedmaker for a five-minute instant love, but Beatrice, descendant of Wangu Makeri who made men tremble with desire at her naked body bathed in moonlight, daughter of Nyang'endo, the founder of modern Ilmorog, of whom they often sang that she had worked several lovers into impotence.

Then she noticed him and he was the opposite of the lover of her

nouveau riches: French, meaning "people who have recently become rich"
Mombasa: Kenya's second-largest city

dreams. He came one Saturday afternoon driving a big five-ton lorry. He carefully parked it beside the Benzes, the Jaguars and the Daimlers, not as a lorry, but as one of those sleek cream-bodied frames, so proud of it he seemed to be. He dressed in a baggy grey suit over which he wore a heavy khaki military overcoat. He removed the overcoat, folded it with care, and put it in the front seat. He locked all the doors, dusted himself a little, then walked round the lorry as if inspecting it for damage. A few steps before he entered Treetop, he turned round for a final glance at his lorry dwarfing the other things. At Treetops he sat in a corner and, with a rather loud defiant voice, ordered a Kenya one.° He drank it with relish, looking around at the same time for a face he might recognize. He indeed did recognize one of the big ones and he immediately ordered for him a quarter bottle of Vat 69.° This was accepted with a bare nod of the head and a patronizing smile; but when he tried to follow his generosity with a conversation, he was firmly ignored. He froze, sank into his Muratina.° But only for a time. He tried again: he was met with frowning faces. More pathetic were his attempts to join in jokes; he would laugh rather too loudly, which would make the big ones stop, leaving him in the air alone. Later in the evening he stood up, counted several crisp hundred shilling notes and handed them to Nyagūthiī behind the counter ostensibly for safekeeping. People whispered; murmured; a few laughed, rather derisively, though they were rather impressed. But this act did not win him immediate recognition. He staggered towards room no. 7 which he had hired. Beatrice brought him the keys. He glanced at her, briefly, then lost all interest.

Thereafter he came every Saturday. At five when most of the big shots were already seated. He repeated the same ritual, except the money act, and always met with defeat. He nearly always sat in the same corner and always rented room 7. Beatrice grew to anticipate his visits and, without being conscious of it, kept the room ready for him. Often after he had been badly humiliated by the big company, he would detain Beatrice and talk to her, or rather he talked to himself in her presence. For him, it had been a life of struggles. He had never been to school although getting an education had been his ambition. He never had a chance. His father was a squatter in the European settled area in the Rift Valley.° That meant a lot in those colonial days. It meant among other things a man and his children were doomed to a future of sweat and toil for the white devils and their children. He had joined the freedom struggle and like the others had been sent to detention. He came from detention the same as his mother had brought him to this world. Nothing. With independence° he found he

Kenya one: a cheap local beverage
Vat 69: an expensive imported whisky
Muratina: a deadly local alcoholic concoction, also known as "kill-me-quick"
the Rift Valley: one of Kenya's most fertile areas, chosen for British colonial settlement
independence: Kenya's independence from Britain in 1963

did not possess the kind of education which would have placed him in one of the vacancies at the top. He started as a charcoal burner, then a butcher, gradually working his own way to become a big transporter of vegetables and potatoes from the Rift Valley and Chiri districts to Nairobi. He was proud of his achievement. But he resented that others, who had climbed to their present wealth through loans and a subsidized education, would not recognize his like. He would rumble on like this, dwelling on education he would never have, and talking of better chances for his children. Then he would carefully count the money, put it under the pillow, and then dismiss Beatrice. Occasionally he would buy her a beer but he was clearly suspicious of women whom he saw as money-eaters of men. He had not yet married.

One night he slept with her. In the morning he scratched for a twenty shilling note and gave it to her. She accepted the money with an odd feeling of guilt. He did this for several weeks. She did not mind the money. It was useful. But he paid for her body as he would pay for a bag of potatoes or a sack of cabbages. With the one pound, he had paid for her services as a listener, a vessel of his complaints against those above, and as a one-night receptacle of his man's burden. She was becoming bored with his ego, with his stories that never varied in content, but somehow, in him, deep inside, she felt that something had been there, a fire, a seed, a flower which was being smothered. In him she saw a fellow victim and looked forward to his visits. She too longed to talk to someone. She too longed to confide in a human being who would understand.

And she did it one Saturday night, suddenly interrupting the story of his difficult climb to the top. She did not know why she did it. Maybe it was the rain outside. It was softly drumming the corrugated iron sheets, bringing with the drumming a warm and drowsy indifference. He would listen. He had to listen. She came from Karatina° in Nyeri. Her two brothers had been gunned down by the British soldiers. Another one had died in detention. She was, so to speak, an only child. Her parents were poor. But they worked hard on their bare strip of land and managed to pay her fees in primary school. For the first six years she had worked hard. In the seventh year, she must have relaxed a little. She did not pass with a good grade. Of course she knew many with similar grades who had been called to good government secondary schools. She knew a few others with lesser grades who had gone to very top schools on the strength of their connections. But she was not called to any high school with reasonable fees. Her parents could not afford fees in a Harambee school. And she would not hear of repeating standard seven. She stayed at home with her parents. Occasionally she would help them in the shamba° and with house chores. But imagine: for the past six years she had led a life with a

Karatina: a village in Kenya
shamba: the courtyard area around the homestead

different rhythm from that of her parents. Life in the village was dull. She would often go to Karatina and to Nyeri in search of work. In every office, they would ask her the same questions: what work do you want? What do you know? Can you type? Can you take shorthand? She was desperate. It was in Nyeri, drinking Fanta° in a shop, tears in her eyes, that she met a young man in a dark suit and sun-glasses. He saw her plight and talked to her. He came from Nairobi. Looking for work? That's easy; in a big city there would be no difficulty with jobs. He would certainly help. Transport? He had a car — a cream-white Peugeot. Heaven. It was a beautiful ride, with the promise of dawn. Nairobi. He drove her to Terrace Bar. They drank beer and talked about Nairobi. Through the window she could see the neon-lit city and knew that here was hope. That night she gave herself to him, with the promise of dawn making her feel light and gay. She had a very deep sleep. When she woke in the morning, the man in the cream-white Peugeot was not there. She never saw him again. That's how she had started the life of a barmaid. And for one and a half years now she had not been once to see her parents. Beatrice started weeping. Huge sobs of self-pity. Her humiliation and constant flight were fresh in her mind. She had never been able to take to bar culture, she always thought that something better would come her way. But she was trapped, it was the only life she now knew, although she had never really learnt all its laws and norms. Again she heaved out and in, tears tossing out with every sob. Then suddenly she froze. Her sobbing was arrested in the air. The man had long covered himself. His snores were huge and unmistakable.

She felt a strange hollowness. Then a bile of bitterness spilt inside her. She wanted to cry at her new failure. She had met several men who had treated her cruelly, who had laughed at her scruples, at what they thought was an ill-disguised attempt at innocence. She had accepted. But not this, Lord, not this. Was this man not a fellow victim? Had he not, Saturday after Saturday, unburdened himself to her? He had paid for her human services; he had paid away his responsibility with his bottle of Tuskers and hard cash in the morning. Her innermost turmoil had been his lullaby. And suddenly something in her snapped. All the anger of a year and a half, all the bitterness against her humiliation were now directed at this man.

What she did later had the mechanical precision of an experienced hand.

She touched his eyes. He was sound asleep. She raised his head. She let it fall. Her tearless eyes were now cold and set. She removed the pillow from under him. She rummaged through it. She took out his money. She counted five crisp pink notes. She put the money inside her brassiere.

She went out of room no. 7. Outside it was still raining. She did not

Fanta: the brand name of a popular orange-flavored soda

want to go to her usual place. She could not now stand the tiny cupboard room or the superior chatter of her roommate. She walked through mud and rain. She found herself walking towards Nyagūthiī's room. She knocked at the door. At first she had no response. Then she heard Nyagūthiī's sleepy voice above the drumming rain.

'Who is that?'

'It is me. Please open.'

'Who?'

'Beatrice.'

'At this hour of the night?'

'Please.'

Lights were put on. Bolts unfastened. The door opened. Beatrice stepped inside. She and Nyagūthiī stood there face to face. Nyagūthiī was in a see-through nightdress: on her shoulders she had a green pullover.

'Beatrice, is there anything wrong?' she at last asked, a note of concern in her voice.

'Can I rest here for a while? I am tired. And I want to talk to you.' Beatrice's voice carried assurance and power.

'But what has happened?'

'I only want to ask you a question, Nyagūthiī.'

They were still standing. Then, without a word, they both sat on the bed.

'Why did you leave home, Nyagūthiī?' Beatrice asked.

Another silent moment. Nyagūthiī seemed to be thinking about the question. Beatrice waited. Nyagūthiī's voice when at last it came was slightly tremulous, unsteady.

'It is a long story, Beatrice. My father and mother were fairly wealthy. They were also good Christians. We lived under regulations. You must never walk with the heathen. You must not attend their pagan customs — dances and circumcision rites, for instance. There were rules about what, how and when to eat. You must even walk like a Christian lady. You must never be seen with boys. Rules, rules all the way. One day instead of returning home from school, I and another girl from a similar home ran away to Eastleigh. I have never been home once this last four years. That's all.'

Another silence. Then they looked at one another in mutual recognition.

'One more question, Nyagūthiī. You need not answer it. But I have always thought that you hated me, you despised me.'

'No, no, Beatrice, I have never hated you. I have never hated anybody. It is just that nothing interests me. Even men do not move me now. Yet I want, I need instant excitement. I need the attention of those false flattering eyes to make me feel myself, myself. But you, you seemed above all this — somehow you had something inside you that I did not have.'

Beatrice tried to hold her tears with difficulty.

Early the next day, she boarded a bus bound for Nairobi. She walked down Bazaar street looking at the shops. Then down Government Road, right into Kenyatta Avenue, and Kimathi street. She went into a shop near Hussein Suleman's street and bought several stockings. She put on a pair. She next bought herself a new dress. Again she changed into it. In a Bata shoeshop, she bought high heeled shoes, put them on and discarded her old flat ones. On to an Akamba kiosk, and she fitted herself with earrings. She went to a mirror and looked at her new self. Suddenly she felt enormous hunger as if she had been hungry all her life. She hesitated in front of Moti Mahal. Then she walked on, eventually entering Fransae. There was a glint in her eyes that made men's eyes turn to her. This thrilled her. She chose a table in a corner and ordered Indian curry. A man left his table and joined her. She looked at him. Her eyes were merry. He was dressed in a dark suit and his eyes spoke of lust. He bought her a drink. He tried to engage her in conversation. But she ate in silence. He put his hand under the table and felt her knees. She let him do it. The hand went up and up her thigh. Then suddenly she left her unfinished food and her untouched drink and walked out. She felt good. He followed her. She knew this without once turning her eyes. He walked beside her for a few yards. She smiled at herself but did not look at him. He lost his confidence. She left him standing sheepishly looking at a glass window outside Gino's. In the bus back to Ilmorog, men gave her seats. She accepted this as of right. At Treetops bar she went straight to the counter. The usual crowd of big men was there. Their conversations stopped for a few seconds at her entry. Their lascivious eyes were turned to her. The girls stared at her. Even Nyagūthiī could not maintain her bored indifference. Beatrice bought them drinks. The manager came to her, rather unsure. He tried a conversation. Why had she left work? Where had she been? Would she like to work in the bar, helping Nyagūthiī behind the counter? Now and then? A barmaid brought her a note. A certain big shot wanted to know if she would join their table. More notes came from different big quarters with the one question; would she be free tonight? A trip to Nairobi even. She did not leave her place at the counter. But she accepted their drinks as of right. She felt a new power, confidence even.

She took out a shilling, put it in the slot and the juke box boomed with the voice of Robinson Mwangi singing Hūnyū wa Mashambani. He sang of those despised girls who worked on farms and contrasted them with urban girls. Then she played a Kamaru and a D.K.° Men wanted to dance with her. She ignored them, but enjoyed their flutter around her. She twisted her hips to the sound of yet another D.K. Her body was free. She was free. She sucked in the excitement and tension in the air.

Then suddenly at around six, the man with the five-ton lorry stormed

---

Kamaru, D.K.: popular Kenyan recording artists

into the bar. This time he had on his military overcoat. Behind him was a policeman. He looked around. Everybody's eyes were raised to him. But Beatrice went on swaying her hips. At first he could not recognize Beatrice in the girl celebrating her few minutes of glory by the juke box. Then he shouted in triumph. 'That is the girl! Thief! Thief!'

People melted back to their seats. The policeman went and handcuffed her. She did not resist. Only at the door she turned her head and spat. Then she went out followed by the policeman.

In the bar the stunned silence broke into hilarious laughter when someone made a joke about sweetened robbery without violence. They discussed her. Some said she should have been beaten. Others talked contemptuously about 'these bar girls.' Yet others talked with a concern noticeable in unbelieving shakes of their heads about the rising rate of crime. Shouldn't the Hanging Bill be extended to all thefts of property? And without anybody being aware of it the man with the five-ton lorry had become a hero. They now surrounded him with questions and demanded the whole story. Some even bought him drinks. More remarkable, they listened, their attentive silence punctuated by appreciative laughter. The averted threat to property had temporarily knit them into one family. And the man, accepted for the first time, told the story with relish.

But behind the counter Nyagūthiī wept.

MALAWI

JACK MAPANJE

Jack Mapanje (1943–) was born in southern Malawi. He studied in Malawi and England and taught at the University of Malawi before his arrest on unspecified charges. After his release, he left Malawi to live in England. Despite heavy censorship in Malawi, several writers have been quietly developing their skills. Although Mapanje's poetry belongs to this school, it also has a strong personal voice that is refreshingly free of echoes of other poets.

Mapanje dips into Chewa orature for his images and motifs, which he uses to make subtle criticism of Malawi's one-party dictatorship. He is incensed by the obsequiousness that his people exhibit for those in authority and parodies it in his writing. He makes equally incisive comments on social issues such as prostitution and the gap between the rich and the poor in his country.

Messages

I

Tell her we still expose our bottoms
Eat unseasoned *nsima* with *bonongwe*°
From a wooden ladle our hands unscented,
We still sleep in slums rolling
In bird-droppings, friends of fleas,   5
Maggots. Tell her our pleasure
Is still in the pattering tin-drums
That convoke these tatters in the cold
Of dawn to quench hangovers. Tell
Her besides, a cat sees best at night   10
Not much at noon and so when time
Comes, while she eats and drinks
While she twists and shouts, rides
And travels, we shall refuse

nsima **with** *bonongwe:* chewa, cornmeal with wild spinach, common Malawian dish
  eaten by the very poor

To reach her our stuff of fortune   15
Even if she called us witches!
We swear by our fathers dead!

   2

The red neon light illuminates
Her loose butterfly skirt
The iron rippled hair°   20
Her pink veneer smile

Her moist hand grips mine
Her forefinger goring my palm
What . . . ? She . . . ? — nail varnish
On my palm . . . 'a beer please . . .'   25

Her back swirls off me
Gassed by reeking perfumes, sitting:
Tattering curtains, doors to bathrooms
Couples in corners unabashed

She comes back thick-lip-cigaretted   30
The chest jutting into the world generously
The lashes greased bluer
'Come from far . . . ? Tired . . . eh . . . ?'

I reply a struck-Portuguese-match laughter
As I try to whisper her navel name   35
'Asawilunda, your mother at Kadango greets you and . . .'
Oh, already floating to the next customer?

   3

Did you think it was a hunting party
Where after a fall from chasing a hare
You laughed together an enemy shaking   40
Dust off your bottom, a friend reaching
You your bow and arrow? Or a game safari
Where you patted your hounds before
The halloo? Did you think this the bush
Where the party would take the best of   45
Their kill to the Chief so he could allow
Them more hunting bush next time? No,
Mother, it's a war here, a lonely war

iron rippled hair: hair straightened with a hot comb to look like a European's fashionable hairstyle

Where you hack your own way single-handed
To make anything up to the Shaka° of   50
The tribe! It's fine the earth's fertile!

On His Royal Blindness
Paramount Chief Kwangala°

I admire the quixotic display of your paramountcy
How you brandish our ancestral shields and spears
Among your warriors dazzled by your loftiness
But I fear the way you spend your golden breath
Those impromptu, long-winded tirades of your might   5
In the heat, do they suit your brittle constitution?

I know I too must sing to such royal happiness
And I am not arguing. Wasn't I too tucked away in my
Loin-cloth infested by jiggers and fleas before
Your bright eminence showed up? How could I quibble   10
Over your having changed all that? How dare I when
We have scribbled our praises all over our graves?

Why should I quarrel when I too have known mask
Dancers making troubled journeys to the gold mines
On bare feet and bringing back fake European gadgets   15
The broken pipes, torn coats, crumpled bowler hats,
Dangling mirrors and rusty tincans to make their
Mask dancing strange? Didn't my brothers die there?

No, your grace, I am no alarmist nor banterer
I am only a child surprised how you broadly disparage   20
Me shocked by the tedium of your continuous palaver. I
Adore your majesty. But paramountcy is like a raindrop
On a vast sea. We should not wait for the children to
Tell us about our toothless gums or our showing flies.

When This Carnival Finally Closes

When this frothful carnival finally closes, brother
When your drumming veins dry, these very officers
Will burn the scripts of the praises we sang to you

Shaka: the founder of the Zulu nation between the eighteenth and nineteenth centuries
Chief Kwangala: a mythical, all-powerful figure

And shatter the calabashes° you drank from. Your
Charms, these drums, and the effigies blazing will   5
Become the accomplices to your lie-achieved world!
Your bamboo hut on the beach they'll make a bonfire
Under the cover of giving their hero a true traditional
Burial, though in truth to rid themselves of another
Deadly spirit that might otherwise have haunted them,   10
And at the wake new mask dancers will quickly leap
Into the arena dancing to tighter skins, boasting
Other clans of calabashes as the undertakers jest:
What did he think he would become, a God? The devil!

calabashes: drinking gourds made from the tropical calabash tree

GABRIEL OKARA

Gabriel Okara (1921–) was born in Nembe in the Ijaw-speaking area of Nigeria and educated at Government College, Umuahia. Through private study and a deep interest in literature and music, in the language and culture of his people, and in their spoken expression, Okara developed into a remarkable poet. His work deals with both the colonial past and the neocolonial present.

The poems here contrast Western and African cultures, yet show the antithesis between the cultures to be superficial. Focusing on the differences underplays the complementarity that is possible between cultures and necessary to create harmony in the world. Okara also decries the mockery and the rejection of his rich and enduring heritage by the West. He focuses, too, on the neocolonial era, which has bred cultural alienation and self-hatred among Africa's new elites.

Piano and Drums

When at break of day at a riverside
I hear jungle drums telegraphing
the mystic rhythm, urgent, raw
like bleeding flesh, speaking of
primal youth and the beginning.   5
I see the panther ready to pounce,
the leopard snarling about to leap
and the hunters crouch with spears poised;

And my blood ripples, turns torrent,
topples the years and at once I'm   10
in my mother's lap a suckling;
at once I'm walking simple
paths with no innovations,
rugged, fashioned with the naked
warmth of hurrying feet and groping hearts   15
in green leaves and wild flowers pulsing.

Then I hear a wailing piano
solo speaking of complex ways
in tear-furrowed concerto;
of far-away lands   20
and new horizons with
coaxing diminuendo, counterpoint,
crescendo. But lost in the labyrinth
of its complexities, it ends in the middle
of a phrase at a daggerpoint.   25

And I, lost in the morning mist
of an age at a riverside keep
wandering in the mystic rhythm
of jungle drums and the concerto.

You Laughed and Laughed and Laughed

In your ears my song
is motor car misfiring
stopping with a choking cough;
and you laughed and laughed and laughed.

In your eyes my ante-   5
natal walk was inhuman, passing
your omnivorous understanding
and you laughed and laughed and laughed.

You laughed at my song,
you laughed at my walk.   10
Then I danced my magic dance
to the rhythm of talking —
drums pleading, but you shut your
eyes and laughed and laughed and laughed.

And then I opened my mystic   15
inside wide like
the sky, instead you entered your
car and laughed and laughed and laughed.

You laughed at my dance,
you laughed at my inside.   20

You laughed and laughed and laughed.
But your laughter was ice-block
laughter and it froze your inside, froze

your voice, froze your ears,
froze your eyes and froze your tongue. 25

And now it's my turn to laugh;
but my laughter is not
ice-block laughter. For I
know not cars, know not ice-blocks.

My laughter is the fire 30
of the eye of the sky, the fire
of the earth, the fire of the air,
the fire of the seas and the
rivers fishes animals trees,
and it thawed your inside, 35
thawed your voice, thawed your
ears, thawed your eyes and
thawed your tongue.

So a meek wonder held
your shadow and you whispered; 40
"Why so?"
And I answered:
"Because my fathers and I
are owned by the living
warmth of the earth 45
through our naked feet."

Once upon a Time

Once upon a time, son,
they used to laugh with their hearts
and laugh with their eyes;
but now they only laugh with their teeth
while their ice-block-cold eyes 5
search behind my shadow.

There was a time indeed
they used to shake hands with their hearts;
but that's gone, son.
Now they shake hands without hearts 10
while their left hands search
my empty pockets.

"Feel at home," "Come again,"
they say, and when I come

again and feel   15
at home, once, twice,
there will be no thrice —
for then I find doors shut on me.

So I have learned many things, son.
I have learned to wear many faces   20
like dresses — homeface,
officeface, streetface, hostface, cock-
tailface, with all their conforming smiles
like a fixed portrait smile.

And I have learned too   25
to laugh with only my teeth
and shake hands without my heart.
I have also learned to say "Goodbye,"
when I mean "Goodriddance";
to say "Glad to meet you,"   30
without being glad; and to say "It's been
nice talking to you," after being bored.

But believe me, son
I want to be what I used to be
when I was like you. I want   35
to unlearn all these muting things.
Most of all, I want to relearn
how to laugh, for my laugh in the mirror
shows only my teeth like a snake's bare fangs!

So show me, son,   40
how to laugh; show me how
I used to laugh and smile
once upon a time when I was like you.

CHINUA ACHEBE

Chinua Achebe (1930–) was born in Ogidi in eastern Nigeria. After studying medicine and literature at the University of Ibadan, he worked for the Nigerian Broadcasting Corporation. He taught at universities in Nigeria and the United States, and is the recipient of numerous prizes. His work reflects the various crisis periods Nigeria has come through, from preconquest times to the present. His contribution to English literature is as significant as that of any other contemporary writer.

Achebe's consummate skill as a storyteller is manifest in his handling of madness in "The Madman." The narrative is richly layered with comedy, irony, and the social customs of the Ibo-speaking people of eastern Nigeria.

The Madman

He was drawn to markets and straight roads. Not any tiny neighbourhood market where a handful of garrulous women might gather at sunset to gossip and buy ogili for the evening's soup, but a huge, engulfing bazaar beckoning people familiar and strange from far and near. And not any dusty, old footpath beginning in this village, and ending in that stream, but broad, black, mysterious highways without beginning or end. After much wandering he had discovered two such markets linked together by such a highway; and so ended his wandering. One market was Af<u>o</u>, the other Eke. The two days between them suited him very well: before setting out for Eke he had ample time to wind up his business properly at Af<u>o</u>. He passed the night there putting right again his hut after a day of defilement by two fat-bottomed market women who said it was their market-stall. At first he had put up a fight but the women had gone and brought their men-folk — four hefty beasts of the bush — to whip him out of the hut. After that he always avoided them, moving out on the morning of the market and back in at dusk to pass the night. Then in the morning he rounded off his affairs swiftly and set out on that long, beautiful boa-constrictor of a road to Eke in the distant town of Ogbu. He held his staff and cudgel at the ready in his right hand, and with the left he steadied the basket of his belongings on his head. He had got himself this cudgel lately to deal with little beasts on the way who threw stones at him and made fun of their mothers' nakedness, not his own.

He used to walk in the middle of the road, holding it in conversation. But one day the driver of a mammy-wagon° and his mate came down on him shouting, pushing and slapping his face. They said their lorry very nearly ran over their mother, not him. After that he avoided those noisy lorries too, with the vagabonds inside them.

Having walked one day and one night he was now close to the Eke market-place. From every little side-road crowds of market people poured into the big highway to join the enormous flow to Eke. Then he saw some young ladies with water-pots on their heads coming towards him, unlike all the rest, away from the market. This surprised him. Then he saw two more water-pots rise out of a sloping footpath leading off his side

mammy-wagon: a common, crowded, cheap mode of transport

of the highway. He felt thirsty then and stopped to think it over. Then he set down his basket on the roadside and turned into the sloping footpath. But first he begged his highway not to be offended or continue the journey without him. 'I'll get some for you too,' he said coaxingly with a tender backward glance. 'I know you are thirsty.'

Nwibe was a man of high standing in Ogbu and was rising higher; a man of wealth and integrity. He had just given notice to all the ozo° men of the town that he proposed to seek admission into their honoured hierarchy in the coming initiation season.

'Your proposal is excellent,' said the men of title. 'When we see we shall believe.' Which was their dignified way of telling you to think it over once again and make sure you have the means to go through with it. For ozo is not a child's naming ceremony; and where is the man to hide his face who begins the ozo dance and then is foot-stuck to the arena? But in this instance the caution of the elders was no more than a formality for Nwibe was such a sensible man that no one could think of him beginning something he was not sure to finish.

On that Eke day Nwibe had risen early so as to visit his farm beyond the stream and do some light work before going to the market at midday to drink a horn or two of palm-wine with his peers and perhaps buy that bundle of roofing thatch for the repair of his wives' huts. As for his own hut he had a couple of years back settled it finally by changing his thatch-roof to zinc. Sooner or later he would do the same for his wives. He could have done Mgboye's hut right away but decided to wait until he could do the two together, or else Udenkwo would set the entire compound on fire. Udenkwo was the junior wife, by three years, but she never let that worry her. Happily Mgboye was a woman of peace who rarely demanded the respect due to her from the other. She would suffer Udenkwo's provoking tongue sometimes for a whole day without offering a word in reply. And when she did reply at all her words were always few and her voice low.

That very morning Udenkwo had accused her of spite and all kinds of wickedness on account of a little dog.

'What has a little dog done to you?' she screamed loud enough for half the village to hear. 'I ask you Mgboye, what is the offence of a puppy this early in the day?'

'What your puppy did this early in the day,' replied Mgboye, 'is that he put his shit-mouth into my soup-pot.'

'And then?'

'And then I smacked him.'

'You smacked him! Why don't you cover your soup-pot? Is it easier to hit a dog than cover a pot? Is a small puppy to have more sense than a woman who leaves her soup-pot about ... ?'

ozo: a lofty title of honor among the Igbo of Nigeria

'Enough from you, Udenkwo.'

'It is not enough, Mgboye, it is not enough. If that dog owes you any debt I want to know. Everything I have, even a little dog I bought to eat my infant's excrement keeps you awake at nights. You are a bad woman, Mgboye, you are a very bad woman!'

Nwibe had listened to all of this in silence in his hut. He knew from the vigour of Udenkwo's voice that she could go on like this till market-time. So he intervened, in his characteristic manner by calling out to his senior wife.

'Mgboye! Let me have peace this early morning!'

'Don't you hear all the abuses, Udenkwo . . . '

'I hear nothing at all from Udenkwo and I want peace in my compound. If Udenkwo is crazy must everybody else go crazy with her? Is one crazy woman not enough in my compound so early in the day?'

'The great jungle has spoken,' sang Udenkwo in a sneering sing-song. 'Thank you, great judge. Udenkwo is mad. Udenkwo is always mad, but those of you who are sane let . . .'

'Shut your mouth, shameless woman, or a wild beast will lick your eyes for you this morning. When will you learn to keep your badness within this compound instead of shouting it to all Ogbu to hear? I say shut your mouth!'

There was silence then except for Udenkwo's infant whose yelling had up till then been swallowed up by the larger noise of the adults.

'Don't cry, my father,' said Udenkwo to him. 'They want to kill your dog, but our people say the man who decides to chase after a chicken, for him is the fall . . .'

By the middle of the morning Nwibe had done all the work he had to do on his farm and was on his way again to prepare for market. At the little stream he decided as he always did to wash off the sweat of work. So he put his cloth on a huge boulder by the men's bathing section and waded in. There was nobody else around because of the time of day and because it was market day. But from instinctive modesty he turned to face the forest away from the approaches.

The madman watched him for quite a while. Each time he bent down to carry water in cupped hands from the shallow stream to his head and body the madman smiled at his parted behind. And then remembered. This was the same hefty man who brought three others like him and whipped me out of my hut in the Afo market. He nodded to himself. And he remembered again: this was the same vagabond who descended on me from the lorry in the middle of my highway. He nodded once more. And then he remembered yet again: this was the same fellow who set his children to throw stones at me and make remarks about their mothers' buttocks, not mine. Then he laughed.

Nwibe turned sharply round and saw the naked man laughing, the deep grove of the stream amplifying his laughter. Then he stopped as suddenly as he had begun; the merriment vanished from his face.

'I have caught you naked,' he said.

Nwibe ran a hand swiftly down his face to clear his eyes of water.

'I say I have caught you naked, with your thing dangling about.'

'I can see you are hungry for a whipping,' said Nwibe with a quiet menace in his voice, for a madman is said to be easily scared away by the very mention of a whip. 'Wait till I get up there. . . . What are you doing? Drop it at once . . . I say drop it!'

The madman had picked up Nwibe's cloth and wrapped it round his own waist. He looked down at himself and began to laugh again.

'I will kill you,' screamed Nwibe as he splashed towards the bank, maddened by anger. 'I will whip that madness out of you today!'

They ran all the way up the steep and rocky footpath hedged in by the shadowy green forest. A mist gathered and hung over Nwibe's vision as he ran, stumbled, fell, pulled himself up again and stumbled on, shouting and cursing. The other, despite his unaccustomed encumbrance steadily increased his lead, for he was spare and wiry, a thing made for speed. Furthermore, he did not waste his breath shouting and cursing; he just ran. Two girls going down to the stream saw a man running up the slope towards them pursued by a stark-naked madman. They threw down their pots and fled, screaming.

When Nwibe emerged into the full glare of the highway he could not see his cloth clearly any more and his chest was on the point of exploding from the fire and torment within. But he kept running. He was only vaguely aware of crowds of people on all sides and he appealed to them tearfully without stopping: 'Hold the madman, he's got my cloth!' By this time the man with the cloth was practically lost among the much denser crowds far in front so that the link between him and the naked man was no longer clear.

Now Nwibe continually bumped against people's backs and then laid flat a frail old man struggling with a stubborn goat on a leash. 'Stop the madman,' he shouted hoarsely, his heart tearing to shreds, 'he's got my cloth!' Everyone looked at him first in surprise and then less surprise because strange sights are common in a great market. Some of them even laughed.

'They've got his cloth he says.'

'That's a new one I'm sure. He hardly looks mad yet. Doesn't he have people, I wonder.'

'People are so careless these days. Why can't they keep proper watch over their sick relations, especially on the day of the market?'

Farther up the road on the very brink of the market-place two men from Nwibe's village recognized him and, throwing down the one his long basket of yams, the other his calabash of palm-wine held on a loop, gave desperate chase, to stop him setting foot irrevocably within the occult territory of the powers of the market. But it was in vain. When finally they caught him it was well inside the crowded square. Udenkwo in tears tore off her top-cloth which they draped on him and led him home by the hand. He spoke just once about a madman who took his cloth in the stream.

'It is all right,' said one of the men in the tone of a father to a crying child. They led and he followed blindly, his heavy chest heaving up and down in silent weeping. Many more people from his village, a few of his in-laws and one or two others from his mother's place had joined the grief-stricken party. One man whispered to another that it was the worst kind of madness, deep and tongue-tied.

'May it end ill for him who did this,' prayed the other.

The first medicine-man his relatives consulted refused to take him on, out of some kind of integrity.

'I could say yes to you and take your money,' he said. 'But that is not my way. My powers of cure are known throughout Olu and Igbo but never have I professed to bring back to life a man who has sipped the spirit-waters of ani-mmọ. It is the same with a madman who of his own accord delivers himself to the divinities of the market-place. You should have kept better watch over him.'

'Don't blame us too much,' said Nwibe's relative. 'When he left home that morning his senses were as complete as yours and mine now. Don't blame us too much.'

'Yes, I know. It happens that way sometimes. And they are the ones that medicine will not reach. I know.'

'Can you do nothing at all then, not even to untie his tongue?'

'Nothing can be done. They have already embraced him. It is like a man who runs away from the oppression of his fellows to the grove of an alusi and says to him: Take me, oh spirit, I am your osu.° No man can touch him thereafter. He is free and yet no power can break his bondage. He is free of men but bonded to a god.'

The second doctor was not as famous as the first and not so strict. He said the case was bad, very bad indeed, but no one folds his arms because the condition of his child is beyond hope. He must still grope around and do his best. His hearers nodded in eager agreement. And then he muttered into his own inward ear: If doctors were to send away every patient whose cure they were uncertain of, how many of them would eat one meal in a whole week from their practice?

Nwibe was cured of his madness. That humble practitioner who did the miracle became overnight the most celebrated mad-doctor of his generation. They called him Sojourner to the Land of the Spirits. Even so it

osu: an untouchable person in the Igbo caste system

remains true that madness may indeed sometimes depart but never with all his clamorous train. Some of these always remain — the trailers of madness you might call them — to haunt the doorway of the eyes. For how could a man be the same again of whom witnesses from all the lands of Olu and Igbo have once reported that they saw today a fine, hefty man in his prime, stark naked, tearing through the crowds to answer the call of the market-place? Such a man is marked for ever.

Nwibe became a quiet, withdrawn man avoiding whenever he could the boisterous side of the life of his people. Two years later, before another initiation season, he made a new inquiry about joining the community of titled men in his town. Had they received him perhaps he might have become at least partially restored, but those ozo men, dignified and polite as ever, deftly steered the conversation away to other matters.

WOLE SOYINKA

Wole Soyinka (1934–) was born in Abeokuta, Nigeria, and educated in Nigeria and England. He was briefly attached to the Royal Court Theatre, London, and subsequently taught at universities in Africa, Europe, and America. Hailed as "one of the finest playwrights ever to write in English," he was awarded the Nobel Prize in 1986. His work employs Yoruba theatrical techniques, myths, and rituals in a way that transcends the work's immediate social context. Soyinka's work often reflects the resilience of Yoruba culture.

The play The Strong Breed *is based on the Yoruba festival of the new year and the ritual of sacrificing a "carrier" of the previous year's evil. It also reflects the social change that comes about as a result of exposure to Western culture. Eman finds that his Western education has rendered him unfit for the traditional task for which he was born.*

The Strong Breed

CHARACTERS

EMAN   a stranger
SUNMA   Jaguna's daughter
IFADA   an idiot
A GIRL
JAGUNA
OROGE
Attendant Stalwarts.   The villagers

from Eman's past —
OLD MAN   his father
OMAE   his betrothed
TUTOR
PRIEST
Attendants.   The villagers

The scenes are described briefly, but very often a darkened stage with lit areas will not only suffice but is necessary. Except for the one indicated place, there can be no break in the action. A distracting scene-change would be ruinous.

A mud house, with space in front of it. Eman, in light buba° and trousers stands at the window, looking out. Inside, Sunma is clearing the table of what looks like a modest clinic, putting the things away in a cupboard. Another rough table in the room is piled with exercise books, two or three worn text-books, etc. Sunma appears agitated. Outside, just below the window crouches Ifada. He looks up with a shy smile from time to time, waiting for Eman to notice him.

SUNMA [*hesitant.*]: You will have to make up your mind soon Eman. The lorry leaves very shortly.
[*As Eman does not answer, Sunma continues her work, more nervously. Two villagers, obvious travellers, pass hurriedly in front of the house, the man has a small raffia° sack, the woman a cloth-covered basket, the man enters first, turns and urges the woman who is just emerging to hurry.*]
SUNMA [*seeing them, her tone is more intense.*]: Eman, are we going or aren't we? You will leave it till too late.
EMAN [*quietly.*]: There is still time — if you want to go.
SUNMA: If I want to go . . . and you?
[*Eman makes no reply.*]
SUNMA [*bitterly.*]: You don't really want to leave here. You never want to go away — even for a minute.
[*Ifada continues his antics. Eman eventually pats him on the head and the boy grins happily. Leaps up suddenly and returns with a basket of oranges which he offers to Eman.*]
EMAN: My gift for today's festival enh?
[*Ifada nods, grinning.*]
EMAN: They look ripe — that's a change.
SUNMA [*she has gone inside the room. Looks round the door.*]: Did you call me?
EMAN: No. [*She goes back.*] And what will you do tonight Ifada? Will you take part in the dancing? Or perhaps you will mount your own masquerade?
[*Ifada shakes his head, regretfully.*]
EMAN: You won't? So you haven't any? But you would like to own one.
[*Ifada nods eagerly.*]

buba: a long, flowing West African robe
raffia: a cultivated palm used for making hats, mats, baskets, and so on

EMAN: Then why don't you make your own?

[*Ifada stares, puzzled by this idea.*]

EMAN: Sunma will let you have some cloth you know. And bits of wool . . .

SUNMA [*coming out.*]: Who are you talking to Eman?

EMAN: Ifada. I am trying to persuade him to join the young maskers.

SUNMA [*losing control.*]: What does he want here? Why is he hanging round us?

EMAN [*amazed.*]: What . . . ? I said Ifada, Ifada.

SUNMA: Just tell him to go away. Let him go and play somewhere else!

EMAN: What is this? Hasn't he always played here?

SUNMA: I don't want him here. [*Rushes to the window.*] Get away idiot. Don't bring your foolish face here any more, do you hear? Go on, go away from here . . .

EMAN [*restraining her.*]: Control yourself Sunma. What on earth has got into you?

[*Ifada, hurt and bewildered, backs slowly away.*]

SUNMA: He comes crawling round here like some horrible insect. I never want to lay my eyes on him again.

EMAN: I don't understand. It *is* Ifada you know. Ifada! The unfortunate one who runs errands for you and doesn't hurt a soul.

SUNMA: I cannot bear the sight of him.

EMAN: You can't do what? It can't be two days since he last fetched water for you.

SUNMA: What else can he do except that? He is useless. Just because we have been kind to him . . . Others would have put him in an asylum.

EMAN: You are not making sense. He is not a madman, he is just a little more unlucky than other children. [*Looks keenly at her.*] But what is the matter?

SUNMA: It's nothing. I only wish we had sent him off to one of those places for creatures like him.

EMAN: He is quite happy here. He doesn't bother anyone and he makes himself useful.

SUNMA: Useful! Is that one of any use to anybody? Boys of his age are already earning a living but all he can do is hang around and drool at the mouth.

EMAN: But he does work. You know he does a lot for you.

SUNMA: Does he? And what about the farm you started for him! Does he ever work on it? Or have you forgotten that it was really for Ifada you cleared that bush. Now you have to go and work it yourself. You spend all your time on it and you have no room for anything else.

EMAN: That wasn't his fault. I should first have asked him if he was fond of farming.

SUNMA: Oh, so he can choose? As if he shouldn't be thankful for being allowed to live.

EMAN: Sunma!

SUNMA: He does not like farming but he knows how to feast his dumb mouth on the fruits.

EMAN: But I want him to. I encourage him.

SUNMA: Well keep him. I don't want to see him any more.

EMAN [*after some moments.*]: But why? You cannot be telling all the truth. What has he done?

SUNMA: The sight of him fills me with revulsion.

EMAN [*goes to her and holds her.*]: What really is it?

[*Sunma avoids his eyes.*] It is almost as if you are forcing yourself to hate him. Why?

SUNMA: That is not true. Why should I?

EMAN: Then what is the secret? You've even played with him before.

SUNMA: I have always merely tolerated him. But I cannot any more. Suddenly my disgust won't take him any more. Perhaps . . . perhaps it is the new year. Yes, yes, it must be the new year.

EMAN: I don't believe that.

SUNMA: It must be. I am a woman, and these things matter. I don't want a mis-shape near me. Surely for one day in the year, I may demand some wholesomeness.

EMAN: I do not understand you.

[*Sunma is silent.*]

It was cruel of you. And to Ifada who is so helpless and alone. We are the only friends he has.

SUNMA: No, just you. I have told you, with me it has always been only an act of kindness. And now I haven't any pity left for him.

EMAN: No. He is not a wholesome being.

[*He turns back to looking through the window.*]

SUNMA [*half-pleading.*]: Ifada can rouse your pity. And yet if anything, I need more kindness from you. Every time my weakness betrays me, you close your mind against me . . . Eman . . . Eman . . .

[*A Girl comes in view, dragging an effigy by a rope attached to one of its legs. She stands for a while gazing at Eman. Ifada, who has crept back shyly to his accustomed position, becomes somewhat excited when he sees the effigy. The girl is unsmiling. She possesses in fact, a kind of inscrutability which does not make her hard but is unsettling.*]

GIRL: Is the teacher in?

EMAN [*smiling.*]: No.

GIRL: Where is he gone?

EMAN: I don't really know. Shall I ask?

GIRL: Yes, do.

EMAN [*turning slightly.*]: Sunma, a girl outside wants to know . . .

[*Sunma turns away, goes into the inside room.*]

EMAN: Oh. [*Returns to the girl, but his slight gaiety is lost.*] There is no one at home who can tell me.

GIRL: Why are you not in?

EMAN: I don't really know. Maybe I went somewhere.

GIRL: All right. I will wait until you get back.

[*She pulls the effigy to her, sits down.*]

EMAN [*slowly regaining his amusement.*]: So you are all ready for the new year.

GIRL [*without turning round.*]: I am not going to the festival.

EMAN: Then why have you got that?

GIRL: Do you mean my carrier? I am unwell you know. My mother says it will take away my sickness with the old year.

EMAN: Won't you share the carrier with your playmates?

GIRL: Oh, no. Don't you know I play alone? The other children won't come near me. Their mothers would beat them.

EMAN: But I have never seen you here. Why don't you come to the clinic?

GIRL: My mother said No.

[*Gets up, begins to move off.*]

EMAN: You are not going away?

GIRL: I must not stay talking to you. If my mother caught me . . .

EMAN: All right, tell me what you want before you go.

GIRL [*stops. For some moments she remains silent.*]: I must have some clothes for my carrier.

EMAN: Is that all? You wait a moment.

[*Sunma comes out as he takes down a buba from the wall. She goes to the window and glares almost with hatred at the girl. The girl retreats hastily, still impassive.*]

By the way Sunma, do you know who that girl is?

SUNMA: I hope you don't really mean to give her that.

EMAN: Why not? I hardly ever use it.

SUNMA: Just the same don't give it to her. She is not a child. She is as evil as the rest of them.

EMAN: What has got into you today?

SUNMA: All right, all right. Do what you wish.

[*She withdraws. Baffled, Eman returns to the window.*]

EMAN: Here . . . will this do? Come and look at it.

GIRL: Throw it.

EMAN: What is the matter? I am not going to eat you.

GIRL: No one lets me come near them.

EMAN: But I am not afraid of catching your disease.

GIRL: Throw it.

[*Eman shrugs and tosses the buba. She takes it without a word and slips it on the effigy, completely absorbed in the task. Eman watches for a while, then joins Sunma in the inner room*]

GIRL: [*after a long, cool survey of Ifada.*]: You have a head like a spider's egg, and your mouth dribbles like a roof. But there is no one else. Would you like to play?

[*Ifada nods eagerly, quite excited.*]

GIRL: You will have to get a stick.

[*Ifada rushes around, finds a big stick and whirls it aloft, bearing down on the carrier.*]

GIRL: Wait. I don't want you to spoil it. If it gets torn I shall drive you away. Now, let me see how you are going to beat it.

[*Ifada hits it gently.*]

GIRL: You may hit harder than that. As long as there is something left to hang at the end.

[*She appraises him up and down.*]

You are not very tall . . . will you be able to hang it from a tree?

[*Ifada nods, grinning happily.*]

GIRL: You will hang it up and I will set fire to it. [*Then, with surprising venom.*] But just because you are helping me, don't think it is going to cure you. I am the one who will get well at midnight, do you understand? It is my carrier and it is for me alone.

[*She pulls at the rope to make sure that it is well attached to the leg.*]

Well don't stand there drooling. Let's go.

[*She begins to walk off, dragging the effigy in the dust. Ifada remains where he is for some moments, seemingly puzzled. Then his face breaks into a large grin and he leaps after the procession, belabouring the effigy with all his strength. The stage remains empty for some moments. Then the horn of a lorry is sounded and Sunma rushes out. The hooting continues for some time with a rhythmic pattern. Eman comes out.*]

EMAN: I am going to the village . . . I shan't be back before nightfall.

SUNMA [*blankly.*]: Yes.

EMAN [*hesitates.*]: Well what do you want me to do?

SUNMA: The lorry was hooting just now.

EMAN: I didn't hear it.

SUNMA: It will leave in a few minutes. And you did promise we could go away.

EMAN: I promised nothing. Will you go home by yourself or shall I come back for you?

SUNMA: You don't even want me here?

EMAN: But you have to go home haven't you?

SUNMA: I had hoped we would watch the new year together — in some other place.

EMAN: Why do you continue to distress yourself?

SUNMA: Because you will not listen to me. Why do you continue to stay where nobody wants you?

EMAN: That is not true.

SUNMA: It is. You are wasting your life on people who really want you out of their way.

EMAN: You don't know what you are saying.

SUNMA: You think they love you? Do you think they care at all for what you — or I — do for them?

EMAN: *Them*? These are your own people. Sometimes you talk as if you were a stranger too.

SUNMA: I wonder if I really sprang from here. I know they are evil and I am not. From the oldest to the smallest child, they are nourished in evil and unwholesomeness in which I have no part.

EMAN: You knew this when you returned?

SUNMA: You reproach me then for trying at all?

EMAN: I reproach you with nothing? But you must leave me out of your plans. I can have no part in them.

SUNMA [*nearly pleading.*]: Once I could have run away. I would have gone and never looked back.

EMAN: I cannot listen when you talk like that.

SUNMA: I swear to you, I do not mind what happens afterwards. But you must help me tear myself away from here. I can no longer do it by myself . . . It is only a little thing. And we have worked so hard this past year . . . surely we can go away for a week . . . even a few days would be enough.

EMAN: I have told you Sunma . . .

SUNMA [*desperately.*]: Two days Eman. Only two days.

EMAN [*distressed.*]: But I tell you I have no wish to go.

SUNMA [*suddenly angry.*]: Are you so afraid then?

EMAN: Me? Afraid of what?

SUNMA: You think you will not want to come back.

EMAN [*pitying.*]: You cannot dare me that way.

SUNMA: Then why won't you leave here, even for an hour? If you are so sure that your life is settled here, why are you afraid to do this thing for me? What is so wrong that you will not go into the next town for a day or two?

EMAN: I don't want to. I do not have to persuade you, or myself about anything. I simply have no desire to go away.

SUNMA [*his quiet confidence appears to incense her.*]: You are afraid. You accuse me of losing my sense of mission, but you are afraid to put yours to the test.

EMAN: You are wrong Sunma. I have no sense of mission. But I have found peace here and I am content with that.

SUNMA: I haven't. For a while I thought that too, but I found there could be no peace in the midst of so much cruelty. Eman, tonight at least, the last night of the old year . . .

EMAN: No Sunma. I find this too distressing; you should go home now.

SUNMA: It is the time for making changes in one's life Eman. Let's breathe in the new year away from here.

EMAN: You are hurting yourself.

SUNMA: Tonight. Only tonight. We will come back tomorrow, as early as you like. But let us go away for this one night. Don't let another year break on me in this place . . . you don't know how important it is to me, but I will tell you, I will tell you on the way . . . but we must not be here today, Eman, do this one thing for me.

EMAN [*sadly.*]: I cannot.

SUNMA: I was a fool to think it would be otherwise. The whole village may use you as they will but for me there is nothing. Sometimes I think you believe that doing anything for me makes you unfaithful to some part of your life. If it was a woman then I pity her for what she must have suffered.
[*Eman winces and hardens slowly. Sunma notices nothing.*]
Keeping faith with so much is slowly making you inhuman.
[*Seeing the change in Eman.*] Eman. Eman. What is it?
[*As she goes towards him, Eman goes into the house.*]

SUNMA [*apprehensive, follows him.*]: What did I say? Eman. Forgive me, forgive me please.
[*Eman remains facing into the slow darkness of the room. Sunma, distressed, cannot decide what to do.*]
I swear I didn't know . . . I would not have said it for all the world.
[*A lorry is heard taking off somewhere nearby. The sound comes up and slowly fades away into the distance. Sunma starts visibly, goes slowly to the window.*]

SUNMA [*as the sound dies off, to herself.*]: What happens now?

EMAN [*joining her at the window.*]: What did you say?

SUNMA: Nothing.

EMAN: Was that not the lorry going off?

SUNMA: It was.

EMAN: I am sorry I couldn't help you.
[*Sunma, about to speak, changes her mind.*]

EMAN: I think you ought to go home now.

SUNMA: No, don't send me away. It's the least you can do for me. Let me stay here until all the noise is over.

EMAN: But are you not needed at home? You have a part in the festival.

SUNMA: I have renounced it; I am Jaguna's eldest daughter only in name.

EMAN: Renouncing one's self is not so easy — surely you know that.

SUNMA: I don't want to talk about it. Will you at least let us be together tonight?

EMAN: But . . .

SUNMA: Unless you are afraid my father will accuse you of harbouring me.

EMAN: All right, we will go out together.

SUNMA: Go out? I want us to stay here.

EMAN: When there is so much going on outside?

SUNMA: Some day you will wish that you went away when I tried to make you.

EMAN: Are we going back to that?

SUNMA: No. I promise you I will not recall it again. But you must know that it was also for your sake that I tried to get us away.

EMAN: For me? How?

SUNMA: By yourself you can do nothing here. Have you not noticed how tightly we shut out strangers? Even if you lived here for a lifetime, you would remain a stranger.

EMAN: Perhaps that is what I like. There is peace in being a stranger.

SUNMA: For a while perhaps. But they would reject you in the end. I tell you it is only I who stand between you and contempt. And because of this you have earned their hatred. I don't know why I say this now, except that somehow, I feel that it no longer matters. It is only I who have stood between you and much humiliation.

EMAN: Think carefully before you say any more. I am incapable of feeling indebted to you. This will make no difference at all.

SUNMA: I ask for nothing. But you must know it all the same. It is true I hadn't the strength to go by myself. And I must confess this now, if you had come with me, I would have done everything to keep you from returning.

EMAN: I know that.

SUNMA: You see, I bare myself to you. For days I had thought it over, this was to be a new beginning for us. And I placed my fate wholly in your hands. Now the thought will not leave me, I have a feeling which will not be shaken off, that in some way, you have tonight totally destroyed my life.

EMAN: You are depressed, you don't know what you are saying.

SUNMA: Don't think I am accusing you. I say all this only because I cannot help it.

EMAN: We must not remain shut up here. Let us go and be part of the living.

SUNMA: No. Leave them alone.

EMAN: Surely you don't want to stay indoors when the whole town is alive with rejoicing.

SUNMA: Rejoicing! Is that what it seems to you? No, let us remain here. Whatever happens I must not go out until all this is over.

[*There is silence. It has grown much darker.*]

EMAN: I shall light the lamp.

SUNMA [*eager to do something.*]: No, let me do it.

[*She goes into the inner room.*

Eman paces the room, stops by a shelf and toys with the seeds in an 'ayo' board, takes down the whole board and places it on a table, playing by himself.

The girl is now seen coming back, still dragging her 'carrier'. Ifada brings up the rear as before. As he comes round the corner of the house two men emerge from the shadows. A sack is thrown over Ifada's head, the rope is pulled tight rendering him instantly help-less. The girl has reached the front of the house before she turns round at the sound of scuffle. She is in time to see Ifada thrown over the shoulders and borne away. Her face betraying no emotion at all, the girl backs slowly away, turns and flees, leaving the 'car-rier' behind. Sunma enters, carrying two kerosene lamps. She hangs one up from the wall.]

EMAN: One is enough.

SUNMA: I want to leave one outside.

[*She goes out, hangs the lamp from a nail just above the door. As she turns she sees the effigy and gasps. Eman rushes out.*]

EMAN: What is it? Oh, is that what frightened you?

SUNMA: I thought . . . I didn't really see it properly.

[*Eman goes towards the object, stoops to pick it up.*]

EMAN: It must belong to that sick girl.

SUNMA: Don't touch it.

EMAN: Let's keep it for her.

SUNMA: Leave it alone. Don't touch it Eman.

EMAN [*shrugs and goes back.*]: You are very nervous.

SUNMA: Let's go in.

EMAN: Wait. [*He detains her by the door, under the lamp.*] I know there is something more than you've told me. What are you afraid of tonight?

SUNMA: I was only scared by that thing. There is nothing else.

EMAN: I am not blind Sunma. It is true I would not run away when you wanted me to, but that doesn't mean I do not feel things. What does tonight really mean that it makes you so helpless?

SUNMA: It is only a mood. And your indifference to me . . . let's go in.

[*Eman moves aside and she enters; he remains there for a moment and then follows.*

She fiddles with the lamp, looks vaguely round the room, then goes and shuts the door, bolting it. When she turns, it is to meet Eman's eyes, questioning.]

SUNMA: There is a cold wind coming in.

[*Eman keeps his gaze on her.*]

SUNMA: It *was* getting cold.

[*She moves guiltily to the table and stands by the 'ayo' board, re-arranging the seeds. Eman remains where he is a few moments, then brings a stool and sits opposite her. She sits down also and they begin to play in silence.*]

SUNMA: What brought you here at all, Eman? And what makes you stay?

[*There is another silence.*]

SUNMA: I am not trying to share your life. I know you too well by now. But at least we have worked together since you came. Is there nothing at all I deserve to know?

EMAN: Let me continue a stranger — especially to you. Those who have much to give fulfil themselves only in total loneliness.

SUNMA: Then there is no love in what you do.

EMAN: There is. Love comes to me more easily with strangers.

SUNMA: That is unnatural.

EMAN: Not for me. I know I find consummation only when I have spent myself for a total stranger.

SUNMA: It seems unnatural to me. But then I am a woman. I have a woman's longings and weaknesses. And the ties of blood are very strong in me.

EMAN [*smiling.*]: You think I have cut loose from all these — ties of blood.

SUNMA: Sometimes you are so inhuman.

EMAN: I don't know what that means. But I am very much my father's son.

[*They play in silence. Suddenly Eman pauses listening.*]

EMAN: Did you hear that?

SUNMA [*quickly.*]: I heard nothing . . . it's your turn.

EMAN: Perhaps some of the mummers are coming this way.

[*Eman, about to play, leaps up suddenly.*]

SUNMA: What is it? Don't you want to play any more?

[*Eman moves to the door.*]

SUNMA: No. Don't go out Eman.

EMAN: If it's the dancers I want to ask them to stay. At least we won't have to miss everything.

SUNMA: No, no. Don't open the door. Let us keep out everyone tonight.

[*A terrified and disordered figure bursts suddenly round the corner, past the window and begins hammering at the door. It is Ifada. Desperate with terror, he pounds madly at the door, dumb-moaning all the while.*]

EMAN: Isn't that Ifada?

SUNMA: They are only fooling about. Don't pay any attention.

EMAN [*looks round the window.*]: That is Ifada. [*Begins to unbolt the door.*]

SUNMA [*pulling at his hands.*]: It is only a trick they are playing on you. Don't take any notice Eman.

EMAN: What are you saying? The boy is out of his senses with fear.

SUNMA: No, no. Don't interfere Eman. For God's sake don't interfere.

EMAN: Do you know something of this then?

SUNMA: You are a stranger here Eman. Just leave us alone and go your own way. There is nothing you can do.

EMAN [*he tries to push her out of the way but she clings fiercely to him.*]: Have you gone mad? I tell you the boy must come in.

SUNMA: Why won't you listen to me Eman? I tell you it's none of your business. For your own sake do as I say.
[*Eman pushes her off, unbolts the door. Ifada rushes in, clasps Eman round the knees, dumb-moaning against his legs.*]

EMAN [*manages to re-bolt the door.*]: What is it Ifada? What is the matter?
[*Shouts and voices are heard coming nearer the house.*]

SUNMA: Before it's too late, let him go. For once Eman, believe what I tell you. Don't harbour him or you will regret it all your life.
[*Eman tries to calm Ifada who becomes more and more abject as the outside voices get nearer.*]

EMAN: What have they done to him? At least tell me that. What is going on Sunma?

SUNMA [*with sudden venom.*]: Monster! Could you not take yourself somewhere else?

EMAN: Stop talking like that.

SUNMA: He could have run into the bush couldn't he? Toad! Why must he follow us with his own disasters!

VOICES OUTSIDE: It's here . . . Round the back . . . Spread, spread . . . this way . . . no, head him off . . . use the bush path and head him off . . . get some more lights . . .
[*Eman listens. Lifts Ifada bodily and carries him into the inner room. Returns at once, shutting the door behind him.*]

SUNMA [*slumps into a chair, resigned.*]: You always follow your own way.

JAGUNA [*comes round the corner followed by Oroge and three men, one bearing a torch.*]: I knew he would come here.

OROGE: I hope our friend won't make trouble.

JAGUNA: He had better not. You, recall all the men and tell them to surround the house.

OROGE: But he may not be in the house after all.

JAGUNA: I know he is here . . . [*to the men.*] . . . go on, do as I say.
[*He bangs on the door.*]

Teacher, open your door . . . you two stay by the door. If I need you I will call you.

[*Eman opens the door.*]

JAGUNA [*speaks as he enters.*]: We know he is here.

EMAN: Who?

JAGUNA: Don't let us waste time. We are grown men, teacher. You understand me and I understand you. But we must take back the boy.

EMAN: This is my house.

JAGUNA: Daughter, you'd better tell your friend. I don't think he quite knows our ways. Tell him why he must give up the boy.

SUNMA: Father, I . . .

JAGUNA: Are you going to tell him or aren't you?

SUNMA: Father, I beg you, leave us alone tonight . . .

JAGUNA: I thought you might be a hindrance. Go home then if you will not use your sense.

SUNMA: But there are other ways . . .

JAGUNA [*turning to the men.*]: See that she gets home. I no longer trust her. If she gives trouble carry her. And see that the women stay with her until all this is over.

[*Sunma departs, accompanied by one of the men.*]

JAGUNA: Now teacher . . .

OROGE [*restrains him.*]: You see, Mister Eman, it is like this. Right now, nobody knows that Ifada has taken refuge here. No one except us and our men — and they know how to keep their mouths shut. We don't want to have to burn down the house you see, but if the word gets around, we would have no choice.

JAGUNA: In fact, it may be too late already. A carrier should end up in the bush, not in a house. Anyone who doesn't guard his door when the carrier goes by has himself to blame. A contaminated house should be burnt down.

OROGE: But we are willing to let it pass. Only, you must bring him out quickly.

EMAN: All right. But at least you will let me ask you something.

JAGUNA: What is there to ask? Don't you understand what we have told you?

EMAN: Yes. But why did you pick on a helpless boy. Obviously he is not willing.

JAGUNA: What is the man talking about? Ifada is a godsend. Does he have to be willing?

EMAN: In my home, we believe that a man should be willing.

OROGE: Mister Eman, I don't think you quite understand. This is not a simple matter at all. I don't know what you do, but here, it is not a cheap task for anybody. No one in his senses would do such a job. Why do you think we give refuge to idiots like him? We don't know where he came from. One morning, he is simply there, just like that. From nowhere at all. You see, there is a purpose in that.

JAGUNA: We only waste time.

OROGE: Jaguna, be patient. After all, the man has been with us for some time now and deserves to know. The evil of the old year is no light thing to load on any man's head.

EMAN: I know something about that.

OROGE: You do? [*Turns to Jaguna who snorts impatiently.*] You see I told you so didn't I? From the moment you came I saw you were one of the knowing ones.

JAGUNA: Then let him behave like a man and give back the boy.

EMAN: It is you who are not behaving like men.

JAGUNA [*advances aggressively.*]: That is a quick mouth you have . . .

OROGE: Patience Jaguna . . . if you want the new year to cushion the land there must be no deeds of anger. What did you mean my friend?

EMAN: It is a simple thing. A village which cannot produce its own carrier contains no men.

JAGUNA: Enough. Let there be no more talk or this business will be ruined by some rashness. You . . . come inside. Bring the boy out, he must be in the room there.

EMAN: Wait.

[*The men hesitate.*]

JAGUNA [*hitting the nearer one and propelling him forward.*]: Go on. Have you changed masters now that you listen to what he says?

OROGE [*sadly.*]: I am sorry you would not understand Mister Eman. But you ought to know that no carrier may return to the village. If he does, the people will stone him to death. It has happened before. Surely it is too much to ask a man to give up his own soil.

EMAN: I know others who have done more.

[*Ifada is brought out, abjectly dumb-moaning.*]

EMAN: You can see him with your own eyes. Does it really have meaning to use one as unwilling as that.

OROGE [*smiling.*]: He shall be willing. Not only willing but actually joyous. I am the one who prepares them all, and I have seen worse. This one escaped before I began to prepare him for the event. But you will see him later tonight, the most joyous creature in the festival. Then perhaps you will understand.

EMAN: Then it is only a deceit. Do you believe the spirit of a new year is so easily fooled?

JAGUNA: Take him out. [*The men carry out Ifada.*] You see, it is so easy to talk. You say there are no men in this village because they cannot provide a willing carrier. And yet I heard Oroge tell you we only use strangers. There is only one other stranger in the village, but I have not heard him offer himself [*spits.*] It is so easy to talk is it not?

[*He turns his back on him.*

They go off, taking Ifada with them, limp and silent. The only sign of life is that he strains his neck to keep his eyes on Eman till the very moment that he disappears from sight. Eman remains where they left him, staring after the group.]

[*A black-out lasting no more than a minute. The lights come up slowly and Ifada is seen returning to the house. He stops at the window and looks in. Seeing no one, be bangs on the sill. Appears surprised that there is no response. He slithers down on his favourite spot, then sees the effigy still lying where the girl had dropped it in her flight. After some hesitation, he goes towards it, begins to strip it of the clothing. Just then the girl comes in.*]

GIRL: Hey, leave that alone. You know it's mine.

[*Ifada pauses, then speeds up his action.*]

GIRL: I said it is mine. Leave it where you found it.

[*She rushes at him and begins to struggle for possession of the carrier.*]

GIRL: Thief! Thief! Let it go, it is mine. You animal, just because I let you play with it. Idiot! Idiot!

[*The struggle becomes quite violent. The girl is hanging on to the effigy and Ifada lifts her with it, flinging her all about. The girl hangs on grimly.*]

GIRL: You are spoiling it . . . why don't you get your own? Thief! Let it go you thief!

[*Sunma comes in walking very fast, throwing apprehensive glances over her shoulder. Seeing the two children, she becomes immediately angry. Advances on them.*]

SUNMA: So you've made this place your playground. Get away you untrained pigs. Get out of here.

[*Ifada flees at once, the girl retreats also, retaining possession of the 'carrier'.*

Sunma goes to the door. She has her hand on the door when the significance of Ifada's presence strikes her for the first time. She stands rooted to the spot, then turns slowly round.]

SUNMA: Ifada! What are you doing here?

[*Ifada is bewildered. Sunma turns suddenly and rushes into the house, flying into the inner room and out again.*]

Eman! Eman! Eman!

[*She rushes outside.*]

Where did he go? Where did they take him?

[*Ifada distressed, points. Sunma seizes him by the arm, drags him off.*]

Take me there at once. God help you if we are too late. You loathsome thing, if you have let him suffer . . .

[*Her voice fades into other shouts, running footsteps, banged tins, bells, dogs, etc., rising in volume.*]

[*It is a narrow passage-way between two mud-houses. At the far end one man after another is seen running across the entry, the noise dying off gradually.*

About half-way down the passage, Eman is crouching against the wall, tense with apprehension. As the noise dies off, he seems to relax, but the alert hunted look is still in his eyes which are ringed in a reddish colour. The rest of his body has been whitened with a floury substance. He is naked down to the waist, wears a baggy pair of trousers, calf-length, and around both feet are bangles.]

EMAN: I will simply stay here till dawn. I have done enough.

[*A window is thrown open and a woman empties some slop from a pail. With a startled cry Eman leaps aside to avoid it and the woman puts out her head.*]

WOMAN: Oh, my head. What have I done! Forgive me neighbour . . . Eh, it's the carrier!

[*Very rapidly she clears her throat and spits on him, flings the pail at him and runs off, shouting.*]

He's here. The carrier is hiding in the passage. Quickly, I have found the carrier!

[*The cry is taken up and Eman flees down the passage. Shortly afterwards his pursuers come pouring down the passage in full cry. After the last of them come Jaguna and Oroge.*]

OROGE: Wait, wait. I cannot go so fast.

JAGUNA: We will rest a little then. We can do nothing anyway.

OROGE: If only he had let me prepare him.

JAGUNA: They are the ones who break first, these fools who think they were born to carry suffering like a hat. What are we to do now?

OROGE: When they catch him I must prepare him.

JAGUNA: He? It will be impossible now. There can be no joy left in that one.

OROGE: Still, it took him by surprise. He was not expecting what he met.

JAGUNA: Why then did he refuse to listen? Did he think he was coming to sit down to a feast. He had not even gone through one compound before he bolted. Did he think he was taken round the people to be blessed? A woman, that is all he is.

OROGE: No, no. He took the beating well enough. I think he is the kind who would let himself be beaten from night till dawn and not utter a sound. He would let himself be stoned until he dropped dead.

JAGUNA: Then what made him run like a coward?

OROGE: I don't know. I don't really know. It is a night of curses Jaguna. It is not many unprepared minds will remain unhinged under the load.

JAGUNA: We must find him. It is a poor beginning for a year when our own curses remain hovering over our homes because the carrier refused to take them.

[*They go. The scene changes. Eman is crouching beside some shrubs, torn and bleeding.*]

EMAN: They are even guarding my house . . . as if I would go there, but I need water . . . they could at least grant me that . . . I can be thirsty too . . . [*he pricks his ears.*] . . . there must be a stream nearby . . . [*as he looks round him, his eyes widen at a scene he encounters.*]

[*An old man, short and vigorous looking is seated on a stool. He also is wearing calf-length baggy trousers, white. On his head, a white cap. An attendant is engaged in rubbing his body with oil. Round his eyes, two white rings have already been marked.*]

OLD MAN: Have they prepared the boat?

ATTENDANT: They are making the last sacrifice.

OLD MAN: Good. Did you send for my son?

ATTENDANT: He's on his way.

OLD MAN: I have never met the carrying of the boat with such a heavy heart. I hope nothing comes of it.

ATTENDANT: The gods will not desert us on that account.

OLD MAN: A man should be at his strongest when he takes the boat my friend. To be weighed down inside and out is not a wise thing. I hope when the moment comes I shall have found my strength.

[*Enter Eman, a wrapper round his waist and a 'danski'° over it.*]

OLD MAN: I meant to wait until after my journey to the river, but my mind is so burdened with my own grief and yours I could not delay it. You know I must have all my strength. But I sit here, feeling it all eaten slowly away by my unspoken grief. It helps to say it out. It even helps to cry sometimes.

[*He signals to the attendant to leave them.*]

Come nearer . . . we will never meet again son. Not on this side of the flesh. What I do not know is whether you will return to take my place.

EMAN: I will never come back.

OLD MAN: Do you know what you are saying? Ours is a strong breed my son. It is only a strong breed that can take this boat to the river

danski: a brief shirt

year after year and wax stronger on it. I have taken down each year's evils for over twenty years. I hoped you would follow me.

EMAN: My life here died with Omae.

OLD MAN: Omae died giving birth to your child and you think the world is ended. Eman, my pain did not begin when Omae died. Since you sent her to stay with me son, I lived with the burden of knowing that this child would die bearing your son.

EMAN: Father . . .

OLD MAN: Don't you know it was the same with you? And me? No woman survives the bearing of the strong ones. Son, it is not the mouth of the boaster that says he belongs to the strong breed. It is the tongue that is red with pain and black with sorrow. Twelve years you were away my son, and for those twelve years I knew the love of an old man for his daughter and the pain of a man helplessly awaiting his loss.

EMAN: I wish I had stayed away. I wish I never came back to meet her.

OLD MAN: It had to be. But you know now what slowly ate away my strength. I awaited your return with love and fear. Forgive me then if I say that your grief is light. It will pass. This grief may drive you now from home. But you must return.

EMAN: You do not understand. It is not grief alone.

OLD MAN: What is it then? Tell me, I can still learn.

EMAN: I was away twelve years. I changed much in that time.

OLD MAN: I am listening.

EMAN: I am unfitted for your work father. I wish to say no more. But I am totally unfitted for your call.

OLD MAN: It is only time you need son. Stay longer and you will answer the urge of your blood.

EMAN: That I stayed at all was because of Omae. I did not expect to find her waiting. I would have taken her away, but hard as you claim to be, it would have killed you. And I was a tired man. I needed peace. Because Omae was peace, I stayed. Now nothing holds me here.

OLD MAN: Other men would rot and die doing this task year after year. It is strong medicine which only we can take. Our blood is strong like no other. Anything you do in life must be less than this, son.

EMAN: That is not true father.

OLD MAN: I tell you it is true. Your own blood will betray you son, because you cannot hold it back. If you make it do less than this, it will rush to your head and burst it open. I say what I know my son.

EMAN: There are other tasks in life father. This one is not for me. There are even greater things you know nothing of.

OLD MAN: I am very sad. You only go to give to others what rightly belongs to us. You will use your strength among thieves. They are thieves because they take what is ours, they have no claim of blood to it. They will even lack the knowledge to use it wisely. Truth is my companion at this moment my son. I know everything I say will surely bring the sadness of truth.

EMAN: I am going father.

OLD MAN: Call my attendant. And be with me in your strength for this last journey. A-ah, did you hear that? It came out without my knowing it; this is indeed my last journey. But I am not afraid.

[*Eman goes out. A few moments later, the attendant enters.*]

ATTENDANT: The boat is ready.

OLD MAN: So am I.

[*He sits perfectly still for several moments. Drumming begins somewhere in the distance, and the old man sways his head almost imperceptibly. Two men come in bearing a miniature boat, containing an indefinable mound. They rush it in and set it briskly down near the old man, and stand well back. The old man gets up slowly, the attendant watching him keenly. He signs to the men, who lift the boat quickly onto the old man's head. As soon as it touches his head, he holds it down with both hands and runs off, the men give him a start, then follow at a trot.*

As the last man disappears Oroge limps in and comes face to face with Eman — as carrier — who is now seen still standing beside the shrubs, staring into the scene he has just witnessed. Oroge, struck by the look on Eman's face, looks anxiously behind him to see what has engaged Eman's attention. Eman notices him then, and the pair stare at each other. Jaguna enters, sees him and shouts, 'Here he is', rushes at Eman who is whipped back to the immediate and flees, Jaguna in pursuit. Three or four others enter and follow them. Oroge remains where he is, thoughtful.]

JAGUNA [*re-enters.*]: They have closed in on him now, we'll get him this time.

OROGE: It is nearly midnight.

JAGUNA: You were standing there looking at him as if he was some strange spirit. Why didn't you shout?

OROGE: You shouted didn't you? Did that catch him?

JAGUNA: Don't worry. We have him now. But things have taken a bad turn. It is no longer enough to drive him past every house. There is too much contamination about already.

OROGE [*not listening.*]: He saw something. Why may I not know what it was?

JAGUNA: What are you talking about?

OROGE: Hm. What is it?

JAGUNA: I said there is too much harm done already. The year will demand more from this carrier than we thought.

OROGE: What do you mean?

JAGUNA: Do we have to talk with the full mouth?

OROGE: S-sh . . . look!

[*Jaguna turns just in time to see Sunma fly at him, clawing at his face like a crazed tigress.*]

SUNMA: Murderer! What are you doing to him. Murderer! Murderer!

[*Jaguna finds himself struggling really hard to keep off his daughter, he succeeds in pushing her off and striking her so hard on the face that she falls to her knees. He moves on her to hit her again.*]

OROGE [*comes between.*]: Think what you are doing Jaguna, she is your daughter.

JAGUNA: My daughter! Does this one look like my daughter? Let me cripple the harlot for life.

OROGE: That is a wicked thought Jaguna.

JAGUNA: Don't come between me and her.

OROGE: Nothing in anger — do you forget what tonight is?

JAGUNA: Can you blame me for forgetting?

[*Draws his hand across his cheek — it is covered with blood.*]

OROGE: This is an unhappy night for us all. I fear what is to come of it.

JAGUNA: Let's go. I cannot restrain myself in this creature's presence. My own daughter . . . and for a stranger . . .

[*They go off, Ifada, who came in with Sunma and had stood apart, horror-stricken, comes shyly forward. He helps Sunma up. They go off, he holding Sunma bent and sobbing.*]

[*Enter Eman — as carrier. He is physically present in the bounds of this next scene, a side of a round thatched hut. A young girl, about fourteen runs in, stops beside the hut. She looks carefully to see that she is not observed, puts her mouth to a little hole in the wall.*]

OMAE: Eman . . . Eman . . .

[*Eman — as carrier — responds, as he does throughout the scene, but they are unaware of him.*]

EMAN [*from inside.*]: Who is it?

OMAE: It is me, Omae.

EMAN: How dare you come here!

[*Two hands appear at the hole and pushing outwards, create a much larger hole through which Eman puts out his head. It is Eman as a boy, the same age as the girl.*]

Go away at once. Are you trying to get me into trouble!

OMAE: What is the matter?

EMAN: You. Go away.

OMAE: But I came to see you.

EMAN: Are you deaf? I say I don't want to see you. Now go before my tutor catches you.

OMAE: All right. Come out.

EMAN: Do what!

OMAE: Come out.

EMAN: You must be mad.

OMAE [sits on the ground.]: All right, if you don't come out I shall simply stay here until your tutor arrives.

EMAN [about to explode, thinks better of it and the head disappears. A moment later he emerges from behind the hut.] What sort of a devil has got into you?

OMAE: None. I just wanted to see you.

EMAN [his mimicry is nearly hysterical.]: 'None. I just wanted to see you.' Do think this place is the stream where you can go and molest innocent people?

OMAE [coyly.]: Aren't you glad to see me?

EMAN: I am not.

OMAE: Why?

EMAN: Why? Do you really ask me why? Because you are a woman and a most troublesome woman. Don't you know anything about this at all. We are not meant to see any woman. So go away before more harm is done.

OMAE [flirtatious.]: What is so secret about it anyway? What do they teach you.

EMAN: Nothing any woman can understand.

OMAE: Ha ha. You think we don't know eh? You've all come to be circumcised.

EMAN: Shut up. You don't know anything.

OMAE: Just think, all this time you haven't been circumcised, and you dared make eyes at us women.

EMAN: Thank you — woman. Now go.

OMAE: Do they give you enough to eat?

EMAN [testily.]: No. We are so hungry that when silly girls like you turn up, we eat them.

OMAE [feigning tears.]: Oh, oh, oh, he's abusing me. He's abusing me.

EMAN [alarmed.]: Don't try that here. Go quickly if you are going to cry.

OMAE: All right, I won't cry.

EMAN: Cry or no cry, go away and leave me alone. What do you think will happen if my tutor turns up now.

OMAE: He won't.

EMAN [mimicking.]: 'He won't.' I suppose you are his wife and he tells you where he goes. In fact this is just the time he comes round to our huts. He could be at the next hut this very moment.

OMAE: Ha-ha. You're lying. I left him by the stream, pinching the girls' bottoms. Is that the sort of thing he teaches you?

EMAN: Don't say anything against him or I shall beat you. Isn't it you loose girls who tease him, wiggling your bottoms under his nose?

OMAE [going tearful again.]: A-ah, so I am one of the loose girls eh?

EMAN: Now don't start accusing me of things I didn't say.

OMAE: But you said it. You said it.

EMAN: I didn't. Look Omae, someone will hear you and I'll be in disgrace. Why don't you go before anything happens.

OMAE: It's all right. My friends have promised to hold your old rascal tutor till I get back.

EMAN: Then you go back right now. I have work to do. [Going in.]

OMAE [runs after and tries to hold him. Eman leaps back, genuinely scared.]: What is the matter? I was not going to bite you.

EMAN: Do you know what you nearly did? You almost touched me!

OMAE: Well?

EMAN: Well! Isn't it enough that you let me set my eyes on you? Must you now totally pollute me with your touch? Don't you understand anything?

OMAE: Oh, that.

EMAN [nearly screaming.]: It is not 'oh that'. Do you think this is only a joke or a little visit like spending the night with your grandmother? This is an important period of my life. Look, these huts, we built them with our own hands. Every boy builds his own. We learn things, do you understand? And we spend much time just thinking. At least, I do. It is the first time I have had nothing to do except think. Don't you see, I am becoming a man. For the first time, I understand that I have a life to fulfil. Has that thought ever worried you?

OMAE: You are frightening me.

EMAN: There. That is all you can say. And what use will that be when a man finds himself alone — like that? [Points to the hut.] A man must go on his own, go where no one can help him, and test his strength. Because he may find himself one day sitting alone in a wall as round as that. In there, my mind could hold no other thought. I may never have such moments again to myself. Don't dare to come and steal any more of it.

OMAE [this time, genuinely tearful.]: Oh, I know you hate me. You only want to drive me away.

EMAN [impatiently.]: Yes, yes, I know I hate you — but go.

OMAE [going, all tears. Wipes her eyes, suddenly all mischief.]: Eman.

EMAN: What now?

OMAE: I only want to ask one thing . . . do you promise to tell me?

EMAN: Well, what is it?

OMAE [gleefully.]: Does it hurt?

[*She turns instantly and flees, landing straight into the arms of the returning tutor.*]

TUTOR: Te-he-he . . . what have we here? What little mouse leaps straight into the beak of the wise old owl eh?

[*Omae struggles to free herself, flies to the opposite side, grimacing with distaste.*]

TUTOR: I suppose you merely came to pick some fruits eh? You did not sneak here to see any of my children.

OMAE: Yes, I came to steal your fruits.

TUTOR: Te-he-he . . . I thought so. And that dutiful son of mine over there. He saw you and came to chase you off my fruit trees didn't he? Te-he-he . . . I'm sure he did, isn't that so my young Eman?

EMAN: I was talking to her.

TUTOR: Indeed you were. Now be good enough to go into your hut until I decide your punishment. [*Eman withdraws.*] Te-he-he . . . now now my little daughter, you need not be afraid of me.

OMAE [*spiritedly.*]: I am not.

TUTOR: Good. Very good. We ought to be friendly. [*His voice becomes leering.*] Now this is nothing to worry you my daughter . . . a very small thing indeed. Although of course if I were to let it slip that your young Eman had broken a strong taboo, it might go hard on him you know. I am sure you would not like that to happen, would you?

OMAE: No.

TUTOR: Good. You are sensible my girl. Can you wash clothes?

OMAE: Yes.

TUTOR: Good. If you will come with me now to my hut, I shall give you some clothes to wash, and then we will forget all about this matter eh? Well, come on.

OMAE: I shall wait here. You go and bring the clothes.

TUTOR: Eh? What is that? Now now, don't make me angry. You should know better than to talk back at your elders. Come now.

[*He takes her by the arm, and tries to drag her off.*]

OMAE: No no, I won't come to your hut. Leave me. Leave me alone you shameless old man.

TUTOR: If you don't come I shall disgrace the whole family of Eman, and yours too.

[*Eman re-enters with a small bundle.*]

EMAN: Leave her alone. Let us go Omae.

TUTOR: And where do you think you are going?

EMAN: Home.

TUTOR: Te-he-he . . . As easy as that eh? You think you can leave here any time you please? Get right back inside that hut!

[*Eman takes Omae by the arm and begins to walk off.*]

TUTOR: Come back at once.

[*He goes after him and raises his stick. Eman catches it, wrenches it from him and throws its away.*]

OMAE [*hopping delightedly.*]: Kill him. Beat him to death.

TUTOR: Help! Help! He is killing me! Help!

[*Alarmed, Eman clamps his hand over his mouth.*]

EMAN: Old tutor, I don't mean you any harm, but you mustn't try to harm me either. [*He removes his hand.*]

TUTOR: You think you can get away with your crime. My report shall reach the elders before you ever get into town.

EMAN: You are afraid of what I will say about you? Don't worry. Only if you try to shame me, then I will speak. I am not going back to the village anyway. Just tell them I have gone, no more. If you say one word more than that I shall hear of it the same day and I shall come back.

TUTOR: You are telling me what to do? But don't think to come back next year because I will drive you away. Don't think to come back here even ten years from now. And don't send your children.

[*Goes off with threatening gestures.*]

EMAN: I won't come back.

OMAE: Smoked vulture! But Eman, he says you cannot return next year. What will you do?

EMAN: It is a small thing one can do in the big towns.

OMAE: I thought you were going to beat him that time. Why didn't you crack his dirty hide?

EMAN: Listen carefully Omae . . . I am going on a journey.

OMAE: Come on. Tell me about it on the way.

EMAN: No, I go that way. I cannot return to the village.

OMAE: Because of that wretched man? Anyway you will first talk to your father.

EMAN: Go and see him for me. Tell him I have gone away for some time. I think he will know.

OMAE: But Eman . . .

EMAN: I haven't finished. You will go and live with him till I get back. I have spoken to him about you. Look after him!

OMAE: But what is this journey? When will you come back?

EMAN: I don't know. But this is a good moment to go. Nothing ties me down.

OMAE: But Eman, you want to leave me.

EMAN: Don't forget all I said. I don't know how long I will be. Stay in my father's house as long as you remember me. When you become tired of waiting, you must do as you please. You understand? You must do as you please.

OMAE: I cannot understand anything Eman. I don't know where you are going or why. Suppose you never came back! Don't go Eman. Don't leave me by myself.

EMAN: I must go. Now let me see you on your way.

OMAE: I shall come with you.

EMAN: Come with me! And who will look after you? Me? You will only be in my way, you know that! You will hold me back and I shall desert you in a strange place. Go home and do as I say. Take care of my father and let him take care of you.

[*He starts going but Omae clings to him.*]

OMAE: But Eman, stay the night at least. You will only lose your way. Your father Eman, what will he say? I won't remember what you said . . . come back to the village . . . I cannot return alone Eman . . . come with me as far as the crossroads.

[*His face set, Eman strides off and Omae loses balance as he increases his pace. Falling, she quickly wraps her arms around his ankle, but Eman continues unchecked, dragging her along.*]

OMAE: Don't go Eman . . . Eman, don't leave me, don't leave me . . . don't leave your Omae . . . don't go Eman . . . don't leave your Omae . . .

[*Eman — as carrier — makes a nervous move as if he intends to go after the vanished pair. He stops but continues to stare at the point where he last saw them. There is stillness for a while. Then the Girl enters from the same place and remains looking at Eman. Startled, Eman looks apprehensively round him. The Girl goes nearer but keeps beyond arm's length.*]

GIRL: Are you the carrier?

EMAN: Yes. I am Eman.

GIRL: Why are you hiding?

EMAN: I really came for a drink of water . . . er . . . is there anyone in front of the house?

GIRL: No.

EMAN: But there might be people in the house. Did you hear voices?

GIRL: There is no one here.

EMAN: Good. Thank you. [*He is about to go, stops suddenly.*] Er . . . would you . . . you will find a cup on the table. Could you bring me the water out here? The water-pot is in a corner.

[*The Girl goes. She enters the house, then, watching Eman carefully, slips out and runs off.*]

EMAN [*sitting.*]: Perhaps they have all gone home. It will be good to rest. [*He hears voices and listens hard.*] Too late. [*Moves cautiously nearer the house.*] Quickly girl, I can hear people coming. Hurry up. [*Looks through the window.*] Where are you? Where is she? [*The truth dawns on him suddenly and he moves off, sadly.*]

[*Enter Jaguna and Oroge, led by the Girl.*]

GIRL [*pointing.*]: He was there.

JAGUNA: Ay, he's gone now. He is a sly one is your friend. But it won't save him for ever.

OROGE: What was he doing when you saw him?

GIRL: He asked me for a drink of water.

JAGUNA,
OROGE } : Ah! [*They look at each other.*]

OROGE: We should have thought of that.

JAGUNA: He is surely finished now. If only we had thought of it earlier.

OROGE: It is not too late. There is still an hour before midnight.

JAGUNA: We must call back all the men. Now we need only wait for him — in the right place.

OROGE: Everyone must be told. We don't want anyone heading him off again.

JAGUNA: And it works so well. This is surely the help of the gods themselves Oroge. Don't you know at once what is on the path to the stream?

OROGE: The sacred trees.

JAGUNA: I tell you it is the very hand of the gods. Let us go.

[*An overgrown part of the village. Eman wanders in, aimlessly, seemingly uncaring of discovery. Beyond him, an area lights up, revealing a group of people clustered round a spot, all the heads are bowed. One figure stands away and separate from them. Even as Eman looks, the group breaks up and the people disperse, coming down and past him. Only three people are left, a man (Eman) whose back is turned, the village priest and the isolated one. They stand on opposite sides of the grave, the man on the mound of earth. The priest walks round to the man's side and lays a hand on his shoulder.*]

PRIEST: Come.

EMAN: I will. Give me a few moments here alone.

PRIEST: Be comforted.

[*They fall silent.*]

EMAN: I was gone twelve years but she waited. She whom I thought had too much of the laughing child in her. Twelve years I was a pilgrim, seeking the vain shrine of secret strength. And all the time, strange knowledge, this silent strength of my child-woman.

PRIEST: We all saw it. It was a lesson to us; we did not know that such goodness could be found among us.

EMAN: Then why? Why the wasted years if she had to perish giving birth to my child? [*They are both silent.*] I do not really know for what great meaning I searched. When I returned, I could not be certain I had found it. Until I reached my home and I found her a full-grown woman, still a child at heart. When I grew to believe it, I thought, this, after all, is what I sought. It was here all the time.

And I threw away my new-gained knowledge. I buried the part of me that was formed in strange places. I made a home in my birth-place.

PRIEST: That was as it should be.

EMAN: Any truth of that was killed in the cruelty of her brief happiness.

PRIEST [*looks up and sees the figure standing away from them, the child in his arms. He is totally still.*] Your father — he is over there.

EMAN: I knew he would come. Has he my son with him?

PRIEST: Yes.

EMAN: He will let no one take the child. Go and comfort him priest. He loved Omae like a daughter, and you all know how well she looked after him. You see how strong we really are. In his heart of hearts the old man's love really awaited a daughter. Go and comfort him. His grief is more than mine.

[*The priest goes. The old man has stood well away from the burial group. His face is hard and his gaze unswerving from the grave. The priest goes to him, pauses, but sees that he can make no dent in the man's grief. Bowed, he goes on his way.*]

[*Eman, as carrier, walking towards the graveside, the other Eman having gone. His feet sink into the mound and he breaks slowly on to his knees, scooping up the sand in his hands and pouring it on his head. The scene blacks out slowly.*]

[*Enter Jaguna and Oroge.*]

OROGE: We have only a little time.

JAGUNA: He will come. All the wells are guarded. There is only the stream left him. The animal must come to drink.

OROGE: You are sure it will not fail — the trap I mean.

JAGUNA: When Jaguna sets the trap, even elephants pay homage — their trunks downwards and one leg up in the sky. When the carrier steps on the fallen twigs, it is up in the sacred trees with him.

OROGE: I shall breathe again when this long night is over.

[*They go out.*]

[*Enter Eman — as carrier — from the same direction as the last two entered. In front of him is a still figure, the old man as he was, carrying the dwarf boat.*]

EMAN [*joyfully.*]: Father.

[*The figure does not turn round.*]

EMAN: It is your son, Eman. [*He moves nearer.*] Don't you want to look at me? It is I, Eman. [*He moves nearer still.*]

OLD MAN: You are coming too close. Don't you know what I carry on my head?

EMAN: But Father, I am your son.

OLD MAN: Then go back. We cannot give the two of us.

EMAN: Tell me first where you are going.

OLD MAN: Do *you* ask that? Where else but to the river?

EMAN [*visibly relieved.*]: I only wanted to be sure. My throat is burning. I have been looking for the stream all night.

OLD MAN: It is the other way.

EMAN: But you said . . .

OLD MAN: I take the longer way, you know how I must do this. It is quicker if you take the other way. Go now.

EMAN: No, I will only get lost again. I shall go with you.

OLD MAN: Go back my son. Go back.

EMAN: Why? Won't you even look at me?

OLD MAN: Listen to your father. Go back.

EMAN: But father!

[*He makes to hold him. Instantly the old man breaks into a rapid trot. Eman hesitates, then follows, his strength nearly gone.*]

EMAN: Wait father. I am coming with you . . . wait . . . wait for me father . . .

[*There is a sound of twigs breaking, of a sudden trembling in the branches. Then silence.*]

[*The front of Eman's house. The effigy is hanging from the sheaves. Enter Sunma, still supported by Ifada, she stands transfixed as she sees the hanging figure. Ifada appears to go mad, rushes at the object and tears it down. Sunma, her last bit of will gone, crumbles against the wall. Some distance away from them, partly hidden, stands the Girl, impassively watching. Ifada hugs the effigy to him, stands above Sunma. The Girl remains where she is, observing.*

Almost at once, the villagers begin to return, subdued and guilty. They walk across the front, skirting the house as widely as they can. No word is exchanged. Jaguna and Oroge eventually appear. Jaguna who is leading, sees Sunma as soon as he comes in view. He stops at once, retreating slightly.]

OROGE [*almost whispering.*]: What is it?

JAGUNA: The viper.

[*Oroge looks cautiously at the woman.*]

OROGE: I don't think she will even see you.

JAGUNA: Are you sure? I am in no frame of mind for another meeting with her.

OROGE: Let's go home.

JAGUNA: I am sick to the heart of the cowardice I have seen tonight.

OROGE: That is the nature of men.

JAGUNA: Then it is a sorry world to live in. We did it for them. It was all for their own common good. What did it benefit me whether the man lived or died. But did you see them? One and all they looked up at the man and words died in their throats.

OROGE: It was no common sight.

JAGUNA: Women could not have behaved so shamefully. One by one they crept off like sick dogs. Not one could raise a curse.

OROGE: It was not only him they fled. Do you see how unattended we are?

JAGUNA: There are those who will pay for this night's work!

OROGE: Ay, let us go home.

[*They go off. Sunma, Ifada and the Girl remain as they are, the light fading slowly on them.*]

THE END

SENEGAL

LEOPOLD SEDAR SENGHOR

Leopold Sedar Senghor (1906–) was born in Senegal. A deputy in the French National Assembly, he became Senegal's first president in 1960 and held that post until 1980. He was a founder and chief spokesperson, with Aimé Césaire from Martinique, of negritude, a movement that seeks to assert the cultural identity of people whose ancestral home is Africa. Senghor's poetry scales the various intensities of negritude, from its aggressive to its serene variations.

With considerable lyricism, Senghor's poetry champions African customs and traditions that have been ridiculed by Europeans. He glorifies his continent's past, implying that Africa, which was great in the past, will be great again. His discourse is anticolonial and critical of Western culture's cold, impersonal, inhibited ways. His full vision, though (see his poem "New York"), portrays an accommodating world enriched by values from all places.

Black Woman

Naked woman, black woman
Dressed in your color that is life, in your form that is beauty!
I grew up in your shadow. The softness of your hands
Shielded my eyes, and now at the height of Summer and Noon,
From the crest of a charred hilltop I discover you, Promised
     Land   5
And your beauty strikes my heart like an eagle's lightning flash.

Naked woman, dark woman
Ripe fruit with firm flesh, dark raptures of black wine,
Mouth that gives music to my mouth
Savanna of clear horizons, savanna quivering to the fervent
     caress   10
Of the East Wind, sculptured tom-tom, stretched drumskin
Moaning under the hands of the conqueror
Your deep contralto voice is the spiritual song of the Beloved.

Naked woman, dark woman
Oil no breeze can ripple, oil soothing the thighs   15
Of athletes and the thighs of the princes of Mali°
Gazelle with celestial limbs, pearls are stars
Upon the night of your skin. Delight of the mind's riddles,
The reflections of red gold from your shimmering skin
In the shade of your hair, my despair   20
Lightens in the close suns of your eyes.

Naked woman, black woman
I sing your passing beauty and fix it for all Eternity
before jealous Fate reduces you to ashes to nourish the roots
        of life.

Translated from the French by Melvin Dixon

Totem°

I must hide in the intimate depths of my veins.
The Ancestors storm-dark skinned, shot with lightning
            And thunder
And my guardian animal! I must hide him
Lest I smash through the boom of scandal.   5
He is my faithful blood and demands fidelity
Protecting my naked pride against
Myself and all the insolence of lucky races.

Translated from the French
by John Reed and Clive Wake

New York

Jazz orchestra: solo trumpet

I

New York! At first your beauty confused me, and your great
        longlegged golden girls.
I was so timid at first under your blue metallic eyes, your
        frosty smile

Mali: a famous West African kingdom from the Middle Ages, for which the present
    state of Mali was named
totem: an animal or plant believed to be the tutelar spirit of a tribe or clan

So timid. And the disquiet in the depth of your skyscraper
    streets
Lifting up owl eyes in the sun's eclipse.
Your sulphurous light and the livid shafts (their heads
    dumbfounding the sky)   5
Skyscrapers defying cyclones on their muscles of steel and their
    weathered stone skins.
But a fortnight on the bald sidewalks of Manhattan
— At the end of the third week the fever takes you with the
    pounce of a jaguar
A fortnight with no well or pasture, all the birds of the air
Fall suddenly dead below the high ashes of the terraces.   10
No child's laughter blossoms, his hand in my fresh hand
No mother's breast. Legs in nylon. Legs and breasts with no
    sweat and no smell.
No tender word for mouths are lipless. Hard cash buys artificial
    hearts.
No book where wisdom is read. The painter's palette flowers
    with crystals of coral.
Insomniac nights O nights of Manhattan, tormented by fatuous
    fires, while the klaxons cry through the empty hours   15
And dark waters bear away hygienic loves, like the bodies of
    children on a river in flood.

    2

It is the time of signs and reckonings
New York! It is the time of manna and hyssop.
Only listen to God's trombones, your heart beating to the
    rhythm of blood your blood.
I have seen Harlem humming with sounds and solemn colour
    and flamboyant smells   20
— (It is tea-time for the man who delivers pharmaceutical
    products)
I have seen them preparing at flight of day, the festival of the
    Night. I proclaim there is more truth in the Night than
    in the day.
It is the pure hour when God sets the life before memory
    germinating in the streets
All the amphibious elements shining like suns.
Harlem Harlem! I have seen Harlem Harlem! A breeze green
    with corn springing from the pavements ploughed by the
    bare feet of dancers in   25
Crests and waves of silk and breasts of spearheads, ballets of
    lilies and fabulous masks

The mangoes of love roll from the low houses under the police
horses' hooves.
I have seen down the sidewalks streams of white rum and
streams of black milk in the blue haze of cigars.
I have seen the sky at evening snowing cotton flowers and wings
of seraphim and wizard's plumes.
Listen, New York, listen to your brazen male voice your vibrant
oboe voice, the muted anguish of your tears falling in great
clots of blood   30
Listen to the far beating of your nocturnal heart, rhythm and
blood of the drum, drum and blood and drum.

3

New York! I say to New York, let the black blood flow into your
blood
Cleaning the rust from your steel articulations, like an oil of life
Giving your bridges the curve of the hills, the liana's suppleness.
See, the ancient times come again, unity is rediscovered the
reconciliation of the Lion the Bull and the Tree   35
The idea is linked to the act the ear to the heart the sign to the
sense.
See your rivers murmuring with musky caymans, manatees with
eyes of mirage. There is no need to invent the Mermaids.
It is enough to open your eyes to the April rainbow
And the ears, above all the ears to God who with a burst of
saxophone laughter created the heavens and the earth in six
days.
And on the seventh day, he slept his great negro sleep.   40

Translated from the French by
John Reed and Clive Wake

Be Not Amazed

Be not amazed beloved, if sometimes my song grows dark,
If I exchange the lyrical reed for the Khalam° or the tama°
And the green scent of the ricefields, for the swiftly galloping
    war drums.
I hear the threats of ancient deities, the furious cannonade of the
    god.
Oh, tomorrow perhaps, the purple voice of your bard will be
    silent for ever.   5
That is why my rhythm becomes so fast, that the fingers bleed
    on the Khalam.
Perhaps, beloved, I shall fall tomorrow, on a restless earth
Lamenting your sinking eyes, and the dark tom-tom of the
    mortars below.
And you will weep in the twilight for the glowing voice that
    sang your black beauty.

Translated from the French by
John Reed and Clive Wake

In What Tempestuous Night

What dark tempestuous night has been hiding your face?
And what claps of thunder frighten you from the bed
When the fragile walls of my breast tremble?
I shudder with cold, trapped in the dew of the clearing.
Oh, I am lost in the treacherous paths of the forest.   5
Are these creepers or snakes that entangle my feet?
I slip into the mudhole of fear and my cry is suffocated in a
    watery rattle.
But when shall I hear your voice again, happy luminous morn?
When shall I recognize myself again in the laughing mirror of
    eyes, that are large like windows?
And what sacrifice will pacify the white mask of the goddess?   10

Khalam: a type of lute
tama: a small drum

Perhaps the blood of chickens or goats, or the worthless blood in
    my veins?
Or the prelude of my song, the ablution of my pride?

Give me propitious words.

Translated from the French by
John Reed and Clive Wake

Prayer to Masks

Black mask, red mask, you black and white masks,
Rectangular masks through whom the spirit breathes,
I greet you in silence!
And you too, my lionheaded ancestor.
You guard this place, that is closed to any feminine laughter, to
    any mortal smile.   5
You purify the air of eternity, here where I breathe the air of my
    fathers.
Masks of markless faces, free from dimples and wrinkles,
You have composed this image, this my face that bends over the
    altar of white paper.
In the name of your image, listen to me!
Now while the Africa of despotism is dying — it is the agony of a
    pitiable princess   10
Like that of Europe to whom she is connected through the
    navel —

Translated from the French by Melvin Dixon

Senegal

Now fix your immobile eyes upon your children who have been
    called
And who sacrifice their lives like the poor man his last garment
So that hereafter we may cry "hear" at the rebirth of the world
    being the leaven that the white flour needs.

For who else would teach rhythm to the world that has died of
    machines and cannons?
For who else should ejaculate the cry of joy, that arouses the
    dead and the wise in a new dawn?   5
Say, who else could return the memory of life to men with a
    torn hope?
They call us cotton heads, and coffee men, and oily men,
They call us men of death.
But we are the men of the dance whose feet only gain
   power when they beat the hard soil.

Translated from the French by
John Reed and Clive Wake

Visit

I dream in the intimate semi-darkness of an afternoon.
I am visited by the fatigues of the day,
The deceased of the year, the souvenirs of the decade,
Like the procession of the dead in the village on the horizon of
    the shallow sun.
It is the same sun bedewed with illusions,   5
The same sky unnerved by hidden presences,
The same sky feared by those who have a reckoning with the
    dead,
And suddenly my dead draw near to me. . . .

Translated from the French by
John Reed and Clive Wake

Luxembourg 1939

This morning at the Luxembourg, this autumn at the
    Luxembourg, as I lived and relived my youth
No loafers, no water, no boats upon the water, no children, no
    flowers.
Ah! The September flowers and the sunburnt cries of children
    who defied the coming winter.

Only two old boys trying to play tennis.
This autumn morning without children — the children's theater
    is shut!   5
This Luxembourg where I cannot trace my youth, those years
    afresh as the lawns.
My dreams defeated, my comrades despairing, can it be so?
Behold them falling like leaves with the leaves, withered and
    wounded trampled to death the color of blood
To be shovelled into what common grave?
I do not know this Luxembourg, these soldiers mourning guard.   10

They have put guns to protect the whispering retreat of Senators,
They have cut trenches under the bench where I first learnt the
    soft flowering of lips.
That notice again! Ah yes, dangerous youth!
I watch the leaves fall into the shelters, into the ditches into the
    trenches
Where the blood of a generation flows   15
Europe is burying the yeast of nations and the hope of newer
    races.

Translated from the French by
John Reed and Clive Wake

SEMBENE OUSMANE

*Sembene Ousmane (1923–), fiction writer and filmmaker, was born in
Senegal. "I have earned my living since I was fifteen," he says. After
service in the French army in World War II, he worked as a docker in
Marseilles, joined the French communist party, became a union organizer, and also began to write. He deals with the problems of workers
and peasants, and he projects an image of Africa that is more reflective
and self-critical and less romanticized, in contrast to his peers, such as
Leopold Sedar Senghor, who glorify the past.*

    *The story offers an implausible explanation of how tribal scars origi-
nated, implying that explanations of African custom supplied by ad-
herents of negritude have little validity. Ousmane sees negritude as di-
versionary, self-serving, idle talk by African elites, with little meaning
in real life.*

Tribal Scars or the Voltaique

In the evenings we all go to Mane's place, where we drink mint tea and discuss all sorts of subjects, even though we know very little about them. But recently we neglected the major problems such as the ex-Belgian Congo, the trouble in the Mali Federation, the Algerian War and the next UNO° meeting — even women, a subject which normally takes up about a quarter of our time. The reason was that Saer, who is usually so stolid and serious, had raised the question, "Why do we have tribal scars?"

(I should add that Saer is half Voltaique,° half Senegalese; but he has no tribal scars.)

Although not all of us have such scars on our faces, I have never heard such an impassioned discussion, such a torrent of words, in all the time we have been meeting together at Mane's. To hear us, anyone would have thought that the future of the whole continent of Africa was at stake. Every evening for weeks the most fantastic and unexpected explanations were put forward. Some of us went to neighboring villages and even farther afield to consult the elders and the griots,° who are known as the "encyclopedias" of the region, in an endeavor to plumb the depths of this mystery, which seemed buried in the distant past.

Saer was able to prove that all the explanations were wrong.

Someone said vehemently that "it was a mark of nobility"; another that "it was a sign of bondage." A third declared that "It was decorative — there was a tribe which would not accept a man or a woman unless they had these distinctive marks on the face and body." One joker told us with a straight face that: "Once upon a time, a rich African chief sent his son to be educated in Europe. The chief's son was a child when he went away, and when he returned he was a man. So he was educated, an intellectual, let us say. He looked down on the tribal traditions and customs. His father was annoyed by this, and wondered how to bring him back into the royal fold. He consulted his chief counselor. And one morning, out on the square and in front of the people, the son's face was marked with cuts."

No one believed that story, and the teller was reluctantly obliged to abandon it.

Someone else said: "I went to the French Institute and hunted around in books, but found nothing. However, I learned that the wives of the gentlemen in high places are having these marks removed from their faces; they go to Europe to consult beauticians. For the new rules for African beauty disdain the old standards of the country; the women are becoming Americanized. It's the spreading influence of the 'darkies' of

UNO: United Nations Organization
Voltaique: a person from the River Volta region of West Africa
griot: a person who is part poet, part historian, part sorcerer

Fifth Avenue, New York. And as the trend develops, tribal scars lose their meaning and importance and are bound to disappear."

We talked about their diversity, too; about the variety even within one tribe. Cuts were made on the body as well as on the face. This led someone to ask: "If these tribal scars were signs of nobility, or of high or low caste, why aren't they ever seen in the Americas?"

"Ah, we're getting somewhere at last!" exclaimed Saer, who obviously knew the right answer to his original question, or thought he did.

"Tell us then. We give up," we all cried.

"All right," said Saer. He waited while the man on duty brought in glasses of hot tea and passed them round. The room became filled with the aroma of mint.

"So we've got around to the Americas," Saer began. "Now, none of the authoritative writers on slavery and the slave trade has ever mentioned tribal scars, so far as I know. In South America, where fetishism° and witchcraft as practiced by slaves still survive to this day, no tribal scars have ever been seen. Neither do Negroes living in the Caribbean have them, nor in Haita, Cuba, the Dominican Republic nor anywhere else. So we come back to Black Africa before the slave trade, to the time of the old Ghana Empire,° the Mali and the Gao Empires, and the cities and kingdoms of the Hausa, Bournou, Benin, Mossi and so on. Now, not one of the travelers who visited those places and wrote about them mentions this practice of tribal scars. So where did it originate?"

By now everyone had stopped sipping hot tea; they were all listening attentively.

"If we study the history of the slave trade objectively we find that the dealers sought blacks who were strong and healthy and without blemish. We find too, among other things, that in the markets here in Africa and on arrival overseas the slave was inspected, weighed and evaluated like an animal. No one was inclined to buy merchandise which had any blemish or imperfection, apart from a small mark which was the stamp of the slave-trader; but nothing else was tolerated on the body of the beast. For there was also the preparation of the slave for the auction market; he was washed and polished — whitened, as they said then — which raised the price. How, then, did these scars originate?"

We could find no answer. His historical survey had deepened the mystery for us.

"Go on, Saer, you tell us," we said, more eager than ever to hear his story of the origin of tribal scars.

And this is what he told us:

fetishism: worship of a fetish, an object in which one's guardian spirit is believed to dwell
old Ghana empire: a famous African kingdom from the Middle Ages for which the present state of Ghana was named

The slave-ship *African* had been anchored in the bay for days, waiting for a full load before sailing for the Slave States. There were already more than fifty black men and thirty Negro women down in the hold. The captain's agents were scouring the country for supplies. On this particular day only a few of the crew were on board; with the captain and the doctor, they were all in the latter's cabin. Their conversation could be heard on deck.

Amoo bent lower and glanced back at the men who were following him. He was a strong, vigorous man with rippling muscles, fit for any manual work. He gripped his axe firmly in one hand and felt his long cutlass with the other, then crept stealthily forward. More armed men dropped lithely over the bulwarks, one after the other. Momutu, their leader, wearing a broad-brimmed hat, a blue uniform with red facings, and high black boots, signalled with his musket to surround the galley. The ship's cooper had appeared from nowhere and tried to escape by jumping into the sea. But the blacks who had remained in the canoes seized him and speared him to death.

Fighting had broken out aboard the *African*. One of the crew tried to get to close quarters with the leading attackers and was struck down. The captain and the remaining men shut themselves in the doctor's cabin. Momutu and his band, armed with muskets and cutlasses, besieged the cabin, firing at it now and again. Meanwhile the vessel was being looted. As the shots rang out, the attackers increased in number; canoes left the shore, glided across the water to the *African,* and returned laden with goods.

Momutu called his lieutenants to him — four big fellows armed to the teeth. "Start freeing the prisoners and get them out of the hold."

"What about him?" asked his second-in-command, nodding towards Amoo who was standing near the hatchway.

"We'll see about him later," replied Momutu. "He's looking for his daughter. Get the hold open — and don't give any arms to the local men. Take the lot!"

The air was heavy with the smell of powder and sweat. Amoo was already battering away at the hatch-covers, and eventually they were broken open with axes and a ram.

Down in the stinking hold the men lay chained together by their ankles. As soon as they had heard the firing they had begun shouting partly with joy, partly from fright. From between-decks, where the women were, came terrified cries. Among all this din, Amoo could make out his daughter's voice. Sweat pouring from him, he hacked at the panels with all his strength.

"Hey, brother, over here!" a man called to him. "You're in a hurry to find your daughter?"

"Yes," he answered, his eyes glittering with impatience.

After many hours of hard work the hold was wide open and Momutu's men had brought up the captives and lined them up on deck, where the ship's cargo for barter had been gathered together: barrels of spirits, boxes of knives, crates containing glassware, silks, parasols and cloth. Amoo had found his daughter, Iome, and the two were standing a little apart from the rest. Amoo knew very well that Momutu had rescued the captives only in order to sell them again. It was he who had lured the *African*'s captain into the bay.

"Now we're going ashore," Momutu told them. "I warn you that you are my prisoners. If anyone tries to escape or to kill himself, I'll take the man next in the line and cut him to pieces."

The sun was winking towards the horizon and the bay had become a silvery, shimmering sheet of water; the line of trees along the shore stood out darkly. Momutu's men began to put the booty into canoes and take it ashore. Momutu, as undisputed leader, directed operations and gave orders. Some of his men still stood on guard outside the cabin, reminding those inside of their presence by discharging their muskets at the door every few minutes. When the ship had been cleared, Momutu lit a long fuse that ran to two kegs of gunpowder. The captain, finding that all was quiet, started to make his way up top; as he reached the deck, a ball from a musket hit him full in the chest. The last canoes pulled away from the ship, and when they were half-way to the shore the explosions began; then the *African* blew up and sank.

By the time everything had been taken ashore it was quite dark. The prisoners were herded together and a guard set over them, although their hands and feet were still tied. Throughout the night their whisperings and sobs could be heard, punctuated now and then by the sharp crack of a whip. Some distance away, Momutu and his aides were reckoning up their haul, drinking quantities of spirits under the starry sky as they found how well they had done for themselves.

Momutu sent for Amoo to join them.

"You'll have a drink with us, won't you?" said Momutu when Amoo approached with his sleeping daughter on his back (but they only appeared as dim shadows).

"I must be going. I live a long way off and the coast isn't a safe place now. I've been working for you for two months," said Amoo, refusing a drink.

"Is it true that you killed your wife rather than let her be taken prisoner by slave-traders?" asked one of the men, reeking of alcohol.

"Ahan!"

"And you've risked your life more than once to save your daughter?"

"She's my daughter! I've seen all my family sold into slavery one after another, and taken away into the unknown. I've grown up with fear, fleeing with my tribe so as not to be made a slave. In my tribe there are no slaves, we're all equal."

"That's because you don't live on the coast," put in a man, which made Momutu roar with laughter. "Go on, have a drink! You're a great fighter. I saw how you cut down that sailor. You're good with an axe."

"Stay with me. You're tough and you know what you want," said Momutu, passing the keg of spirits to him. Amoo politely declined a drink. "This is our work," Momutu went on. "We scour the grasslands, take prisoners and sell them to the whites. Some captains know me, but I entice others to this bay and some of my men lure the crew off the ship. Then we loot the ship and get the prisoners back again. We kill any whites left on board. It's easy work, and we win all round. I've given you back your daughter. She's a fine piece and worth several iron bars."

(Until the seventeenth century on the west coast of Africa slaves were paid for with strings of cowries° as well as with cheap goods; later, iron bars took the place of cowries. It is known that elsewhere in other markets iron bars have always been the medium of exchange.)

"It's true that I've killed men," said Amoo, "but never to take prisoners and sell them as slaves. That's your work, but it isn't mine. I want to get back to my village."

"He's an odd fellow. He thinks of nothing but his village, his wife and his daughter."

Amoo could only see the whites of their eyes. He knew that these men would not think twice of seizing himself and his daughter and selling them to the first slave-trader encountered. He was not made in their evil mold.

"I wanted to set off tonight."

"No," snapped Momutu. The alcohol was beginning to take effect, but he controlled himself and softened his voice. "We'll be in another fight soon. Some of my men have gone with the remaining whites to collect prisoners. We must capture them. Then you'll be free to go."

"I'm going to get her to lie down and have some sleep. She's had a bad time," said Amoo, moving away with his daughter.

"Has she had something to eat?"

"We've both eaten well. I'll be awake early."

The two disappeared into the night; but a shadowy figure followed them.

"He's a fine, strong fellow. Worth four kegs."

"More than that," added another. "He'd fetch several iron bars and some other stuff as well."

"Don't rush it! After the fight tomorrow we'll seize him and his daughter too. She's worth a good bit. We mustn't let them get away. There aren't many of that kind to be found along the coast now."

A soothing coolness was coming in from the sea. Night pressed close, under a starry sky. Now and then a scream of pain rose sharply, followed by another crack of the whip. Amoo had settled down with Iome some

cowries: glossy seashells used as currency

distance away from the others. His eyes were alert, though his face looked sleepy. During the dozen fights he had taken part in to redeem his daughter, Momutu had been able to judge his qualities, his great strength and supple body. Three times three moons ago, slave-hunters had raided Amoo's village and carried off all the able-bodied people. He had escaped their clutches because that day he had been out in the bush. His mother-in-law, who had been spurned because of her elephantiasis,° had told him the whole story.

When he had recovered his daughter from the slave-ship, his tears had flowed freely. Firmly holding the girl's wrist and clutching the blood-stained axe in his other hand, his heart had beat fast. Iome, who was nine or ten years old, had wept too.

He had tried to soothe away her fears. "We're going back to the village. You mustn't cry, but you must do what I tell you. Do you understand?"

"Yes, father."

"Don't cry any more. It's all over now! I'm here with you."

And there in the cradle of the night, Iome lay asleep with her head on her father's thigh. Amoo unslung his axe and placed it close at hand. Sitting with his back against a tree, his whole attention was concentrated on the immediate surroundings. At the slightest rustle, his hand went out to grasp his weapon. He dozed a little from time to time.

Even before a wan gleam had lighted the east, Momutu roused his men. Some of them were ordered to take the prisoners and the loot to a safe place. Amoo and Iome kept out of the way. The girl had deep-set eyes and was tall for her age; her hair was parted in the middle and drawn into two plaits which hung down to her shoulders. She clung to her father's side; she had seen her former companions from the slave-ship, and although she may not have known the fate in store for them, the sound of the whips left her in no doubt as to their present state.

"They'll wait for us farther on," said Momutu, coming across to Amoo. "We mustn't let ourselves be surprised by the whites' scouting party. Why are you keeping your child with you? You could have left her with one of my men."

"I'd rather keep her with me. She's very frightened," answered Amoo, watching the prisoners and escort moving off.

"She's a beautiful girl."

"Yes."

"As beautiful as her mother?"

"Not quite."

Momutu turned away and got the rest of his men, about thirty, on the move. They marched in single column. Momutu was well known among

elephantiasis: a disease that causes thickening and hardening of the skin and usually affects lower extremities slave-traders, and none of them trusted him. He had previously acted as an agent for some of the traders, then had become a "master of language" (interpreter), moving between the forts and camps where the captured Negroes were held.

They marched all that morning, with Amoo and his daughter following in the rear. When Iome was tired, her father carried her on his back. He was well aware that a watch was being kept on him. The men ahead of him were coarse, sorry-looking creatures; they looked ridiculous, trailing their long muskets. They began to leave the grasslands behind and soon were among tall trees where flocks of vultures perched. No one spoke. All that could be heard was the chattering of birds and now and again a distant, echoing howling. Then they reached the forest, humid and hostile, and Momutu called a halt; he dispersed his men and told them to rest.

"Are you tired, brother?" one of them asked Amoo. "And what about her?"

Iome raised her thick-lashed eyes towards the man, then looked at her father.

"She's a bit tired," said Amoo, looking round for a resting-place. He saw a fallen trunk at the foot of a tree and took Iome to it. The man set to keep watch on them remained a little distance away.

Momutu had a few sweet potatoes distributed to the men, and when this meager meal was over he went to see Amoo.

"How's your daughter?"

"She's asleep," said Amoo, who was carving a doll out of a piece of wood.

"She's a strong girl," said Momutu, sitting down beside him and taking off his broad-brimmed hat. His big black boots were all muddy. "We'll have a rest and wait for them here. They're bound to come this way."

Amoo was more and more on his guard. He nodded, but kept his eyes on Iome in between working at the piece of wood, which was gradually taking shape.

"After that you'll be free to go. Do you really want to go back to your village?"

"Yes."

"But you haven't anybody left there," said Momutu, and without waiting for Amoo to reply went on, "I once had a village, too, on the edge of a forest. My mother and father lived there, many relatives — a whole clan! We had meat to eat and sometimes fish. But over the years, the village declined. There was no end to lamentations. Ever since I was born I'd heard nothing but screams, seen mad flights into the bush or the forest. You go into the forest, and you die from some disease; you stay in the open, and you're captured to be sold into slavery. What was I to do? Well, I made my choice. I'd rather be with the hunters than the hunted."

Amoo, too, knew that such was life. You were never safe, never sure of seeing the next day dawn. But what he did not understand was the use made of the men and women who were taken away. It was said that the whites used their skins for making boots.

They talked for a long time, or rather Momutu talked without stopping. He boasted of his exploits and his drinking bouts. As Amoo listened, he became more and more puzzled about Momutu's character. He was like some petty warlord, wielding power by force and constraint. Eventually, after what seemed a very long time to Amoo, a man came to warn the chief that the whites were approaching. Momutu gave his orders — kill them all, and hold their prisoners. In an instant the forest fell silent; only the neutral voice of the wind could be heard.

The long file of black prisoners came into view, led by four Europeans each armed with two pistols and a culverin.° The prisoners, men and women, were joined together by a wooden yoke bolted round the neck and attached to the man in front and the one behind. Three more Europeans brought up the rear, and a fourth, probably ill, was being carried in a litter by four natives.

A sudden burst of firing from up in the trees echoed long and far. This was followed by screams and confused fighting. Amoo took advantage to fell the man guarding him and, taking his daughter by the hand, slipped away into the forest.

They crossed streams and rivers, penetrating ever deeper into the forest but heading always to the south-east. Amoo's knife and axe had never been so useful as during this time. They traveled chiefly at night, never in broad daylight, avoiding all human contact.

Three weeks later they arrived at the village — about thirty huts huddled together between the bush and the source of a river. There were few inhabitants about at that hour of the day; besides, having been frequently drained of its virile members, the village was sparsely populated. When Amoo and Iome reached the threshold of his mother-in-law's hut, the old woman limped out and her cries drew other people, many of them feeble. They were terrified at first, but stood uttering exclamations of joy and surprise when they saw Amoo and Iome. Tears and questions mingled as they crowded round. Iome's grandmother gathered her up and took her into the hut like a most precious possession, and the girl replied to her questions between floods of tears.

The elders sent for Amoo to have a talk and tell them of his adventures.

"All my life, and since before my father's life," said one of the oldest present, "the whole country has lived in the fear of being captured and sold to the whites. The whites are barbarians."

"Will it ever end?" queried another. "I have seen all my children car-

culverin: a long cannon used in the sixteenth and seventeenth centuries ried off, and I can't remember how many times we have moved the village. We can't go any farther into the forest . . . there are the wild beasts, diseases . . . "

"I'd rather face wild beasts than slave-hunters," said a third man. "Five or six rains ago, we felt safe here. But we aren't any longer. There's a slave camp only three-and-a-half days' march from the village."

They fell silent; their wrinkled, worn and worried faces bore the mark of their epoch. They discussed the necessity to move once again. Some were in favor, others pointed out the danger of living in the heart of the forest without water, the lack of strong men, and the family graves that would have to be abandoned. The patriarch, who had the flat head and thick neck of a degenerate, proposed that they should spend the winter where they were but send a group to seek another suitable site. It would be sheer madness to leave without having first discovered and prepared a place to go to. There were also the customary sacrifices to be made. Finally, all the men agreed on this course of action. During the short time they would remain there, they would increase cultivation and hold all the cattle in common, keeping the herd in an enclosure. The patriarch was of the opinion that the old women could be used to keep a watch on the village.

The return of Amoo and Iome had put new life into them. They started working communally, clearing and weeding the ground and mending the fences. The men set off for work together and returned together. The women busied themselves too; some did the cooking while others kept a look-out for any surprise visit by "procurers." (Procurers were native agents, recognizable by their uniform in the colors of the nation they worked for; they were commonly called "slave-hunters.") No one looked in the direction of the sea without a feeling of apprehension.

The rains came, and the fertile, bountiful earth gave life to the seeds that had been sown. Although the villagers went about their work with no visible sign of worry or fear, they were always on the alert for an attack, knowing it was bound to come sooner or later.

Amoo shared his hut with Iome and always slept with a weapon close at hand. Even a harmless gust of wind sent the girl into a panic. Amoo put his whole heart into his work; Iome, by general agreement, was allowed to rest as much as possible, and she gradually recovered from her ordeal. Her black cheeks shone again, tiny folds formed round her neck and her flat little breasts began to fill out.

Days and weeks slipped by peacefully. The narrow, cultivated strips of land, wrenched from the grip of nature after long struggles, were giving promise of a good harvest. The cassava plants° were in bud; the people were beginning to get in stocks of palm-oil, butter, beans and honey, in fact everything they would need in the new village. The prospecting

cassava plants: tropical plants cultivated for their edible roots

party returned, having discovered an excellent site at the foot of the mountains but above the grasslands, and not far from a running stream. The soil was good, there was plenty of pasture, and the children would be safe from the "procurers."

Everyone was very pleased with the prospect. The patriarch named the day for departure, and the feeling of safety in the near future led to a relaxation of precautions. Fires, previously forbidden during the hours of darkness for fear of betraying the village, now glowed at night; laughter rang out, and children dared to wander out of sight of their parents, for the adults were thinking only of the departure. They could count the days now. In the council hut there were discussions on which was the favorable sign for the move. Each and everyone was attending to the household gods, the totems and the family graves.

Yet it was not a sacred day, but one like any other. The sun was shining brightly, the tender green leaves of the trees were rustling in the wind, the clouds frolicked in the sky, the humming-birds were gaily seeking food, and the monkeys especially were gambolling in the trees. The whole village was enjoying this glorious day, the kind that can tempt a traveler to stay awhile, a long while.

And it happened on that particular day! On that day the "procurers" suddenly appeared. The frightened animals instinctively fled madly into the forest; men, women and children gave terrified screams on hearing the firing and scattered in panic, having but one thought, to flee to the only retreat open to them — the forest.

Amoo, grasping his axe, pushed Iome and her grandmother before him. But the old, handicapped woman could make only slow progress. They had fled between the huts and the enclosure and gained the edge of the village, and then Amoo had come face to face with one of Momutu's lieutenants. Amoo was the quicker, and struck him down. But now a whole pack was in pursuit.

Amoo went deeper into the forest, where the thick undergrowth and overhanging branches made progress even slower. Still, if Amoo had been alone, he could have escaped. But he could not abandon his child. He thought of his wife. He had killed her so that she should not be taken. His mother-in-law reminded him of his wife. To abandon the old woman would be abandoning his wife. Time and again, the old woman stopped to get her breath; her thick leg was becoming ever weightier to drag along. Amoo helped her as best he could, while Iome stuck to his side, not saying a word.

An idea came to Amoo. He stopped, took Iome gently by the chin and gazed at her for a long time, for what seemed an eternity. His eyes filled with tears.

"Mother," he said, "we can't go any farther. Ahead, there's death for all three of us. Behind, there's slavery for Iome and me."

"I can't go a step farther," said the old woman, taking her granddaughter by the hand. She raised a distraught face to Amoo.

"Mother, Iome can escape them. You both can. Your skin is no longer any use, the whites can't make boots with it."

"But if Iome's left alone, she'll die. And what about you?"

"You go free. What happens to me is my affair."

"You're not going to kill us?" exclaimed the woman.

"No, mother. But I know what to do so that Iome stays free. I must do it quickly. They're getting near, I can hear their voices."

A thunderbolt seemed to burst in his head and the ground to slip away from him. He took a grip on himself, seized his knife and went to a particular bush (the Wolof° call it *Bantamare;* its leaves have antiseptic properties), wrenched off a handful of the large leaves and returned to the other two, who had been watching him wonderingly.

His eyes blurred with tears as he looked at his daughter. "You mustn't be afraid, Iome."

"You're not going to kill her as you did her mother?" exclaimed his mother-in-law again.

"No. Iome, this is going to hurt, but you'll never be a slave. Do you understand?"

The child's only answer was to stare at the blade of the knife. She remembered the slave-ship and the bloodstained axe.

Swiftly, Amoo gripped the girl between his strong legs and began making cuts all over her body. The child's cries rang through the forest; she screamed till she had no voice left. Amoo just had time to finish before the slave-hunters seized him. He had wrapped the leaves all round the girl. With the other captured villagers, Amoo was taken down to the coast. Iome returned to the village with her grandmother, and thanks to the old woman's knowledge of herbs Iome's body soon healed; but she still bore the scars.

Months later, the slave-hunters returned to the village; they captured Iome but let her go again. She was worth nothing, because of the blemishes on her body.

The news spread for leagues around. People came from the remotest villages to consult the grandmother. And over the years and the centuries a diversity of scars appeared on the bodies of our ancestors.

And that is how our ancestors came to have tribal scars. They refused to be slaves.

Translated from the French by Len Ortzen

Wolof: one of the largest ethnic groups in West Africa, mainly in Senegal

SOUTH AFRICA

NADINE GORDIMER

Nadine Gordimer (1926–), novelist and short story writer, was born in the town of Springs in South Africa. Among the literary prizes she has received are the Booker Prize and the 1992 Nobel Prize. A member of the African National Congress, her work exposes the absurdity and the inhumanity of apartheid and the impotence of white liberalism in the social context of South Africa.

The story "Comrades" is concerned with the uneasy relations between South African blacks and whites — even when they belong to the same political camp — as a result of a long history of racial inequality and exploitation. It illustrates the difficulties of interracial communication, a communication gap that is manifest in the inability of characters from different racial groups to speak one another's languages. The white, affluent woman in the story finds the African boys inscrutable and their situation "undecipherable": they have been boycotting schools under apartheid for two years, and yet they are attending a conference on People's Education. The story presents the anomalies of life under apartheid, especially during the era of youth revolt.

Comrades

As Mrs. Hattie Telford pressed the electronic button that deactivates the alarm device in her car a group of youngsters came up behind her. Black. But no need to be afraid; this was not a city street. This was a non-racial enclave of learning, a place where tended flowerbeds and trees bearing botanical identification plates civilized the wild reminder of campus guards and dogs. The youngsters, like her, were part of the crowd loosening into dispersion after a university conference on People's Education. They were the people to be educated; she was one of the committee of white and black activists (convenient generic for revolutionaries, leftists secular and Christian, fellow-travellers and liberals) up on the platform.

— Comrade . . . — She was settling in the driver's seat when one so slight and slim he seemed a figure in profile came up to her window. He drew courage from the friendly lift of the woman's eyebrows above blue eyes, the tilt of her freckled white face: — Comrade, are you going to town? —

No, she was going in the opposite direction, home . . . but quickly, in the spirit of the hall where these young people had been somewhere, somehow present with her (ah no, she with them) stamping and singing Freedom songs, she would take them to the bus station their spokesman named. — Climb aboard! —

The others got in the back, the spokesman beside her. She saw the nervous white of his eyes as he glanced at and away from her. She searched for talk to set them at ease. Questions, of course. Older people always start with questioning young ones. Did they come from Soweto?°

They came from Harrismith, Phoneng Location.°

She made the calculation: about two hundred kilometres distant . . . How did they get here? Who told them about the conference?

— We are Youth Congress in Phoneng. —

A delegation. They had come by bus; one of the groups and stragglers who kept arriving long after the conference had started. They had missed, then, the free lunch?

At the back, no-one seemed even to be breathing. The spokesman must have had some silent communication with them, some obligation to speak for them created by the journey or by other shared experience in the mysterious bonds of the young — these young. — We are hungry. — And from the back seats was drawn an assent like the suction of air in a compressing silence.

She was silent in response, for the beat of a breath or two. These large gatherings both excited and left her overexposed, open and vulnerable to the rub and twitch of the mass shuffling across rows of seats and loping up the aisles, babies' fudge-brown soft legs waving as their napkins are changed on mothers' laps, little girls with plaited loops on their heads listening like old crones, heavy women swaying to chants, men with fierce, unreadably black faces breaking into harmony tender and deep as they sing to God for his protection of Umkhonto we Sizwe,° as people on both sides have always, everywhere, claimed divine protection for their soldiers, their wars. At the end of a day like this she wanted a drink, she wanted the depraved luxury of solitude and quiet in which she would be restored (enriched, oh yes! by the day) to the familiar limits of her own being.

Hungry. Not for iced whisky and feet up. It seemed she had scarcely hesitated: — Look, I live nearby, come back to my house and have something to eat. Then I'll run you into town. —

— That will be very nice. We can be glad for that. — And at the back the tight vacuum relaxed.

Soweto: an acronym for "southwestern townships," the segregated residential area for Africans near Johannesburg

Harrismith, Phoneng Location: an African segregated area near the all-white town of Harrismith

Umkhonto we Sizwe: literally, "spear of the nation"; the liberation army of the African National Congress

They followed her in through the gate, shrinking away from the dog — she assured them he was harmless but he was large, with a fancy collar by which she held him. She trooped them in through the kitchen because that was the way she always entered her house, something she would not have done if they had been adult, her black friends whose sophistication might lead them to believe the choice of entrance was an unthinking historical slight. As she was going to feed them, she took them not into her livingroom with its sofas and flowers but into her diningroom, so that they could sit at table right away. It was a room in confident taste that could afford to be spare: bare floorboards, matching golden wooden ceiling, antique brass chandelier, reed blinds instead of stuffy curtains. An African wooden sculpture represented a lion marvellously released from its matrix in the grain of a Mukwa tree-trunk. She pulled up the chairs and left the four young men while she went back to the kitchen to make coffee and see what there was in the refrigerator for sandwiches. They had greeted the maid, in the language she and they shared, on their way through the kitchen, but when the maid and the lady of the house had finished preparing cold meat and bread, and the coffee was ready, she suddenly did not want them to see that the maid waited on her. She herself carried the heavy tray into the diningroom.

They are sitting round the table, silent, and there is no impression that they stopped an undertone exchange when they heard her approaching. She doles out plates, cups. They stare at the food but their eyes seem focused on something she can't see; something that overwhelms. She urges them — Just cold meat, I'm afraid, but there's chutney if you like it . . . milk everybody? . . . is the coffee too strong, I have a heavy hand, I know. Would anyone like to add some hot water? —

They eat. When she tries to talk to one of the others, he says *Ekskuus?*° And she realizes he doesn't understand English, of the white man's languages knows perhaps only a little of that of the Afrikaners in the rural town he comes from. Another gives his name, as if in some delicate acknowledgement of the food. — I'm Shadrack Nsutsha. — She repeats the surname to get it right. But he does not speak again. There is an urgent exchange of eye-language, and the spokesman holds out the emptied sugar-bowl to her. — Please. — She hurries to the kitchen and brings it back refilled. They need carbohydrate, they are hungry, they are young, they need it, they burn it up. She is distressed at the inadequacy of the meal and then notices the fruit bowl, her big copper fruit bowl, filled with apples and bananas and perhaps there is a peach or two under the grape leaves with which she likes to complete an edible still life. — Have some fruit. Help yourselves. —

Ekskuus: corruption of "excuse"

They are stacking their plates and cups, not knowing what they are expected to do with them in this room which is a room where apparently people only eat, do not cook, do not sleep. While they finish the bananas and apples (Shadrack Nsutsha had seen the single peach and quickly got there first) she talks to the spokesman, whose name she has asked for: Dumile. — Are you still at school, Dumile? — Of course he is not at school — *they* are not at school; youngsters their age have not been at school for several years, they are the children growing into young men and women for whom school is a battle-ground, a place of boycotts and demonstrations, the literacy of political rhetoric, the education of revolt against having to live the life their parents live. They have pompous titles of responsibility beyond childhood: he is chairman of his branch of the Youth Congress, he was expelled two years ago — for leading a boycott? Throwing stones at the police? Maybe burning the school down? He calls it all — quietly, abstractly, doesn't know many ordinary, concrete words but knows these euphemisms — 'political activity'. No school for two years? No. — So what have you been able to do with yourself, all that time? —

She isn't giving him a chance to eat his apple. He swallows a large bite, shaking his head on its thin, little-boy neck. — I was inside. Detained from this June for six months. —

She looks round the others. — And you? —

Shadrack seems to nod slightly. The other two look at her. She should know, she should have known, it's a common enough answer from youths like them, their colour. They're not going to be saying they've been selected for the 1st Eleven at cricket° or that they're off on a student tour to Europe in the school holidays.

The spokesman, Dumile, tells her he wants to study by correspondence, 'get his matric'° that he was preparing for two years ago; two years ago when he was still a child, when he didn't have the hair that is now appearing on his face, making him a man, taking away the childhood. In the hesitations, the silences of the table, where there is nervously spilt coffee among plates of banana skins, there grows the certainty that he will never get the papers filled in for the correspondence college, he will never get the two years back. She looks at them all and cannot believe what she knows: that they, suddenly here in her house, will carry the AK 47s° they only sing about, now, miming death as they sing. They will have a career of wiring explosives to the undersides of vehicles, they will go away and come back through the bush to dig holes not to plant trees to shade home, but to plant land mines. She can see they have been terribly harmed but cannot believe they could harm. They are wiping their fruit-sticky hands furtively palm against palm.

1st eleven at cricket: first cricket team
matric: twelfth-grade college entry examination
AK 47s: firearms used mainly by the liberation army

She breaks the silence; says something, anything.

— How d'you like my lion? Isn't he beautiful? He's made by a Zimbabwean artist, I think the name's Dube. —

But the foolish interruption becomes revelation. Dumile, spokesman, in his gaze — distant, lingering, speechless this time — reveals what has overwhelmed them. In this room, the space, the expensive antique chandelier, the consciously simple choice of reed blinds, the carved lion: all are on the same level of impact, phenomena undifferentiated, undecipherable. Only the food that fed their hunger was real.

NJABULO SIMAKAHLE NDEBELE

Njabulo Simakahle Ndebele (1948–) grew up in Charterston on the East Rand and was educated in South Africa, England, and the United States. After many years in exile, he returned to South Africa to teach at the University of the Witwatersrand. He was appointed deputy rector at the University of the Western Cape, then vice chancellor at the University of the North, and won the Noma Award in 1983.

Like much of Ndebele's work, "Death of a Son" is concerned with coping with life under apartheid, which sometimes drives a wedge between those whom it afflicts. He examines the humiliation that comes from defeat and how it strains personal relations among victims of the system. The story portrays women as the heroines of continuity who sustain life from one era to the next — the glue that holds together even the most fragmented societies.

Death of a Son

At last we got the body. Wednesday. Just enough time for a Saturday funeral. We were exhausted. Empty. The funeral still ahead of us. We had to find the strength to grieve. There had been no time for grief, really. Only much bewilderment and confusion. Now grief. For isn't grief the awareness of loss?

That is why when we finally got the body, Buntu said: "Do you realize our son is dead?" I realized. Our awareness of the death of our first and only child had been displaced completely by the effort to get his body. Even the horrible events that caused the death: we did not think of them, as such. Instead, the numbing drift of things took over our minds: the pleas, letters to be written, telephone calls to be made, telegrams to be dispatched, lawyers to consult, "influential" people to "get in touch with," undertakers to be contacted, so much walking and driving. That is what suddenly mattered: the irksome details that blur the goal (no matter how terrible it is), each detail becoming a door which, once unlocked, revealed yet another door. Without being aware of it, we were distracted by the smell of the skunk and not by what the skunk had done.

We realized something too, Buntu and I, that during the two-week effort to get our son's body, we had drifted apart. For the first time in our marriage, our presence to each other had become a matter of habit. He was there. He'll be there. And I'll be there. But when Buntu said: "Do you realize our son is dead?" he uttered a thought that suddenly brought us together again. It was as if the return of the body of our son was also our coming together. For it was only at that moment that we really began to grieve; as if our lungs had suddenly begun to take in air when just before, we were beginning to suffocate. Something with meaning began to emerge.

We realized. We realized that something else had been happening to us, adding to the terrible events. Yes, we had drifted apart. Yet, our estrangement, just at that moment when we should have been together, seemed disturbingly comforting to me. I was comforted in a manner I did not quite understand.

The problem was that I had known all along that we would have to buy the body anyway. I had known all along. Things would end that way. And when things turned out that way, Buntu could not look me in the eye. For he had said: "Over my dead body! Over my dead body!" as soon as we knew we would be required to pay the police or the government for the release of the body of our child.

"Over my dead body! Over my dead body!" Buntu kept on saying.

Finally, we bought the body. We have the receipt. The police insisted we take it. That way, they would be "protected." It's the law, they said.

I suppose we could have got the body earlier. At first I was confused, for one is supposed to take comfort in the heroism of one's man. Yet, inwardly, I could draw no comfort from his outburst. It seemed hasty. What sense was there to it when all I wanted was the body of my child? What would happen if, as events unfolded, it became clear that Buntu would not give up his life? What would happen? What would happen to him? To me?

For the greater part of two weeks, all of Buntu's efforts, together with friends, relatives, lawyers and the newspapers, were to secure the release of the child's body without the humiliation of having to pay for it. A "fundamental principle."

Why was it difficult for me to see the wisdom of the principle? The worst thing, I suppose, was worrying about what the police may have been doing to the body of my child. How they may have been busy prying it open "to determine the cause of death"?

Would I want to look at the body when we finally got it? To see further mutilations in addition to the "cause of death"? What kind of mother would not want to look at the body of her child? people will ask. Some will say: "It's grief." She is too grief-stricken.

"But still . . . ," they will say. And the elderly among them may say: "Young people are strange."

But how can they know? It was not that I would not want to see the body of my child, but that I was too afraid to confront the horrors of my own imagination. I was haunted by the thought of how useless it had been to have created something. What had been the point of it all? This body filling up with a child. The child steadily growing into something that could be seen and felt. Moving, as it always did, at that time of day when I was all alone at home waiting for it. What had been the point of it all?

How can they know that the mutilation to determine "the cause of death" ripped my own body? Can they think of a womb feeling hunted? Disgorged?

And the milk that I still carried. What about it? What had been the point of it all?

Even Buntu did not seem to sense that that principle, the "fundamental principle," was something too intangible for me at that moment, something that I desperately wanted should assume the form of my child's body. He still seemed far from ever knowing.

I remember one Saturday morning early in our courtship, as Buntu and I walked hand-in-hand through town, window-shopping. We cannot even be said to have been window-shopping, for we were aware of very little that was not ourselves. Everything in those windows was merely an excuse for words to pass between us.

We came across three girls sitting on the pavement, sharing a packet of fish and chips after they had just bought it from a nearby Portuguese café. Buntu said: "I want fish and chips too." I said: "So seeing is desire." I said: "My man is greedy!" We laughed. I still remember how he tightened his grip on my hand. The strength of it!

Just then, two white boys coming in the opposite direction suddenly rushed at the girls, and, without warning, one of them kicked the packet of fish and chips out of the hands of the girl who was holding it. The second boy kicked away the rest of what remained in the packet. The girl stood up, shaking her hand as if to throw off the pain in it. Then she pressed it under her armpit as if to squeeze the pain out of it. Meanwhile, the two boys went on their way laughing. The fish and chips lay scattered on the pavement and on the street like stranded boats on a river that had gone dry.

"Just let them do that to you!" said Buntu, tightening once more his grip on my hand as we passed on like sheep that had seen many of their own in the flock picked out for slaughter. We would note the event and wait for our turn. I remember I looked at Buntu, and saw his face was somewhat glum. There seemed no connection between that face and the words of reassurance just uttered. For a while, we went on quietly. It was then that I noticed his grip had grown somewhat limp. Somewhat reluctant. Having lost its self-assurance, it seemed to have been holding on because it had to, not because of a confident sense of possession.

It was not to be long before his words were tested. How could fate work this way, giving to words meanings and intentions they did not carry when they were uttered? I saw that day, how the language of love could so easily be trampled underfoot, or scattered like fish and chips on the pavement, and left stranded and abandoned like boats in a river that suddenly went dry. Never again was love to be confirmed with words. The world around us was too hostile for vows of love. At any moment, the vows could be subjected to the stress of proof. And love died. For words of love need not be tested.

On that day, Buntu and I began our silence. We talked and laughed, of course, but we stopped short of words that would demand proof of action. Buntu knew. He knew the vulnerability of words. And so he sought to obliterate words with acts that seemed to promise redemption.

On that day, as we continued with our walk in town, that Saturday morning, coming up towards us from the opposite direction, was a burly Boer° walking with his wife and two children. They approached Buntu and me with an ominously determined advance. Buntu attempted to pull me out of the way, but I never had a chance. The Boer shoved me out of the way, as if clearing a path for his family. I remember, I almost crashed into a nearby fashion display window. I remember, I glanced at the family walking away, the mother and the father each dragging a child. It was for one of those children that I had been cleared away. I remember, also, that as my tears came out, blurring the Boer family and everything else, I saw and felt deeply what was inside of me: a desire to be avenged.

But nothing happened. All I heard was Buntu say: "The dog!" At that very moment, I felt my own hurt vanish like a wisp of smoke. And as my hurt vanished, it was replaced, instead, by a tormenting desire to sacrifice myself for Buntu. Was it something about the powerlessness of the curse and the desperation with which it had been made? The filling of stunned silence with an utterance? Surely it ate into him, revealing how incapable he was of meeting the call of his words.

And so it was, that that afternoon, back in the township,° left to ourselves at Buntu's home, I gave in to him for the first time. Or should I say I offered myself to him? Perhaps from some vague sense of wanting to heal something in him? Anyway, we were never to talk about that event.

Boer: Dutch word meaning "farmer"; used to describe descendants of Dutch settlers in South Africa
township: segregated black residential area, also called "location"

Never. We buried it alive deep inside of me that afternoon. Would it ever be exhumed? All I vaguely felt and knew was that I had the keys to the vault. That was three years ago, a year before we married.

The cause of death? One evening I returned home from work, particularly tired after I had been covering more shootings by the police in the East Rand.° Then I had hurried back to the office in Johannesburg° to piece together on my typewriter the violent scenes of the day, and then to file my report to meet the deadline. It was late when I returned home, and when I got there, I found a crowd of people in the yard. They were those who could not get inside. I panicked. What had happened? I did not ask those who were outside, being desperate to get into the house. They gave way easily when they recognized me.

Then I heard my mother's voice. Her cry rose well above the noise. It turned into a scream when she saw me. "What is it, mother?" I asked, embracing her out of a vaguely despairing sense of terror. But she pushed me away with an hysterical violence that astounded me.

"What misery have I brought you, my child?" she cried. At that point, many women in the room began to cry too. Soon, there was much wailing in the room, and then all over the house. The sound of it! The anguish! Understanding, yet eager for knowledge, I became desperate. I had to hold onto something. The desire to embrace my mother no longer had anything to do with comforting her; for whatever she had done, whatever its magnitude, had become inconsequential. I needed to embrace her for all the anguish that tied everyone in the house into a knot. I wanted to be part of that knot, yet I wanted to know what had brought it about.

Eventually, we found each other, my mother and I, and clasped each other tightly. When I finally released her, I looked around at the neighbors and suddenly had a vision of how that anguish had to be turned into a simmering kind of indignation. The kind of indignation that had to be kept at bay only because there was a higher purpose at that moment: the sharing of concern.

Slowly and with a calmness that surprised me, I began to gather the details of what had happened. Instinctively, I seemed to have been gathering notes for a news report.

It happened during the day, when the soldiers and the police that had been patrolling the township in their Casspirs° began to shoot in the streets at random. Need I describe what I did not see? How did the child come to die just at that moment when the police and the soldiers began to shoot at random, at any house, at any moving thing? That was how one of our windows was shattered by a bullet. And that was when my mother, who looked after her grandchild when we were away at work,

East Rand: the area to the east of Johannesburg
Johannesburg: South Africa's largest city
Casspirs: armoured vehicles used by South African army

panicked. She picked up the child and ran to the neighbors. It was only when she entered the neighbor's house that she noticed the wetness of the blanket that covered the child she held to her chest as she ran for the sanctuary of neighbors. She had looked at her unaccountably bloody hand, then she noted the still bundle in her arms, and began at that moment to blame herself for the death of her grandchild . . .

Later, the police, on yet another round of shooting, found people gathered at our house. They stormed in, saw what had happened. At first, they dragged my mother out, threatening to take her away unless she agreed not to say what had happened. But then they returned and, instead, took the body of the child away. By what freak of logic did they hope that by this act their carnage would never be discovered?

That evening, I looked at Buntu closely. He appeared suddenly to have grown older. We stood alone in an embrace in our bedroom. I noticed, when I kissed his face, how his once lean face had grown suddenly puffy.

At that moment, I felt the familiar impulse come upon me once more, the impulse I always felt when I sensed that Buntu was in some kind of danger, the impulse to yield something of myself to him. He wore the look of someone struggling to gain control of something. Yet, it was clear he was far from controlling anything. I knew that look. Had seen it many times. It came at those times when I sensed that he faced a wave that was infinitely stronger than he, that it would certainly sweep him away, but that he had to seem to be struggling. I pressed myself tightly to him as if to vanish into him; as if only the two of us could stand up to the wave.

"Don't worry," he said. "Don't worry. I'll do everything in my power to right this wrong. Everything. Even if it means suing the police!" We went silent.

I knew that silence. But I knew something else at that moment: that I had to find a way of disengaging myself from the embrace.

Suing the police? I listened to Buntu outlining his plans. "Legal counsel. That's what we need," he said. "I know some people in Pretoria,"° he said. As he spoke, I felt the warmth of intimacy between us cooling. When he finished, it was cold. I disengaged from his embrace slowly, yet purposefully. Why had Buntu spoken?

Later, he was to speak again, when all his plans had failed to work: "Over my dead body! Over my dead body!"

He sealed my lips. I would wait for him to feel and yield one day to all the realities of misfortune.

Ours was a home, it could be said. It seemed a perfect life for a young couple: I, a reporter; Buntu, a personnel officer at an American factory manufacturing farming implements. He had traveled to the United States and returned with a mind fired with dreams. We dreamed together. Much time we spent, Buntu and I, trying to make a perfect home. The occasions

Pretoria: South Africa's administrative capital

are numerous on which we paged through *Femina, Fair Lady, Cosmopolitan, Home Garden, Car,* as if somehow we were going to surround our lives with the glossiness in the magazines. Indeed, much of our time was spent window-shopping through the magazines. This time, it was different from the window-shopping we did that Saturday when we courted. This time our minds were consumed by the things we saw and dreamed of owning: the furniture, the fridge, TV, videocassette recorders, washing machines, even a vacuum cleaner and every other imaginable thing that would ensure a comfortable modern life.

Especially when I was pregnant. What is it that Buntu did not buy, then? And when the boy was born, Buntu changed the car. A family, he would say, must travel comfortably.

The boy became the center of Buntu's life. Even before he was born, Buntu had already started making inquiries at white private schools. That was where he would send his son, the bearer of his name.

Dreams! It is amazing how the horrible findings of my newspaper reports often vanished before the glossy magazines of our dreams, how I easily forgot that the glossy images were concocted out of the keys of typewriters, made by writers whose business was to sell dreams at the very moment that death pervaded the land. So powerful are words and pictures that even their makers often believe in them.

Buntu's ordeal was long. So it seemed. He would get up early every morning to follow up the previous day's leads regarding the body of our son. I wanted to go with him, but each time I prepared to go he would shake his head.

"It's my task," he would say. But every evening he returned, empty-handed, while with each day that passed and we did not know where the body of my child was, I grew restive and hostile in a manner that gave me much pain. Yet Buntu always felt compelled to give a report on each day's events. I never asked for it. I suppose it was his way of dealing with my silence.

One day he would say: "The lawyers have issued a court order that the body be produced. The writ of *habeas corpus.*"

On another day he would say: "We have petitioned the Minister of Justice."

On yet another he would say: "I was supposed to meet the Chief Security Officer. Waited the whole day. At the end of the day they said I would see him tomorrow if he was not going to be too busy. They are stalling."

Then he would say: "The newspapers, especially yours, are raising the hue and cry. The government is bound to be embarrassed. It's a matter of time."

And so it went on. Every morning he got up and left. Sometimes alone, sometimes with friends. He always left to bear the failure alone.

How much did I care about lawyers, petitions and Chief Security Officers? A lot. The problem was that whenever Buntu spoke about his efforts, I heard only his words. I felt in him the disguised hesitancy of someone who wanted reassurance without asking for it. I saw someone who got up every morning and left not to look for results, but to search for something he could only have found with me.

And each time he returned, I gave my speech to my eyes. And he answered without my having parted my lips. As a result, I sensed, for the first time in my life, a terrible power in me that could make him do anything. And he would never ever be able to deal with that power as long as he did not silence my eyes and call for my voice.

And so, he had to prove himself. And while he left each morning, I learned to be brutally silent. Could he prove himself without me? Could he? Then I got to know, those days, what I'd always wanted from him. I got to know why I have always drawn him into me whenever I sensed his vulnerability.

I wanted him to be free to fear. Wasn't there greater strength that way? Had he ever lived with his own feelings? And the stress of life in this land: didn't it call out for men to be heroes? And should they live up to it even though the details of the war to be fought may often be blurred? They should.

Yet it is precisely for that reason that I often found Buntu's thoughts lacking in strength. They lacked the experience of strife that could only come from a humbling acceptance of fear and then, only then, the need to fight it.

Me? In a way, I have always been free to fear. The prerogative of being a girl. It was always expected of me to scream when a spider crawled across the ceiling. It was known I would jump onto a chair whenever a mouse blundered into the room.

Then, once more, the Casspirs came. A few days before we got the body back, I was at home with my mother when we heard the great roar of truck engines. There was much running and shouting in the streets. I saw them, as I've always seen them on my assignments: the Casspirs. On five occasions they ran down our street at great speed, hurling tear-gas canisters at random. On the fourth occasion, they got our house. The canister shattered another window and filled the house with the terrible pungent choking smoke that I had got to know so well. We ran out of the house gasping for fresh air.

So, this was how my child was killed? Could they have been the same soldiers? Now hardened to their tasks? Or were they new ones being hardened to their tasks? Did they drive away laughing? Clearing paths for their families? What paths?

And was this our home? It couldn't be. It had to be a little bird's nest waiting to be plundered by a predator bird. There seemed no sense to the wedding pictures on the walls, the graduation pictures, birthday pictures, pictures of relatives, and paintings of lush landscapes. There seemed no sense anymore to what seemed recognizably human in our house. It took only a random swoop to obliterate personal worth, to blot out any value there may have been to the past. In desperation, we began to live only for the moment. I do feel hunted.

It was on the night of the tear gas that Buntu came home, saw what had happened, and broke down in tears. They had long been in the coming . . .

My own tears welled out too. How much did we have to cry to refloat stranded boats? I was sure they would float again.

A few nights later, on the night of the funeral, exhausted, I lay on my bed, listening to the last of the mourners leaving. Slowly, I became conscious of returning to the world. Something came back after it seemed not to have been there for ages. It came as a surprise, as a reminder that we will always live around what will happen. The sun will rise and set, and the ants will do their endless work, until one day the clouds turn gray and rain falls, and even in the township, the ants will fly out into the sky. Come what may.

My moon° came, in a heavy surge of blood. And, after such a long time, I remembered the thing Buntu and I had buried in me. I felt it as if it had just entered. I felt it again as it floated away on the surge. I would be ready for another month. Ready as always, each and every month, for new beginnings.

And Buntu? I'll be with him, now. Always. Without our knowing, all the trying events had prepared for us new beginnings. Shall we not prevail?

moon: menstrual cycle

UGANDA

OKOT P' BITEK

Okot p' Bitek (1931–1982) was born in Gulu in northern Uganda, and educated in Uganda, England, and Wales. Exiled from Uganda in the era of Idi Amin's dictatorship, he taught abroad before returning to Makerere, Uganda, as a professor of creative writing. He wrote in English and Acholi — he translated his own work, celebrated for its satire on both tradition and modernity — and was a leading authority on Luo oral tradition, which informs his work.

"My Husband's Tongue Is Bitter" (part of the long dramatic mono-logue Song of Lawino*) registers the complaints of an alcoholic woman whose husband has rejected her in favor of modern ways and another, Westernized, woman. "What Is Africa to Me?" (part of the sequel* Song of Ocol*) is a rejoinder by her husband, who has turned his back on his culture and embraced Western culture. Taken separately, their vitri-olic, extremist statements constitute a pair of one-sided pictures. What is lacking, p' Bitek suggests, is a syncretic vision — a synthesis of both cultures that is not based on blanket rejection or uncritical accept-ance.*

My Husband's Tongue Is Bitter

Husband, now you despise me
Now you treat me with spite
And say I have inherited the stupidity of my aunt;
Son of the Chief,
Now you compare me   5
With the rubbish in the rubbish pit,
You say you no longer want me
Because I am like the things left behind
In the deserted homestead.
You insult me   10
You laugh at me
You say I do not know the letter A
Because I have not been to school
And I have not been baptized

You compare me with a little dog,   15
A puppy.

My friend, age-mate of my brother,
Take care,
Take care of your tongue,
Be careful what your lips say.   20

First take a deep look, brother,
You are now a man
You are not a dead fruit!
To behave like a child does not befit you!

Listen Ocol, you are the son of a Chief,   25
Leave foolish behavior to little children,
It is not right that you should be laughed at in a song!
Songs about you should be songs of praise!

Stop despising people
As if you were a little foolish man,   30
Stop treating me like saltless ash°
Become barren of insults and stupidity;
Who has ever uprooted the Pumpkin?

My clansmen, I cry
Listen to my voice: 35
The insults of my man
Are painful beyond bearing.

My husband abuses me together with my parents;
He says terrible things about my mother
And I am so ashamed!   40

He abuses me in English
And he is so arrogant.

He says I am rubbish,
He no longer wants me!
In cruel jokes, he laughs at me,   45
He says I am primitive
Because I cannot play the guitar,
He says my eyes are dead
And I cannot read,
He says my ears are blocked   50
And cannot hear a single foreign word,
That I cannot count the coins.

saltless ash: the ash that remains after salt has been extracted

He says I am like sheep,
The fool,

Ocol treats me   55
As if I am no longer a person,
He says I am silly
Like the *ojuu* insects that sit on the beer pot°
My husband treats me roughly.
The insults!   60
Words cut more painfully than sticks!
He says my mother is a witch,
That my clansmen are fools
Because they eat rats,
He says we are all Kaffirs.°   65
We do not know the ways of God,
We sit in deep darkness
And do not know the Gospel,
He says my mother hides her charms
In her necklace   70
And that we are all sorcerers.

My husband's tongue
Is bitter like the roots of the *lyonno* lily,
Is is hot like the penis of the bee,
Like the sting of the *kalang*!   75
Ocol's tongue is fierce like the arrow of the scorpion,
Deadly like the spear of the buffalo-hornet.
It is ferocious
Like the poison of a barren woman
And corrosive like the juice of the gourd.   80

My husband pours scorn
On Black People,
He behaves like a hen
That eats its own eggs
A hen that should be imprisoned under a basket.   85

His eyes grow large
Deep black eyes
Ocol's eyes resemble those of the Nile Perch!
He becomes fierce
Like a lioness with cubs,   90
He begins to behave like a mad hyena.

beer pot: a gourd, or container, for traditionally brewed beer
Kaffir: an Arabic word meaning "non-believer," and an abusive term for Africans

He says Black People are primitive
And their ways are utterly harmful,
Their dances are mortal sins
They are ignorant, poor, and diseased!   95

Ocol says he is a modern man,
A progressive and civilized man,
He says he has read extensively and widely
And he can no longer live with a thing like me
Who cannot distinguish between good and bad,   100

He says I am just a village woman,
I am of the old type,
And no longer attractive.

He says I am blocking his progress,
My head, he says,   105
Is as big as that of an elephant
But it is only bones,
There is no brain in it,
He says I am only wasting his time.

Translated from the Acholi by Okot p' Bitek

What Is Africa to Me?

What is Africa
To me?

Blackness,
Deep, deep fathomless
Darkness;   5

Africa,
Idle giant
Basking in the sun,
Sleeping, snoring,
Twitching in dreams;   10

Diseased with a chronic illness,
Choking with black ignorance,
Chained to the rock
Of poverty,

And yet laughing,   15
Always laughing and dancing,
The chains on his legs
Jangling;

Displaying his white teeth
In bright pink gum,   20
Loose white teeth
That cannot bite,
Joking, giggling, dancing . . .

Stuck in the stagnant mud
Of superstitions,   25
Frightened by the spirits
Of the bush, the stream,
The rock,
Scared of corpses . . .

He hears eerie noises   30
From the lakeside
And from the mountain top,
Sees snakes
In the whirlwind
And at both ends   35
Of the rainbow;

The caves house his gods
Or he carries them
On his head
Or on his shoulder   40
As he roams the wilderness,
Led by his cattle,
Or following the spoor
Of the elephant
That he has speared   45
But could not kill;

Child,
Lover of toys,
Look at his toy weapons,
His utensils, his hut . . .   50
Toy garden, toy chickens,
Toy cattle,
Toy children . . .

Timid,
Unadventurous,   55
Scared of the unbeaten track,

Unweaned,
Clinging to mother's milkless breasts
Clinging to brother,
To uncle, to clan,   60
To tribe

To blackness,

To Africa,

Africa
This rich granary   65
Of taboos, customs,
Traditions . . .

Mother, mother,
Why,
Why was I born   70
Black?

Translated from the Acholi by Okot p' Bitek

THE
MIDDLE
EAST

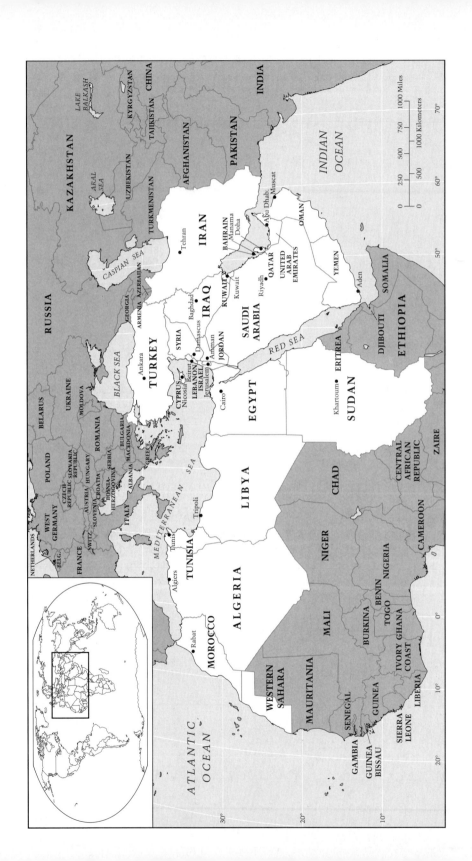

THE
MIDDLE
EAST

From Morocco to Iran, from Turkey to Yemen, North Africa and the Middle East have one thing in common: an Islamicate culture. This does not mean that all North Africans and Middle Easterners are Muslims, but rather that, with the exception of the modern state of Israel, their cultures bear the mark of long contact with Islam as a civilization and a religion.

THE ISLAMIC TRADITION

In seventh-century Arabia, a trader from Mecca called Muhammad received revelations through the angel Gabriel. He shared these visions with family and friends, and soon he had acquired a considerable following as well as concerted opposition. The venture of Islam had begun. Muhammad's Companions recorded the Prophet's words, for he himself could neither read nor write. Soon after his death in 632, these inspired utterances were organized into the Qur'an, the scripture of Islam. Until today, Arabs consider the Arabic of the Qur'an, Allah's uncreated word, to be the touchstone of faith and the acme of prose eloquence.

It may seem odd that the mediator of this influential text should have been illiterate. However, Muhammad was the norm, and his case is instructive in understanding seventh-century Arabian society. Poetry abounded, and poets had a moral authority almost unimaginable by current Western standards. Tribal leaders were generally expected to be accomplished poets even before being effective military leaders. However, a standard script did not yet exist, beyond the minimal code necessary for the purposes of trading, and poetry was not recorded in writing. Poetry was recited, improvised upon as recited, and passed on through generations of reciters. Memorization was the principal means of learning, and today some Muslim children are still expected to memorize the entire text of the Qur'an as well as some pre-Islamic poetry. Despite its secular nature, this seventh-century poetry is still held in reverence as the highest form of poetic expression in Arabic.

Within one hundred years of the death of the Prophet, Islam and its by then fully encoded scriptural language had spread through North Africa as far west as Spain and as far east as Iran. Peninsula Arabs, many of nomadic descent, came into contact with the sophisticated cultures of the Sassanian and Byzantine empires. Many became enculturated, adopting new customs and behaviors. One of the most visible and long-lasting of these cultural accretions was the imposition of the veil on women, which designated a man's superior social standing. It was only later that the veil was interpreted as a religious symbol. The capital of the Muslim empire moved from the Arabian Peninsula to Damascus, Syria, and then in 750 to Baghdad, Iraq. Both of these powerful, cosmopolitan cities became important centers of Arabic culture and learning. Best known is the ninth-century court of the Abbasid ruler Harun al-Rashid, which provided the setting for *The Thousand and One Nights*. It was here that Greek and Latin classics were translated and preserved, later forming the basis for the European Renaissance.

Between the twelfth and fourteenth centuries, Arabic literature reached its formal peak with the *maqama*, a prose-poetry genre distinguished by verbal artifice and telling the story of a witty rogue. Meanwhile, Persian and Turkish cultures were dominated by the Persian-language works of mystical masters such as Shams al-Din Muhammad Hafiz and Jalal al-Din Rumi. Thereafter, cultural energy in the western and central parts of the Islamicate world seems to have waned. Arabic, Turkish, and Persian literatures became refined forms of belles lettres whose purpose was to edify and educate the artistocratic reader, while displaying the craft and knowledge of the writer. Although individuals like the protosociologist Ibn Khaldun did leave their mark, they were few and far between. The Ottoman Empire, which remained the prevalent force in the area until the end of the nineteenth century, was known more for its military exploits than for its cultural achievements. It was finally undermined and then defeated in its confrontation with the newly industrialized countries of Europe.

EUROPEAN INFLUENCES

Literature as we have known it in Europe since the eighteenth century only began to be accepted in the Middle East and North Africa at around the turn of this century. Drama, the novel, the short story, and experimentation with conventional poetic structures were alien concepts. Writers believed that engagement with everyday life and its problems was to be eschewed; it revealed the author's deficient grasp on the classics and the need to resort to the ordinary. They had been educated to believe that targeting a general readership indicated absence of sophistication.

Contact with Europe challenged such attitudes. In the nineteenth century, the French and the British established colonial enclaves throughout North Africa and the Middle East, while the Russians exerted pressure on the northern borders of Iran. These imperial powers brought with them their cultural and intellectual institutions, which the elites they dominated first admired and emulated and later learned to distrust. Above all, they introduced progressive liberal and democratic ideas that would eventually be used against them. At the same time, and as a result of these contacts, some of these African and Asian elites began to travel to Europe to drink at the source.

Cairo became an intellectual magnet, attracting writers, artists, and political activists who were coming under pressure at home. Muhammad Ali, the Albanian governor whom the Ottoman sultan Selim III had sent to drive the invading French out of Egypt in 1805 and who had then remained in power, encouraged all efforts to modernize and to become more like the Europeans. He brought in European military and technical consultants and sent scientific missions to England and France who collected and translated critical texts into Arabic, to gain information about the technological accomplishments and scientific discoveries that had made European civilization the driving force in the modern era.

The delegations of translators who stayed for long periods in the capitals of Europe spent their spare time reading and eventually translating literature. They were intrigued by the straightforward language and the realism and romanticism of the fiction and drama that they were encountering for the first time. Many of these official translators, as well as other Europhiles, were drawn in particular to the translations of Russian literature that abounded in Europe in the late 1800s; they recognized in the malaise of these new middle classes a situation analogous to their own. Some even began to write their own versions of the stories they had read, substituting Arab, Persian, and Turkish names for those of the French, English, and Russian characters.

Simultaneous with this pro-European activity, a group of Muslim reformers emerged who warned against unthinking westernization. Aware of the colonizers' contempt for Islam, they urged its virtues and relevance in the process of modernization. But many modernists were convinced that to become part of the brave new world they had to turn their backs on religion. In the relatively open climate of Egypt, Arab Muslim reformers and secularists became locked in a polemical debate that produced its own canon, while also inspiring writers like Taha Husayn to write fiction and biographies on the subject.

In the first decade of this century, revolutions broke out in Iran and Turkey to oust autocratic, religiously sanctioned, ineffectual rulers and to establish liberal democracies. The Iranian revolution was quenched by the British and the Russians, who divided Iran between them. In 1921, Reza Khan became king, or shah, and for twenty years all middle-class and working-class political aspirations and literary endeavors were closely monitored. In contrast, the Turkish revolution continued to smolder until Mustafa Kemal, better known as Ataturk, came to power. In 1924, Ataturk abolished the Islamic Ottoman Caliphate and launched his secularization program; its echoes resounded throughout the Middle East and North Africa. Although many applauded such a drastic move, some, particularly the religiously minded, were profoundly disturbed. In 1928, the Egyptian Hasan al-Banna founded the Muslim Brothers. This religiously conservative, politically active association inspired the formation of other such organizations. They have survived the vicissitudes of a strife-torn century to remain a force with which governments and their leaders have constantly had to contend, not always successfully, as in the Iranian case. However, these Islamic apologists remained a minority.

In general, interest in Europe remained high. One of the more outspoken enthusiasts was Nasir al-Din Shah, who ruled Iran toward the end of the nineteenth century. This literary dilettante traveled extensively, and he wrote two diaries recounting his adventures using the unadorned and direct style that he had discovered in the new literature he was reading. After initial embarrassment at his apparent lack of rhetorical eloquence, other writers followed his lead. Many wrote of their travels, but some also invented narratives inspired by these new experiences. One such was the Egyptian Muhammad Husain Haikal, who spent some time in Paris where in 1913 and 1914 he wrote *Zaynab*. This love story is said to be the first novel produced in Arabic. He used a pseudonym so he could write about what was considered to be a controversial topic — about a woman, particularly one who was not from the elite, who falls in love above her class. He also wrote in a controversial form — a work of simple, extended prose. The success of the novel signaled the fact that entrenched attitudes were changing.

It was not only the writing of literature that was changing, but also literary criticism. Around the time of World War I, a group of Egyptian intellectuals who were also poets and had received at least part of their education in England formed a school called the *Diwan*. Using principles learned from their study of the great nineteenth-century English literary critics, they attacked the romanticism and neoclassicism that had shaped earlier attempts to reform the region's outworn literary norms. They urged greater attention to the cultural and social context of literary subjects. Literature was not merely an art to be written for its own sake; it had a political role to play in reflecting and thereby changing society. However, the conflicting influences of the early classics on the one hand and of European and Russian literature on the other were hard to break.

Throughout the Middle East, poetry remained the bastion of classical accomplishment until well into the twentieth century. In terms of subject matter, traditional poetry was generally an individualistic project with mystical overtones. Conventional structures of rhyme and rhythm and traditional imagery were considered sacrosanct. Nazim Hikmet Ran of Turkey was one of the first poets in the Middle East to succeed in introducing the free verse style that many have associated with the Soviet poet Vladimir Vladimirovich Mayakovsky. He exploited this new form of poetic expression to criticize Turkey's Kemalist government, particularly its savage treatment of the Armenians in 1915 and 1922. His poetic experiments did not garner a large following. It was only after World War II that this kind of new poetry, with its sociopolitical orientation, gained acceptance elsewhere in the Middle East and North Africa. The controversial modernist experiments in Persian poetry of Nima Yushij that had been rejected in the 1920s, 1930s, and 1940s, were widely adopted in the 1960s as models by social critics like Forugh Farrokhzad. In the Arab world at the end of the 1940s, it was a woman, the Iraqi Nazik al-Malaika, who is considered to be the first successful practitioner of free verse. Intellectuals recognized in this new poetry a special space in which to express anxiety and anger. Palestinian poets in exile all over the world became militant in their calls for resistance, claiming that the martyrs' blood that had soaked the land would give birth to new warriors. This mythic claim was taken up by other Arab writers as Palestine became the emblem of continued oppression. Like several others, the Iraqi Badr Shakir al-Sayyab used Christian symbology to write of the resurrection of the Arab nation. More recently, women like the Kuwaiti Suad al-Mubarak al-Sabah have expressed in surprisingly explicit verse their anger with and their rejection of patriarchal values.

NEW TOPICS

The two topics that galvanized the emergence of authentic Middle Eastern literatures were women and technology. Reformers had for some time been declaring that gender segregation and related lack of education were as harmful to society as they were to the women themselves. They argued that women, generally upper-class women, should be educated so that they might better educate their sons. Men whose mothers were illiterate and isolated from society could not hope to become strong leaders of strong nations. Education for women of the middle and upper classes became a priority item for intellectuals throughout the Middle East. As focus centered on the education question, other women's issues emerged. Men and women writers and reformers from all over the Islamicate world took up the campaign against seclusion and the veil, which was equated with a kind of segregation that deprived women of the opportunities to be educated. A turning point came in 1923 when Huda Sharawi, the leader of the Egyptian Feminist Union, publicly unveiled. Sharawi and her colleagues argued that as long as women remained segregated, uneducated, and veiled, they would be subject to other forms of oppression. They would continue to be married off as children. They would remain subject to impetuous divorces that usually left the women without resources. When they were sexually dishonored, it was they and not the men who were brutally punished. Short story writers took up these issues in their literary experiments.

The other topic that freed writers from their reliance on traditional forms and imported themes was the Middle East's accommodation to technology. It was often symbolized by the arrival of a train or a steamship at an outpost that until then had been oblivious to the existence of a wider world and its technology. After initial fascination with these toys of the West, the colonized began to reconsider their early enthusiasms. From the 1920s onward, writers depict characters who become unwitting victims of a technology that had promised to improve their lives. Bringing technology into lands not yet prepared for it often signaled the end of a particular way of life — it could even be fatal. Tayeb Salih's model of a village that is able to repel modernization and its agents is a refreshing alternative to stories of victimization. Middle Eastern literatures were pushing down their own roots as they engaged with problems that they felt to be uniquely theirs.

Publishing this early literature was not easy. Few publishing houses were prepared to take on risky literary ventures, so it became the task of the recently established journals and newspapers to sponsor these new writings. During the nineteenth century, journals sprang up throughout the Middle East, and by the 1920s there were over a dozen women's journals in the Arab world alone. Most of these publications had, and in many cases still have, literary pages or supplements where fiction and poetry appear for the first time and to a wide audience.

Publication in newspapers gave birth to chapter-by-chapter novels. Sadeq Hedayat in Iran, with his kafkaesque *Blind Owl* (1936), and Naguib Mahfouz in Egypt, the 1988 Nobel laureate, pioneered and brought to maturity this unusual genre. The early novels grew out of the short story genre — although the short story as it was known in the West did not have any direct parallel in classical Middle Eastern literatures, it was more easily incorporated than the novel because it did resemble some classical forms, like the *maqama,* and it was short. Because the early novels were published serially they often had an episodic structure. Eventually novelists began to consider the broad spectrum of their societies. They traced the influence of political and social change through the evolution of particular characters and even of generations within a single family.

FROM COLONY TO NATION-STATE

During the middle and late 1940s, the countries of the Middle East were beginning to shake off the rule of imperial powers; World War II had distracted them from their colonial interests. The Palestinians liberated themselves from the British, only to find themselves in conflict with European Zionists. The movement had emerged as a response to anti-Semitic activity in Europe that had culminated in the Holocaust. After 1948, the new state of Israel was established on the land of Palestine. The

Palestinian struggle for a homeland or for rights within Israel remains a thorny international issue. Elsewhere in the Middle East and North Africa, nationalist resistance movements were gaining strength and successes.

In tandem with the emergence of nationalism was a turn to study indigenous languages and cultures. Language academies were founded. In several countries, literary language was purged of foreign terms and made more flexible to allow the introduction of oral elements, including the heretofore despised colloquial expression. Anything imported was subject to increasing criticism as people prepared for self-rule. The superpower rivalry between the Americans and the Soviets may have divided the Middle East and North Africa into zones of influence, but it did not brake the drive toward independence.

During this turbulent period, Hedayat continued to write morbid satires that arose out of the frustration of his liberal nationalist hopes for Iran and his compassion for the wretched of the earth. Mahfouz painted the canvas of popular life in Cairo, depicting in particular the problems of living in a society in transition. Although others before them had touched on the spiritual costs of modernization, none had centered their attention so fully and painfully on the moral desolation of modernity. Like his short story "Zaabalawi," the novels that Mahfouz wrote in the late 1950s and mid-1960s all speak of a quest journey that ends in disappointment or death. After 1967, Mahfouz's writing changed radically; the long socio-realistic novels give way to short, abstract, fragmented prose. The defeat inflicted on the Arabs by Israel during the Six Day War of 1967 had an overwhelming effect on the entire Arab world and particularly on the writers.

If it was women and technology that galvanized Middle Eastern literatures in the first third of the twentieth century, it is nationalism and wars in the middle and late decades of this century that influenced the later development of Middle Eastern literatures. During the 1940s, the end of Reza Shah's dictatorship and the ascendancy of the working-class Tudeh Party allowed for the emergence of progressive, socialist literature deeply rooted in Iranian reality. After 1948, the Palestinian-Israeli conflict preoccupied Arab politicians, and intellectuals as well. The Algerian War of Independence, 1954–1962, presented a model for justified violence. The Lebanese Civil War, 1975–1992, represented the dystopia of ideologies run amok.

Palestine and Israel

The repercussions of the Palestinian situation spread far beyond the geographical boundaries of the area involved. When the state of Israel was established in 1948, most of the Palestinians who had been living on the land left. However, a small number, many of them peasants, did remain. The literature that they produced in the early 1950s indicates a desire to come to terms with the new inhabitants while maintaining individual and national dignity. Although this desire is reflected in some contemporary left-wing Israeli writing, most of the Israeli writers of the pioneering generation, like the 1966 Nobel laureate S. Y. Agnon, were not yet concerned with the Arabs in their midst. Their memories of life in the European and Russian diasporas and the dreadful memory of the Holocaust overshadow their writings. However, in the 1950s and 1960s, Israeli poets like Dahlia Rabikovich looked to European writers, including Rainer Maria Rilke, Paul Valéry, William Butler Yeats, and T. S. Eliot for inspiration as they became increasingly alienated from the political scene. Contemporary fiction writers also were beginning to ask difficult ethical questions about their recently formed nation-state.

After 1967, the writing within Israel changed. Palestinians, like Emile Habibi in *The Secret Life of Saeed, the Ill-Fated Pessoptimist* (1974) and Anton Shammas in *Arabesques* (1986), express the crisis of a minority that had sought but failed to find acceptance by the new, primarily European, occupants of the land. On the other hand, Israelis like Amos Oz and Abraham Yehoshua build on the burgeoning angst of their immediate predecessors. But their writings are more concretely engaged with reality. They create characters who struggle to come to terms with the meaning of Israel. Meanwhile, the Palestinians who had left in 1948 were experimenting with ways in which to articulate their sense of loss. Ghassan Kanafani, the doyen of Palestinian prose literature, writes of individuals stranded without community and confronted by impossible choices. After 1967 and the Israeli occupation of the West Bank and Gaza, new writers from the territories appeared, such as novelist Sahar Khalifa.

Algeria

In 1954, six years after the founding of the Israeli state and two years after the success of the Egyptian Free Officers' Revolution, the Algerians launched their war of independence from 130 years of French rule. They wanted to drive the French settlers out, but they also wanted to reestablish contact with what they presumed to be their authentic culture, which was both Arab and Berber. Like other North African writers, Algerians were concerned by their inability to express themselves in their "mother tongue" of Arabic and their need to rely on French, the language of the colonizers. During and after the war, writers complained of the "white page" that symbolized the need to write and the simultaneous impossibility of writing in French.

The hallmarks of this war were the mobilization of all the people, particularly the women, and the glorification of violence. Algerian male writers and outsiders like the Martinican Frantz Fanon were awed by the unprecedented public role that women played. The women who wrote at the time did not seem to be aware that they were doing anything out of the ordinary. It was only twenty years later in the 1980s, after the women activists had returned home unthanked, that writers like Assia Djebar began to realize that these women had not been politically aware at the time of their participation. Like the Palestinian women in the West Bank, they should have talked and written of what they had done for their country. While they were still active and needed, they should have demanded rewards for their services.

The novels and short stories that Algerian women had in fact been writing during the war, between 1954 and 1962, were closer in subject and spirit to those written by contemporary Lebanese, Syrian, Turkish, and Iranian women. Like the Lebanese Layla Baalbaki, they were writing of the confusing messages girls received as they grew up. Middle- and upper-class girls were sent to school, where they were led to expect an interesting future and even a career, and then they were forced into an unwanted marriage, often described as a prison. Baalbaki was the first Middle Eastern woman writer to gain international fame, or rather notoriety, when her story "Space Ship of Tenderness to the Moon" (1964) earned her an obscenity trial. She had described the naked body of a man who happened to be the protagonist's husband. She was eventually acquitted. In Iran, Forugh Farrukhzad was attracting wide criticism not only for her outspoken poems about love and sex, but also for her unconventional lifestyle. These women opened the way for others to criticize misogynist tendencies in their society and to suggest alternative models of behavior for both men and women.

Lebanon

The Lebanese Civil War that broke out in 1975 allowed women the kind of literary space they could not have otherwise enjoyed. For the first time anywhere in the Middle East, there were more women than men writing and getting their works published. The Beirut Decentrists were a group of women who wrote about the chaos and the meaninglessness of the war, and its impact on the lives of men and women both in Beirut and outside. They created women whom the war had empowered to demand a role in shaping the contours of the new, postbellum society. Emily Nasrallah attacked the ideal of emigration: the people, most of them men, who had left Lebanon for economic gain before and during the war were not, contrary to common expectation, coming back. By the early 1980s, the Decentrists had discursively transformed the meaning of women's passive waiting in war-torn Lebanon into survival and resistance. With the memory of Algerian women's unacknowledged participation still vivid, they inscribed their activism into the war story.

After 1982, the civil war took on an explicitly international character. The Israelis, the Iranians, and the Syrians became more directly involved. The Israeli army invaded the south and then moved on to Beirut, which they besieged. Literary reactions in Lebanon and Israel were immediate and passionate. In Israel itself, there was a crisis of confidence in the government as intellectuals and left-wing activists began to question what the army was doing in Lebanon. The Syrians became entrenched in Beirut. Meanwhile, Ayatollah Khomeini was consolidating power at home in Iran and abroad. The Islamic Revolutionary Guards policed public morality in Iran, and they tried to influence the course of the war in Lebanon. Writers, poets, artists, and film directors were guarded in their criticism.

TRANSLATION AND RECOGNITION

The 1980s were an important decade for Middle Eastern literatures. There were several wars that spawned a whole new literary corpus. There was also international recognition. Mahfouz won the Nobel Prize in 1988; the following year the Moroccan Tahar Benjelloun became the first Arab to win the coveted French honor, the Prix Goncourt. At the same time, Arabic, Persian, Turkish, and Hebrew fiction and poetry were being translated into European languages. Whereas previously the translation process had been idiosyncratic, with random works sporadically translated into one language or another, by the mid-1980s European and American publishing houses were adopting Middle Eastern literary series as well as individual authors, and the process became more systematic. The first International Feminist Bookfair, which took place in London in 1986, launched the Lebanese writer Hanan al-Shaykh and established as classics the radical feminist novels and short stories of the Egyptian activist Nawal Saadawi. Some writers who have had a greater share of recognition abroad are writing with the awareness that their works will be translated into other languages. This fact has in some cases affected both the subject matter and the literary style of the author. It remains to be seen how Middle Eastern and North African writers will react to the knowledge that they are now working within an international community.

Miriam Cooke

FOR FURTHER READING

Primary Works

Agnon, Shmuel Yosef. *A Guest for the Night.* London: Gollancz, 1968.
——. *In the Heart of the Sea.* New York: Schocken, 1947.
——. *The Bridal Canopy.* Garden City: Doubleday, 1937.
Djebar, Assia. *Women of Algiers in Their Apartment.* Charlottesville: University of Virginia Press, 1992.
——. *Fantasia: An Algerian Cavalcade.* Portsmouth, N. H.: Heinemann, 1994.
Farrokhzad, Forugh. *Another Birth.* Emeryville, Calif.: Albany Press, 1982.

Habibi, Emile. *The Secret Life of Saeed, the Ill-Fated Pessoptomist.* New York: Vantage Press, 1982.

Hedayat, Sadeq. *The Blind Owl.* New York: Grove Press, 1957.

Mahfouz, Naguib. *Midaq Alley.* Washington, D.C.: Three Continents Press, 1981.

———. *Trilogy: Palace Walk, Palace of Desire, Sugar Street.* Translated by William Maynard Hutchins and Olive E. Kenny. New York: Doubleday, 1990, 1991, 1992.

Nasrallah, Emily. *A House Not Her Own.* Charlottestown, P.E.I., Canada: Gynergy Books, 1992.

———. *Flight Against Time.* Charlottestown, P.E.I., Canada: Ragweed Press, 1987.

Saadawi, Nawal. *The Innocence of the Devil.* London: Methuen, 1994.

———. *Memoirs of a Woman Doctor.* London: Saqi, 1988.

———. *Woman at Point Zero.* London: Zed, 1983.

Salih, Tayeb. *Season of Migration to the North.* Washington, D.C.: Three Continents Press, 1980.

Secondary Works

Badawi, Mustafa. *Modern Arabic Literature.* Cambridge: Cambridge University Press, 1993.

Hamalian, Leo, and John D. Yohannan. *New Writing from the Middle East.* New York: Mentor Press, 1978.

Hodgson, Marshall. *The Venture of Islam.* Chicago: University of Chicago Press, 1977.

Ricks, Thomas M. *Critical Perspectives on Modern Persian Literature.* Washington, D.C.: Three Continents Press, 1984.

ALGERIA

ASSIA DJEBAR

The Algerian Revolution, the muse of nearly all contemporary Algerian writers, broke out when Assia Djebar (1936–) was eighteen years old. She wrote her first novel, The Thirst, *in 1957 and her second,* The Impatient, *the next year. Djebar became caught up in political events, and in 1959 she fled to Tunis where she wrote "There Is No Exile." She did not publish the story until 1980, as though she did not want to voice her doubts about the war at the time. She wrote two novels on the war,* Children of the New World *(1962) and* The Naive Larks *(1967) five years later. In both of these novels, women characters become active in the military along with the men but experience little sense of consequent empowerment. This portrayal contradicts writings by men like Muhammad Dib and Malek Haddad, who represent women's military involvement as a growing danger.*

Djebar has been prolific, writing six novels in French and producing films. Like many of her compatriots, she has lamented her inability to write in Arabic because of the colonial repression of Arabic in Algerian schools. Because her work is considered feminist, hence westernized, it has not been translated into Arabic in Algeria. She is currently working on a quartet of novels; the first two have appeared under the titles Fantasia, an Algerian Cavalcade *(1985) and* A Sister to Sheherazade *(1987). These novels are pessimistic assessments of women's ability to change an overbearing patriarchy.*

There Is No Exile

That particular morning, I'd finished the housework a little earlier, by nine o'clock. Mother had put on her veil, taken her basket; in the opening of the door, she repeated as she had been repeating every day for three years: "Not until we had been chased out of our own country did I find myself forced to go out to market like a man."

"Our men have other things to do," I answered, as I'd been answering every day for three years.

"May God protect us!"

I saw Mother to the staircase, then watched her go down heavily because of her legs: "May God protect us," I said again to myself as I went back in.

The cries began around ten o'clock, more or less. They were coming from the apartment next door and soon changed into shrieks. All three of us, my two sisters — Aïcha, Anissa, and I — recognized it by the way in which the women received it: it was death.

Aïcha, the eldest, ran to the door, opened it in order to hear more clearly: "May misfortune stay away from us," she mumbled. "Death has paid the Smaïn family a visit."

At that moment, Mother came in. She put the basket on the floor, stopped where she stood, her face distraught, and began to beat her chest spasmodically with her hands. She was uttering little stifled cries, as when she was about to get sick.

Anissa, although she was the youngest of us, never lost her calm. She ran to close the door, lifted Mother's veil, took her by the shoulders and made her sit down on a mattress.

"Now don't get yourself in that state on account of someone else's misfortune," she said. "Don't forget you have a bad heart. May God shelter and keep us always."

While she repeated the phrase several more times, she went to get some water and sprinkled it on Mother, who now, stretched out full length on the mattress, was moaning. Then Anissa washed her entire face, took a bottle of cologne from the wardrobe, opened it, and put it under her nostrils.

"No!" Mother said. "Bring me some lemon."

And she started to moan again.

Anissa continued to bustle about. I was just watching her. I've always been slow to react. I'd begun to listen to the sobs outside that hadn't ceased, would surely not cease before nightfall. There were five or six women in the Smaïn family, and they were all lamenting in chorus, each one settling, forever it seemed, into the muddled outbreak of their grief. Later, of course, they'd have to prepare the meal, busy themselves with the poor, wash the body. . . . There are so many things to do, the day of a burial.

For now, the voices of the hired mourners,° all alike without any one of them distinguishable from the other if only by a more anguished tone, were making one long, gasping chant, and I knew that it would hang over the entire day like a fog in winter.

"Who actually died over there?" I asked Mother, who had almost quieted down.

"Their young son," she said, inhaling the lemon deeply. "A car drove over him in front of the door. I was coming home when my eyes saw him

hired mourners: women paid to keen during funerals

twisting one last time, like a worm. The ambulance took him to the hospital, but he was already dead."

Then she began to sigh again.

"Those poor people," she was saying, "they saw him go out jumping with life and now they're going to bring him back in a bloodstained sheet."

She raised herself halfway, repeated: "jumping with life." Then she fell back down on the mattress and said nothing other than the ritual formulas to keep misfortune away. But the low voice she always used to address God had a touch of hardness, vehemence.

"This day has an evil smell," I said, still standing in front of Mother, motionlessly. "I've sensed it since this morning, but I didn't know then that it was the smell of death."

"You have to add: May God protect us!" Mother said sharply. Then she raised her eyes to me. We were alone in the room, Anissa and Aïcha had gone back to the kitchen.

"What's the matter with you?" she said. "You look pale. Are you feeling sick, too?"

"May God protect us!" I said and left the room.

At noon, Omar was the first one home. The weeping continued. I'd attended to the meal while listening to the threnody and its modulations. I was growing used to them. I thought Omar would start asking questions. But no. He must have heard about it in the street.

He pulled Aïcha into a room. Then I heard them whispering. When some important event occurred, Omar spoke first to Aïcha in this way, because she was the eldest and the most serious one. Previously, Father used to do the same thing, but outside, with Omar, for he was the only son.

So there was something new; and it had nothing to do with death visiting the Smaïn family. I wasn't curious at all. Today is the day of death, all the rest becomes immaterial.

"Isn't that so?" I said to Anissa, who jumped.

"What's the matter now?"

"Nothing," I said without belaboring the point, for I was familiar with her always disconcerted answers whenever I'd start thinking out loud. Even this morning . . .

But why this sudden, blatant desire to stare at myself in a mirror, to confront my own image at some length, and to say, while letting my hair fall down my back so that Anissa would gaze upon it: "Look. At twenty-five, after having been married, after having lost my two children one after the other, having been divorced, after this exile and after this war,°

this exile . . . this war: the 1954–62 war of Independence for Algeria, during which many Algerians left home

here I am busy admiring myself, smiling at myself like a young girl, like you . . ."

"Like me!" Anissa said, and she shrugged her shoulders.

Father came home a little late because it was Friday and he'd gone to say the prayer of *dhor*° at the mosque. He immediately asked why they were in mourning.

"Death has visited the Smaïns," I said, running toward him to kiss his hand. "It has taken their young son away."

"Those poor people," he said after a silence.

I helped him get settled in his usual place, on the same mattress. Then, as I put his meal in front of him and made sure he didn't have to wait for anything, I forgot about the neighbors for a while. I liked to serve Father; it was, I think, the only household task I enjoyed. Especially now. Since our departure, Father had aged a great deal. He gave too much thought to those who weren't with us, even though he never spoke of them, unless a letter arrived from Algeria and he asked Omar to read it.

In the middle of the meal I heard Mother murmur: "They can't possibly feel like eating today."

"The body is still at the hospital," someone said.

Father said nothing. He rarely spoke during meals.

"I'm not really hungry," I said, getting up, to excuse myself.

The sobs outside seemed more muffled, but I could still distinguish their singsong. Their gentle singsong. This is the moment, I said to myself, when grief becomes familiar, and pleasurable, and nostalgic. This is the moment when you weep almost voluptuously, for this gift of tears is a gift without end. This was the moment when the bodies of my children would turn cold fast, so fast, and when I knew it. . . .

At the end of the meal, Aïcha came into the kitchen, where I was by myself. First she went to close the windows that looked out over the neighboring terraces, through which the weeping reached me. But I could still hear it. And, oddly, it was that which made me so tranquil today, a little gloomy.

"There are some women coming this afternoon to see you and to propose marriage," she began. "Father says the candidate is suitable in every way."

Without answering, I turned my back to her and went to the window.

"Now what's your problem?" she said a little sharply.

"I need some air," I said and opened the window all the way, so that the song could come in. It had already been a while since the breathing of death had become, for me, "the song."

Aïcha remained a moment without answering. "When Father goes out, you'll attend to yourself a little," she said at last. "These women know

dhor: the midday prayer (Muslims pray five times a day)

very well that we're refugees like so many others, and that they're not going to find you dressed like a queen. But you should look your best, nevertheless."

"They've stopped weeping," I remarked, "or perhaps they're already tired," I said, thinking of that strange fatigue that grasps us at the depth of our sorrow.

"Why don't you keep your mind on the women who're coming?" Aïcha replied in a slightly louder voice.

Father had left. Omar too, when Hafsa arrived. Like us, she was Algerian and we'd known her there, a young girl of twenty with an education. She was a teacher but had been working only since her mother and she had been exiled, as had so many others. "An honorable woman doesn't work outside her home," her mother used to say. She still said it, but with a sigh of helplessness. One had to live, and there was no man in their household now.

Hafsa found Mother and Anissa in the process of preparing pastries, as if these were a must for refugees like us. But her sense of protocol was instinctive in Mother; an inheritance from her past life that she could not readily abandon.

"These women you're waiting for," I asked, "who are they?"

"Refugees like us," Aïcha exclaimed. "You don't really think we'd give you away in marriage to strangers?" Then with heart and soul: "Remember," she said, "the day we return to our own country, we shall all go back home, all of us, without exception."

"The day that we return," Hafsa, standing in the middle of the room, suddenly cried out, her eyes wide with dreams. "The day that we return to our country!" she repeated. "How I'd like to go back there on foot, the better to feel the Algerian soil under my feet, the better to see all our women, one after the other, all the widows, and all the orphans, and finally all the men, exhausted, sad perhaps, but free — free! And then I'll take a bit of soil in my hands, oh, just a tiny handful of soil, and I'll say to them: 'See, my brothers, see these drops of blood in these grains of soil in this hand, that's how much Algeria has bled throughout her body, all over her vast body, that's how much Algeria has paid for our freedom and for this, our return, with her own soil. But her martyrdom now speaks in terms of grace. So you see, my brothers . . .'"

"The day that we return," Mother repeated softly in the silence that followed . . . "if God wills it."

It was then that the cries began again through the open window. Like an orchestra that brusquely starts a piece of music. Then, in a different tone, Hafsa reminded us: "I'm here for the lesson."

Aïcha pulled her into the next room.

During their meeting, I didn't know what to do. The windows of the kitchen and of the other two rooms looked out over the terraces. I went from one to the other, opening them, closing them, opening them again. All of this without hurrying, as if I weren't listening to the song.

Anissa caught me in my rounds.

"You can tell they're not Algerian," she said. "They're not even accustomed to being in mourning."

"At home, in the mountains," Mother answered, "the dead have nobody to weep over them before they grow cold."

"Weeping serves no purpose," Anissa was stoic, "whether you die in your bed or on the bare ground for your country."

"What do you know about it?" I suddenly said to her. "You're too young to know."

"Soon they're going to bury him," Mother whispered.

Then she raised her head and looked at me. I had once again closed the window behind me. I couldn't hear anything anymore.

"They're going to bury him this very day," Mother said again a little louder, "that's our custom."

"They shouldn't," I said. "It's a hateful custom to deliver a body to the earth when beauty still shines on it. Really quite hateful. . . . It seems to me they're burying him while he's still shivering, still . . ." (but I couldn't control my voice any longer).

"Stop thinking about your children!" Mother said. "The earth that was thrown on them is a blanket of gold. My poor daughter, stop thinking about your children!" Mother said again.

"I'm not thinking about anything," I said. "No, really. I don't want to think about anything. About anything at all."

It was already four o'clock in the afternoon when they came in. From the kitchen where I was hiding, I heard them exclaim, once the normal phrases of courtesy had been uttered: "What is that weeping?"

"May misfortune stay far away from us! May God protect us!"

"It gives me goose bumps," the third one was saying. "I've almost forgotten death and tears, these days. I've forgotten them, even though our hearts are always heavy."

"That is the will of God," the second one would respond.

In a placid voice, Mother explained the reason for the mourning next door as she invited them into the only room we had been able to furnish decently. Anissa, close by me, was already making the first comments on the way the women looked. She was questioning Aïcha, who had been with Mother to welcome them. I had opened the window again and watched them exchange their first impressions.

"What are you thinking?" Anissa said, her eye still on me.

"Nothing," I said feebly; then, after a pause: "I was thinking of the different faces of fate. I was thinking of God's will. Behind that wall, there is a dead person and women going mad with grief. Here, in our house, other women are talking of marriage . . . I was thinking of that difference."

"Just stop 'thinking,'" Aïcha cut in sharply. Then to Hafsa, who was coming in: "You ought to be teaching *her*, not me. She spends all her time thinking. You'd almost believe she's read as many books as you have."

"And why not?" Hafsa asked.

"I don't need to learn French," I answered. "What purpose would it serve? Father has taught us all our language. 'That's all you need,' he always says."

"It's useful to know languages other than your own," Hafsa said slowly. "It's like knowing other people, other countries."

I didn't answer. Perhaps she was right. Perhaps you ought to learn and not waste your time letting your mind wander, like mine, through the deserted corridors of the past. Perhaps I should take lessons and study French, or anything else. But I, I never felt the need to jostle my body or my mind. . . . Aïcha was different. Like a man: hard and hardworking. She was thirty. She hadn't seen her husband in three years, who was still incarcerated in Barberousse prison,° where he had been since the first days of the war. Yet, she was getting an education and didn't settle for household work. Now, after just a few months of Hafsa's lessons, Omar no longer read her husband's infrequent letters, the few that might reach her. She managed to decipher them by herself. Sometimes I caught myself being envious of her.

"Hafsa," she said, "it's time for my sister to go in and greet these ladies. Please go with her."

But Hafsa didn't want to. Aïcha insisted, and I was watching them play their little game of politeness.

"Does anyone know if they've come for the body yet?" I asked.

"What? Didn't you hear the chanters just now?" Anissa said.

"So that's why the weeping stopped for a moment," I said. "It's strange, as soon as some parts of the Koranic verses° are chanted, the women immediately stop weeping. And yet, that's the most painful moment, I know it all too well myself. As long as the body is there in front of you, it seems the child isn't quite dead yet, can't be dead, you see? . . . Then comes the moment when the men get up, and that is to take him, wrapped in a sheet, on their shoulders. That's how he leaves, quickly, as on the day that he came. . . . For me, may God forgive me, they can chant Koranic verses all they want, the house is still empty after they've gone, completely empty. . . ."

Hafsa was listening, her head leaning toward the window. With a shiver, she turned toward me. She seemed younger even than Anissa, then.

Barberousse prison: a French-run prison in Algeria where revolutionaries were incarcerated

Koranic verses: parts of the Koran, the Muslims' holy book which is divided into chapters and verses

"My God," she said, emotion in her voice, "I've just turned twenty and yet I've never encountered death. Never in my whole life!"

"Haven't you lost anyone in your family in this war?" Anissa asked.

"Oh yes," she said, "but the news always comes by mail. And death by mail, you see, I can't believe it. A first cousin of mine died under the guillotine as one of the first in Barberousse. Well, I've never shed a tear over him because I cannot believe that he's dead. And yet he was like a brother to me, I swear. But I just can't believe he's dead, you understand?" she said in a voice already wrapped in tears.

"Those who've died for the Cause° aren't really dead," Anissa answered with a touch of pride.

"So, let's think of the present. Let's think about today," Aïcha said in a dry voice. "The rest is in God's hand."

There were three of them: an old woman who had to be the suitor's mother and who hastily put on her glasses as soon as I arrived; two other women, seated side by side, resembled each other. Hafsa, who'd come in behind me, sat down next to me. I lowered my eyes.

I knew my part, it was one I'd played before; stay mute like this, eyes lowered, and patiently let myself be examined until the very end: it was simple. Everything is simple, beforehand, for a girl who's being married off.

Mother was talking. I was barely listening. I knew the themes to be developed all too well: Mother was talking about our sad state as refugees; then they'd be exchanging opinions on when the end might be announced: ". . . another Ramadan° to be spent away from home . . . perhaps this was the last one . . . perhaps, if God wills it! Of course, we were saying the same thing last year, and the year before that . . . Let's not complain too much. . . . In any event, victory is certain, all our men say the same thing. And we, we know the day of our return will come. . . . We should be thinking of those who stayed behind. . . . We should be thinking of those who are suffering. . . . The Algerian people are a people whom God loves. . . . And our fighters are made of steel. . . ." Then they'd come back to the tale of the flight, to the different means by which each one had left her soil where the fires were burning. . . . Then they'd evoke the sadness of exile, the heart yearning for its country. . . . And the fear of dying far from the land of one's birth. . . . Then. . . . "But may God be praised and may he grant our prayers!"

This time it lasted a bit longer; an hour perhaps, or more. Until the time came to serve coffee. By then, I was hardly listening at all. I too was thinking in my own way of this exile, of these somber days.

I was thinking how everything had changed, how on the day of my

the Cause: the Algerian War of Independence
Ramadan: the month during which Muslims fast

first engagement we had been in the long, bright living room of our house in the hills of Algiers; how we'd been prosperous then, we had prosperity and peace; how Father used to laugh, how he used to give thanks to God for the abundance of his home . . . And I, I wasn't as I was today, my soul grey, gloomy and with this idea of death beating faintly inside me since the morning. . . . Yes, I was thinking how everything had changed and that, still, in some way everything remained the same. They were still concerned with marrying me off. And why exactly? I suddenly wondered. And why exactly? I repeated to myself, feeling something like fury inside me, or its echo. Just so I could have worries that never change whether it's peace or wartime, so I could wake up in the middle of the night and question myself on what it is that sleeps in the depths of the heart of the man sharing my bed. . . . Just so I could give birth and weep, for life never comes unaccompanied to a woman, death is always right behind, furtive, quick, and smiling at the mothers. . . . Yes, why indeed? I said to myself.

Coffee had now been served. Mother was inviting them to drink.

"We won't take even one sip," the old woman began, "before you've given us your word about your daughter."

"Yes," the other one said, "my brother impressed upon us that we weren't to come back without your promising to give her to him as his wife."

I was listening to Mother avoid answering, have herself be begged hypocritically, and then again invite them to drink. Aïcha joined in with her. The women were repeating their request. . . . It was all as it should be.

The game went on a few minutes longer. Mother invoked the father's authority: "I, of course, would give her to you. . . . I know you are people of means. . . . But there is her father."

"Her father has already said yes to my brother," one of the two women who resembled each other replied. "The question remains only to be discussed between us."

"Yes," said the second one, "it's up to us now. Let's settle the question."

I raised my head; it was then, I think, that I met Hafsa's gaze.

There was, deep in her eyes, a strange light, surely of interest or of irony, I don't know, but you could feel Hafsa as an outsider, attentive and curious at the same time, but an outsider. I met that look.

"I don't want to marry," I said. "I don't want to marry," I repeated, barely shouting.

There was much commotion in the room: Mother got up with a deep sigh; Aïcha was blushing, I saw. And the two women who turned to me, with the same slow movement of shock: "And why not?" one of them asked.

"My son," the old woman exclaimed with some arrogance, "my son is a man of science. In a few days he is leaving for the Orient."

"Of course," Mother said with touching haste. "We know he's a scholar. We know him to have a righteous heart. . . . Of course. . . ."

"It's not because of your son," I said. "But I don't want to get married. I see the future before my eyes, it's totally black. I don't know how to explain it, surely it must come from God. . . . But I see the future totally black before my eyes!" I said again, sobbing, as Aïcha led me out of the room in silence.

Later, but why even tell the rest, except that I was consumed with shame and I didn't understand. Only Hafsa stayed close to me after the women had left.

"You're engaged," she said sadly. "Your mother said she'd give you away. Will you accept?" and she stared at me with imploring eyes.

"What difference does it make?" I said and really thought inside myself: What difference does it make? "I don't know what came over me before. But they were all talking about the present and its changes and its misfortunes. And I was saying to myself: of what possible use is it to be suffering like this, far away from home, if I have to continue here as before in Algiers, to stay home and sit and pretend. . . . Perhaps when life changes, everything should change with it, absolutely everything. I was thinking of all that," I said, "but I don't even know if that's bad or good. . . . You, you're smart, and you know these things, perhaps you'll understand. . . ."

"I do understand," she said, hesitating as if she were going to start talking and then preferred to remain silent.

"Open the window," I said. "It's almost dark."

She went to open it and then came back to my bed where I'd been lying down to cry, without reason, crying for shame and fatigue all at the same time. In the silence that followed, I was feeling distant, pondering the night that little by little engulfed the room. The sounds from the kitchen, where my sisters were, seemed to be coming from somewhere else.

Then Hafsa began to speak: "Your father," she said, "once spoke of exile, of our present exile, and he said — oh, I remember it well, for nobody speaks like your father — he said: 'There is no exile for any man loved by God. There is no exile for the one who is on God's path. There are only trials.'"

She went on a while, but I've forgotten the rest except that she repeated *we* very often with a note of passion. She said that word with a peculiar vehemence, so much so that I began to wonder toward the end whether that word really meant the two of us alone, or rather other women, all the women of our country.

To tell the truth, even if I'd known, what could I have answered? Hafsa was too knowledgeable for me. And that's what I would have liked to have told her when she stopped talking, perhaps in the expectation that I would speak.

But it was another voice that answered, a woman's voice that rose, through the open window, rose straight as an arrow toward the sky, that rounded itself out, spread out in its flight, a flight ample as a bird's after the storm, then came falling back down in sudden torrents.

"The other women have grown silent," I said. "The only one left to weep now is the mother. . . . Such is life," I added a moment later. "There are those who forget or who simply sleep. And then there are those who keep bumping into the walls of the past. May God take pity on them!"

"Those are the true exiles," said Hafsa.

Translated from the French
by Marjolijn de Jager

NAGUIB MAHFOUZ

When he was young, the family of Naguib Mahfouz (1911–) lived in two popular districts of Cairo, al-Jamaliya and al-Abbasiya, which provide the backdrop for most of his writings. In 1931, Mahfouz matriculated at Egyptian University, a mere three years after it had become the first Arab university to open its doors to women. Forty years later, in his collection entitled Mirrors *(1972), he mocks himself and his classmates for thinking that these women were seeking husbands and not an education.*

Mahfouz began writing in the late 1930s. Many believe that his greatest work is the Trilogy, *a three-volume family saga that he wrote in the early 1950s, at the time of the nationalist revolution. In 1959, he produced the controversial* Children of Our Alley, *which was banned because of what was said to be its anti-Islamic message. The novel's message, that humanity in its greed for material gain is moving further and further away from God, remained an important theme in the shorter, existentialist novels he wrote in the 1960s. Particularly well received was* The Thief and the Dogs *(1962), which follows a Marxist thief from his release from prison, through his disappointments with former Marxist colleagues, to his Kafkaesque murder in a cemetery.*

After the defeat of the Arabs by Israel in the 1967 war, Mahfouz turned from long, intricately descriptive, accessible novels to short, elliptical, experimental prose, like Love in the Rain *(1973). In the 1980s, Mahfouz published fiction devoted to leadership at home and abroad. He was awarded the Nobel Prize in literature in 1988, the first Arab writer to be thus honored.*

Mahfouz wrote "Zaabalawi" in 1965. It epitomizes the search-for-God motif that dominates his writings between 1959 and 1967.

Zaabalawi

Finally I became convinced that I had to find Sheikh° Zaabalawi.
   The first time I had heard of his name had been in a song:

What's wrong with the world, O Zaabalawi?
They've turned it upside down and made it insipid.

sheikh: a religious person's honorific title

It had been a popular song in my childhood and one day it had occurred to me — in the way children have of asking endless questions —
to ask my father about him.

"Who is Zaabalawi, father?"

He had looked at me hesitantly as though doubting my ability to understand the answer. However, he had replied:

"May his blessing descend upon you, he's a true saint of God, a re-
mover of worries and troubles. Were it not for him I would have died miserably — "

In the years that followed I heard him many a time sing the praises of
his good saint and speak of the miracles he performed. The days passed
and brought with them many illnesses from each one of which I was able,
without too much trouble and at a cost I could afford, to find a cure, until
I became afflicted with that illness for which no one possesses a remedy.
When I had tried everything in vain and was overcome by despair, I remembered by chance what I had heard in my childhood: Why, I asked
myself, should I not seek out Sheikh Zaabalawi? I recollected that my father had said that he had made his acquaintance in Khan Gaafar° at the
house of Sheikh Kamar, one of those sheikhs who practiced law in the religious courts, and I therefore took myself off to his house. Wishing to
make sure that he was still living there, I made enquiries of a vendor of
beans whom I found in the lower part of the house.

"Sheikh Kamar!" he said, looking at me in amazement. "He left the
quarter ages ago. They say he's now living in Garden City and has his office in al-Azhar Square."

I looked up the office address in the telephone book and immediately
set off to the Chamber of Commerce Building where it was located. On
asking to see him I was ushered into a room just as a beautiful woman
with a most intoxicating perfume was leaving it. The man received me
with a smile and motioned me towards a fine leather-upholstered chair.
My feet were conscious of the costly lushness of the carpet despite the
thick soles of my shoes. The man wore a lounge suit and was smoking
a cigar; his manner of sitting was that of someone well satisfied both
with himself and his worldly possessions. The look of warm welcome he
gave me left no doubt in my mind that he thought me a prospective
client, and I felt acutely embarrassed at encroaching upon his valuable
time.

"Welcome!" he said, prompting me to speak.

"I am the son of your old friend Sheikh Ali al-Tahtawi," I answered so
as to put an end to my equivocal position.

A certain languor was apparent in the glance he cast at me; the languor
was not total in that he had not as yet lost all hope in me.

"God rest his soul," he said. "He was a fine man."

Khan Gaafar: a popular district in Cairo

The very pain that had driven me to go there now prevailed upon me to stay.

"He told me," I continued, "of a devout saint named Zaabalawi whom he met at Your Honor's. I am in need of him, sir, if he be still in the land of the living."

The languor became firmly entrenched in his eyes and it would have come as no surprise to me if he had shown the door to both me and my father's memory.

"That," he said in the tone of one who has made up his mind to terminate the conversation, "was a very long time ago and I scarcely recall him now."

Rising to my feet so as to put his mind at rest regarding my intention of going, I asked:

"Was he really a saint?"

"We used to regard him as a man of miracles."

"And where could I find him today?" I asked, making another move towards the door.

"To the best of my knowledge he was living in the Birgawi Residence in al-Azhar," and he applied himself to some papers on his desk with a resolute movement that indicated he wouldn't open his mouth again. I bowed my head in thanks, apologized several times for disturbing him and left the office, my head so buzzing with embarrassment that I was oblivious to all sounds around me.

I went to the Birgawi Residence which was situated in a thickly populated quarter. I found that time had so eaten into the building that nothing was left of it save an antiquated facade and a courtyard which, despite it being supposedly in the charge of a caretaker, was being used as a rubbish dump. A small insignificant fellow, a mere prologue to a man, was using the covered entrance as a place for the sale of old books on theology and mysticism.

On asking him about Zaabalawi he peered at me through narrow, inflamed eyes and said in amazement:

"Zaabalawi! Good heavens, what a time ago that was! Certainly he used to live in this house when it was livable in, and many was the time he would sit with me talking of bygone days and I would be blessed by his holy presence. Where, though, is Zaabalawi today?"

He shrugged his shoulders sorrowfully and soon left me to attend to an approaching customer. I proceeded to make enquiries of many shopkeepers in the district. While I found that a large number of them had never even heard of him, some, though recalling nostalgically the pleasant times they had spent with him, were ignorant of his present whereabouts, while others openly made fun of him, labeled him a charlatan, and advised me to put myself in the hands of a doctor — as though I had not already done so. I therefore had no alternative but to return disconsolately home.

With the passing of the days like motes in the air my pains grew so severe that I was sure I would not be able to hold out much longer. Once again I fell to wondering about Zaabalawi and clutching at the hopes his venerable name stirred within me. Then it occurred to me to seek the help of the local Sheikh of the district; in fact, I was surprised I hadn't thought of this to begin with. His office was in the nature of a small shop except that it contained a desk and a telephone, and I found him sitting at his desk wearing a jacket over his striped *galabia*.° As he did not interrupt his conversation with a man sitting beside him, I stood waiting till the man had gone. He then looked up at me coldly. I told myself that I should win him over by the usual methods, and it wasn't long before I had him cheerfully inviting me to sit down.

"I'm in need of Sheikh Zaabalawi," I answered his enquiry as to the purpose of my visit.

He gazed at me with the same astonishment as that shown by those I had previously encountered.

"At least," he said, giving me a smile that revealed his gold teeth, "he is still alive. The devil of it is, though, he has no fixed abode. You might well bump into him as you go out of here, on the other hand you might spend days and months in fruitless search of him."

"Even you can't find him!"

"Even I! He's a baffling man, but I thank the Lord that he's still alive!"

He gazed at me intently, and murmured:

"It seems your condition is serious."

"Very!"

"May God come to your aid! But why don't you go about it rationally?"

He spread out a sheet of paper on the desk and drew on it with unexpected speed and skill until he had made a full plan of the district showing all the various quarters, lanes, alleyways, and squares. He looked at it admiringly and said, "These are dwelling houses, here is the Quarter of the Perfumers, here the Quarter of the Coppersmiths, the Mouski,° the Police and Fire Stations. The drawing is your best guide. Look carefully in the cafés, the places where the dervishes° perform their rites, the mosques and prayer-rooms, and the Green Gate, for he may well be concealed among the beggars and be indistinguishable from them. Actually, I myself haven't seen him for years, having been somewhat preoccupied with the cares of the world and was only brought back to those most exquisite times of my youth by your enquiry."

I gazed at the map in bewilderment. The telephone rang and he took up the receiver.

galabia: a floor-length shirt worn by Egyptian men
Mouski: a market in Cairo
dervishes: religious ascetics in Islam

"Take it," he told me, generously. "We're at your service."

Folding up the map, I left and wandered off through the quarter, from square to street to alleyway, making enquiries of everyone I felt was familiar with the place. At last the owner of a small establishment for ironing clothes told me:

"Go to the calligrapher Hassanein in Umm al-Ghulam° — they were friends."

I went to Umm al-Ghulam where I found old Hassanein working in a deep, narrow shop full of signboards and jars of color. A strange smell, a mixture of glue and perfume, permeated its every corner. Old Hassanein was squatting on a sheepskin rug in front of a board propped against the wall: in the middle of it he had inscribed the word "Allah" in silver lettering. He was engrossed in embellishing the letters with prodigious care. I stood behind him, fearful to disturb him or break the inspiration that flowed to his masterly hand. When my concern at not interrupting him had lasted some time, he suddenly enquired with unaffected gentleness:

"Yes?"

Realizing that he was aware of my presence, I introduced myself.

"I've been told that Sheikh Zaabalawi is your friend and I'm looking for him," I said.

His hand came to a stop. He scrutinized me in astonishment.

"Zaabalawi! God be praised!" he said with a sigh.

"He is a friend of yours, isn't he?" I asked eagerly.

"He was, once upon a time. A real man of mystery: he'd visit you so often that people would imagine he was your nearest and dearest, then would disappear as though he'd never existed. Yet saints are not to be blamed."

The spark of hope went out with the suddenness of a lamp by a power-cut.

"He was so constantly with me," said the man, "that I felt him to be a part of everything I drew. But where is he today?"

"Perhaps he is still alive?"

"He's alive, without a doubt. He had impeccable taste and it was due to him that I made my most beautiful drawings."

"God knows," I said, in a voice almost stifled by the dead ashes of hope, "that I am in the direst need of him and no one knows better than you of the ailments in respect of which he is sought."

"Yes — yes. May God restore you to health. He is, in truth, as is said of him, a man, and more — "

Smiling broadly, he added: "And his face is possessed of an unforgettable beauty. But where is he?"

Reluctantly I rose to my feet, shook hands and left. I continued on my way eastwards and westwards through the quarter, enquiring about him

---

Umm al-Ghulam: a district in Cairo

from everyone who, by reason of age or experience, I felt was likely to help me. Eventually I was informed by a vendor of lupine that he had met him a short while ago at the house of Sheikh Gad, the well-known composer. I went to the musician's house in Tabakshiyya where I found him in a room tastefully furnished in the old style, its walls redolent with history. He was seated on a divan, his famous lute lying beside him, concealing within itself the most beautiful melodies of our age, while from within the house came the sound of pestle and mortar and the clamor of children. I immediately greeted him and introduced myself, and was put at my ease by the unaffected way in which he received me. He did not ask, either in words or gesture, what had brought me, and I did not feel that he even harbored any such curiosity. Amazed at his understanding and kindness, which boded well, I said:

"O Sheikh Gad, I am an admirer of yours and have long been enchanted by the renderings of your songs."

"Thank you," he said with a smile.

"Please excuse my disturbing you," I continued timidly, "but I was told that Zaabalawi was your friend and I am in urgent need of him."

"Zaabalawi!" he said, frowning in concentration, "You need him? God be with you, for who knows, O Zaabalawi, where you are?"

"Doesn't he visit you?" I asked eagerly.

"He visited me some time ago. He might well come now; on the other hand I mightn't see him till death!"

I gave an audible sigh and asked:

"What made him like that?"

He took up his lute. "Such are saints or they would not be saints," he said laughing.

"Do those who need him suffer as I do?"

"Such suffering is part of the cure!"

He took up the plectrum and began plucking soft strains from the strings. Lost in thought, I followed his movements. Then, as though addressing myself, I said:

"So my visit has been in vain!"

He smiled, laying his cheek against the side of the lute.

"God forgive you," he said, "for saying such a thing of a visit that has caused me to know you and you me!"

I was much embarrassed and said apologetically:

"Please forgive me; my feelings of defeat made me forget my manners!"

"Do not give in to defeat. This extraordinary man brings fatigue to all who seek him. It was easy enough with him in the old days when his place of abode was known. Today, though, the world has changed and after having enjoyed a position attained only by potentates, he is now pursued by the police on a charge of false pretenses. It is therefore no longer an easy matter to reach him, but have patience and be sure that you will do so."

He raised his head from the lute and skillfully led into the opening bars of a melody. Then he sang:

I make lavish mention, even though I blame myself, of those I have
    loved,
For the words of lovers are my wine.

With a heart that was weary and listless I followed the beauty of the melody and the singing.

"I composed the music to this poem in a single night," he told me when he had finished. "I remember that it was the night of the Lesser Bairam.° He was my guest for the whole of that night and the poem was of his choosing. He would sit for a while just where you are, then would get up and play with my children as though he were one of them. Whenever I was overcome by weariness or my inspiration failed me he would punch me playfully in the chest and joke with me, and I would bubble over with melodies and thus I continued working till I finished the most beautiful piece I have ever composed."

"Does he know anything about music?"

"He was the epitome of things musical. He had an extremely beautiful speaking voice and you had only to hear him to want to burst into song. His loftiness of spirit stirred within you — "

"How was it that he cured those diseases before which men are powerless?"

"That is his secret. Maybe you will learn it when you meet him."

But when would that meeting occur? We relapsed into silence and the hubbub of children once more filled the room.

Again the Sheikh began to sing. He went on repeating the words "and I have a memory of her" in different and beautiful variations until the very walls danced in ecstasy. I expressed my wholehearted admiration and he gave me a smile of thanks. I then got up and asked permission to leave and he accompanied me to the outer door. As I shook him by the hand he said, "I hear that nowadays he frequents the house of Hagg Wanas al-Damanhouri. Do you know him?"

I shook my head, a modicum of renewed hope creeping into my heart.

"He is a man of private means," he told me, "who from time to time visits Cairo, putting up at some hotel or other. Every evening, though, he spends at the Negma Bar in Alfi Street."

I waited for nightfall and went to the Negma Bar. I asked a waiter about Hagg Wanas and he pointed to a corner which was semi-secluded

Lesser Bairam: an Islamic holy feast

because of its position behind a large pillar with mirrors on its four sides. There I saw a man seated alone at a table with a bottle three-quarters empty and another empty one in front of him; there were no snacks or food to be seen and I was sure that I was in the presence of a hardened drinker. He was wearing a loosely flowing silk *galabia* and a carefully wound turban; his legs were stretched out towards the base of the pillar, and as he gazed into the mirror in rapt contentment the sides of his face, rounded and handsome despite the fact that he was approaching old age, were flushed with wine. I approached quietly till I stood but a few feet away from him. He did not turn towards me, or give any indication that he was aware of my presence.

"Good evening, Mr. Wanas," I said with amiable friendliness.

He turned towards me abruptly as though my voice had roused him from slumber and glared at me in disapproval. I was about to explain what had brought me to him when he interrupted me in an almost imperative tone of voice which was none the less not devoid of an extraordinary gentleness:

"First, please sit down, and, second, please get drunk!"

I opened my mouth to make my excuses but, stopping up his ears with his fingers, he said:

"Not a word till you do what I say."

I realized that I was in the presence of a capricious drunkard and told myself that I should go along with him at least halfway.

"Would you permit me to ask one question?" I said with a smile, sitting down.

Without removing his hands from his ears he indicated the bottle.

"When engaged in a drinking bout like this I do not allow any conversation between myself and another unless, like me, he is drunk, otherwise the session loses all propriety and mutual comprehension is rendered impossible."

I made a sign indicating that I didn't drink.

"That's your look-out," he said offhandedly. "And that's my condition!"

He filled me a glass which I meekly took and drank. No sooner had it settled in my stomach than it seemed to ignite. I waited patiently till I had grown used to its ferocity, and said:

"It's very strong, and I think the time has come for me to ask you about — "

Once again, however, he put his fingers in his ears.

"I shan't listen to you until you're drunk!"

He filled up my glass for the second time. I glanced at it in trepidation; then, overcoming my innate objection, I drank it down at a gulp. No sooner had it come to rest inside me than I lost all willpower. With the third glass I lost my memory and with the fourth the future vanished.

The world turned round about me and I forgot why I had gone there. The man leaned towards me attentively but I saw him — saw everything — as a mere meaningless series of colored planes. I don't know how long it was before my head sank down on to the arm of the chair and I plunged into deep sleep. During it I had a beautiful dream the like of which I had never experienced. I dreamed that I was in an immense garden surrounded on all sides by luxuriant trees and the sky was nothing but stars seen between the entwined branches, all enfolded in an atmosphere like that of sunset or a sky overcast with cloud. I was lying on a small hummock of jasmine petals which fell upon me like rain, while the lucent spray of a fountain unceasingly sprinkled my head and temples. I was in a state of deep contentedness, of ecstatic serenity. An orchestra of warbling and cooing played in my ear. There was an extraordinary sense of harmony between me and my inner self, and between the two of us and the world, everything being in its rightful place without discord or distortion. In the whole world there was no single reason for speech or movement, for the universe moved in a rapture of ecstasy. This lasted but a short while. When I opened my eyes consciousness struck at me like a policeman's fist and I saw Wanas al-Damanhouri regarding me with concern. In the bar only a few drowsy people were left.

"You have slept deeply," said my companion; "you were obviously hungry for sleep."

I rested my heavy head in the palms of my hands. When I took them away in astonishment and looked down at them I found that they glistened with drops of water.

"My head's wet," I protested.

"Yes, my friend tried to rouse you," he answered quietly.

"Somebody saw me in this state?"

"Don't worry, he is a good man. Have you not heard of Sheikh Zaabalawi?"

"Zaabalawi!" I exclaimed, jumping to my feet.

"Yes," he answered in surprise. "What's wrong?"

"Where is he?"

"I don't know where he is now. He was here and then he left."

I was about to run off in pursuit but found I was more exhausted than I had imagined. Collapsed over the table, I cried out in despair:

"My sole reason for coming to you was to meet him. Help me to catch up with him or send someone after him."

The man called a vendor of prawns and asked him to seek out the Sheikh and bring him back. Then he turned to me.

"I didn't realize you were afflicted. I'm very sorry — "

"You wouldn't let me speak," I said irritably.

"What a pity! He was sitting on this chair beside you the whole time. He was playing with a string of jasmine petals he had round his neck, a gift from one of his admirers, then, taking pity on you, he began to sprin-kle some water on your head to bring you round."

"Does he meet you here every night?" I asked, my eyes not leaving the doorway through which the vendor of prawns had left.

"He was with me tonight, last night and the night before that, but be-fore that I hadn't seen him for a month."

"Perhaps he will come tomorrow," I answered with a sigh.

"Perhaps."

"I am willing to give him any money he wants."

Wanas answered sympathetically:

"The strange thing is that he is not open to such temptations, yet he will cure you if you meet him."

"Without charge?"

"Merely on sensing that you love him."

The vendor of prawns returned, having failed in his mission.

I recovered some of my energy and left the bar, albeit unsteadily. At every street corner I called out, "Zaabalawi!" in the vague hope that I would be rewarded with an answering shout. The street boys turned con-temptuous eyes on me till I sought refuge in the first available taxi.

The following evening I stayed up with Wanas al-Damanhouri till dawn, but the Sheikh did not put in an appearance. Wanas informed me that he would be going away to the country and wouldn't be returning to Cairo until he'd sold the cotton crop.

I must wait, I told myself; I must train myself to be patient. Let me content myself with having made certain of the existence of Zaabalawi, and even of his affection for me, which encourages me to think that he will be prepared to cure me if a meeting between us takes place.

Sometimes, however, the long delay wearied me. I would become beset by despair and would try to persuade myself to dismiss him from my mind completely. How many weary people in this life know him not or regard him as a mere myth! Why, then, should I torture myself about him in this way?

No sooner, however, did my pains force themselves upon me than I would again begin to think about him, asking myself as to when I would be fortunate enough to meet him. The fact that I ceased to have any news of Wanas and was told he had gone to live abroad did not deflect me from my purpose; the truth of the matter was that I had become fully con-vinced that I had to find Zaabalawi.

Yes, I have to find Zaabalawi.

Translated from the Arabic
by Denys Johnson-Davies

NAWAL SAADAWI

The controversial novelist, physician, and feminist activist Nawal Saadawi (1931–) studied medicine at the University of Cairo. She practiced psychiatry in cities and in the countryside for several years and was appointed director of health education in Egypt. In 1957, her Memoirs of a Woman Doctor *was serialized. The publication of* Woman and Sex *in 1972 incensed the government, which banned the book and dismissed her from her post. She has written more than thirty books, most of them novels, which have been translated into twenty languages. The best known is* Woman at Point Zero *(1975), a psychiatrist's interview with a woman prisoner on the eve of her execution for killing her pimp. Saadawi has also produced nonfiction books on the condition of women in the Arab world. More recently, she has examined in her novels the impact on women of the growth of Islamic fundamentalism. This focus has earned her the ire of religious extremist groups who published* Nawal Saadawi in the Dock *(1993), a book that tries her as a heretic and condemns her to death.*

"She Has No Place in Paradise" is a short story taken from a 1987 collection by the same title, which was first anthologized in English translation. It is one of her darkest pieces, presenting a woman's life in this world and the next as utterly desperate.

She Has No Place in Paradise

With the palm of her hand, she touched the ground beneath her but did not feel soil. She looked upwards, stretching her neck towards the light. Her face appeared long and lean, the skin so dark it was almost black.

She could not see her own face in the dark and held no mirror in her hand. But the white light fell onto the back of her hand so that it became white in turn. Her narrow eyes widened in surprise and filled with light. Thus widened and full of light, her eyes looked like those of a *houri.*°

In astonishment, she turned her head to the right and to the left. A vast expanse between the leafy trees above her head as she sat in the shade and the stream of water like a strip of silver, its clusters of droplets like pearls, then that deep plate full of broth to the rim.

Her eyelids tightened to open her eyes to the utmost. The scene remained the same, did not alter. She touched her robe and found it to be as soft as silk. From the neck of her gown wafted the scent of musk or good perfume.

---

houri: according to Islam, a virgin of paradise

Her head and eyes were motionless for she feared that any blink of her eyelids would change the scene or that it would disappear as it had done before.

But from the corner of her eye, she could see the shade stretching endlessly before her, and green trees between the trunks of which she saw a house of red brick like a palace, with a marble staircase leading up to the bedroom.

She remained fixed to the spot, able neither to believe nor disbelieve. Nothing upset her more than the recurrence of the dream that she had died and woken to find herself in paradise. The dream seemed to her impossible, for dying seemed impossible, waking after death even more impossible and going to paradise the fourth impossibility.

She steadied her neck still more and from the corner of her eye stared into the light. The scene was still the same, unaltered. The red brick house, like that of the *Omda*,° the towering staircase leading to the bedroom, the room itself bathed in white light, the window looking out onto distant horizons, the wide bed, its posts swathed in a curtain of silk, all were still there.

It was all so real it could not be denied. She stayed where she was, fearing to move and fearing to believe. Was it possible to die and waken so quickly and then go to paradise?

What she found hardest to believe was the speed of it all. Death, after all, was easy. Everybody died and her own death was easier than anyone's, for she had lived between life and death, closer to death than to life. When her mother gave birth to her, she lay on top of her with all her weight until she died; her father beat her on the head with a hoe until she died; she had gone into fever after each birth, even until the eighth child; when her husband kicked her in the stomach; when the blows of the sun penetrated under the bones of her head.

Life was hard and death for her was easier. Easier still was waking after death, for no one dies and no one wakens; everyone dies and awakens, except an animal which dies and remains dead.

Her going to paradise was also impossible. But if not her, who would go to paradise? Throughout her life she had never done anything to anger Allah or His Prophet.° She used to tie her frizzy black hair with a skein of wool into a plait; the plait she wrapped up in a white headscarf and her head she wrapped in a black shawl. Nothing showed from under her robe except the heel of her foot. From the moment of her birth until her death, she knew only the word: Okay.

Before dawn, when her mother slapped her as she lay, to go and carry

Omda: the village mayor
Allah or His Prophet: God (in Islam), and Muhammad, the seventh-century Arabian prophet of Islam

dung-pats° on her head, she knew only: Okay. If her father tied her to the water mill in place of the sick cow, she said only: Okay. She never raised her eyes to her husband's and when he lay on top of her when she was sick with fever, she uttered only the words: Okay.

She had never stolen or lied in her life. She would go hungry or die of hunger rather than take the food of others, even if it were her father's or brother's or husband's. Her mother would wrap up food for her father in a flat loaf of bread and make her carry it to the field on her head. Her husband's food was also wrapped up in a loaf by his mother. She was tempted, as she walked along with it, to stop under the shade of a tree and open the loaf; but she never once stopped. Each time she was tempted, she called on God to protect her from the Devil, until the hunger became unbearable and she would pick a bunch of wild grass from the side of the road which she would chew like gum, then swallow with a sip of water, filling the cup of her hand from the bank of the canal and drinking until she had quenched her thirst. Then, wiping her mouth on the sleeve of her robe, she would mutter to herself: Thank God, and repeat it three times. She prayed five times a day, her face to the ground, thanking God. If she were attacked by fever and her head filled with blood like fire, she would still praise Allah. On fast days, she would fast; on baking days, she would bake; on harvest days, she would harvest; on holy days, she would put on her mourning weeds and go to the cemetery.

She never lost her temper with her father or brother or husband. If her husband beat her to death and she returned to her father's house, her father would send her back to her husband. If she returned again, her father would beat her and *then* send her back. If her husband took her back and did not throw her out, and then beat her, she returned to her mother who would tell her: Go back, Zeinab. Paradise will be yours in the hereafter.

From the time she was born, she had heard the word "paradise" from her mother. The first time she'd heard it, she was walking in the sun, a pile of dung on her head, the soles of her feet scorched by the earth. She pictured paradise as a vast expanse of shade without sun, without dung on her head, on her feet shoes like those of Hassanain, the neighbor's son, pounding the earth as he did, his hand holding hers, the two of them sitting in the shade.

When she thought of Hassanain, her imagination went no further than holding hands and sitting in the shade of paradise. But her mother scolded her and told her that neither their neighbor's son Hassanain, nor any other neighbor's son, would be in paradise, that her eyes would not fall on any man other than her father or brother, that if she died after getting married and went to paradise, only her husband would be there, that

---

dung-pats: cow dung commonly used in Egypt for fuel and in building if her soul was tempted, awake or asleep, and her eye fell on a man other than her husband and even before he held her hand in his, she would not so much as catch a glimpse of paradise or smell it from a thousand meters . . .

From that time, whenever she lay down to sleep, she saw only her husband. In paradise, her husband did not beat her. The pile of dung was no longer on her head; neither did the earth burn the soles of her feet. Their black mud house became one of red brick, inside it a towering staircase, then a wide bed on which her husband sat, holding her hand in his.

Her imagination went no further than holding his hand in paradise. Never once in her life had her hand held her husband's. Eight sons and daughters she had conceived with him without once holding his hand. On summer nights, he lay in the fields; in the winter, he lay in the barn or above the oven. All night long, he slept on his back without turning. If he did turn, he would call to her in a voice like a jackal's: Woman! Before she could answer "yes" or "okay," he would have kicked her over onto her back and rolled on top of her. If she made a sound or sighed, he would kick her again. If she did not sigh or make a sound, she would get a third kick, then a fourth until she did. His hand never chanced to hold hers nor his arm happen to stretch out to embrace her.

She had never seen a couple, human or otherwise, embrace except in the dovecot. When she went up there, on the top of the wall appeared a pair of doves, their beaks close together; or when she went down to the cattle pen or from behind the wall there appeared a pair — bull and cow or buffalo or dogs — and her mother brandishing a bamboo stick and whipping them, cursing the animals.

Never in her life had she taken the black shawl off her head nor the white scarf tied under the shawl, except when someone died, when she untied the scarf and pulled the black shawl around her head. When her husband died, she knotted the black shawl twice around her forehead and wore mourning weeds for three years. A man came to ask for her in marriage without her children. Her mother spat in disgust and pulled the shawl down over her forehead, whispering: It's shameful! Does a mother abandon her children for the sake of a man? The years passed by and a man came to ask for her hand in marriage, with her children. Her mother yelled at the top of her voice: What does a woman want in this world after she has become a mother and her husband dies?

One day, she wanted to take off the black shawl and put on a white scarf, but she feared that people would think she'd forgotten her husband. So she kept the black shawl and the mourning weeds and remained sad for her husband until she died of sadness.

She found herself wrapped in a silken shroud inside a coffin. From behind the funeral procession, she heard her mother's wailing like a howl in the night or like the whistle of a train: You'll meet up with your husband in paradise, Zeinab.

Then the noise stopped. She heard nothing but silence and smelled nothing but the soil. The ground beneath her became as soft as silk. She said: It must be the shroud. Above her head, she heard rough voices, like two men fighting. She did not know why they were fighting until she heard one of them mention her name and say that she deserved to go directly to paradise without suffering the torture of the grave. But the other man did not agree and insisted that she should undergo some torture, if only a little: She cannot go directly up to paradise. Everyone must go through the torture of the grave. But the first man insisted that she had done nothing to merit torture, that she had been one hundred percent faithful to her husband. The second man argued that her hair had shown from under her white headscarf, that she had dyed her hair red with henna, that the hennaed heels of her feet had shown from under her robe.

The first man retorted that her hair had never shown, that what his colleague had seen was only the skein of wool, that her robe had been long and thick, under it even thicker and longer underskirts, that no one had seen her heels red.

But his colleague argued, insisting that her red heels had enticed many of the village men.

The dispute between the two of them lasted all night. She lay face down on the ground, her nose and mouth pressed into the earth. She held her breath pretending to be dead. Her torture might be prolonged if it became clear that she had not died; death might save her. She heard nothing of what passed between them; nobody, human or spirit, can hear what happens in the grave after death. If one did happen to hear, one had to pretend not to have heard or not to have understood. The most serious thing to understand is that those two men are not angels of the grave or angels of any type, for it is not possible for angels to ignore the truth which everyone in the village with eyes to see could know: that her heels had never been red like those of the *Omda*'s daughter, but like her face and palms, were always cracked and as black as the soil.

The argument ended before dawn without torture. She thanked God when the voices stopped. Her body grew lighter and rose up as if in flight. She hovered as if in the sky, then her body fell and landed on soft, moist earth and she gasped: Paradise.

Cautiously, she raised her head and saw a vast expanse of green, and thick leafy trees, shade beneath them.

She sat up on the ground and saw the trees stretching endlessly before her. Fresh air entered her chest, expelling the dirt and dust and the smell of dung.

With a slight movement, she rose to her feet. Between the tree trunks she could see the house of red brick, the entrance before her very eyes.

She entered quickly, panting. She climbed the towering staircase panting. In front of the bedroom, she stopped for a moment to catch her breath. Her heart was beating wildly and her chest heaved.

The door was closed. She put out her hand carefully and pushed it. She saw the four posts of the bed, around them a silken curtain. In the middle, she saw a wide bed, on top of it her husband, sitting like a bridegroom. On his right, was a woman. On his left, another woman. Both of them wore transparent robes revealing skin as white as honey, their eyes filled with light, like the eyes of *houris*.

Her husband's face was not turned towards her, so he did not see her. Her hand was still on the door. She pulled it behind her and it closed. She returned to the earth, saying to herself: There is no place in paradise for a black woman.

Translated from the Arabic by Shirley Eber

IRAN

SADEQ HEDAYAT

Sadeq Hedayat (1903–1951) was a member of the Iranian nobility. He studied in Paris in the late 1920s where he was influenced by the current literary trends, particularly surrealism. He wrote critical essays on Omar Khayyam and Franz Kafka, several novels, and a number of plays. He is considered the father of the Iranian short story, and he produced six collections of short stories. His best-known work is The Blind Owl *(1938), which encapsulates many themes that are typical of his work. This novel presents life as a prison that subjects its inmate to isolation experienced as barriers, walls, dead ends, and insane asylums. In 1951, he committed suicide while in France.*

"The Stray Dog" is the title story of a collection that appeared in 1942. Hedayat tells, through the eyes of a dog, a tragic human story of rejection and alienation. This use of animals is quite common in Persian literature and emerges out of a long tradition of animal allegories in folktales.

The Stray Dog

A few small stores: a bakery, a butcher's stall, a grocery, two tea houses, and a barber shop contributed to the basic requisites of the primitive way of life that made up Varamin Square.°

The merciless sun had nearly grilled and half-broiled the traffic circle and its inhabitants, who anxiously waited for the first evening breeze and the shades of night.

The people, the stores, the trees and the beasts were exhausted. A sultry heat weighed heavily overhead and a soft dust wavered in the azure blue sky.

The traffic of cars thickened the dust. On one side of the Square was an old sycamore whose innards had rotted away but which had spread its misshapen rheumatic branches with a strange persistence. Beneath the shade of its dust-laden leaves on a wide spacious platform, two street urchins with loud cries hawked their wares of rice pudding and pumpkin

Varamin Square: a square in Teheran

seeds. A dense, muddy stream pushed its way through the gutter in front of the tea house. The only building that attracted the eye was the well-known tower of Varamin with its cracked cylindrical body and its conical top. The sparrows had built their nests in the crevices made by the fallen bricks. Silent, they slumbered in the intense heat. Only the whimpering of a dog broke the silence.

This was a Scottish setter with sooty muzzle and black spots on its legs as if splashed by muddy water. He had drooping ears, a pointed tail, and a dirty coat, but two intelligent human-like eyes shone in his shaggy snout. In the depth of his eyes a human spirit was discernible. In his be-nighted life something eternal undulated in his eyes and had a message that could not be conveyed, for it had been trapped just behind his pupils — it was neither the glimmer nor the color, some other unbelievable thing, like what you might see in the eyes of a wounded gazelle. Not only was there a similarity between his eyes and the eyes of a man but a same-ness and equality. A pair of greenish-blue eyes filled with pain and hope-ful waiting discernible only in the visage of a lost and wayward dog.

But no one saw or heeded his painful beseeching looks! The errand boy of the bakery beat him when he found him in front of the shop. The butcher's apprentice threw stones at him if he saw him near his stall.

If he took refuge in the shade of a car, the driver was sure to entertain him with a rough kick of his spiked boots, and when one and all tired of victimizing him, it was the turn of the urchin who sold rice pudding to take special pleasure in torturing him.

At each cry of pain that escaped the dog, the rice-pudding vendor boy threw another stone, which invariably hit with devilish accuracy and brought out his noisy laughter with cries of "You untouchable cur!" It seemed that the others were his accomplices, for they encouraged the boy in an underhanded, sly way and burst into laughter.

One and all, all of them beat him to please their Almighty God. To them it was natural to torture the dirty untouchable dog which their reli-gion had set a curse upon. At last the rice-pudding boy chastised him so much that the animal was forced to run away through the narrow alley leading to the tower.

He pulled himself with difficulty on an empty stomach and took refuge in a *jube.*° Once there he laid his head on his pasterns, put out his tongue, and in a state verging on wakefulness and dreaming, watched the green fields that waved in the wind. He was tired out and his nerves ached.

In the damp air of the *jube* a certain unnameable feeling of well-being pervaded his whole body. Diverse smells of the dead and the living things resuscitated in his muzzle a confusion of faraway memories.

Whenever he fixed his eyes on the green fields, his instinctive urges were roused, reviving old memories in his brain.

jube: an open channel for water in the streets of Iranian cities

But this time, the feeling was so strong that it seemed as if an unknown voice urged him to movement; to jump and frolic. He felt a great urge to run and jump about in these green fields.

This feeling was hereditary, for all his ancestors had been bred in the open spaces of the Scottish meadows and green forests.

But now his whole being was so sore that he could not move. A painful feeling mixed with weakness and lethargy pervaded him. A whole file of forgotten and lost sensations were excited.

Formerly he had different checks and different requirements. He had bound himself to the beck and call of his Master; to drive out strange persons and dogs from his Master's premises: to play with his Master's child. He knew how to behave with the known and the authorized people and how to treat strangers; to eat on time; and when to expect fondling.

But now all these checks were removed. Now his whole life had narrowed to the permanent quest for food, which he got by rummaging fearfully in garbage piles; to being beaten throughout the day; and howls and whimpering had become his sole means of defense.

Once upon a time he had been brave, fearless, clean, and full of life, but now he had become a yellow timid scapegoat. He had become a bag of nerves: if he heard a voice, or something near him moved, he would nearly jump out of his skin and shiver.

He even dreaded his own voice. He had got used to dirt and refuse. His body itched, and he did not have the guts to hunt out the lice, or enough self-respect to lick himself clean. He felt that he had become a part of the garbage. Something in him had died, had burnt out.

Two winters had passed since he landed in this out-of-the-way hell of a place, and all this time he had not eaten a full meal, nor slept a happy comfortable sleep. His passions and feelings were strangled. None had pampered him. No one had looked into his eyes. Although the people here resembled his Master in appearance, his Master's feelings and character were a world apart from these people. It was as if the people he knew before were nearer to his world. They seemed to understand his pains and feelings better, and they backed him up.

Of the smells that reached his nostrils and made him light-headed, there was the smell of the rice pudding coming from the pot set in front of the street boy. The white liquid so much resembled his mother's milk that it brought back memories of puppyhood.

Suddenly he went numb, remembering when he was a tiny thing sucking that warm invigorating liquid from his mother's breasts while his mother licked him clean with her strong tongue. The strong smell that came from his mother's bosom and from his pup-brother, the poignant and the heavy smell of his mother and her milk, revived in his nostrils. When he was fully satisfied, his body used to become warm and relaxed; a liquid warmth would run through his veins and arteries. His head would feel heavy and drop from his mother's breasts and a deep slumber would follow, filled with sensual feelings for the nearness of that fount of life; so close and so full of abundance.

His pup-brother's downy body, his mother's bark, all these were treasured in his mind. He remembered his old wooden kennel, the games he used to play with his pup-brother in that small garden. He would bite the tips of his brother's ears and they would both fall, get up again, and run. Then he found a new playmate. This was his Master's son. At the end of the garden he ran after him and barked and bit his clothes.

He could never forget his Master's caresses nor the lumps of sugar the Master used to feed him with his own hands, never; but he loved his Master's son even more, for he was his playmate and never beat him.

Then after some time he lost all traces of his mother and pup-brother. There remained only his Master, the Master's son, the Master's wife and their old servant. How well he recognized their individual scents and their footsteps from a distance!

When lunch or dinner was served he would walk round the table smelling different dishes of food, and sometimes his Master's wife would throw him a choice morsel despite the strong protests of her husband. Then the old servant would come and would call him "Pat, Pat" and pile his food in a special dish which lay near his wooden kennel.

Pat's troubles started when his rut came on, for his Master would not let him out of the house to run after bitches. As fate would have it, one day in the fall, his Master, with two other people whom Pat knew well and who often came to their house, got into a car and called Pat and made him sit next to them in the car. Pat had been in cars with his Master before, but this time he was in heat and was beset with a strong, disturbing urge.

After a few hours of driving they got off at this same square. His Master with the other two men made their way through this same street that passes by the tower, but suddenly the scent of a bitch, the traces of her scent, turned him mad. He sniffed and followed the scent and at last through a *jube* entered a garden.

Near evening twice he heard his Master calling him, "Pat, Pat!" Was it really his Master's voice or an echo of it? He could not be sure, for he did not want it to be. His Master's voice always had a strange effect on him: it was a reminder of what he knew were his duties. But a Power over and above other forces had made him oblivious to all but the bitch. He was deaf to all external sounds. He felt an intense sensation, and the bitch's scent was so strong, heavy, and poignant that he felt light-headed.

His nerves, muscles, and senses were no longer at his command. In the face of the new and unique experience, he was powerless, but his delectation was short-lived. The owner of the garden and his men assailed him with clubs and spade handles and routed him through the water channel.

Once out, Pat, confused and tired but light and relieved, jolted himself into reality and began to look for the Master.

In some back alleys he could smell thin traces of his Master's scent, which he inspected elaborately, leaving his own scent at regular intervals.

He even explored the ruins outside the village. Then he came back, for he was sure that his Master had returned to the square. But there in the traffic circle his Master's thin scent got lost in other scents.

Was it possible that his Master had gone and left him there? He felt a sensational anxiety mixed with fear.

How could he live without his Master, without his god? His Master was a god to him. He was sure his Master would come and seek him out.

Panicked, he ran down several roads. It was useless.

Night came and Pat, tired out and disappointed, returned to the square. There was no trace of his Master.

He rounded the village a few more times and at last went to the *jube* which led to the bitch, but they had obstructed the way with heavy stones.

He set to digging the ground with gusto to open a hole to the garden, but it was impossible.

When he saw that it was hopeless, he napped there.

In the middle of the night the sound of his own wailing in his dreams woke him up. In a panic, he was soon on his feet, went through several alleys, sniffed the walls, and strayed here and there.

He felt starved, and when he returned to the square, the smell of various foods reached his nostrils — the smell of the left-over meat, the fresh bread and yoghurt. All of the odors had commingled.

He must beg food from these people who looked like his Master, and if he was lucky enough to have no rival to drive him out, perhaps one of these creatures who held food in his possession would take care of him.

Cautiously and with much foreboding he went towards a bakery which had just opened.

The strong smell of baked dough pervaded the air. Someone who held some bread under his arm called to him "Come . . . Come . . ."

How strange this voice seemed to his ears. The stranger threw him a piece of the warm bread. After a little hesitation Pat ate the bread and shook his tail for him.

The stranger put his bread on the shop's platform, and then timidly and with much caution, caressed Pat's head, and using his two hands opened his collar. How relieved he felt!

It was as if all the responsibilities, checks and duties were lifted off his neck. But when again he shook his tail and neared the owner of the bakery shop, a heavy shoe shot into his groin, and whimpering he ran away.

The owner religiously dipped his hands in the gutter water three times to wash off the ill effects of having touched the unclean dog.

Pat recognized his neck band which still hung in front of the shop.

Since that day, save kicks, stones and a good taste of the club. Pat had not received anything from these people.

It was as if they were all his sworn enemies and took pleasure in tormenting him.

Pat felt that he had entered into a new world which was not his and contained no one who cared a whit about his sentiments and idiosyncrasies.

The first days were passed with much difficulty but by and by he adjusted. In addition to this, he had found a place at the bend of the alley on the right-hand side where people emptied refuse cans and where he could find tasty morsels in the garbage, such as bones, fat, skin, fish heads and many other foods that he could not recognize.

The rest of the day he spent in front of the bakery and the butcher's stall.

His eyes were fixed on the hands of the butcher, but he received more beatings than delicious bits. Altogether he had made peace with his new mode of life.

Of his past life there remained only a hodge-podge of ambiguous and erased traces and only some distant scents. When he had it hard, he found a sort of refuge and solace in this lost paradise and automatically gave himself up to the memories of those bygone days.

But the thing that tortured him more than anything was his craving to be fondled.

He was like a child who had been constantly used roughly and been constantly abused but retained his tender feelings. Especially now in his new pain-ridden life, more than ever before he felt the need for kindness and attention.

His eyes begged for such treatment and he was prepared to give his life to the first person who was kind to him or caressed his head.

He was in dire need to show his sincerity to someone, to sacrifice his life for that someone.

He longed to show his adoration and fidelity, but no one cared two straws for him. The eyes he looked into had nothing in them save enmity and evil designs. Any movement he made to attract the attention of these people only increased their rage and anger.

When Pat was having his forty winks inside the *jube,* he moaned, and this wakened him up several times, as if he were beset by nightmares.

He felt a great hunger; there was the smell of grilled mutton meat in the air. A cruel hunger tortured his insides, so much so that he forgot his weakness and other pains, with difficulty got to his feet, and wearily set out towards the traffic circle.

Now at this time one of those noisy cars, followed by a whirlwind of dust, drove into Varamin Square.

A man got out, went to Pat and stroked his head. He was not his Master. Pat was not deceived, for he knew his Master's scent very well.

But why did he pat him? Pat shook his tail and threw the man a suspicious look.

Wasn't he being deceived? But no, for he no longer had a collar round his neck so that he would pat him for it.

The man turned and again caressed him. Pat followed the man. His surprise increased as the man entered a room that Pat knew very well, from where the smell of food always emanated.

The man sat on a bench near the wall. They brought him fresh bread, yoghurt, eggs and other foods.

The man dipped bits and pieces of bread in yoghurt and threw them in front of him.

At first Pat gulped these in a hurry, then ate them at his leisure.

At the same time his soulful emerald eyes, beautiful and full of supplication and gratitude, were fixed on the face of the man and all the while he shook his tail.

Was he dreaming or was he awake? Unbelievably, he had eaten his fill without having his meal interrupted by severe punishment.

Was it possible that he had found a new Master? Despite the heat, the man got up, went towards the alley leading to the tower.

Once there, he hesitated, then crossed several labyrinthine winding alleys.

Pat followed him. The man went to the ruins that had some walls. His Master had also gone there.

Perhaps these men were also after picking up the scent of females of their own species. Pat waited for him in the shade of a wall.

After a while, through another route, they returned to the Square.

There again the man patted him, and after taking a short walk round the circle, went and sat in one of the cars that Pat knew.

Pat did not dare to climb in: he sat near the car and looked at the man.

Suddenly the car started in a burst of dust and Pat without any hesitation began to run after it.

No, he had learned his lesson, he did not want to lose his benefactor again. Notwithstanding the pain he felt throughout his body, his tongue was out and he ran in leaps and bounds after the car.

The car had left the village and was crossing a desert.

Two or three times Pat overtook the car but again lagged behind.

Despair made him summon all his power and burst into sudden leaps, but the car was faster. He could not reach the car and the running greatly weakened him.

He felt a great weakness at the pit of his stomach and all at once sensed that his limbs no longer obeyed his commands and could not make the slightest movement.

All his efforts were pointless. He didn't know why he had run or where he was going.

He could neither go ahead nor back. He stopped, short of breath, his tongue hanging out.

His eyes had darkened. With bent head and with much labor, he pulled himself out of the middle of the road and went and laid his belly on wet and hot sand near a ditch on the edge of a field.

By means of his instinct that had never lied to him, he felt that he would never be able to move from that place.

Translated from the Farsee
by Siavosh Danesh

FORUGH FARROKHZAD

Forugh Farrokhzad (1935–1967) was married off at age sixteen, and a year later, she had a child. Two years later she was divorced. Her subsequent public involvement with a married man earned her society's disapproval. Matters were not improved when she started to write, for she was the first woman in Iran to rebel against the traditional content of Persian poetry and to express herself openly, some say autobiographically, in criticizing social norms. Her first poem, "Captive," was published when she was seventeen, and three years later she brought out what was considered to be a "scandalously frank" anthology with the same title. Many have esteemed Another Birth (1964), with its open yet lyrical evocation of love, loneliness, and alienation, to be her best writing. In it she breaks with conventional quatrain stanzas to compose verses of unequal length and untraditional meter. During the late 1950s, Farrokhzad studied filmmaking in England. She produced several documentaries, including The House Is Black (1963), a film about a leper colony in Tabriz, which won the prize for documentaries at the Uberhausen Film Festival. She died in a car accident at the age of thirty-two.

"Window" and "Friday" are taken from Another Birth. Like many other Middle Eastern women, she describes the home as a prison.

Window

one window for seeing
one window for hearing
one window that as a tubular body of a well
reaches at its depth into the heart of the earth
and opens to the vastness of this blue-colored recurrent kindness   5
one windows that fills the little hands of loneliness

with the nocturnal gift
of the fragrance of the generous stars.
And thence, it is possible
to invite the sun to the desolation of the little geraniums 10
one window is enough for me.

I come from the realm of dolls
from beneath the shadow of paper trees
in the garden of an illustrated book
from the dry seasons of the barren experiences of friendship
and love 15
in the dirt-alleys of innocence
from the years of the growth of the pale letters of the alphabet
behind the desks of the tubercular schools
from the moment that the children could
spell "stone" on the blackboard 20
and the startled starlings flew off the aged tree.

I come from within the roots of the carnivorous plants
and my brain still
overflows with the cry of horror of the butterfly
that they had crucified 25
in a notebook with a pin

When my faith hung from the frail rope of justice
and throughout the town
they tore to pieces the heart of my lights
when they blind-folded the childish eyes of my love 30
with the dark kerchief of laws
and from the anxious temples of my dreams
sprang out fountains of blood
when my life amounted to nothing, any longer
nothing except the tic toc of the clock on the wall 35
I understood that madly I must, must, must
love

One window is enough for me
one window into the moment of consciousness and observation
and silence
Now the walnut plant 40
has grown tall enough to explain the meaning of the wall
for its younger leaves
Ask the mirror
the name of your savior
the earth that trembles beneath your feet 45
is it not more alone than you?
The prophets delivered the message of destruction

to our century
Are these continuous explosions
and poisoned clouds   50
the echoes of holy verses?
Oh friend, oh brother, oh blood-kin
When you reach the moon
record the history of the massacre of the flowers.

The dreams, always   55
fall from the height of their naivete and they die
I would smell the fragrance of a four-leaf clover
that has grown upon the grave of old concepts.
The woman that was buried in the shroud of her expectations
    and her chastity
was she my youth?   60
Will I again ascend the steps of my curiosity
to greet the good God who walks upon the roof top?

I feel that the time has passed
I feel that "the moment" of my portion is of the pages of history
I feel that the table is a false distance between my hair and   65
the hands of this sad stranger.

Speak a word to me
The person that bestows upon you the kindness of a living body
Would want from you what else but the perception of the sense
    of existence?

Speak a word to me   70
I, in the shelter of my window,
have communication with the sun.

Translated from the Farsee
by Ardavan Davaran

Friday

Silent Friday
deserted Friday
Friday of back streets, old miseries
Friday's languorous, languishing thoughts
Friday's spasms of yawns and stretching   5
futile Friday
sacrificed Friday

the house vacant
dismal house
house shuttered against the coming of the young   10
gloomed house vainly recalling the sun
house of desolations, doubting, divinings
curtains house, books house, closets and pictures house

O how my life passed, calmly proud
a strange and foreign stream   15
flowing through the heart of these mute, deserted Fridays
the heart of these vacant, desolating houses
O how my life passed calmly proud . . .

Translated from the Farsee by
Jascha Kessler and Amin Banani

BADR SHAKIR AL-SAYYAB

Critics consider Badr Shakir al-Sayyab (1926–1964) to be one of the greatest modern Arab poets. A great admirer of T. S. Eliot's The Waste Land, *he revolutionized poetic style while, as a committed socialist, politicizing content and urging a realist approach. With his country-woman Nazik al-Malaika, he is credited with launching the free verse movement at the end of the 1940s, publishing "Was It Love?" in his first anthology,* Wilted Flowers *(1947), and then several free verse poems in* Legends *(1950). In the 1950s he was one of the Tammuz poets, whose nationalist writings invoked the Adonis myth with its emphasis on rejection, crucifixion, and resurrection. In 1960 he published* Song of Rain, *an anthology that was to have considerable impact throughout the Arab world.*

When he learned that he had been struck by a degenerative nervous disease, al-Sayyab traveled to Beirut, London, and Paris in search of a cure. His last poems which include the figures of Sinbad and Job, are filled with nostalgia, despair, and fear; he even composed elegies for himself. He died in poverty at the age of thirty-eight. He produced seven collections of poetry and translations into Arabic of several writers including Edith Sitwell, whose work he greatly admired, and Nazim Hikmet Ran.

Rain Song

Your eyes are two palm tree forests in early light,
Or two balconies from which the moonlight recedes
When they smile, your eyes, the vines put forth their leaves,
And lights dance . . . like moons in a river
Rippled by the blade of an oar at break of day;   5
As if stars were throbbing in the depths of them . . .

And they drown in a mist of sorrow translucent
Like the sea stroked by the hand of nightfall;
The warmth of winter is in it, the shudder of autumn,
And death and birth, darkness and light;   10
A sobbing flares up to tremble in my soul

And a savage elation embracing the sky,
Frenzy of a child frightened by the moon.
It is as if archways of mist drank the clouds
And drop by drop dissolved in the rain . . .   15
As if children snickered in the vineyard bowers,
The song of the rain
Rippled the silence of birds in the trees . . .
Drop, drop, the rain . . .
Drip . . .   20
Drop . . . the rain . . .

Evening yawned, from low clouds
Heavy tears are streaming still.
It is as if a child before sleep were rambling on
About his mother (a year ago he went to wake her, did not find
    her,   25
Then was told, for he kept on asking,
"After tomorrow, she'll come back again . . .")
That she must come back again,
Yet his playmates whisper that she is there
In the hillside, sleeping her death for ever,   30
Eating the earth around her, drinking the rain;
As if a forlorn fisherman gathering nets
Cursed the waters and fate
And scattered a song at moonset,
Drip, drop, the rain . . .   35
Drip, drop, the rain . . .

Do you know what sorrow the rain can inspire?
Do you know how gutters weep when it pours down?
Do you know how lost a solitary person feels in the rain?
Endless, like spilt blood, like hungry people, like love,   40
Like children, like the dead, endless the rain.
Your two eyes take me wandering with the rain,
Lightnings from across the Gulf° sweep the shores of Iraq
With stars and shells,
As if a dawn were about to break from them,   45
But night pulls over them a coverlet of blood.
I cry out to the Gulf: "O Gulf,
Giver of pearls, shells and death!"
And the echo replies,
As if lamenting: 50
"O Gulf,
Giver of shells and death . . ."

the Gulf: the Persian Gulf, sometimes also called the Arabian Gulf

I can almost hear Iraq husbanding the thunder,
Storing lightning in the mountains and plains,
So that if the seal were broken by men   55
The winds would leave in the valley not a trace of Thamud.°
I can almost hear the palmtrees drinking the rain,
Hear the villages moaning and emigrants
With oar and sail fighting the Gulf
Winds of storm and thunder, singing   60
"Rain . . . rain . . .
Drip, drop, the rain . . ."

And there is hunger in Iraq,
The harvest time scatters the grain in it,
That crows and locusts may gobble their fill,   65
Granaries and stones grind on and on,
Mills turn in the fields, with them men turning . . .
Drip, drop, the rain . . .
Drip . . .
Drop . . .   70

When came the night for leaving, how many tears we shed,
We made the rain a pretext, not wishing to be blamed
Drip, drop, the rain . . .
Drip, drop, the rain . . .
Since we had been children, the sky   75
Would be clouded in wintertime,
And down would pour the rain,
And every year when earth turned green the hunger struck us.
Not a year has passed without hunger in Iraq.
Rain . . .   80
Drip, drop, the rain . . .
Drip, drop . . .

In every drop of rain
A red or yellow color buds from the seeds of flowers,
Every tear wept by the hungry and naked people,   85
Every spilt drop of slaves' blood,
Is a smile aimed at a new dawn,
A nipple turning rosy in an infant's lips,
In the young world of tomorrow, bringer of life.
Drip, drop, the rain . . .   90
Drip . . .
Drop . . . the rain . . .
Iraq will blossom one day in the rain.

Thamud: an ancient Arabian tribe described in the Koran as having been destroyed by
   God; a symbol for the temporality of power

I cry out to the Gulf: "O Gulf,
Giver of pearls, shells and death!"   95
The echo replies
As if lamenting:
"O Gulf,
Giver of shells and death."
And across the sands from among its lavish gifts   100
The Gulf scatters fuming froth and shells
And the skeletons of miserable drowned emigrants
Who drank death forever
From the depths of the Gulf, from the ground of its silence,
And in Iraq a thousand serpents drink the nectar   105
From a flower the Euphrates has nourished with dew.
I hear the echo
Ringing in the Gulf:
"Rain . . .
Drip, drop, the rain . . .   110
Drip, drop."
In every drop of rain
A red or yellow color buds from the seeds of flowers.
Every tear wept by the hungry and naked people
And every spilt drop of slaves' blood   115
Is a smile aimed at a new dawn,
A nipple turning rosy in an infant's lips
In the young world of tomorrow, bringer of life.

And still the rain pours down.

Translated from the Arabic by
Lena Jayyusi and Christopher Middleton

Song in August

Tammuz° dies on the skyline,
His blood seeps away with twilight
In the dim cavern. Darkness
Is a black ambulance,

Night a flock of women: 5
Kohl,° black cloaks.
Night, an enormous tent.
Night, a blocked day.

Tammuz: a mythical figure; the equivalent of Adonis who symbolizes resurrection
kohl: antimony

I called to my negro maid:
"Murjana,° it's dark now,   10
Switch the light on. You know what? I'm hungry.
There's a song, I forgot, some sort of a song.
What's this chatter on the radio?
From London, Murjana, a
Jazz concert so   15
Find it, I'm happy, jazz,
Blood rhythm."

Tammuz dies and Murjana
Crouches cold like the forest.
She says, breathless: 20
"The night, wild pig,
How miserable the night is."
"Murjana, was that the doorbell?"
So she says, breathless:
"There are women at the door."   25
And Murjana makes the coffee.

Fur over white shoulders:
Wolf covers woman.
On her breasts a whole sheen of tiger skin
Filling the forest, stealing from the trees.   30
Night stretches,
Distraction, night
An earth-oven, radiant from ghosts,
Bread inhaling the night fires,
And the visitor eats, famished.   35
Murjana crouches
Cold like the forest.

The visitor laughs, she says: "Suʾad's boyfriend,
Been giving her a bad time, broke the engagement,
The dog disowned the bitch . . ."   40

Tammuz dies, never to return.
Coldness drips from the moon,
The visitor huddles at the fire gossiping, sharp-tongued.
Night has extinguished the coasts,
The visitor crouches, cold, robed   45
With wolf fur.
The fire she lit with bloody talk
Goes out.

Murjana: the name for a black woman slave in ancient Arabian culture

Night and ice,
Across them a sound falls, clank of iron   50
Muffled by wolf howls.
Distant sound,
The visitor, like me, is cold.

So come on over and share my cold,
Come by God,   55
Husband, I'm alone here,
The visitor is cold as I am —
So come on over,
Only with you can I talk about everyone.
And there are so many people to be talked about.   60
The dark is a hearse, the driver blind
And your heart is a burial ground.

Translated from the Arabic by
Lena Jayyusi and Christopher Middleton

SHMUEL YOSEF AGNON

When he was ten, the family of Shmuel Yosef Agnon (1888–1970) immigrated to Jaffa, Palestine. He went to Germany five years later, where he lived throughout World War I. In 1924, he returned to Jerusalem and remained there for the rest of his life. His first published writings were poems, which appeared in 1903. Five years later he started to publish short stories.

He published his first, and some say best, novel, The Bridal Canopy, *in 1919. This picaresque novel, which tells of the ups and downs of a turn-of-the-century Hasidic family, is an allegory on the decline of Jewish religious life in Poland.* Yesterday and the Day Before *(1945) anticipates the emergence of Israel out of the Holocaust. Agnon recaptures traditional lives of the Jewish diaspora in eastern Europe as well as the rebellion of the young who start a pioneering life in Palestine. Agnon's twenty-four volumes of novels, novellas, and short stories gained him the reputation of being the best writer of Hebrew fiction. He was awarded the Nobel Prize for literature in 1966. His unique style and language — a blend of classic and rabbinic Hebrew and Yiddish revived in a spoken Hebrew — have been highly influential.*

"At the Outset of the Day" was published in 1951, three years after the establishment of the State of Israel. It evokes a mood of loss for the destruction of the Torah, the book of Jewish law that contains the souls of the people, and signifies the destruction of the Jewish community.

At the Outset of the Day

After the enemy destroyed my home I took my little daughter in my arms and fled with her to the city. Gripped with terror, I fled in frenzied haste a night and a day until I arrived at the courtyard of the Great Synagogue one hour before nightfall on the eve of the Day of Atonement.° The hills and mountains that had accompanied us departed, and I and the child entered into the courtyard. From out of the depths rose the Great

Day of Atonement: the Jewish day of fasting and praying for forgiveness for the past year's sins

Synagogue, on its left the old House of Study and directly opposite that, one doorway facing the other, the new House of Study.

This was the House of Prayer and these the Houses of Torah that I had kept in my mind's eye all my life. If I chanced to forget them during the day, they would stir themselves and come to me at night in my dreams, even as during my waking hours. Now that the enemy had destroyed my home I and my little daughter sought refuge in these places; it seemed that my child recognized them, so often had she heard about them.

An aura of peace and rest suffused the courtyard. The Children of Israel had already finished the afternoon prayer and, having gone home, were sitting down to the last meal before the fast to prepare themselves for the morrow, that they might have strength and health enough to return in repentance.

A cool breeze swept through the courtyard, caressing the last of the heat in the thick walls, and a whitish mist spiraled up the steps of the house, the kind children call angels' breath.

I rid my mind of all that the enemy had done to us and reflected upon the Day of Atonement drawing ever closer, that holy festival comprised of love and affection, mercy and prayer, a day whereon men's supplications are dearer, more desired, more acceptable than at all other times. Would that they might appoint a reader of prayers worthy to stand before the Ark,° for recent generations have seen the decline of emissaries of the congregation who know how to pray; and cantors° who reverence their throats with their trilling, but bore the heart, have increased. And I, I needed strengthening — and, needless to say, my little daughter, a babe torn away from her home.

I glanced at her, at my little girl standing all atremble by the memorial candle in the courtyard, warming her little hands over the flame. Growing aware of my eyes, she looked at me like a frightened child who finds her father standing behind her and sees that his thoughts are muddled and his heart humbled.

Grasping her hand in mine, I said, "Good men will come at once and give me a prayer shawl with an adornment of silver just like the one the enemy tore. You remember the lovely prayer shawl that I used to spread over your head when the priests would rise up to bless the people. They will give me a large festival prayerbook filled with prayers, too, and I will wrap myself in the prayer shawl and take the book and pray to God, who saved us from the hand of the enemy who sought to destroy us.

"And what will they bring you, my dearest daughter? You, my darling, they will bring a little prayerbook full of letters, full of all of the letters of the alphabet and the vowel-marks, too. And now, dearest daughter, tell

---

the Ark: the Ark of the Covenant, a sacred, gold-covered, wooden chest identified by the Hebrews with God
cantors: singers in a synagogue

me, an *alef*° and a *bet*° that come together with a *kametz*° beneath the *alef* — how do you say them?"

"*Av*," my daughter answered.

"And what does it mean?" I asked.

"Father," my daughter answered, "like you're my father."

"Very nice, that's right, an *alef* with a *kametz* beneath and a *bet* with no dot in it make '*Av*.'

"And now, my daughter," I continued, "what father is greater than all other fathers? Our Father in Heaven, who is my father and your father and the father of the whole world. You see, my daughter, two little letters stand there in the prayerbook as if they were all alone, then they come together and lo and behold they are '*Av*.' And not only these letters but all letters, all of them join together to make words and words make prayers and the prayers rise up before our Father in Heaven who listens very, very carefully, to all that we pray, if only our hearts cling to the upper light like a flame clings to a candle."

Even as I stood there speaking of the power of the letters a breeze swept through the courtyard and pushed the memorial candle against my daughter. Fire seized hold of her dress. I ripped off the flaming garment, leaving the child naked, for what she was wearing was all that remained of her lovely clothes. We had fled in panic, destruction at our heels, and had taken nothing with us. Now that fire had consumed her dress I had nothing with which to cover my daughter.

I turned this way and that, seeking anything my daughter could clothe herself with. I sought, but found nothing. Wherever I directed my eyes, I met emptiness. I'll go to the corner of the storeroom, I said to myself, where torn sacred books are hidden away, perhaps there I will find something. Many a time when I was a lad I had rummaged about there and found all sorts of things, sometimes the conclusion of a matter and sometimes its beginning or its middle. But now I turned there and found nothing with which to cover my little girl. Do not be surprised that I found nothing. When books were read, they were rent; but now that books are not read, they are not rent.

I stood there worried and distraught. What could I do for my daughter, what could I cover her nakedness with? Night was drawing on and with it the chill of the night, and I had no garment, nothing to wrap my daughter in. I recalled the home of Reb° Alter, who had gone up to the Land of Israel. I'll go to his sons and daughters, I decided, and ask clothing of them. I left my daughter as she was and headed for the household of Reb Alter.

---

alef: the first letter of the Hebrew alphabet
bet: the second letter of the Hebrew alphabet
kametz: a diacritical mark placed above or below Hebrew letters
reb: a religious leader in Judaism

How pleasant to walk without being pursued. The earth is light and comfortable and does not burn beneath one's feet, nor do the Heavens fling thorns into one's eyes. But I ran rather than walked, for even if no man was pursuing me, time was: the sun was about to set and the hour to gather for the evening prayer was nigh. I hurried lest the members of Reb Alter's household might already be getting up to leave for the House of Prayer.

It is comforting to remember the home of a dear friend in time of distress. Reb Alter, peace be with him, had circumcised me, and a covenant of love bound us together. As long as Reb Alter lived in his home I was a frequent visitor there, the more so in the early days when I was a classmate of his grandson Gad. Reb Alter's house was small, so small that one wondered how such a large man could live there. But Reb Alter was wise and made himself so little that his house seemed large.

The house, built on one of the low hills surrounding the Great Synagogue, had a stucco platform protruding from it. Reb Alter, peace be with him, had been in the habit of sitting on that platform with his long pipe in his mouth, sending wreaths of smoke gliding into space. Many a time I stood waiting for the pipe to go out so I could bring him a light. My grandfather, peace be with him, had given Reb Alter that pipe at my circumcision feast. "Your grandfather knows pipes very well," Reb Alter told me once, "and knows how to pick just the right pipe for every mouth."

Reb Alter stroked his beard as he spoke, like one well aware that he deserved that pipe, even though he was a modest man. His modesty showed itself one Friday afternoon before sunset. As he put out the pipe, and the Sabbath was approaching, he said, "Your grandfather never has to put out his pipe; he knows how to smoke more or less as time necessitates."

Well, then, I entered the home of Reb Alter and found his daughter, together with a small group of old men and old women, sitting near a window while an old man with a face like a wrinkled pear stood reading them a letter. All of them listened attentively, wiping their eyes. Because so many years had passed I mistook Reb Alter's daughter for her mother. What's going on? I asked myself. On the eve of the Day of Atonement darkness is falling, and these people have not lit a "candle of life." And what sort of letter is this? If from Reb Alter, he is already dead. Perhaps it was from his grandson, my friend Gad, perhaps news had come from Reb Alter's grandson Gad, who had frequented the House of Study early and late. One day he left early and did not return.

It is said that two nights prior to his disappearance his wetnurse had seen him in a dream sprouting the plume of a peculiar bird from his head, a plume that shrieked, "A, B, C, D!" Reb Alter's daughter folded the letter and put it between the mirror and the wall. Her face, peeking out of the mirror, was the face of an aged woman bearing the burden of her years. And alongside her face appeared my own, green as a wound that has not formed a scab.

I turned away from the mirror and looked at the rest of the old people in Reb Alter's home and tried to say something to them. My lips flipped against each other like a man who wishes to say something but, upon seeing something bizarre, is seized with fright.

One of the old men noticed the state of panic I was in. Tapping one finger against his spectacles, he said, "You are looking at our torn clothing. Enough that creatures like ourselves still have skin on our flesh." The rest of the old men and old women heard and nodded their heads in agreement. As they did so their skin quivered. I took hold of myself, walked backwards, and left.

I left in despair and, empty-handed, with no clothing, with nothing at all, returned to my daughter. I found her standing in a corner of the court-yard pressed against the wall next to the purification board on which the dead are washed. Her hair was loose and wrapped about her. How great is Thy goodness, O God, in putting wisdom into the heart of such a little girl to enable her to wrap herself in her hair after her dress has burned off, for as long as she had not been given a garment it was good that she covered herself with her hair. But how great was the sadness that enveloped me at that moment, the outset of this holy festival whose joy has no parallel all the year. But now there was no joy and no sign of joy, only pain and anguish.

The stone steps sounded beneath feet clad in felt slippers and long stockings, as Jews bearing prayer shawls and ritual gowns streamed to the House of Prayer. With my body I covered my little girl, trembling from the cold, and I stroked her hair. Again I looked in the storeroom where the torn pages from sacred books were kept, the room where in my youth I would find, among the fragments, wondrous and amazing things. I remember one of the sayings, it went approximately like this: "At times she takes the form of an old woman and at times the form of a little girl. And when she takes the form of a little girl, don't imagine that your soul is as pure as a little girl; this is but an indication that she passionately yearns to recapture the purity of her infancy when she was free of sin. The fool substitutes the *form* for the *need*; the wise man substitutes *will* for *need*."

A tall man with a red beard came along, picking from his teeth the last remnants of the final meal, pushing his wide belly out to make room for himself. He stood about like a man who knew that God would not run away and there was no need to hurry. He regarded us for a moment, ran his eyes over us, then said something with a double meaning.

My anger flowed into my hand, and I caught him by the beard and began yanking at his hair. Utterly astonished, he did not move. He had good cause to be astonished too: a small fellow like me lifting my hand against a brawny fellow like him. Even I was astonished: had he laid hold of me, he would not have let me go whole.

Another tall, husky fellow came along, one who boasted of being my dearest friend. I looked up at him, hoping that he would come between us. He took his spectacles, wiped them, and placed them on his nose. The whites of his eyes turned green and his spectacles shone like moist scales. He stood looking at us as though we were characters in an amusing play.

I raised my voice and shouted, "A fire has sprung up and has burned my daughter's dress, and here she stands shivering from the cold!" He nodded his head in my direction and once more wiped his spectacles. Again they shone like moist scales and flashed like green scum on water. Once more I shouted, "It's not enough that no one gives her any clothing, but they must abuse us, too!" The fellow nodded his head and repeated my words as though pleased by them. As he spoke he turned his eyes away from me so that they might not see me, and that he might imagine he had made up the story on his own. I was no longer angry with my enemy, being so gripped with fury at this man: though he had prided himself on being my friend, he was repeating all that had befallen me as though it were a tale of his own invention.

My daughter began crying. "Let's run away from here."

"What are you saying?" I answered. "Don't you see that night has fallen and that we have entered the holy day? And if we were to flee, where would we flee and where could we hide?"

Where could we hide? Our home lay in ruins and the enemies covered all the roads. And if by some miracle we escaped, could we depend upon miracles? And here were the two Houses of Study and the Great Synagogue in which I studied Torah° and in which I prayed and here was the corner where they had hidden away sacred books worn with age. As a little boy I rummaged about here frequently, finding all sorts of things. I do not know why, on this particular day, we found nothing, but I remember that I once found something important about *need* and *form* and *will.* Were it not for the urgency of the day I would explain this matter to you thoroughly, and you would see that it is by no means allegorical but a simple and straightforward affair.

I glanced at my little girl who stood trembling from the cold, for she had been stripped of her clothing, she didn't even have a shirt, the night was chill and the song of winter birds resounded from the mountains. I glanced at my daughter, the darling of my heart, like a father who glances at his little daughter, and a loving smile formed on my lips. This was a very timely smile, for it rid her of her fear completely. I stood then with my daughter in the open courtyard of the Great Synagogue and the two

Torah: the written law that comprises all the teachings of Judaism

Houses of Study which all my life stirred themselves and came to me in my dreams and now stood before me, fully real. The gates of the Houses of Prayer were open, and from all three issued the voices of the readers of prayer. In which direction should we look and whither should we bend our ears?

He who gives eyes to see with and ears to hear with directed my eyes and ears to the old House of Study. The House of Study was full of Jews, the doors of the Ark were open and the Ark was full of old Torah scrolls, and among them gleamed a new scroll clothed in a red mantle with silver points. This was the scroll that I had written in memory of the souls of days that had departed. A silver plate was hung over the scroll, with letters engraved upon it, shining letters. And even though I stood far off I saw what they were. A thick rope was stretched in front of the scroll that it might not slip and fall.

My soul fainted within me, and I stood and prayed as those wrapped in prayer shawls and ritual gowns. And even my little girl, who had dozed off, repeated in her sleep each and every prayer in sweet melodies no ear has ever heard.

I do not enlarge. I do not exaggerate.

Translated from the Hebrew
by David S. Segal

EMILE HABIBI

At age nineteen, the fiction writer, playwright, journalist, and political activist Emile Habibi (1921–) joined the Palestine Communist Party. He was chosen to be the editor-in-chief of the party's biweekly newspaper. In 1948, he became a founding member of the Israeli Communist Party. Three times he was elected to represent the party in the Israeli parliament, serving a total of nineteen years. Although he had started to write fiction in the 1950s, it was not until 1968 that he published a short story volume entitled Six Stories for the Six Day War. *Six years later, he published* The Secret Life of Saeed, the Ill-Fated Pessoptomist. *This tragicomic novel tells the story of Palestinians living under Israeli rule from the perspective of a luckless "fool." It has been translated into several languages and was staged in both Arabic and Hebrew in Israel. In 1983, he published a play,* Luka, the Son of Luka.

"The Gipsy" gives a poignant look into the life of a grocer who is reluctant to part with his dreams, despite their impossibility. The story is filled with nostalgia but also with the sense that writing is critical to the preservation of a cultural legacy.

The Gipsy (a song in three movements)

1. The Bride's Tears

"Father, how do you weep?"

"From my pen-nib, daughter. The tips of my pens are my tearducts."

"But what you write lightens our cares."

"That's how tears are. The disasters we make lightest of are the ones which afflict other people. And when we weep with them it's first of all to relieve our own sorrows and only then to console them."

"Are all tears like that?"

"All except the bride's tears when she looks back. They burn like bleach, searing her mother's heart, paining her bridegroom, angering his mother and making the girls in the neighborhood curl their lips in surprise and distaste."

"What sort of tears are you shedding now?"

"Tears like the bride's."

2. Zennouba

If he had been the only one to see her on that bright April morning, he would have hugged this new vision to himself in the belief that it was one more of his daydreams. In recent months his daydreams had encroached so much on the events of his everyday life that they had become inextricably part of it.

How cruelly old age was mocking him! She had held her wrinkled hand, leaving his black hair untouched, but only to plague him with childish fancies. He was reminded of the old man who, panting from exhaustion, had reached his hundredth birthday. Old age could find no scope for her jokes except his gaping mouth, so she planted new milk teeth in it.

He remembered how, when the first fuzz appeared on his cheeks, he used to come back from school to his house in this alley, his head full of the conquests of Alexander of Macedon. As he walked along Wadi Street° he would be building an empire even greater than Alexander's, or crossing the Straits of Gibraltar at the head of the Arab fleets to win back Spain.° One day, passing the grocer's, he was conquering the whole of Europe with Napoleon Bonaparte, and as it later turned out he really was leaping and jumping as he attacked the enemy. The news spread through the alley that the boy was "abnormal." When it came to his middle-aged

---

Wadi Street: a street in Haifa, Israel

to win back Spain: the hope to return to Spain, from which Jews and Muslims were ousted

father's ears his older brother tied him to a doorpost and his father went for him with his belt, beating him into a "normal" boy again.

From then on he had no more fantasies. His youth passed in a dream-like flash, fathering boys and girls with their own fantasies, but he dared not think about the past lest he brand as naive a childhood in which his spirit had been ready to capture the wind.

Here he was now, on the verge of sixty, watching the never-ending stream of life's travelers in the old Wadi Street, with the barber, the baker, the fishmonger, the grocer, the wild herbs seller and the dairy-woman from Tira. Nothing new had appeared on this scene except the plastic goods seller and the policeman. Again daydreams assailed him, even more vigorously than in his boyhood. Now he was thoroughly con-fused and he kept them jealously to himself, even though he no longer had an older brother to tie him to the doorpost and his father's bones had long since turned to dust. He too had become a father.

If the truth be told, there was a great difference between yesterday's dreams and the dreams of today, even though he liked to make believe that life surrounded itself with the same aura of dreams whether it was coming or going. His boyhood dreams seized life as a rebellious young giant seizes a mountain, lifting it up and swaggering along with it in front of his astonished bride and the rest of mankind. The dreams of old age were a groan stifled under a towering mountain of "if onlys" which had wrung his heart. Each fantasy began with an "if only" like a rock rolling down from the summit and tearing away all the fences he had set up round his monotonous existence. "If I'd done something different some-thing else would have happened. Why didn't I take that course, then?"

He had long been convinced of the futility of that maxim expressing the essence of resignation: nothing can ever be better than what has been. But he now realized that this conviction held true not only for the future but also for the past. What had been could have been better than it was. How many nights had he spent as a boy punching his pillows with his fists for hours, out of anger that he had not dared to counter his oppo-nent's attack blow for blow that day. These "if onlys" went back a long way in his life, if the truth be told.

But he was not the only one to see her on the bright April morning. She descended on the Wadi from the gate to the steep street as dew falls on the branches of an old fig tree — Zennouba the beautiful gipsy, the same as she had been thirty years before, quite unchanged, with her lean body and her bright embroidered dress. In her hand she held the small tambourine with the big brass jingles just like the big brass earrings she wore. Her smile was playful, her eyes were green with naturally dark lashes in her brown face, and she had a well-turned figure. Hey, Zen-nouba! We agreed to call you by this name thirty years ago when you walked proudly through our streets, sometimes alone (and how fine those times were!) and sometimes with your father (*was* he your father, Zennouba?), his monkey and his amazing bear. Zennouba! It may not have been your name (have you got a name, Zennouba?) but we settled on it and it suited you and us. This name was so woven into our childhood games and jokes that it became a part of them, to be mentioned in the same breath with things like the school wall which served as our fort when we fought other children, or the master we caught kissing the headmistress (neither of them reappeared the following term) or the window at which the neighbor's daughter, the pretty Greek girl, would sit with a needle in one hand and thread in the other. But she only wove dreams of love with her eyes. He used to walk by under her window at least seven times a day, craning his neck so as to see her eyes. Would she bestow a glance on him? Just one, my God! What had happened to this window now? He sighed as he walked past it. The neighbor was gone and so was her daughter. And what surprised him was that when he passed the window now he no longer needed to look up to see it as he had in his childhood. No, he now had to look down. What had come over it? Had it subsided till it was at shoulder-level, or had the road risen in the course of time, years accumulating on it until it had almost reached the height of the window? God bless the memories of childhood, Zennouba! God bless those days when he wore baggy trousers, patched and patched till they outdid Abu Qasim's shoes° before his mother declared that he had grown out of them. In our minds everything gets bigger or smaller except ourselves. We stay as we were, Zennouba!

She descended on the Wadi from the gate to the steep street, Zennouba, the beautiful gipsy, the same as she had been thirty years before, quite unchanged. She left behind her along the whole length of Wadi Street the turmoil that a passing whirlwind leaves when it catches up and sweeps along all the goods on display in the potters' bazaar.

Old Hind, the seller of wild herbs, was the first to see her. She called out to her: "Zennouba!" The beautiful gipsy turned to look at her with laughing eyes. The much-loved name went from mouth to mouth, repeated by all the elderly people in the Wadi like an echo reverberating in a cavern deep in the bowels of a mountain. They gathered round her in a circle, the barber, the baker, the fishmonger, the grocer, Hind the wild herbs seller, the dairywoman from Tira, the retired teacher who made a living from the fish he caught in the Tell es-Samak and the man on the verge of sixty who sat watching the never-ending stream of life's travelers. Even the Wadi's doctor, its one remaining treasure, saw her, called out to her and joined the circle round her. The plastic goods seller, the policemen and the neighborhood children stood gazing in astonishment, unable to grasp what was happening at all.

Abu Qasim's shoes: patched shoes, used proverbially

Old Hind, the seller of wild herbs, started.

"I'm Hind, Zennouba, Hind with the brown skin who used to work in the bakery. I used to gather round me more young men than you did with your tambourine. What mother didn't ask herself then, Zennouba, what the hidden reason was for her son's eagerness to carry her loaves to the oven to be baked. I was the reason, Zennouba. But now my herbs only pick up a few unpierced piastres.° They've even blocked up the holes in the piastres against us, Zennouba! Play your tambourine and dance, Zennouba, and maybe the children will gather round and we'll both make some money."

"When the dough in your houses rises and Abu Jamila dances again in your squares, I'll play my tambourine, Hind, I'll dance, my orphan girl."

The old people of the Wadi gathered round her chuckled. The plastic goods seller understood nothing of what was going on round him, and neither did the policemen. But the children came closer, playfully fingering her embroidered dress. And the man on the verge of sixty laughed till the tears came into his eyes.

"Abu Jamila!"
"Abu Jamila, among this beauty I've let my life go by."
"Abu Jamila, all I have is love, I've a right to this love!"
"Abu Jamila!"
"Abu Jamila, I can bear it no longer, my death is close by."
"Abu Jamila!"

Then it was the turn of the bald fishmonger, who always maintained that youth is to be measured not by the luxuriance of one's head of hair but by the solid implantation of one's moustache, and who altered the price of his fish not according to its quality or freshness but according to the attractiveness of the customer. He called out:

"I'm the boy Curly, Zennouba, all the girls' sweetheart. I used to steal the biggest orange from my father's shop for you in exchange for a kiss from you in the blind alley leading off the Wadi and a thrashing from my father in his shop doorway. Where's the bear, Najla's friend, Zennouba?"

"When you've all grown wiser than the bear, you Curly who got thrashed so often in your father's shop doorway and in the alley leading off the Wadi, and when you've learnt to love Samiya too, then the bear will come back and play in your squares."

The old people of the Wadi gathered round her chuckled. The plastic goods seller was annoyed that everyone was neglecting his wares. And the policemen debated whether they should ask her to produce her license. The children talked with bated breath about the bear and how

piastres: old coins that had a hole in the middle

scared they were of him. And the man on the verge of sixty laughed till the tears came into his eyes.

Najla, Samiya and Najla's friend the bear.

Najla . . . was the daughter of the hotel-proprietor and used to a life of luxury. The servant used to bring her to school and collect her when it was over. In the classroom she had a special chair different from all our chairs. She was lazy at her lessons, but her golden hair and her father's prestige ensured her the highest marks.

Samiya . . . was a thin, wall-eyed girl, the daughter of Hafiza the school cleaner. The efforts she made to learn her lessons were a permanent source of amusement to us.

When we played hide-and-seek the boys never hid anywhere except where Najla was. Samiya was always alone in her hiding-place. One day we went on playing hide-and-seek till after sunset, pushing and shoving each other to share the hiding-place of the "pet," Najla. Samiya called out in tears: "Why doesn't anyone hide with me, I'm frightened."

Did Samiya find someone later on to hide with her, comfort her and allay her fears, someone to comfort her sense of exile in the land of her exile?

Najla's friend the bear . . . One day we left the classroom to watch the gipsy with her bear — it was before the great earthquake, if I remember rightly, and certainly before the Graf Zeppelin.° Her father was making the bear dance and walk on his hindlegs, and the bear was carrying a staff to lean on. We were laughing and pushing forward, daring each other to get closer to the bear. Najla was the boldest of us, because her golden hair and her father's influence shielded her from any harm. Suddenly the bear dropped his staff, got down on all fours and wrapped his paw round the leg of Najla, the girl we used to hide with in hide-and-seek. For the first time we saw Najla cry, and we let out a shout as we stood round her. The gipsy's father spent more than an hour trying to get the bear to loosen his grip, while the bear clung to his prize, but at last he got him to release her. In those days an hour passed much more quickly than now. From then on we called the gipsy's bear "Najla's bear." And Najla's standing in our eyes was enhanced; after her special hair, her special father and her special chair she now had a special bear.

Did Najla later find her human bear to warm her leg and comfort her, to comfort her sense of exile in the land of her exile?

Ali the grocer shuddered, regaining his youth in an elemental moment of fate:

"Dance for your friends, just once, Zennouba, once more! Dance for

---

Graf Zeppelin: the first rigid airship, built in 1906

your father, for the bear, the monkey, the autumn dew, the ice-cream seller, the children's noise, for us, Zennouba."

"I've only ever danced for those who look to the future and for the children who just have what lies before them. I shall dance for the children again, for your children, Ali, Curly and Hind, and for yours, you who are on the verge of sixty, when you tell them about me and I'm no longer a stranger to them. Then I shall dance, and hand in hand we'll dance out of the Wadi into the open country."

The old people of the Wadi gathered round her chuckled. The plastic goods seller turned to the policemen: "When are you going to perform your duty?" The policemen asked each other: "How can we?" The children looked questioningly into their parents' faces. And the man on the verge of sixty laughed till the tears came into his eyes.

"Rain, sky, rain!"

"Rain, sky, rain! Our house is built of stone. Uncle Abdallah broke a jug. His master beat him with a club. He had to sleep out in the mud! Ho!"

"Mummy, mummy! Muummy!"

"Real ice cream! Today it costs money, tomorrow it's free!"

"This is the way we knead the dough, like our granny does. This is the way we swagger in school, like the teacher does."

"My son! A bomb's gone off at the end of the street!"

"Your son's all right. It's Masoud's boy who's been killed."

"Granny's legs are bandy, she can't run. Her legs are just as crooked as the trigger of a gun."

"Take care not to be out after sunset, otherwise you may get blown up!"

"I hid it in the casket. My uncle came and took it. He took it, he stole it, and to stop my tears, he gave me earrings to wear in my ears."

"There's a strike!"

"The earrings are silly, they dangle willy-nilly. Princess of this land, they're asking for your hand. At the city gate, they've brought you cake. Damascus cakes are dear. God keep my uncle in his care. My uncle's in the country, eating dates with honey. I asked him for a few. He took a knife to run me through."

"Police!"

The Wadi's doctor, our one remaining treasure, wanted nothing so much as to feel her pulse. In reality he was testing his heart to see if it still throbbed.

"I wasn't a boy then, Zennouba, I used to come back from Damascus University, and you would come to my room to tell my fortune. The copper basin is ready and the room is just as it was. I can fill it with my own hands. Come on, tell me what the future holds."

"Even a blind man can tell what the future still holds for you, treasure. Turn the basin upside down and tap out a rhythm on it!"

The old people of the Wadi gathered round her chuckled, and so did the one remaining treasure. Even the plastic goods seller and the policemen laughed. The children copied the doctor's laugh because they loved him just as he loved them. And the man on the verge of sixty laughed till the tears came into his eyes.

Ever since his student days he had been keen on cleanliness and preserving appearances. When the gipsy came to his room he used to call the landlady and she would bring him a basin full of water. Then he would begin by washing the gipsy. "What do you want the water for, neighbor?" "So she can tell my fortune, neighbor." "With *water*?" "Gipsies have all kinds of ways of telling fortunes."

The fact was that no-one loved the gipsy as our friend did, and he knew her through and through. And she loved him, too.

The man on the verge of sixty did not want to rake up the past. He knew her too and he loved her. But he had begun to know himself.

But she, the gipsy, didn't leave him alone. Pointing at him she burst out laughing. Then she turned to the lemonade and fizzy drinks kiosk in front of him and broke into laughter again.

"What's happened to the trio of geniuses and the room where you were born, which was to be turned into a museum?"

The old people of Wadi street gathered round her chuckled. The owner of the fizzy drinks kiosk rushed over to the plastic goods seller and conferred with him in a whisper. They both went over to the policemen and murmured something to them. The children's mouths watered at the mention of lemonade. And the man on the verge of sixty laughed so hard that he had to wipe the tears from his eyes.

They were three clever boys at school. Their teacher nicknamed them the trio of geniuses and put the idea into their heads that they had a great future. He had heard that one had become a professor of Arabic in a university in Khartoum, and people said the second was being treated in a sanatorium in Lebanon. And he was here, on the verge of sixty, watching the never-ending stream of life's travelers.

He used to confide all his dreams to Zennouba. He dreamed that he would become a great man, and then the nation would turn the room in this alley in which he had been born into a museum where mementos and literary remains of his would be collected. But his nation was busy looking for its own remains, and one wall of the room in which he had been born had been knocked down to make way for a lemonade and fizzy drinks kiosk.

What had happened to the garrulous barber to keep him from joining in the conversation till now? Leaving his shop he had been one of the first to go over to her, with his scissors in one hand and his comb in the other. He had brought out the client who was in his shop too. It might have been supposed that he was laughing with the others at the beautiful memories Zennouba evoked with her sudden return. But that might well have been a mistake. He was known to have besmirched himself with politics in his bygone youth. And for that reason he took a serious view of things. Since the beginning of the situation we are now in he had not opened his mouth to discuss politics, devoting all his attention to plumbing the depths of his customers' and friends' personal secrets. He only laughed and joked in earnest.

But in the whirlwind unleashed by the gipsy he couldn't keep silent. He wanted to say something and join in making the others laugh, while making clear, especially in the presence of the police, that he had abandoned politics fifteen years earlier. Yet the poor man only succeeded in giving himself a bloody nose.

"You're a gipsy and this isn't your country. Why have you come back instead of all those who are absent?"

"And have you still got a country, you barber of brains? What do you cut off in this country of yours, people's hair or their roots? Falafel° have got deeper roots than you. They've outlived Turkish rule and British rule and they're still going strong."

The man on the verge of sixty didn't know whether the old people of Wadi Street chuckled at the barber or not, because he had to get up from his seat and merge into the never-ending stream of life's travelers after the police had begun to break up the crowd.

The children separated, going to buy falafel from a stall at the end of Wadi street. The falafel there were made in the modern way, but they were still falafel, the falafel of old.

"Falafel hom!"°
   "Oriental falafel!"
   "Falafel with half a loaf!"
   "Falafel and a whole loaf!"
   "The king of falafel!"

"Where are you off to, Zennouba?"
   "I'm going back where I came from."
   "Just a moment, Zennouba."
   "What about the police?"
   "Don't leave us, Zennouba!"

falafel: deep-fried vegetable patties
falafel hom: Hebrew for "hot falafel"

"I've never left you. Tell your children about me, so that when I come back it won't just be Hind who remembers me, and Curly and Ali the grocer, and the one remaining treasure, and the man on the verge of sixty — where's he gone? — and the barber of politics. Then your children will remember me too. And I shall come back and dance, dance with you hand in hand out of the Wadi and into the open country, with the children of the plastic goods seller and the policemen too."

She left the Wadi as she had descended on it, from the gate to the steep street — Zennouba the beautiful gipsy, the same as she had been thirty years before, quite unchanged. She left behind her the whole length of Wadi Street the turmoil a passing whirlwind leaves when it catches up and sweeps along all the goods on display in the potters' bazaar.

If he had been the only one to see her he would have hugged the vision to himself and kept it for his very own. But he was not the only one to see her. And if the truth be told, he isn't alone.

3. Milk Teeth

"Why are you weeping now, father? Are those tears like the bride's?"

"I saw your little sister out on the balcony as the sun came up, throwing the sun her milk teeth and calling out: 'Little sun, little sun, take my donkey's teeth and give me gazelle's teeth.' We did the same at her age. We may have been sorry to say goodbye to our milk teeth but we looked forward to gazelle's teeth."

"And now what?"

"There's no stranger theory than the one propounded by a gloomy friend of mine. He says that if a human being were to come from another planet to our earth he would think it was a world of the dead and the orphans, with the number of the living a mere drop in the ocean of the dead. Tread lightly on their bones! There's no child born who doesn't lose its parents."

"What then?"

"That's one way of looking at our world, with your eyes fixed on the past. But there's another way of looking, with your eyes turned to the future. Every death is followed by life, children become parents and the stream of life's travelers never ends."

"And then?"

"The wise man uses both his eyes to look at life."

"And then?"

"One step follows another. This is the road trodden by the never-ending stream of life's travelers. Throw your milk teeth to the sun."

Translated from the Arabic
by Hilary Kilpatrick

DAHLIA RABIKOVICH

Considered Israel's leading woman poet, Dahlia Rabikovich (1936–) was raised on a collective farm, went to school in Haifa, served in the Israeli army, and studied English literature at the Hebrew University in Jerusalem. She was deeply affected by the loss of her father, who was killed by a drunk driver. This loss, suffered when she was a child of six, pervades her poetry. She published her first anthology of poetry, The Love of an Orange, *when she was twenty-three. In 1972, she brought out* All Thy Breakers and Waves; *her fifth and most recent collection is* Real Love *(1986).*

"The Dress" is the title poem of a collection that was published in English in 1976 (the book's full title is A Dress of Fire*). These poems reflect her rejection of authority regardless of the cost.*

The Dress

(For Yitzhak Livini)

You know, she said,
they've sewn you a dress
of fire.

Remember how Jason's wife
burned in her dress?   5
It's Medea, she said. Medea did her in.
You have to watch out, she said,
they've sewn you a dress that glows like an ember
and burns like coals.

Will you wear it? she said, don't wear it.   10
It's not the wind whistling,
it's the poison seeping in
You're not even a princess,
what will you do to Medea?
You must learn to know voices, she said,   15
it's not the wind whistling.

Do you remember, I said to her, when I was six?
They shampooed my hair and I went out into the street.
The smell of the shampoo followed me like a cloud.
Afterwards I was sick from the wind and the rain.   20
I didn't yet understand Greek tragedies,
but the smell of the perfume wafted
and I was very sick.
Today I understand that it's an unnatural perfume.

What will become of you, she said,   25
they've sewn you a burning dress.
They've sewn me a burning dress, I said, I know.
So why are you standing there, she said.
You should be careful.
Don't you know what a burning dress is?   30

I know, I said, but not how to be careful.
The smell of that perfume confuses me.
I said to her: No one has to agree with me.
I put no faith in Greek tragedies.

But the dress, she said, the dress burns with fire.   35
What are you saying, I screamed,
what are you saying?
I'm not wearing a dress at all.
It's me who's burning.

Translated from the Hebrew by Marcia Falk

The Sound of Birds at Noon

This chirping
is certainly not malicious.
They sing without giving us a thought
and they are many
as the seed of Abraham.   5
They have their own life,
flight is a thing they take for granted.
Some of them are precious,
some are common,
but the wing is all grace.   10
Their heart is never heavy
even when they're pecking at worms.
Perhaps they're just lightheaded.
They were given the sky to rule
over day and night   15
and when they touch a branch
the branch too is theirs.
This chirping is completely free of malice.
Over the years, it even seems
to bear a note of compassion.   20

Translated from the Hebrew by Marcia Falk

Pride

Even rocks break, I tell you,
and not from old age.
For years they lie on their backs
in the heat and the cold,
so many years   5
it almost seems peaceful.
They don't move from their place
and so the cracks are hidden.
A kind of pride.
Year after year passes over them   10
expectant, waiting.
The one who will shatter them later
has not yet come.
And so the moss grows,
the seaweeds are tossed about,   15
the sea pounces in, and returns.
And they, it seems, do not move.
Until a little seal comes
to rub against the rocks,
comes and goes away.   20
And suddenly the stone is wounded.
I told you, when rocks break
it comes as a surprise.
And all the more with people.

Translated from the Hebrew by Marcia Falk

From Day to Night

Every day I get up again from sleep
as if it were my last awakening.
I don't know what awaits me —
from this one might say, perhaps,
that nothing awaits me.   5
This year's spring is like the one before.
The month of Iyar — I know what it is
but it doesn't matter to me.
I don't notice when day
passes into night —   10
just that the night is colder

and silence equal to them both.
In the morning, I hear the sound of birds.
Affection for them
eases me to sleep. 15
The one who is dear to me isn't here
and perhaps he isn't anywhere.
I go from day to day,
from day to night,
like a feather 20
that the bird doesn't feel
as it falls.

Translated from the Hebrew by Marcia Falk

Distant Land

Tonight, in a sailing boat, I came back
From the isles of the sun, and their coral clusters.
There were girls with combs of gold
Left on the shore in the isles of the sun.

For four years of milk and honey 5
I roamed the shores on the isles of the sun.
The fruit stalls were heavily laden
And cherries glistened in the sun.

Oarsmen and boatmen from seventy lands
Sailed towards the isles of the sun. 10
Through four years by shining light
I kept counting ships of gold.

For four years, rounded like apples,
I kept stringing coral beads.
In the isles of the sun merchants and pedlars 15
Spread out sheets of crimson silk.

And the sea was unfathomable, deeper than any depth,
As I returned from the isles of the sun.
Heavy sundrops, with the weight of honey,
Dripped on the island before sunset. 20

Translated from the Hebrew by A. C. Jacobs

KUWAIT

SUAD AL-MUBARAK AL-SABAH

Suad al-Mubarak al-Sabah (1942–), a member of the ruling family in Kuwait, is a poet and a human rights activist. She studied in Cairo and then in England, earning her Ph.D. in planning and development from the University of Surrey in 1982. She has authored several economic studies, including Kuwait, Anatomy of a Crisis Economy *(1983). Her poetry is filled with* joie de vivre *as well as anger and frustration with the state of the Arab world today. She is a patron of literary activity and has sponsored the republication of the forty volumes of* Al-Risala, *an important journal that published the works of leading Arab intellectuals in the 1930s and 1940s.*

A New Definition of the Third World

Because love with us
Is a third-rate emotion
And because women are third-class citizens
And volumes of poetry are literature of the third rank
They call us the peoples of the Third World.   5

Translated from the Arabic by
Salwa Jabsheh and John Heath-Stubbs

A Thousand Times More Beautiful

Because in long black hair you take delight
They let it down like curtains of the night
Those Eastern girls, to greet you, prince, they say
We would not have those tresses shorn away.

Because you love a countenance sun-burnt   5
To bathe in the sun's rays those girls have learnt
To bid you welcome these things they have done
You who on love's steed come riding on.

Because you love my face simple and plain
They bathe in rose water and tropic rain,   10
Because you love my beauty's simple dower
Simple as is the morning lily flower
God, to honor you, has given his grace
To Singapore, perfecting its bright face.

The world is larger for your loving me   15
The sky's more wide, a deeper blue the sea
The birds are freer flying in that sky
A thousand times more beautiful am I.

Translated from the Arabic by
Salwa Jabsheh and John Heath-Stubbs

A Covenant

1

Come, let us sign together
A covenant of peace
Whereby I reclaim my days under your sway
And my lips besieged by yours
Whereby you reclaim your fragrance   5
That courses beneath my skin.

2

Write down whatever form of words you choose
Whatever terms you deem right
And I will unconditionally sign
Draw up what covenant suits you best   10
So I be eliminated from the numbers
In your notebooks
From the furniture in your office
And you depart from the glass in my mirror.

3

Come, let us try to play this impossible game   15
If only for a day

So I will go to my hairdresser to kill time
And you to your smoking room to play cards.

Translated from The Arabic by
Salwa Jabsheh and John Heath-Stubbs

Sojourn Forever

I deliver to you all the keys of my city
And appoint you its governor
Expel all its counselors and take the chains
Of fear from off my wrists.

I have worn my robe woven with threads of care   5
And have made from the light of your eyes my eye shadow
And in my hair I placed a sprig of orange blossom
You once gave me
And I sat waiting on my throne
And asked to sojourn forever in the gardens of your breast.   10

Your fragrance drifts in my fancy
Like a sword of steel
It pierces the walls and the curtains
And it pierces me
Annihilating the fragments of time   15
And annihilating me
        Then you leave me to walk barefoot
On the broken glass of mirrors and depart.

Translated from the Arabic by
Salwa Jabsheh and John Heath-Stubbs

Free Harbor

Many ships have asked for sanctuary
In the harbor of my eyes
I refused asylum to all of them
Your ships alone
Have the right to take refuge   5
In my territorial waters
Your ships alone

Have the right to sail in my blood
Without prior permission.

Translated from the Arabic by
Salwa Jabsheh and John Heath-Stubbs

You Alone

You alone . . . control my history
And write your name on the first page
And on the third, and the tenth,
And on the last.
You alone are allowed to sport with my days   5
From the first century of my birth
To the twenty-first century after love.
You alone can add to my days what you wish
And delete what you wish
My whole history flows from the palms of your hands   10
And pours into your palms.

Translated from the Arabic by
Salwa Jabsheh and John Heath-Stubbs

LEBANON

LAYLA BAALBAKI

*Layla Baalbaki (1936–) was one of the first Arab women to write
without reserve about the situation of women in the Arab world. In
1958, she published her well-known novel,* I Live, *which tells the story
of a middle-class young woman who is rebelling against her family
and societal norms. Baalbaki wrote some short stories in the 1960s and
her second novel,* Distorted Gods *(1965), which expresses her frustration with traditional expectations of women's behavior, especially the
exaggerated focus on virginity at marriage. With the outbreak of the
civil war in her native country in 1975, she ceased to publish.*

*"A Space Ship of Tenderness to the Moon" was published in a col-
lection by that name in 1964. Baalbaki presents succinctly a complex
relationship between two people trying to hold on to love and independence within the traditional expectations of their society. It also tells a
mildly erotic story of a wife's appreciation of her husband's body. Nine
months after its publication, the government declared the work to be
pornographic. A trial was held to judge whether the story "had harmed
public morality." After an initial deferred sentence of prison for one to
six months, Baalbaki was acquitted.*

A Space Ship of Tenderness to the Moon

When I closed my eyes I was able to see everything around me, the long
settee which fills one vast wall in the room from corner to corner; the
shelves on the remaining walls; the small table; the colored cushions on
the carpet; the white lamp, in the shape of a large kerosene one, that
hung from a hole in the wall and rested on the tiled floor. Even the windows we had left curtainless. In the second room was a wide sofa; a table
supporting a mirror; a wall-cupboard and two chairs upholstered in velvet. Since our marriage we hadn't changed a thing in the little house, and
I refused to remove anything from it.

I opened my eyelids a little as I heard my husband mumble, "It's light
and we alone are awake in the city." I saw him rising up in front of the
window as the silver light of dawn spread over his face and naked body. I
love his naked body.

Once again I closed my eyes; I was able to see every little bit of him, every minute hidden detail: his soft hair, his forehead, nose, chin, the veins of his neck, the hair on his chest, his stomach, his feet, his nails. I called to him to come back and stretch out beside me, that I wanted to kiss him. He didn't move and I knew, from the way he had withdrawn from me and stood far off, that he was preparing himself to say something important. In this way he becomes cruel and stubborn, capable of taking and carrying through decisions. I am the exact opposite: in order to talk things over with him I must take hold of his hand or touch his clothes. I therefore opened my eyes, threw aside the cushion I was hugging and seized hold of his shirt, spreading it across my chest. Fixing my gaze on the ceiling I asked him if he saw the sea.

"I see the sea," he answered.

I asked him what color it was.

"Dark blue on one side," he said, "and on the other a grayish white."

I asked him if the cypress trees were still there.

"They are still there among the houses that cling close together," he answered, "and there's water lying on the roofs of the buildings."

I said I loved the solitary date-palm which looked, from where we were, as though it had been planted in the sea and that the cypress trees put me in mind of white cemeteries.

For a long while he was silent and I remained staring up at the ceiling. Then he said, "The cocks are calling," and I quickly told him I didn't like chickens because they couldn't fly and that when I was a child I used to carry them up to the roof of our home and throw them out into space in an attempt to teach them to fly, and both cocks and hens would always land in a motionless heap on the ground.

Again he was silent for a while, after which he said that he saw a light come on at the window of a building opposite. I said that even so we were still the only two people awake in the city, the only two who had spent the night entwined in each other's arms. He said that he had drunk too much last night. I quickly interrupted him by saying I hated that phrase — I drank too much — as though he regretted the yearning frenzy with which he had made love to me. Sensing that I was beginning to get annoyed he changed the subject, saying: "The city looks like a mound of sparkling precious stones of all colors and sizes."

I answered that I now imagined the city as colored cardboard boxes which would fall down if you blew on them; our house alone, with its two rooms, was suspended from a cloud and rode in space. He said that his mouth was dry and he wanted an orange. I concluded what I had been saying by stating that though I had never lived in any other city, I hated this one and that had I not dreamt that I would one day meet a man who would take me far, far away from it I would have died of dejection long, long ago. Pretending that he had not heard my last remark he repeated: "I want an orange, my throat's dry." I disregarded his request and went on to say that with him I paid no heed to where I was: the earth with its trees, its mountains, rivers, animals and human beings just vanished. Unable to wait further, he burst out at me, "Why do you refuse to have children?"

I was sad, my heart was wrung, the tears welled up into my eyes, but I didn't open my mouth.

"How long is it since we married?" he asked. I uttered not a word as I followed him round with my eyes. He stiffened and continued, "It's a year and several months since we married and you've been refusing and refusing, though you were crazy about children before we married; you were dying for them."

He swerved and struck the settee with his hands as he burst out, "Hey chair, don't you remember her entreaties? And you lamp, didn't you hear the sound of her wailing? And you cushions, did she not make of you tiny bodies that she hugged to herself and snuggled up to as she slept? Speak, O things inanimate. Speak. Give back to her her voice which is sunk into you."

Quietly I said that inanimate things don't feel, don't talk, don't move. Angrily he enquired: "How do you know they're dead?" I replied that things weren't dead, but that they drew their pulse beats from people. He interrupted me by saying that he wouldn't argue about things now and wouldn't allow me to escape solving the problem as I always did. Absent-mindedly I explained to him that the things around me, these very things — this settee, this carpet, this wall, this lamp, this vase, the shelves and the ceiling — are all a vast mirror that reflects for me the outside world: the houses, the sea, the trees, the sky, the sun, the stars and the clouds. In them I see my past with him, the hours of misery and dejection, the moments of meeting and of tenderness, of bliss and of happiness, and from them I now deduce the shapes of the days to come. I would not give them up.

He became angry and shouted, "We're back again with things. I want to understand here and now why you refuse to have children." No longer able to bear it, I shouted that he too at one time refused to have them. He was silent for a while, then he said, "I refused before we were married, when it would have been foolish to have had one." Sarcastically I told him that he was afraid of them, those others, those buffoons in the city. He used to beg for their assent, their blessing, their agreement, so that he might see me and I him, so that he might embrace me and I him, so that we might each drown the other in our love. They used to determine for us our places of meeting, the number of steps to be taken to get there, the time, the degree to which our voices could be raised, the number of breaths we took. And I would watch them as they secretly scoffed at us, shamelessly slept with the bodies they loved, ate three meals a day, smoked cigarettes with the cups of coffee and carafes of arak,° and guf-

arak: anise-flavored alcohol popular in the Eastern Mediterranean

fawed as they vulgarly chewed over stories about us and thought up patterns of behavior for us to put into effect the following day. His voice was choked as he mumbled: "I don't pay attention to others. I was tied to another woman."

Ah, how can I bear all this torture, all this passionate love for him? He used to be incapable of confessing the bitter truth to her, that he didn't love her, wouldn't love her. Choking, he said that it wasn't easy, he wasn't callous enough to be able to stare into another human being's face and say to her, after nine years of getting up each and every day and finding her there, "Now the show's over," and turn his back and walk off. I told him to look at my right hand and asked him if my blood was still dripping from it hot on to the floor? "You were mad," he mumbled, "mad when you carried out the idea. I opened this door, entered this room and saw you stretched out on this settee, the veins of your hand slashed, your fingers trailing in a sea of blood. You were mad. I might have lost you." I smiled sadly as I pulled the shirt up to my chest, my face breathing in the smell of it. I said that my part in the play required that I should take myself off at the end, and the form of absence possible for me, the form I could accept and bear, was a quick death rather than a slow, cruel crawling, like that of the turtle in the film *Mondo Cane* that lost its way in the sands, held in the sun's disc, as it searched for the river-bank. He repeated sadly that he didn't know I was serious about him. I asked him sarcastically whether he was waiting for me to kill myself in order to be sure that I was telling the truth. I told him that I had lost myself in my love for him; oblivious to all else, I slipped unseen, like a gust of wind, through people's fingers, scorching their faces as I passed through the street. All I was conscious of was the weight of bodies, the height of buildings and of his hands. I asked him to draw closer and give me his hand which I craved to hold. He remained standing far off, inflexible, and at once accused me that after all that misery and triumph I was refusing to become pregnant from him, had refused again and again and again, and that from my refusal he understood I no longer loved him.

What? I cried out that he could never accuse me of that. Only yesterday I was stretched out beside him and he gave himself up to deep sleep while I was open-eyed, rubbing my cheeks against his chin, kissing his chest, snuggling up under his arm, searching in vain for sleep. I told him frankly that I was upset by the speed with which he got to sleep, and by my being left alone and awake at his side. He hastened to deny this, saying that he had never been aware of my having remained sleepless. He believed that I dozed off the moment he did. I revealed maliciously that it wasn't the first time he had left me alone. I then related in full yesterday's incident, telling of how he had been asleep breathing quietly, with me stretched close up against him smoking a cigarette, when suddenly in the emptiness of the room through the smoke I had seen a foot fleeing from under the sheets. I moved my own but it didn't move and a coldness ran through the whole of my body. I moved it but it didn't move. It occurred to me to shout. I moved it but it didn't move. I hurriedly hid my face in his hair. I was afraid. He moved and the foot moved. I cried silently. I had imagined, had felt, had been unable to tell the difference between his foot and mine. In a faint voice he said: "In this age people don't die of love." Quickly seizing the opportunity I said that in this age people didn't beget children. In olden times they knew where the child would be born, who it would be likely to resemble, whether it would be male or female; they would knit it woollen vests and socks, would embroider the hems, pockets and collars of its dresses with colored birds and flowers. They would amass presents of gold crucifixes for it and medallions with "Allah bless him" on them, opened palms studded with blue stones, and pendants with its name engraved on them. They would reserve a midwife for it, would fix the day of the delivery, and the child would launch out from the darkness and be flung into the light at the precise time estimated. They would register a piece of land in the child's name, would rent it a house, choose companions for it, decide which school it would be sent to, the profession it would study for, the person it could love and to whom it could bind its destiny. That was a long, long time ago, in the time of your father and my father. He asked, "Do you believe that twenty years ago was such an age away? What has changed since? What has changed? Can't you and can't I provide everything that is required for a child?" To soften the blow I explained that before I married I was like a child that lies down on its back in front of the window, gazes up at the stars and stretches out its tiny arm in a desire to pluck them. I used to amuse myself with this dream, with this impossibility, would cling to it and wish it would happen. He asked me: "Then you were deceiving me?"

Discovering he had changed the conversation into an attack on me so as to win the battle, I quickly told him that only the woman who is unfulfilled with her man eagerly demands a child so that she can withdraw, enjoy being with her child and so be freed. He quickly interrupted me: "And were you unsatisfied?" I answered him that we had been afraid, had not traveled to the last sweet unexplored regions of experience; we had trembled in terror, had continually bumped against the faces of others and listened to their voices. For his sake, for my own, I had defied death in order to live. He was wrong, wrong, to doubt my being madly in love with him.

"I'm at a loss. I don't understand you," he muttered. I attacked him by saying that was just it, that he also wouldn't understand me if I told him I didn't dare become pregnant, that I would not perpetrate such a mistake.

"Mistake?" he shrieked. "Mistake?" I clung closer to his shirt, deriving strength from it, and slowly, in a low voice, I told him how scared I was about the fate of any child we might cast into this world. How could

I imagine a child of mine, a being nourished on my blood, embraced within my entrails, sharing my breathing, the pulsations of my heart and my daily food, a being to whom I give my features and the earth, how can I bear the thought that in the future he will leave me and go off in a rocket to settle on the moon? And who knows whether or not he'll be happy there. I imagine my child with white ribbons, his fresh face flushed; I imagine him strapped to a chair inside a glass ball fixed to the top of a long shaft of khaki-colored metal ending in folds resembling the skirt of my Charleston dress.° He presses the button, a cloud of dust rises up and an arrow hurls itself into space. No, I can't face it. I can't face it.

He was silent a long, long time while the light of dawn crept in by his face to the corners of the room, his face absent-minded and searching in the sky for an arrow and a child's face. The vein between his eyebrows was knotted; perplexity and strain showed in his mouth. I, too, remained silent and closed my eyes.

When he was near me, standing like a massive tower at a rocket-firing station, my heart throbbed and I muttered to him that I adored his naked body. When he puts on his clothes, especially when he ties his tie, I feel he's some stranger come to pay a visit to the head of the house. He opened his arms and leaned over me. I rushed into his embrace, mumbling crazily: "I love you, I love you, I love you, I love you, I love you." He whispered into my hair: "You're my pearl." Then he spread the palm of his hand over my lips, drawing me to him with the other hand, and ordered: "Let us take off, you and I, for the moon."

Translated from the Arabic
by Denys Johnson-Davies

EMILY NASRALLAH

When Emily Nasrallah (1938–) was still a girl in a South Lebanese village, she wrote to her uncle who had emigrated to the United States, asking him to sponsor her education. He agreed, and upon completing her secondary education in her hometown, Nasrallah moved to the capital where she worked her way through the American University at Beirut. In 1962, she published her first, somewhat autobiographical novel, September Birds. *It tells the story of village girls who are supposed to stay at home to await suitors from afar and who are ostracized if they do otherwise. Over the following seventeen years, she*

Charleston dress: a low-waisted, often fringed dress worn in the 1920s to dance the Charleston

published some children's books and a short story collection. When the civil war broke out in Lebanon in 1975, she wrote Those Memories *(1980), in which a woman who has stayed in Beirut through the fighting confronts one who had left and who therefore understands nothing about the conflict. The following year she came out with* Flight Against Time, *in which she exposes the reality of emigration: those who left to gain fame and fortune overseas were not coming back.*

"Our Daily Bread" came out in 1986 in a volume of short stories on the war by the same title. It tells the story of close friendship between two women. In this war, to escape death once was no guarantee of survival.

Our Daily Bread

We would sit together and talk about the war,° Sana' and I. Sometimes pessimism and hopelessness descended upon us, covering us like a tent. Then we would grow silent, as though cement blocks and sand bags had blocked the way for words. Our words sank and hid within the depths of our throats.

But in untroubled times of tranquillity, we would sit around and analyze the situation, in our simple way that depended on theories.

At the end of one of our sessions, Sana' stood up, and with a mocking smile on her face and a sigh from the depth of her heart, she said, "And now that we've put to rest all the unresolved matters of the world and put an end to the war, I have to go back home and cook for my family."

And with a wink she added sarcastically, "You do know, of course, that a woman's role is not restricted to theorizing and finding political solutions and discussing philosophical matters. We have to cook and clean and take care of everything in order to deserve our title of real women!"

She threw out her words in a funny, endearing way, and took her leave of me in a loving manner. The war had not changed her, nor hardened her, as it had so many people.

Sana' had her own unique way of welcoming friends or bidding them farewell. She hugged warmly and affectionately. Without reservations, she poured all her love into them, and coated their hearts with her ever-present joy of life. She gave everyone around her a feeling of warmth and well being; a promise of better things to come in spite of the darkness of war, in spite of the walls of anger, hatred and resentment erected around us. She made us feel that the world she inhabited, and us with it, would always be alright.

the war: the Lebanese Civil War, 1975–1992

Some time ago she came to visit me, after a forced absence that had lasted months. I hugged her, my heart soaring with the joy of seeing her again safe and sound, with the relief that she had—that we all had—made it out of our basement prisons, out of our damp and smelly shelters.

"I was afraid we would not meet again," I said to her, looking at the changes the war had wrought on her already slim figure. "I . . . was . . ." I choked on my tears.

She realized my words would drag us into the tragedy of what had happened. She jumped out of her seat and with a laugh she twirled around in a little dance to show she was still the same, then returned to her place, and laughed. . . . She laughed until her eyes filled with tears. That was Sana'. Always using laughter to mask the tears in every delicate situation, holding her smile up like a shield in the face of tragedy. And she often cried with laughter, but she never cried with pain or sadness.

That was Sana', sweet and unique and funny.

Then she and I sat and talked, just like we had always done in the days of peace and good living.

It was the first time we had seen each other after the invasion of Beirut. We did not talk much, for the sound of rockets and explosions still deafened us; the smell of fire and smoke burned our nostrils; and the names of victims filled the distance between us. After a while we sat in silence — she smoking her cigarette and sipping her bitter coffee and I looking out at the remnants and rubble of the homes around us.

I tried to interrupt our silence and bring her back to the present. "Where to from here . . . ?"

She looked at me at length and said nothing.

I repeated my question, "When will salvation finally come our way, Sana'? Do you think we have reached the limit, that this is the beginning of the end?"

Again she looked at me, silently, and the silence filled more empty moments. I respected her feelings and withdrew into the hidden pockets of myself. There I saw a pencil moving of its own volition in the distance between us, drawing a caricature of our little session.

I shuddered. Then I started laughing out loud, bringing her out of her silence. She looked towards me and said, "I hope to God that only good things are making you laugh. What is so funny?"

Actually, I did not really know why I was laughing, for the situation was rather sad. Or was I crying, hiding my tears with laughter? I still do not know the meaning of my laughter at that time. I do not want to dwell on that confusing moment when everything around us had collapsed, and we were trying to reconnect the broken lines of friendship and human relations.

Yesterday she appeared anew, after a long absence outside the country. Her presence reminded me of a saying by an Indian philosopher, "Sometimes we see the face of God in the presence of our friends."

I was cooped up inside my house, walking through rooms empty save for the holes in the walls made by the flying shrapnel of continuous war. They were like slap marks on the face of memory. I no longer remembered what corner would provide me with some semblance of peace and tranquillity, in which to remember friends now scattered around the globe, who only yesterday had taken refuge in each others' hearts.

I lived in a circle of anxiety, the sounds of distant artillery fire echoing around me. They coincided with sounds of sirens, speaking of yet more victims falling on every front, until the very earth groaned with the burden and the rocks crumbled from the weight. The radio stations still competed to get the terrible news out to their listeners.

Suddenly, Sana' arrived. She looked healthier than I had seen her before, her face had regained its color. But when we embraced I could feel her tremble against me.

"Congratulate me on my narrow escape . . . " she said, before I had a chance to ask her anything. "You could have been walking in your friend's funeral procession . . . this morning."

I backed away from her and whispered, "May God send nothing but good!"

"Oh, no, it's only good," she said, mocking me. "A small explosion, is all. A booby-trapped car and it nearly ended my life."

"You?"

"Yes, me. What's so strange about it being me? How am I different from anyone else? Why not me . . . "

"Tell me. Calmly tell me what happened," I interrupted.

"The explosion at the bank," she said. "Didn't you hear about it?"

"Of course, I heard about it. Once and twice and ten times."

"I was there!" she said quietly.

I cried out in disbelief, "There, there? At the bank, or on the road?"

"I was on the road, and I had just entered the building next to the bank. I heard the explosion as I was getting on the elevator. My ears still ring with the sound of it."

I had little to say, except to murmur the prayers that come automatically, as though they were my only salvation and my last shelter. "Thank God for your escape . . ."

"It was luck," she said calmly, "I escaped injury, others did not. It was just their turn and not mine. Next time might be my turn, who knows? We cannot afford to forget that for a single minute."

I tried to pull her out of the cloud of pessimism that had enveloped her. "Every day brings its own provisions. It is enough to deal with the evils one day at a time."

She watched me for a while. Then without saying a word she walked to the front door. Quietly she opened the door and stood on the threshold for a few seconds. Then she disappeared out the door, leaving me with that strange confusion, the mysterious sensation one has when confronted with someone who "nearly left the land of the living." Someone who will never again be able to take life for granted; someone for whom the incident becomes an obsession, feeding on the mind and nurtured by the heart. It is as if that person had received a sign and the sign had been drawn invisibly on his forehead.

I do not remember what farewell she bade me. Except that she had murmured something about having work to do, having an important rendezvous to go to.

I prayed for her and followed the prayers with a thousand "God be with you's." And I returned to the nucleus of my home, my office. But before I opened my book and took up my pen, I turned on the radio. The news-flash music was on, the tune that makes hearts jump in a panic: "Here is the latest news flash on the situation." My blood turned to ice as I listened to the voice pant at the enormity of the news it was delivering: "A huge car bomb exploded a few minutes ago, resulting in a large number of casualties. We will keep you posted as more news comes in . . ."

A few minutes ago! In that district? That's the same neighborhood where Sana' lives. Did she go home? No, no . . . she said she was going to an important rendezvous. She said she was busy.

I reached for the phone to dial her home number. It was impossible. The hotter the war situation, the colder the telephones become. No sign of life, no dial tone. Dead. Below zero temperature.

But *Sana'*! How do I get to her? Could she be among the wounded? Or one of the d . . . No . . . no . . .

The radio announcer again. With numbers and the names of victims this time. More than twenty killed and tens more injured. I listened carefully; an endless list of names. None of them Sana'. Maybe she had already passed that area before the explosion. Or maybe she took another route. She must have taken another route if she was going to that meeting of hers. But where . . . ? Where was that meeting taking place? Why hadn't I asked her? What if she went home to change her clothes before going to the meeting? I should have asked her. Maybe . . . What if . . . ?

Doubt is a vicious killer. It always attacks when you're down. And once your defenses have gone down you can only sink further into despair.

I spent the next few minutes in the shadow of my doubts, guessing. My only contact with the explosion was the needle on my radio moving from one station to the next, all of them delivering the same news to their listeners.

I was still in that state when my phone gave a strangled ring. I jumped on it, took up the receiver with trembling hands.

A stranger's voice on the other end said, "Mrs. Muna Al Ghazal?"

"Are you Mrs. Muna?" asked the voice again and only my lips answered that indeed I was, while in my head a devil rampaged.

"Yes, yes, that's me. And you are . . . ?" He did not give me a chance to finish the question.

"I am Dr. Nouman, from the University Hospital . . ."

"Dr. Nouman, yes. What is it? Why are you calling me?"

"I would like you to come to the hospital immediately. Your friend indicated — before she — well, that her family was out of the country and that you are the person closest to her. Come immediately."

"No . . . I don't know you, Doctor. You must have the wrong number. You know how the phones are these days. Besides, my phone is not even working, you couldn't have called me. You don't know me and everything is so mixed up, the telephone lines, the names, the numbers, the faces . . . You dialed the wrong number, Doctor!"

No . . . no . . . I won't believe it. Only a little while ago she left here, in perfect health and spirit. She told me she had escaped an explosion by a miracle. She came to tell me that.

She left saying she had an appointment. An important appointment. And I know her: she never breaks a promise. She never misses a rendezvous.

Translated from the Arabic
by Thuraya Khalil-Khouri

PALESTINE

GHASSAN KANAFANI

During the 1948 war, Ghassan Kanafani (1936–1972) and his family left Palestine and settled in a refugee camp in Syria. In 1955, because of his political activities, Kanafani was expelled from Damascus University where he had been studying Arabic literature. He taught in Kuwait for four years and then he moved to Beirut and worked as a journalist. In 1969, he became spokesperson for the Popular Front for the Liberation of Palestine (PFLP) and editor-in-chief of the PFLP's periodical. At age thirty-six, he was killed by a car bomb. In 1975, he was posthumously awarded the Lotus Prize for Literature by the Conference of Afro-Asian Writers.

Kanafani's writings are committed to building resistance in exile. He wrote five novels, two plays, and five collections of short stories. His first novel, Men in the Sun *(1963), tells of the tragedy of three Palestinian refugees trying to reach Kuwait across the desert. Their failure serves as a lesson to others who would leave. This novel was translated into several languages and made into a film, which was banned in some Arab countries for its criticism of Arab regimes. His second novel,* All That's Left to You *(1966), is considered one of the earliest and most successful modernist experiments in Arabic fiction.*

"The Death of Bed Number 12" was published in 1961. It weaves the imagined life of a destitute hospital patient.

The Death of Bed Number 12

Dear Ahmed,

I have chosen you in particular to be the recipient of this letter for a reason which may appear to you commonplace, yet since yesterday my every thought has been centered on it. I chose you in particular because when I saw him yesterday dying on the high white bed I remembered how you used to use the word "die" to express anything extreme. Many is the time I've heard you use such expressions as "I almost died laughing," "I was dead tired," "Death itself couldn't quench my love," and so on. While it is true that we all use such words, you use them more than anybody. Thus it was that I remembered you as I saw him sinking down in the bed and clutching at the coverlet with his long, emaciated fingers, giving a convulsive shiver and then staring out at me with dead eyes.

But why have I not begun at the beginning? You know, no doubt, that I am now in my second month at the hospital. I have been suffering from a stomach ulcer, but no sooner had the surgeon plugged up the hole in my stomach than a new one appeared in my head, about which the surgeon could do nothing. Believe me, Ahmed, that an "ulcer" on the brain is a lot more stubborn than one in the stomach. My room leads on to the main corridor of the Internal Diseases Wing, while the window overlooks the small hospital garden. Thus, propped up by a pillow, I can observe both the continuous flow of patients passing the door as well as the birds which fly past the window incessantly. Amidst this hubbub of people who come here to die in the serene shadow of the scalpel and whom I see, having arrived on their own two feet, leaving after days or hours on the death trolley, wrapped round in a covering of white; in this hubbub I find myself quite unable to make good those holes that have begun to open up in my head, quite incapable of stopping the flow of questions that mercilessly demand an answer of me.

I shall be leaving the hospital in a few days, for they have patched up my insides as best they can. I am now able to walk leaning on the arm of an old and ugly nurse and on my own powers of resistance. The hospital, however, has done little more than transfer the ulcer from my stomach to my head, for in this place, as the ugly old woman remarked, medicine may be able to plug up a hole in the stomach but it can never find the answers required to plug up holes in one's thinking. The day she said this the old woman gave a toothless laugh as she quietly led me off to the scales.

What, though, is such talk to do with us? What I want to talk to you about is death. Death that takes place in front of you, not about that death of which one merely hears. The difference between the two types of death is immeasurable and cannot be appreciated by someone who has not been a witness to a human being clutching at the coverlet of his bed with all the strength of his trembling fingers in order to resist that terrible slipping into extinction, as though the coverlet can pull him back from that colossus who, little by little, wrests from his eyes this life about which we know scarcely anything.

As the doctors waited around him, I examined the card that hung at the foot of his bed. I had slipped out of my room and was standing there, unseen by the doctors, who were engaged in a hopeless attempt to save the dying man. I read: "Name: Mohamed Ali Akbar. Age: 25. Nationality: Omani." I turned the card over and this time read: "Leukemia." Again I stared into the thin brown face, the wide frightened eyes and the lips that trembled like a ripple of purple water. As his eyes turned and came to rest on my face it seemed that he was appealing to me for help. Why? Because I used to give to him a casual greeting every morning? Or was it that he saw in my face some understanding of the terror that he was undergoing? He went on staring at me and then — quite simply — he died.

It was only then that the doctor discovered me and dragged me off angrily to my room. But he would never be able to banish from my mind the scene that is ever-present there. As I got on to my bed I heard the voice of the male nurse in the corridor alongside my door saying in a matter-of-fact voice:

"Bed number 12 has died!"

I said to myself: "Mohamed Ali Akbar has lost his name, he is Bed number 12." What do I mean now when I talk of a human being whose name was Mohamed Ali Akbar? What does it matter to him whether he still retains his name or whether it has been replaced by a number? Then I remembered how he wouldn't allow anyone to omit any part of his name. Every morning the nurse would ask him, "And how are you, Mohamed Ali?" and he would not reply, for he regarded his name as being Mohamed Ali Akbar — just like that, all in one — and that this Mohamed Ali to whom the nurse was speaking was some other person.

Though the nurses found a subject for mirth in this insistence on his whole name being used, Mohamed Ali Akbar continued to demand it; perhaps he regarded his right to possessing his name in full as being an insistence that he at least owned something, for he was poor, extremely poor, a great deal more so than you with your fertile imagination could conceive as you lounge around in the café; poverty was something engraved in his face, his forearms, his chest, the way he ate, into everything that surrounded him.

When I was able to walk for the first time after they had patched me up, I paid him a visit. The back of his bed was raised and he was sitting up, lost in thought. I sat on the side of the bed for a short while, and we exchanged a few brief, banal words. I noticed that alongside his pillow was an old wooden box with his name carved on it in semi-Persian style writing; it was securely tied with twine. Apart from this he owned nothing except his clothes, which were kept in the hospital cupboard. I remembered that on that day I had asked the nurse:

"What's in the old box?"

"No one knows," she answered, laughing. "He refuses to be parted from the box for a single instant."

Then she bent over me and whispered:

"These people who look so poor are generally hiding some treasure or other — perhaps this is his!"

During my stay here no one visited him at the hospital. As he knew no one I used to send him some of the sweets with which my visitors inundated me. He accepted everything without enthusiasm. He was not good at expressing gratitude and his behavior over this caused a certain fleeting resentment in me.

I did not concern myself with the mysterious box. Though Mohamed

Ali Akbar's condition steadily worsened, his attitude towards the box did not change, which caused the nurse to remark to me that if there had been some treasure in it he would surely have given it away or willed it to someone, seeing that he was heading for death at such speed. Like some petty philosopher I had laughed that day saying to myself that the stupidity of this nurse scarcely knew any bounds, for how did she expect Mohamed Ali Akbar to persuade himself that he was inevitably dying, that there was not a hope of his pulling through? His insistence on keeping the box was tantamount to hanging on to his hope of pulling through and being reunited with his box.

When Mohamed Ali Akbar died I saw the box at his side, where it had always been, and it occurred to me that the box ought to be buried unopened with him. On going to my room that night I was quite unable to sleep. While Mohamed Ali Akbar had been deposited in the autopsy room, wrapped up in a white covering, he was, at the same time, sitting in my room and staring at me, passing through the hospital wards and searching about in his bed; I could almost hear the way he would gasp for breath before going to sleep. When day dawned across the trees of the hospital garden, I had created a complete story about him for myself.

Mohamed Ali Akbar was a poor man from the western quarter of the village of Abkha in Oman; a thin, dark-skinned young man, with aspirations burning in his eyes that could find no release. True he was poor, but what does poverty matter to a man if he has never known anything else? The whole of Abkha suffered from being poor, a poverty identical to Mohamed Ali Akbar's; it was, however, a contented poverty, a poverty that was deep-seated and devoid of anything that prompted one to feel that it was wrong and that there was something called "riches." And so it was that the two water-skins° Mohamed Ali Akbar carried across his shoulders as he knocked on people's doors to sell them water, were the two scales which set the balance of his daily round. Mohamed Ali Akbar was aware of a certain dizziness when he laid down the water-skins, but when taking them up again the next morning he would feel that his existence was progressing tranquilly and that he had ensured for himself a balanced, undeviating journey through life.

Mohamed Ali Akbar's life could have continued in this quiet and ordered fashion, had fate emulated civilization — in not reaching faraway Oman. But fate was present even in far-off Oman and it was inevitable that Mohamed Ali Akbar should suffer a little from its capricious ways.

It happened on a scorchingly hot morning. Though the sun was not yet at the meridian, the surface of the road was hot and the desert blew gusts of dust-laden wind into his face. He knocked at a door which was answered by a young, brown-skinned girl with wide black eyes, and every-

water-skins: vessels made of goatskin and containing water

thing happened with the utmost speed. Like some clumsy oaf who has lost his way, he stood in front of the door, the water-skins swinging to and fro on his lean shoulders. Abstractedly he stared at her, hoping like someone overcome with a mild attack of sunstroke that his eyes would miraculously be capable of clasping her to him. She stared back at him in sheer astonishment, and, unable to utter a word, he turned his back on her and went off home with his water-skins.

Though Mohamed Ali Akbar was exceptionally shy even with his own family, he found himself forced to pour out his heart to his elder sister. As his mother had died of smallpox a long time ago and his father was helplessly bedridden, it was to his sister that he turned for help, for he had unswerving confidence that Sabika possessed the necessary intelligence and judgment for solving a problem of this sort. Seated before him on the rush mat, shrouded in her coarse black dress, she did not break her silence till Mohamed Ali Akbar had gasped out the last of his story.

"I shall seek her hand in marriage," she then said. "Isn't that what you want?"

"Yes, yes, is it possible?"

Removing a straw from the old rush mat, his sister replied:

"Why not? You are now a young man and we are all equal in Abkha."

Mohamed Ali Akbar spent a most disturbed night. When morning came he found that his sister was even more eager than himself to set off on her mission. They agreed to meet up at noon when she would tell him of the results of her efforts, and from there they would both make the necessary arrangements for bringing the matter to completion.

Mohamed Ali Akbar did not know how to pass the time wandering through the lanes with the water-skins on his shoulders. He kept looking at his shadow and beseeching God to make it into a circle round his feet so that he might hurry back home. After what seemed an eternity, he made his way back and was met at the door by his sister.

"It seems that her mother is agreeable. But it must all be put to her father, who will give his answer in five days."

Deep down within him Mohamed Ali Akbar felt that he was going to be successful in making the girl his wife. As far as he was able to imagine he began from henceforth to build up images of his future with this young and beautiful brown-skinned girl. His sister Sabika looked at the matter with a wise and experienced eye, but she too was sure they would be successful, for she was convinced that her brother's name was without blemish among the people of Abkha; she had, in addition, given a lot of attention to gaining the approval of the girl's mother, knowing as she did how a woman was able to put over an idea to her husband and make him believe that it was his own. Sabika, therefore, awaited the outcome of the matter with complete composure.

On the fifth day Sabika went to the girl's house in order to receive the answer. When she returned, however, her disconsolate face showed that she had failed. She stood in a corner of the room, unable to look Mohamed Ali Akbar in the eye, not knowing how to begin recounting what had happened.

"You must forget her, Mohamed Ali," she said when she had managed to pluck up her courage.

Not knowing what to say, he waited for his sister to finish.

"Her father died two days ago," continued Sabika, finding an opportunity in his silence to continue. "His dying wish to his family was that they should not give her to you in marriage."

Mohamed Ali Akbar heard these words as though they were addressed to someone else.

"But why, Sabika — why?" was all he could ask.

"He was told that you were a scoundrel, that you lived by stealing sheep on the mountain road, trading what you steal with the foreigners."

"I?"

"They think you are Mohamed Ali," said Sabika in a trembling voice she was unable to control. "You know — the scoundrel Mohamed Ali? Her father thought that you were he. . . ."

"But I am not Mohamed Ali," he replied, palms outstretched like a child excusing himself for some misdeed he has not committed. "I'm Mohamed Ali Akbar."

"There's been a mistake — I told them at the beginning that your name was Mohamed Ali. I didn't say Mohamed Ali Akbar because I saw no necessity for doing so."

Mohamed Ali Akbar felt his chest being crushed under the weight of the blow. However, he remained standing where he was, staring at his sister Sabika without fully seeing her. Blinded by anger, he let fly a final arrow:

"Did you tell her mother that I'm not Mohamed Ali but Mohamed Ali Akbar?"

"Yes, but the father's last wish was that they shouldn't marry her to you."

"But I'm Mohamed Ali Akbar the water-seller, aren't I?"

What was the use, though, of being so stricken? Everything had, quite simply, come to an end, a single word had lodged itself in the gullet of his romance and it had died. Mohamed Ali Akbar, however, was unable to forget the girl so easily and spent his time roaming about near her house in the hope of seeing her once again. Why? He did not know. His failure brought in its wake a savage anger which turned to hate; soon he was no longer able to pass along that road for fear that his fury would overcome him and he would pelt the window of her house with stones.

From that day onwards he refused to be called by anything but his name in full: Mohamed Ali Akbar, all in one. He refused to answer to anyone who called him Mohamed or Mohamed Ali and this soon became a habit with him. Even his sister Sabika did not dare to use a contracted form of his name. No longer did he experience his former contentment, and Abkha gradually changed to a forbidding graveyard in his eyes. Refusing to give in to his sister's insistence that he should marry, a worm called "wealth" began to eat its way into his brain. He wanted to take revenge on everything, to marry a woman with whom he could challenge the whole of Abkha, all those who did not believe that he was Mohamed Ali Akbar but Mohamed Ali the scoundrel. Where, though, to find wealth? Thus he decided to sail away to Kuwait.

The distance between Abkha and Ras al-Khaima° is two hours by foot, and from Ras al-Khaima to Kuwait by sea is a journey of three days, the fare for which, on an antiquated boat, was seventy rupees.° After a year or two he would be able to return to Oman and strut about proudly in the alleyways of Abkha wearing a snow-white *aba*° trimmed with gold, like the one he had seen round the shoulders of a notable from Ras al-Khaima who had come to his village to take the hand of a girl the fame of whose beauty had reached all the way there.

The journey was a hard one. The boat which took that eager throng across the south and then made its way northwards to the corner of the Gulf was continually exposed to a variety of dangers. But ebullient souls accustomed to life's hardships paid no heed to such matters; all hands cooperated in the task of delivering safely that small wooden boat floating on the waves of the great sea. And when the sails of the ships lying in Kuwait's quiet harbor came into view, Mohamed Ali Akbar experienced a strange feeling: the dream had now fallen from the colored world of fantasy into the realm of reality and he had to search around for a starting point, for a beginning to his dream. It seemed to him that the fantasies nourished by his hate for Abkha and for which he now sought vengeance were not of sufficient moment. As the frail craft approached, threading its way among the anchored boats, he was slowly drained of his feeling and it appeared to him that his long dreams of wealth were merely a solace for his sudden failure and that they were quite irrational. The packed streets, the buildings with their massive walls, the gray sky, the scorching heat, the warm air of the north wind, the roads crammed with cars, the serious faces, all these things appeared to him as barriers standing between him and his dream. He hurried aimlessly through this ocean of people, conscious of a deep feeling of loss which resembled vertigo, almost convinced that these many faces which did not glance at him were his first enemy, that all these people were the walls obstructing the very beginning of the road to his dream. The story was not as simple as in Abkha. Here it was without beginning, without end, without landmarks. It seemed to him that all the roads along which he walked were endless,

Ras al-Khaima: a small country, part of the United Arab Emirates
rupees: the currency used in the Indian subcontinent
aba: a cloak

that they circuited a rampart that held everything — every single thing — within its embrace. When, at sunset, a road led him to the seashore and he once again saw the sea, he stood staring across at the far horizon that joined up with the water: out there was Abkha, enveloped in tranquillity. It existed, every quarter had its beginning and its end, every wall carried its own particular lineaments; despite everything it was close to his heart. He felt lost in a rush of scalding water and for the first time he had no sense of shame as he lifted his hand to wipe salty tears from his cheeks.

Mohamed Ali Akbar wept without embarrassment, perhaps for the first time since he grew up; involuntarily, he had been overcome by a ferocious yearning for the two water-skins he used to carry across his shoulders. He was still staring out at the horizon while night gradually settled down around him. It made him feel in a way that he was present in a certain place at a certain time and that this night was like night in Abkha: people were sleeping behind their walls, the streets bore the lineaments of fatigue and silence, the sea rumbled heavily under the light of the moon. He felt relief. Wanting to laugh and yet unable to, he wept once again.

Dawn brought him an upsurge of fresh hope. He rose and went running through the streets. He realized that he must find someone from Oman with whom he could talk and that he would, sooner or later, find such a person, and from there he would learn where he was destined to proceed, from where to make a start.

And so Mohamed Ali Akbar attained his position as errand boy at a shop and was provided with a bicycle on which to carry out his duties. It was from this bicycle that the features of the streets, the qualities of the walls, registered themselves in his head. He felt a certain intimacy with them, but it was an intimacy imposed upon a background of a forbidding impression that he was being dogged by the eyes of his sister Sabika, the chinks in the girl's window, and Mohamed Ali the scoundrel who, unwittingly, had caused such dire disaster.

Months passed with the speed of a bicycle's wheels passing over the surface of a road. The wealth he had dreamed of began to come in and Mohamed Ali Akbar clung to this tiny fortune with all his strength, lest some passing whim should sweep it away or some scoundrel lay his hands on it. Thus it was that it occurred to him to make a sturdy wooden box in which to keep his fortune.

But what did Mohamed Ali Akbar's fortune consist of? Something that could not be reckoned in terms of money. When he had collected a certain amount of money he had bought himself a diaphanous white *aba* with gold edging. Every evening, alone with his box, he would take out the carefully folded *aba*, pass his thin brown fingers tenderly over it and spread it before his eyes; on it he would spill out his modest dreams, tracing along its borders all the streets of his village, the low, latticed windows from behind which peeped the eyes of young girls. There, in a corner of the *aba*, reposed the past which he could not bring himself to return to but whose existence was necessary in order to give the *aba* its true value. The thin fingers would fold it gently once again, put it safely back in its wooden box, and tie strong cord round the box. Then, and only then, did sleep taste sweet.

The box also contained a pair of china earrings for his sister Sabika, which he would give her on his return to Abkha, a bottle of pungent perfume, and a white purse holding such money as God in His bounty had given him and which he hoped would increase day by day.

As for the end, it began one evening. He was returning his bicycle to the shop when he felt a burning sensation in his limbs. He was alarmed at the thought that he had grown so weak, and with such speed, but did not take a great deal of notice, having had spells of trembling whenever he felt exceptionally homesick for Sabika and Abkha; he had already experienced just such a sensation of weakness when savagely yearning for all those things he hated and loved and had left behind, those things that made up the whole of his past. And so Mohamed Ali Akbar hastened along the road to his home with these thoughts in mind. But his feeling of weakness and nostalgia stayed with him till the following midday. When he made the effort to get up from bed, he was amazed to find that he had slept right through to noon instead of waking up at his usual early hour. What alarmed him even more was that he was still conscious of the feeling of weakness boring into his bones. Slightly afraid, he thought for a while and imagined himself all at once standing on the seashore with the glaring sun reflected off the water almost blinding him, the two waterskins on his shoulders, conscious of a sensation of intense exhaustion. The reflection of the sun increased in violence, yet he was unable to shut his eyes — they were aflame. Abruptly he slid back into sleep.

Here time as usually understood came to an end for Mohamed Ali Akbar. From now on everything happened as though he were raised above the ground, as though his legs were dangling in midair: like a man on a gallows, he was moving in front of Time's screen, a screen as inert as a rock of basalt. His part as a practicing human had been played out; his part as a mere spectator had come. He felt that there was no bond tying him to anything, that he was somewhere far away and that the things that moved before his eyes were no more than fish inside a large glass tumbler; his own eyes, too, were open and staring as though made of glass.

When he woke up again he realized that he was being carried by his arms and legs. Though he felt exhausted, he found the energy to recall that there was something which continued to be necessary to him and called out in a faint voice:

"The box . . . the box!"

No one, however, paid him any attention. With a frenzied movement he rose so as to get back to his box. His chest panting with the effort of getting to his feet, he called out:

"The box!"

But once again no one heard him. As he reached the door he clung to it and again gasped out in a lifeless voice:

"The box . . ."

Overcome by his exertions, he fell into a trance that was of the seashore itself. This time he felt that the tide was rising little by little over his feet and that the water was intensely cold. His hands were grasping a square-shaped rock with which he plunged downwards. When he awoke again he found himself clasping his old box tied round with cord. While specters passed to and fro in front of him, a needle was plunged into his arm, and a face bent over him.

Long days passed. But for Mohamed Ali Akbar nothing really happened at all. The mercilessness of the pain continued on its way, and he was not conscious of its passing. He was conscious only of its constant presence. The sea became dissolved into windows behind wooden shutters low against the side of the street, a pair of china earrings, an *aba* wet with salt water, a ship suspended motionless above the waves, and an old wooden box.

Only once was he aware of any contact with the world. This was when he heard a voice beside him say:

"What's in the old box?"

He looked at the source of the voice and saw, as in a dream, the face of a young, clean-shaven man with fair hair who was pointing at the box and looking at something.

The moment of recollection was short. He returned to gazing silently at the sea, though the face of the clean-shaven, blond young man also remained in front of him. After this he felt a sudden upsurge of energy; for no particular reason things had become clear to him. He distinctly saw, for the first time since he had collapsed, the rising of the sun. It seemed to him that he was capable of getting up from his bed and returning to his bicycle. Everything had grown clear to him: the box was alongside him, bound round as it had always been. Feeling at peace, he moved so as to get up, when a crowd of men in white clothes suddenly descended upon him, standing round him and regarding him with curiosity. Mohamed Ali Akbar tried to say something but was unable to. Suddenly he felt that the tide had risen right up to his waist and that the water was unbearably cold. He could feel nothing. He stretched out his arms to seize hold of something lest he should drown, but everything slid away from under his fingers. Suddenly, he saw the clean-shaven face of the blond young man again; he stared at him, somewhat frightened of him on account of his box, while the water continued to rise higher and higher until it had screened off that fair, clean-shaven face from his gaze.

"Bed number 12 has died."

As the male nurse called out I was unable to free myself from Mohamed Ali Akbar's eyes staring out at me before he died. I imagined that Mohamed Ali Akbar, who refused to have his name mutilated, would now be satisfied at being merely "Bed number 12" if only he could be assured about the fate of his box.

This, my dear Ahmed, is the story of Mohamed Ali Akbar, Bed number 12, who died yesterday evening and is now lying wrapped round in a white cloth in the autopsy room — the thin brown face that shifted an ulcer from my intestines to my brain and who caused me to write to you, so you don't again repeat your famous phrase "I almost died laughing" in my presence.

Ever yours,

I haven't yet left the hospital. My health is gradually getting back to normal and the method by which I gauge this amuses me. Do you know how I measure my strength? I stand smoking on the balcony and throw the cigarette end with all my strength so that it falls along the strips of green grass in the garden. In past weeks the cigarette would fall just within the fourth strip, but today it was much nearer the sixth.

From your letter I understand you to say that you were in no need of being a witness to Mohamed Ali Akbar's death to know what death is. You wrote saying that the experience of death does not require the tragic prologues with which I described Mohamed Ali Akbar's and that people die with far greater matter-of-factness: the man who fell down on the pavement and so let off the loaded pistol he had with him, whose bullet ripped open his neck (he was in the company of a strikingly beautiful girl), or the one who had a heart attack in the street one April evening, having become engaged to be married only a week before. Yes, that's all very true, my dear Ahmed, all very true, but the problem doesn't lie here at all, the problem of death is in no way that of the dead man, it is the problem of those who remain, those who bitterly await their turn so that they too may serve as a humble lesson to the eyes of the living. Of all the things I wrote in my last letter what I want to say now is that we must transfer our thinking from the starting-point to the end. All thinking must set forth from the point of death, whether it be, as you say, that of a man who dies contemplating the charms of the body of a wonderfully beautiful girl, or whether he dies staring into a newly shaven face which frightens him because of an old wooden box tied round with string. The unsolved question remains that of the end; the question of nonexistence, of eternal life — or what? Or what, my dear Ahmed?

Anyway, let's stop pouring water into a sack with a hole in it. Do you know what happened after I sent you my last letter? I went to the doctor's room and found them writing a report about Mohamed Ali Akbar. And they were on the point of opening the box. Oh, Ahmed, how imprisoned we are in our bodies and minds! We are always endowing others with our own attributes, always looking at them through a narrow fissure of our own views and way of thinking, wanting them, as far as we can, to become "us." We want to squeeze them into our skins, to give them our eyes to see with, to clothe them in our past and our own way of facing up to life. We place them within a framework outlined by our present understanding of time and place.

Mohamed Ali Akbar was none of the things I imagined. He was the father of three boys and two girls. We have forgotten that over there men marry early. Also, Mohamed Ali Akbar was not a water-seller, water being plentiful in Oman, but had been a sailor on one of the sailing ships that ply between the ports of the south and the Gulf, before settling down here quite a time ago.

It was in fact four years ago that Mohamed Ali Akbar arrived in Kuwait. After unimaginably hard effort he managed — only two months ago — to open what passed for a shop on one of the pavements of New Street. As to how he provided for his children in Oman, we simply don't know.

I read in the doctor's report that the patient had lost his sight six hours before death and so it would seem that Mohamed Ali Akbar had not in fact been staring into my face at the moment of his death as he was then blind. The doctor also wrote that as the address of the patient's family was not known, his burial would be attended solely by the hospital grave-diggers.

The doctor read out the report to his colleague. It was concise and extremely condensed, merely dealing in technical terms with the man's illness. The doctor's voice was lugubrious and colorless. When he had finished reading he proceeded to untie the string round the box. At this point I thought of leaving the room, for it was none of my business: the Mohamed Ali Akbar I knew had died and this person they had written about was someone else; this box, too, was some other box. I knew for certain what Mohamed Ali Akbar's box contained. Why should I bother myself about some new problem?

And yet I was unable to go to the door, but stood in the corner, trembling slightly.

The box was soon opened and the doctor quickly ran his fingers through the contents. Then he pushed it to one side.

Fearfully I looked into the box: it was filled with recent invoices for sums owed by the shop to the stores which supplied it; in one corner was an old photo of a bearded face, an old watch strap, some string, a small candle and several rupees among the papers.

I must be truthful and say that I was sadly disappointed. Before leaving the room, though, I saw something that stunned me: the nurse had pushed aside Mohamed Ali Akbar's invoices and revealed a long china earring that glittered. In a daze I went to the box and picked up the earring. I don't know why it was that I looked at the nurse and said:

"He bought this earring for his sister Sabika — I happen to know that."

For a brief instant she stared at me in some surprise — then she laughed uproariously. The doctor, too, laughed at the joke.

You are no doubt aware that nurses are required to humor patients with stomach ulcers in case they should suffer a relapse.

Yours ever —

Translated from the Arabic
by Denys Johnson-Davies

SUDAN

TAYEB SALIH

Born in a village in the Northern Province of Sudan and educated in a traditional Koranic school, Tayeb Salih (1929–) did not experience city life until he entered the British-founded Gordon College in the Sudanese capital of Khartoum. From there he went to London to complete his education. There he worked for the British Broadcasting Corporation, becoming head of the drama section of the Arabic program. Salih went from London to Qatar, where he was director-general of information, and from there to Paris, where he now works for UNESCO. *He first started to publish fiction in the 1960s. His best-known and most highly acclaimed work is* Season of Migration to the North *(1967). It is a novel that explores north-south relations and has often been contrasted with Shakespeare's* Othello *and Joseph Conrad's* Heart of Darkness.*

"The Doum Tree of Wad Hamid" was first published in 1960. Like all of Salih's works, the classical Arabic is suffused with an oral narrative flavor. This story celebrates the power of popular traditions to resist modernization.

The Doum Tree° of Wad Hamid

Were you to come to our village as a tourist, it is likely, my son, that you would not stay long. If it were in winter time, when the palm trees are pollinated, you would find that a dark cloud had descended over the village. This, my son, would not be dust, nor yet that mist which rises up after rainfall. It would be a swarm of those sand flies which obstruct all paths to those who wish to enter our village. Maybe you have seen this pest before, but I swear that you have never seen this particular species. Take this gauze netting, my son, and put it over your head. While it won't protect you against these devils, it will at least help you to bear them. I remember a friend of my son's, a fellow student at school, whom my son invited to stay with us a year ago at this time of the year. His

---

doum tree: doom palm, or a gingerbread tree of Africa

people come from the town. He stayed one night with us and got up next day, feverish, with a running nose and swollen face; he swore that he wouldn't spend another night with us.

If you were to come to us in summer you would find the horseflies with us — enormous flies the size of young sheep, as we say. In comparison to these the sand flies are a thousand times more bearable. They are savage flies, my son: they bite, sting, buzz, and whirr. They have a special love for man and no sooner smell him out than they attach themselves to him. Wave them off you, my son — God curse all sand flies.

And were you to come at a time which was neither summer nor winter you would find nothing at all. No doubt, my son, you read the papers daily, listen to the radio, and go to the cinema once or twice a week. Should you become ill you have the right to be treated in hospital, and if you have a son he is entitled to receive education at a school. I know, my son, that you hate dark streets and like to see electric light shining out into the night. I know, too, that you are not enamored of walking and that riding donkeys gives you a bruise on your backside. Oh, I wish, my son, I wish — the asphalted roads of the towns — the modern means of transport — the fine comfortable buses. We have none of all this — we are people who live on what God sees fit to give us.

Tomorrow you will depart from our village, of this I am sure, and you will be right to do so. What have you to do with such hardship? We are thick-skinned people and in this we differ from others. We have become used to this hard life, in fact we like it, but we ask no one to subject himself to the difficulties of our life. Tomorrow you will depart, my son — I know that. Before you leave, though, let me show you one thing — something which, in a manner of speaking, we are proud of. In the towns you have museums, places in which the local history and the great deeds of the past are preserved. This thing that I want to show you can be said to be a museum. It is one thing we insist our visitors should see.

Once a preacher, sent by the government, came to us to stay for a month. He arrived at a time when the horseflies had never been fatter. On the very first day the man's face swelled up. He bore this manfully and joined us in evening prayers on the second night, and after prayers he talked to us of the delights of the primitive life. On the third day he was down with malaria, he contracted dysentery, and his eyes were completely gummed up. I visited him at noon and found him prostrate in bed, with a boy standing at his head waving away the flies.

"O Sheikh," I said to him, "there is nothing in our village to show you, though I would like you to see the doum tree of Wad Hamid." He didn't ask me what Wad Hamid's doum tree was, but I presumed that he had heard of it, for who has not? He raised his face which was like the lung of a slaughtered cow; his eyes (as I said) were firmly closed: though I knew that behind the lashes there lurked a certain bitterness.

"By God," he said to me, "if this were the doum tree of Jandal,° and you the Moslems who fought with Ali and Mu'awiya, and I the arbitrator between you, holding your fate in these two hands of mine, I would not stir an inch!" and he spat upon the ground as though to curse me and turned his face away. After that we heard that the Sheikh had cabled to those who had sent him, saying: "The horseflies have eaten into my neck, malaria has burnt up my skin, and dysentery has lodged itself in my bowels. Come to my rescue, may God bless you — these are people who are in no need of me or of any other preacher." And so the man departed and the government sent us no preacher after him.

But, my son, our village actually witnessed many great men of power and influence, people with names that rang through the country like drums, whom we never even dreamed would ever come here — they came, by God, in droves.

We have arrived. Have patience, my son; in a little while there will be the noonday breeze to lighten the agony of this pest upon your face.

Here it is: the doum tree of Wad Hamid. Look how it holds its head aloft to the skies; look how its roots strike down into the earth; look at its full, sturdy trunk, like the form of a comely woman, at the branches on high resembling the mane of a frolicsome steed! In the afternoon, when the sun is low, the doum tree casts its shadow from this high mound right across the river so that someone sitting on the far bank can rest in its shade. At dawn, when the sun rises, the shadow of the tree stretches across the cultivated land and houses right up to the cemetery. Don't you think it is like some mythical eagle spreading its wings over the village and everyone in it? Once the government, wanting to put through an agricultural scheme, decided to cut it down: they said that the best place for setting up the pump was where the doum tree stood. As you can see, the people of our village are concerned solely with their everyday needs and I cannot remember their ever having rebelled against anything. However, when they heard about cutting down the doum tree they all rose up as one man and barred the district commissioner's way. That was in the time of foreign rule. The flies assisted them too — the horseflies. The man was surrounded by the clamoring people shouting that if the doum tree were cut down they would fight the government to the last man, while the flies played havoc with the man's face. As his papers were scattered in the water we heard him cry out: "All right — doum tree stay — scheme no stay!" And so neither the pump nor the scheme came about and we kept our doum tree.

Let us go home, my son, for this is no time for talking in the open. This hour just before sunset is a time when the army of sand flies becomes particularly active before going to sleep. At such a time no one

Jandal: the place where the Caliph Ali and Mu'awiya, the future ruler of the Omayyad dynasty, fought in the seventh century C.E.

who isn't well-accustomed to them and has become as thick-skinned as we are can bear their stings. Look at it, my son, look at the doum tree: lofty, proud, and haughty as though — as though it were some ancient idol. Wherever you happen to be in the village you can see it; in fact, you can even see it from four villages away.

Tomorrow you will depart from our village, of that there is no doubt, the mementoes of the short walk we have taken visible upon your face, neck and hands. But before you leave I shall finish the story of the tree, the doum tree of Wad Hamid. Come in, my son, treat this house as your own.

You ask who planted the doum tree?

No one planted it, my son. Is the ground in which it grows arable land? Do you not see that it is stony and appreciably higher than the river bank, like the pedestal of a statue, while the river twists and turns below it like a sacred snake, one of the ancient gods of the Egyptians? My son, no one planted it. Drink your tea, for you must be in need of it after the trying experience you have undergone. Most probably it grew up by itself, though no one remembers having known it other than as you now find it. Our sons opened their eyes to find it commanding the village. And we, when we take ourselves back to childhood memories, to that dividing line beyond which you remember nothing, see in our minds a giant doum tree standing on a river bank; everything beyond it is as cryptic as talismans, like the boundary between day and night, like that fading light which is not the dawn but the light directly preceding the break of day. My son, do you find that you can follow what I say? Are you aware of this feeling I have within me but which I am powerless to express? Every new generation finds the doum tree as though it had been born at the time of their birth and would grow up with them. Go and sit with the people of this village and listen to them recounting their dreams. A man awakens from sleep and tells his neighbor how he found himself in a vast sandy tract of land, the sand as white as pure silver; how his feet sank in as he walked so that he could only draw them out again with difficulty; how he walked and walked until he was overcome with thirst and stricken with hunger, while the sands stretched endlessly around him; how he climbed a hill and on reaching the top espied a dense forest of doum trees with a single tall tree in the center which in comparison with the others looked like a camel amid a herd of goats; how the man went down the hill to find that the earth seemed to be rolled up before him so that it was but a few steps before he found himself under the doum tree of Wad Hamid; how he then discovered a vessel containing milk, its surface still fresh with froth, and how the milk did not go down though he drank until he had quenched his thirst. At which his neighbor says to him, "Rejoice at release from your troubles."

You can also hear one of the women telling her friend: "It was as though I were in a boat sailing through a channel in the sea, so narrow that I could stretch out my hands and touch the shore on either side. I found myself on the crest of a mountainous wave which carried me upwards till I was almost touching the clouds, then bore me down into a dark, bottomless pit. I began shouting in my fear, but my voice seemed to be trapped in my throat. Suddenly I found the channel opening out a little. I saw that on the two shores were black, leafless trees with thorns, the tips of which were like the heads of hawks. I saw the two shores closing in upon me and the trees seemed to be walking towards me. I was filled with terror and called out at the top of my voice, "O Wad Hamid!" As I looked I saw a man with a radiant face and a heavy white beard flowing down over his chest, dressed in spotless white and holding a string of amber prayer-beads. Placing his hand on my brow he said: "Be not afraid," and I was calmed. Then I found the shore opening up and the water flowing gently. I looked to my left and saw fields of ripe corn, waterwheels turning, and cattle grazing, and on the shore stood the doum tree of Wad Hamid. The boat came to rest under the tree and the man got out, tied up the boat, and stretched out his hand to me. He then struck me gently on the shoulder with the string of beads, picked up a doum fruit from the ground and put it in my hand. When I turned round he was no longer there."

"That was Wad Hamid," her friend then says to her, "you will have an illness that will bring you to the brink of death, but you will recover. You must make an offering to Wad Hamid under the doum tree."

So it is, my son, that there is not a man or woman, young or old, who dreams at night without seeing the doum tree of Wad Hamid at some point in the dream.

You asked me why it was called the doum tree of Wad Hamid and who Wad Hamid was. Be patient, my son — have another cup of tea.

At the beginning of home rule a civil servant came to inform us that the government was intending to set up a stopping place for the steamer. He told us that the national government wished to help us and to see us progress, and his face was radiant with enthusiasm as he talked. But he could see that the faces around him expressed no reaction. My son, we are not people who travel very much, and when we wish to do so for some important matter such as registering land, or seeking advice about a matter of divorce, we take a morning's ride on our donkeys and then board the steamer from the neighboring village. My son, we have grown accustomed to this, in fact it is precisely for this reason that we breed donkeys. It is little wonder, then, that the government official could see nothing in the people's faces to indicate that they were pleased with the news. His enthusiasm waned and, being at his wit's end, he began to fumble for words.

"Where will the stopping place be?" someone asked him after a period of silence. The official replied that there was only one suitable place — where the doum tree stood. Had you that instant brought along a woman and had her stand among those men as naked as the day her mother bore her, they could not have been more astonished.

"The steamer usually passes here on a Wednesday," one of the men quickly replied; "if you made a stopping place, then it would be here on Wednesday afternoon." The official replied that the time fixed for the steamer to stop by their village would be four o'clock on Wednesday afternoon.

"But that is the time when we visit the tomb of Wad Hamid at the doum tree," answered the man; "when we take our women and children and make offerings. We do this every week." The official laughed. "Then change the day!" he replied. Had the official told these men at that moment that every one of them was a bastard, that would not have angered them more than this remark of his. They rose up as one man, bore down upon him, and would certainly have killed him if I had not intervened and snatched him from their clutches. I then put him on a donkey and told him to make good his escape.

And so it was that the steamer still does not stop here and that we still ride off on our donkeys for a whole morning and take the steamer from the neighboring village when circumstances require us to travel. We content ourselves with the thought that we visit the tomb of Wad Hamid with our women and children and that we make offerings there every Wednesday as our fathers and fathers' fathers did before us.

Excuse me, my son, while I perform the sunset prayer — it is said that the sunset prayer is "strange": if you don't catch it in time it eludes you. *God's pious servants — I declare that there is no god but God and I declare that Mohamed is His Servant and His Prophet — Peace be upon you and the mercy of God!*

Ah, ah. For a week this back of mine has been giving me pain. What do you think it is, my son? I know, though — it's just old age. Oh to be young! In my young days I would breakfast off half a sheep, drink the milk of five cows for supper, and be able to lift a sack of dates with one hand. He lies who says he ever beat me at wrestling. They used to call me "the crocodile." Once I swam the river, using my chest to push a boat loaded with wheat to the other shore — at night! On the shore were some men at work at their waterwheels, who threw down their clothes in terror and fled when they saw me pushing the boat towards them.

"Oh people," I shouted at them, "what's wrong, shame upon you! Don't you know me? I'm "the crocodile." By God, the devils themselves would be scared off by your ugly faces."

My son, have you asked me what we do when we're ill?

I laugh because I know what's going on in your head. You townsfolk hurry to the hospital on the slightest pretext. If one of you hurts his finger you dash off to the doctor who puts a bandage on and you carry it in a sling for days; and even then it doesn't get better. Once I was working in the fields and something bit my finger — this little finger of mine. I jumped to my feet and looked around in the grass where I found a snake lurking. I swear to you it was longer than my arm. I took hold of it by the head and crushed it between two fingers, then bit into my finger, sucked out the blood, and took up a handful of dust and rubbed it on the bite.

But that was only a little thing. What do we do when faced with real illness?

This neighbor of ours, now. One day her neck swelled up and she was confined to bed for two months. One night she had a heavy fever, so at first dawn she rose from her bed and dragged herself along till she came — yes, my son, till she came to the doum tree of Wad Hamid. The woman told us what happened.

"I was under the doum tree," she said, "with hardly sufficient strength to stand up, and called out at the top of my voice: 'O Wad Hamid, I have come to you to seek refuge and protection — I shall sleep here at your tomb and under your doum tree. Either you let me die or you restore me to life; I shall not leave here until one of these two things happens.'

"And so I curled myself up in fear," the woman continued with her story, "and was soon overcome by sleep. While midway between wakefulness and sleep I suddenly heard sounds of recitation from the Koran and a bright light, as sharp as a knife edge, radiated out, joining up the two river banks, and I saw the doum tree prostrating itself in worship. My heart throbbed so violently that I thought it would leap up through my mouth. I saw a venerable old man with a white beard and wearing a spotless white robe come up to me, a smile on his face. He struck me on the head with his string of prayer-beads and called out: 'Arise.'

"I swear that I got up I know not how and went home I know not how. I arrived back at dawn and woke up my husband, my son, and my daughters. I told my husband to light the fire and make tea. Then I ordered my daughters to give trilling cries of joy, and the whole village prostrated themselves before us. I swear that I have never again been afraid, nor yet ill."

Yes, my son, we are people who have no experience of hospitals. In small matters such as the bites of scorpions, fever, sprains, and fractures, we take to our beds until we are cured. When in serious trouble we go to the doum tree.

Shall I tell you the story of Wad Hamid, my son, or would you like to sleep? Townsfolk don't go to sleep till late at night — I know that of them. We, though, go to sleep directly the birds are silent, the flies stop harrying the cattle, the leaves of the trees settle down, the hens spread their wings over their chicks, and the goats turn on their sides to chew the cud. We and our animals are alike: we rise in the morning when they rise and go to sleep when they sleep, our breathing and theirs following one and the same pattern.

My father, reporting what my grandfather had told him, said: "Wad

Hamid, in times gone by, used to be the slave of a wicked man. He was one of God's holy saints but kept his faith to himself, not daring to pray openly lest his wicked master should kill him. When he could no longer bear his life with this infidel he called upon God to deliver him and a voice told him to spread his prayer-mat on the water and that when it stopped by the shore he should descend. The prayer-mat put him down at the place where the doum tree is now and which used to be waste land. And there he stayed alone, praying the whole day. At nightfall a man came to him with dishes of food, so he ate and continued his worship till dawn."

All this happened before the village was built up. It is as though this village, with its inhabitants, its waterwheels and buildings, had become split off from the earth. Anyone who tells you he knows the history of its origin is a liar. Other places begin by being small and then grow larger, but this village of ours came into being at one bound. Its population neither increases nor decreases, while its appearance remains unchanged. And ever since our village has existed, so has the doum tree of Wad Hamid; and just as no one remembers how it originated and grew, so no one remembers how the doum tree came to grow in a patch of rocky ground by the river, standing above it like a sentinel.

When I took you to visit the tree, my son, do you remember the iron railing round it? Do you remember the marble plaque standing on a stone pedestal with "The doum tree of Wad Hamid" written on it? Do you remember the doum tree with the gilded crescents above the tomb? They are the only new things about the village since God first planted it here, and I shall now recount to you how they came into being.

When you leave us tomorrow — and you will certainly do so, swollen of face and inflamed of eye — it will be fitting if you do not curse us but rather think kindly of us and of the things that I have told you this night, for you may well find that your visit to us was not wholly bad.

You remember that some years ago we had Members of Parliament and political parties and a great deal of to-ing and fro-ing which we couldn't make head or tail of. The roads would sometimes cast down strangers at our very doors, just as the waves of the sea wash up strange weeds. Though not a single one of them prolonged his stay beyond one night, they would nevertheless bring us the news of the great fuss going on in the capital. One day they told us that the government which had driven out imperialism had been substituted by an even bigger and noisier government.

"And who has changed it?" we asked them, but received no answer. As for us, ever since we refused to allow the stopping place to be set up at the doum tree no one has disturbed our tranquil existence. Two years passed without our knowing what form the government had taken, black or white. Its emissaries passed through our village without staying in it, while we thanked God that He had saved us the trouble of putting them up. So things went on till, four years ago, a new government came into power. As though this new authority wished to make us conscious of its presence, we awoke one day to find an official with an enormous hat and small head, in the company of two soldiers, measuring up and doing calculations at the doum tree. We asked them what it was about, to which they replied that the government wished to build a stopping place for the steamer under the doum tree.

"But we have already given you our answer about that," we told them. "What makes you think we'll accept it now?"

"The government which gave in to you was a weak one," they said, "but the position has now changed."

To cut a long story short, we took them by the scruffs of their necks, hurled them into the water, and went off to our work. It wasn't more than a week later when a group of soldiers came along commanded by the small-headed official with the large hat, shouting, "Arrest that man, and that one, and that one," until they'd taken off twenty of us, I among them. We spent a month in prison. Then one day the very soldiers who had put us there opened the prison gates. We asked them what it was all about but no one said anything. Outside the prison we found a great gathering of people; no sooner had we been spotted than there were shouts and cheering and we were embraced by some cleanly dressed people, heavily scented and with gold watches gleaming on their wrists. They carried us off in a great procession, back to our own people. There we found an unbelievably immense gathering of people, carts, horses, and camels. We said to each other, "The din and flurry of the capital has caught up with us." They made us twenty men stand in a row and the people passed along it shaking us by the hand: the Prime Minister — the President of the Parliament — the President of the Senate — the member for such and such constituency — the member for such and such other constituency.

We looked at each other without understanding a thing of what was going on around us except that our arms were aching with all the handshakes we had been receiving from those Presidents and Members of Parliament.

Then they took us off in a great mass to the place where the doum tree and the tomb stand. The Prime Minister laid the foundation stone for the monument you've seen, and for the dome you've seen, and for the railing you've seen. Like a tornado blowing up for a while and then passing over, so that mighty host disappeared as suddenly as it had come without spending a night in the village — no doubt because of the horseflies which, that particular year, were as large and fat and buzzed and whirred as much as during the year the preacher came to us.

One of those strangers who were occasionally cast upon us in the village later told us the story of all this fuss and bother.

"The people," he said, "hadn't been happy about this government since it had come to power, for they knew that it had got there by bribing a number of the Members of Parliament. They therefore bided their time and waited for the right opportunities to present themselves, while the opposition looked around for something to spark things off. When the doum tree incident occurred and they marched you all off and slung you into prison, the newspapers took this up and the leader of the government which had resigned made a fiery speech in Parliament in which he said:

"To such tyranny has this government come that it has begun to interfere in the beliefs of the people, in those holy things held most sacred by them." Then, taking a most imposing stance and in a voice choked with emotion, he said: "Ask our worthy Prime Minister about the doum tree of Wad Hamid. Ask him how it was that he permitted himself to send his troops and henchmen to desecrate that pure and holy place!"

The people took up the cry and throughout the country their hearts responded to the incident of the doum tree as to nothing before. Perhaps the reason is that in every village in this country there is some monument like the doum tree of Wad Hamid which people see in their dreams. After a month of fuss and shouting and inflamed feelings, fifty members of the government were forced to withdraw their support, their constituencies having warned them that unless they did so they would wash their hands of them. And so the government fell, the first government returned to power and the leading paper in the country wrote: "The doum tree of Wad Hamid has become the symbol of the nation's awakening."

Since that day we have been unaware of the existence of the new government and not one of those great giants of men who visited us has put in an appearance; we thank God that He has spared us the trouble of having to shake them by the hand. Our life returned to what it had been: no water-pump, no agricultural scheme, no stopping place for the steamer. But we kept our doum tree which casts its shadow over the southern bank in the afternoon and, in the morning, spreads its shadow over the fields and houses right up to the cemetery, with the river flowing below it like some sacred legendary snake. And our village has acquired a marble monument, an iron railing, and a dome with gilded crescents.

When the man had finished what he had to say he looked at me with an enigmatic smile playing at the corners of his mouth like the faint flickerings of a lamp.

"And when," I asked, "will they set up the water-pump, and put through the agricultural scheme and the stopping place for the steamer?"

He lowered his head and paused before answering me, "When people go to sleep and don't see the doum tree in their dreams."

"And when will that be?" I said.

"I mentioned to you that my son is in the town studying at school," he replied. "It wasn't I who put him there; he ran away and went there on his own, and it is my hope that he will stay where he is and not return.

When my son's son passes out of school and the number of young men with souls foreign to our own increases, then perhaps the water-pump will be set up and the agricultural scheme put into being — maybe then the steamer will stop at our village — under the doum tree of Wad Hamid."

"And do you think," I said to him, "that the doum tree will one day be cut down?" He looked at me for a long while as though wishing to project, through his tired, misty eyes, something which he was incapable of doing by word.

"There will not be the least necessity for cutting down the doum tree. There is not the slightest reason for the tomb to be removed. What all these people have overlooked is that there's plenty of room for all these things: the doum tree, the tomb, the water-pump, and the steamer's stopping place."

When he had been silent for a time he gave me a look which I don't know how to describe, though it stirred within me a feeling of sadness, sadness for some obscure thing which I was unable to define. Then he said: "Tomorrow, without doubt, you will be leaving us. When you arrive at your destination, think well of us and judge us not too harshly."

Translated from the Arabic
by Denys Johnson-Davies

TURKEY

NAZIM HIKMET RAN

Nazim Hikmet Ran (1920–1963) is considered the most outstanding poet of twentieth-century Turkey. He transmitted into Turkish literature Marxist ideology as well as the free verse style of the Soviet poet Mayakovsky. His writings are filled with social criticism and anti-imperialist sentiment. He was the only major Turkish writer to speak out against the Armenian massacres in 1915 and 1922. He was jailed by Ataturk in the 1930s. Upon his release in 1950, Hikmet Ran exiled himself to the Soviet Union, where he died. His books were banned in Turkey from the late 1930s to the late 1940s and again from 1951 until his death. Posthumously, his work has gained a new popularity.

The poems selected cover a long period and reflect the kinds of concerns that pervade all of his writings, particularly fear and the circumstances surrounding his experiences of imprisonment.

On Living

I

Living is no laughing matter:
   you must live with great seriousness
      like a squirrel, for example —
I mean without looking for something beyond and above living.
      I mean living must be your whole occupation.   5
Living is no laughing matter:
   you must take it seriously
   so much so and to such a degree that,
for example, your hands tied behind your back, your back to the
      wall,   10
or else in a laboratory
   in your white coat and thick glasses,
   you'll be able to die for people —
even for people whose faces you've never seen,
even though you know living   15
   is the most real, the most beautiful thing.

I mean you must take living so seriously
that even at seventy, for example, you will plant olives —
and not so they'll be left for your children either,
but because even though you fear death you don't believe it,   20
because living, I mean, weighs heavier.

2

Let's say we're seriously ill, need surgery —
which is to say there's a chance we won't get up
            from the white table.
Even though it's impossible not to feel sad about going a little
            too soon,   25
we'll still laugh at the jokes being told,
we'll look out the window to see if it's raining,
or we'll still wait anxiously
            for the latest newscast . . .
Let's say we're at the front,   30
            for something worth fighting for, say.
There, in the first offensive, on that very day,
            we might fall on our face, dead.
We'll know this with a curious anger,
            but we'll still worry ourselves to death   35
            about the outcome of the war, which might go on for years.

Let's say we're in prison
and close to fifty,
and we have eighteen more years, say, before the iron doors will
            open.
We'll still live with the outside,   40
with its people and animals, struggle and wind —
            I mean with the outside beyond the walls.
I mean, however and wherever we are,
            we must live as if one never dies.

3

This earth will grow cold,   45
a star among stars
            and one of the smallest —
a gilded mote on the blue velvet, I mean,
            I mean *this*, our great earth.
This earth will grow cold one day,   50
not like a heap of ice
or a dead cloud even,

but like an empty walnut it will roll along
   in pitch-black space . . .
You must grieve for this right now,   55
you have to feel this sorrow now,
for the world must be loved this much
   if you're going to say "I lived" . . .

Translated from the Turkish by
Randy Blasing and Mutlu Konuk

The Strangest Creature on Earth

You're like a scorpion, my brother,
you live in cowardly darkness
    like a scorpion.
You're like a sparrow, my brother,
always in a sparrow's flutter.   5
You're like a clam, my brother,
closed like a clam, content.
And you're frightening, my brother, like the mouth of an extinct
   volcano.
Not one,
   not five,   10
you are millions, unfortunately.
You're like a sheep, my brother.
    When the cloaked drover raises his stick,
       you quickly join the herd
and run, almost proudly, to the slaughterhouse.   15
I mean, you're the strangest creature on earth —
stranger, even, than that fish
    that couldn't see the ocean for the water.
And the oppression in this world
    is thanks to you.   20
And if we're hungry, if we're tired, if we're covered with blood,
and if we're still being crushed like grapes for our wine,
      the fault is yours
 — I can hardly bring myself to say it —
but most of the fault, my dear brother, is yours.   25

Translated from the Turkish by
Randy Blasing and Mutlu Konuk

Some Advice to Those Who Will Serve Time in Prison

If instead of being hanged by the neck
   you're thrown inside
   for not giving up hope
in the world, in your country, in people,
   if you do ten or fifteen years   5
   apart from the time you have left,
you won't say
     "Better I had swung from the end of a rope
                    like a flag" —
you'll put your foot down and live.   10
It might not be a pleasure exactly,
but it's your solemn duty
   to live one more day
       to spite the enemy.
Part of you may live alone inside,   15
     like a stone at the bottom of a well.
But the other part
   must be so caught up
   in the flurry of the world
   that you shiver there inside   20
when outside, at forty days' distance, a leaf moves.
To wait for letters inside,
or to sing sad songs,
or to lie awake all night staring at the ceiling
     is sweet, but dangerous.   25
Look at your face from shave to shave,
forget your age,
watch out for lice,
     and for spring nights;
and always remember   30
   to eat every last piece of bread —
also, don't forget to laugh heartily.
And, who knows,
the woman you love may no longer love you.
Don't say it's no big thing —   35
it's like the snapping of a green branch
               to the man inside.
To think of roses and gardens inside is bad,
to think of seas and mountains is good.
Read and write without stopping to rest,   40
and I also advise weaving,

and also making mirrors.
I mean it's not that you can't pass
    ten or fifteen years inside,
        and more even —   45

you can,
as long as the jewel
in the left side of your chest docsn't lose its luster!

*Translated from the Turkish by
Randy Blasing and Mutlu Konuk*

Awakening

You woke up.
Where are you?
At home.
You're still
        not used to waking up   5
        in your own house.
This is the kind of daze
        thirteen years of prison leaves you in.
Who's sleeping next to you?
It's not loneliness — it's your wife.   10
She's sleeping peacefully, like an angel.
Pregnancy becomes the lady.
What time it is?
Eight.
You're safe till night.   15
Because it's the custom:
        the police don't raid houses in broad daylight.

*Translated from the Turkish by
Randy Blasing and Mutlu Konuk*

Evening Walk

You no sooner got out of prison
than you made your wife
        pregnant;
she's on your arm,
        and you're out for an evening walk around the neighborhood.   5

The lady's belly comes up to her nose.
She carries her sacred charge coyly.
You're respectful and proud.
The air is cool
— cool like baby hands.   10
You'd like to take it in your palms

      and warm it up.
The neighborhood cats are at the butcher's door,
and upstairs his curly wife
has settled her breasts on the window ledge   15
        and is watching the evening.
Half-light, spotless sky:
smack in the middle sits the evening star,
     sparkling like a glass of water.
Indian summer lasted long this year —   20
the mulberry trees are yellow,
       but the figs are still green.
Refik the typesetter and the milkman Yorgi's middle daughter
     have gone out for an evening stroll,
      their fingers locked.   25
The grocer Karabet's lights are on.
This Armenian citizen has not forgiven
     the slaughter of his father in the Kurdish mountains.
But he loves you,
because you also won't forgive   30
     those who blackened the name of the Turkish people.
The tuberculars of the neighborhood and the bedridden
     look out from behind the glass.
The washwoman Huriye's unemployed son,
      weighed down by his sadness,   35
      goes off to the coffeehouse.
Rahmi Bey's radio is giving the news:
in a country in the Far East,
moon-faced yellow people
     are fighting a white dragon.   40
Of your people,
     four thousand five hundred Mehmets
      have been sent there to murder their brothers.
You blush
     with rage and shame   45
and not in general either —
   this impotent grief
   is all yours.

It's as if they'd knocked your wife down from behind and killed
  her child,
or as if you were back in jail   50
and they were making the peasant guards
           beat the peasants again.

All of a sudden it's night.
The evening walk is over.
A police jeep turned into your street,   55
your wife whispered:
   "To our house?"

          Translated from the Turkish by
          Randy Blasing and Mutlu Konuk

SOUTH ASIA

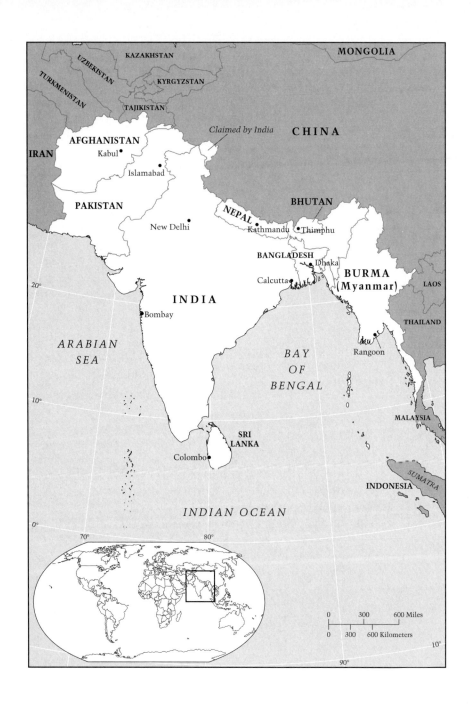

SOUTH ASIA

Many twentieth-century South Asian writers use home and family to develop the primary settings for their stories and poems. In a short story called "Purvai — The Easterly Wind," for example, the emigré Pakistani writer Zamiruddin Ahmad gives us a vivid picture of a nuclear family (a woman, her husband, and their young son) at home in a modern urban environment. In his relatively long poem entitled "Small-Scale Reflections on a Great House," the multilingual Indian writer A. K. Ramanujan evokes the daily life and the larger life cycle of an extended family over several generations. Ahmad's story and Ramanujan's poem differ from each other, because the former is about a Muslim family in a small home that is apparently isolated from the outside world, whereas the latter is about a large Hindu household that is open on every side, so that nothing really stays out.

Despite their cultural differences, however, Ahmad's story and Ramanujan's poem share a vital feature: both works use home, house, family life, and familial relations as metaphors for society as a whole. Ahmad's realistic narrative is not just a representation of a particular modern Muslim woman in an unusual family situation, but a candid portrait of contemporary middle-class Islamic society in Pakistan, India, Bangladesh, and elsewhere. Correspondingly, Ramanujan's allegory is not just about a particular extended family in southern India, but about a large part of modern Indian society in its entirety. By using home and family as metaphors for the outside world, such writers compress a great deal of cultural information, historical context, and social commentary into a compact text. But in order to understand how such metaphors work, we need to acquaint ourselves with South Asian society, history, politics, and culture on a more factual and critical level, as follows.

DIVERSITY AND UNITY

The region called South Asia consists at present of seven sovereign nations: Pakistan, Afghanistan, India, Nepal, Bhutan, Bangladesh, and Sri Lanka. As the accompanying map shows, this region is bounded to the west by Iran and the Arabian Sea; to the north by the former U.S.S.R. and

China, the latter now including Tibet; to the east by Myanmar (formerly Burma) and the Bay of Bengal; and to the south by the Indian Ocean. The British, who ruled a large part of the region directly or indirectly as a European colonial power from about 1757 onward, divided it into separate nations when they left in 1947. At that time, Afghanistan, India, Nepal, Bhutan, and Sri Lanka appeared on the political map more or less as they appear today. But what are now Pakistan and Bangladesh then constituted West Pakistan and East Pakistan, respectively, and were the two unequal halves of a single nation, separated by more than one thousand miles. Sikkim formed a tiny independent kingdom situated between Nepal and Bhutan. In 1971, with India's help, East Pakistan broke away from West Pakistan to establish itself as the independent nation of Bangladesh, and in the 1980s India annexed Sikkim for strategic military reasons.

The division and redivision of South Asia into various modern nations since World War II is only the most recent phase in a long and complicated process of state formation in the region. In fact, for a long time before the middle of the twentieth century, the region as a whole was called "Indos," "Hind," or "Hindustan," words that are best translated by the phrase "the Indian subcontinent." Taken as a unit, the subcontinent has a continuous cultural history, recorded in numerous written and orally transmitted texts, material artifacts, and architectural monuments, among other forms of evidence, stretching back more than three thousand years. During the past three millennia, the subcontinent has been the site of a great number and variety of small and large political entities. These range from dozens of ancient local republics around 500 B.C., to hundreds of modern princely states between about A.D. 1750 and 1950; from an ancient Buddhist empire around 250 B.C. and a classical Hindu empire between roughly A.D. 400 and 600, to a powerful Islamic empire between 1526 and 1707 and a comparable British empire between 1757 and 1947.

Despite the fluctuations in political organization over thirty centuries or more, the subcontinent has managed to sustain several kinds of linkages among its parts. One is the network of interacting and evolving languages from two major language families, among others, which has survived the countless upheavals of South Asian history. Another is the ongoing series of relationships among various racial and ethnic populations on the subcontinent, including numerous immigrants from outside the region, who have coexisted separately or adapted and intermingled gradually in spite of sharp, even violent, mutual differences. A third is the web of connections arising from shared as well as distinct but interdependent historical circumstances, such as imperial rule or colonization, that brings together the different languages and peoples of the subcontinent. These and other such continuities make South Asia a single, though internally diverse, cultural region with permeable boundaries between its parts, rather than a cluster of separate nations with hard walls between them, as it may seem to be on a contemporary map.

HISTORY AND SOCIETY

In the contexts of literature and culture, the history of South Asia can be split into three broad, overlapping periods. The ancient period lasted from around 1200 B.C. to A.D. 1200; the middle period, which began at different times in different language communities throughout the subcontinent, stretched from approximately A.D. 800 to 1800; and the modern period, which also began at different points in different places and cultures across the region, ran from about 1750 to the present.

Religion, cosmology, and worldview have played decisive roles in the histories of South Asia. The ancient period began around 1200 B.C. with the emergence of a worldview that later became what we now call Hinduism, the religion of the Hindus. As the story by Mahasweta Devi and the poems by A. K. Ramanujan, Gagan Gill, and Indira Sant below indicate, Hindu beliefs and practices still shape a large portion of Indian society today. Around 600 B.C., two other major religions, Jainism and Buddhism, appeared in the western and eastern parts of the subcontinent. Both these religions seriously questioned and rejected many of the philosophical, theological, and ritual bases of early Hinduism. Whereas Buddhism was almost completely driven out of India (to Sri Lanka, Tibet, Southeast Asia, and East Asia) within several hundred years of its initial formation, Jainism has remained on the subcontinent down to the present time, integrated deeply in Hindu literature, art, philosophy, religious practice, and society.

In what are now Pakistan, Afghanistan, and northern India, the so-called middle period of South Asian cultural history began at around the time Muslim invaders first entered or settled in the region in the eighth through twelfth centuries, bringing the religion of Islam with them. Throughout the present millennium, Muslim and Hindu societies on the subcontinent have been locked in a series of interdependences, as well as in ongoing, often violent conflicts. The differences between the two societies range from those concerning religious beliefs and practices to those regarding social organization and everyday customs and manners. Islam, for instance, promotes universal brotherhood, monotheism, iconoclasm, circumcision, and *purdah* (secluding women from public view), whereas Hinduism supports a caste hierarchy, untouchability, polytheism, and the worship of idols. The polarization of Islam and Hinduism was modified late in the middle period, when Christianity arrived on a significant scale on the subcontinent, with Portuguese, Dutch, English, and French missionaries in the sixteenth century. Around the same time, Sikhism appeared as another important indigenous religion in north India, including parts of present-day Pakistan. It rejected both Hinduism and Islam, yet combined key elements from the two in its syncretistic doctrine, so that it brought together, for example, the iconoclasm of Islam and the deification of the *guru*, or spiritual master, found in Hinduism.

The religious, political, and social developments of the ancient and middle periods described above have had decisive effects on modern South Asia. Hinduism is now the religion of the majority of the populations in India and Nepal; Buddhism, of the majority in Sri Lanka; and Islam, of the majority in Pakistan, Afghanistan, and Bangladesh. Also, Christianity and Sikhism are the faiths of sizable minority communities in present-day India. In the first half of the twentieth century, the old unresolvable differences of belief and practice between Hindus and Muslims created a massive rift within the national freedom movement directed against British rule. The ideological divide led to the partition of the subcontinent in 1947, and the establishment of East Pakistan and West Pakistan as a physically divided but ideologically and politically unified Muslim state and India as a secular state with a Hindu majority and a Muslim minority. Partition also resulted in the large-scale, mostly panic-stricken migrations of Muslims to Pakistan and Hindus to India across the new borders, and led to violence, especially over property, which resulted in the deaths of about three million people attempting to resettle during those months. As shown in poems like Shrikant Verma's "Process of Change" and Dhoomil's "A City, Evening, and an Old Man: Me," Hindu-Muslim conflicts continue into the present.

In the postcolonial period, Pakistani, Afghan, and Bangladeshi national politics and international relations have been shaped largely by Islamic issues, and all three of these nations are strongly aligned today with the Islamic nations of the Middle East. In contrast, local and national politics in the Hindu segments of contemporary India has been dominated by Hindu institutions of caste and traditional Hindu views of law, administration, social hierarchy, and power. Within India, in specific local and national contexts, this has resulted in violence between Hindus and Muslims (as in Ayodhya, Kashmir, and Bombay in the early 1990s), as well as between Hindus and Sikhs (in Punjab, since the early 1980s). Internationally, it has fueled two major wars between India and Pakistan, in 1965 and 1971, as well as ongoing tension between the two nations (such as the "liberation" of Kashmir, a state in north India with a majority Muslim population). In Sri Lanka, since the late 1970s, similar conflicts between Tamil settlers (a Hindu minority) in the northern parts of the island and Sinhala inhabitants in the south (a Buddhist majority) have snowballed into guerrilla warfare and civil war with international ramifications.

LANGUAGES

The complications in contemporary South Asian societies arising from religious, national, and ethnic differences are intensified by the presence of a large number of languages, literatures, and cultures. In general, the indigenous languages are associated with particular subnational regions, specific populations or communities, and fairly well-defined historical situations. In the ancient period (that is before about A.D. 1200), South Asian literatures were composed mainly in varieties of Sanskrit, in Pali and classical Tamil, and in groups of lesser languages called the Prakrits and the Apabhramshas. Sanskrit was predominantly the language of Hindu society; Buddhist hybrid-Sanskrit and Pali were the languages of Buddhist culture; whereas the Prakrits and the Apabhramshas were used by the Jain and Hindu communities. All of the above languages were used mainly across northern India during the first half of the ancient period. Around the beginning of the common era, classical Tamil appeared as a literary language in the southernmost part of the peninsula, but until about A.D. 600 it remained outside the influence of Hinduism; in the next two or three centuries, Tamil culture began to enter the Hindu religious world, and the language itself was affected by classical Sanskrit. This transition toward the end of the ancient period, however, took place across radical differences between two distinct language families. Tamil belongs to the Dravidian language family, the fourth largest in the world, with twenty-five languages, whereas Sanskrit, Pali, and the Prakrits and the Apabhramshas belong to the Indo-European language family (Sanskrit therefore bears a strong resemblence to Greek and Latin, but classical Tamil does not).

Toward the end of the ancient period and the beginning of the middle period, the old Indo-Aryan languages mentioned above began to give way to new vernacular and regional languages all over South Asia. Early in the present millennium, literary and discursive texts began to be composed in Maithili, Hindawi, Rajasthani, and Marathi; by about A.D. 1500, orally transmitted and written literatures had emerged in Bengali and Oriya in the east; Hindi, Urdu, Punjabi, and Kashmiri across the north; and Gujarati and Marathi in the west. In the south, four Dravidian languages — Tamil, Kannada, Telugu, and Malayalam — had developed new local, vernacular literatures. With the exception of Hindi and Urdu, all these languages were used for literary purposes in predominantly Hindu communities (Hindi and Urdu were split more evenly between Hindu and Muslim writers). Meanwhile, by the middle of the present millennium, Islam had complicated this literary map by introducing three older "foreign" languages into South Asia: Arabic and Persian, and, to a much lesser extent, Turkish. Since Arabic and Persian were used variously for religious, administrative, educational, and literary purposes under Muslim state patronage, they began to permanently influence not only Hindi and Urdu, but also languages like Bengali, Gujarati, Marathi, and Punjabi. By the end of the eighteenth century, most of the South Asian languages had acquired Persianized and Arabicized vocabularies, especially for bureacratic, legal, and commercial purposes.

Soon after 1750, when the British started to militarily, diplomatically, and commercially colonize different parts of India (particularly around

Calcutta, Bombay, and Madras), the East India Company as well as Christian missions and private enterprises introduced English into South Asia. With the creation of an English-language press and an English-medium education system, English began to interact regularly with not only Sanskrit and Persian, the classical languages of Hindu and Muslim learning, respectively, but also with the regional languages: Bengali in Bengal, Hindi and Urdu across the north, Marathi in the Bombay Presidency, and Tamil in the Madras Presidency. After the middle of the nineteenth century, English influenced the lexicon, grammar, syntax, styles, textual forms, and literary genres of each modern Indian language; it provided concrete models for writers attempting to "modernize" their Indian-language literatures; and it participated in the shaping of distinctly modern "hybrid" Indian minds, sensibilities, and cultures. The modern Indian languages originated in ancient Sanskrit, Prakrits, Apabhramshas, and Tamil (among other sources), and developed under the shadow of Arabic and Persian, but they became recognizably modern primarily because of the linguistic, literary, and cultural effects of English.

The modern Indian literary works we read in translation at the end of the twentieth century come out of this tangle of languages, societies, religions, and histories. The stories and poems reproduced here come from ten different South Asian literary languages (including English), and translation may make them seem more homogeneous than they are in the original mediums. As suggested in the stories by Zamiruddin Ahmad, Anita Desai, and C. S. Lakshmi and the poems by Nissim Ezekiel, Vinda Karandikar, and G. Shankara Kurup, the cultural milieus and assumptions of people who speak different languages can be rather different.

POSTCOLONIAL POETRY

The major modern South Asian literary languages have poetic traditions going back continuously to the early or middle centuries of the present millennium. Since they either originated in Sanskrit and the Dravidian language family, or have been influenced since the middle period by one or more classical Indian languages, their poetic traditions and histories are linked also to the poetry and poetics of the ancient period. Thus, modern verse in Marathi, an Indo-Aryan language, is related to poetic practices that started in western India around the twelfth century, as well as to precedents and models in classical Sanskrit. In the case of Tamil, modern poetry is continuous, despite many historical changes and mediations, with a classical period in the language nearly 2,000 years ago.

Against such a background, modern poetry emerged in the indigenous languages of the subcontinent between the mid-nineteenth and early twentieth centuries strongly affected by specific historical conditions. Toward the end of the eighteenth century and at the beginning of the nineteenth, British scholars and administrators, working together with

South Asian scholars and collaborators, started a process of standardizing the languages by creating modern dictionaries, grammars, and textbooks. A little later, in the course of modernizing education on the subcontinent, the British introduced the English language and its literature into school, college, and university curricula. These two kinds of innovation gave modern Indian writers newly reconstituted linguistic media to write in and new literary models to learn from and imitate. As a result, by the second half of the nineteenth century, English and European poetic genres, verse forms, conventions of metrical composition, and subjects had become an essential part of the native South Asian poets' imaginative resources. Western models provided new ways of composing lines, rhymes, and stanzas; unprecedented forms, ranging from the sonnet, the romantic lyric, and the long contemplative poem, to the Miltonic epic and the Tennysonian elegy; and novel themes, such as the poet's autobiography, nature, the industrial world, economic exploitation, and alienation. In addition, the changes in the linguistic and literary environment introduced by British colonial rule provoked South Asian poets to reexamine, retrieve, and revitalize their indigenous pasts in fresh ways. Many poets between about 1850 and 1950 thus adapted the rules of classical Sanskrit prosody for composition in the modern Indian languages, revived or modified ancient and middle-period South Asian verse forms and genres for present use, and productively tested traditional Indian themes and modern Western subjects and attitudes against each other.

During the last one hundred years of British rule, South Asian poetry evolved through several distinct phases and movements. Between about 1860 and 1910, many poets in languages like Bengali, Hindi, and Marathi worked in two concurrent, interacting movements, one aimed at a revival of classical Indian (specifically Hindu) culture, and the other at a long-term reform of Indian social institutions and cultural values in order to achieve emancipation of one kind or another. Between about 1910 and 1950, the majority of popular poets in languages ranging from Assamese and Gujarati to Malayalam and Urdu was involved in the nationalist movement, which used a variety of means to dislodge British colonial power from South Asia. The revivalist and reformist poets of the late nineteenth century and the nationalist poets of the early twentieth century also participated in other movements, some influenced by the English and European romantic poets and others by the Anglo-American modernists. After about 1935, the latter group proved to be particularly important for subsequent South Asian poetry as a whole, since it produced two subcontinentwide poetic movements: experimentalism, broadly modernist and avant-garde in its orientation, and progressivism, generally committed to a socialist, Marxist, or communist criticism and reconstruction of modern South Asian society. Immediately after decolonization, these two radical movements merged in different languages to produce the "new poetry" of the postcolonial decades. Different degrees of poetic experimentalism and political progressivism are noticeable, for example, in Kunwar Narayan's "Preparations of War," M. Gopalakrishna Adiga's "Do Something, Brother," and Yasmine Gooneratne's "Menika."

Since about 1960, the new poetry of the subcontinental languages, together with South Asian poetry written originally in English, has been associated with a range of specific themes, innovations, and issues. One issue, for example, has been that of Indianness, or national and cultural identity, in the context of westernization and internationalism. In general, several Indian-English poets, like poets in English from Pakistan and Sri Lanka, have been concerned strongly with discovering or constructing a national or local identity for themselves. A poet like Ezekiel does this by identifying himself with the contemporary city of Bombay, as in "Minority Poem," and with certain features of urban India and its historical contexts, as in "In India." A poet like Ramanujan accomplishes something similar by exploring extensively the worlds of south Indian and Dravidian domesticity, family, and kinship, together with Indian immigrant or diasporic experience, as in "Small-Scale Reflections on a Great House" and "Love Poem for a Wife 1." Poets in the indigenous languages, such as Hindi, Marathi, and Kannada, also discover and articulate such connections with local and national cultures, but their access to self, society, and tradition may be different from that of the poets writing in English. In "The Master Carpenter," a poem written in Malayalam, for example, Shankara Kurup uses local history, myth, and legend to construct a detailed and distinctive account of cultural identity that may not be available poetically to a writer like Ezekiel.

A second important network of issues centers around history and politics. A large number of poets working in the experimental and progressive traditions of modern South Asian writing attempt to critically reexamine the histories of the region, to demystify historical and social processes, and to satirize and thereby change inherited social codes, customs, and institutions. In Hindi, which possesses a highly developed tradition of political verse, Narayan ("Preparations of War") reconfigures the violence that underlies South Asian political history, Verma ("Process of Change") critically dramatizes Hindu-Muslim relations, and Dhoomil ("The City, Evening, and an Old Man: Me") depicts the failures of liberal democracy and points to the effects of alienation on citizenship in modern Indian society. In Marathi, Karandikar ("The Knot") reveals the conflict-ridden nature of modern urban India, whereas in Kannada, Adiga ("Do Something, Brother") employs modernist verse satire to question, dismantle, and reframe contemporary attitudes toward modernity, modernization, and the natural environment.

A third set of issues in recent South Asian poetry, particularly targeted by feminists, has been the situation of women in society, especially in relation to men and male power, the structure of home and family, widowhood, female desire, and the functions of motherhood. Sant ("Household

Fires," "Her Dream"), writing in Marathi, gives us powerful insights into the subjection and powerlessness of housewives in urban Hindu households, as well as the painful experience of widowhood in traditional and modern Indian society, where social prejudices still force widows not to remarry. In contrast, Gagan Gill ("A Desire in Her Bangles"), a younger woman poet writing in Hindi, uses the confessional mode and widowhood as a metaphor to dramatize a modern Indian woman's anguish in an undissolvable marriage to a faithless and insensitive man. In further contrast, Amrita Pritam ("The Process of Creation"), the most important contemporary writer in the Punjabi language, conflates the act of creating poetry, sexual desire and fantasy, and the fear of violation as well as of motherhood and miscarriage, to allegorize a variety of contemporary women's situations. In each such grouping of issues, texts, and poets, we find a vital reexamination and critique of present-day South Asian society.

POSTCOLONIAL FICTION

In the course of the twentieth century, many of the major South Asian languages have each produced hundreds of competent fiction writers. To experience modern Bengali or Urdu fiction in all its variety and at its finest, for example, a reader would have to sample the work of fifty or sixty notable writers in the language. The difficulties of dealing with a large number of excellent writers and a wide range of styles are compounded by the variety of forms. Contemporary South Asian fiction is published in popular as well as literary forms ranging over the short story, the novella, the novel, and the novel-sequence. It appears in privately published small literary magazines, state-sponsored and institutional journals, regionally and nationally circulated periodicals, and in books published by small presses as well as by large publishing houses. Since there are many large communities of South Asian immigrants in different parts of the world now, popular and literary fiction in the various languages reaches a broad spectrum of readers both on and outside the subcontinent.

In the postcolonial period (since the late 1940s), South Asian fiction writers have produced work in a wide range of styles, some relatively old and others more experimental and new. The fiction of the post-1960 period therefore can be divided into several coexisting kinds, though in any given decade one or two of these may be more common than the rest. Of the important styles of fiction produced in South Asia today, four are especially widespread: social realism, psychological realism, fiction based on myth, and allegorical fiction (including magic realism).

To analyze the four basic styles of fiction, it is useful to distinguish generally between realistic writing and nonrealistic writing. Realism involves the attempt to represent things as they are in the world of actual, everyday experience. Nonrealistic writing employs narrative structures that do not merely imitate real life, but actively impose specific types of meaning on characters, actions, situations, and events (which in themselves can be interpreted in a number of ways). Any kind of writing actually imposes an order on its materials that is not inherent in them, but we can pragmatically differentiate between texts that seek to represent things as they are and those that emphasize the fact that the writer's imagination transforms its material. The latter kind of text may use narrative structures provided by myth or elaborately constructed allegories. Realistic fiction can take the shape of social realism or psychological realism, and social realism in turn can be subdivided into socialist realism and humanist realism. In any case, such distinctions can only be provisional, since complex works of fiction frequently combine a number of different styles, strategies, and techniques to produce their effects, and such a combination may well include realistic as well as nonrealistic representations, social realism as well as psychological realism, and myth as well as allegory.

In postcolonial South Asian fiction, social realism offers a narrative in which the author is concerned primarily with depicting, as accurately and comprehensively as possible, the actual social life of a group, class, community, nation, or people. Capturing particular settings in great detail, the writer conveys the local color of a particular village, region, or city, or of a certain community of characters in a specific social and natural environment, often with the help of empirical information. Some South Asian social realists use some version of the Marxist analysis of society and history, and offer a materialist diagnosis of life on the subcontinent that may be called socialist realism. A Bengali woman writer like Mahasweta Devi, for instance, uses a highly refined variety of socialist realism to expose the exploitation, domination, and patriarchal chauvinism at work in Indian and Hindu society, and to dramatize their horrifying consequences, as at the tragic end of the story "Breast-Giver." Similarly, a male writer in Kannada, such as P. Lankesh, employs the strategies of socialist realism in combination with other techniques — such as cinematic montage — to highlight class differences, class conflicts, and the consequences of poverty in contemporary southern Indian society.

Another branch of social realism might be called humanist realism, which is based on a liberal rather than a Marxist understanding of social and historical phenomena. Postcolonial humanist realism from the subcontinent tends to be middle-class fiction about the lives, experiences, and moral shortcomings of middle-class characters. In modern South Asia, the middle class is a relatively privileged and protected class, economically and psychologically alienated from the mass of lower-class and subaltern citizens as well as from the small upper class. The subcontinental middle class frequently sees itself, and is seen by others, as a parasitical, practically useless segment of society. Humanist social realism, which often mixes with psychological realism, often deals with middle-class life by constructing an ironic comedy of manners. An Indian-English woman writer like Anita Desai, for example, develops bittersweet tragicomedies of middle-class manners (as in "The Farewell Party"), and hence stands in sharp contrast to a practitioner of socialist realism like Mahasweta Devi, whose fictions are starker, more brutal, and more engaged with larger economic and political issues.

Psychological realism differs from the varieties of social realism described above because it emphasizes the exploration or dramatization of the mind of one or more characters, either because those characters are unique and therefore interesting individuals, or because they are social types, and hence representative of an entire class or group. In postcolonial South Asian fiction, psychological realism is rarely separated from social realism, because its characters are often caught in a complex web of social relations, even when they are alienated from the world around them. This is evident again in Desai's "The Farewell Party," for example, which combines a psychological exploration of the heroine as well as the hero, but only as their mental states and thought processes unfold in a humanistically represented middle-class social situation. The conjuncture of social and psychological realism is also manifest in an Urdu story from Pakistan, Zamiruddin Ahmad's "Purvai — The Easterly Wind," which with great precision examines the sensibilities of a contemporary Muslim housewife and her husband, who seem to be isolated from the society around them. The story makes its impact on a reader from the subcontinent precisely because the Muslim couple are part of an urban nuclear family, so different from the extended family typical of India, Pakistan, and Bangladesh, which still tends to repress and erase women's identities, desires, and fantasies.

In most examples of twentieth-century South Asian social and psychological realism, the plot structure of a story or a novel would be an open-ended slice of life, whether confined to so-called scenes from provincial life (as in the works of Shankar Lamichhane and P. Lankesh) or to urban and cosmopolitan life (as in the stories by Amrita Pritam and C. S. Lakshmi). A fiction that claims to represent a slice of real life begins and ends *in media res*, inviting the reader's hospitable imagination to construct for itself the "before" and the "after" of the story line. In what I have called humanist social realism, irony often provides a reversal and a discovery that generate narrative closure, despite the open-endedness of the depicted scenes. In socialist realism, a covert or explicit economic, historical, or political argument provides a beginning, a middle, and an end for the narrative, the end coming with a resolution of the contradictions in a character's actions or in a specific social situation.

In contrast to realistic writing, nonrealistic fiction in South Asia uses plot structures derived from a variety of sources independent of the materials of representation. As suggested earlier, two sources of story lines are especially common in the postcolonial period. In one instance, a writer may produce a story set in the modern world of the Indian subcontinent and may represent particular characters, situations, settings, or events with realistic immediacy and precision, but structure the narrative according to a preexisting *myth*, that is, a typical, often heroic story from a prehistorical, nonhistorical, or ahistorical past. Some South Asian fiction writers use classical Indian (mostly Hindu) or early Arabic and Persian (often Islamic) myths, invented in epics like the *Mahabharata* or in classics like *The Thousand and One Nights*. Other writers use myths found in South Asian folklore and oral traditions, which circulate archetypal stories that define or capture certain recurrent human attitudes, situations, or experiences. Shankara Kurup's "The Master Carpenter," though a poem rather than a work of prose fiction, employs an anti-Oedipal myth to shape its narrative in the mode of psychological realism.

In addition to employing myth, recent South Asian authors commonly choose allegory as a mode and a structural device. In the 1970s and 1980s especially, following developments in Latin America, Europe, and elsewhere, writers in languages like Urdu, Hindi, and Marathi have taken to combining allegorical narratives with fantastic, surreal, or marvelous material. In early postcolonial instances, such as Kahlida Asghar's story "The Wagon" from Pakistan, we find an allegory of modernization and urbanization that is skeptical of material progress and technological advancement. The city Asghar conjures up so phantasmagorically is Any City, at once unreal and terribly real, equally locatable in the first world as it is in the third world. It could be a story of some unimaginable natural disaster, but most likely it is a tale about something like a meltdown at a nuclear plant, like the one that occurred at Chernobyl in 1986, nearly twenty years after the story was written. In more recent stories like Enver Sajjad's "The Bird" and Naiyer Masud's "The Color of Nothingness," the allegorical mode moves much closer to magical realism, in which fantastic events occur under otherwise perfectly ordinary circumstances, such as a tourist's visit to a new city or a boy's interactions with various elders in the family and in the neighborhood while growing up.

CONNECTIONS AND DISCONTINUITIES

A close reading of the following stories and poems by twenty-two writers working in ten different languages will highlight several aspects of contemporary South Asian literature. The different national cultures, linguistic communities, and literary traditions on the subcontinent intermesh in a variety of ways, creating commonalities across the entire region while at the same time asserting their distinctive identities. Each South Asian language thus takes us into a different world, in which we find familiar elements as well as unexpected new ones. Within this network of connections and discontinuities, each language world seems to have specific literary tendencies. Hindi poetry, for example, often inclines toward political themes, whereas Marathi poetry tends to be more aesthetic. A high proportion of Indian-English fiction stands closer to liberal humanism, whereas a large amount of Bengali fiction is aligned with progressive left-wing politics. In spite of such differences, however, the various traditions within South Asian writing come together to make up a cultural whole that is recognizably distinct from that of the Caribbean, the Middle East, or East Asia.

Vinay Dharwadker

FOR FURTHER READING

Primary Works

Adiga, M. Gopalakrishna. *Song of the Earth and Other Poems*. Calcutta: Writers Workshop, 1974.

Desai, Anita. *Games at Twilight and Other Stories*. New York: Harper and Row, 1978.

Devi, Mahasweta. Six short stories in *Of Women, Outcastes, Peasants, and Rebels: A Selection of Bengali Short Stories*. Edited by Kalpana Bardhan. Berkeley: University Press of California, 1990.

Ezekiel, Nissim. *Collected Poems 1952–1988*. New Delhi: Oxford University Press, 1989.

Karandikar, Vinda. "Himayoga," in *The Penguin New Writing in India*. Edited by Aditya Behl and David Nicholls. New Delhi: Penguin, 1994.

Pritam, Amrita. "Two Poems," *World Literature Today*. Vol. 68, no. 2 (Spring 1994).

Ramanujan, A. K. *Collected Poems*. New Delhi: Oxford University Press, 1994.

Sant, Indira. *The Snake-skin and Other Poems*. Bombay: Nirmala Sadanand, 1975.

Secondary Works

Alter, Stephen, and Dissanayake, Wimal, eds. *The Penguin Book of Modern Indian Short Stories*. New Delhi: Penguin, 1989.

Dharwadker, Vinay. "Twenty-nine Modern Indian Poems," *TriQuarterly*. No. 77 (Winter 1990).

Dharwadker, Vinay, and Ramanujan, A. K., eds. *The Oxford Anthology of Modern Indian Poetry*. New Delhi: Oxford University Press, 1994.

Hutt, Michael James, ed. *Himalayan Voices: An Introduction to Modern Nepali Literature*. Berkeley: University Press of California, 1991.

Memon, Muhammad Umar, ed. *The Color of Nothingness: Modern Urdu Short Stories*. New Delhi: Penguin, 1991.

Tharu, Susie, and Lalita, K., eds. *Women Writing in India*, 2 vols. New York: Feminist Press at CUNY, 1993.

G. SHANKARA KURUP

G. Shankara Kurup (1901–1972) was born in the state of Kerala. Over the course of a writing career of more than fifty years, he became one of the principal innovators of modern poetry in the language of Malayalam. His poetry combined lyricism with narrative skill and a dramatic imagination and drew on the conventions of traditional Indian literature and poetics, Indian folk and oral traditions, and modern English and European writing.

"The Master Carpenter" reveals several facets of Kurup's sensibility. It is a relatively long narrative poem, which retells a folk story in a modern literary idiom. The story itself is dramatic, with fully developed characters interacting in a richly visualized setting and with the plot moving steadily toward a climax and a resolution. The story holds our interest because it focuses on a drama of character and a conflict of ideas and ideals that exceed the particularities of the plot. The poem, in fact, presents a striking contemporary version of the Indian anti-Oedipus. In the original Oedipus story, as told in classical Greek tragedy, Oedipus unknowingly kills his own father and marries his mother. In Kurup's poem, this structure is inverted in a provocative way.

The Master Carpenter

I feel a little better today.
But how long shall I lie
coiled here?
The marrow of my bones is gouged out and eaten.
I'm a mere ghost. I just breathe.   5

This is April!.
The jackfruit tree that shines
like slashed gold at the touch of a chisel,
and the honey-mango tree that always tempts the hand
to carve a toy boat from its trunk,   10
will be shaking now
with blossom, with fruit.

If only I could creep up to the window
and take a look at them!
There's not a plantain stump in my garden,   15
and my heart beats when I see a tree,
any tree, anywhere.

That single *champak* tree near the Uliyannur temple.°
O it's huge, it's so straight.
Nine men can't hug it with joined hands.   20
No bend, no crack, not a hole in it, not a hole.
I can measure it with my eyes:
it's more than eighty *kols*.°
If you cut it down, you can change the bamboo thatch
of every mother's son in the village.   25
Or else we could make rafters for houses
that would be the envy of chieftains.
But this stump's now rotten.
What's the use of wishing for things?
I can't even sink the edge of my chisel   30
into wood any more.

Nani, she sits on the doorstep,
her stomach caved in, bent double,
fumbling for bits and pieces of dry betel leaf,°
a chunk of betel nut, a stalk of tobacco.   35
Fire a cannon in her ear, she won't hear it.
She's an old crone now.
I remember the day she stood by my side,
straight as a *champak* tree in bloom,
a body fresh from under the chisel,   40
her smile a sparkle of new silver.

   The old eyes came out of the gray bush of the eyebrows,
   went out through the back door all eaten up by white ants
   and wandered there for a while.
   "If only I could get up, I could crawl.   45
   O the hand that could have held up an old man ..."
   The old carpenter shook with sobs.
   As if to wipe it all away, memory and all,
   his hand passed slowly over the furrows of his forehead.

If only I could somehow totter up to the workshop,   50
I could at least sit there,

Uliyannur temple: a Hindu place of worship
kol: a length measure used by Indian carpenters
betel leaf: an aromatic leaf chewed as a stimulant and narcotic

and taste the gladness
that only scale and chisel can bring.

That temple, like a huge inverted bowl
carved in black wood, shining under the sky —   55
it rose under these working hands.
With my chisel I put in his hands,
my child made that sacred eagle now there
on the flagmast of burnished brass,
and those wings that look as if they're moving.   60

They say I'm green with envy.
What father won't beam with pride
on hearing the praises of his son?
But then, you can stop the clappers of a thousand bells,
but you can't stop one wagging tongue.   65
We two made teakwood images
of the guardsmen of the eight directions,
and placed them on the twin towers:
one made with this hand, the other with his.
They said his image had more life than mine.   70
My son wins, but what does it matter
for a father to lose to his son?
Isn't his glory my glory too?

But look, they said, my face darkened
to hear the boy praised.   75
I may be a carpenter, but am I not also a father?
They said, the old man knows the carpentry and the craft,
but it's the son who has the sculptor's art.
Why should these village idiots gabble like this?
We sat near each other at work in the shop,   80
but there was silence between us.
Let them slight me and say what they will.
Can I, can I, his real father,
really wish for this dreadful end?
He may be clever, may even be a genius,   85
but he got it all from his father.
That old Nayar said, when I went to his house,
"When the moon arrives, the sun must fade."
Why did he have to say such things?

Once, for fun, I made a moving doll   90
and fixed it below the bridge.
At the first footfall the doll would dance like a water goddess;
when a man came to the middle of the bridge,
she would come up on the water inch by inch

and open her mouth and spit   95
at the unsuspecting man,
taking him completely by surprise.
There were milling crowds at the river to see this wonder.

Young sandalwood trees emit their fragrance
if they are chafed,   100
but, let me tell you,
my child proved his mettle again mine
without scorn or ill will.
In four days, another doll rose in his name
on the lips of the people everywhere.   105
When my doll came up to spit,
his doll would slowly turn and lift her hand;
and when mine opened her mouth to spit,
his would slap her smartly in the face.
I felt that slap.   110
Even in the sky there isn't room enough for two moons.
He left the house. Nani was in tears.
My heart burned inside me like a heap of paddy husk,°
but I held my tongue.

Then came the elephant *pandal*° for the temple.   115
Why on earth did I have to call
on this great son of mine for it?
My master said to me,
"Consult your son and make the pandal beautiful."
I felt like turning back at once.   120
But I didn't.
Consult! No one so far had said that to me.

It might look like envy.
But isn't a son's glory the father's?
Though the carpenter may work with wood,   125
he himself isn't wood.
The pandal came up well.
As you know, a pandal needs artistic work on the facade.
He said, "I'll look after that, if you wish,
and my father can work on putting up the gables."   130
Does he, my son, have to tell me,
his father, to put up the gables?
Do I need his nod for this?

---

paddy husk: a husk of rice grain, usually burned as waste after threshing
elephant pandal: a large tent with the effigy of an elephant mounted on it, used for a
   public festival at a temple

His hands were working
on Goddess Lakshmi's lotus,°   135
carving sandalwood.
And I was shaping a wooden rivet
with the broad chisel,
its blade glittering in the sun
like the edge of a sword.   140
And then, unawares,
unawares it slipped out of my hand,
that chisel!

I began to pray at once
and begged of God that it shouldn't fall on my son.   145

In the flick of an eyelash
I saw my son reeling to the ground,
head almost severed from body.
People gathered around.
Eyes, like long sharp needles, looked at me.   150
How could I find my feet on the ladder?
I somehow plunged to the ground.
It seems my son then said, "Forgive me."
I didn't hear the words.
Curly hair gummed to the neck with blood,   155
in blood he lay.
Those staring eyes
that had swallowed all pain, that sight
is always with me, it doesn't leave me.

And no one has seen Nani smile since then.   160
Scalding tears flowed from her eyes
till they could flow no more.
Who will believe that it was a slip of the hand?
Whatever one might say, who will ever believe it?

O Nani, you don't believe it, do you,   165
will a father ever do this?
My son would now have been the staff of my life,
if only it hadn't happened.
"Happened? Made to happen!"
a little voice says inside me,   170
correcting me again and again.
Can a father do it?
Something hammers away at my heart with a mallet,

Goddess Lakshmi's lotus: in Indian temple sculpture, the lotus on which the Goddess
    Lakshmi rests her feet

something tries to pull out that nail
hammered in so deep.   175

   Nani broke the old man's chain of memories
as she pounded away at her little hand mill
of betel leaf and betel nut,
"It's some time since those cobwebs
were swept from the ceiling.   180
Did something fall into your eyes?
Why're they watering?"

Translated from the Malayalam by
K. M. George and A. K. Ramanujan

INDIRA SANT

Indira Sant (1914–) was born in Pune in the state of Maharashtra. In the mid-1930s she married N. M. Sant, also a young poet, who left her a widow at a young age. For the next three decades Indira Sant supported herself and her children by working full-time as a teacher in Belgaum. During this period she wrote fiction for children as well as nearly five hundred poems.

*   Shortly after Indian Independence in 1947, Sant became famous for the emotional intensity of her short, lyrical poems. In the next three decades, she emerged as a feminist poet who spoke powerfully on behalf of middle- and lower-class women in contemporary Maharashtrian society. Her treatment of the psychological and social condition of Indian women is evident in both "Her Dream" and "Household Fires." The first of these poems is autobiographical and quasi-confessional. It represents the frame of mind of a widow who dreams of happiness but knows, at the same time, that such happiness is merely a dream — in traditional Hindu society widows cannot remarry and therefore cannot share in even the simple benefits and pleasures of family life. The second poem juxtaposes the situations of different members of a modern nuclear family in India (husband/father, daughters, sons), as seen by the woman (wife/mother) who takes care of them constantly. The poem reveals the subjection in which Indian housewives continue to live.*

Her Dream

Her dream, like the dream of a dozen other women.
A full plate, deliciously full.
Places to go, things to do, morning and evening.
Neatly ironed clothes. A nicely furnished home.
Sometimes a play, sometimes a concert — with the best seats.   5
All the happiness in the world on a meager income.
Laughter and teasing. Talk and chatter.
Her dream, like the dream of a dozen other women.

But she woke up before the dream began.
And then she never fell asleep again.   10

Translated from the Marathi
by Vinay Dharwadker

Household Fires

The daughter's job: without a murmur
to do the chores piling up around the house
until she leaves for work,
to pay her younger brother's fees,
to buy her sister ribbons,   5
to get her father's spectacles changed.
To take the others to the movies on holidays,
to keep back a little and hand over the rest
on payday.

The son's job: fresh savory snacks   10
for the whole household to eat:
to bring back the clothes from the washerman,
to clean and put away the bicycle,
to sing out of key while packing his father's lunch
at the stroke of the hour,   15
to open the door sulkily
whenever someone comes home from the movies,
to wrinkle his brow
when he puts out his hand for money
and is asked instead, "How much? For what?"   20

The younger daughter's job:
to savor the joys of shyness,
to shrink back minute by minute.
The younger son's job:

to choke all the while, grow up slowly
in states of wet and dry.   25

Four children learning in her fold,
her body drained by hardship,
what's left of her? A mass of tatters,
five tongues of flame   30
licking and licking at her on every side,
fanning and fanning the fire in her eyes
till her mind boils over,
gets burned.

*Translated from the Marathi
by Vinay Dharwadker*

M. GOPALAKRISHNA ADIGA

*Gopalakrishna Adiga (1918–1992) taught English literature in Mysore
and Udipi, and served as the principal of Lal Bahadur College, Sagar.
He was the editor of* Sakshi, *a literary magazine that started in 1967,
and also a translator of Henrik Ibsen and Walt Whitman into the
language of Kannada. Shortly before his death in 1992, he received the
Kabir Samman, one of the highest forms of recognition for poets in India.*

*Adiga's early verse — from the 1940s — was metrical and conven-
tional, but by the following decade he had begun to experiment vigorously with theme as well as form. His mature poetry is often dense and
verbally innovative, and may seem difficult in the modernist way (that
is, complex, obscure, reticent, and impersonal). He usually compresses
several themes into a single poem, developing them with suggestion,
allusion, or oblique reference, rather than direct statement. Among his
recurrent themes are the ambiguous presence of the past in contemporary times and the troubled relationships among nature, human culture, and the modern world. "Do Something, Brother" is a poem in this
group, and is intended as a satire on human restlessness, incessant
(and often mindless) activity, and unwitting destruction.*

Do Something, Brother

Do something, brother:
keep doing something, anything;
you mustn't be idle.

Pull out this plant, nip this little leaf,
crush that flower.   5
There's grass,
run a burning brand through it,
burn it like Lanka.°
Tiny butterflies, parrots, sparrows —
chase them, catch them,   10
pluck their wings,
pull out their fur and feather.
There, in the garden,
jasmine and the banana's gold
grow for the wild elephant's feet.   15
All over the walls
virility's master switches
itch for your fingers;
close your eyes
and pull down twenty of them.   20
Earth, water, the skies,
they're all your geese with golden eggs:
gouge them out, slash them.
"Do, or die," they say.
Disasters are the test   25
for your genius's galloping dance:
something must crash every minute.
Brother, act, act at once, do something.
Thought's weights and measures
are all for the past,   30
for the undying ghostly treasures of the dead.

There's the forest,
cut it clean to the stump,
slit it for your buntings.
You have the axe, the sickle,   35
the saw, and the knife;
go, harvest all the world
with a flourish of your hand.
But you meet
winter mists, walls of fog,   40
walls that line the space between face and face,
and the road that sighs and breaks in two
under your eyes,
a couple of mountain peaks that rear their hoods

Lanka: in the ancient Indian epic *Ramayana,* the city ruled by a demon king and set on
fire by a monkey-warrior fighting for the hero

and lower upon your head, 45
or lightning winks from sirens
that sing in every tree:
do they plunge you into anxieties
and dilemmas of reason?
No, no, this won't do. 50
You're a simple man, and that's your strength.
Horse sense and the blinkers
are your forte.

Eat what comes to hand; crush what you touch;
cut the hindering vines. 55
Mother Earth herself, though tired,
lies open to the skies;
there's still flesh on her bone,
marrow for your hunger.
Come, come, brother, 60
never forget that you're a man!

Then there's the Well of Life.°
Rope the wheel and axle,
pull out all the water.
Reach the last dryness of the rock; 65
grope, grope with the grappling iron.
"V for Victory," brother.
Break down the atom,
reach for the ultimate world within.
Find God's own arrow 70
and aim it straight at the heart
of God's own embryo world.
Do something, brother,
do anything.
Idle men 75
are burdens on the land.
Do something, brother.
Keep doing something all the time
to lighten Mother Earth's loads.
This is right, This is natural. 80
This is the one thing needful.

Translated from the Kannada
by A. K. Ramanujan

Well of Life: a satirical symbol of human life taking place inside a well, in darkness and
in isolation from the environment

VINDA KARANDIKAR

Vinda Karandikar (1918–) was born in a village in Ratnagiri District, in the southwestern coastal region of Maharashtra. He was educated at Rajaram College, Kolhapur, and at the University of Bombay, receiving an M.A. in English in 1946. He taught literature for more than thirty years in Bombay. He has published more than twenty books, among which are collections of poems, children's verse, and essays and criticism, as well as translations into the language of Marathi of Aristotle's Poetics, *Goethe's* Faust *(Part One), and Shakespeare's* King Lear.*

Karandikar's poetry is rigorously intellectual and deftly brings together a left-wing political perspective on social and economic issues and a humanistic perspective on literary forms, poetic traditions, and the social functions of writing. Much of his output is at once philosophical and satirical and attempts to bring complicated historical and political issues into the arena of public debate and popular culture in contemporary India. "Traitor" is a satire that attacks the kind of patriotism and slavish cultural nationalism that became commonplace in the Indian urban middle class between the 1920s and the 1950s. "The Knot," a longer poem written from an existentialist viewpoint, gives us an anatomy of romantic indecisiveness, which leads to failure in practical and political action as well as in love.

Traitor

A crazy man who lives in one of Bombay's narrow lanes
Says that even if you pour blood enough to fill the Indian Ocean
On a mound of soil as big as the Himalayas, it won't sprout a
    fistful of green grass.
When the dogs in the neighborhood bark in a fight, he trembles
    with a nameless fear
And goes in to relieve himself. Don't call him crazy, call him a
    coward.   5
In the morning he eagerly drinks up the dose of fire offered by
    the newspapers,
And runs his fingers through his children's hair to make amends.
Having read the *Bhagavad-gita°* he warns himself, "Don't you
    ever
Touch a weapon." When he opens his umbrella in the street, he
    remembers

Bhagavad-gita: an ancient Indian philosophical and religious poem that explains human action in the context of war

The mushrooming umbrella of a nuclear explosion — an
    umbrella of dogs around him —   10
And puts his hand on the shoulder of any passerby to steady
    himself.
And when he hears the battle songs in khaki uniform, he weeps
    like a eunuch.
Don't call him a eunuch, call him a traitor.
He chews on the betelnut° of his unchanging destiny with his
    rotten molars,
And mutters even when he's wide awake, "I still want to live,
To see Picasso's dove° flying through the cloudless sky."

Translated from the Marathi
by Vinay Dharwadker

The Knot

        Balancing
its weight on the horizon's balustrade
for a moment, the leukemic evening
disappeared into the hospital in the west.
        The fronds   5
of the coconut palm behind the public bench
were shivering at the wind's touch.
        She said,
"Eight years ago the green fronds
of this tree used to brush against our backs.   10
You remember, don't you?"
        He remembered
how he'd started when the fronds had touched
his back while he was kissing her passionately,
how suddenly a fear had shaken him —   15
like the abominable snowman wandering
on the edge of the mind's precipice —
        "Yes, I remember,"
he said — "Have you noticed how many
coconuts there are on this small palm?"   20
        He didn't realize it,
but his words touched her sense of inadequacy
without meaning to. She drew the end

betelnut: the hard nut of the betel plant, chewed as a stimulant and narcotic
Picasso's dove: the dove of peace designed by Pablo Picasso for the United Nations
    shortly after World War II

of her sari° around herself and hugged
the plastic purse close to her flat chest.   25
            "Can I ask you something?"
she said — "How long are we going
to keep meeting each other like this?"
He fidgeted with the finger he was holding
in Sartre's *God and Satan*° to mark a page   30
and muttered, "Who knows?"
A little troubled, confused, crestfallen.
            Irritated,
she said, "You! You ought to know!"
The certainty with which he had known things   35
eight years ago had dissolved
in the cesspool of his circumstances.
He remembered the great critique of the War°
he'd composed; the expectations
he'd built up; the castles he'd built   40
on the future's mist — now all crumbling.
      A parade celebrating the fourth
      anniversary of the end of the War
      was passing down the street in front of them,
      cheering the reign of peace in its voice of steel.   45
            Just then
he was struck by an earlier memory —
another girl — another ruptured moment —
those days, premature, twisted out of shape,
running around in circles round the fire.   50
Their endless wealth of anguish,
now lost. "No! Impossible!" he said to himself,
laughing at his own dead self.
"I couldn't have done it! But if I had —
if I had — if only I were man enough!"   55
He muttered, "What's bound to happen, happens."
The late April sun had beaded
the two furrows on his brow with sweat.
            "You know,"
she said, "you ought to know,"   60
in a provocative tone. (In other words,
a tone of voice she'd learnt by heart
while going around with Eknath Samant.

sari: a traditional garment worn by Indian women
Sartre's *God and Satan*: an existential play on the biblical theme of good and evil by
    French writer Jean-Paul Sartre
the War: World War II

— If Eknath hadn't won himself
a permanent commission — then maybe —   65
but why — the lousy bastard!)
                    "You know,"
she said, "you know. It seems you've forgotten —
'When the War has ended,' you'd said."
                    "Yes, I'd said it.   70
When my health has improved a little,
when my life has become stable."
                    Playing with her buttons,
she pretended that she wasn't angry,
and muttered something inaudible.   75
She was really very tired; very weary;
that's why it wasn't going to do her any good
to be so impatient now.
            Now there were workers
            marching towards a factory   80
            shouting, "Long live the Revolution!"
            and demanding two months' extra pay as a bonus.
                    She spluttered,
"Tell me once and for all —
when will your great war end?"   85
                    He said,
"Who knows, who knows" —
"Go ask that madman there,"
she said with amazing sarcasm.
— Across the street a local idiot   90
was walking around with rags
bundled up on his head, looking for more.
                    He thought,
we're both trapped in a huge wheel —
we're stuck in it — and it's hurtling down   95
the steep slope of time,
without direction, without will —
in that great headlong plunge of destiny
he saw the freedom of his own desire,
like a whirlpool — the desire to know,   100
not to live; to choose, not to act.
                    In that moment of clarity
he drew the retrenchment notice°
from his plastic wallet — he'd received it
earlier that day — and placed the piece of paper,   105
this paper sob, in her hand — the hand

retrenchment notice: a letter indicating termination of employment

with which she was playing with a button.
   That day
she went away with the resolve
never to come back again. In her heart,   110
she drew strength from her shattered hopes;
when she saw the future's skeleton,
her fear of uncertainty melted away.
That day for the first time she found
strength in loneliness. She found the courage   115
that comes from hopelessness.
   And he too
found a little unexpected satisfaction
when she turned her back to him —
for the first time in eight years   120
he saw in her braided hair
the knot of a braid of artificial hair.

Translated from the Marathi
by Vinay Dharwadker

Amrita Pritam

Amrita Pritam (1919–) was born in Gujranwala, which is now in Pakistan. Her mother, a school teacher, died when Pritam was eleven years old. Pritam started writing early and published her first book of poems when she was sixteen. At that age she also married Gurbaksh Singh, to whom she had been engaged at age four, and with whom subsequently she had two children. This marriage, however, ended in divorce in 1960. Since 1947 Pritam has lived in New Delhi. She was the first woman writer to win the annual award given by the Sahitya Akademi, India's national academy of letters, which she received for her poetry in 1956. She has published more than seventy books in Punjabi.

In her prose as well as verse, Pritam is frequently concerned with women's experiences and situations in Indian society. "Process of Creation," a poem written in the 1970s, reconceives female writing as a bodily process that involves sexual desire, fear, reproductive conception, and possible miscarriage. "The Weed," a short story written in the 1980s, portrays the multifaceted relationship between an educated, middle-class Indian woman and a poor, illiterate girl from a village, who works as a domestic servant in a city. Whereas the poem links writing, creation, and birth to ideals of justice, the story relates the constraints of illiteracy, patriarchal subjection, and arranged marriages to the prospects of freedom, fulfillment, and emancipation.

Process of Creation

Sometimes the poem looks at the sheet of paper
and averts her face
as if the paper were a strange man

But sometimes
as when a girl fasts faithfully on *karva chauth*°   5
and that night she has what seems to be a dream
suddenly a man touches her body
and even in the dream her body shudders

But sometimes   licking fire
she starts   wakes up   10
touches her limbs ripe with womanhood
undoes the buttons of her blouse
splashes handfuls of moonlight on her body
and the hand that wrings her body dry
seems to tremble   15

Her body's darkness spreads like a mat
she lies face down on it
breaks off pieces of its straw
and every part of her catches fire
and she feels that her body's darkness wants to break   20
in someone's strong arms

Suddenly a sheet of paper moves forward
and touches her trembling hands
one part burns   one part melts
and she smells an unfamiliar fragrance   25
and her hand stares at the lines
that have inscribed her body

Her hand goes to sleep   her body shakes
and something like sweat breaks out on her brow
a long line breaks   30
and her breath
soaks in the double fragrance of life and death

All these thin black lines
as though they were pieces of a single line
she stands wrung out   silent and astonished   35
looking   thinking

karva chauth: in the Hindu calendar, the fourth day of the month of Kartik (October-
   November), on which a married woman fasts for her husband's well-being and eats
   only after the first sighting of the moon in the evening

This is a miscarriage of justice
a part of her is dead
maybe this is exactly how
a young woman miscarries her child   40

Translated from the Punjabi
by Vinay Dharwadker

The Weed

Angoori was the new bride of the old servant of my neighbor's neighbor's
neighbor. Every bride is new, for that matter; but she was new in a different way: the second wife of her husband who could not be called new because he had already drunk once at the conjugal well. As such, the pre-
rogatives of being new went to Angoori only. This realization was further
accentuated when one considered the five years that passed before they
could consummate their union.

About six years ago Prabhati had gone home to cremate his first wife.
When this was done, Angoori's father approached him and took his wet
towel, wringing it dry, a symbolic gesture of wiping away the tears of
grief that had wet the towel. There never was a man, though, who cried
enough to wet a yard-and-a-half of calico. It had got wet only after Prabhati's bath. The simple act of drying the tear-stained towel on the part of
a person with a nubile daughter was as much as to say, "I give you my
daughter to take the place of the one who died. Don't cry anymore. I've
even dried your wet towel."

This is how Angoori married Prabhati. However, their union was postponed for five years, for two reasons: her tender age, and her mother's
paralytic attack. When, at last, Prabhati was invited to take his bride
away, it seemed he would not be able to, for his employer was reluctant
to feed another mouth from his kitchen. But when Prabhati told him that
his new wife could keep her own house, the employer agreed.

At first, Angoori kept *purdah*° from both men and women. But the veil
soon started to shrink until it covered only her hair, as was becoming to
an orthodox Hindu woman. She was a delight to both ear and eye. A
laughter in the tinkling of her hundred ankle-bells and a thousand bells
in her laughter.

"What are you wearing Angoori?"

"An anklet. Isn't it pretty?"

"And what's on your toe?"

kept *purdah*: followed the Indian women's custom of remaining veiled (or keeping the
  face covered) in the presence of all but members of the immediate family

"A ring."

"And on your arm?"

"A bracelet."

"What do they call what's on your forehead?"

"They call it *aliband.*"°

"Nothing on your waist today, Angoori?"

"It's too heavy. Tomorrow I'll wear it. Today, no necklace either. See! The clasp is broken. Tomorrow I'll go to the city to get a new clasp . . . and buy a nose-pin. I had a big nose-ring. But my mother-in-law kept it."

Angoori was very proud of her silver jewelry, elated by the mere touch of her trinkets. Everything she did seemed to set them off to maximum effect.

The weather became hot with the turn of the season. Angoori too must have felt it in her hut where she passed a good part of the day, for now she stayed out more. There were a few huge *neem* trees° in front of my house; underneath them an old well that nobody used except an occasional construction worker. The spilt water made several puddles, keeping the atmosphere around the well cool. She often sat near the well to relax.

"What are your reading, *bibi?*"° Angoori asked me one day when I sat under a *neem* tree reading.

"Want to read it?"

"I don't know reading."

"Want to learn?"

"Oh, no!"

"Why not? What's wrong with it?"

"It's a sin for women to read!"

"And what about men?"

"For them, it's not a sin."

"Who told you this nonsense?"

"I just know it."

"I read. I must be sinning."

"For city women, it's no sin. It is for village women."

We both laughed at this remark. She had not learned to question all that she was told to believe. I thought that if she found peace in her convictions, who was I to question them?

Her body redeemed her dark complexion, an intense sense of ecstasy always radiating from it, a resilient sweetness. They say a woman's body is like a lump of dough, some women have the looseness of under-kneaded dough while others have the clinging plasticity of leavened dough. Rarely does a woman have a body that can be equated to rightly kneaded dough, a baker's pride. Angoori's body belonged to this category,

aliband: an ornamental band worn by women on the forehead

neem: common north Indian tree

bibi: a term of respectful address for a woman in a superior position by age, class, or status

her rippling muscles impregnated with the metallic resilience of a coiled spring. I felt her face, arms, breasts, legs with my eyes and experienced a profound langor. I thought of Prabhati: old, short, loose-jawed, a man whose stature and angularity would be the death of Euclid.° Suddenly a funny idea struck me: Angoori was the dough covered by Prabhati. He was her napkin, not her taster. I felt a laugh welling up inside me, but I checked it for fear that Angoori would sense what I was laughing about. I asked her how marriages are arranged where she came from.

"A girl, when she's five or six, adores someone's feet. He is the husband."

"How does she know it?"

"Her father takes money and flowers and puts them at his feet."

"That's the father adoring, not the girl."

"He does it for the girl. So it's the girl herself."

"But the girl has never seen him before!"

"Yes, girls don't see."

"Not a single girl ever sees her future husband!"

"No . . . ," she hesitated. After a long, pensive pause, she added, "Those in love . . . they see them."

"Do girls in your village have love-affairs?"

"A few."

"Those in love, they don't sin?" I remembered her observation regarding education for women.

"They don't. See, what happens is that a man makes the girl eat the weed and then she starts loving him."

"Which weed?"

"The wild one."

"Doesn't the girl know that she has been given the weed?"

"No, he gives it to her in a *paan*.° After that, nothing satisfies her but to be with him, her man. I know. I've seen it with my own eyes."

"Whom did you see?"

"A friend; she was older than me."

"And what happened?"

"She went crazy. Ran away with him to the city."

"How do you know it was because of the weed?"

"What else could it be? Why would she leave her parents? He brought her many things from the city: clothes, trinkets, sweets."

"Where does this weed come in?"

"In the sweets: otherwise how could she love him?"

"Love can come in other ways. No other way here?"

"No other way. What her parents hated was that she was that way."

"Have you seen the weed?"

Euclid: an ancient Greek mathematician and physicist
paan: the aromatic leaf of the betel plant, chewed as a stimulant and narcotic

"No, they bring it from a far country. My mother warned me not to take *paan* or sweets from anyone. Men put the weed in them."

"You were very wise. How come your friend ate it?"

"To make herself suffer," she said sternly. The next moment her face clouded, perhaps in remembering her friend. "Crazy. She went crazy, the poor thing," she said sadly. "Never combed her hair, singing all night. . . ."

"What did she sing?"

"I don't know. They all sing when they eat the weed. Cry too."

The conversation was becoming a little too much to take, so I retired.

I found her sitting under the *neem* tree one day in a profoundly abstracted mood. Usually one could hear Angoori coming to the well; her ankle-bells would announce her approach. They were silent that day.

"What's the matter, Angoori?"

She gave me a blank look and then, recovering a little, said, "Teach me reading, *bibi*."

"What has happened?"

"Teach me to write my name."

"Why do you want to write? To write letters? To whom?"

She did not answer, but was once again lost in her thoughts.

"Won't you be sinning?" I asked, trying to draw her out of her mood. She would not respond. I went in for an afternoon nap. When I came out again in the evening, she was still there singing sadly to herself. When she heard me approaching, she turned around and stopped abruptly. She sat with hunched shoulders because of the chill in the evening breeze.

"You sing well, Angoori." I watched her great effort to turn back the tears and spread a pale smile across her lips.

"I don't know singing."

"But you do, Angoori!"

"This was the . . ."

"The song your friend used to sing." I completed the sentence for her.

"I heard it from her."

"Sing it for me."

She started to recite the words. "Oh, it's just about the time of year for change. Four months winter, four months summer, four months rain! . . ."

"Not like that. Sing it for me," I asked. She wouldn't, but continued with the words.

Four months of winter reign in my heart;
My heart shivers, O my love.
Four months of summer, wind shimmers in the sun.
Four months come the rains; clouds tremble in the sky.

"Angoori!" I said loudly. She looked as if in a trance, as if she had eaten the weed. I felt like shaking her by the shoulders. Instead, I took her by the shoulders and asked if she had been eating regularly. She had not; she cooked for herself only, since Prabhati ate at his master's. "Did you cook today?" I asked.

"Not yet."

"Did you have tea in the morning?"

"Tea? No milk today."

"Why no milk today?"

"I didn't get any. Ram Tara . . ."

"Fetches the milk for you?" I added. She nodded.

Ram Tara was the night-watchman. Before Angoori married Prabhati, Ram Tara used to get a cup of tea at our place at the end of his watch before retiring on his cot near the well. After Angoori's arrival, he made his tea at Prabhati's. He, Angoori and Prabhati would all have tea together sitting around the fire. Three days ago Ram Tara went to his village for a visit.

"You haven't had tea for three days?" I asked. She nodded again. "And you haven't eaten, I suppose?" She did not speak. Apparently, if she had been eating, it was as good as not eating at all.

I remembered Ram Tara: good-looking, quick-limbed, full of jokes. He had a way of talking with smiles trembling faintly at the corner of his lips.

"Angoori?"

"Yes, *bibi*."

"Could it be the weed?"

Tears flowed down her face in two rivulets, gathering into two tiny puddles at the corners of her mouth.

"Curse on me!" she started in a voice trembling with tears, "I never took sweets from him . . . not a betel° even . . . but tea. . . ." She could not finish. Her words were drowned in a fast stream of tears.

Translated from the Punjabi by Raj Gill

NISSIM EZEKIEL

Nissim Ezekiel (1924–) was born into a Jewish family in Bombay. In the 1950s he worked in journalism, broadcasting, and advertising, before becoming a college teacher of English and American literature in Bombay. He has published plays, art criticism, newspaper columns, and book reviews.

Ezekiel, who writes only in English, began publishing his poems soon after India gained independence in 1947. Early in his career he developed a distinctive style, which is characterized by a cosmopolitan

---

betel: leaf or nut of the betel plant

sensibility, a spare diction, a frequently skeptical viewpoint, and irreverent humor mixed with satirical wit. His themes usually center around urban India, especially the city of Bombay. "Minority Poem," written in the mid-1970s, weaves introspection, self-criticism, and social observation into a philosophical vision of the poet's contemporary situation. "In India," written a decade earlier, brings together past and present-day issues, autobiography and satire, as well as social drama and the drama of conflicting perspectives.

Minority Poem

In my room, I talk
to my invisible guests:
they do not argue, but wait

Till I am exhausted,
then they slip away   5
with inscrutable faces.

I lack the means to change
their amiable ways,
although I love their gods.

It's the language really   10
separates, whatever else
is shared. On the other hand,

Everyone understands
Mother Teresa;° her guests
die visibly in her arms.   15

It's not the mythology
or the marriage customs
that you need to know,

It's the will to pass
through the eye of a needle   20
to self-forgetfulness.

The guests depart, dissatisfied;
they will never give up
their mantras,° old or new.

Mother Teresa: an Indian nun famous for her charitable work with the poor and homeless of Calcutta and winner of the 1979 Nobel Peace Prize
mantra: in Hinduism, a sacred formula or phrase believed to have magical power, used in prayer and incantation

And you, uneasy
orphan of their racial
memories, merely   25

Polish up your alien
techniques of observation,
while the city burns.   30

In India

1

Always, in the sun's eye,
Here among the beggars,
Hawkers, pavement sleepers,
Hutment dwellers, slums,
Dead souls of men and gods,   5
Burnt-out mothers, frightened
Virgins, wasted child
And tortured animal,
All in noisy silence
Suffering the place and time,   10
I ride my elephant of thought,
A Cézanne° slung around my neck.

2

The Roman Catholic Goan boys°
The whitewashed Anglo-Indian° boys
The musclebound Islamic boys   15
Were earnest in their prayers.

They copied, bullied, stole in pairs
They bragged about their love affairs
They carved the tables, broke the chairs
But never missed their prayers.   20

The Roman Catholic Goan boys
Confessed their solitary joys

a Cézanne: a painting by Paul Cézanne, a late-nineteenth-century French Impressionist
Roman Catholic Goan boys: boys from Roman Catholic families in Goa, on the Indian
    west coast, colonized by the Portuguese between the sixteenth and twentieth cen-
    turies
Anglo-Indian: of mixed British and Indian descent

Confessed their games with high-heeled toys
And hastened to the prayers.

The Anglo-Indian gentlemen   25
Drank whisky in some Jewish den
With Muslims slowly creeping in
Before or after prayers.

3

To celebrate the year's end:
men in grey or black,   30
women, bosom semi-bare,
twenty-three of us in all,
six nations represented.

The wives of India sit apart.
They do not drink,   35
they do not talk,
of course, they do not kiss.
The men are quite at home
among the foreign styles
(What fun the flirting is!),   40
I myself, decorously,
press a thigh or two in sly innocence.
The party is a great success.

Then someone says: we can't
enjoy it, somehow, don't you think?   45
The atmosphere corrupt,
and look at our wooden wives . . .
I take him out to get some air.

4

This, she said to herself,
As she sat at table   50
With the English boss,
Is IT. This is the promise:
The long evenings
In the large apartment
With cold beer and Western music,   55
Lucid talk of art and literature,
And of all 'the changes India needs'.

At the second meeting
In the large apartment

After cold beer and the music on,   60
She sat in disarray.
The struggle had been hard
And not altogether successful.
Certainly the blouse
Would not be used again.   65
But with true British courtesy
He lent her a safety pin
Before she took the elevator down.

MAHASWETA DEVI

*Mahasweta Devi (1926–) was born in Dhaka (Dacca), then in East
Bengal and now the capital of Bangladesh. She began writing fiction in
Bengali in the mid-1950s, and has published forty novels, eighteen collections of short stories, and several volumes of plays and children's
fiction. During the past four decades, she has also been a teacher, a
freelance journalist, and a social activist, participating in organizations and programs designed to help women, poor farmers, factory
workers, untouchables in the Hindu caste system, and the subcontinent's indigenous peoples. Her work has been translated and discussed
critically in Gayatri Spivak's* In Other Worlds *(1987) and Kalpana
Bardhan's* Of Women, Outcasts, Peasants, and Rebels *(1990).*

*Since the late 1980s, Devi has become internationally famous for
her experimental social-documentary short stories. These stories are
often based on carefully researched historical records, investigative
journalism, and activist fieldwork in the Indian countryside. "Breast-
Giver," written in the mode of social realism, is part social satire and
part tragic allegory. Its main character is Jashoda, a Brahmin woman.
When Jashoda's husband loses his legs in an accident, the couple and
their children become dependent for their support on the Haldars, a
rich but lower-caste Hindu family who employ Jashoda as a wet-nurse.
Devi tells Jashoda's story in such a way that it becomes an allegorical
narrative of "Mother" India after Independence in 1947.*

Breast-Giver

My aunties they lived in the woods, in the forest their home they did
   make.
Never did Aunt say here's a sweet dear, eat, sweetie, here's a piece of
   cake.

Jashoda doesn't remember if her aunt was kind or unkind. It is as if she were Kangalicharan's wife from birth, the mother of twenty children, living or dead, counted on her fingers. Jashoda doesn't remember at all when there was no child in her womb, when she didn't feel faint in the morning, when Kangali's body didn't *drill* her body like a geologist in a darkness lit only by an oil-lamp. She never had the time to calculate if she could or could not bear motherhood. Motherhood was always her way of living and keeping alive her world of countless beings. Jashoda was a mother by profession, *professional mother.* Jashoda was not an *amateur* mama like the daughters and wives of the master's house. The world belongs to the professional. In this city, this kingdom, the amateur beggar-pickpocket-hooker has no place. Even the mongrel on the path or sidewalk, the greedy crow at the garbage don't make room for the upstart *amateur.* Jashoda had taken motherhood as her profession.

The responsibility was Mr. Haldar's new son-in-law's Studebaker and the sudden desire of the youngest son of the Haldar-house to be a driver. When the boy suddenly got a whim in mind or body, he could not rest unless he had satisfied it instantly. These sudden whims reared up in the loneliness of the afternoon and kept him at slave labor like the khalifa of Bagdad.° What he had done so far on that account did not oblige Jashoda to choose motherhood as a profession.

One afternoon the boy, driven by lust, attacked the cook and the cook, since her body was heavy with rice, stolen fishheads, and turnip greens, and her body languid with sloth, lay back, saying, "Yah, do what you like." Thus did the incubus of Bagdad get off the boy's shoulders and he wept repentant tears, mumbling, "Auntie, don't tell." The cook — saying, "What's there to tell?" — went quickly to sleep. She never told anything. She was sufficiently proud that her body had attracted the boy. But the thief thinks of the loot. The boy got worried at the improper supply of fish and fries in his dish. He considered that he'd be fucked if the cook gave him away. Therefore on another afternoon, driven by the Bagdad djinn,° he stole his mother's ring, slipped it into the cook's pillowcase, raised a hue and cry, and got the cook kicked out. Another afternoon he lifted the radio set from his father's room and sold it. It was difficult for his parents to find the connection between the hour of the afternoon and the boy's behavior, since his father had created him in the deepest night by the astrological calendar and the tradition of Haldars of Harisal. In fact you enter the sixteenth century as you enter the gates of this house. To

the khalifa of Bagdad: until modern times, the head of state of the Muslim kingdom of Baghdad (now in Iraq); a central character of the stories from the Arabic classic *The Thousand and One Nights*
Bagdad djinn: a genie or spirit capable of exercising a supernatural power over human beings and their affairs

this day you take your wife by the astrological almanac. But these matters are mere blind alleys. Motherhood did not become Jashoda's profession for these afternoon-whims.

One afternoon, leaving the owner of the shop, Kangalicharan was returning home with a handful of stolen samosas° and sweets under his dhoti.° Thus he returns daily. He and Jashoda eat rice. Their three offspring return before dark and eat stale samosas and sweets. Kangalicharan stirs the seething vat of milk in the sweet shop and cooks and feeds "food cooked by a good Brahmin"° to those pilgrims at the Lionseated goddess's° temple who are proud that they are not themselves "fake Brahmins by sleight of hand." Daily he lifts a bit of flour and such and makes life easier. When he puts food in his belly in the afternoon he feels a filial inclination toward Jashoda, and he goes to sleep after handling her capacious bosom. Coming home in the afternoon, Kangalicharan was thinking of his imminent pleasure and tasting paradise at the thought of his wife's large round breasts. He was picturing himself as a farsighted son of man as he thought that marrying a fresh young thing, not working her overmuch, and feeding her well led to pleasure in the afternoon. At such a moment the Haldar son, complete with Studebaker, swerving by Kangalicharan, ran over his feet and shins.

Instantly a crowd gathered. It was an accident in front of the house after all, "otherwise I'd have drawn blood," screamed Nabin, the pilgrim-guide. He guides the pilgrims to the Mother goddess of Shakti-power,° his temper is hot in the afternoon sun. Hearing him roar, all the Haldars who were at home came out. The Haldar chief started thrashing his son, roaring, "You'll kill a Brahmin, you bastard, you unthinking bull?" The youngest son-in-law breathed relief as he saw that his Studebaker was not much damaged and, to prove that he was better human material than the money-rich, *culture*-poor in-laws, he said in a voice as fine as the finest muslin, "Shall we let the man die? Shouldn't we take him to the hospital?" — Kangali's boss was also in the crowd at the temple and, seeing the samosas and sweets flung on the roadway was about to say, "Eh Brahmin!! Stealing food?" Now he held his tongue and said, "Do that *sir*." The youngest son-in-law and the Haldar-chief took Kangalicharan quickly to the hospital. The master felt deeply grieved. During the Second War, when he helped the anti-Fascist struggle of the Allies by buying and selling scrap iron — then Kangali was a mere lad. Reverence for Brah-

samosa: a crisp, fried snack, like a large dumpling stuffed with spicy potato
dhoti: an Indian man's traditional lower garment
Brahmin: a learned priest, a member (by birth) of the highest caste group in the Hindu caste system
Lionseated goddess: the Goddess Kali, who rides a lion and represents the violent and terrifying aspect of maternal-female divinity
Mother goddess of Shakti-power: the maternal Goddess Kali, who is also known as Shakti (literally, "power")

mins crawled in Mr. Haldar's veins. If he couldn't get chatterjeebabu° in the morning he would touch the feet of Kangali, young enough to be his son, and put a pinch of dust from his chapped feet on his own tongue. Kangali and Jashoda came to his house on feast days and Jashoda was sent a gift of cloth and vermillion when his daughters-in-law were pregnant. Now he said to Kangali — "Kangali! don't worry son. You won't suffer as long as I'm around." Now it was that he thought that Kangali's feet, being turned to ground meat, he would not be able to taste their dust. He was most unhappy at the thought and he started weeping as he said, "What has the son of a bitch done." He said to the doctor at the hospital, "Do what you can! Don't worry about cash."

But the doctors could not bring the feet back. Kangali returned as a lame Brahmin. Haldarbabu had a pair of crutches made. The very day Kangali returned home on crutches, he learned that food had come to Jashoda from the Haldar house every day. Nabin was third in rank among the pilgrim-guides. He could only claim thirteen percent of the goddess's food and so had an inferiority complex. Inspired by seeing Rama-Krishna in the movies a couple of times, he called the goddess "my crazy one" and by the book of the Kali-worshippers° kept his consciousness immersed in local spirits. He said to Kangali, "I put flowers on the crazy one's feet in your name. She said I have a share in Kangali's house, he will get out of the hospital by that fact." Speaking of this to Jashoda, Kangali said, "What? When I wasn't there, you were getting it off with Nabin?" Jashoda then grabbed Kangali's suspicious head between the two hemispheres of the globe and said, "Two maid servants from the big house slept here every day to guard me. Would I look at Nabin? Am I not your faithful wife?"

In fact Kangali heard of his wife's flaming devotion at the big house as well. Jashoda had fasted at the mother's temple, had gone through a female ritual, and had traveled to the outskirts to pray at the feet of the local guru.° Finally the Lionseated came to her in a dream as a midwife carrying a *bag* and said, "Don't worry. Your man will return." Kangali was most overwhelmed by this. Haldarbabu said, "See, Kangali? The bastard unbelievers say, the Mother gives a dream, why togged as a midwife? I say, she creates as mother, and preserves as midwife."

Then Kangali said, "Sir! How shall I work at the sweetshop any longer. I can't stir the vat with my kerutches.° You are god. You are feeding so many people in so many ways. I am not begging. Find me a job."

chatterjeebabu: used satirically as a generic Bengali name for a member of the priestly caste; *Chatterjee* is a common modern Bengali upper-caste last name, and *babu* is a term of respectful address for men in a superior social position, used as a suffix
Kali-worshippers: Hindu worshippers or devotees of the Goddess Kali, who elevate her above her male consort, Lord Shiva (one of the three main gods in Hinduism)
local guru: the most influential spiritual master or religious teacher in the city
kerutches: Bengali pronunciation of the English "crutches"

Haldarbabu said, "Yes Kangali! I've kept you a spot. I'll make you a shop in the corner of my porch. The Lionseated is across the way! Pilgrims come and go. Put up a shop of dry sweets. Now there's a wedding in the house. It's my bastard seventh son's wedding. As long as there's no shop, I'll send you food."

Hearing this, Kangali's mind took wing like a rainbug in the rainy season. He came home and told Jashoda, "Remember Kalidasa's° poem? You eat because there isn't, wouldn't have got if there was? That's my lot, chuck.° Master says he'll put up a shop after his son's wedding. Until then he'll send us food. Would this have happened if I had legs? All is Mother's will, dear!"

Everyone is properly amazed that in this fallen age the wishes and wills of the Lionseated, herself found by a dream-command a hundred and fifty years ago, are circulating around Kangalicharan Patitundo.° Haldarbabu's change of heart is also Mother's will. He lives in independent India, the India that makes no distinctions among people, kingdoms, languages, varieties of Brahmins, varieties of Kayasthas° and so on. But he made his cash in the British era, when *Divide and Rule* was the policy. Haldarbabu's mentality was constructed then. Therefore he doesn't trust anyone — not a Punjabi-Oriya-Bihari-Gujarati-Marathi-Muslim.° At the sight of an unfortunate Bihari child or a starvation-ridden Oriya beggar his flab-protected heart, located under a forty-two inch Gopal° brand vest, does not itch with the rash of kindness. He is a successful son of Harisal. When he sees a West Bangali fly he says, "Tchah! at home even the flies were fat — in the bloody West everything is pinched-skinny." All the temple people are struck that such a man is filling with the milk of humankindness toward the West Bengali Kangalicharan. For some time this news is the general talk. Haldarbabu is such a patriot that, if his nephews or grandsons read the lives of the nation's leaders in their schoolbook, he

Kalidasa: fifth-century poet and dramatist, the most famous Sanskrit writer in Indian history; one of his major poems, *Ritusamhara*, describes each of the Indian seasons in detail

chuck: term of familiar address

Kangalicharan Patitundo: satirically, "Kangalicharan the Fallen One"

Kayastha: genealogically a low caste in the Hindu hierarchy, but traditionally high in social status because its members are literate professionals (scribes, administrators, writers, etc.)

Punjabi-Oriya-Bihari-Gujarati-Marathi-Muslim: Haldarbabu, a Bengali or resident of Bengal, is suspicious of the other kinds of Indians, whether Punjabis (residents of Punjab, in northwestern India), Oriyas (residents of Orissa, just south of Bengal), Biharis (residents of Bihar, just west of Bengal), Gujaratis (residents of Gujarat, in western India), Marathis (residents of Maharashtra, on India's west coast), or Muslims (the preceding categories refer to Hindus)

Gopal brand: satirically, a clothing brand-name derived from "Gopal," one of the common names of Lord Krishna, who is one of the incarnations of Lord Vishnu (one of the three main gods in Hinduism)

says to his employees, "Nonsense! why do they make 'em read the lives of characters from Dhaka, Mymansingh, Jashore? Harisal is made of the bone of the martyr god. One day it will emerge that the *Vedas* and the *Upanishads*° were also written in Harisal." Now his employees tell him, "You have had a *change of heart,* so much kindness for a West Bengali, you'll see there is divine *purpose* behind this." The Boss is delighted. He laughs loudly and says, "There's no East or West for a Brahmin. If there's a sacred thread around his neck you have to give him respect even when he's taking a shit."

Thus all around blow the sweet winds of sympathy-compassion-kindness. For a few days, whenever Nabin tries to think of the Lion-seated, the heavy-breasted, languid-hipped body of Jashoda floats in his mind's eye. A slow rise spreads in his body at the thought that perhaps she is appearing in his dream as Jashoda just as she appeared in Jashoda's as a midwife. The fifty percent pilgrim-guide says to him, "Male and female both get this disease. Bind the root of a white forget-me-not in your ear when you take a piss."

Nabin doesn't agree. One day he tells Kangali, "As the Mother's son I won't make a racket with Shakti-power. But I've thought of a plan. There's no problem with making a Hare Krishna racket.° I tell you, get a Gopal in your dream. My Aunt brought a stony Gopal from Puri.° I give it to you. You announce that you got it in a dream. You'll see there'll be a to-do in no time, money will roll in. Start for money, later you'll get devoted to Gopal."

Kangali says, "Shame, brother! Should one joke with gods?"

"Ah get lost," Nabin scolds. Later it appears that Kangali would have done well to listen to Nabin. For Haldarbabu suddenly dies of heart failure. Shakespeare's *welkin*° breaks on Kangali and Jashoda's head.

2

Haldarbabu truly left Kangali in the lurch. Those wishes of the Lion-seated that were manifesting themselves around Kangali *via-media* Haldarbabu disappeared into the blue like the burning promises given by a political party before the elections and became magically invisible like

Vedas and Upanishads: The four Vedas are the earliest Hindu collections of revealed, magical, and ritual texts; the Upanishads are attached to the Vedas as speculative and mystical discourses on the meaning of Vedic revelation and the ultimate essence of reality; both the Vedas and the Upanishads were composed in north-western India, in early forms of the Sanskrit language.
Hare Krishna racket: a loud noise (racket) and a dishonest business (racket) based on religious devotion to, say, Lord Krishna (also known as Gopal)
Puri: one of the holiest cities in Hinduism, now in the eastern Indian state of Orissa, famous for its temples to Lord Krishna or Gopal
welkin: in Shakespeare's language, "the vault of heaven"

the heroine of a fantasy. A European witch's *bodkin°* pricks the colored balloon of Kangali and Jashoda's dreams and the pair falls in deep trouble. At home, Gopal, Nepal, and Radharani whine interminably for food and abuse their mother. It is very natural for children to cry so for grub. Ever since Kangalicharan's loss of feet they'd eaten the fancy food of the Haldar household. Kangali also longs for food and is shouted at for trying to put his head in Jashoda's chest in the way of Gopal, the Divine Son. Jashoda is fully an Indian woman, whose unreasonable, unreasoning, and unintelligent devotion to her husband and love for her children, whose unnatural renunciation and forgiveness have been kept alive in the popular consciousness by all Indian women from Sati-Savitri-Sita° through Nirupa Roy and Chand Osmani.° The creeps of the world understand by seeing such women that the old Indian tradition is still flowing free — they understand that it was with such women in mind that the following aphorisms have been composed — "a female's life hangs on like a turtle's" — "her heart breaks but no word is uttered" — "the woman will burn, her ashes will fly / Only then will we sing her / praise on high." Frankly, Jashoda never once wants to blame her husband for the present misfortune. Her mother-love wells up for Kangali as much as for the children. She wants to become the earth and feed her crippled husband and helpless children with a fulsome harvest. Sages did not write of this motherly feeling of Jashoda's for her husband. They explained female and male as Nature and the Human Principle. But this they did in the days of yore — when they entered this *peninsula* from another land. Such is the power of the Indian soil that all women turn into mothers here and all men remain immersed in the spirit of holy childhood. Each man the Holy Child and each woman the Divine Mother. Even those who deny this and wish to slap *current posters* to the effect of the *"eternal she"* — "Mona Lisa" — "La passionaria" — "Simone de Beauvoir,"° et cetera, over the old ones and look at women that way are, after all, Indian cubs. It is notable that the educated Babus° desire all this from women outside the home. When they cross the threshold they want the Divine Mother in the words and conduct of the revolutionary ladies. The *process* is most

bodkin: dagger, stiletto, or sharply pointed instrument for piercing holes in cloth and leather

Sati-Savitri-Sita: three archetypal "pure women" and "ideal wives" in ancient Indian mythology and literature, who made superhuman sacrifices for their husbands and families

Nirupa Roy and Chand Usmani: mid-twentieth-century Indian actresses who frequently played self-sacrificing wives and mothers in commercial Hindi films

"La passionara"—"Simone de Beauvoir": images or examples of "liberated" Western women who stand in contrast to traditional Indian stereotypes of self-sacrificing women (such as Sati, Savitri, or Sita)

educated Babus: Westernized, middle-class Indian bureaucrats or modern professionals who claim to reject traditional Indian norms of behavior

complicated. Because he understood this the heroines of Saratchandra° always fed the hero an extra mouthful of rice. The apparent simplicity of Saratchandra's and other similar writers' writings is actually very complex and to be thought of in the evening, peacefully after a glass of wood-apple juice.° There is too much influence of fun and games in the lives of the people who traffic in studies and intellectualism in West Bengal and therefore they should stress the wood-apple correspondingly. We have no idea of the loss we are sustaining because we do not stress the wood-apple-type-herbal remedies correspondingly.

However, it's incorrect to cultivate the habit of repeated incursions into *bye-lanes* as we tell Jashoda's life story. The reader's patience, unlike the cracks in Calcutta streets, will not widen by the decade. The real thing is that Jashoda was in a cleft stick. Of course they ate their fill during the Master's funeral days, but after everything was over Jashoda clasped Radharani to her bosom and went over to the big house. Her aim was to speak to the Mistress and ask for the cook's job in the vegetarian kitchen.°

The Mistress really grieved for the Master. But the lawyer let her know that the Master had left her the proprietorship of this house and the right to the rice warehouse. Girding herself with those assurances, she has once again taken the rudder of the family empire. She had really felt the loss of fish and fish-head. Now she sees that the best butter, the best milk sweets from the best shops, heavy cream, and the best variety of bananas can also keep the body going somehow. The Mistress lights up her easychair. A six-months' babe in her lap, her grandson. So far six sons have married. Since the almanac approves of the taking of a wife almost every month of the year, the birth rooms in a row on the ground floor of the Mistress's house are hardly ever empty. The *lady doctor* and Sarala the midwife never leave the house. The Mistress has six daughters. They too breed every year and a half. So there is a constant *epidemic* of blanket-quilt-feeding spoon-bottle-oilcloth-*Johnson's baby powder*-bathing basin.

The Mistress was out of her mind trying to feed the boy. As if relieved to see Jashoda she said, "You come like a god! Give her some milk, dear, I beg you. His mother's sick — such a brat, he won't touch a bottle." Jashoda immediately suckled the boy and pacified him. At the Mistress's special request Jashoda stayed in the house until nine p.m. and suckled the Mistress's grandson again and again. The Cook filled a big bowl with rice and curry for her own household. Jashoda said as she suckled the boy, "Mother! The Master said many things. He is gone, so I don't think of them. But Mother! Your Brahmin-son does not have his two feet. I

Saratchandra: Saratchandra Chatterjee, major early-twentieth-century Bengali fiction writer who practiced social realism

don't think for myself. But thinking of my husband and sons I say, give me any kind of job. Perhaps you'll let me cook in your household?"

"Let me see dear! Let me think and see." The Mistress is not as sold on Brahmins as the Master was. She does not accept fully that Kangali lost his feet because of her son's afternoon whims. It was written for Kangali as well, otherwise why was he walking down the road in the blazing sun grinning from ear to ear? She looks in charmed envy at Jashoda's *mammal projections* and says, "The good lord sent you down as the legendary Cow of Fulfillment. Pull the teat and milk flows! The ones I've brought to my house, haven't a quarter of this milk in their nipples!"

Jashoda says, "How true Mother! Gopal was weaned when he was three. This one hadn't come to my belly yet. Still it was like a flood of milk. Where does it come from, Mother? I have no good food, no pampering!"

This produced a lot of talk among the women at night and the menfolk got to hear it too at night. The second son, whose wife was sick and whose son drank Jashoda's milk, was particularly uxorious. The difference between him and his brothers was that the brothers created progeny as soon as the almanac gave a good day, with love or lack of love, with irritation or thinking of the accounts at the works. The second son impregnates his wife at the same *frequency*, but behind it lies deep love. The wife is often pregnant, that is an act of God. But the second son is also interested in that the wife remains beautiful at the same time. He thinks a lot about how to *combine* multiple pregnancies and beauty, but he cannot fathom it. But today, hearing from his wife about Jashoda's surplus milk, the second son said all of a sudden, "Way found."

"Way to what?"

"Uh, the way to save you pain."

"How? I'll be out of pain when you burn me.° Can a year-breeder's health mend?"

"It will, it will, I've got a divine engine in my hands! You'll breed yearly *and* keep your body."

The couple discussed. The husband entered his Mother's room in the morning and spoke in heavy whispers. At first the Mistress hemmed and hawed, but then she thought to herself and realized that the proposal was worth a million rupees. Daughters-in-law *will* be mothers. When they are mothers, they will suckle their children. Since they will be mothers as long as it's possible — progressive suckling will ruin their shape. Then if the sons look outside, or harass the maidservants, she won't have a voice to object. Going out because they can't get it at home — this is just. If Jashoda becomes the infants' suckling-mother, her daily meals, clothes on feast days, and some monthly pay will be enough. The Mistress is constantly occupied with women's rituals. There Jashoda can act as the fruit-

burn me: cremate me (Hindus cremate their dead)

ful Brahmin wife. Since Jashoda's misfortune is due to her son, that sin too will be lightened.

Jashoda received a portfolio when she heard her proposal. She thought of her breasts as most precious objects. At night when Kangalicharan started to give her a feel she said, "Look. I'm going to pull our weight with these. Take good care how you use them." Kangalicharan hemmed and hawed that night, of course, but his Gopal frame of mind disappeared instantly when he saw the amount of grains — oil — vegetables coming from the big house. He was illuminated by the spirit of Brahma the Creator and explained to Jashoda, "You'll have milk in your breasts only if you have a child in your belly. Now you'll have to think of that and suffer. You are a faithful wife, a goddess. You will yourself be pregnant, be filled with a child, rear it at your breast, isn't this why Mother came to you as a midwife?"

Jashoda realized the justice of these words and said, with tears in her eyes, "You are husband, you are guru. If I forget and say no, correct me. Where after all is the pain? Didn't Mistress-Mother breed thirteen? Does it hurt a tree to bear fruit?"

So this rule held. Kangalicharan became a professional father. Jashoda was by *profession* Mother. In fact to look at Jashoda now even the skeptic is convinced of the profundity of that song of the path of devotion. The song is as follows:

Is a Mother so cheaply made?
Not just by dropping a babe!

Around the paved courtyard on the ground floor of the Haldar house over a dozen auspicious milch cows live in some state in large rooms. Two Biharis look after them as Mother Cows. There are mountains of rind-bran-hay-grass-molasses. Mrs. Haldar believes that the more the cow eats, the more milk she gives. Jashoda's place in the house is now above the Mother Cows. The Mistress's sons become incarnate Brahma and create progeny. Jashoda preserves the progeny.

Mrs. Haldar kept a strict watch on the free flow of her supply of milk. She called Kangalicharan to her presence and said, "Now then, my Brahmin son? You used to stir the vat at the shop, now take up the cooking at home and give her a rest. Two of her own, three here, how can she cook at day's end after suckling five?"

Kangalicharan's intellectual eye was thus opened. Downstairs the two Biharis gave him a bit of chewing tobacco and said, "Mistress Mother said right. We serve the Cow Mother as well — your woman is the Mother of the World."

From now on Kangalicharan took charge of the cooking at home. Made the children his assistants. Gradually he became an expert in cooking plantain curry, lentil soup, and pickled fish, and by constantly feeding

Nabin a head-curry with the head of the goat dedicated to the Lionseated he tamed that ferocious cannabis-artist° and drunkard. As a result Nabin inserted Kangali into the temple of Shiva the King.° Jashoda, eating well-prepared rice and curry every day, became as inflated as the *bank account* of a Public Works Department *officer*. In addition, Mistress-Mother gave her milk gratis. When Jashoda became pregnant, she would send her preserves, conserves, hot and sweet balls.

Thus even the skeptics were persuaded that the Lionseated had appeared to Jashoda as a midwife for this very reason. Otherwise who has ever heard or seen such things as constant pregnancies, giving birth, giving milk like a cow, without a thought, to others' children? Nabin too lost his bad thoughts. Devotional feelings came to him by themselves. Whenever he saw Jashoda he called out "Mother! Mother! Dear Mother!" Faith in the greatness of the Lionseated was rekindled in the area and in the air of the neighborhood blew the *electrifying* influence of goddess-glory.

Everyone's devotion to Jashoda became so strong that at weddings, showers, namings, and sacred-threadings they invited her and gave her the position of chief fruitful woman. They looked with a comparable eye on Nepal-Gopal-Neno-Boncha-Patal etc. because they were Jashoda's children, and as each grew up, he got a sacred thread and started catching pilgrims for the temple. Kangali did not have to find husbands for Radha-rani, Altarani, Padmarani and such daughters. Nabin found them husbands with exemplary dispatch and the faithful mother's faithful daughters went off each to run the household of her own Shiva! Jashoda's worth went up in the Haldar house. The husbands are pleased because the wives' knees no longer knock when they riffle the almanac. Since their children are being reared on Jashoda's milk, they can be the Holy Child in bed at will. The wives no longer have an excuse to say "no." The wives are happy. They can keep their figures. They can wear blouses and bras of "European cut." After keeping the fast of Shiva's night by watching all-night picture shows they are no longer obliged to breast-feed their babies. All this was possible because of Jashoda. As a result Jashoda became vocal and, constantly suckling the infants, she opined as she sat in the Mistress's room, "A woman breeds, so here medicine, there blood-peshur,° here doctor's visits. Showoffs! Look at me! I've become a year-breeder! So is my body failing, or is my milk drying? Makes your skin crawl? I hear they are drying their milk with injishuns.° Never heard of such things!"

cannabis-artist: a person addicted to one or more drugs derived from the cannabis plant, such as hashish
Shiva the King: Lord Shiva, one of the three major gods in Hinduism, here regarded as the god of gods
bloodpeshur: Bengali pronunciation of English "blood pressure"
injishun: Bengali pronunciation of English "injection"

The fathers and uncles of the current young men of the Haldar house used to whistle at the maidservants as soon as hair grew on their upper lips. The young ones were reared by the Milk-Mother's milk, so they looked upon the maid and the cook, their Milk-Mother's friends, as mothers too and started walking around the girls' school. The maids said, "Joshi! You came as The Goddess! You made the air of this house change!" So one day as the youngest son was squatting to watch Jashoda's milking, she said, "There dear, my Lucky! All this because you swiped him in the leg! Whose wish was it then?" "The Lionseated's," said Haldar junior.

He wanted to know how Kangalicharan could be Brahma without feet? This encroached on divine area, and he forgot the question.

All is the Lionseated's will!

3

Kangali's shins were cut in the fifties, and our narrative has reached the present. In twenty-five years, sorry in thirty, Jashoda has been confined twenty times. The maternities toward the end were profitless, for a new wind entered the Haldar house somehow. Let's finish the business of the twenty-five or thirty years. At the beginning of the narrative Jashoda was the mother of three sons. Then she became gravid seventeen times. Mrs. Haldar died. She dearly wished that one of her daughters-in-law should have the same good fortune as her mother-in-law. In the family the custom was to have a second wedding if a couple could produce twenty children. But the daughters-in-law called a halt at twelve-thirteen-fourteen. By evil counsel they were able to explain to their husbands and make arrangements at the hospital. All this was the bad result of the new wind. Wise men have never allowed a new wind to enter the house. I've heard from my grandmother that a certain gentleman would come to her house to read the liberal journal *Saturday Letter*. He would never let the tome enter his home. "The moment wife, or mother, or sister reads that paper," he would say, "she'll say 'I'm a woman! Not a mother, not a sister, not a wife.'" If asked what the result would be, he'd say, "They would wear shoes while they cooked." It is a perennial rule that the power of the new wind disturbs the peace of the women's quarter.

It was always the sixteenth century in the Haldar household. But at the sudden significant rise in the *membership* of the house the sons started building new houses and splitting. The most objectionable thing was that in the matter of motherhood, the old lady's granddaughters-in-law had breathed a completely different air before they crossed her threshold. In vain did the Mistress say that there was plenty of money, plenty to eat. The old man had dreamed of filling half Calcutta with Haldars. The granddaughters-in-law were unwilling. Defying the old lady's tongue, they took off to their husbands' places of work. At about this time, the pilgrim-guides of the Lionseated had a tremendous fight and some unknown person or persons turned the image of the goddess around. The Mistress's heart broke at the thought that the Mother had turned her back. In pain she ate an unreasonable quantity of jackfruit in full summer and died shitting and vomiting.

4

Death liberated the Mistress, but the sting of staying alive is worse than death. Jashoda was genuinely sorry at the Mistress's death. When an elderly person dies in the neighborhood, it's Basini who can weep most elaborately. She is an old maidservant of the house. But Jashoda's meal ticket was offered up with the Mistress. She astounded everyone by weeping even more elaborately.

"Oh blessed Mother!," Basini wept. "Widowed, when you lost your crown, you became the Master and protected everyone! Whose sins sent you away Mother! Ma, when I said, don't eat so much jackfruit, you didn't listen to me at all Mother!"

Jashoda let Basini get her breath and lamented in that pause, "Why should you stay, Mother! You are blessed, why should you stay in this sinful world! The daughters-in-law have moved the throne! When the tree says I won't bear, alas it's a sin! Could you bear so much sin, Mother! Then did the Lionseated turn her back, Mother! You knew the abode of good works had become the abode of sin, it was not for you Mother! Your heart left when the Master left Mother! You held your body only because you thought of the family. O mistresses, o daughters-in-law! take a vermillion print of her footstep! Fortune will be tied to the door if you keep that print! If you touch your forehead to it every morning, pain and disease will stay out!"

Jashoda walked weeping behind the corpse to the burning ghat° and said on return, "I saw with my own eyes a chariot descend from heaven, take Mistress-Mother from the pyre, and go on up."

After the funeral days were over, the eldest daughter-in-law said to Jashoda, "Brahmin sister! the family is breaking up. Second and Third are moving to the house in Beleghata. Fourth and Fifth are departing to Maniktala-Bagmari. Youngest will depart to our Dakshireswar house."

"Who stays here?"

"I will. But I'll let the downstairs. Now must the family be folded up. You reared everyone on your milk, food was sent every day. The last child was weaned, still Mother sent you food for eight years. She did what pleased her. Her children said nothing. But it's no longer possible."

"What'll happen to me, elder daughter-in-law-sister?"

burning ghat: cremation ground, especially on the bank of a river

"If you cook for my household, your board is taken care of. But what'll you do with yours?"

"What?"

"It's for you to say. You are the mother of twelve living children! The daughters are married. I hear the sons call pilgrims, eat temple food, stretch out in the courtyard. Your Brahmin-husband has set himself up in the Shiva temple, I hear. What do you need?"

Jashoda wiped her eyes. "Well! Let me speak to the Brahmin."

Kangalicharan's temple had really caught on. "What will you do in my temple?" he asked.

"What does Naren's niece do?"

"She looks after the temple household and cooks. You haven't been cooking at home for a long time. Will you be able to push the temple traffic?"

"No meals from the big house. Did that enter your thieving head? What'll you eat?"

"You don't have to worry," said Nabin.

"Why did I have to worry for so long? You're bringing it in at the temple, aren't you? You've saved everything and eaten the food that sucked my body."

"Who sat and cooked?"

"The man brings, the woman cooks and serves. My lot is inside out. Then you ate my food, now you'll give me food. Fair's fair."

Kangali said on the beat, "Where did you bring in the food? Could you have gotten the Haldar house? Their door opened for *you* because *my* legs were cut off. The Master had wanted to set *me* up in business. Forgotten everything, you cunt?"

"Who's the cunt, you or me? Living off a wife's carcass, you call that a man?"

The two fought tooth and nail and cursed each other to the death. Finally Kangali said, "I don't want to see your face again. Buzz off!"

"All right."

Jashoda too left angry. In the meantime the various pilgrim-guide factions conspired to turn the image's face forward, otherwise disaster was imminent. As a result, penance rituals were being celebrated with great ceremony at the temple. Jashoda went to throw herself at the goddess's feet. Her aging, milkless, capacious breasts are breaking in pain. Let the Lionseated understand her pain and tell her the way.

Jashoda lay three days in the courtyard. Perhaps the Lionseated has also breathed the new wind. She did not appear in a dream. Moreover, when, after her three days' fast, Jashoda went back shaking to her place, her youngest came by. "Dad will stay at the temple. He's told Naba and I to ring the bells. We'll get money and holy food every day."

"I see! Where's dad?"

"Lying down. Golapi-auntie is scratching the prickly heat on his back. Asked us to buy candy with some money. So we came to tell you."

Jashoda understood that her usefulness had ended not only in the Haldar house but also for Kangali. She broke her fast in name and went to Nabin to complain. It was Nabin who had dragged the Lionseated's image the other way. After he had settled the dispute with the other pilgrim-guides re the overhead income from the goddess Basanti ritual, the goddess Jagaddhatri ritual, and the autumn Durgapuja,° it was he who had once again pushed and pulled the image the right way. He'd poured some liquor into his aching throat, had smoked a bit of cannabis, and was now addressing the local electoral candidate: "No offerings for the Mother from you! Her glory is back. Now we'll see how you win!"

Nabin is the proof of all the miracles that can happen if, even in this decade, one stays under the temple's power. He had turned the goddess's head himself and had himself believed that the Mother was averse because the pilgrim-guides were not organizing like all the want-votes groups. Now, after he had turned the goddess's head he had the idea that the Mother had turned on her own.

Jashoda said, "What are you babbling?"

Nabin said, "I'm speaking of Mother's glory."

Jashoda said, "You think I don't know that you turned the image's head yourself?"

Nabin said, "Shut up, Joshi. God gave me ability, and intelligence, and only then could the thing be done through me."

"Mother's glory has disappeared when you put your hands on her."

"Glory disappeared! If so, how come, the fan is turning, and you are sitting under the fan? Was there ever an elettiri° fan on the porch ceiling?"

"I accept. But tell me, why did you burn my luck? What did I ever do to you?"

"Why? Kangali isn't dead."

"Why wait for death? He's more than dead to me."

"What's up?"

Jashoda wiped her eyes and said in a heavy voice, "I've carried so many, I was the regular milk-mother at the Master's house. You know everything. I've never left the straight and narrow."

"But of course. You are a portion of the Mother."

"But Mother remains in divine fulfillment. Her 'portion' is about to die for want of food. Haldar-house has lifted its hand from me."

"Why did you have to fight with Kangali? Can a man bear to be insulted on grounds of being supported?"

---

the goddess Basanti ritual, the goddess Jagaddhatri ritual, and the autumn Durgapuja:
   annual religious festivals popular especially in Bengal, dedicated to female deities
elettiri: Bengali pronunciation of English "electric"

"Why did you have to plant your niece there?"

"That was divine play. Golapi used to throw herself in the temple. Little by little Kangali came to understand that he was the god's companion-incarnate and she *his* companion."

"Companion indeed! I can get my husband from her clutches with one blow of a broom!"

Nabin said, "No! that can't be any more. Kangali is a man in his prime, how can he be pleased with you any more? Besides, Golapi's brother is a real hoodlum, and he is guarding her. Asked *me* to *get out*. If I smoke ten pipes, he smokes twenty. Kicked me in the midriff. I went to speak for you. Kangali said, don't talk to me about her. Doesn't know her man, knows her master's house. The master's house is her household god, let her go there."

"I will."

Then Jashoda returned home, half crazed by the injustice of the world. But her heart couldn't abide the empty room. Whether it suckled or not, it's hard to sleep without a child at the breast. Motherhood is a great addiction. The addiction doesn't break even when the milk is dry. Forlorn Jashoda went to the Haldaress. She said, "I'll cook and serve, if you want to pay me, if not, not. You must let me stay here. That sonofabitch is living at the temple. What disloyal sons! They are stuck there too. For whom shall I hold my room?"

"So stay. You suckled the children, *and* you're a Brahmin. So stay. But sister, it'll be hard for you. You'll stay in Basini's room with the others. You mustn't fight with anyone. The master is not in a good mood. His temper is rotten because his third son went to Bombay and married a local girl. He'll be angry if there's noise."

Jashoda's good fortune was her ability to bear children. All this misfortune happened to her as soon as that vanished. Now is the downward time for Jashoda, the milk-filled faithful wife who was the object of the reverence of the local houses devoted to the Holy Mother. It is human nature to feel an inappropriate vanity as one rises, yet not to feel the *surrender* of "let me learn to bite the dust since I'm down" as one falls. As a result one makes demands for worthless things in the old way and gets kicked by the weak.

The same thing happened to Jashoda. Basini's crowd used to wash her feet and drink the water. Now Basini said easily, "You'll wash your own dishes. Are you my master, that I'll wash your dishes. You are the master's servant as much as I am."

As Jashoda roared, "Do you know who I am?" she heard the eldest daughter-in-law scold, "That is what I feared. Mother gave her a swelled head. Look here, Brahmin sister! I didn't call you, you begged to stay, don't break the peace."

Jashoda understood that now no one would attend to a word she said. She cooked and served in silence and in the late afternoon she went to the temple porch and started to weep. She couldn't even have a good cry. She heard the music for the evening worship at the temple of Shiva. She wiped her eyes and got up. She said to herself, "Now save me, Mother! Must I finally sit by the roadside with a tin cup? Is that what you want?

The days would have passed in cooking at the Haldar-house and complaining to the Mother. But that was not enough for Jashoda. Jashoda's body seemed to keel over. Jashoda doesn't understand why nothing pleases her. Everything seems confused inside her head. When she sits down to cook she thinks she's the milk-mother of this house. She is going home in a showy sari with a free meal in her hand. Her breasts feel empty, as if wasted. She had never thought she wouldn't have a child's mouth at her nipple.

Joshi became bemused. She serves nearly all the rice and curry, and forgets to eat. Sometimes she speaks to Shiva the King, "If Mother can't do it, you take me away. I can't pull any more."

Finally it was the sons of the eldest daughter-in-law who said, "Mother! Is the milk-mother sick? She acts strange."

The eldest daughter-in-law said, "Let's see."

The eldest son said, "Look here? She's a Brahmin's daughter, if anything happens to her, it'll be a sin for us."

The eldest daughter-in-law went to ask. Jashoda had started the rice and then lain down in the kitchen on the spread edge of her sari. The eldest daughter-in-law, looking at her bare body, said, "Brahmin sister! Why does the top of your left tit look so red? God! flaming red!"

"Who knows? It's like a stone pushing inside. Very hard, like a rock."

"What is it?"

"Who knows? I suckled so many, perhaps that's why?"

"Nonsense! One gets breast-stones or pus-in-the-tit if there's milk. Your youngest is ten."

"That one is gone. The one before survived. That one died at birth. Just as well. This sinful world!"

"Well the doctor comes tomorrow to look at my grandson. I'll ask. Doesn't look good to me."

Jashoda said with her eyes closed, "Like a stone tit, with a stone inside. At first the hard ball moved about, now it doesn't move, doesn't budge."

"Let's show the doctor."

"No, sister daughter-in-law, I can't show my body to a male doctor."

At night when the doctor came the eldest daughter-in-law asked him in her son's presence. She said, "No pain, no burning, but she is keeling over."

The doctor said, "Go ask if the *nipple* has shrunk, if the armpit is swollen like a seed."

Hearing "swollen like a seed," the eldest daughter-in-law thought, "How crude!" Then she did her field investigations and said, "She says all that you've said has been happening for some time."

"How old?"

"If you take the eldest son's age she'll be about fifty-five."

The doctor said, "I'll give medicine."

Going out, he said to the eldest son, "I hear your *Cook* has a problem with her *breast*. I think you should take her to the *cancer hospital*. I didn't see her. But from what I heard it could be *cancer* of the *mammary gland*."

Only the other day the eldest son lived in the sixteenth century. He has arrived at the twentieth century very recently. Of his thirteen offspring he has arranged the marriages of the daughters, and the sons have grown up and are growing up at their own speed and in their own way. But even now his grey cells are covered in the darkness of the eighteenth- and the pre-Bengal-Renaissance nineteenth centuries. He still does not take smallpox vaccination and says, "Only the lower classes get smallpox. I don't need to be vaccinated. An upper-caste family, respectful of gods and Brahmins, does not contract that disease."

He pooh-poohed the idea of cancer and said, "Yah! Cancer indeed! That easy! You misheard, all she needs is an ointment. I can't send a Brahmin's daughter to a hospital just on your word."

Jashoda herself also said, "I can't go to hospital. Ask me to croak instead. I didn't go to hospital to breed, and I'll go now? That corpse-burning devil returned a cripple because he went to hospital!"

The elder daughter-in-law said, "I'll get you a herbal ointment. This ointment will surely soothe. The hidden boil will show its tip and burst."

The herbal ointment was a complete failure. Slowly Jashoda gave up eating and lost her strength. She couldn't keep her sari on the left side. Sometimes she felt burning, sometimes pain. Finally the skin broke in many places and sores appeared. Jashoda took to her bed.

Seeing the hang of it, the eldest son was afraid, if at his house a Brahmin died! He called Jashoda's sons and spoke to them harshly, "It's your mother, she fed you so long, and now she is about to die! Take her with you! She has everyone and she should die in a Kayastha household?"

Kangali cried a lot when he heard this story. He came to Jashoda's almost-dark room and said, "Wife! You are a blessed auspicious faithful woman! After I spurned you, within two years the temples dishes were stolen, I suffered from boils in my back, and that snake Golapi tricked Napla, broke the safe, stole everything and opened a shop in Tarakeswar. Come, I'll keep you in state."

Jashoda said, "Light the lamp."

Kangali lit the lamp.

Jashoda showed him her bare left breast, thick with running sores and said, "See these sores? Do you know how these sores smell? What will you do with me now? Why did you come to take me?"

"The Master called."

"Then the Master doesn't want to keep me." — Jashoda sighed and said, "There is no solution about me. What can you do with me?"

"Whatever, I'll take you tomorrow. Today I clean the room. Tomorrow for sure.

"Are the boys well? Noblay and Gaur used to come, they too have stopped."

"All the bastards are selfish. Sons of my spunk after all. As inhuman as I."

"You'll come tomorrow?"

"Yes — yes — yes."

Jashoda smiled suddenly. A heart-splitting nostalgia-provoking smile. Jashoda said, "Dear, remember?"

"What, wife?"

"How you played with these tits? You couldn't sleep otherwise? My lap was never empty, if this one left my nipple, there was that one, and then the boys of the Master's house. How I could, I wonder now!"

"I remember everything, wife!"

In this instant Kangali's words are true. Seeing Jashoda's broken, thin, suffering form even Kangali's selfish body and instincts and belly-centered consciousness remembered the past and suffered some empathy. He held Jashoda's hand and said, "You have fever?"

"I get feverish all the time. I think by the strength of the sores."

"Where does this rotten stink come from?"

"From these sores."

Jashoda spoke with her eyes closed. Then she said, "Bring the holy doctor. He cured Gopal's *typhoid* with *homeopathy*."

"I'll call him. I'll take you tomorrow."

Kangali left. That he went out, the tapping of his crutches, Jashoda couldn't hear. With her eyes shut, with the idea that Kangali was in the room, she said spiritlessly, "If you suckle you're a mother, all lies! Nepal and Gopal don't look at me, and the Master's boys don't spare a peek to ask how I'm doing." The sores on her breast kept mocking her with a hundred mouths, a hundred eyes. Jashoda opened her eyes and said, "Do you hear?"

Then she realized that Kangali had left.

In the night she sent Basini for *Lifebuoy* soap and at dawn she went to take a bath with the soap. Stink, what a stink! If the body of a dead cat or dog rots in the garbage can you get a smell like this. Jashoda had forever scrubbed her breasts carefully with soap and oil, for the master's sons had put the nipples in their mouth. Why did those breasts betray her in the end? Her skin burns with the sting of soap. Still Jashoda washed herself with soap. Her head was ringing, everything seemed dark. There was fire in Jashoda's body, in her head. The black floor was very cool. Jashoda spread her sari and lay down. She could not bear the weight of her breast standing up.

As Jashoda lay down, she lost sense and consciousness with fever. Kangali came at the proper time: but seeing Jashoda he lost his grip. Finally Nabin came and rasped, "Are these people human? She reared all the boys with her milk and they don't call a doctor? I'll call Hari the doctor."

Haribabu took one look at her and said, "Hospital."

Hospitals don't admit people who are so sick. At the efforts and recommendations of the eldest son, Jashoda was admitted.

"What's the matter? O Doctorbabu, what's the problem?" — Kangali asked, weeping like a boy.

"Cancer."

"You can get cancer in a tit?"

"Otherwise how did she get it?"

"Her own twenty, thirty boys at the Master's house — she had a lot of milk — "

"What did you say? How many did she *feed*?"

"About fifty for sure."

"Fif-ty!"

"Yes sir."

"She had twenty children?"

"Yes sir."

"God!"

"Sir!"

"What?"

"Is it because she suckled so many — ?"

"One can't say why someone gets cancer, one can't say. But when people breast-feed too much — didn't you realize earlier? It didn't get to this in a day?"

"She wasn't with me, sir. We quarreled — "

"I see."

"How do you see her? Will she get well?"

"Get well! See how long she lasts. You've brought her in the last stages. No one survives this stage."

Kangali left weeping. In the late afternoon, harassed by Kangali's lamentations, the eldest son's second son went to the doctor. He was minimally anxious about Jashoda — but his father nagged him and he was financially dependent on his father.

The doctor explained everything to him. It happened not in a day, but over a long time. Why? No one could tell. How does one perceive breast cancer? A hard lump inside the breast toward the top can be removed. Then gradually the lump inside becomes large, hard, and like a congealed pressure. The skin is expected to turn orange, as is expected a shrinking of the nipple. The gland in the armpit can be inflamed. When there is *ulceration*, that is to say sores, one can call it the final stages. Fever? From the point of view of seriousness it falls in the second or third category. If there is something like a sore in the body, there can be fever. That is *secondary.*

The second son was confused with all this specialist talk. He said, "Will she live?"

"No."

"How long will she suffer?"

"I don't think too long."

"When there's nothing to be done, how will you treat her?"

"*Painkiller, sedative, antibiotic* for the fever. Her body is very, very *down.*"

"She stopped eating."

"You didn't take her to a doctor?"

"Yes."

"Didn't he tell you?"

"Yes."

"What did he say?"

"That it might be cancer. Asked us to take her to the hospital. She didn't agree."

"Why would she? She'd die!"

The second son came home and said, "When Arun-doctor said she had *cancer*, she might have survived if treated then."

His mother said, "If you know that much then why didn't you take her? Did I stop you?"

Somewhere in the minds of the second son and his mother an unknown sense of guilt and remorse came up like bubbles in dirty and stagnant water and vanished instantly.

Guilt said — she lived with us, we never took a look at her, when did the disease catch her, we didn't take it seriously at all. She was a silly person, reared so many of us, we didn't look after her. Now, with everyone around her she's dying in hospital, so many children, husband living, when she clung to us, then we had _____! What an alive body she had, milk leaped out of her, we never thought she would have this disease.

The disappearance of guilt said — who can undo Fate? It was written that she'd die of *cancer* — who'd stop it? It would have been wrong if she had died here — her husband and sons would have asked, how did she die? We have been saved from that wrongdoing. No one can say anything.

The eldest son assured them, "Now Arun-doctor says no one survives *cancer*. The cancer that Brahmin-sister has can lead to cutting of the tit, removing the uterus, even after that people die of *cancer*. See, Father gave us a lot of reverence toward Brahmins — we are alive by father's grace. If Brahmin-sister had died in our house, we would have had to perform the penance-ritual."

Patients much less sick than Jashoda die much sooner. Jashoda astonished the doctors by hanging on for about a month in hospital. At first Kangali, Nabin, and the boys did indeed come and go, but Jashoda remained the same, comatose, cooking with fever, spellbound. The sores on her breast gaped more and more and the breast now looks like an open wound. It is covered by a piece of thin *gauze* soaked in *antiseptic lotion,* but the sharp smell of putrefying flesh is circulating silently in the room's air like incense-smoke. This brought an ebb in the enthusiasm of Kangali and the other visitors. The doctor said as well, "Is she not responding? All for the better. It's hard to bear without consciousness, can anyone bear such death-throes consciously?"

"Does she know that we come and go?"

"Hard to say."

"Does she eat."

"Through tubes."

"Do people live this way?"

"Now your very_____"

The doctor understood that he was unreasonably angry because Jashoda was in this condition. He was angry with Jashoda, with Kangali, with women who don't take the signs of breast-cancer *seriously* enough and finally die in this dreadful and hellish pain. Cancer constantly defeats patient and doctor. One patient's cancer means the patient's death and the defeat of science, and of course of the doctor. One can medicate against the secondary symptom, if eating stops one can *drip glucose* and feed the body, if the lungs become incapable of breathing there is *oxygen* — but the advance of *cancer,* its expansion, spread, and killing, remain unchecked. The word *cancer* is a general signifier, by which in the different parts of the body is meant different *malignant growths.* Its characteristic properties are to destroy the infected area of the body, to spread by *metastasis,* to return after *removal,* to create *toximeia.*

Kangali came out without a proper answer to his question. Returning to the temple, he said to Nabin and his sons, "There's no use going any more. She doesn't know us, doesn't open her eyes, doesn't realize anything. The doctor is doing what he can."

Nabin said, "If she dies?"

"They have the *telephone number* of the old Master's eldest son, they'll call."

"Suppose she wants to see you. Kangali, your wife is a blessed auspicious faithful woman! Who would say the mother of so many. To see her body — but she didn't bend, didn't look elsewhere."

Talking thus, Nabin became gloomily silent. In fact, since he'd seen Jashoda's infested breasts, many a philosophic thought and sexological argument have been slowly circling Nabin's drug-and-booze-addled dim head like great rutting snakes emptied of venom. For example, I lusted after her? This is the end of that intoxicating bosom? Ho! Man's body's a zero. To be crazy for that is to be crazy.

Kangali didn't like all this talk. His mind had already *rejected* Jashoda. When he saw Joshoda in the Haldar-house he was truly affected and even after her admission into hospital he was passionately anxious. But now that feeling is growing cold. The moment the doctor said Jashoda wouldn't last, he put her out of mind almost painlessly. His sons are his sons. Their mother had become a distant person for a long time. Mother meant hair in a huge topknot, blindingly white clothes, a strong personality. The person lying in the hospital is someone else, not Mother.

Breast *cancer* makes the *brain comatose,* this was a solution for Jashoda.

Jashoda understood that she had come to hospital, she was in the hospital, and that this desensitizing sleep was a medicated sleep. In her weak, infected, dazed brain she thought, has some son of the Haldar-house become a doctor? No doubt he sucked her milk and is now repaying the milk-debt? But those boys entered the family business as soon as they left high school! However, why don't the people who are helping her so much free her from the stinking presence of her chest? What a smell, what treachery? Knowing these breasts to be the rice-winner, she had constantly conceived to keep them filled with milk. The breast's job is to hold milk. She kept her breast clean with perfumed soap, she never wore a top, even in youth, because her breasts were so heavy.

When the *sedation* lessens, Jashoda screams, "Ah! Ah! Ah!" — and looks for the *nurse* and the doctor with passionate bloodshot eyes. When the doctor comes, she mutters with hurt feelings, "You grew so big on my milk, and now you're hurting me so?"

The doctor says, "She sees her milk-sons all over the world."

Again injection and sleepy numbness. Pain, tremendous pain, the cancer is spreading *at the expense of the human host.* Gradually Jashoda's left breast bursts and becomes like the *crater* of a volcano. The smell of putrefaction makes approach difficult.

Finally one night, Jashoda understood that her feet and hands were getting cold. She understood that death was coming. Jashoda couldn't open her eyes, but she understood that some people were looking at her hand. A needle pricked her arm. Painful breathing inside. Has to be. Who is looking? Are these her own people? The people whom she suckled because she carried them, or those she suckled for a living? Jashoda thought, after all, she had suckled the world, could she then die alone? The doctor who sees her every day, the person who will cover her face with a sheet, will put her on a cart, will lower her at the burning ghat, the untouchable who will put her in the furnace, are all her milk-sons. One must become Jashoda if one suckles the world. One has to die friendless, with no one left to put a bit of water in the mouth. Yet someone was supposed to be there at the end. Who was it? It was who? Who was it?

Jashoda died at 11 p.m.

The Haldar-house was called on the phone. The phone didn't ring. The Haldars *disconnected* their phone at night.

Jashoda Devi, Hindu female, lay in the hospital morgue in the usual way, went to the burning ghat in a van, and was burnt. She was cremated by an untouchable.

Jashoda was God manifest, others do and did whatever she thought. Jashoda's death was also the death of God. When a mortal masquerades as God here below, she is forsaken by all and she must always die alone.

Translated from the Bengali by
Gayatri Chakravorty Spivak

KUNWAR NARAYAN

Kunwar Narayan (1927–) was born in Faizabad, which is now in the state of Uttar Pradesh, and received an M.A. in English literature from Lucknow University. He is a businessman and lives in Lucknow. He has published literary essays in Hindi, as well as four collections of poetry and one volume of short fiction.

Narayan was one of the innovative modernist poets who appeared in the Hindi literary world shortly after Indian Independence. In his early verse of the 1950s and 1960s, he experimented with symbolism as well as historical and philosophical material. In his more recent poetry, he is frequently concerned with psychological processes and social types and with the intersection of the mythic and the modern. Both "Preparations of War" and "Archaeological Find" are poems of the latter kind. They offer a view of human agents in history and politics whose actions repeat the past cyclically and in unsuspected ways, transforming the present moment into a mythic time that is here and now, but also everywhere and always. Such a conception enables Narayan to explain the violence of contemporary political life, especially in the guise of authoritarian rule, as a phenomenon with multiple origins in the near and remote historical past.

Preparations of War

After thousands of years
like the same beaten-up question
the same beaten-up man is still being asked
      "Who are you?
      Where do you live?   5
      What's your name?"

The prisoner who patrols
a motionless octagonal cell
holds three guards captive at the same time.

Everywhere outside   10
a forest of iron bars has spread its stranglehold
like a magnet's invisible lines of force.

And this is the solid proof of the success
of a massive buildup of arms
that as soon as we have a gun in our hands   15
enemy heads
begin to appear all around us.

Translated from the Hindi by
Vinay Dharwadker and Aparna Dharwadker

Archaeological Find

When I began to have doubts
about making headway in our search
       I was very close to home.

    It wasn't a hill but a valley
    we'd dug up.   5
    Engrossed in the digging
    we were buried
    several hundred years back in time
    so far and so deep
    we'd become hard to find.   10

Maybe at that moment
when I first found it hard to breathe
the past of an entire culture
broke away from us,
and I panicked and ran   15
towards the barely visible present, its sky and open air
that were being slowly shut out.

    A man begins his search
    when he knows what exists and what doesn't
    because he has learnt where a search begins and ends,   20
    his constant effort is to stay alive
    in the midst of all those battles
    that aren't his — or even for him —
    in which he's neither hero nor coward,
    he can only go on doing what he should   25
    with honesty and honor
    and yet not be bricked up alive
    in the walls of his own home.

I met him unexpectedly.
For reasons of his own   30
he gave me his number but not his name.
When he grew tired of years of watching history
he built himself a tomb,
closed the entrance with a heavy rock
                    and went to sleep.   35

He never woke up again, though looking at him
you wouldn't think he'd ever gone to sleep.
The force of his steady gaze, his face,
his language that spoke to no one —
in that cold, dank room   40
these were some of the signs still left
to say he wasn't a piece of stone but a man
who'd been trying for several thousand years
                    to survive as a man.

Translated from the Hindi
by Vinay Dharwadker

A. K. RAMANUJAN

A. K. Ramanujan (1929–1993) was born in Mysore, a city now in the state of Karnataka in India. He taught English literature at various colleges in India in the 1950s before moving to the United States to earn his Ph.D. in linguistics. After 1962 he taught mainly at the University of Chicago.

Over a period of four decades, Ramanujan published three collections of poems in English, two volumes of poetry, a novella, and short stories in the Kannada language, and a large number of scholarly and critical essays in English. He also translated poetry, fiction, and folklore extensively, especially from Kannada and Tamil into English and from English into Kannada.

Ramanujan's poems in English combine dramatic scenes with narrative vignettes and lyrical expression with philosophical insight. "Love Poem for a Wife 1" is part of a large group of poems about family life, extended families, and the difficulties of love and harmony in marriage. "Small-Scale Reflections on a Great House" uses the extended family as a metaphor for Indian society. It draws on concrete, everyday details as well as large-scale comic and tragic patterns to paint a vivid picture of life in a modern Indian household across sev-

eral generations. At the same time, the poem suggests parallels be-
tween the history and mythology of the family and those of the nation,
and hence constructs a miniature allegory of modern India.

Love Poem for a Wife 1

Really what keeps us apart
at the end of years is unshared
childhood. You cannot, for instance,
meet my father. He is some years
dead. Neither can I meet yours: 5
he has lately lost his temper
and mellowed.

In the transverse midnight gossip
of cousins' reunions among
brandy fumes, cashews and the Absences   10
of grandparents, you suddenly grow
nostalgic for my past and I
envy you your village dog-ride
and the mythology

of the seven crazy aunts.   15
You begin to recognize me
as I pass from ghost to real
and back again in the albums
of family rumours, in brothers'
anecdotes of how noisily   20
father bathed,

slapping soap on his back;
find sources for a familiar
sheep-mouth look in a sepia wedding
picture of father in a turban,   25
mother standing on her bare
splayed feet, silver rings
on her second toes;

and reduce the entire career
of my recent unique self   30
to the compulsion of some high
sentence in His Smilesian diary.
And your father, gone irrevocable
in age, after changing every day
your youth's evenings,   35

he will acknowledge the wickedness
of no reminiscence: no, not
the burning end of the cigarette
in the balcony, pacing
to and fro as you came to the gate,   40
late, after what you thought
was an innocent

date with a nice Muslim friend
who only hinted at touches.
Only two weeks ago, in Chicago,   45
you and brother James started
one of your old drag-out fights
about where the bathroom was
in the backyard,

north or south of the well   50
next to the jackfruit tree
in your father's father's house
in Alleppey.° Sister-in law
and I were blank cut-outs
fitted to our respective   55
slots in a room

really nowhere as the two of you
got down to the floor to draw
blueprints of a house from memory
of everything, from newspapers   60
to the backs of envelopes
and road-maps of the United States
that happened

to flap in the other room
in a midnight wind: you wagered heirlooms   65
and husband's earnings on what
the Uncle in Kuwait
would say about the Bathroom
and the Well, and the dying,
by now dead,   70

tree next to it. Probably
only the Egyptians had it right:
their kings had sisters for queens
to continue the incests
of childhood into marriage.   75

Alleppey: a small town in the state of Kerala, near the tip of the Indian peninsula

Or we should do as well-meaning
Hindus did,

betroth us before birth,
forestalling separate horoscopes
and mothers' first periods,   80
and wed us in the oral cradle
and carry marriage back into
the namelessness of childhoods.

Small-Scale Reflections
on a Great House

Sometimes I think that nothing
that ever comes into this house
goes out. Things come in every day

to lose themselves among other things
lost long ago among   5
other things lost long ago;

lame wandering cows from nowhere
have been known to be tethered,
given a name, encouraged

to get pregnant in the broad daylight   10
of the street under the elders'
supervision, the girls hiding

behind windows with holes in them.

Unread library books
usually mature in two weeks   15
and begin to lay a row

of little eggs in the ledgers
for fines, as silverfish
in the old man's office room

breed dynasties among long legal words   20
in the succulence
of Victorian parchment.

Neighbours' dishes brought up
with the greasy sweets they made
all night the day before yesterday   25

for the wedding anniversary of a god,

never leave the house they enter,
like the servants, the phonographs,
the epilepsies in the blood,

sons-in-law who quite forget   30
their mothers, but stay to check
accounts or teach arithmetic to nieces,

or the women who come as wives
from houses open on one side
to rising suns, on another   35

to the setting, accustomed
to wait and to yield to monsoons
in the mountains' calendar

beating through the hanging banana leaves.

And also, anything that goes out   40
will come back, processed and often
with long bills attached,

like the hooped bales of cotton
shipped off to invisible Manchesters°
and brought back milled and folded   45

for a price, cloth for our days'
middle-class loins, and muslin
for our richer nights. Letters mailed

have a way of finding their way back
with many re-directions to wrong   50
addresses and red ink marks

earned in Tiruvilla and Sialkot.°

And ideas behave like rumours,
once casually mentioned somewhere
they come back to the door as prodigies   55

born to prodigal fathers, with eyes
that vaguely look like our own,
like what Uncle said the other day:

invisible Manchesters: Between the early nineteenth and early twentieth centuries, the
   British ruling in India dismantled the strong, 2,000-year-old Indian cotton-weaving
   (handloom) industry by shipping the cotton grown in the Deccan Plateau region to
   Manchester, England, where it was woven into cloth in large steam-powered weav-
   ing mills.
Tiruvilla and Sialkot: small Indian towns in the far south and far north, respectively

that every Plotinus° we read
is what some Alexander° looted   60
between the malarial rivers.

A beggar once came with a violin
to croak out a prostitute song
that our voiceless cook sang

all the time in our backyard.   65

Nothing stays out: daughters
get married to short-lived idiots;
sons who run away come back

in grandchildren who recite Sanskrit
to approving old men, or bring   70
betelnuts° for visiting uncles

who keep them gaping with
anecdotes of unseen fathers,
or to bring Ganges water°

in a copper pot   75
for the last of the dying
ancestors' rattle in the throat.

And though many times from everywhere,

recently only twice:
once in nineteen-forty-three°   80
from as far away as the Sahara,

half-gnawed by desert foxes,
and lately from somewhere
in the north, a nephew with stripes

on his shoulder was called   85
an incident on the border
and was brought back in plane

and train and military truck
even before the telegrams reached,
on a perfectly good   90

chatty afternoon.

Plotinus: ancient Egyptian-born Roman philosopher
Alexander: Alexander the Great, who conquered Egypt, Persia, and western India
betelnut: hard nut of the betel plant, chewed as a stimulant and narcotic
Ganges water: water from the River Ganges, the holiest of rivers; the holy water is used
    ritually by Hindus for purification, rites of passage, etc.
nineteen-forty-three: the year during World War II when Indian soldiers fought in the
    British army against the Germans invading north Africa

SHRIKANT VERMA

Shrikant Verma (1931–1986) was born in Bilaspur, which is now in Madhya Pradesh. After receiving an M.A. from Nagpur University in 1956, he moved to New Delhi, where he worked as a journalist and in various political organizations. In 1976 he was elected to the upper house of the Indian Parliament. During the late 1970s and early 1980s, he was a general secretary and spokesman of the Congress (I) Party under Indira Gandhi's leadership. He published nearly twenty books in Hindi, including a novel and collections of short stories, essays, interviews with writers, and poems.

In the late 1950s and early 1960s, Verma wrote verse that was often metrical and lyrical in form and conventionally poetic in theme. After about 1965 he experimented extensively with imagistic short poems and fragmentary long poems, creating a distinctively dense and allusive texture. Both "Process of Change" and "Half-an-Hour's Argument" are representative of this approach, dealing with some of Verma's long-term political and historical concerns. The first of these poems focuses on the phenomenon of political complicity and guilt, using the ongoing conflicts between Hindus and Muslims in post-Independence India as its frame of reference. The latter poem, which is a condensed, fragmentary epic in the modernist style, deals with colonialism and its effects on the modern Indian mind and postcolonial Indian culture.

Process of Change

Where was I
when everyone was cheering?
I too was there
cheering,
fearing the consequence   5
of silence,
            like everyone else.

What did I do
when everyone said
we're Hindus,   10
            Muslims like Aziz
            are our enemies?
I too agreed,
I'm a true Hindu,
            Aziz is my enemy.   15

What did I say
when everyone murmured,
keep your mouth shut,
                silence is safe?

I too concurred,   20
don't risk words
since words betray,
                say
only what the others say.

The cheering is over now,   25
Aziz has been lynched,
the mouths are silent.

                Aghast,
everyone asks,
how could this have happened?   30

And I,
        like everyone else,
repeat the question.
How did this happen?
                Why?   35

*Translated from the Hindi
by Vinay Dharwadker*

Half-an-Hour's Argument

To take a beating at the office, to get knocked down in the world,
to be thrown out —
                what happens afterwards,
when you come home after the beating,
I think of it, I tell myself   5
I've nothing to do with this world,
I've only to become what they became
who went before me,
                beaten up, knocked down, thrown out.

I've only to write, that's all —   10
but I fail to rise,
so does my sunken brow.
To write is to pass through hell.
Why should I pass this way
                away?   15

Go then,
wade into the Vaitarni,°
the river you cross at death,
holding on to the tail of the one before you —
the tail still remains.   20
Or go find some virtue in the gift of a cow
to a poor brahmin priest. Go fix yourself up
for research at some university.
The taste of salt in food,
honesty in politics,   25
the fun of being alive
are gone,
          gone are the things that should have been
in the sixty-eighth year of the twentieth century
after Christ.   30

Filled with joy, a young girl watches her father return
beaten by the world, still walking homeward steadily,
no, don't smother it,
                    let that pyre burn.
Widows, chaste as virgins, are walking towards the flames,   35
shame and shamelessness have blossomed
and borne fruit.

Spring was born in the season of spring, winter in winter,
here at autumn's end
the bitch in heat   40
prowls around,
her tail tucked in.

Get up, the referee says to the fallen wrestler, get up,
helping the fallen to rise
is fun. He rises, to be knocked down again —   45
we got our money's worth!
                    This frittered time.

I too want a seat in the gallery. My greatgrandad
was beaten by a heavyweight,   50
my grandad by a welterweight,
my father by a bout
of malaria,
          and I by Duryodhan.°

Vaitarni: a river in Hindu mythology that corresponds to the River Styx, one of the
rivers of Hades in Greek mythology
Duryodhan: the principal villain of the ancient Indian epic the *Mahabharata*, whose
ambition and duplicity divide his clan and cause a war over the division of a kingdom

Death to Duryodhan!
Malaria has disappeared from the country,   55
so has my family's plot of land.

To whom shall I present my case?
Before whom shall I wave
my affidavit?
                    Is anyone around?   60
Or is this only a wilderness?

This is the home of that profiteering merchant
whose three sons were knocked off
by cholera, elections,
and sloth. The nation is observing Martyrs' Day.°   65
Are you going to join in or not?
Get on to the battlefronts!
A war could break out any moment —
possibilities never end

whether it's Kashmir° or the ocean at Cape Comorin.°   70
When the Bull at the temple in Mahabalipuram° belched
the immortal clan of brahmins got alarmed,
O Yajnavalkya,° giver of Hindu laws,
legislate again,
the Bull has belched —   75

honor the untouchable.°
Honor me as well!
But the public passed me up at the polls, saying,
he's bright all right, but very unruly.
Only twenty votes! Ten that came in before my time,   80
and ten that will come when I am gone.

Martyrs' Day: a national day in India honoring the war dead and those who lost their
    lives in the freedom struggle against the British; corresponds to Memorial Day in
    the United States
Kashmir: the northernmost state of India
Cape Comorin: the southernmost tip of the Indian peninsula
the Bull at the temple in Mahabalipuram: the holy city of Mahabalipuram has a large,
    famous temple dedicated to Lord Shiva (one of the three major gods in Hinduism);
    outside the temple is a large stone icon of the bull Nandi, Shiva's mythological gate-
    keeper and mount
Yajnavalkya: in Hindu tradition, a visionary thinker who lived around 800 B.C. and
    wrote some of the laws that govern the caste system
the untouchable: untouchables are outcasts from the Hindu caste system, which con-
    sists of four main caste groups; untouchables traditionally fill the "polluting" occu-
    pations, such as tanning, garbage-removal, cremation, etc., and cannot exchange
    food or have physical contact with members of the four caste-groups

In Hyderabad I saw Tipu Sultan,° the delicate filigree work
from Bidar,°
        in the same way one day I'll become
a lost thing with a lost name.   85

That's how the law is framed for these things, for the crime
of breaking it, ten thousand years
of exile in disguise,
but who ever lives through it,
who endures such endlessness?   90
Maybe in the end there will still be some air left on earth
as in a punctured bicycle wheel,
I'll live on in tedium,
whatever it is, this much is sure this much is sure that time
might pass more pleasantly which otherwise   95
just rattles away.

Having lived through the eighteen days of battle at Kurukshetra,°
how could the last two thousand years be set aside
so easily? Something to think about.
A lightning bolt for India . . . a rush lead . . .   100
Jawaharlal Nehru° has passed away . . . repeat . . .
Prime Minister Nehru
is no more. . . .
        (Please stay tuned in. There's more to follow).

All my life I had to fight the impudence   105
of those piddling hacks
who passed so close to me.

Poor to pauper, luck from lucky, that's how words are composed,
says grammar.

Don't break the rules,   110
there'll be nothing left.

Tipu Sultan: Sultan Tipu (1749–1799) was a Muslim ruler of the Mysore region, now in
    Karnataka state, who fought heroically against British military expansion in south
    India during the early decades of the East India Company rule
Bidar: a town situated near the city of Hyderabad in the state of Andhra Pradesh in
    southeastern India; famous for its silversmiths, who produce distinctive filigree
    work
Kurukshetra: in the epic *Mahabharata*, the battle-ground for the eighteen-day war be-
    tween the armies of two sets of cousins, the Pandavas (the "heroes") and the Kau-
    ravas (the "villains")
Jawaharlal Nehru: 1889–1964; the first Prime Minister of India after its independence
    from British colonial rule

Nothing was left, I had to battle
with Panini's° Sanskrit grammar,
Vincent Smith's° colonial history,
the geography of Dudley Stamp,°   115
Macaulay's° India is wrong, all wrong,
which — what shall I say —
I accept!

Your Honor, my son is innocent, have me hanged instead,
I've already paid the court fee.   120
Have mercy, my lord.
                              Stop this nonsense!

Saying this, I took my leave,
I can no longer bear to grapple with history.
Let me be forgotten. If justice is possible,   125
let the verdict only be
                              that there was one
who tried to turn this dumb charade into poetry.

Translated from the Hindi by
Vinay Dharwadker and Aparna Dharwadker

KEDARNATH SINGH

Kedarnath Singh (1934–) was born in Chakia, Ballia District, Uttar
Pradesh. He was educated at Banaras Hindu University, Varanasi (also
known as Banaras), from where he received an M.A. in Hindi literature
in 1956 and a Ph.D. in 1964. Since 1978 he has been a professor of
Hindi at Jawaharlal Nehru University, New Delhi. In the past three
decades, he has published two books of scholarly criticism on modern
Hindi literature, as well as several volumes of poetry.

Singh was the first poet to develop a playful, postmodernist style in

Panini: ancient Indian scholar who composed a definitive grammar of the Sanskrit language around 400 B.C.
Vincent Smith: late-nineteenth and early-twentieth-century British colonial historian
of India
Dudley Stamp: British colonial geographer, whose textbook of world geography remained standard in the British empire for several decades around the middle of the
twentieth century
Macaulay: Thomas Babington Macaulay, British writer, scholar, and political figure
whose *Minute on Indian Education* (1835) determined the basic colonial cultural
policy

free verse in Hindi. He writes his poems most often in a colloquial idiom, giving them an open form or structure. He frequently uses a free-flowing syntax, verbal repetition, and even cliché in order to capture some of the features of a casual, conversational voice. He also often combines these oral elements with fantastic symbols, urban themes, and rural images to create a uniquely cosmopolitan contemporary world in his poetry. His various strategies and devices as a craftsman are linked to his progressive left-wing politics, through which he aims to reach common readers or listeners and their everyday concerns. "On Reading a Love Poem" is one of his most successful attempts at bringing these factors together in a single text.

On Reading a Love Poem

When I'd read that long love poem
I closed the book and asked —
Where are the ducks?

I was surprised that they were nowhere
even far into the distance   5

It was in the third line of the poem
or perhaps the fifth
that I first felt
there might be ducks here somewhere

I'd heard the flap flap of their wings   10
but that may have been my illusion

I don't know for how long
that woman
had been standing in the twelfth line
waiting for a bus   15

The poem was completely silent
about where she wanted to go
only a little sunshine
sifted from the seventeenth line
was falling on her shoulders   20

The woman was happy
at least there was nothing in her face to suggest
that by the time she reached the twenty-first line
she'd disappear completely   25
like every other woman

There were *sakhu* trees
standing where the next line began
the trees were spreading
a strange dread through the poem
Every line that came next   30
was a deep disturbing fear and doubt
about every subsequent line

If only I'd remembered —
it was in the nineteenth line
that the woman was slicing potatoes   35

She was slicing
large round brown potatoes
inside the poem
and the poem was becoming
more and more silent   40
more solid

I think it was the smell
of freshly chopped vegetables
that kept the woman alive
for the next several lines   45

By the time I got to the twenty-second line
I felt that the poem was changing its location
like a speeding bullet
the poem had whizzed over the woman's shoulder
towards the *sakhu* trees   50

There were no lines after that
there were no more words in the poem
there was only the woman
there were only
her shoulders her back   55
her voice —
there was only the woman
standing whole outside the poem now
and breaking it to pieces

Translated from the Hindi
by Vinay Dharwadker

DHOOMIL

Dhoomil was the pen name of Sudama Pandeya (1935–1975), who was born in a village near Varanasi (Banaras). He taught electrical engineering at an industrial institute there and published one collection of poems in his lifetime, From the Parliament to the Street *(1972). His later poems were collected by his wife and published posthumously in 1977.*

In his poetry as well as in his public discussions of poetry (for instance, at writers' conferences), Dhoomil advocated political action on the extreme left-wing in India. He attacked British imperialism and European colonialism, but he criticized even more strongly the whole literary, intellectual, and political tradition of Western liberalism and liberal democracy. From this standpoint, he viewed the Indian nationalist elite as well as the post-Independence middle class as collaborators and oppressors deeply alienated from the Indian common people. He therefore felt that the nationalists' and middle-class intellectuals' liberal-democratic principles betrayed the cause of the people, whether farmers in the countryside, factory workers and daily-wage laborers in towns and cities, or the lowest castes and the untouchables. "The City, Evening, and an Old Man: Me" is a medium-length dramatic monologue by a character or persona who finds constructive action impossible in the hopelessly complicated Indian social and political world. The poem is at once a despairing self-portrait and an impersonal, satirical picture of a common type of political failure.

The City, Evening, and an Old Man: Me

I've taken the last drag
and stubbed out my cigarette in the ashtray,
and now I'm a respectable man
with all the trappings of civility.

When I'm on vacation
I don't hate anyone.
I don't have any protest march to join.
I've drunk all the liquor
in the bottle marked
FOR DEFENCE SERVICES ONLY°   10
and thrown it away in the bathroom.

For defence services only: a standard label on bottles of liquor sold at subsidized prices
   to members of the Indian armed forces

That's the sum total of my life.
(Like every good citizen
I draw the curtains across my windows
the moment I hear the air-raid siren.°   15
These days it isn't the light outside
but the light inside that's dangerous.)

I haven't done a thing to deserve
a statue whose unveiling
would make the wise men of this city   20
waste a whole busy day.
I've been sitting in a corner of my dinner plate
and leading a very ordinary life.

What I inherited were citizenship
in the neighborhood of a jail   25
and gentlemanliness
in front of a slaughterhouse.
I've tied them both to my own convenience
and hauled them two steps forward.
The municipal government has taught me   30
to stay on the left side of the road.
(To succeed in life you don't need
to read Dale Carnegie's book
but to understand traffic signs.)

Other than petty lies   35
I don't know the weight of a gun.
On the face of the traffic policeman
doing his drill in the square
I've always seen the map of democracy.

And now I don't have a single worry,   40
I don't have to do a thing.
I've reached the stage in life
when files begin to close.
I'm sitting in my own chair on the verandah
without any qualms.   45
The sun's setting on the toe of my shoe.
A bugle's blowing in the distance.
This is the time when the soldiers come back,
and the possessed city
is now slowly turning its madness   50
into windowpanes and lights.

Translated from the Hindi
by Vinay Dharwadker

P. LANKESH

P. Lankesh (1935–) was born in Konagavalli, in what is now the state of Karnataka. He earned his M.A. in English literature from Mysore University in 1959. He has taught at the University of Bangalore, has produced and directed films, and has worked as an editor and journalist; he also publishes his own newspaper in the language of Kannada. He has published nearly twenty books of poetry, short and novelistic fiction, and drama, as well as an edited anthology of modern Kannada poetry. He has also translated Sophocles and Baudelaire into Kannada.

Lankesh's "Bread," like some of his other fiction, emphasizes quick narrative movement, sharp social and psychological observation, and concern for social dilemmas, inequities, and injustices. The story represents the consciousness and point of view of an aging lower-middle-class woman, who has been visiting her daughter and son-in-law in a small town in southern India, on the occasion of a birth in their family. On the way back alone, she gets trapped involuntarily in a violent confrontation with a beggar and a crowd at the railway station. Lankesh gives us a cinematic eyewitness account of the incident, in which several typical contemporary Indian polarities come into play, including those between the middle class and the extremely poor, a helpless individual and an aggressive crowd, an isolated woman and a large number of men, compassion and cruelty, and fairness and injustice.

Bread

Summer. Wherever it was shady, there were people. Wherever it was damp, there were houseflies. When she got down at Singarapete° railway station, she hadn't noticed lots of things: coolies° scurrying here and there; a station full of dirty-limbed, ragged people, babies clutched in their armpits. Colorful pieces of paper, meaningless to her, were stuck all over the walls. Behind the station, on one side, smoke was rising from earth to sky. On the way into town, there were several processions. She'd tried to read the banners and posters of many of the processions, but couldn't. She'd tried to discuss some things with her daughter who'd just had a baby but the daughter seemed a bit scared. Afraid that her mother was trying to probe into her husband's affairs, she had dodged the questions. The son-in-law gave her no chance to speak when he came home from the office. She gave her daughter the foodstuffs and everything she had brought for her, nursed her after the delivery for a week. She was

---

Singarapete: small town in the state of Karnataka in south India
coolie: a porter, who carries a passenger's luggage for a price

now on her way back to the railway station with her tiny trunk and traveling bag. Her daughter had given her fruit and flat bread for the journey.

It was about four miles from her daughter's house to the station. She did think of taking a horse-cart instead of trying to walk the distance in the hot sun. But she had walked all the way, unwilling to fork out two rupees° for a cart.

"Walked four miles. They say this dump is a station. There's not even standing room," she grumbled to the person next to her, standing near a pillar on the crowded platform. But that person just stood there, unmoved.

At her foot was a gob of someone's snot covered with a swarm of flies — when they came close to her own feet, she felt queasy. She looked around, but decided to stay put as there seemed to be no place of refuge from the invasion of flies. She got very curious about the silent motionless person who stood there under a full head of hair; long hair falling from the crown of the head; from shoulder to ankle a dirty green cloth. She coughed, to attract attention. The person turned around slowly, mechanically. It was a man, not a woman. A face spent in fever, big pits under his eyes, countless lines on his face — a face full of anger and pain. She felt uneasy. She quietly dragged her trunk and bag a little away from the pillar. But he too moved a little and looked her in the eyes. She tried to look away, but couldn't. If she started out from there, he might follow her. There were people milling all around — people going about their own business indifferent to her problem. She wanted to stop some of them and tell them about this man. But she couldn't find the courage. Well, she said to herself, and stood there stubbornly. There were many others like her, waiting near other pillars with baskets, bags, cooking vessels. Dirty people, they sit anywhere at all, spit any place; the more she looked, the dizzier she seemed to get. Then a gong struck, announcing an arriving train. She thought of asking someone when approximately the train might arrive, but her tongue stuck in her mouth. A railway clerk was writing something on a blackboard near the gate. After he left, she could see what it was: "TRAIN DELAYED BY ONE HOUR."

The man was looking elsewhere. She felt a little better.

She wished she could join her children at once, and hear their voices. She was also famished. She was unaccustomed to eating in public, with everybody looking on. Still the belly accepts only one answer. Quietly she opened the bag and drew out the bread. She undid the packet and put it on her lap, thinking of saving at least two pieces of bread for her little baby. As she put aside one and started folding up the paper packet, the man with the long hair gazed at her, his eyes popping. Then she knew that his eyes were not fevered or unhappy, just hungry. She thought she could give him one of the pieces of bread. But she didn't want to get too

---

rupee: the basic unit of currency in modern India

familiar with him. She had suspicions, fears. So she tried wrapping up the bread in some haste, when he directly pounced on her, grabbed all of it and started cramming it into his mouth. She was startled out of her skin by what happened so fast. "Ho! Ho! Thief! Thief!" she screamed.

People slowly gathered around her. One of them, a thin tall cruel-eyed man, stared at her and asked, "What happened?"

She was trembling. "This man stole my — my — "

"Stole your what?"

"My bread. That's what he's eating."

The long-haired hungry man had already bitten off and finished half of it. He didn't seem to be aware of the world around him. His *dhoti°* didn't quite cover his thighs, his shirt was open at the chest. Long matted hair, unkempt beard. The world seemed dumb-struck at his single-mindedness. Some men grumbled something; some left the scene; others were neutral. The tall thin man with the cruel eyes asked again: "Why scream so loud for such a small thing? You know why he stole it, don't you?"

Some people laughed at his dry-voiced question.

Her helplessness grew. She shivered uncontrollably. Trying to force a sound out of her throat, she said: "Can't you see it, he grabbed it from my hand?"

"He was hungry, that's why." The answer was very direct. He got hungry, so he took it: a proper answer. But the roused, disturbed mind fumbled for something that had to be said, and made her say:

"If he'd asked me, I'd have given it to him myself. He needn't have grabbed . . ." But her words dissolved in the hubbub around her. Some laughed, some sneered. Down her neck, close to her chest, hot breaths and teasing voices that made her break out in a sweat. A weak-limbed wide-eyed creature raised his voice and said: "We know all about people like you. This has gone on too long. Don't try and fool us now. Tell us, take an oath on your baby's head and tell us: would you really have given it if he'd asked for it, would you really?"

"Anyone can take any oath," sneered another man.

She got into a rage at these country dogs barking at a woman instead of coming to her help; it didn't matter even if she died now. She cried out bravely:

"Who are you to get me to take oaths? I would have given it if I wished; if not, I wouldn't have. Aren't you ashamed to scold a poor woman when this cur grabs food from her hand and devours it? Don't any of you have wives, children?" She spat. "Dogs!"

"So we're dogs, are we?"

"What else? Get out of my way. Don't touch me."

"Why do dogs need wives and children?" "Give that whore one in the face!" "Look, look at this woman's cheek!"

dhoti: an Indian man's traditional lower garment

"If you touch my hand, I'll pick up my sandals. Will you move aside, or else . . ." As she said this, her voice grew louder. It became a scream. Trampled underfoot, her bag and trunk seemed to have disappeared. Numberless people from all over the station crowded there. "Thu!" she spat out viciously. The gathered crowd laughed, clapped hands; a thousand eyes stared at her. This was her first such experience. She had a feeling she was standing stark naked, she was scared she'd do something vile in the pressure of circumstance. Then began the people's murmur, panic. Someone said, "Police!" At a distance, a policeman was coming towards her, parting the crowd on both sides. She felt the breath of new life. Her fear turned into a fit of weeping. She wept helplessly in a loud voice. The policeman came in a hurry, asking something. His face and body were sweating. He had an ugly devouring look. As soon as he came near enough, he seized her bag, went straight to the beggar, grabbed the bread in his hand, and hit him on the head with his stick.

The crowd had stood motionless so far. But when the stick struck the bread-thief, there was a wave of anger. The anger was itching to become action. The policeman struck the beggar again. Blood began to flow. He stood there stunned by the blow. The policeman, too, was probably scared. He started pushing people with his stick, saying, "Go now, get away from here." She was staring at the thief; there was blood running down him. The crowd held the policeman by his stick and asked, "Why did you hit him?" It looked as if any minute the policeman would be torn to pieces by the crowd, when she said, "Please, don't hit anyone, please." She went closer to the "thief" who was bleeding badly. She couldn't touch him though she wanted to. Shivering, she looked around for her trunk and bag.

The policeman stood by, scared himself. "Look here, madam. It's you that's responsible for this mess. You'd better leave." Trying to please the crowd, he added, "We lose our heads because of people like you." But she couldn't have left then. She wanted to take out fruit from her handbag and distribute it to the "thief" and to the whole crowd. She took the fruit out of the bag, and took out the face cream, the powder, the baby socks and dolls that were in the bag along with the fruit, and held them out, her hands in a gesture of giving — but no one took anything. She tried to say, "Excuse me." But the words didn't come. From her faint hands, the fruit and the socks fell to the ground.

Then a distant whistle and a fearful military cry was heard. The crowd tried to disperse. But it wasn't easy to get through a dense milling crowd. Everyone scrambled, everyone got into everyone else's way. The policeman, who had begun to adopt a somewhat neutral position in the meantime, plucked up new spirit and started beating the crowd with his stick. She said, "No, no, please." Nobody heard her say it.

The reserve force was soon on the crowd. The policeman said to her, "Look here, these people are always getting into trouble, come away.

They'll all run now," and pulled her by the hand. A police hand curved around her shoulders and caressed a breast. She tried to escape it. "Why are they beating up the people? Please. No. Don't beat them. No, I won't come. You leave me alone and go your way." But he didn't let her go, his khaki chest pressed against her sweating breasts. The policeman said, "Have you gone off your head? Come, woman, or we'll be hurt. Come away."

The reserve force kept up a fierce pressure. The people moved back far away and watched, with cruel, revengeful eyes. But the bread-thief stood bleeding near the same old pillar and still stared at her. The policeman dragged her brutally across and gave her over to the reserve force. They stood guard around her as if she were some princess. She wished she could run from there and join the crowd. She wished she could scream out what she felt.

But the police surrounded her, behind her a van. Left right, left, right. As if they'd conquered a country, they marched with her. "Where to?" she asked. "O come with us. We'll send you home," said one of them. Tears welled up in her eyes. She turned around. Between the bars of the station, the walls and the sacks, she could see the beggar. His eyes, full of anger, fever, and hunger still seemed to look only at her. As she looked on, he seemed to walk straight in her direction. She wiped her eyes and looked again. There was no one there. The filthy body odor of policemen. When she closed her eyes, he was there again — a green shirt, a *dhoti* that didn't quite cover his thighs, hunger in his eyes, and drenched with blood.

Translated from the Kannada
by A. K. Ramanujan

NAIYER MASUD

Naiyer Masud (1936–) was born in Lucknow, Uttar Pradesh. He has two doctoral degrees, one in Persian and the other in Urdu literature, and is currently a professor of Persian at Lucknow University. Among his publications are two collections of short stories in Urdu, as well as Urdu translations of Franz Kafka and of several contemporary Iranian writers (whose language is Persian).

Masud mixes psychological realism and fantasy, creating a style that can be broadly classified as magical realism. In "The Color of Nothingness" he combines surreal images of decay with unexpected compressions in time. The cuts in time are such that the main character, who is also the first-person narrator of the story, starts out as a boy

but is transformed suddenly, near the end, into a full-grown man. The
story uses this character's consciousness to convey the experience of
growing up, of dealing with one's own and someone else's pain and suf-
fering, and of coping with loss, loneliness, and death. These themes are
commonplace in modern writing, but Masud's narrative makes them
fresh and memorable by placing them in an unfamiliar context. For his
distinctive setting, he employs a large, prosperous Muslim household
at the height of its social power, and subsequently in decline, around
the third quarter of the twentieth century. He also creates an unusual
cast of characters, which includes the enigmatic and unpredictable
narrator, the eccentric but humane retired surgeon next door, and the
lonely old woman named Nusrat.

The Color of Nothingness

I do not remember the story of the bad woman now, but back in those
days I took a keen interest in it. I remember I was overjoyed learning that
her case would be heard at our place, and that she would herself come
over to see it settled. Prior to this, the case of another notoriously bad
woman had also been heard at our house, and my elders had brought it to
a neat conclusion. But that happened when I was still in my nonage.° I
had only heard others speak of her, and they kept discussing her case
amongst themselves until the case of this second bad woman came along
and absorbed their attention.

On the day she was due to arrive, the outer room of our house was
given a thorough clean-up and later furnished with additional seats. Several curios, some of them centuries old, were added to enhance the
room's decor. The elders also called on me to help tidy up the place, and I
did what was required of me with considerable enthusiasm. As I was
moving a chair, I guessed from the conversation of my elders that that
was the chair the bad woman would have to sit in. My heart began to
pound. I could almost see her sitting right there. In fact, what aroused my
interest in the matter was the opportunity it offered of looking squarely
at a bad woman.

The elders alone were not going to try her; a number of outsiders were
also expected to take part in the proceedings. These were honorable men
to whom we had played host in the past as well. All those sumptuous reception arrangements were, as a matter of fact, intended primarily for
their sake. My instructions, trickling in from the elders every now and
then, focused chiefly on ensuring that the honorable guests were properly
looked after. But that was not where my interests lay.

nonage: period during which a person is legally underage

A flurry of nervous activity swept over the elders as the time when everybody was set to arrive drew near. This obliged me to scurry back and forth several times from the side door of the house to the rather distant outer room which formed a part of the house's facade. In the space between the side door and the outer room was a courtyard, the better part of which was overshadowed by a sprawling ancient tree bearing unusually tiny leaves. As the barrage of commands showed no sign of letting up, I too was infected by this same nervous tension and became somewhat breathless from my repeated rushed trips to the outer room. And yet each time I passed under the tree I didn't fail to raise my hand and give its branches a bit of a shake — it was an urge I could never resist, no less now, when I was quite beside myself amid all that excitement — and my eyes would rise to look at the portico with the run-down roof which stood in a corner of the courtyard. The old surgeon lived in that portico. Every time I laid my hand on the branches he would call out:

"Why do you meddle with that tree for no earthly reason at all?"

But today he did not utter those words, not even once. He just sat there amid God knows what kind of medicines and ointments. He was so preoccupied with the paraphernalia before him that he forgot to defend the tree against my onslaughts. That day I saw him, for the first time ever, with the full array of his armamentarium; in fact, he had already given up the practice of surgery when I was still very young. He was an accomplished surgeon in his time, but I had only heard about his great expertise. To me he was merely an old man who pestered us with question after annoying question about everything and anything that ever transpired in the house. If anything, old age had enhanced his curiosity. But most of his inquiries didn't bring him any joy: the elders rebuffed him, and I, for my part, gave him only incomplete and wrong answers which confused and befuddled him even more. As soon as the case of the bad woman surfaced, the old man came alive with curiosity. Every day he dragged himself out of the portico several times, only to walk back in, angrily mumbling away. Today, however, when he should have been more excited than ever before, he was just quietly engrossed in his work, as if nothing else mattered.

For this I would certainly have teased him a bit. But by now I was feeling quite worked up — mainly because it was well past the time the invitees should have arrived, and in fact none had. The elders began to feel increasingly jittery; once more I found myself scrambling out the side door on my way to the outer room, giving the branches of the tree a tug as I made my way along. The tree, as always, sent a torrent of tiny yellow leaves over me. Brushing them off my hair and shoulders as I made to the outer room . . . I saw there was nobody there.

I remained in the outer room for quite some time. Eventually the hushed stillness of the extravagantly decorated room began to get to me. Bored with the delay of the guests, I felt I no longer wanted to think about the bad woman, or the honorable guests either. It was then that I remembered Nusrat.

Hurrying past the tree on my errands I had seen her, every single time indeed, sitting there, leaning against it, staring straight ahead at the old surgeon, or looking sideways at the ground, as her fingers traced lines in the dirt. And now I even seemed to recall that the first time I passed under the tree — or was it the second time? — she had turned to look at me. Perhaps she also greeted me. But right then I was too flustered to have returned her greeting or even realize that she had actually raised her hand to greet me.

She had a sweet voice and she moved about nimbly. From time to time she came to our house to look after some sick relative of hers. Often I would notice how, upon being called by someone, she would pick her way from one part of the house to another with extreme caution, as if afraid she might step on something fragile and crush it. When she was present in the house, one heard her name quite often. But I rarely spoke to her: for one thing she talked in an exceedingly low voice, and for another, she kept her eyes lowered when she spoke. But she never failed to greet me.

Anyway, I started from the outer room, came to the tree and stopped and stood near it. I tugged lightly at the branches. The tree was in the throes of autumn and most of the leaves had turned pale and fallen. Here and there the branches were covered with spider webs, which caught many of the leaves as they came spiraling down. I looked at Nusrat. She sat leaning forward now, her head resting on her knees, her fingers still tracing lines busily. But then I saw her hand slacken and become motionless. Tiny yellow leaves covered her hair and shoulders, and she was dressed in white. It was bright and sunny under the tree, but too warm to sit outside.

"It isn't chilly outside," I said.

She raised her head to look at me, and I asked, "Are you feeling cold, Nusrat?"

She sat up, her eyes still glued to the old surgeon.

"Are you feeling cold, Nusrat?"

"Not really," she said with a faint smile.

"Then why are you sitting here, in the sun?"

She didn't answer.

"Why don't you go in?" I said, pointing to the side door. "It's very hot here in the sun."

"Baba asked me to be here," she said looking at the old surgeon.

"Come on then. We'll go and sit with him," I said.

And although it seemed as if she was willing to follow my suggestion, she made no attempt to get up. I repeated my words and waited for quite a while for her to rise.

"I am not able to walk," she said softly and with a slight nod of her head pointed to her feet.

Only then did I notice. Her feet had been badly crushed, blackish-green and so swollen it was difficult to attribute them to a human body. The skin had split open in several places with a light red showing between the cracks. The right foot had been totally knocked out of shape and the left toes, bloated and curling round, were buried to half their length in the right sole. It seemed they were being sucked into the right foot with a tremendous force and, before long, would break off and completely vanish into it. All of this looked like a murderous struggle, the sheer tension of which had caused a mesh of protruding blue veins to erupt ominously all across her calves.

"What happened, Nusrat?" I asked her again and again.

"Everybody says both feet will just have to be amputated," she said. "But Baba wants me to let him . . ." here her voice became so faint I could not hear the words that followed. I looked at the old surgeon. He was busy picking up some iron instruments one by one and peering at them, drawing them close to his eyes. Something was coming to a boil in a clay pot close by and the portico was filled with smoke.

"Baba said I'm not to let anyone know," I heard Nusrat say. "He said he would do it today, because everyone would be busy elsewhere."

"But, Nusrat, what did really happen?"

Thereupon she told me the whole story. I've already forgotten some of the details, others I couldn't make out as her voice, every now and then, dropped to a whisper. Perhaps she was in too much pain. She mentioned some men who were in a vehicle and wanted to get to a certain destination in a hurry. Perhaps there had been an accident. But something was blocking the vehicle and had to be removed. Nusrat promptly pushed, whatever it was, aside. But before she could get out of the way the vehicle lurched forward and crushed both her feet. It rolled on without bothering to stop and Nusrat lay there unattended for a long time.

"What kind of people were they?" I exclaimed after hearing her out. "Didn't they even notice they'd run you over?"

"As a matter of fact, they did," she said. "That's why only the front wheel passed over my feet. They quickly veered the vehicle over to one side, maneuvering the rear wheel away from the path of my feet."

"But they didn't stop?"

"They were in a hurry."

"You didn't stop them either?"

"They were in a hurry. Still I managed to say . . ." her voice faded out.

"What did you say, Nusrat?"

"But maybe they could not hear me."

"What did you say, Nusrat?"

"I said: you see how helpless I am."

I couldn't help laughing at this.

"What a pointless thing to say!" I said. "What purpose could it possibly serve! It wouldn't have mattered at all — would it? — even if they had heard it."

"But what else could I have said?"

I had no answer to that. All the same I said, "Men like them are not likely to be affected by such a remark. *You see how helpless I am*," I mimicked the way she'd said it. "Did you not even realize the sort of people they were?"

"That's what people are like," she said, and once again put her face back on her knees.

Sensing she was not going to cry, I continued. "So what happened then? How did you get out of there?"

Just as she started to tell me about it I heard a few sharp sounds. I turned round and looked at the old surgeon. He was getting up, clutching his waist with his hands. Obviously, he was not the source of those sounds. I looked back at Nusrat. Her lips were moving but the raucous sounds drowned out her soft voice. Finally I did manage to guess where they were coming from. I moved a few steps back to get a better view. I saw vehicles pulling up in front of the outer room. The bad woman had arrived.

I sprinted off.

Most of the seats in the outer room had been taken. Nearly all the honorable guests had also arrived. Their faces looked unusually serious, almost grim in fact. My elders, being the hosts as well, were in something of a fix: whether to look more hospitable or more grim. A number of women were also present. The bad woman was there too, as part of the audience. Contrary to my expectations, she didn't look significantly different from the others. She had draped herself in several mantles, one on top of the other, and the only expression her face betrayed was one of exhaustion. Although she was literally buried under her clothing, a part of her belly with prominent blue veins could still be seen clearly. Her lips parted a little as she breathed, exposing fully two of her front teeth, which remained in view as she kept breathing quick and fast. I was disappointed when I saw her. A girl was sitting right close to her, and every now and then the bad woman leaned toward her to say something. Following one of her remarks the girl began to look around and her eyes fell on me. She got up and walked over to me. Then she said, "Could one get a drink of water?"

I hurried off at once. As I passed under the tree on my way to the side door I saw the old surgeon sitting in front of Nusrat and examining her feet very closely. Hearing my footsteps he raised his head and squinted at me in an effort to make out who I might be. Had I tugged at the branches, he would have recognized me at once. As I hastened to the outer room after fetching the glass of water from the house, I saw the old man still busily looking at Nusrat's feet.

The bad woman drained the glass in a single draught and then handed it back to the girl, who then returned it to me. I had to bring her water three times over. And all of this could go on just because some honorable guests still hadn't turned up. Time and again a sudden silence would descend on the room, prompting one or another of the elders to dispel it by clearing his throat and uttering some stuffy pleasantry to the guests seated near him.

The fourth time I brought the water it was the girl who took the glass from my hand and began to drink from it in unhurried, small sips. Two of her teeth, refracted and distorted by the glass and the water, appeared enormous. When she handed the glass back to me I put it down nonchalantly on the floor near the door, and the girl returned to the bad woman.

By now the atmosphere in the room had become so intolerably thick that I thought I might just as well withdraw for a while.

As I was passing under the tree I heard the voice of the old surgeon.

"Come here," he was calling me. I turned to walk over to him.

"Come closer."

I drew nearer. He put his hand on my shoulder, pulling me down toward him.

"Her feet are stuck together," he whispered. "The first thing is to separate them. That usually is exceedingly painful. She may writhe and thrash about. Perhaps I won't be able to hold her still by myself. Perhaps I no longer have the strength to do so."

I looked at Nusrat. There was panic in her eyes; all the same, she was trying to smile.

"Maybe if you talked to her and somehow kept her occupied . . ." the old man whispered again. "Said things that would take her mind off me, completely off me. For if she suddenly jerked her feet, things would go badly for her. I mean her left toes would snap off. Don't let that happen. When I gesture to you, keep her mind off what I'm doing. Make sure she remains absolutely still, I mean absolutely still."

Next he said something funny but couldn't make her laugh, and I, on my part, told her some anecdotes from earlier in the old man's life. I spoke of his achievements in the field of surgery about which I'd heard, while in the meantime the old man went on examining her feet from various angles and placing them on the ground in different ways.

I talked for a long time. I told her interesting tidbits about our family. Then I began to talk about her. But it could not have amounted to much, or been very coherent. What did I really know about her? All the same, I tried not to let her guess that. I now had the distinct impression that she no longer was thinking about the old surgeon. Throughout I would glance at him intermittently. I saw him indicate that I should be ready.

"And do you know, Nusrat, what came to my mind the very first time I saw you?" I couldn't even remember when that first time had been. Nonetheless I continued: "Do you know what crossed my mind that day? It seemed to me that you were walking on flowers." Just then I realized how awful a mistake this was and hastily proceeded to say, "Should I tell you something about your hands, Nusrat — something I believe nobody else could ever tell you?"

Right then I saw the old man make that unmistakable sign. I quickly took hold of both her hands and pressed them hard.

"Should I tell you?" I whispered. Almost at once I heard harsh voices rise from the direction of the outer room and then melt into the distance. Precisely then her hands trembled in my grasp. I saw her face turn blue, then red, and then ashen white. She bit her lips and her eyes expressed terrible agony.

"It's all right," I heard the old man say. "It's absolutely right. Well done! I will be able to cure her now. Just wait and see."

I turned towards the old man. He had spread his hands over Nusrat's feet, hiding them completely. I wanted to see what exactly he had done, but he refused harshly.

"Don't look at her feet," he said, "and don't you let her look at them either."

I turned my face away and looked up at the spider webs stuck to the branches of the tree. It was absolutely quiet all around, except for a soft clink coming every now and then from the surgical instruments. In anxious anticipation I waited for the old man to say something. And he did, finally:

"You may go now, if you like, and attend to your own business. I can handle the rest myself."

Only then did I realize I was still holding her hands. She had put her face back down on her knees and her hands were damp with sweat. I let go of them, got up and, even though aware that I was already too late, began to walk towards the outer room.

A deathly hush had now swept over the room. The chairs were in total disarray, and some hastily scribbled-on scraps of paper lay near some of them. I collected the scraps. The scrawled writing marked the consultations which had taken place among the elders and honorable guests. I put the chairs back in order. I had a hard time deciphering the writings on the scraps, but once I had mastered it I tried to ascertain the events that had taken place during my absence. I arranged and rearranged the scraps in many different ways but failed completely to make any sense of them; as soon as I changed their order the events they were supposed to represent also underwent a complete change. I wasted a considerable amount of time juggling those scraps and was none the wiser for my effort. My interest, tremendously aroused by the sight of them, began to dampen and then vanish altogether. The room, lined with antiques, began to suffocate me. I felt I couldn't stay there any longer. As I was leaving the room I noticed that the glass lay totally undisturbed near the door where I had set it. I didn't bother to pick it up; instead I headed directly for the tree.

But there was only the carpet of yellow leaves beneath it. I furtively looked at the portico of the old surgeon. It was empty, although still filled with smoke.

Soon afterwards my house began to empty out. My people, all of them, began to expire, one by one and in quick succession; the end of the elders was even swifter: as though they were a heap of rice pressed by a damp hand, lifting them clear off. I looked on at all this, thinking that I was in a dream and hoping that I'd wake up from it. Occasionally I felt frightened. Anyway, in the end I found myself all alone in a rambling mansion, trying somehow to get used to my loneliness. I would visit each and every part of the house, anxious, always anxious not to let even the smallest space remain unoccupied by me for too long. Had anyone watched me in those days, he certainly would have thought I was looking for something I had lost.

But one day it occurred to me that I had somehow completely neglected the outer room. So I went there. The main door stood open as usual and the heavy curtain across it stirred slowly. The light inside the room was rather dim, which made the farthest chairs appear hazy. In spite of the poor light I could still see the heavy layer of dust which had settled on the precious curios. The walls too had become coated with dust and the portraits of the elders looked faded and dull. I touched the curios one at a time, leaving my fingerprints on them. I wiped the dust off the portraits of my elders with my hand. They became so vivid that I felt like talking to them. And when I spoke I could hear my voice resonate inside the room. I talked for a long time. Coming to one portrait I broke my stride and stopped. The kind face peered at me with apprehension. A sense of loss overwhelmed me and I gently touched the portrait with my forehead.

"I remember everything," I said. "Everything."

Those anxious eyes just kept gazing at me.

"But nothing can be done now. I had no idea until right now how the same house could look so completely deserted, and yet so full of people. This very room . . ." I swept the room with my glance, "this very room, once upon a time . . ." my eyes caught the glass on the floor near the door, "why, even the bad woman . . ." Right then I heard the rustle of a dress, forcing me to turn around and look.

Someone had just got up from a chair in the distant gloom and was walking toward me. It was a woman. Is she the bad woman? I wondered. But then I heard her voice.

"You wouldn't have recognized me," she said softly. She had drawn nearer now. I bent down and touched her feet to see if they were completely healed.

"That's wonderful!" I said. "I am happy, Nusrat, that your feet are better now."

A long silence ensued during which neither of us said a word. Then I said, "I hope there are no scars."

One after the other she put her feet forward in the light filtering through the bottom of the heavy curtain.

"Even the scars have disappeared," she said.

Another long silence followed which I felt compelled to break.

"After a few days," I began, "you won't even remember what terrible pain you had to endure. The scars would have been a reminder."

"But I *shall*."

"That's what everyone imagines in the beginning. Without scars, though, one couldn't remember — neither the pain, nor even the old surgeon."

That probably disturbed her a bit and when she spoke again she did so hesitantly, as if trying to explain a mistake of hers.

"The scars would certainly have been there, but Baba himself . . . he said there should be no scars." Then, after a while, she added, repeating her words two or three times, "I didn't say anything to him."

"You don't have to explain anything," I said, raising my hand. "I'm not blaming you at all. But the fact is though, there are no scars now."

The stiff manner in which I spoke was all too obvious to me. It was not the right thing to do — I conceded to myself. But I couldn't help it. The loss of so many had left me saddened.

"You must be wondering, Nusrat, why I'm talking this way," I said. "You must be thinking it isn't the way I spoke to you that day under the tree."

"That was another day," Nusrat said, looking intently at her feet. Her voice grew softer as she added, "I was in a pitiable state that day."

She lifted her head to look at me. After a brief silence she said in a voice that was softer still, "That was a day of commiseration."

"And today?" I asked, my voice growing louder. "Is it not a day of commiseration also? Weren't you really looking forward to it?" I took a few quick steps forward and came quite close to her. "But, Nusrat, let me tell you, my state is not pitiable."

"When did I ever say that?" There was sheer torment in her eyes and her voice sounded tremulous. "I couldn't even imagine it would turn out like this."

Suddenly her voice choked. She seemed ready to collapse. I caught her arm to support her. After I had steadied her, I released her and moved back. Her face lost all its color and she stood there so perfectly still and lost for such a long time that she herself looked like one of the antiques in the room. The marks left by my dusty fingers remained on her arm.

I now began to feet a bit contrite. "I am sorry, Nusrat," I said. "The room is full of dust and you are so fond of white clothes. And white does look lovely on you. I've heard many people admire you for it. As for me, I like black more. Do you know why?"

She raised her head to look at me. I repeated a line I had read somewhere — one I never quite managed to forget: "Because black is the color of nothingness."

And the sense of loss overwhelmed me once again. I have no idea how much longer Nusrat stood there, waiting for me to say something more. But finally I saw her turn around slowly and walk towards the door. I heard the muted sound of the glass breaking and saw Nusrat hesitate for a moment near the door. Then she lifted the heavy curtain. Outside light invaded the room and, just as suddenly, vanished.

She was a soft-footed girl. I didn't hear the sound of her receding footsteps.

I remembered that my prolonged stay in the room had caused me to neglect other parts of the house, and this prompted me to leave at once. Coming to the door my eyes caught the glass. It was broken now. I swept the pieces aside with my foot. The edges of some of the jagged pieces, I noticed, were stained with something — fresh blood, I recognized at once, in spite of the faint light.

Afterwards I had the opportunity to pass under the tree many times. It had again filled out with dense foliage. The branches, unable to cope with the heavy burden of the leaves, had dropped so low over the ground that I literally had to crawl under them to get across. And if on occasion I walked totally absorbed in my thoughts, the soft leaves invariably struck me across the face. This prompted me to think: why not prune these branches which always get in my way?

One day I was going towards the side door. As I approached the tree I automatically bent a little. But the leaves struck me in the face all the same and I noticed that the branches had dropped lower still. I was irritated. I thrust out my hand and pushed them away right and left, only to have them bounce back and strike me more forcefully than before. I began to feel terribly itchy on my face and neck and snapped off quite a few branches, yanking them vigorously. I had to bend low to free myself from the tangle. As I straightened up and brushed the twigs and leaves off my body, I noticed someone sitting huddled against the trunk. It was not possible to make out the face of the figure because of the gloom cast by the thick foliage, but I recognized her all the same.

"Nusrat!" I called out, picking my way toward her. As I drew near I saw that she was dressed in black.

"Nusrat!" I called softly and my eyes fell on her. Her features were not visible. I couldn't understand why it was so. I leaned forward and took a closer look. Dry yellow leaves covered her face like a veil. I wanted to remove the leaves from her face but saw that they were held together by cobwebs and my hand stopped halfway.

"Nusrat!" I called again in a voice growing fainter. I saw that the black mantle covered her from her shoulders down to her feet. One of her hands was free of the cape and appeared resting on the ground. Her fingers were coated with dust and there was a maze of lines drawn in the dirt.

"Nusrat!" I said, but in a manner suggestive of a man talking only to himself. I shook her in an effort to wake her up. I made an attempt to move her feet slowly. It was then that I saw:

Her feet under the black mantle formed an odd protuberance. I didn't touch her. Somehow I knew that beneath the mantle her feet were again misshapen.

I looked around. My sweeping eyes came to rest on the portico of the old surgeon. The floor was covered with the debris of the caved-in roof. There was no voice to be heard anywhere. Not a thing seemed to move. The chill under the tree increased suddenly and a severe trembling seized my body.

I stood up and ran through the side door. I had only taken a few steps inside when I turned back to close it. I firmly grabbed hold of the two sides of the door and brought them close together. As it was about to close I peered through the slit that remained to find out whether Nusrat was still sitting in the same way. She was.

I shut the door and was never able to open it again.

Translated from the Urdu by
Muhammad Umar Memon

ANITA DESAI

Anita Desai (1937–) was born in Mussoorie, Uttar Pradesh, the daughter of a Bengali father and a German mother. She received her B.A. in English literature from Miranda House, University of Delhi. Since the 1950s she has lived in New Delhi, Calcutta, Bombay, and other Indian cities. She has also been a frequent visitor abroad, serving as a visiting fellow at Girton College, Cambridge, England, in 1986–87, and as a professor at Smith College in the United States in 1987–89. Since 1989 she has been a professor at Mount Holyoke College, teaching creative writing there for one semester each year and spending the rest of her time in India. She started publishing her fiction in English in the early 1960s.

The fiction that Desai wrote in the 1960s and 1970s is often a lyrical and existentialist exploration of the minds and lives of individual characters as well as social types. Most of these characters belong to the middle class in post-Independence India and inhabit a social world that is rather westernized and therefore detached from traditional society on the subcontinent. "The Farewell Party," taken from Games at Twilight, *portrays distinctive as well as stereotypical characters and situations in a middle-class professional community in contemporary small-town India. It is a story that combines social and psychological realism, though it emphasizes the latter. It provides a fairly sympathetic account of the thought processes and feelings of the main characters (a housewife and her husband) and a more satirical account of the society around them.*

The Farewell Party

Before the party she had made a list, faintheartedly, and marked off the items as they were dealt with, inexorably — cigarettes, soft drinks, ice, *kebabs* and so on. But she had forgotten to provide lights. The party was to be held on the lawn: on these dry summer nights one could plan a lawn party weeks in advance and be certain of fine weather, and she had thought happily of how the roses would be in bloom and of the stars and perhaps even fireflies, so decorative and discreet, all gracefully underlining her unsuspected talent as a hostess. But she had not realized that there would be no moon and therefore it would be very dark on the lawn. All the lights on the veranda, in the portico and indoors were on, like so many lanterns, richly copper and glowing, with extraordinary beauty as though aware that the house would soon be empty and these were the last few days of illumination and family life, but they did very little to light the lawn which was vast, a still lake of inky grass.

Wandering about with a glass in one hand and a plate of cheese biscuits in another, she gave a start now and then to see an acquaintance emerge from the darkness which had the gloss, the sheen, the coolness but not the weight of water, and present her with a face, vague and without outlines but eventually recognizable. 'Oh,' she cried several times that evening, 'I didn't know you had arrived. I've been looking for you,' she would add with unaccustomed intimacy (was it because of the gin and lime, her second, or because such warmth could safely be held to lead to nothing now that they were leaving town?). The guest, also having had several drinks between beds of flowering balsam and torenias° before launching out onto the lawn, responded with an equal vivacity. Sometimes she had her arm squeezed or a hand slid down the bareness of her back — which was athletic: she had once played tennis, rather well —

torenias: subtropical flowering plants

and once someone said, 'I've been hiding in this corner, watching you,' while another went so far as to say, 'Is it true you are leaving us, Bina? How can you be so cruel?' And if it were a woman guest, the words were that much more effusive. It was all heady, astonishing.

It was astonishing because Bina was a frigid and friendless woman. She was thirty-five. For fifteen years she had been bringing up her children and, in particular, nursing the eldest who was severely spastic. This had involved her deeply in the workings of the local hospital and with its many departments and doctors, but her care for this child was so intense and so desperate that her relationship with them was purely professional. Outside this circle of family and hospital — ringed, as it were, with barbed wire and lit with one single floodlight — Bina had no life. The town had scarcely come to know her for its life turned in the more jovial circles of mah-jong, bridge, coffee parties, club evenings and, occasionally, a charity show in aid of the Red Cross. For these Bina had a kind of sad contempt and certainly no time. A tall, pale woman, heavy-boned and sallow, she had a certain presence, a certain dignity, and people, having heard of the spastic child, liked and admired her, but she had not thought she had friends. Yet tonight they were coming forth from the darkness in waves that quite overwhelmed.

Now here was Mrs Ray, the Commissioner's wife, chirping inside a nest of rustling embroidered organza. 'Why are you leaving us so soon, Mrs Raman? You've only been here — two years, is it?'

'Five,' exclaimed Bina, widening her eyes, herself surprised at such a length of time. Although time dragged heavily in their household, agonizingly slow, and the five years had been so hard that sometimes, at night, she did not know how she had crawled through the day and if she would crawl through another, her back almost literally broken by the weight of the totally dependent child and of the three smaller ones who seemed perpetually to clamour for their share of attention, which they felt they never got. Yet now these five years had telescoped. They were over. The Raman family was moving and their time here was spent. There had been the hospital, the girls' school, the boys' school, picnics, monsoons, birthday parties and measles. Crushed together into a handful. She gazed down at her hands, tightened around glass and plate. 'Time has flown,' she murmured incredulously.

'Oh, I wish you were staying, Mrs Raman,' cried the Commissioner's wife and, as she squeezed Bina's arm, her fragrant talcum powder seemed to lift off her chalky shoulders and some of it settled on Bina who sneezed. 'It's been so nice to have a family like yours here. It's a small town, so little to do, at least one must have good friends . . .'

Bina blinked at such words of affection from a woman she had met twice, perhaps thrice before. Bina and her husband did not go in for society. The shock of their first child's birth had made them both fanatic parents. But she knew that not everyone considered this vital factor in their lives, and spoke of 'social duties' in a somehow reproving tone. The Commissioner's wife had been annoyed, she always felt, by her refusal to help out at the Red Cross fair. The hurt silence with which her refusal had been accepted had implied the importance of these 'social duties' of which Bina remained so stubbornly unaware.

However, this one evening, this last party, was certainly given over to their recognition and celebration. 'Oh, everyone, everyone is here,' rejoiced the Commissioner's wife, her eyes snapping from face to face in that crowded aquarium, and, at a higher pitch, cried 'Renu, why weren't you at the mah-jong party this morning?' and moved off into another powdery organza embrace that rose to meet her from the night like a moth and then was submerged again in the shadows of the lawn. Bina gave one of those smiles that easily frightened people found mocking, a shade too superior, somewhat scornful. Looking down into her glass of gin and lime, she moved on and in a minute found herself brought up short against the quite regal although overweight figure, in raw silk and homespun and the somewhat saturnine air of underpaid culture, of Bose, an employee of the local museum whom she had met once or twice at the art competitions and exhibitions to which she was fond of hauling her children, whether reluctant or enthusiastic, because 'it made a change,' she said.

'Mrs Raman,' he said in the fruity tones of the culture-bent Bengali, 'how we'll miss you at the next children's art competitions. You used to be my chief inspiration — '

'Inspiration?' she laughed, incredulously, spilling some of her drink and proffering the plate of cheese biscuits from which he helped himself, half-bowing as though it were gold she offered, gems.

'Yes, yes, inspiration,' he went on, even more fruitily now that his mouth was full. 'Think of me — alone, the hapless organizer — surrounded by mammas, by primary school teachers, by three, four, five hundred children. And the judges — they are always the most trouble, those judges. And then I look at you — so cool, controlling your children, handling them so wonderfully and with such superb results — my inspiration!'

She was flustered by this unaccustomed vision of herself and half-turned her face away from Bose the better to contemplate it, but could find no reflection of it in the ghostly white bush of the Queen of the Night, and listened to him murmur on about her unkindness in deserting him in this cultural backwater to that darkest of dooms — guardian of a provincial museum — where he saw no one but school teachers herding children through his halls or, worse, Government officials who periodically and inexplicably stirred to create trouble for him and made their official presences felt amongst the copies of the Ajanta frescoes° (in which even the mouldy and peeled-off portions were carefully reproduced) and

Ajanta frescoes: paintings on the walls of rock-caves at Ajanta, done by Buddhist monks around the middle of the first millennium A.D.

the cupboards of Indus Valley seals.° Murmuring commiseration, she left him to a gloomy young professor of history who was languishing at another of the institutions of provincial backwaters that they so deplored and whose wife was always having a baby, and slipped away, still feeing an unease at Bose's unexpected vision of her which did not tally with the cruder reality, into the less equivocal company provided by a ring of twittering 'company wives'.

These women she had always encountered in just such a ring as they formed now, the kind that garden babblers form under a hedge where they sit gabbling and whirring with social bitchiness, and she had always stood outside it, smiling stiffly, not wanting to join and refusing their effusively nodded invitation. They were the wives of men who represented various mercantile companies in the town — Imperial Tobacco, Brooke Bond, Esso and so on — and although they might seem exactly alike to one who did not belong to this circle, inside it were subtle gradations of importance according to the particular company for which each one's husband worked and of these only they themselves were initiates. Bina was, however unwillingly, an initiate. Her husband worked for one of these companies but she had always stiffly refused to recognize these gradations, or consider them. They noted the rather set sulkiness of her silence when amongst them and privately labelled her queer, proud, boring and difficult. Also, they felt she belonged to their circle whether she liked it or not.

Now she entered this circle with diffidence, wishing she had stayed with the more congenial Bose (why hadn't she? What was it in her that made her retreat from anything like a friendly approach?) and was taken aback to find their circle parting to admit her and hear their cries of welcome and affection that did not, however, lose the stridency and harshness of garden babblers' voices.

'Bina, how do you like the idea of going back to Bombay?'

'Have you started packing, Bina? Poor you. Oh, are you having packers over from Delhi? Oh well then it's not so bad.'

Never had they been so vociferous in her company, so easy, so warm. They were women to whom the most awful thing that had every happened was the screw of a golden ear ring disappearing down the bathroom sink or a mother-in-law's visit or an ayah° deserting just before the arrival of guests: what could they know of Bina's life, Bina's ordeal? She cast her glance at the drinks they held — but they were mostly of orange squash. Only the Esso wife, who participated in amateur dramatics and ran a boutique and was rather taller and bolder than the rest, held a whisky and soda. So much affection generated by just orange squash? Im-

Indus Valley seals: seals surviving from the early civilization that flourished in the valley of the River Indus (now in central Pakistan) about 4,000 years ago

ayah: in middle- and upper-class modern Indian households, a nanny or children's nurse

possible. Rather tentatively, she offered them the remains of the cheese biscuits, found herself chirping replies, deploring the nuisance of having packing crates all over the house, talking of the flat they would move into in Bombay, and then, sweating unobtrusively with the strain, saw another recognizable fish swim towards her from the edge of the liquescent lawn, and swung away in relief, saying, 'Mrs D'Souza! How late you are, but I'm so glad — ' for she really was.

Mrs D'Souza was her daughter's teacher at the convent school and had clearly never been to a cocktail party before so that all Bina's compassion was aroused by those school-scuffed shoes and her tea-party best — quite apart from the simple truth that she found in her an honest individuality that all those beautifully dressed and poised babblers lacked, being stamped all over by the plain rubber stamps of their husbands' companies — she hurried off to find Mrs D'Souza something suitable to drink. 'Sherry? Why yes, I think I'll be able to find you some,' she said, a bit flabbergasted at such an unexpected fancy of the pepper-haired schoolteacher, 'and I'll see if Tara's around — she'll want to see you,' she added, vaguely and fraudulently, wondering why she had asked Mrs D'Souza to a cocktail party, only to see, as she skirted the rose bed, the admirable Bose appear at her side and envelop her in this strange intimacy that marked the whole evening, and went off, light-hearted, towards the table where her husband was trying, with the help of some hired waiters in soggy white uniforms with the name of the restaurant from which they were hired embroidered in red across their pockets, to cope with the flood of drinks this party atmosphere had called for and released.

Harassed, perspiring, his feet burning, Raman was nevertheless pleased to be so obviously employed and be saved the strain of having to converse with his motley assembly of guests: he had no more gift for society than his wife had. Ice cubes were melting on the tablecloth in sopping puddles and he had trouble in keeping track of his bottles: they were, besides the newly bought dozens of beer bottles and Black Knight whisky, the remains of their five years in this town that he now wished to bring to their end — bottles brought by friends from trips abroad, bottles bought cheap through 'contacts' in the army or air force, some gems, extravaganzas bought for anniversaries such as a nearly full bottom of Vat 69, a bottle with a bit of crème de menthe growing sticky at the bottle, some brown sherry with a great deal of rusty sediment, a red Golconda wine from Hyderabad, and a bottle of Remy Martin that he was keeping guiltily to himself, pouring small quantities into a whisky glass at his elbow and gulping it down in between mixing some very weird cocktails for his guests. There was no one at the party he liked well enough to share it with. Oh, one of the doctors perhaps, but where were they? Submerged in grass, in dark, in night and chatter, clatter of ice in glass, teeth on biscuit, teeth on teeth. Enamel and gold. Crumbs and dregs. All awash, all soaked in night. Watery sound of speech, liquid sound of drink. Water and ice and night. It occurred to him that everyone had forgotten him, the host, that it was a mistake to have stationed himself amongst the waiters, that he ought to move out, mingle with the guests. But he felt himself drowned, helplessly and quite delightfully, in Remy Martin, in grass, in a border of purple torenias.

Then he was discovered by his son who galloped through the ranks of guests and waiters to fling himself at his father and ask if he could play the new Beatles record, his friends had asked to hear it.

Raman considered, taking the opportunity to pour out and gulp down some more of the precious Remy Martin. 'All right,' he said, after a judicious minute or two, 'but keep it low, everyone won't want to hear it,' not adding that he himself didn't, for his taste in music ran to slow and melancholy, folk at its most frivolous. Still, he glanced into the lighted room where his children and the children of neighbours and guests had collected, making themselves tipsy on Fanta° and Coca-Cola, the girls giggling in a multicoloured huddle and the boys swaggering around the record-player with a kind of lounging strut, holding bottles in their hands with a sophisticated ease, exactly like experienced cocktail party guests, so that he smiled and wished he had a ticket, a passport that would make is possible to break into that party within a party. It was chillingly obvious to him that he hadn't one. He also saw that a good deal of their riotousness was due to the fact that they were raiding the snack trays that the waiters carried through the room to the lawn, and that they were seeing to it that the trays emerged half-empty. He knew he ought to go in and see about it but he hadn't the heart, or the nerve. He couldn't join that party but he wouldn't wreck it either so he only caught hold of one of the waiters and suggested that the snack trays be carried out from the kitchen straight onto the lawn, not by way of the drawing-room, and led him towards a group that seemed to be without snacks and saw too late that it was a group of the company executives that he loathed most. He half-groaned, then hiccuped at his mistake, but it was too late to alter course now. He told himself that he ought to see to it that the snacks were offered around without snag or error.

Poor Raman was placed in one of the lower ranks of the companies' hierarchy. That is, he did not belong to a British concern, or even to an American-collaboration one, but merely to an Indian one. Oh, a long-established, prosperous and solid one but, still, only Indian. Those cigarettes that he passed around were made by his own company. Somehow it struck a note of bad taste amongst these fastidious men who played golf, danced at the club on Independence Eve° and New Year's Eve, invited at least one foreign couple to every party and called their decorative

Fanta: the brand name of a popular orange-flavored soda
Independence Eve: the evening of August 14, preceding the day of India's independence
    from British colonial rule (August 15, 1947)

wives 'darling' when in public. Poor Raman never had belonged. It was so obvious to everyone, even to himself, as he passed around those awful cigarettes that sold so well in the market. It had been obvious since their first disastrous dinner party for this very ring of jocular gentlemen, five years ago. Nono had cried right through the party, Bina had spent the evening racing upstairs to see to the babies' baths and bed-time and then crawling reluctantly down, the hired cook had got drunk and stolen two of the chickens so that there was not enough on the table, no one had relaxed for a minute or enjoyed a second — it had been too sad and harrowing even to make a good story or a funny anecdote. They had all let it sink by mutual consent and the invitations to play a round of golf on Saturday afternoon or a rubber of bridge on Sunday morning had been issued and refused with conspiratorial smoothness. Then there was that distressing hobby of Raman's: his impossibly long walks on which he picked up bits of wood and took them home to sandpaper and chisel and then call wood sculpture. What could one do with a chap who did that? He himself wasn't sure if he pursued such odd tastes because he was a social pariah or if he was one on account of this oddity. Not to speak of the spastic child. Now that didn't even bear thinking of, and so it was no wonder that Raman swayed towards them so hesitantly, as though he were wading through water instead of over clipped grass, and handed his cigarettes around with such an apologetic air.

But, after all, hesitation and apology proved unnecessary. One of them — was he Polson's Coffee or Brooke Bond Tea? — clasped Raman about the shoulders as proper men do on meeting, and hearty voices rose together, congratulating him on his promotion (it wasn't one, merely a transfer, and they knew it), envying him his move to the metropolis. They talked as if they had known each other for years, shared all kinds of public schoolboy fun. One — was he Voltas or Ciba? — talked of golf matches at the Willingdon as though he had often played there with Raman, another spoke of *kebabs* eaten on the roadside after a party as though Raman had been one of the gang. Amazed and grateful as a schoolboy admitted to a closed society, Raman nodded and put in a few cautious words, put away his cigarettes, called a waiter to refill their glasses and broke away before the clock struck twelve and the golden carriage turned into a pumpkin, he himself into a mouse. He hated mice.

Walking backwards, he walked straight into the soft barrier of Miss Dutta's ample back wrapped and bound in rich Madras silk.

'Sorry, sorry, Miss Dutta, I'm clumsy as a bear,' he apologized, but here, too, there was no call for apology for Miss Dutta was obviously delighted at having been bumped into.

'My dear Mr Raman, what can you expect if you invite the whole town to your party?' she asked in that piercing voice that invariably made her companions drop theirs self-consciously. 'You and Bina have been so popular — what are we going to do without you?'

He stood pressing his glass with white-tipped fingers and tried to think what he or Bina had provided her with that she could possibly miss. In any case, Miss Dutta could always manage, and did manage, everything single-handedly. She was the town busy-body, secretary and chairman of more committees than he could count: they ranged from the Film Society to the Blood Bank, from the Red Cross to the Friends of the Museum, for Miss Dutta was nothing if not versatile. 'We hardly ever saw you at our film shows of course,' her voice rang out, making him glance furtively over his shoulder to see if anyone were listening, 'but it was so nice *knowing* you were in town and that I could count on you. So few people here *care*, you know,' she went on, and affectionately bumped her comfortable middle-aged body into his as someone squeezed by, making him remember that he had once heard her called a man-eater, and wonder which man she had eaten and even consider, for a moment, if there were not, after all, some charm in those powdered creases of her creamy arms, equalling if not surpassing that of his worn and harassed wife's bony angles. Why did suffering make for angularity? he even asked himself with uncharacteristic unkindness. But when Miss Dutta laid an arm on top of his glass-holding one and raised herself on her toes to bray something into his ear, he loyally decided that he was too accustomed to sharp angles to change them for such unashamed luxuriance, and, contriving to remove her arm by grasping her elbow — how one's fingers sank into the stuff! — he steered her towards his wife who was standing at the table and inefficiently pouring herself another gin and lime.

'This is my third,' she confessed hurriedly, 'and I can't tell you how gay it makes me feel. I giggle at everything everyone says.'

'Good,' he pronounced, feeling inside a warm expansion of relief at seeing her lose, for the moment, her tension and anxiety. 'Let's hear you giggle,' he said, sloshing some more gin into her glass.

'Look at those children,' she exclaimed, and they stood in a bed of balsam, irredeemably crushed, and looked into the lighted drawing room where their daughter was at the moment the cynosure of all juvenile eyes, having thrown herself with abandon into a dance of monkey-like movements. 'What is it, Miss Dutta?' the awed mother enquired. 'You're more up in the latest fashions than I am — is it the twist, the rock or the jungle?' and all three watched, enthralled, till Tara began to totter and, losing her simian grace, collapsed against some wildly shrieking girl friends.

A bit embarrassed by their daughter's reckless abandon, the parents discussed with Miss Dutta whose finger by her own admission, was placed squarely on the pulse of youth, the latest trends in juvenile culture on which Miss Dutta gave a neat sociological discourse (all the neater for having been given earlier that day at the convocation of the Home Science College) and Raman wondered uneasily at this opening of floodgates in his own family — his wife grown giggly with gin, his daughter performing wildly to a Chubby Checkers record — how had it all come about? Was it the darkness all about them, dense as the heavy curtains about a stage, that made them act, for an hour or so, on the tiny lighted stage of brief intimacy with such a lack of inhibition? Was it the drink, so freely sloshing from end to end of the house and lawn on account of his determination to clear out his 'cellar' (actually one-half of the sideboard and the top shelf of the wardrobe in his dressing-room) and his muddling and mixing them, making up untried and experimental cocktails and lavishly pouring out the whisky without a measure? But these were solid and everyday explanations and there was about this party something out of the ordinary and everyday — at least to the Ramans, normally so austere and unpopular. He knew the real reason too — it was all because the party had been labelled a 'farewell party', everyone knew it was the last one, that the Ramans were leaving and they would not meet up again. There was about it exactly that kind of sentimental euphoria that is generated at a ship-board party, the one given on the last night before the end of the voyage. Everyone draws together with an intimacy, a lack of inhibition not displayed or guessed at before, knowing this is the last time, tomorrow they will be dispersed, it will be over. They will not meet, be reminded of it or be required to repeat it.

As if to underline this new and Cinderella's ball–like atmosphere of friendliness and gaiety, three pairs of neighbours now swept in (and three kochias° lay down and died under their feet, to the gardener's rage and sorrow): the couple who lived to the Ramans' left, the couple who lived to their right, and the couple from across the road, all crying, 'So sorry to be late, but you know what a long way we had to come,' making everyone laugh identically at the identical joke. Despite the disparity in their looks and ages — one couple was very young, another middle-aged, the third grandparents — they were, in a sense, as alike as the company executives and their wives, for they too bore a label if a less alarming one: Neighbours, it said. Because they were neighbours, and although they had never been more than nodded to over the hedge, waved to in passing cars or spoken to about anything other than their children, dogs, flowers and gardens, their talk had a vivid immediacy that went straight to the heart.

'Diamond's going to miss you so — he'll be heartbroken,' moaned the grandparents who lived alone in their spotless house with a black labrador who had made a habit of visiting the Ramans whenever he wanted young company, a romp on the lawn or an illicit biscuit.

'I don't know what my son will do without Diamond,' reciprocated Bina with her new and sympathetic warmth. 'He'll force me to get a dog of his own, I know, and how will I ever keep one in a flat in Bombay?'

'When are you going to throw out those rascals?' demanded a father of

kochias: flowering plants

Raman, pointing at the juvenile revellers indoors. 'My boy has an exam tomorrow, you know, but he said he couldn't be bothered about it — he had to go to the Ramans' farewell party.'

One mother confided in Bina, winning her heart forever, 'Now that you are leaving, I can talk to you about it at last: did you know my Vinod is sweet on your Tara? Last night when I was putting him to bed, he said "Mama, when I grow up I will marry Tara. I will sit on a white horse and wear a turban and carry a sword in my belt and I will go and marry Tara." What shall we do about that, eh? Only a ten year difference in age, isn't there — or twelve?' and both women rocked with laughter.

The party had reached its crest, like a festive ship, loud and illuminated for that last party before the journey's end, perched on the dizzy top of the dark wave. It could do nothing now but descend and dissolve. As if by simultaneous and unanimous consent, the guests began to leave (in the wake of the Commissioner and his wife who left first, like royalty) streaming towards the drive where cars stood bumper to bumper — more than had visited the Ramans' house in the previous five years put together. The light in the portico fell on Bina's pride and joy, a Chinese orange tree, lighting its miniature globes of fruit like golden lanterns. There was a babble, an uproar of leavetaking (the smaller children, already in pyjamas, watched open-mouthed from a dark window upstairs). Esso and Caltex left together, arms about each other and smoking cigars, like figures in a comic act. Miss Dutta held firmly to Bose's arm as they dipped, bowed, swayed and tripped on their way out. Bina was clasped, kissed — ear rings grazed her cheek, talcum powder tickled her nose. Raman had his back slapped till he thrummed and vibrated like a beaten gong.

It seemed as if Bina and Raman were to be left alone at last, left to pack up and leave — now the good-byes had been said, there was nothing else they could possibly do — but no, out popped the good doctors from the hospital who had held themselves back in the darkest corners and made themselves inconspicuous throughout the party, and now, in the manner in which they clasped the host by the shoulders and the hostess by the hands, and said 'Ah *now* we have a chance to be with you at last, now we can begin *our* party,' revealed that although this was the first time they had come to the Ramans' house on any but professional visits, they were not merely friends — they were almost a part of that self-defensive family, the closest to them in sympathy. Raman and Bina both felt a warm, moist expansion of tenderness inside themselves, the tenderness they had till today restricted to the limits of their family, no farther, as though they feared it had not an unlimited capacity. Now its close horizons stepped backwards, with some surprise.

And it was as the doctors said — the party now truly began. Cane chairs were dragged out of the veranda onto the lawn, placed in a ring next to the flowering Queen of the Night which shook out flounces and frills of white scent with every rustle of night breeze. Bina could give in now to her two most urgent needs and dash indoors to smear her mosquito-bitten arms and feet with Citronella and fetch Nono to sit on her lap, to let Nono have a share, too, in the party. The good doctors and their wives leant forward and gave Nono the attention that made the parents' throats tighten with gratitude. Raman insisted on their each having a glass of Remy Martin — they must finish it tonight, he said, and would not let the waiter clear away the ice or glasses yet. So they sat on the veranda steps, smoking and yawning.

Now it turned out that Dr Bannerji's wife, the lady in the Dacca sari° and the steel-rimmed spectacles, had studied in Shantiniketan,° and she sang, at her husband's and his colleagues' urging, Tagore's sweetest, saddest songs.° When she sang, in heartbroken tones that seemed to come from some distance away, from the damp corners of the darkness where the fireflies flitted,

> 'Father, the boat is carrying me away,
> Father, it is carrying me away from home,'

the eyes of her listeners, sitting tensely in that grassy, inky dark, glazed with tears that were compounded equally of drink, relief and regret.

C. S. LAKSHMI

C. S. Lakshmi (1944–), who publishes much of her work under the pseudonym Ambai, was born into a large middle-class Tamil-speaking family in Bangalore, Karnataka. In 1963 she went to Madras, where she earned a master's degree in political science and worked briefly as a school teacher. Between 1967 and 1978 she lived in New Delhi, where she worked on a Ph.D. degree and conducted research on women writers. Since 1978 she has lived with her filmmaker husband, Vishnu Mathur, in Bombay, where she is actively involved in research on women and in several women's organizations. Lakshmi began writ-

Dacca sari: an expensive silk sari, with distinctive colors and patterns, made in Dacca (now the capital of Bangladesh)

Shantiniketan: town in the state of West Bengal in India; Vishwabharati, a distinguished university founded by the Bengali writer Rabindranath Tagore, who won the Nobel Prize for literature in 1913, is located there

Tagore's sweetest, saddest songs: Rabindranath Tagore (1861–1941), who won the Nobel Prize for literature in 1913, was a Bengali poet, dramatist, fiction-writer, and lyricist, as well as a painter and a musician; several hundred of the songs he wrote and set to music (in a semiclassical North Indian style) are extremely popular among middle-class Indians.

ing fiction in Tamil as a teenager and published her first two novels be-
fore she was twenty. Besides fiction in Tamil, she has published nonfic-
tional works in English and articles and critical essays on the situation
of women in Indian history, society, culture, and politics.

"A Rat and a Sparrow" evokes the metropolis of Bombay in the
1980s and gives us a lively picture of its cosmopolitan community of
young adults. Except for Susan, a visitor from France, the men and
women come from different parts of India. The story identifies Hindus,
Sikhs, and Christians, as well as speakers of Bengali, Hindi, Malay-
alam, and Tamil. Despite some prejudices and misunderstandings, the
characters learn to negotiate their linguistic, ethnic, and cultural dif-
ferences with mutual respect. The story uses the symbols of rat and
sparrow to create a multilayered parable of life in the contemporary
big city, especially in a society divided by inequities of power between
the old and the young, northerners and southerners, predators and vic-
tims, men and women, and the aggressive and the meek.

A Rat and a Sparrow

When she woke up and turned her face, the rat's face was right next to
her cheek. When she screamed, jumped up and shivered, the rat also
jumped up, assaulted by the scream, and cowered in the window. It lifted
its nose as if to say, "How you startled me with that scream!" Each time
it tried to move, there was another scream. Finally, it sat down where it
was, absolutely still. She stood there, staring at it, dazed.

It's hard to relate to rats. Especially to this rat. It must be this one that
gnaws and eats only the autobiographies on the top shelf. Because some
of the covers of the autobiographies have been eaten at random, without
any method, some titles are left with remnants like "MY AUTOB," "MY
ST," and "MEMOI." In the book titled in big letters "THE AUTOBIOGRAPHY
OF A DONKEY," only the word "DONKEY" remained. When one looked at it
from below, only the word DONKEY in thick dark print appeared under
the smiling picture of the author. Though some people might think it's
the right epithet for the author, it's not clear how far they would leave
such judgments to a rat. It occurred to her that, though he might have referred to himself as a donkey in mock-humility, the author might still
object to underlining it this way. Therefore, when she heard the KRK KRK
sounds at night from the top shelf, she turned her flashlight on it. The rat
had settled on the autobiography and had begun to gnaw around the donkey. It looked down at her. It seemed to smile at her. Her tongue twisted
in a scream. Her friends who had celebrated their Saturday night with
them in the usual way and had now fallen into a slumber, suddenly woke
up. They chased away the two-inch rat. It ran and hid in the bathroom.

Paramveer went in there with a coconut frond broom and shut the door behind him.

"Param, do not murder it. Just stun it."

"It's only two inches long. How would I know how to stun it with the right blow?"

"What wilt thou do if it doth not perish after thou hast given it chase?" said Susan in high chaste Tamil. She had come from Paris. She was Param's girl-friend. She had come to India to research Hindu goddesses. She says that Lakshmi° sitting at the feet of Vishnu and rubbing them is not a sign of male domination: it's only to give Vishnu the energy and enthusiasm he needs to create the world and to protect it. When she asked, "If this Lakshmi has the power to rouse such fervor in the god, why doesn't she rub her own feet and do Vishnu's job herself?" Susan said, "Thou art making me laugh," in chaste Tamil. And now she stood there outside the bathroom, saying Aiyaho! listening to the sounds of Param's struggles with the rat.

Param came out of the bathroom with the rat lying on its back on the coconut frond broom.

"It's just fainted," he said to her. Then he went down to the street and let it go. When this Sardarji with his hair in a top-knot went down with a broom and a rat at one o-clock in the morning, the watchmen of the building were a little disturbed. Next day, they avoided looking at her directly.

Just when she was sleeping peacefully, imagining that the rat had recovered from its swoon and moved away to a world without autobiographies, right next to her cheek sat this rat.

Was it the same rat? Did it return here as soon as it recovered from its fainting fit? Or is this the other one's companion?

Several people had warned her that this big city had lots of rats and bandicoots.° As these people were artists and intellectuals, there was good reason to think that they were describing human beings in this symbolic fashion. And then, here — in Gita's and Sukhdev's apartment with one room and a kitchen, the odor of pickles in mustard oil, mixed with the sweaty smells of clothes hanging on the clothesline — when she had to spend her first night in the city there with Amulyo, the rat image seemed quite appropriate. That kitchen did look like a rat-hole. She had a dream that night.

Buildings touching the sky on all four sides, like hills. Narrow streets. As you enter a building, looking for a place to live, the houses turn into rat-holes. Some people are lying on their backs, some on their sides. Some people are sleeping with their heads on their knees, some are talk-

Lakshmi: in Hindu mythology, the Goddess Lakshmi, who is the consort of Lord Vishnu, one of the three major gods
bandicoot: a large rat or rat-like creature

ing, others are laughing. A woman comes home from her office, casually enters a rat-hole. In disembodied voices, they talk about the conveniences of their apartments. When she tried to hold on to a hanging rope in order to stand comfortably, she finds it's the rough-textured tail of a rat . . .

She must have uttered something in her sleep. She woke up. Amulyo was fast asleep. He had come into this world with the gift of sleep. She shook him.

"Amul . . . Amul . . ."

"Ha . . ." he said, startled, opening his eyes.

"Amul, I had a dream."

"Mm."

"It was a terrifying dream, Amul. My whole body went cold."

Amul sat up and drank water from a bottle. He poured some into a glass and gave it to her. After she drank it, he said, "Tell me."

When she described it, he laughed.

"How is it you dream of such lovely images? Complete with symbols and all, and you don't even agree with Freud!"

She hit him in the stomach. "You are a hooligan. You're a wretch. You're a sleepy head like Kumbhakarna.° You're just an idiot." With each epithet, she gave him another blow.

Laughing, he stretched and lay down. She climbed over him and sat on his stomach, her legs on either side of him, like a goddess about to slay a demon.

Amulyo held her uplifted hand. Quite gently. Her eyes filled. Amulyo's eyes also welled up.

Above their heads, shelves blackened by kitchen smoke. Aluminum vessels that could be discarded anytime they wished to pack up. A kerosene stove. Roach powder scattered around the edges of walls. Ten feet away, the kitchen drain. He looked at them and then at her and fell silent.

She softly played with his belly button.

"It was just a dream, Amul," she said.

She remembered her Coimbatore° house, its spaciousness, its backyard. Some places come twined with certain images. That house brought with it the image of Patti. Patti, who had borne children since she was thirteen. Patti who had cooked vegetables and sweet *halvas*° in large frypans. Patti who had vigorously massaged her thin-fleshed grandchildren (she was also one among them) with caster oil and told them the Ramayana°

Kumbhakarna: the brother of Ravana, the "villain" of the *Ramayana*; in the epic story, Kumbhakarna is a prodigious sleeper, hibernating for six months at a time
Coimbatore: a town in the western part of Tamil Nadu state in south India
halva: a sweet snack or dessert
the Ramayana: an ancient Indian epic, the first poem *(kavya)* in the Sanskrit language

while she did so. Patti with a tongue like a whip. One word from her would sting like a lash.

Animals surrounded her, like cows around Krishna's flutesong.°

Patti woke up suddenly from an afternoon nap one hot day. She went to the backyard. On the wall behind the well, a monkey was shrieking in a most horrible voice.

"Hey, what's the matter?" asked Patti.

"Urr," it said.

Auntie's children cried out to her, "Don't go near it, Patti!"

Patti stared at the monkey. She went to the woodpile next to the bathroom, and brought a coconut shell, dipped it in the cistern, filled it with water and went near the money. When she stretched out her hand with the shell, the monkey snatched it from her and drank up the water in one breath. She filled it again. The animal drank three times from her shell and darted away swirling its tail.

"It's thirsty," said Patti.

The house had cats. Black, white, brown, at least a dozen cats. A line of granddaughters and grandsons. After feeding a line of the males first according to custom, she would sit down, stretching out a leg, to eat with a line of the girls and women, when the cats would come running.

"Meaow," one would say.

"It wants a *papadam*,"° Patti would translate. The cats had a taste for *papadam*, *rasam*,° cooked rice, roast potatoes and so on. She would feed rice mixed with *ghee*° to the cat that had just given birth to a litter and survived, poor thing. As soon as milk was delivered in the morning, the cats would get their share.

"Do you want a cat?" asked Amulyo.

"Unh unh. Do you want one? You've a dog at home, don't you?"

"It's utterly wrong to shut up animals in these cage-like flats," he said.

"Children too," she added.

Since that dream about the rat, she had glimpses, *darshans*,° of the rat, and heard rat legends. The rat experiences of Gita and Sukhdev. Once when they were watching a movie, munching on popcorn, something bit Gita in the leg. As she shook it off, Sukhdev also shook his leg. When they looked down, they saw a bandicoot running. Their feet were bloody. After several tetanus shots, he expressed his righteous indignation to a journalist friend of his, and asked him to write about it in his newspaper. The friend smiled most patiently and told Sukhdev what had happened to

Krishna's flutesong: In Hindu mythology, Lord Krishna, one of the ten incarnations of Lord Vishnu, is portrayed as a cowherd who plays a flute and lures all the cowgirls to himself.
papadam: a fried or roasted snack, like a crisp tortilla
rasam: a spicy broth made with tomatoes, lentils, and other ingredients
ghee: clarified butter
darshan: a glimpse, sighting, or vision

the film critic: when she missed the press showing of the movie, she went to see it in the regular theater where it was playing. As she was making notes, she felt something tugging at her *dupatta.*° She ignored it and continued to write on her pad resting it on the arm of the seat. When the lights came on at the intermission, she saw a rat in her lap. When she started up and let out a scream, people said, "All this fuss about a rat!" The person next to her told a long elaborate rat joke. A woman learned judo. She also learned karate and *kalaripayirru,* the martial art of Kerala.° But when she sighted a little mouse in her kitchen, she screamed and stood on a chair! The man who told the joke laughed like a hyena at his own joke. We don't know if any bandicoot had ever nipped at his foot.

She knew a story about a Rat Prince. Once upon a time, there were three princes. One of them was the Rat Prince. The other two drive him away. After several hardships, he meets a princess. As soon as she kisses him, he is transformed into a handsome young man . . . She later added a footnote to the story, when she grew up. That kiss turned the rat into a prince. But the princess turned into a rat. How weird! No prince ever came forward to kiss her, not even our Rat Prince.

After Gita and Sukhdev had gone away for a year, and these people had lived in that flat for a whole year, this rat had returned to do battle. Big cities usually have a symbol. Like the Big Apple for New York. The only symbol for this city, she thought, would be Rat. The city of rats. Rat people. Rat people who will still be rats even after a kiss. There might be a history to this rat cowering on the window. Maybe it had got tired of being a rat for ages, sick of eating all those autobiographies. Maybe it had come here all the way to kiss her and change himself into a prince.

She got up and pushed the windowpane out with a stick. The rat jumped out and ran.

When Amulyo returned from his trip the next day, she told him about the rat. Shall we buy rat poison? he asked her. This is such a literary rat, it shouldn't die in agony, she thought. There must be other ways to die. Come to think of it, she had a nonsensical praise-poem in her collection. A poem sung in praise of a leader in Tamilnadu.° His opponents in the party had spread a rumor that the poem had been sung in front of him a few hours before his death, that he had to be moved to the hospital soon after, and that the poem had something to do with it. She thought that this rat would surely die if it ate that poem. But would it writhe in agony? She felt like laughing.

"Do you happen to have a book that would finish it off?"

"Look here, don't you make fun of Tamil. Your books are so useless, even rats won't touch it."

---

dupatta: a woman's long, scarf-like garment, usually draped over a loose shirt or tunic
kalaripayirru: a centuries-old martial art developed in the state of Kerala
Tamilnadu: state in modern south India

"Is this a border issue?"

"What else? How can an idiot who can't even pronounce a ZHA make fun of Tamil? Come say TAMIZH, TAMIZH, say ZH let me see."

Amulyo pronounced ZH perfectly.

"Is it enough to pronounce it just once? Say VAZHAIPPAZHAM VAZHUKKI KIZHAVI NAZHUVI KUZHIYL KIZHE VIZHUNDAL.° Say it."

"Look here, I haven't slept all night in the train. I couldn't get a sleeper. First get me a cup of tea and then give me TamiZH — see I said TAMIZH — then give me TamiZH lessons."

They say this is a city where people of all kinds live. There was one big group labeled Madrasis.° One of Amulyo's friends would make his mouth a little crooked whenever he saw her and say, *"Namaskaram ji."*° He would grind that word pretty hard. He believed that adding -AM to the end of any world would make it Tamil. So he would say, "Tea-Am, Coffee-Am, Chappatti-Am . . ." in a drawled out list and ask, "How's that?"

After he had done this once or twice, she said with great pity, "Vijay, this speech defect of yours, have you had it from childhood? Is there any remedy for it? You have so much trouble speaking, poor thing!"

Vijay was startled. He stammered, "No . . . This . . . is Madrasi . . ."

"Oh, I was worried all these days that something was wrong with your tongue. You see, the rest of us don't speak like that."

Vijay looked at Amulyo, as if asking for help.

"What, Vijay? What will you drink? Tea-AM?"

Vijay said, in a small voice, "Tea."

Another friend, as soon as he had put away three good pegs of rum, had insisted on telling a joke. "I'm going to act like a Madrasi," he said in a loud voice. Before others could control him, he had become a Madrasi. "I'm going to eat like a Madrasi," he announced. He rolled up his sleeves, imagined he had a leaf full of food in front of him, scooped up a handful and sucked it in with a big hissing noise. Another big scoop of imagined food and another huge hiss of suction. Then he pretended he was filling his mouth noisily. Then he put out his tongue and pretended to lick the palm and then the back of his hand. Then he laughed at his own act, though no one else did.

VAZHAIPPAZHAM . . . VIZHUNDAL: The Tamil and Malayalam languages contain a retroflex consonant ZH, pronounced somewhat like an American R in "card" or "barn," which non-Tamil and non-Malayalam speakers find hard to say. Here Amulyo, a Bengali-speaker (from West Bengal, the state in eastern India), is asked by his wife to utter a Tamil tongue-twister which means, "The old woman slipped on a banana and fell into a pit."

Madrasis: natives of Madras, the capital of the state of Tamil Nadu; generic label for any natives of the Tamil-speaking region of south India

Namaskaram ji: traditional Indian greeting, meaning "I bow to you"

Vijay went up to him and whispered something. He looked at her and said, grinning all the while, "Just for fun . . . I love the temples in Tamil-nadu. I like the *ddosa, vadda, iddli*° and all," stressing the dd's.

She said, "Wretch!" in Tamil.

Only Amulyo understand what she said. He quickly gave his friend his bag and sent him home. Vijay didn't say as usual, *"Namaskaram ji,"* but said "Good night" to her, weakly, giving her a hug.

She was in a frenzy. She felt like embracing the plantain leaf seller in the Tamils-speaking colony of the city. When their Tamil dialect with words like *avuka* and *ivuka*° fell on her ears, it felt as if the Tamraparni river itself had rolled over its banks. Tamil dishes like *dosai, idli, vadai, rasam,*° and the chicken curry of Chettinad seemed like the very staple of life. Forgotten Tamil songs began to appear in her memory suddenly at night, in the afternoon sun, or when wiping off sweat in the heat of buses and trains — it went through her like a lightning of pain. She heard her grandfather sing a folksong at night as he walked up and down the open terrace, looking up at the stars:

> *This rotting body, of no use for anything*
> *like a torn sieve — O parrot,*
> *it's forever a thing of pain.*

A frenzy possessed and shook her till she reached the Tamil bookstore. When she saw the colorful covers of books in the bookstore with their pictures of women looking up or lying down, her legs twined around themselves.

It looked as if the owner of the store would never remove his hand from within his *dhoti*.° She couldn't think what great treasure was there inside. Whenever he saw a woman, his hand would go hide itself there. With the other hand, he spoke emphatically about Tamil culture.

"We're maintaining a culture, madam. I've been stoned in the cause of Tamil. (He pointed to a bald spot on his head.) We're now trying hard to put up a statue of Bharati° and one of Tiruvalluvar.° I've proposed that we should inscribe stanzas from the *Kural*° all over the walls. As soon as you enter, your eyes should fall on a *Kural* stanza. It should pierce your eyes. You come in like this now. There should be a stanza:

---

ddosa, vadda, iddli: south Indian foods
avuka, ivuka: Tamil-dialect words as examples of the musical quality of the language
rasam: spicy broth made with tomatoes, lentils, and other ingredients
dhoti: an Indian man's traditional lower garment
Bharati: Subramania Bharati, major twentieth-century Tamil poet
Tiruvalluvar: major ancient Tamil poet who flourished in the third or fourth century
Kural: short-title for *Tirukkural*, classical Tamil poem by Tiruvalluvar; written in hemistichs that are also called *kurals*

Even if she doesn't worship a god,
if she worships her husband,
if she says, "Rain!" it will rain.

"How do you like that? It would thrill you. We must praise our women. In our *Kural-* and *Tevaram*-singing competitions,° if a woman wins, we won't give her some random prize. We'll give her a brass lamp-stand, we'll give her a book on the place of women in Tamil culture." Bending forward, he continued, "Look, our entire culture is entirely in the hands of women."

His voice was full of the satisfaction of having given over the entire culture into the hands of women. It occurred to her that if this man's hand would give up its cultural searches and come out, we could burden it also with a little of our culture.

Outside the bookstore, a man was speaking. He was a singer in the association where all South Indians came to learn the arts.

"They threw me out. You know that, don't you?"

"Is that so? Why?"

He quickly undid the buttons of his white starched shirt and showed his bare chest.

"I don't have a scared thread."°

The two of them brought home a rather virulent rat poison. They spread it on pieces of bread and left them in corners. She put one piece behind *The Autobiography of a Donkey.* One couldn't tell which piece it ate. It lay peacefully dead inside the soft blue cotton bag. It touched her to the quick. Did it suffer agony, did it writhe? It spoiled her sleep. It ruined her books. It died alone writhing in the blue bag. Amulyo took it to the beach and shook it out.

This rat will no longer stand up to them, as the other one they saw once on the seashore. A man was walking in front of them with a rat-trap in his hand on the beach, one evening. There was a squealing little rat in it, looking through the trap. They opened the trap towards the sea. The rat was scared by the ocean. It refused to leave the trap. Squealing away, it grabbed the rods of the trap. He tried to shake the trap, turn it upside down, beat its sides. But the rat was obstinate, wouldn't come out. The man sat next to the trap, praying, waiting for the rat to come out. When she and Amulyo were leaving the beach, they looked back and found that the man was still sitting there, waiting. The rat didn't seem to appreciate

Kural- and Tevaram-singing competitions: competitions in which trained singers display their skills in performing the text of the *Tirukkural* and the hymns to Lord Shiva in the ancient *Tevaram* tradition
sacred thread: a cotton thread worn by a male brahmin around his torso, signifying his priestly status

his stubbornness. In the last night of the sunset, they saw the silhouette of the man and the rat trap. Around the horizon stood buildings like hills.

The sparrow arrived some days after these events. When she stood in the verandah that was big enough only to hold one person, she looked first at the garbage heap below and the children sitting down in the road to defecate, and then turned to the old movie house in front. An old Hindi movie was running there. To compensate for the failure of the electric fans, they had opened all the balcony doors. Through the heavy black curtains, a song sung by Mukesh° for Raj Kapoor° floated towards her. It seemed to fall down, fluttering against her shoulders. Startled, she turned around: it was a sparrow. A little one. Its wing broken and crooked. Its mouth was red as a berry. She was afraid to touch it. She found an ink-filler, filled it with water, and dropped some in its mouth. It opened its eyes. She picked it up on cardboard and set it in a corner. At night she covered it with a net basket.

When she lifted the basket in the morning, the sparrow let out a chirp. With little squeaks, it turned in circles, and struck the ink-filler with its beak. Before she could turn, two sparrows had come and perched on the verandah parapet. They flew quickly down to the baby sparrow and inserted little grubworms into its mouth. The smart little one made appreciative chirping noises and swallowed them. Then it lay down.

Flying lessons began that very afternoon. One of the sparrows flew upwards, first slowly, then quickly. As soon as it sat down, the other one flew. The little sparrow tried to rise in the air with its crooked wing and fell down. Till five o'clock, both sparrows tried. The little one gave up on flying and began to walk. The sparrows left the little one in her care and left for the day. The little one couldn't fly more than five or six feet. It made its dwelling near the first iron bracket of the bookshelf. Unlike the stealthy rat that laid siege in the middle of the night, this one put droppings on one set of books even during the day. She kneeled one day in front of it and sang the old rhyme, "Little sparrow, little sparrow, do you know, do you know, my man who has left me hasn't come home yet?" The sparrow made sharp KRK noises and showed its displeasure. It also liked red things. It scattered its droppings freely on books with red covers. When she opened the door at night after a long absence, it squeaked from its corner and showed its disapproval.

When the window next to the book shelf was opened, it went and perched on the cross bar. Against the background of buildings darkened

---

Mukesh: a famous singer in the Indian commercial film industry, whose career peaked between the late 1940s and the early 1970s; in musical films, he sang most often for the actor Raj Kapoor

Raj Kapoor: a major mid-century Indian film actor and producer; his "singing voice" in musical films was provided by the singer Mukesh

by mill-smoke, and the smell and din of vehicles, a small crooked-winged sparrow was foregrounded. A little sparrow looking out of eyes like beads.

When a curtain of rain dimmed the outlines of everything, the sparrow was still on the bar. If one screwed one's eyes and looked at it sideways, the sparrow filled one's vision. Behind its head, there was a stretch of the ash-smeared city. As if it was placed on the sparrow's head. Like a crown.

When she leaned her head on the window and dozed off for a second and woke up, the sparrow wasn't there. She searched for it all over the flat, calling it, "Little One, Little One." When she called again loudly and looked out of the veranda, it showed its head from a hole in the building opposite. She could see its crooked wing. Just when she was worrying how she would save it if a hawk or eagle or vulture should attack it, the little one rose lightly and flew out and returned to the whole in the wall. Then again it demonstrated how it could fly. When she and Amulyo stood in the verandah, it flew a third time rhythmically up and down and hid in the tree that was fifty feet away. There were many sparrows in that tree.

As far as the eye could reach, there were long rows of buildings, without any interval. Unfinished walls with cracks. On some curvy lines of cement over the cracks. Walls smeared with tar to keep them from getting soaked with rain-water. Colorful clothes hanging from long hooks attached to the verandahs. In a few windows there were green leaves sprouting from planters. With all this, the city looked like a demon. In the middle of it all, in a tree that had somehow grown and branched out randomly, a little sparrow.

Then one evening something happened. Street lights, shop lights, and neon ads had begun to shine. The road was a sea of vehicles. Double decker buses roared by. Autorickshaws° sliding and twisting noisily between them, impatient scooters and cars. It was a deluge of noises. Somehow Amulyo entered the stream, ran and scrambled on to the other side of the road. She got stuck on the one-foot stone division that cut the road in two. Amulyo summoned her to cross, making gestures with his hands. The eyes were mobbed by big bright posters stuck everywhere without wasting even a square foot. A doubledecker bus passed, almost rubbing against her back. It was covered with monstrous patches of blue, green and black advertisements. Idiotic vehicles that screeched, came to a halt and then moved on. She took a couple of steps and retreated before a shrieking black car. Horn sounds drummed in her ear. Face, neck, armpits and thighs streamed with sweat. A woman clutching two empty fishbaskets full of fish in one hand approached her. The baskets reeked. With her one free hand, the woman caught her by the waist. Lifting her two baskets with one hand, she dragged her through the medley of vehicles

---

autorickshaws: compact, three-wheel taxis in India, like automated rickshaws

till they reached the other side. Once she joined Amulyo, the fisher-woman moved on.

In that sidewalk filled with spittle, gutters, cigarette stubs, and smalltime traders, overflowing with all the sounds of the city, while she stood for a second getting her breath back, the man came towards her. He would be called *Bevda* ("drunk") in city lingo. The city treated *Bevdas* with compassion. If a *Bevda* lies down and sleeps in a bus or train, no one will wake him up. They would say, *Bevda Bevda,* and walk across forgivingly. Once, at midnight, a *Bevda* boarded a bus and refused to buy a ticket from the conductor. He sputtered in Hindi, "Drink drink drink. Drink in the morning, drink in the afternoon, drink at night. Drink drink drink." The conductor himself bought a ticket for him. The man lay down with a thud, saying, "Poor fellow, *Bevda.*"

When this *Bevda* came in front of her, she saw that he was middle-aged. About ten feet away from her, he fell down on the sidewalk in "slow motion." No one noticed it. People walked around him.

When Amulyo and she went near him, he tried to get up but failed. Extending his index finger and thumb in a two-inch angle, he said, "Had a little too much," and smiled happily. They roused him a little from the sidewalk and made him lie down next to a wall. He said, "Do I have my sandals on my feet? Could you hand them to me? The hooligans will snatch them and throw them away." Once he had his sandals in his hand, he hugged them and shut his eyes. A peaceful smile on his face.

They stood in the long line at the bus stop. She leaned against the street lamp and started laughing. After a moment, Amulyo joined her. The two of them could not contain their laughter.

Translated from the Tamil
by A. K. Ramanujan

GAGAN GILL

Gagan Gill (1959–) was born in New Delhi, where she currently lives with her husband, the Hindu novelist Nirmal Verma. She works as a journalist in Hindi and Punjabi. Her first collection of poems, The Girl Will Return One Day, *appeared in 1989. Gill is one of the foremost poets among the writers of a new generation, who were born in India after Independence and began publishing their work in the 1980s. Equally at home in Hindi, Punjabi, and English, she writes from a postmodernist and feminist position. Many of her poems deal with a girl's sense of identity, constraint, and freedom in the process of grow-*

ing up. Some of her poems also boldly explore women's desires and fantasies, treating sexuality with a seriousness that prevents it from becoming merely sensational.

"A Desire in Her Bangles" is one in a group of confessional poems written in an impersonal style. This poem plays with the northern Indian Hindu convention that green glass bangles are tokens of a woman's married state. On the death of her husband, the woman has to undergo a rite of passage in which she inaugurates her widowhood by breaking the bangles on the threshold of the home she shared with him. In Gill's poem, the young woman imagines herself as a wife with an unfaithful husband and plans to get her revenge by symbolically passing through the rite of widowhood. Not only would the woman thus be free of the emotional distress of the man's betrayal, but by inaugurating her own widowhood she would, in effect, ritually enact his "death."

A Desire in Her Bangles

A desire circulates
in the girl's bangles
that they should break
first on her bed
and then on the threshold of her home   5

But why on the threshold?

Because inside the girl
there's a grieving woman
who's a widow
who isn't a widow yet   10
but who'll become one

The girl's fear
runs trembling from her veins
to her bangles
her desire trembles in them   15
her grief trembles in them

Grief?

Where's the girl's man?
The man for whom
there's mourning in her veins   20
for whom
desire circulates in her bangles?

Her man is trapped
in some other body
some other dream   25
in some other sorrow
some other tears
every sorrow, dream, and tear of his
lies beyond the girl's grieving reach . . .

But the girl's a girl   30
she's still full
of that original innocence
madness, mortality,
for which
she's going to punish this man   35

when she breaks her bangles tomorrow . . .

Translated from the Hindi
by Vinay Dharwadker

NEPAL

SHANKAR LAMICHHANE

Shankar Lamichhane (1928–1975) was born in Kathmandu, the capital of Nepal. He spent his early childhood living with an uncle's family in Banaras, one of the principal cities now in the state of Uttar Pradesh, India. He worked for a number of government and cultural institutions in Kathmandu, and in his later years he became the manager of a handicrafts store.

Lamichhane's story satirizes the Western tourist who comes to Nepal with a variety of preconceptions. Such tourists often assume that they are culturally superior to the native people, that they know more about the country than its own inhabitants, and that Nepal is simply an exotic Eastern land. Lamichhane mocks such a visitor by making him speak in his own voice in the first half of the story, hence revealing his prejudices. In the second half, Lamichhane lets a Nepali host speak on his own behalf, as he guides the tourist through the reality of everyday life in modern Nepal. The second speaker paints a bitter, ultimately tragic portrait of Nepal's economic, cultural, and spiritual condition, representing it allegorically with the figure of a child.

The Half-Closed Eyes of the Buddha and the Slowly Setting Sun

Oh guide, you do not, you cannot understand the joy we Westerners feel when we first set foot upon the soil of your country!

As the Dakota° crosses the Four Passes,° we see this green valley with its geometric fields, its earthen houses of red, yellow, and white. The scent of soil and mountains is in the air, and there's an age-old peacefulness in the atmosphere. You were born amongst all of this, and so perhaps you feel that the embrace of these blue hills' outspread arms confines you. But we live in the plains or beside the sea. Our vision founders

---

Dakota: a commercial airplane used commonly in India between the 1940s and the 1970s

the Four Passes: translation of Char Bhanjyang, a Nepali name for the Kathmandu Valley

on an horizon of land or sea, and so we know the affection with which the breast of these hills forever clings to your sight. You have never had to suffer the feeling of insignificance that is caused by a vast distance. Perhaps we are always adrift in vastness, my friend; perhaps that is why this, your enclosure, appeals to us! Has it ever occurred to you that the half-closed eyes of the Buddha seem to welcome you, even at the airport? It is as if one acquires a calmness, as if one is returning once more to a resting place.

You have always known only how to give to the West. You've given us religion and the Purāṇas,° images of brass and ornaments of ivory, manuscripts of palm leaves and inscriptions on copperplate. You gave us a civilization and its wisdom and garlands of jasmine flowers around our necks. You have continued in your giving, ignorant of what others call "taking," innocent of the notion of ownership. The very word *indulgence* is unknown to you. My friend, I know your history. Before I came here I spent several years in our libraries, leafing through the pages of your priceless volumes. You are a guide who will lead me down the streets and alleyways of the present, but I could take you along your ancient ways. Even now I can see it clearly: the valley is filled with water,° and a lotus flower blooms where Swyambhūnāth° now stands. Manjushrī strikes with his sword at Chobhār.° I see monks and nuns receiving alms and spreading the law in the nooks and crannies of the Kāsthamaṇḍapa.° Behold the eyes of these shaven-headed monks. You cannot meet their gaze! It is called the *samyak* gaze.° Do you know what that means? It is perception, pure and without contamination; sight that perceives everything in its true form. I'll have just one more drink before dinner. . . .

You live in a house like a temple, but you are unaware of its beauty, its enchantment. In these wooden images, these multifarious ornamentations, these many styles, there is the flowing music of a chisel in the hands of an artist. Do you not feel it? Tell me about those happy, prosperous young artists working in the fields all day and creating beautiful im-

the Purāṇas: literally, "the ancient books," which contain large quantities of classical Hindu mythology, cosmology, and theology
Swyambhūnāth, Manjushrī, Chobhār: Swyambhūnāth is the name of the hill that stands in the middle of the Kathmandu Valley in Nepal. According to Buddhist legend, in remote times the valley was filled by a lake. Once, a miraculous flame appeared on the surface of the lake. Manjushrī, a legendary bodhisttva (an enlightened being, like the Buddha himself) came down to earth to see the miracle. He took it as a sign that the lake should be drained, so that human beings could inhabit the valley. He used his sword to cleave the hills at Chobhār, south of the valley, to let the waters escape.
   Kāsthamaṇḍapa: the name of a temple, said to have been built with the wood of a single tree; probably the oldest building in Kathmandu (the capital of Nepal), after which the city itself is named
samyak gaze: a pure, contemplative gaze, achieved by means of Buddhist spiritual exercises

ages of their personal deities in their spare time, who are now covered by the dusts of the past.

Once, an artist was adding the finishing touches to a wooden image when his fair, tiny wife came by, carrying her baby on her back, and poured him *raksī°* from a jug. The foam bubbled over and congealed. Is it true that it was that foam that inspired the artist to construct a roof of tiles? Oh, your land is truly great, this country where so many different cultures found their home. Aryans, non-Aryans, Hindus, and Buddhists all came and obtained a rebirth here. It must be the effect of your country's soil, my friend; it was the soil that enabled all these races to flourish together here. Come, I'll drink one more small one, it's not dinnertime yet. . . .

I am greatly indebted to you for you have served me both Nepali and Newārī° food. Ah, *mo-mos!°* . . . Just picture the scene: it is winter and an old man sits in the upper story of his house, lit only by the fire. Perhaps the smoke is filling the room like fog from floor to ceiling. Perhaps he is telling his grandson about each and every Nepali item that Princess Bhrikutī took with her when King Amshuvarmān sent her off to Tibet.° The old lady smokes tobacco from a bamboo hookah, and, mindful of the old man, she carries on making fresh *mo-mos*. The son's wife puts some of them onto a brass plate, and the old man's words are garbled and obscured by his mouthful. The grandson laughs, and the old man tries to swallow quickly, so he burns his tongue and, unabashed, pours out a stream of ribald curses. . . . These are scenes that cannot be read in an old book in a library, and that is why I've had to come to Kathmandu and soak myself in its atmosphere, for which I'm greatly obliged to you. . . . Now, cheers once again, to your great country, and to mine!

Oh, and another thing that is not to be found in any book is the smile on the faces of these people. It is a smile of welcome, as if our meeting were neither accidental nor our first. It's as if I was the farmer's eldest son, coming home after a long day's work in the fields, as if my labors had been fruitful and I was content and at ease with my father. It's as if I have taken the world's most beautiful woman for my wife and have brought her along behind me, and my mother is smiling a welcome from the door. It's as if my sister's husband and I were the closest of friends

---

raksī: a common Nepali brew or drink

Nepali and Newārī: "Nepali" refers to the language and culture of the dominant Hindu population of Nepal, ethnically also known as the Gurkhas; "Newārī" refers similarly to the Newars, the earliest inhabitants of the Kathmandu Valley

mo-mo: Tibetan food; steamed dumpling stuffed with meat

Princess Bhrikutī, King Amshuvarmān, Tibet: The Tibetan king Songsten Gampo, who ruled around A.D. 627–650 and established Buddhism in Tibet, had two wives. One was a Chinese princess, and the other was Bhrikutī, daughter of Nepalese king Amshuvarmān. Both princesses are credited with converting the Tibetan king to Buddhism.

'and we, her brother and her husband, were coming along with our arms around one another, singing songs of drunkenness. It's as if — I cannot explain; however much I try, I cannot describe it fully. That smile is full of wisdom; it is a smile from the soul, a smile peculiar to this place. . . . One more drink, to your Nepalese smile, that sweet smile!

And then there are the eyes. The eyes of the carved lattice windows, the eyes painted on the door panels. The eyes on the *stūpas,*° the eyes of the people. And the eyes of the Himalaya, which peep out from the gaps between the hills like those of a neighbor's boy when he jumps up to see the peach tree in your garden. This is a land of eyes, a land guarded by the half-closed eyes of the Lord Buddha.

Even if all of the world's history books were destroyed today, your eyes would build a new culture; they would reassemble a civilization. My appetite for eyes is still not satiated. Tomorrow I shall go to a lonely place where there is a *stūpa* with eyes that are clear. There I want to see the pleasant lift of sunset reflected in the eyes of the Buddha. Show me beautiful, full eyes, eyes without equal, eyes whose memory will make this journey of mine unforgettable. . . . Come, let's go to eat dinner.

Come, my guest; today I am to show you some eyes.

This is Chobhār hill, where you people come to see the cleft that was made by Manjushrī's sword and the outflow of the Bāgmati River. Today I'll take you up the hill where few of our guests ever go and no tourist's car can proceed. There (in your words) the dust of time has not yet covered the culture of the past. Do you see this worn old rock? A young village artist has drawn some birds on it. Nearby, he has sketched a temple, leaving out any mention of the religion to which it belongs. Further up the hill, in the middle of the village, stands the temple of Ādināth.° In the temple courtyard there is a shrine of Shiva,° several Buddha images, and many prayer wheels,° inscribed *Om mani padme hum.*° You say it is a living example of Nepalese tolerance and coexistence. Children play happily there, unconcerned by the variety of their gods, religions, and philosophies. But my guest, I will not take you there.

You have already seen much of such things, and you have understood them and even preached them. Today I'll take you to a house where I feel sure you will find the pulse of our reality. They are a farmer's family, probably owning a few fields here and there, where they work and sweat

stūpa: a domed Buddhist monument

Ādināth, Shiva: Lord Shiva, one of the three main gods in Hinduism, is worshipped widely in Nepal; Ādināth is one of his common epithets, meaning "the first (or prime) lord and master"

prayer wheel: an icon of a chariot wheel, signifying the Buddhist law *(dhamma),* used in prayer and meditation

Om mani padme hum: famous Buddhist-Sanskrit spiritual formula, meaning "hail to the jewel in the lotus"

to pay off half the proceeds to someone in the city. There is no smoke to fill their upstairs room, they cook no *mo-mo*s in their hearth, nor do they discuss Bhrikutī's dowry in their winters. There is a child in the home, who is certainly no divine incarnation, either. Attacked by polio and born into a poor farmer's household, the child is surely incapable of spreading the law or of making any contribution to this earth. He has taken birth here in one of his maker's strangest forms of creation. And moreover, my friend — oh, the climb has tired you; would you like some filtered water from the thermos flask? — my intention is not to show him to you as any kind of symbol. Yesterday you were swept along by waves of emotion, inspired by your "Black and White" whisky, and you urged me to show you eyes that would forever remind you of your visit to Nepal. So I have brought you here to show you eyes like that.

The child's whole body is useless; he cannot speak, move his hands, chew his food, or even spit. His eyes are the only living parts of his body and it is only his eyes that indicate that he is actually alive. I don't know whether his eyes have the *samyak* gaze or not. I don't even understand the term, but his face is certainly devoid of all emotion. His gaze is uninterested, without resolution or expression; it is inactive and listless, unexercised and lacking any measure of contemplation. (Perhaps I have begun to speak unwittingly in the terms of the Aryan eightfold path,° which will either be your influence or a virtue bestowed upon me by the child.)

My guest, these are the eyes you wanted. A living being accumulates many capabilities in one lifetime. It feels happy and it smiles; it feels sad and it weeps. If it feels cold, it seeks warmth, and if it is hungry, it prepares food to eat. It seeks to learn what it doesn't already know, and it succeeds or it fails. It has many experiences, some bitter, some sweet, and these it relates when company, occasion, and mood seem suited. How commonplace all of these actions are! My guest, yesterday you said that we Eastern peoples were always making contributions to the West, did you not? (Shall I give you some water? Are you out of breath?) Here is a child who can neither give nor take anything at all. Just put yourself in his position for a moment. You want your finger to do something, but your finger refuses. You want to speak, but speech will not come to you. Every vein, nerve, and bone is powerless to heed the commands of your brain, and yet . . . you are alive. I know that this disease occurs in your country, too. But the ability to endure it and to maintain a total indifference in the eyes, even, perhaps, to foster the *samyak* gaze, this capacity for remaining speechless, inactive, powerless, and immobile, and yet to survive without complaint . . . this can surely only be found in an Easterner!

Aryan eightfold path: the spiritual path of the eight-part "golden mean" preached by the Buddha

Come, come closer. I have lied to his parents; I have told them that you are a doctor. Look . . . their faith in you shows in their eyes. There is intimacy, kindliness, and gratitude in their eyes, as if your coming here were preordained. That smile you described is on their faces, as if you were their eldest son who has brought a life-restoring remedy across the seven seas for your brother. The old peasant woman is smiling, isn't she? It's as if she's rejoicing at the birth of her first grandchild from your wife, the beauty of the world. I know that this same smile will remain on their faces as long as you are here. I know that it will be extinguished when you turn to go. Once you've gone they'll sink back into the same old darkness.

The child has a sister whose body functions properly. He watches her as she crawls around, picking up everything she comes across and putting it into her mouth, knocking over the beer, overturning the cooking stone. Just for an instant, the ambition to emulate her is reflected in his eyes, but then it is reabsorbed into the same old indifference. Once his mother was scolding his sister, and a light gleamed in his eyes. I couldn't tell you to which era its vision belonged, but I realized that he wanted to speak. With a gaze devoid of language, gesture, or voice, he wanted to say, "Mother, how can you appreciate what fun it is to fall over? To crawl through the green dub grass and rub the skin off your knees, to shed a couple of drops of blood like smeared tears, and graze your flesh a little. To feel pain and to cry, to call out for help. That pain would be such a sweet experience. She can rub her snot or spittle into her own grazes, or pull out the thorn that has pricked her, and throw it away. Or she could pull off a scab that has healed over a buried splinter of glass or spend a few days resting under her quilt. She can climb up onto the storage jar to try to pull a picture down from the wall, and when the peg slips out and the picture falls and the glass smashes with a wonderful noise, she feels a wave of fear as she realizes her guilt. She has grown up, learning from experience the facts that fire can burn her and water makes her wet, that nettles cause blisters and beer makes her dizzy. That if she falls she might be hurt or break a bone, that if something else falls it will probably break. That if someone dies, she is able to weep, and if someone laughs, she can laugh right back; if someone makes fun of her, she can strike them, and if someone steals from her, she can steal from them. My sister, who learns and remembers each and every new word she hears, is the result of the self-sacrificing practice of thousands of years of human language. She embodies a history, a tradition, and a culture, and it is in her very ability to speak that the future is born. But not in one like me, who cannot even move his lips. In my body, in its strength and gestures, an unbroken cycle of historical and human development has come to its conclusion. A long labor, a chain of events, a lengthy endeavor, and an endlessness are all at an end. The future ends and is broken abruptly."

And these are the eyes, my guest, that look at you but see nothing; this is the gaze that is incapable of self-manifestation. This is beauty that is complete and has no other expression.

These are eyes surrounded by mountains; their lashes are rows of fields where rice ripens in the rains and wheat ripens in the winter. These are the eyes that welcome you, and these are eyes that build. And in these eyes hides the end of life. Look! They are just as beautiful as the setting sun's reflection in the eyes of the Buddha!

Translated from the Nepali
by Michael James Hutt

PAKISTAN

ZAMIRUDDIN AHMAD

Zamiruddin Ahmad (1925–1990) was born in Fatehgarh, India. When the subcontinent was partitioned in 1947, he migrated to Pakistan. In 1971 he moved to London, where he lived and worked until his death. He worked as a journalist in India, Pakistan, the Middle East, and the United Kingdom, and also as a radio and television broadcaster in Pakistan and England.

During his lifetime Ahmad published about forty short stories in Urdu literary magazines. Besides fiction, he wrote a large number of critical essays, a study of the representations of female sexuality in Urdu literature, as well as radio plays and scripts for television serials. At the time of his death he was working on his first novel.

"Purvai — The Easterly Wind," first published in Urdu around 1987, is one of Ahmad's late stories. It is a work of psychological realism. It deals with a Muslim nuclear family in a contemporary urban setting and focuses on the woman, who is not only a housewife but also a working mother. The male author uses a point of view strongly sympathetic to the woman and portrays the gentle awakening or reawakening of her desire, in middle age and as a married woman, for a man she had known before her marriage. All these elements combine with Ahmad's intimate treatment of character and situation to produce an unusual story, since the more conventional setting in modern Urdu fiction tends to be an extended family network in which female consciousness and female sexuality are not highlighted.

Purvai — The Easterly Wind

The boy lifted his head from the notebook and looked at the closed door behind which his father was changing his clothes.

"Father," he said, "what does *purva°* mean?"

The answer came from the kitchen instead, where his mother was frying *parathas°* for breakfast: *"Purvai."°*

---

purva: east
paratha: a thick, unleavened, whole-wheat bread, like a pan-fried tortilla
purvai, purvayya: an easterly wind

"The wind that blows in an easterly direction?"

"No," she answered, lifting the paratha from the skillet and stacking it on the pile in the breadcloth, "rather, the wind that blows from the east."

"It's also called *purvayya* — isn't it?"

The door opened. The father, buttoning up the front of his shirt, walked onto the veranda where one three-legged chair and three perfectly good ones stood flanking a round table covered with a plastic cover. A schoolbag lay open on the table before the boy who sat in one of the chairs, bent over a notebook on which he was writing something.

The father buttoned his right sleeve and asked, "What's this all about?"

"Oh, I've got to make a sentence."

"So have you made one?"

The boy gently pushed the notebook toward his father. The latter looked down at it and read out loud: "If the wind blows from the east, it's called purvai." After a pause he remarked, "But that's the meaning!"

"So?" the boy scratched his head.

In walked the mother holding a plate with a paratha and a small serving of spiced scrambled eggs. She set the plate before the boy and said, "Write!"

The boy promptly bowed his head over the notebook again.

"One of the effects of purvai is that it cheers up the saddest person, for a while at least, and . . ."

The boy lifted his eyes from the notebook and fixed them on his mother's face. She thought for some time and then said, "That'll do. Get rid of the 'and'!"

The boy dutifully struck out the word.

Meanwhile she quickly returned to the kitchen adjoining the veranda with its door opening onto a small courtyard.

The boy shut the notebook, stuffed it into his schoolbag, and began hurriedly eating his breakfast. After he was done eating, he walked to the water-tank in the courtyard by the kitchen door and rinsed his mouth a few times. He dried his hands on a small towel hung on a clothesline in the courtyard, slung the schoolbag on his shoulder, and said, "Mother, I'll be late this evening. There's a field hockey match."

He then said goodbye to her, unlatched the courtyard door and scurried out.

Not long afterwards she returned with a plate: a couple of parathas and a small portion of some gravied meat dish left over from the previous evening. She put the plate before her husband, who was now ensconced in the same chair earlier occupied by the boy.

He stared at the plate. "No scrambled eggs for me?"

"There was just one egg," she answered, walking back to the kitchen. "I'll get some more in the evening, on my way home from work. Today's payday."

Back in the kitchen she sat down on the low wicker stool. She took out a piece of stale bread from the breadcloth, broke off a morsel, dipped it in the gravy left over in the pan, popped it into her mouth and started to slowly chew. After a couple of mouthfuls, she put the bread into the cloth.

"Aren't you going to eat breakfast?" he called, mopping the plate clean with the last of his bread.

"Oh, I've already eaten," she replied from the kitchen, removing the pot from the stove and pouring the boiling water into the tea kettle.

"When?"

"While you were bathing."

He heard the sound of a spoon being twirled in a cup and asked, "You'll at least make me some tea, or . . . ?"

In response she promptly walked in with two cups neatly placed on saucers. She put one down before him and the other before herself, then settled into an empty chair.

He took a sip of the steaming brew and absent-mindedly began to scratch at the plastic tablecloth with his fingernail, trying to take off the stubborn stain left there by lentil gravy.

She too took a sip and said, "Never mind, I'll clean it off."

They sipped their tea for a while. After some time he said, "This is the second day in a row that I've had to wear the same shirt."

"Oh well. The laundryman never shows up on time. We'll have to find another."

"But maybe a couple of shirts could be washed at home."

"Why not?" There was a sharp sound as the teacup hit the saucer. "The whole pile of dirty laundry could be washed at home."

He was stunned. "Now you're cross with me."

She didn't bother to respond.

He gently took her hand and began to caress it. But she pulled it away — brusquely. He rose and strode toward the back of her chair and installed himself behind her, so close that only the thin wooden back of the chair separated their bodies. He put his palms on her pale cheeks, stooped over her and kissed her matted hair. Then he raised his right finger and touched her gently across her firmly closed lips. Both his hands slid down along her loose hair, lingered awhile on her shoulders and then wandered slyly further down.

She drew back and sprang to her feet. "I have a lot of things to do . . ."

He snickered — out of embarrassment.

"I've got to do the dishes, make the beds, take a bath . . ."

He grabbed her shoulders and pressed on them to force her to sit down. Then he pulled over a chair, sat down in it facing her and said, "What's the matter?"

"Nothing," she said, fixing her gaze on her unadorned nails.

"Look at me!"

But she didn't; instead, she said, "This isn't the right time."

"And last night?"

"I had a headache."

He laughed. "You're a great one for making excuses." There was a trace of sarcasm in his voice.

She collected the teacups and started off for the kitchen. Her ample buttocks, swaying beneath the folds of her sari,° touched off a wave of excitement throughout his body before they dissolved into the grey darkness of the kitchen.

Just as she was stepping out of the store her eyes fell on a chauffeur-driven car parking some distance away on the opposite side of the street. A man sat in the rear, his head resting comfortably against the back of the seat. She started. The chauffeur got out, walked back and opened the rear door. She quickly slipped behind a tree next to the sidewalk. A tallish man, with a slightly dark complexion, wearing a suit and tie and a pair of shiny shoes, stepped out. After exchanging a few words with the chauffeur he walked away from the car and entered a nearby lane. The chauffeur returned to sit in the car.

Her throat constricted and went completely dry; her feet felt incredibly heavy; and she broke into a fine sweat. She felt as though her eyes were ready to pop out of their sockets and follow the man into the lane. She swallowed uneasily once or twice and nervously rubbed first her forehead and then her temples. She took the end of her sari lying over her shoulders and carefully covered her head with it and came out from behind the tree. She took a few hesitant steps toward the other side of the street, but faltered. She stood still, vacantly staring at the car for a few moments. Then she hastily crossed the street, walked up to the parked car, and stopped a couple of feet away from the chauffeur, unable to make up her mind whether she wanted to stop or move on ahead.

The chauffeur examined her from head to toe. Her grip on the shopping-bag tightened. She started to walk over, but then suddenly midway she did an about-face and began to walk away.

This time the chauffeur looked only at her face.

She turned around again and took a deep breath. Then she walked back to the car and asked the chauffeur, "Who was that gentleman?"

Her question had the casualness of one pedestrian asking another for the time or an address.

The chauffeur eyed her over again and replied, "He's our guest."

"Your guest?"

"Yes. I mean he's visiting my boss. He's from Pakistan."

She hesitated for a bit, then asked, "His name is Masrur Ahmad — isn't it?"

The chauffeur, who had meanwhile started to light a cigarette, blew

---

sari: a traditional garment worn by Indian women

out the match and tossed it out the window. It landed a few inches from her sandals.

"Don't know," he said. "The boss calls him Qazi-ji."

"Qazi Masrur Ahmad," she said, as if to herself. "His full name is Qazi Masrur Ahmad."

"Could be," the driver said indifferently, and through the windshield he quickly fixed his gaze on a girl in tight clothes who was walking up ahead.

A car, driven by a young woman, passed by. Another young woman sat next to the driver, her radiant hair blowing in the wind. The rear seat was occupied by a frail man and a portly woman.

She squashed the burnt match-stub with the tip of her sandal, opened the shopping bag, peered around in it, and, walking in a semi-circle around the rear of the car, came to a clothes store and stopped in front of it. After a while she walked back to the chauffeur by the same route.

"He's brought his wife along too — hasn't he?" she asked, in the manner of a child asking for something nearly impossible to get.

The chauffeur looked at her as though she was crazy. He was apparently irritated at her for coming back and pestering him with yet another question. But, being basically a courteous man, he replied gently, "Wife! No. Qazi Sahib is still a bachelor."

She quickly thanked him. She turned around, cast a sweeping look down the lane and started off toward the bus station with soft, brisk steps.

When the father, carrying a bundle of files, came into the house, he found the boy at the table doing homework. He put the bundle on the table, sat down in a chair, looked around and asked, "Where's your mother?"

"Bathing."

He heard the sound of water splashing in the bathroom.

"This time of day?"

The boy didn't answer.

The plastic tablecloth suddenly caught the man's eye. It looked spotlessly clean and shiny. The floor in the veranda too looked immaculate, still slightly wet. Perhaps it's just been mopped — he thought. The courtyard floor also looked a bit wet here and there. The house had only three rooms, each with its door opening onto the veranda. He looked at the first door, then at the second, and then at the third: each looked clean, thoroughly wiped, he speculated, with a duster. The same naked light bulb still hung directly above the table, still covered with its tenacious pile of dust, but somehow he felt it burnt much brighter today.

The sound of bathing ceased. Presently the door opened and she emerged, wearing fully starched, light green *pajama*-trousers and a *kurta*-shirt° of the same color, with her wet hair wrapped up in a towel.

---

kurta-shirt: loose-fitting Indian shirt, often worn with a trouser-like garment called *pajama*

"It's late," she said, stopping by her husband. "I missed the six o'clock bus."

Waves of perfume wafted from her body. Her cheeks were flushed. The naked light bulb in the veranda seemed to have set off a whole array of tiny sparks in her eyes.

"Didn't you take a bath in the morning?" he asked, tearing his eyes away from the flashing pink of her cheeks.

"I couldn't. I was running late."

She proceeded toward the same door from which her husband had come out buttoning his shirt earlier in the morning.

"How about getting me a cup of tea?"

"Sure. But let me dry my hair first."

She went into the room. He yanked out a pack of cigarettes and a box of matches from his coat pocket, lit a cigarette and puffed on it.

In the meantime the boy finished his homework, picked up his school things and left for the middle room.

After the last drag the husband threw the cigarette butt down on the floor and squashed it with his shoe. Just as he was getting up, she came out of the room, her hair free of the towel and now spread loosely on her shoulders. The folds of her stiff, starched *dupatta*° seemed to have frozen over her breasts. Holding the wet towel in her hand she walked to the courtyard and hung it on the clothesline.

She was about to step into the kitchen when the boy called, "Mother."

"Yes, Munna?"

"I'm hungry."

"All right."

"He hasn't eaten yet?" the father asked.

She shook her head.

"How come?"

"Oh, he had a cup of tea with a couple of pieces of toast after he got home from school. He said he wasn't feeling very hungry."

The boy came in and said, "Mother, I want supper."

"Come on Munna. Don't be so impatient. Let me fix tea for your father. Then I'll feed you."

The boy returned to his room. As she was just stepping into the kitchen, her husband got up from his chair and said, "Never mind."

"Why?"

"Let's eat supper instead. I'm hungry too."

Sounds of banging pots and pans started to pour out of the kitchen. The boy turned on the radio. The father went into the room to change, then into the bathroom.

In the meantime, she set the table and brought out the food. "All right Munna," she called out, taking the middle chair, "dinner's on."

dupatta: a woman's long, scarf-like garment, usually draped over a loose shirt or tunic

The boy turned off the radio and came onto the veranda. His eyes fell on the platter in the middle of the table. "Wow!" he let out a joyous cry, "Pilaf today!"

The husband had just dried his hand and mouth on the wet towel hanging on the clothesline in the courtyard and was back on the veranda. "Pilaf?" he said, somewhat surprised.

She held out the platter to him and said, "I got off from work a little early today; so I thought I might cook something special." She then offered him the bowl of spicy yoghurt *raita.*°

He took a generous helping of the pilaf and poured some raita on it. She served more than half of the remaining pilaf to the boy and dumped the rest on her plate, then pushed the raita toward the boy. The boy took some and set the bowl before his mother.

"Very tasty," the husband remarked after the first mouthful.

"Yeah," the boy, his mouth full, chimed in.

She smiled.

After the supper dishes were cleared away, she went into the kitchen and promptly returned with a cardboard box which she set on the table.

"My, my, what a treat!" the husband exclaimed, opening the box. "What's the occasion? Did you get a raise or something?"

He picked up a *gulab-jaman*° and popped it into his mouth.

"Oh no," she said, suddenly feeling a little embarrassed. "For days now Munna has been begging for sweets. So I thought I might just as well get some. That's all."

Then, looking at the boy, she said, "Have some."

The boy picked out a *laddu.*° So did the father. But she took a square of *barfi.*°

Presently the boy took a gulab-jaman but, before stuffing it into his mouth, said, "Mother Siraj Sahib was telling us that the purvai also has another effect . . ."

"I know," she said, very softly.

"And what's that?" the father asked.

"When it blows, it causes old hurts to start aching again . . . Is that really true?"

"Yes," she answered, again very softly.

"Have some more," her husband offered, holding the box.

"That's enough for me," she said.

A half hour or so later she went into the kitchen, but returned right away. "What's the rush?" she said. "I can always do the dishes in the morning."

raita: yogurt blended with spices and other ingredients, served as an accompaniment to the main dishes in a north Indian and Pakistani meal
gulab-jaman: a north Indian sweet food served as a snack or dessert
laddu, barfi: north Indian sweet foods served as snacks and desserts, particularly on festive occasions

"Yes," the husband, bent over a file, said, without lifting his head.

After some time she went into the boy's room. When she returned she said, settling back in her chair, "He's fast asleep."

"Yes," he nodded, again without bothering to lift his head.

After a while she got up and brought a magazine from her room and started reading it. But when he bent down to pick up a fresh file from the floor he looked at her out of the corner of his eye and realized that she really wasn't reading the magazine at all; instead, she was looking intently into the yawning darkness of the courtyard.

When he lifted his head again to light a cigarette, he found her reading the magazine. She looked at him over the magazine, smiled sweetly, and resumed her reading.

After a bit, she slapped the magazine shut and got up. "Well, I'm going to bed."

"You go on. I'll be there in a while."

She went into her room. The sound of her humming continued for a while, then the quiet was absolute.

The moist, thick darkness oozing down from the sky had covered the length of the courtyard; the noise of the traffic outside on the street had grown progressively fainter and ultimately died down; and the bark of a solitary dog arose somewhere far away. He decided it was time to turn in. He closed the last of the files and placed it on top of the pile, rubbed his aching eyes, lit a cigarette and got up. He then turned off the veranda light, noiselessly pushed her door open and went in.

His eyes fell on their twin beds, headboards snug against the back wall. The small shaded lamp on the low sidetable lodged between the beds was still on, its dim glow barely reaching above their beds.

She was sleeping in the bed on the right; her clothes — the same pajama-kurta suit and dupatta which only a few hours ago had sent a surge of excitement through him — and her bra lay all crumpled and bunched on the easy chair to the right of her bed. So unlike her! — he wondered, a trifle surprised. Wasn't she, after all, in the habit of neatly folding her clothes and putting them carefully away in the closet every time she changed?

He edged closer to the bed and lifted the lightweight comforter pulled over her body all the way to her shoulders. He was stunned. Free of the last restraint of modesty, her sleeping body somehow seemed fully awake in anticipation of someone. He had the curious feeling that he didn't know that body, that he was looking at it for the first time ever.

He quickly stubbed out the cigarette and, every so gently, noiselessly, sat down on the edge of her bed. She shifted; and her face, turned slightly toward the easy chair, came directly under the lamp's subdued glow. Then, as he stood watching, a faint smile swept over her sealed lips.

He put one hand over the pillow cushioning her head and the other over the pillow lodged under her arm and lowered himself over her face.

His parted lips stopped inches away from her closely pressed ones. Her eyelids seemed moist. This vague suspicion was confirmed when he detected a wet spot on her pillow close by her head.

He straightened up, staring tensely for a while at her face and her breasts facing him. Then, ever so gently, he raised his index finger and touched her on the lips. Her breathing altered, as did the rhythm of her heaving chest. That faint smile abruptly departed from her lips. He held his breath and waited for a few moments. After her breathing returned to normal and the heaving in her chest subsided, he got up, taking care not to make the slightest sound. For the next few moments he stared vacantly at her body as it lay there comfortably stretched out, awash in its gentle, radiant heat.

Carefully he folded her clothes — her kurta-pajama suit, her dupatta, her bra — and put them neatly on the easy chair before retiring to his bed. He sat on it for quite a while.

She turned over in bed. Her face was now turned toward him. A smile — the sign of some rich, honeyed dream — was radiating from her lips and the corners of her eyes, bringing to the fresh pink of her cheeks a more vibrant color. The other pillow was hugged tight to her bosom.

He stretched out his arm and pulled the comforter over her nakedness. Then he turned off the lamp and went to sleep.

Translated from the Urdu by
Muhammad Umar Memon

ENVER SAJJAD

Enver Sajjad (1935–) was born in Lahore, which is now in Pakistan. He was trained as a physician, and besides practicing medicine, he paints, writes and performs in plays for Pakistan radio and television, and writes fiction in Urdu. He is also a political activist. He founded the Pakistan Artists' Equity in 1972 and later served as its president. He was the secretary and the general secretary of the Pakistan People's Party, Lahore Division, from 1975 to 1980. The military government of General Zia-ul-Haq viewed his politics unfavorably, banning him from state-owned radio and television in the 1970s and 1980s and imprisoning him twice for his dissidence.

Sajjad is primarily an experimental prose writer, whose work has been influenced strongly by European and Western avant-garde movements. "The Bird" is a violent parable of colonialism and its aftermath, particularly of the "neocolonialism" at work in the modern tourist trade. It attacks Western travelers who seek out exotic experiences and trophies at all costs and remain insensitive to the societies and cultures that they raid. The parable dramatizes the confrontation between cultures by enacting a conflict between an unnamed "White Tourist" and a birdlike creature.

The Bird

"YU BLADI BASTIK!"°

The watchman spat poison on the ground, rubbed his mouth clean against his shirtsleeve and stuffed his fist, still rolled over a rupee note, into his pocket. His eyes were glued to the door opening out into the yard. On the way out, the White Tourist, or W.T., spun around to wave him goodbye. Again a drop of poison formed on the watchman's tongue; again he spat out the bitter taste and rubbed his lips dry. Throwing a quick, guilty look at the people nearby, he waved back with a smile; then returned to his seat under the arch of the mausoleum, his fingers furtively twisting the note in his pocket. He was happy — and then, not.

W.T. was very happy. All the mysteries of this land seemed caught in the tinted glass. He turned and snapped a picture of the archway, then removed the overshoes and walked out into the yard. The raw, fresh smell of dust arose from the unpaved ground. He took a deep breath and filled his lungs with the smell; but the next moment it escaped with his breath and became diffused in the air.

"I cannot capture this fragrance with my camera!"

W.T. shook his head in disappointment and began to walk with heavy steps. His shoes crunched the bird-feed scattered in the yard. He didn't sense anything unnatural about the flock of birds pecking grains nearby. Was not the bird's world, as usual, just that grain under the beak? Beyond the grain, nothing else seemed to exist. Who had scattered these grains? Did the birds know where they had come from? Were they certain that the grains did not hide a trap beneath them?

"These, at any rate, are unimportant questions. Why in the world should I worry my head over them? They're the birds' headache. Why, of course, some generous soul has thrown the grain here for the birds. Who else?"

With a carefree toss of his head, W.T. shook off all the questions. He moved cautiously beside the birds and was about to step out of the gate when a rock landed right in the middle of the flock. For a moment the birds seemed ready to fly off, then resumed pecking at the grains. But they had obviously lost their former confidence. Every now and then they craned their necks in the direction the rock had come from. W.T., too,

Yu bladi bastik: the north Indian underclass pronunciation of the English curse, "you bloody bastard"

looked in that direction and saw an innocent-looking boy, his cheeks still free of any fuzz, perched on a fence. A series of images of the young Christ flashed across W.T.'s mind; all of them, however, seemed alien here. That innocent face was this very land: smell of fresh clay, color of ripe wheat, half the earth.

"If I were a painter, I would take him to my studio right away." His hand reached for the camera.

"Heavens, no. Gadgets won't do the job. The fire let loose in the mind by the boy will simply set the celluloid aflame."

With the hem of his shirt, the boy wiped his runny nose and began toying with another rock as he studied the flock. Before he could throw it, W.T. cried out:

"O, you — Judas!"

The boy caught a glimpse of his angry face and, clambering down the fence, scurried away. W.T. moistened his dried throat with a liberal gulp of saliva and heaved a sigh of relief.

"Hell, how I allowed myself to be tricked into that show of sentimentality by the smell and color of the earth! He was Judas; indeed, he was."

He looked at the flock. The birds still seemed a trifle nervous. He had hardly taken a step forward when the infinite mysteries caught in the blue glass leapt up before his eyes. Something strange, resembling a bird, hopped out of the flock and moved forward, sniffing the ground. Featherless, if anything, bristly, the bare stubs of its wings hung from both sides of its crooked body. The colors of the setting sun seemed to slip off it and bounce back to the sun. A shroud of onion skin clung to its body, a pair of chariot-wheel eyes embedded in a large head at the end of a long scrawny neck, a sawtooth in place of a beak: it almost dug into the ground as it walked on its emaciated legs in a measured, studied gait. For one long moment its beak would examine a grain, pick it up, then drop it and move ahead to the next grain. The bare stubs of its wings kept coming in the way and in its effort to grab the grain with its beak, the bird almost wound up spinning like a top on its claws. Then, tired out, it threw its beak to the next grain. Other birds in the flock, oblivious of its existence, went on hurriedly pecking at the grains, getting ready to fly off to their nests. This bird, however, was in no particular hurry as it went on scrutinizing the grains.

W.T. gaped.

Never before had he seen such a bird — bird, because it had emerged from a flock of birds. He had traveled far and wide on the earth, flown across its numerous skies: there was that dark, chilly sky that stretched over a roaring jungle covered with red flowers, and now this onion sky, wrapped in a light-green gauze that gave out a mixed odor of sweat, paddy fields and gunpowder. He had on his suitcase all kinds of stickers picked up as souvenirs of his many travels in distant lands, yet never before had he seen such a bird anywhere in the sky. His hands impulsively reached out for the camera then dropped as he suddenly remembered that he had already used up his last roll of film.

"Then . . ."

He furtively ran his tongue over his lips.

"Then — why not take the bird along? That's it, take it along. In a golden cage, it'll make an excellent present for Mom on her birthday. It may be a talking bird for all I know. Maybe its voice is as lovely as its body is strange. Sure, Mom would love such a fabulous gift."

Suddenly he remembered the joke about the wealthy tycoon who spent a fortune to have a singing bird sent home as a gift. The next day he telephoned to learn whether the bird had arrived safely. He asked his wife, "The bird, darling. Did you like it?" and heard her smack her lips with delight. "Honey, it was delicious!"

W.T. smiled to himself.

"I don't think that would happen; I'll be taking the bird along myself. And even if such a thing happened and Mother's craving for nice food overcame her love of sweet sounds, at least I would be there to relish it with her."

He backed a bit, came opposite the bird and knelt down. The bird threw a look at him, turned round and glanced at the flock. One by one they were leaving the ground, some for the trees, others for the arch. The last ray was dying out, giving a final dab of onion color to the bird's skin. Once again, the bird was looking intently at W.T. Darkness crept down from the trees to the ground. Eager to grab this newly discovered treasure, W.T. picked up a few grains and held them out on his palm to lure the bird. The bird took a few steps and came quite close to him, scanned the grains in W.T.'s palm, then turned away its beak to look at the sky now dyed a darkish red.

"Is it sick or something? If it won't eat the grain, the paddy water will dry out of its onion flesh and then . . . But more than anything else how will I take it into my confidence if it won't peck the feed?"

W.T. impatiently held out his palm to the bird again. The featherless, scraggy bird turned its head and once again peered searchingly at the grains spread out before it on the open palm, stretched its neck and . . .

"Ouch!"

The beak ripped a chunk of flesh from W.T.'s little finger.

He jumped up, shaking his hand; his eyes showed anger and disappointment as he hastily sucked at the wound. Then he yanked out his handkerchief and wrapped it around the bleeding finger. The bird was already busy with the grain and indifferent to the man. No one was in the yard. Hearing W.T.'s cry, the watchman had hurried over to the gate. W.T. gestured to him that he wanted to catch the bird. The watchman spun around to see if anyone was watching. Visitors were passing by. Just then the same innocent-looking boy strolled by, throwing probing glances at the two of them. He still held a rock in his hand. Seeing the boy, the watchman felt embarrassed. Then he shrugged his shoulders in resignation and gestured back to tell W.T. how he could catch the bird. After that, he returned to his place under the arch.

W.T. stretched out his arm and shaded the bird with his hands; he wanted to see if the bird would notice his arms and try to slip out from under them. But the bird, in search of food, was again spinning around on its claws chasing after its own wing. This gave W.T. his chance. Cautiously extending his arms, he deftly closed in on the bird, grabbed its neck, pinched the beak shut with the same hand and with the other clutched its claws.

"I am taking you home. There I will give you nice food to eat. Within days, feathers will grow on your body again and you will warble spring songs, sitting as you would be, in your golden cage. That will make Mom happy, infinitely happy."

One last flutter and the bird became motionless in his grasp.

W.T. turned back to thank the watchman but could not see him against the darkness that swooped down from the vaults of the tomb. Without caring to look for him a second time, W.T. tucked the bird under his arm and strode out of the yard.

His chauffeur was about to slam the door shut when his glance fell on W.T.'s lap. Terrified, he could feel the hair rise on his body.

"Sir, what's that?" he nearly shrieked.

"A bird — I caught it in the cemetery."

The chauffeur didn't pay much attention to what W.T. had to say; he was watching instead the handkerchief, wrapped around the latter's finger, turning red.

"What . . . What happened to your finger?"

"Oh, nothing," W.T. smiled. "The friend bit me. Not a bad bargain even in return for the little finger, not at all — wouldn't you say so?"

"Sir, let go of it, please. It looks like a dangerous beast."

"Beast? Dummy, it's a bird, a local bird. Haven't you seen one before?"

"No, sir, never. What big eyes it has! One could almost see oneself mirrored in them. And this saw of a beak — I am scared."

"Don't be scared. Now it won't do any harm. No more foolish talk, please; just take me to the hotel."

"Your finger! Shouldn't we go to the hospital first?"

"No. It isn't much of a wound."

"Sir, I would say . . . "

"Oh, come on. Let's go."

The chauffeur opened the door, got in behind the wheel, and stuck the key in the ignition, then, as an afterthought, said, "Sir, I guess you will get a lot of money for it in one of the zoos back in your country?"

W.T. gave a gentle, loving look to the bird.

"Maybe. Right now all I want is to take it home and feed it well. Seems the poor thing has starved for centuries."

The chauffeur started the engine. The bird now had its beady eyes fixed on W.T. As the car got moving, it leapt forward and cut across W.T.'s lips, ripping part of his cheek as well.

"Hold it! The damned thing is loose again."

The chauffeur turned off the ignition, got out of the car and opened the rear door.

"Sir, throw it out please."

The bird was fluttering violently in W.T.'s lap, whose hands had become terribly scratched in an effort to subdue it.

"Give me a hand, will you! I almost have it . . . "

"I won't touch it, no, sir. For God's sake, hurl the beast out of the window. Look, sir, you are bleeding all over."

"How can I let it go! Not now. Don't you see, it's all I've got left from these travels. My prize!"

The bird kept charging violently. In the meantime, the handkerchief had come loose and the torn finger dangled from the hand by only a shred of skin.

"Enough, that's enough. Cut it out, now. Look, I'll feed you like a king."

But the bird had no ears. It now tore into W.T.'s shoulders, savagely. Its eyes were crimson and one could almost see its blood throb fitfully underneath its onion skin.

"Help!" W.T. cried out.

Hesitantly the chauffeur reached out to W.T.'s lap, grabbed the bird and hurled it out on the pavement. The bird fell on its back. For one brief moment its claws quivered in the air, then with the speed of lightning it was back on them again. The chauffeur raised his foot to kick it, but the bird charged ferociously back at the new opponent. The chauffeur retreated behind the car. A crowd had meanwhile gathered near the scene, and watched with a feeling of amusement. All of a sudden the bird raced up to the open door of the car and hopped inside. Across W.T.'s eyes danced colors dipped in the smell of sweat, paddy fields and gunpowder, and roaring jungles, dark and chilly, full of red flowers.

He tried to fend off the attack with his arms, but the bird swooped down, deftly avoiding his hands, and began tearing at his chest. W.T. could barely manage to get up and kick the bird out; he then fell back on the seat soaked in his own blood.

From behind the slowly falling curtains on the deluge of mysteries that flowed out of the blue glass, W.T. dimly saw the chauffeur hoist the bird up by its claws and smash it on the pavement. Suddenly a rock hit the chauffeur, and his forehead cracked open. That innocent-looking boy, whose cheeks were still free of any fuzz, whose face was this very land — smell of fresh clay, color of ripe wheat, half the earth — stepped forward. He tore the bird away from the chauffeur and, holding it against his breast and kissing its head, walked out of sight.

"Judas!"

W.T.'s lips moved weakly.

"So, doc, that's the whole story!"

"You bloody bastard!" the physician muttered under his breath, and released the clamp from the tube attached to the bottle of native blood.

Translated from the Urdu by
Muhammad Umar Memon and C. M. Naim

KHALIDA ASGHAR

Khalida Asghar (1938–) was born in Lahore, which is now in Pakistan. She started writing fiction in Urdu in 1963 and published half a dozen short stories, including "The Wagon," in the next two years. After her marriage in 1965, however, she published nothing for about twelve years. Her first book of short fiction appeared in 1981, and since then she has published two more collections. Unlike her early stories, her later stories are concerned mainly with the identity of women in the male-dominated, traditional Islamic society of contemporary Pakistan. She now lives in Rawalpindi, where she teaches English at the Military College of Engineering and Technology. Some of her work has appeared under her married name, Khalida Husain.

"The Wagon," written around 1963, is considered a classic of modern Urdu fiction. At the time of its publication, the story appeared boldly experimental in subject and style. It succeeded in dealing with experiences and phenomena that are difficult to pinpoint precisely, and it risked the mode of fantasy and hallucination at a time when Urdu prose was dominated by social and psychological realism. The story imagines the effects of a large-scale industrial or technological catastrophe on an ordinary individual's life and on an entire region. In the course of the calamity, the citizens of the metropolis in which the story is set become victims of phenomena they cannot even name. "The Wagon" is an allegory of modernization and its consequences, and of urban experience in the nuclear age.

The Wagon

In a rush to get back to the city, I quickly crossed the dirt road and walked onto the Ravi bridge, looking indifferently at the blazing edge of the sun steadily falling into the marsh. I had a queer feeling, as though I saw something. I spun around. There they were, three of them, leaning over the bridge's guard rails and gazing straight into the sunset. Their deathly concentration made me look at the sunset myself, but I found nothing extraordinary in the scene; so I looked back at them instead. Their faces, although not at all similar, still looked curiously alike. Their outfits suggested that they were well-to-do villagers, and their dust-coated shoes that they had trudged for miles just to watch the sun as it set over the marshes of the receding Ravi. Impervious to the traffic on the bridge, they went on staring at the marshes which were turning a dull, deep red in the sun's last glow.

I edged closer to them. The sun had gone down completely; only a dark red stripe remained on the far horizon. Suddenly the three looked at each other, lowered their heads, and silently walked away, toward the villages outside the city. For some time I stood watching their tired figures recede into the distance. Soon the night sounds coming to life in the city reminded me that it was getting late and I'd better rush home. I quickened my pace and walked on under the blue haze of the night sky, pierced here and there by the blinking lights of the city ahead.

The next evening when I reached the bridge, the sunset was a few minutes away. I suddenly recalled the three men and stopped to watch the sunset even though I knew Munna would be waiting on the front porch for sweets and Zakiya, my wife, would be ready for us to go to the movies. I couldn't budge. An inexorable force seemed to have tied me to the ground. Through almost all the previous night I'd wondered what it was about the marsh and the sunset that had engrossed those strange men so entirely.

And then, just as the blazing orange disc of the sun tumbled into the marsh, I saw the three walk up the road. They were coming from villages outside the city limits. They wore identical clothes and resembled each other in their height and gait. Again they walked up to the bridge, stood at the same spot they had the previous evening and peered into the sunset with their flaming eyes filled with a dull sadness. I watched them and wondered why, despite their diverse features, they looked so much alike. One of them, who was very old, had a long, bushy snow-white beard. The second, somewhat lighter in complexion than the other, had a face that shone like gold in the orange glow of sunset. His hair hung down to his shoulders like a fringe, and he had a scar on his forehead. The third was dark and snub-nosed.

The sun sank all the way into the marsh. As on the previous day, the men glanced at each other, let their heads drop and, without exchanging a word, went their way.

That evening I felt terribly ill at ease. In a way I regretted not asking them about their utter fascination with the sunset. What could they be looking for in the sun's fading light? — I wondered. I told Zakiya about the strange threesome. She just laughed and said, "Must be peasants, on their way to the city to have a good time."

An air of strangeness surrounded these men. Zakiya, of course, could not have known it: one really had to look at them to feel the weird aura.

The next day I waited impatiently for the evening. I walked to the bridge, expecting them to show up. And they did, just as the daylight ebbed away. They leaned over the bridge and watched the sun go down, indifferent to the sound of traffic. Their absorption in the scene made it impossible to talk to them. I waited until the sun had gone down completely and the men had started to return. This would be the time to ask them what it was they expected to find in the vanishing sun and the marshes of the receding river.

When the sun had sunk all the way, the men gave one another a sad, mute look, lowered their heads and started off. But, instead of returning to the village, they took the road to the city. Their shoes were covered with dust and their feet moved on rhythmically together.

I gathered my faltering courage and asked them, "Brothers! what village do you come from?"

The man with the snub nose turned around and stared at me for a while. Then the three exchanged glances, but none of them bothered to answer my question.

"What do you see over there . . . on the bridge?" I asked. The mystery about the three men was beginning to weigh heavily upon me now. I felt as though molten lead had seeped into my legs — indeed into my whole body, and that it was only a matter of time before I'd crumble to the ground reeling from a spell of dizziness.

Again they did not answer. I shouted at them in a choking voice, "Why are you always staring at the sunset?"

No answer.

We reached the heavily congested city road. The evening sounds grew closer. It was late October, and the air felt pleasantly cool. The sweet scent of jasmine wafted in, borne by the breeze. As we passed the octroi post,° the old man with snow-white hair suddenly spoke, "Didn't you see? Has nobody in the city seen . . . ?"

"Seen what?"

"When the sun sets, when it goes down all the way . . . ?" asked the hoary old man, rearranging his mantle over his shoulders.

"When the sun goes down all the way?" I repeated. "What about it? That happens every day!"

I said that very quickly, afraid that the slightest pause might force them back into their impenetrable silence.

"We knew that, we knew it would be that way. That's why we came. That other village, there, too . . ." He pointed toward the east and lowered his head.

octroi post: a station or post on a highway, or at the entrance to a city or state, where officials assess local taxes (octroi duties) on select goods and materials

"From there we come . . ." said the snub-nosed man.

"From where?" I asked, growing impatient. "Please tell me clearly."

The third man peered back at me over his shoulder. The scar on his forehead suddenly seemed deeper than before. He said, "We didn't notice, nor, I believe, did you. Perhaps nobody did. Because, as you say, the sun rises and sets every day. Why bother to look? And we didn't, when day after day, there, over there," he pointed in the direction of the east, "the sky became blood-red and so bright it blazed like fire even at nightfall. We just failed to notice . . ." He stopped abruptly, as if choking over his words. "And now this redness," he resumed after a pause, "it keeps spreading from place to place. I'd never seen such a phenomenon before. Nor my elders. Nor, I believe, did they hear their elders mention anything quite like that ever happening."

Meanwhile the darkness had deepened. All I could see of my companions were their white flowing robes; their faces became visible only when they came directly under the pale, dim light of the lampposts. I turned around to look at the stretch of sky over the distant Ravi. I was stunned: it was glowing red despite the darkness.

"You are right," I said, to hide my puzzlement, "we really did fail to notice that." Then I asked, "Where are you going?"

"To the city, of course. What would be the point of arriving there *afterwards?*"

A sudden impulse made me want to stay with them, or to take them home with me. But abruptly, they headed off on another road, and I remembered I was expected home soon. Munna would be waiting on the front porch for his daily sweets and Zakiya must be feeling irritated by my delay.

The next day I stopped at the bridge to watch the sunset. I was hoping to see those three men. The sun went down completely, but they didn't appear. I waited impatiently for them to show up. Soon, however, I was entranced by the sunset's last magical glow.

The entire sky seemed covered with a sheet soaked in blood, and it scared me that I was standing all alone underneath it. I felt an uncanny presence directly behind me. I spun around. There was nobody. All the same, I felt sure there was someone — standing behind my back, within me, or perhaps, somewhere near.

Vehicles, of all shapes and sizes, rumbled along in the light of the street-lamps. Way back in the east, a stretch of evening sky still blazed liked a winding sheet of fire, radiating heat and light far into the closing darkness. I was alarmed and scurried home. Hastily I told Zakiya all I'd seen. But she laughed off the whole thing. I took her up to the balcony and showed her the red and its infernal bright glow against the dark night sky. That sobered her up a little. She thought for a while, then remarked, "We're going to have a storm any minute — I'm sure."

The next day in the office, as I worked, bent over my files, I heard

Mujibullah ask Hafiz Ahmad, "Say, did you see how the sky glows at sunset these days? Even after it gets dark? Amazing, isn't it?"

All at once I felt I was standing alone and defenseless under that blood-sheet of a sky. I was frightened. Small drops of sweat formed on my forehead. As the evening edged closer, a strange restlessness took hold of me. The receding Ravi, the bridge, the night sky and the sun frightened me; I wanted to walk clear out of them. And yet, I also felt irresistibly drawn toward them.

I wanted to tell my colleagues about the three peasants who in spite of their distinctly individual faces somehow looked alike; about how they had come to the city accompanying this strange redness, had drawn my attention to it, and then dropped out of sight; and about how I'd searched in vain for them everywhere. But I couldn't. Mujibullah and Hafiz Ahmad, my office-mates, had each borrowed about twenty rupees° from me some time ago, which they conveniently forgot to return, and, into the bargain, had stopped talking to me ever since.

On my way home when I entered the bridge, a strange fear made me walk briskly, look away from the sun, and try to concentrate instead on the street before me. But the blood-red evening kept coming right along. I could feel its presence everywhere. A flock of evening birds flew overhead in a "V" formation. Like the birds, I too was returning home. Home — yes, but no longer my haven against the outside world; for the flame-colored evening came pouring in from its windows, doors, even through its walls of solid masonry.

I now wandered late in the streets, looking for the three peasants. I wanted to ask them where that red came from. What was to follow? Why did they leave the last settlement? What shape was it in? But I couldn't find them anywhere. Nobody seemed to care.

A few days later I saw some men pointing up to the unusual red color of the evening. Before long, the whole city was talking about it. I hadn't told a soul except Zakiya. How they had found out about it was a puzzle to me. Those three peasants must be in the city — I concluded. They have got to be.

The red of evening had now become the talk of the town.

Chaudhri Sahib, who owns a small bookshop in Mozang Plaza, was an old acquaintance of mine. People got together at his shop for a friendly chat every evening. Often, so did I. But for some time now, since my first encounter with those mantle-wrapped oracular figures, I had been too preoccupied with my own thoughts to go there. No matter where I went, home or outside, I felt restless. At home, an inexorable urge drove me outdoors; outdoors, an equally strong urge sent me scrambling back home, where I felt comparatively safer. I became very confused about where I wanted to be. I began to feel heavy and listless.

rupee: an Indian and Pakistani unit of currency

All the same, I did go back to the bookshop once again that evening. Most of the regulars had already gathered. Chaudhri Sahib asked, "What do you think about it, fellows? Is it all due to the atomic explosions as they say? The rumor also has it that pretty soon the earth's cold regions will turn hot and the hot ones cold and the cycle of seasons will also be upset."

I wanted to tell them about my encounter with the three villagers but felt too shy to talk before so many people. Just then a pungent smell, the likes of which I'd never smelled before, wafted in from God knows where. My heart sank and a strange, sweet sort of pain stabbed my body. I felt nauseous, unable to decide whether it was a stench, a pungent aroma, or even a wave of bitter-sweet pain. I threw the newspaper down and got up to leave.

"What's the matter?" asked Chaudhri Sahib.

"I must go. God knows what sort of smell that is."

"Smell? What smell?" Chaudhri Sahib sniffed the air.

I didn't care to reply and walked away. That offensive smell, the terrifying wave of pain, followed me all the way home. It made me giddy. I thought I might fall any minute. My condition frightened Zakiya, who asked, "What's the matter — you look so pale?"

"I'm all right. God knows what that smell is." I said, wiping sweat off my brow, although it was the month of November.

Zakiya also sniffed the air, then said, "Must be coming from the house of Hakim Sahib. Heaven knows what strange herb concoctions they keep making day and night. Or else it's from burnt food. I burnt some today accidentally."

"But it seems to be everywhere . . . in every street and lane . . . throughout the city."

"Why, of course. The season's changed. It must be the smell of winter flowers," she said inattentively, and became absorbed in her knitting.

With great trepidation I again sniffed the air, but couldn't decide whether the sickening odor still lingered on or had subsided. Perhaps it had subsided. The thought relieved me a bit. But there was no escape from its memory, which remained fresh in my mind, like the itching that continues for some time even after the wound has healed. The very thought that it might return gave me the chills.

By next morning I'd forgotten all about that rotten, suffocating smell. In the office, I found a mountain of files waiting for me. But Mujibullah and Hafiz Ahmad went on noisily discussing some movie. I couldn't concentrate on the work and felt irritated. So I decided to take a break. I called our office boy and sent him to the cafeteria for a cup of tea. Meanwhile I pulled out a pack of cigarettes from my pocket and lit up.

Just then I felt a cracking blow on my head, as if I had fallen off a cliff and landed on my head, which fused everything before my eyes in a swirling blue and yellow streak. It took my numbed senses some time to realize that I was being assaulted once again by the same pain, the same terrible stench. It kept coming at me in waves, and it was impossible to know its source. I found myself frantically shutting every single window in the office, while both Mujibullah and Hafiz Ahmad gawked at me uncomprehendingly.

"Let the sun in! Why are you slamming the windows?" asked Hafiz Ahmad.

"The stench . . . the stench! My God, it's unbearable! Don't you smell it?"

Both of them raised their noses to their air and sniffed. Then Hafiz Ahmad remarked. "That's right. What sort of stench . . . or fragrance is that? It makes my heart sink."

Soon, many people were talking about the stink-waves which came in quick succession and then receded, only to renew their assault a little while later. At sundown they became especially unbearable.

Within a few weeks the stinking odor had become so oppressive that I often found it difficult to breathe. People's faces, usually quite lively and fresh, now looked drained and wilted. Many complained of constant palpitation and headaches. The doctors cashed in. Intellectuals hypothesized that it must be due to nuclear blasts, which were producing strange effects throughout the world, including this foul odor in our city, which attacked people's nerves and left them in a mess. People scrambled to buy tranquilizers, which sold out instantly. Not that the supply was inadequate, but a sudden frenzy to stock up and horde had seized people. Even sleeping pills fetched the price of rare diamonds.

I found both tranquilizers and sleeping pills useless. The stench cut sharper than a sword and penetrated the body like a laser. The only way to guard against it was to get used to it — I thought; and people would do well to remember that. But I was too depressed to tell them myself. Within a few weeks, however, they themselves came to live with the stench.

Just the same, the stench struck terror in the city. People were loath to admit it, but they could not have looked more tense: their faces contorted from the fear of some terrible thing happening at any moment. Nor was their fear unreasonable, as a subsequent event showed a few weeks later.

On a cold mid-December evening, I was returning home from Chaudhri Sahib's. The street was full of traffic and jostling crowds. The stores glittered with bright lights, and people went about their business as usual. Every now and then a stench-wave swept in, made me giddy, and receded. I would freeze in my stride the instant it assailed me and would start moving again as soon as it had subsided. It was the same with others. An outsider would surely have wondered why we suddenly froze, closed our eyes, stopped breathing, then took a deep breath and got started again. But that was our custom now.

That December evening I'd just walked onto the bridge when I felt as if a lance had hit me on the head. My head whirled and my legs buckled. Reeling, I clung on to a lamppost and tried to support my head with my hands. There was no lance, nor was there a hand to wield it. It was that smell — that same rotten smell — I realized with terror. In fact, it seemed that the source of the oppressive stench had suddenly moved very close to me, between my shoulder blades, near my back, immediately behind me — so close that it was impossible to think of it as apart from me.

It was then that my eyes fell on the strange carriage, rambling along in front of me. It was an oversized wagon pulled by a pair of scrawny white oxen with leather blinders over their eyes and thick ropes strung through their steaming nostrils. A wooden cage sat atop the base of the wagon, its interior hidden behind black curtains — or were they just swaying walls of darkness?

Two men, sitting outside the cage enclosure in the front of the wagon, drove the two emaciated, blindfolded animals. I couldn't make out their faces, partly because of the darkness, but partly also because they were buried in folds of cloth thrown loosely around them. Their heads drooped forward and they seemed to have dozed off, overcome by fatigue and sleep.

Behind them the interior of the curtained wagon swelled with darkness and from the heart of that darkness shot out the nauseating stench which cut sharper than a sword . . . Before I knew it, the wagon had creaked past me, flooding my senses with its cargo of stink. My head swirled. I jumped off the main road onto the dirt sidewalk . . . and vomited.

I had no idea whether the people in the city had also seen the eerie wagon. If they had, what must have they endured? I had the hardest time getting home after what I had seen. Once inside the house, I ran to my bed and threw myself on it. Zakiya kept asking me what had happened, but a blind terror sealed my lips.

A few days later a small news item appeared in the local papers. It railed against the local Municipal Office for allowing garbage carts to pass through busy streets in the evening. Not only did muck-wagons pollute the air, they also hurt the fine olfactory sense of the citizenry.

I took a whole week off from work. During those seven days, though hardly fit to go out and observe firsthand the plight of the city, I was nonetheless kept posted of developments by local newspapers. Groups of concerned citizens demanded that the municipal authorities keep the city clear of the muck-wagons or, if that was impossible, assign them routes along less busy streets.

On the seventh day I ventured out. A change was already visible. Wrecked by insomnia and exhaustion, people strained themselves to appear carefree and cheerful, but managed only to look painfully silly. Suddenly I recalled that in the morning I had myself looked no different in the mirror.

About this time, the number of entertainment programs and movies shot up as never before. People swarmed to box offices — often hours before a show — where they formed long lines and patiently waited to be let in, and then filed out from the entertainment still looking pale and ridiculous.

In the office, no matter how hard I tried, I couldn't concentrate on work. Intermittently, the image of the muck-wagon lumbering down the streets flashed across my mind. Was it really one of those municipal dump-carts? No. It couldn't be. Municipal dump-carts never looked like that eerie wagon, with its sleepy drivers, a pair of blindfolded bony oxen, black curtains and the outrageously nauseating smell. What on earth could give off such an odd smell — at once fragrant and foul!

An insane desire suddenly overwhelmed me: to rush up to the wagon, lift up those swaying curtains, and peek inside. I must discover the source of the stench!

Coming to the bridge my feet involuntarily slowed down. There was still some time before sunset and the waves of the pain-filled odor came faster and stronger. I leaned over the bridge, an unknown fear slowly rising in my throat. The bottomless swamp, its arms ominously outstretched, seemed to be dragging me down toward it. I was afraid I might jump into the swamp, sink with the sun and become buried forever in that sprawling sheet of blood.

I became aware of something approaching me — or was I myself drawing closer to something? . . . Something awaited by all men — those before and those after us. My whole body felt as though it was turning into a piece of granite, with no escape from the bridge, the miasma, the sun, for now they all seemed inseparable from my being. Helplessly, I looked around myself and almost dropped dead.

The three men were coming towards me from the direction of the countryside. As before, they were wrapped in their flowing white robes and walked with their amazingly identical gait. I kept staring at them with glassy eyes until they walked right up to me and stopped. The hoary old man was crying, and his snow-white beard was drenched in tears. The other two couldn't look up; their eyes were lowered mournfully, their teeth clenched and their faces withered by a deathly pallor.

"Where were you hiding all these days?" I said between gasps and stammers. "I searched for you everywhere. Tell me, please, what's happening to the city?"

"We were waiting. Trying to hold ourselves back. We had tied ourselves with ropes. Here, look!" They spread their arms before me and bared their shoulders and backs, revealing the deep marks of the rope.

"We did not want to come . . ." the old man said, drowned out by a fit of sobs.

"But there was no choice . . ." the second man said. Before he had finished, he doubled over. His companions also doubled over, as if unable to control a sudden surge of pain. The same wave of pain-filled stench stabbed the air about us, cutting us into halves, flooding our senses, as it scrambled past us.

"There! Look!" said the old man, pointing in the direction of the distant villages and turning deathly pale.

In the distance, I saw the wagon come up the road from behind a cloud of dust. The drowsing coachmen had wrapped their faces because of their nearness to the cutting stench.

A cold shiver ran through my spine. The eyes of the three men suddenly became dull. They were approaching their end — perhaps.

The wagon rumbled close — the stench from it draining the blood from our bodies — and then passed us. Its sinister, jet-black curtains, fluttering in the gentle breeze, appeared, oddly enough, entirely motionless.

The three men ran after the wagon, caught up to it and lifted the curtains. A split second later, a nonhuman scream burst from their gaping mouths. They spun around and bolted toward the distant fields.

"What was it? What did you see?" I asked, running after them. But they did not reply and kept running madly. Their eyes had frozen in a glazed stare.

I followed them until we had left the city several miles behind us, then grabbed the old man's robe and implored, "Tell me! Please tell me!"

He turned his deathly gaze and threw open his mouth. His tongue had got stuck to his palate.

All three had become dumb.

My head whirled, and I collapsed. The three men continued to run, soon disappearing in the distance behind a spiraling cloud of dust. Slowly the dust settled and I returned home.

For months now I have searched in vain for those men. They have vanished without a trace. And the wagon . . . from that fateful evening, it too has changed its route. It no longer passes through the city. After crossing the bridge, it now descends onto the dirt trail leading to villages in the countryside.

The cityfolk are no longer bothered by the slashing stench. They have become immune to it and think it has died, like an old, forgotten tale.

But it continues to torment my body, and day and night a voice keeps telling me, "Now, your turn! Now you shall *see!*"

And this evening I find myself on the bridge, waiting for the wagon . . . waiting.

Translated from the Urdu by
Muhammad Umar Memon

SRI LANKA

YASMINE GOONERATNE

Yasmine Gooneratne (1935–) was born in the island country of Ceylon, which is now called Sri Lanka. She studied English literature at the University of Sri Lanka and at Cambridge University, England. Since the 1970s she has been teaching British and Commonwealth literatures at Macquire University, Australia. She has published collections of her poetry in English, as well as scholarly studies of Alexander Pope, Jane Austen, and Ruth Prawer Jhabvala.

"Menika," the title of Gooneratne's quasi-dramatic poem, is taken from the name of its main character. She is a lower-class woman from a village in the countryside, who now works as a domestic servant in a middle-class household in a Sri Lankan city, such as Colombo or Kandy. The name Menika comes into modern Sinhala (the language of Sri Lanka) from ancient Pali and Sanskrit, where it takes the form Menaka. In classical Sanskrit literature and Hindu and Buddhist mythology, Menaka is the well-known name of a beautiful celestial nymph. Although there are some parallels between the two figures, the servant-woman in Gooneratne's poem stands in contrast to the Menaka of ancient mythology. The modern Menika has been victimized by an abusive, unfaithful husband, has worked her way menially through very hard times, and yet is unable or unwilling to have her husband punished by a court of law.

Menika

Deft-handed, swirling rice-grains in clear water,
pouring the white stream from pot to pot
She said:
I would like to go back to the village next week
There is a court case   5
I am reclaiming my children, two daughters, from their father
He has another woman

Neat-handed, kneading coriander and cumin
on the smooth stone
She said: 10

My father made the marriage
There were good fields and much fine property
My father inspected the fields, my brother went with him
They all agreed it was a good match
Two weeks after the marriage he brought her back to the house   15

The pestle rising, falling, in her practised hands
the grain in the mortar crumbling to powder
She said:
We lived eighteen years in that house
My children with me in one room, she with him in the other   20
One day a relation of his came in, asking for a measure of rice
I did not think to refuse it
That night he came home drunk, and said I was giving away the
          household goods.

Spreading the grain in the sun to dry
She said: 25
When he beat me before the neighbours I sent for my father
He came and took me away
When we signed the Register at the Police Station
the Sergeant said: What a man is this!
To make such a shameful to-do over a measure of rice!   30
She looks after my children well, they tell me
But they are daughters, can I allow them to become women
and far away from me?

On the day of the court case, her skin smoothly powdered,
a crimson sari knotted at her neat waist, her hair   35
combed into shining coils on her slender neck
She said:
He is a good man
There is no fault in him.

EAST ASIA

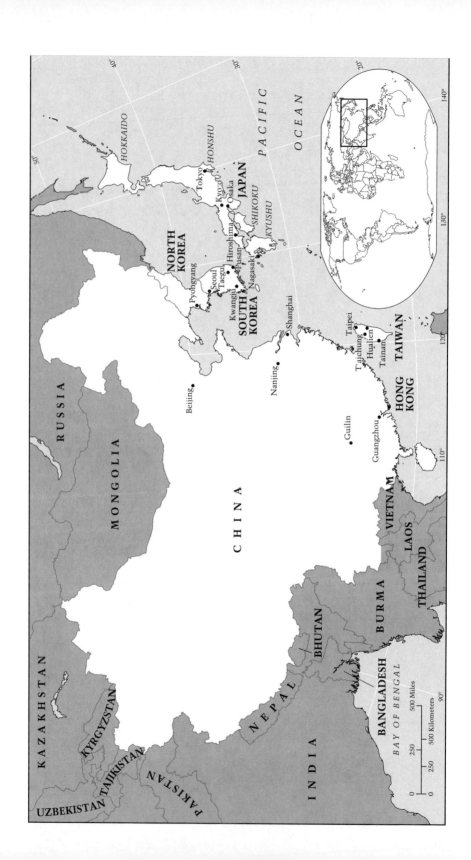

EAST ASIA

Writing is in itself a joy,
Yet saints and sages have long since held it in awe.
For it is Being, created by tasking the Great Void,
And 'tis sound rung out of Profound Silence.
In a sheet of paper is contained the Infinite,
And, evolved from an inch-sized heart, an endless panorama.

— LU CHI, *"Essay on Literature"* (300 A.D.)

The literature of East Asia flows in a living stream from a long and rich tradition. It is a record of innocence and experience, joy and delight, pain and sorrow, profundity and frivolity, which connects the past to the present in spite of wars and upheavals. East Asia comprises China, Mongolia, Korea, and the islands of Taiwan and Japan on the present-day political map. Although there is great diversity among and within these countries, they share historical and cultural traditions that make it possible to speak of the region as a unit.

HISTORICAL TRADITIONS

China

China is by far the largest and oldest civilization in East Asia. Starting in the valley of the Yellow River during the second millennium B.C., it had developed sophisticated art, history, philosophy, and literature by the sixth century B.C. In 221 B.C. the numerous states in the central plain of China were unified by a warrior who declared himself Qin Shi Huang, the First Emperor of Qin. The name China comes from another spelling of Qin. After his death a period of chaos followed before the founding of the Han dynasty (205 B.C.–A.D. 220). The Han dynasty flourished, declined, then fell, leading to a period of division that lasted over three centuries before another short-lived dynasty unified the country, then gave way to the next great dynasty, the Tang (A.D. 618–960). This cycle of the rise and decline of dynasties, of unity and division, characterizes Chinese history, which is discussed by dynasties rather than by centuries. The incursion of nomadic peoples into the central plain and their subsequent sinicization is another pattern of Chinese history. The Yuan dynasty (1280–1368) was founded by the Mongols under Genghis Khan. After their brief rule, the Mongols became Chinese subjects until 1911. In 1945 China relinquished its claim to Mongolia in a treaty with Russia. The Qing dynasty was established in 1644 by the Manchu people from northeast China and ruled until the founding of the Republic of China in 1911.

Today 95 percent of the Chinese people belong to the Han ethnic group. Four other major groups, Manchu, Mongol, Tibetan, and Hui (a Turkish people who follow Islam) occupy resource-rich and strategically important border areas; each has its own written language and literature. Over fifty minority groups, each with its own language and customs, live in China, mostly in the southwest.

For many centuries Chinese civilization dominated that of its neighbors. Thousands of students from Japan, Korea, and other neighboring countries went to China to study its literature, philosophy, art, government, and even technology and science. China called itself Zhongguo, or Middle Kingdom, not only because of its location in a central plain, but because it was the center of a cultural universe.

Japan

Japan occupies an archipelago off the coast of East Asia. Legends place the founding of the Japanese empire in 660 B.C. Its history is very distinct from that of China and Korea, as the emperor of Japan was believed to be a direct lineal descendant of the Sun Goddess. Thus the emperor was chief priest as well as head of state, and it was believed that one family occupied the imperial throne throughout Japanese history. Political authority, however, was often in the hands of other powerful families. From the twelfth to the nineteenth centuries, Japan was under military dictatorship as the samurai warriors held sway under the leadership of a shogun.

The Japanese people are thought to have migrated to the archipelago from North Asia and Southeast Asia in prehistoric times. Except for the Ainu, who have some similarities to Caucasians but constitute a tiny minority, the Japanese are a homogeneous group. Non-Japanese, mostly Koreans, make up less than 1 percent of the population.

Korea

Korea is a mountainous peninsula on the northern border of China; it also shares eleven miles of border with Russia. The Koreans are descended from Tungustic tribes, a distinct racial and cultural group. By the twelfth century B.C. Chinese immigrants had brought their language, culture, and customs, and made the first documented history of Korea. Korea derives its name from the first native state, the Koguryo, established near the Yalu River in the first century A.D. In the seventh century the Silla kingdom to the south conquered Koguryo with Chinese help and unified the peninsula. The Silla dynasty was replaced by the Koryo in the tenth century. In the thirteenth century, after a period of struggle, the Koryo accepted Mongol rule. They were overthrown by the Yi dynasty in 1392, again with Chinese help. Although the Yi ruled until 1910, Korea had become a vassal of the Manchu Qing dynasty in 1637. It was so isolated from other contacts that it became known as the Hermit Kingdom.

CULTURAL TRADITIONS

Confucianism

The greatest cultural influence China had on its neighbors can loosely be called Confucianism. Confucianism was incorporated into the official ideology of Korea and Japan, and to this day reaches deep into the upbringing and education of the Koreans and Japanese as well as the Chinese.

Confucianism developed from the teachings of Confucius (551–479 B.C.), who, living in the period of Warring States, valued social harmony above all else. He declared himself "a transmitter, not a maker" of a tradition that valued personal integrity, devotion to family, and service to the state. Personal integrity was to be achieved through education and self-cultivation, which included knowing one's rightful place in the family. The state was seen as a macrocosm of the family, so the values that served self and family also served the state; each was a hierarchical order in which each member knew his or her place (and her place was invariably lower than his).

Confucianism had become the state ideology in China by the time of the Han dynasty (second century B.C.). Those who wished to serve the state as officials, or mandarins, had to learn the Confucian texts by heart; officials were selected from those who wrote the best essays based on lines extracted from those texts. Those texts influenced not only the ideas, but also the writing styles of the literature elite. This system of selecting civil officials was spread to Korea and Japan. It was abolished in Korea in 1894, and in China only in 1905.

Taoism

In China, Confucianism is balanced with a system of thought known as Taoism. Whereas Confucianism puts humanity at the center of values, Taoism stresses the value of nature. Confucians did their utmost to serve the state; Taoists retired to the mountains to commune with nature. Although Taoists might regard Confucians as worldly title-chasers and busybody do-gooders, and Confucians might regard Taoists as irresponsible hippies, few Chinese were completely consistent in their thought.

Staunch Confucians appreciated and commented on the Taoist texts; Taoist ascetics allowed themselves to be called back into government service. On the popular level, Taoism merged with various native religions and to a certain extent with Buddhism.

Buddhism and Other Religions

When Buddhism entered China from India, it was interpreted from the point of view of Taoism, which provided many of the terms for translating Buddhist texts. Buddhism complemented Confucianism and Taoism in addressing the questions of suffering and death. Since its advocacy of the monastic life is a direct contradiction to the Confucian emphasis on having children to continue the family line and ancestral sacrifices, in time a new type of Buddhist, called "Buddhists at home," or lay Buddhists, emerged to include Confucian and Buddhist scholars. In this syncretic process the harmony of the three teachings became emphasized; they became seen as different paths to the same destination. In addition to the three major teachings of Confucianism, Taoism, and Buddhism, every village in China had one or more local guardian gods. A host of gods in myth and lore, often organized in a bureaucracy that reflected society on earth, presided over every aspect of life. Perhaps the absence of belief in a single, omnipotent, and jealous god contributed to this eclecticism.

The Koreans and Japanese are similarly eclectic in their religious practices. Just as the Chinese modified Buddhism, the Koreans and Japanese have modified the religions and philosophies transmitted from China. Most Koreans are Confucians and Buddhists, although in the last century Christianity has made a number of converts. In Japan, Confucianism and numerous sects of Buddhism exist alongside the native religious tradition, Shinto, "the Way of the Gods." Shinto invests a spirit (*kami*) in every living and inanimate thing, even in rocks and trees.

CONTACT WITH THE WEST

China's contact with the West extends through the centuries from Greek and Roman times. In the thirteenth century, the Venetian Marco Polo was awestruck at China's splendors. In the seventeenth and eighteenth centuries, Jesuit missionaries had access to the imperial court and wrote detailed descriptions of a civilization they admired. Japan's contact with Europeans began in the sixteenth century when Portuguese and Dutch traders, and then Christian missionaries reached Japanese shores. The ruling shoguns were able to confine them to one port. By the nineteenth century, when Western imperialism reached its height, however, both the Qing dynasty in China and the shogunate in Japan were in decline.

Contact with Western imperialism in the nineteenth century drastically changed the relations among the countries of East Asia. After suffering a series of humiliating defeats as Western powers forced ports open, first for the opium trade, then for missionaries and entrepreneurs, by the turn of the century China had been reduced to a semicolonial status vis-a-vis the West. Japan had also been forced by gunboats under the command of the American naval officer Commodore Matthew Perry in 1853 to open ports to Western trade, but quickly learned from the West, transforming itself into an industrial, military, and imperialist power. Japan annexed the island of Taiwan, then known under its Portuguese name of Formosa, after a war with China in 1895. It then easily overcame Chinese domination of Korea and annexed that country outright in 1910. By the turn of the century, Japan had become the dominant power in East Asia, and Chinese students were going to Japan to learn modern science, technology, and institutions. By 1915, Japan had presented its Twenty-One Demands, intended to reduce China to a virtual protectorate. The Chinese students' protest on May 4, 1919, against this and against part of the Versailles Treaty ending World War I became known as the May Fourth Movement.

In the 1930s Japan's relations with China went beyond economic and political encroachment to the use of military force. The Sino-Japanese war, begun with the Japanese invasion of China in 1937, became part of World War II, ending only in 1945 with the explosion of atomic bombs by the United States over the Japanese cities of Hiroshima and Nagasaki. Taiwan was returned to China, Korea was made independent, and Japan was occupied by American forces until 1952.

The war with Japan was followed in China by civil war between the Nationalist and Communist parties. In spite of support from the United States, the Nationalists were defeated and withdrew to the island of Taiwan, where they still claimed to be the legitimate government of all of China. The People's Republic of China, established in 1949 under Mao Zedong, chairman of the Communist Party, struggled to build a new socialist society. Literature was made to serve political purposes and kept under tight control by the government. Many intellectuals fled to every part of the world to escape communist rule. They write from exile in Taiwan, Hong Kong, Southeast Asia, Australia, New Zealand, Europe, and the Americas.

Korea had failed in an independence movement against Japan in 1919. Japan's invasion of China in 1937 brought further restrictions in Korea and eventually led to conscription of Korean workers for Japan's war effort. After World War II, Korea was arbitrarily divided at the Thirty-eighth Parallel, with the Soviet Union dominating the north and U.S. troops stationed in the south. The Democratic People's Republic of Korea was established with its capital at Pyongyang, under the control of the Communist Party under Kim Il Sung in the north, and the Republic of Korea was established in the south, with its capital at Seoul. A civil war followed, which ended in the division between North Korea and South Korea in 1951.

LANGUAGES

Chinese, Korean, and Japanese are three very different languages, but the Chinese writing system was shared by all three. Based on ideographs evolved from pictographs, it is a beautiful and intriguing system in which each syllable it represented by a separate graph or character, which may take from one to more than twenty strokes of the pen to write. True literacy requires knowledge of several thousand characters; the time and effort required simply to learn characters resulted in confining literary education to an elite class in China, Korea, and Japan.

Classical Chinese is extremely concise and largely monosyllabic. Literary models generally date from the Han and Tang dynasties (second century B.C. to ninth century A.D.). Spoken Chinese is tonal; different tones distinguish syllables, which are otherwise pronounced alike. For example, in modern standard Chinese, "*wen*, pronounced in a high rising tone, can mean "literature," but pronounced in a falling tone it can mean "to ask." The many dialects of Chinese differ enough in pronunciation to be considered different languages in a language family, but their speakers are united by a shared writing system.

The place of the Chinese language in traditional Korea and Japan is comparable to that of Latin in the Romance language countries during the Middle Ages. It was the common means of expression among the educated elite. Korean and Japanese men wrote literary works entirely in the Chinese language.

The Japanese language is polysyllabic, and in contrast with the Chinese, sentences are very long; some can be literally interminable. To treat these differences, two phonetic syllabaries were developed and used alongside the Chinese characters. In the eleventh century, while the educated elite were writing entirely in Chinese, the woman writer Murasaki Shikibu wrote Japan's greatest novel, *The Tale of Genji*, entirely in Japanese phonetic script. But the practice of combining Chinese characters with the two systems of Japanese script continues to this day. After World War II, when universal literacy became a goal, the Japanese simplified Chinese characters, prescribing only two thousand for general use.

The Korean language is similar to Japanese in being polysyllabic. Starting around the seventh century A.D., the Koreans also borrowed the monosyllabic Chinese characters to record their literature. A separate Korean writing system with phonetic letters was invented in the fifteenth century. It is celebrated each October 15, National Alphabet Day in Korea.

Classical Chinese was declared a "dead language" in China in the May Fourth Movement of the 1920s. The use of the vernacular played an important role in the movement. It not only accommodated new terms and new ideas but was more flexible in translating from other languages, as the leaders of the movement attacked all aspects of the Chinese tradition and offered an enthusiastic reception to Western ideas and literatures. In more recent decades, a system of simplified characters has been promoted in the People's Republic of China.

LITERARY TRADITIONS

Literature is regarded by the Chinese as one of the great achievements of their civilization, and poetry is regarded as the greatest achievement of Chinese literature. Confucius himself is said to have edited the oldest extant collections of poetry, *The Book of Songs*, or *Classic of Odes*. But the highest achievement in poetry was reached in the Tang dynasty with the work of such poets as Wang Wei, Li Po, Tu Fu, and Po Chü-i. They wrote in *shih* forms, most commonly the *chüeh-chü* in four lines, and the *lü-shih* in eight; the lines were of five or seven syllables, with strict prescriptions for matching lines and syllables with tone, part of speech, type of imagery, and rhyme. Whether their styles were delicate or vigorous, the poets strove to evoke feeling and thoughts that would continue after their words had ended. The Chinese believed *wen yi tsai tao*: literature is to convey the Way, whether it is the Way of the Taoists or of the Confucians. The quiet, contemplative Chinese poetry admired by the American imagists and beatniks was balanced by much didactic poetry. And though every educated Chinese person could recite hundreds of poems by the masters, they did not hesitate to take up the brush and compose their own, whether it was to celebrate a beautiful scene or a friend's birthday.

Fiction, called *"hsiao shuo*, or "small talk," was not regarded as serious literature in traditional China, but a large body of work developed, and every educated person has read such novels as *Water Margin, Journey to the West*, or *The Dream of the Red Chamber* at least once. Many stories were written in the classical Chinese by the literati, and with the invention of printing, the story cycles developed by professional storytellers were recorded in the vernacular and disseminated. The elevation of fiction to a serious genre may be seen as an effect of contact with the West. In the 1920s Lu Hsun (1881–1936), generally regarded as the greatest modern Chinese writer, wrote *A Brief History of Chinese Fiction* to raise the status of the genre. His own powerful short stories probe the causes of China's weakness, social malaise, and moral decadence. The short story is generally regarded as the most successful genre in modern and contemporary Chinese literature.

The Asian verse form best known in the West is the haiku, which dates from the sixteenth century in Japan. Its most famous practitioner is Bashō (1644–1694). Although in modern times the haiku went through many transformations in both form and content, a basic definition of the form has evolved, requiring three lines with 5, 7, and 5 syllables and a word indicating the season for which the poem was written. The modern haiku is represented by Kaneko Tōta in the current selection.

Traditional Japanese drama had three major forms: the Noh, the Kyogen, and the Kabuki. The Noh plays are short, concise, and symbolical, but the highly stylized performances seem very long, integrating speech, dance, mime, singing, and instrumental music. A chorus sits on stage in dark costumes, commenting on the action and sometimes singing lines for the principal performers, who wear wooden masks and extravagant costumes. Generally there is one central character, the *shite*, and his or her foil, the *waki*, each with one or two attendants. Chinese and Japanese poetry arc often central to the theme, but one need not understand the language to experience the highly emotional charge of the performance. A modern Noh play by Mishima Yukiō is included in the present selection. The Kyogen is a short play performed as comic relief between Noh plays. More popular in modern Japan is the Kabuki, which requires less background knowledge to understand, has more excitement and conflict in the plot, and provides more action on stage. As in China, only men appeared on the traditional stage, even in women's roles.

Japanese fiction, after its brilliant start in the eleventh and twelfth centuries, did not develop into a serious genre again until the nineteenth century. A few outstanding examples of comic and picaresque novels were written in a special literary language, but the impetus to write serious novels in the vernacular probably came from contact with the West. As realistic and proletarian fiction were developed by major writers, the most interesting and enduring form has been the *shihosetsu*, the "I-novel" or "ego-novel," a highly personal narrative told in the first person, in which the hero and author are closely identified.

Traditional Korean literature has been characterized as an integration of indigenous and foreign, low and high, folk and literate sources. Two genres of poetry in the Korean language are the *sijo*, a three-line lyric that is still practiced today, and the *kasa*, a narrative and discursive poem of varying length compared to the Chinese rhyme-prose. Both forms were meant to be sung. Prose narrative includes tales, romances, and fables written both in Korean and in Chinese. As in Japan, while men wrote in Chinese, women writers made important contributions to the refinement of the vernacular.

THE CONTEMPORARY SCENE

Contemporary East Asian literature has not completely broken with its long and varied literary tradition. Although writers in each country rebel against tradition and embrace Western literary values to greater and lesser degrees, some traditional forms, themes, and motives continue. The Chinese *chüeh-chü* and *lüshi*, the Japanese haiku, and the Korean *sijo* are still practiced. The fractured, dissonant view of life is not unique to modern times, and the alienation expressed by some writers is still balanced by others who describe the life of simple folk living close to the land. Stories of human relations often still reveal a Confucian outlook, remaining identifiably Asian even without local color.

China

Contemporary literature in China may be said to have had a definite starting date. The central experience informing the current generation of writers was the Great Proletarian Cultural Revolution, begun in 1966. The nationwide movement, directed by Mao Zedong, the chairman of the Chinese Communist Party, sought to create a totally egalitarian, classless society, in which manual work would be just as highly regarded and rewarded as mental work. People were urged not to put their own families first, but to "serve society," as the politicized language of the communists described it. Children denounced their own parents as "rightists," and educated families were separated as they were sent to different farms to learn from the peasants. Political study replaced the usual school curriculum, and students were chosen for higher education not through competitive examinations but through election by their coworkers.

Experienced writers were attacked for being "rightist" or "bourgeois," paraded through the streets in dunce caps, and sent to the countryside to "learn from the peasants." Those who remained in the cities often were assigned to clean latrines. China lost many talented writers and thinkers who found their health and spirits broken by this experiment. By the time the movement reached its end with Mao's death in September 1976, people looked back on the experience as "ten years of chaos."

Literary censorship has had a long history in China, but rarely has it been as effective as it was during the Cultural Revolution. During this period, only Premier Zhou Enlai succeeded in protecting some of the writers and artists. It seems fitting that the first sign of literary rebirth was an outpouring of poetry mourning his death in April 1976. The poems, offered with wreaths at the great square in front of Tiananmen (the Gate of Heavenly Peace), were removed overnight by the authorities, but a movement for democracy grew nonetheless. In 1979 dissidents again publicly posted demands for democracy; the movement was suppressed by arrests and imprisonment, but it continued to grow in underground literary journals. A decade later, the world watched on television as massive public demonstrations were suppressed by tanks and guns in what is now known in the West as the Tiananmen Incident. The number killed in the 1989 demonstrations remains unknown. Perhaps the one positive effect is that interest in contemporary Chinese literature has now moved beyond the narrow circle of academic specialists.

The first generation of poets to emerge after the Cultural Revolution are known in the West as the "Misty" poets. Works by Bei Dao, Gu Cheng, and Shu Ting are presented here. "Misty" is a prettified translation of *menglong,* used by Chinese critics to castigate this type of poetry as obscure or obscurantist. Although the poetry is not difficult to understand for Western readers or for readers of traditional Chinese poetry or the poetry of the May Fourth period, for the Chinese reader accustomed to ditties published in recent decades for workers, peasants, and soldiers, it seems ambiguous, self-absorbed, and overly pessimistic. When the literary image promoted by the party is the optimistic peasant hero selflessly serving society, self-absorption and pessimism can be regarded as political dissent. Political criticism veiled in literature has long been part of the Chinese tradition, and ambiguity often cloaks such criticism.

In the burst of literary creativity that marked the end of the Cultural Revolution in China, writers explored themes, motives, and styles that had been taboo, and a remarkable number of women writers have appeared. Even though discrimination against women still exists in every sphere, including the education that would prepare them to become writers, many have made good use of the stereotyping that invests them with heightened sensitivity, psychological awareness, and attention to detail, family, and social relations. Numerous anthologies of Chinese women writers now exist in English. Cheng Naishan represents them here.

That is not to suggest that literature after the Cultural Revolution is created primarily by dissidents. Liu Xinwu, a state-supported writer, wrote stories that have been classified as "literature of the wounded," or "scar literature," depicting the evil excesses of the Cultural Revolution. Invited to lecture at Columbia University in 1987, he was asked whether or not he and other contemporary Chinese writers were really concerned with the creation of literature for its own sake. Liu is reported to have replied in a voice choked with emotion, "Our country is so poor, how can we think solely of literature? We feel we must do something to help our motherland!" The dissidents now living abroad also speak feelingly of love for their country.

The obsession with China is shared by compatriots of Taiwan and Hong Kong, where some writers devoted themselves to keeping tradition alive, while others continued the experiments with modernism and other Western-influenced modes of writing that had been practiced in China before the war. Exile was a constant theme until the last two decades, when authors such as Hwang Chun-ming and Cheng Ying-chen pursued a "back to the roots" movement, to depict the lives of people whose homes were in Taiwan before the influx of exiles from the mainland.

Japan

In Japan, there has been no dramatic break in literary development in recent decades. Contemporary writers, that is, those born after the American occupation, are overshadowed by the previous generation, which includes such giants as Natsume Soseki (1867–1916), Tanizaki Junichiro

(1886–1965), Kawabata Yasunari (1899–1972), and Mishima Yukiō (1925–1970). These novelists explored the problems of aesthetics; the nature of literature; the process of self-discovery and personal growth; the relation of reality and human perception; the problems of the individual in a changing or hostile world; continuity and change in Japanese customs, values, and society; problems attending urbanization — themes shared by many literatures in the world.

Although the Japanese are viewed in the present century by their Asian neighbors as militaristic aggressors, this image does not appear in their literature, at least not in literature available in English. Mishima stunned his compatriots as well as international readers in 1970 when, dressed in full military uniform, he addressed a crowd from a balcony, then committed *seppuku,* the traditional form of honorable suicide. Not only did the act seem anachronistic, but for many, it was an unpleasant reminder of the part of Japanese history represented by the twin symbols of the chrysanthemum and the sword. Writers were far more inclined to express alienation from the society and values that had led to the war. The literature about the atomic bomb has been much studied and discussed, but its best examples transcend that subject to offer images of humanity in extremis.

The first East Asian to win a Nobel Prize in literature, Kawabata Yasunari was known in the West by only two of his novels, *Thousand Cranes* and *Snow Country.* He presents a world of geishas and aesthetes into which industrialism and modernity intrude very little, if at all. His essay *Japan the Beautiful and Myself* further illustrates the continuity with the Japanese tradition that is represented by his work. Some of his compatriots are said to be "embarrassed by the cherry blossom quaintness" of Kawabata's work, and to think Tanizaki, with his more muscular style and broader view of society, as represented by *Some Prefer Nettles* and *Makioka Sisters,* should have won the prize. Kawabata is represented in the present selections by some very short stories that he called "palm-of-the-hand" stories.

While Japanese writers dedicate themselves to the type of literature that China's Liu despaired of having the leisure to pursue, the same writers often write detective fiction and swashbuckling samurai stories. Turning out potboilers is not a risk to their reputations, which remain secure on the strength of their best work.

The current generation of Japanese writers grew up after the American occupation. They are more internationally oriented than their elders and are more likely to travel to Europe or America than to the hot springs closer to home. They make references to American pop music and Hollywood movies more often than to the Kabuki or Noh. The view of life in many of their works is so fractured, frenzied, or energetic that it would be hard to imagine these writers pausing to sigh over a fallen blossom or to enjoy the strains of a single lute string.

Yet poetry is flourishing in Japan. The once moribund haiku form has been revived and flourishes in hundreds of haiku magazines and clubs. Poets are also experimenting with many Western forms. Among these is the prose poem — similar forms existed in traditional literature — but as in China and Korea, more recent practice of the form is inspired more by French symbolist poetry than by traditional Asian examples.

Japanese women writers are beginning to return after several centuries of near silence to the prominent place they held in the classical period. Readers with the least knowledge of classical Japanese literature will know, in addition to the novelist Murasaki, the diarist Sei Shonagon, and the poets Ono no Komachi and Izumi Shikibu. But like her counterparts in China, the Japanese woman has been restricted by the ideals of quiet submissiveness and by the roles of "good wife and wise mother." Like her sisters the world over, she has lacked access to education, independence, or leisure to devote herself fully to literary creation. She has often paid a heavy price, including ostracism, wrecked marriages, and poverty, to establish herself as a writer. Still, since the mid-1960s, a number of important women writers have emerged who have found translators to introduce them to English language readers.

Korea

Contemporary Korean literature has emerged out of a century of political, social, and spiritual crises. Artists and writers were barred from involvement in political and social issues after an independence movement against Japanese rule failed in 1919. The use of the Korean language was banned in 1940; those caught speaking Korean in public could be imprisoned; Koreans were ordered to adopt Japanese names. When Korea was liberated in 1945, writers must have felt an urge both to express themselves and to ensure cultural survival by writing once more in the Korean language. The civil war and the division of the country into North Korea and South Korea have inspired moving poetry and fiction. In 1960, the regime of President Syngman Rhee was overthrown by a student-led movement. The poet Hwang Tonggyu sees the event as a significant social, political, and poetical milestone, which enabled the voice of poets to become socially and politically relevant even while they strove for a pure poetry. The Korean literary scene was reinvigorated in the 1970s, and a series of translations sponsored by UNESCO is making it available to the American reading public.

A NOTE ON NAMES AND ROMANIZATION

Names are given in the order customary in East Asia, that is, the family name is followed by the given name. In Japan, poets are often referred to by their given names, especially if there is more than one poet with the same name. Hence Kaneko Tōta, whose father was already known as a haiku poet, is referred to as Tōta, but Tanikawa Shuntarō is called Tanikawa. The spelling of Chinese names here reflects the preference of their owners, with the older Wade-Giles system used for writers from Taiwan, and the *pinyin* ("spell sounds") system for writers from the People's Republic of China. Chinese in Hong Kong, including Yu Kwang-chung, often use a third system known as the Post Office System. References to traditional literature here are spelled in Wade-Giles. These are only three among more than forty romanization systems that exist for Chinese. As a comparison, the capital of China is spelled Pei-ching in Wade-Giles, Beijing in *pinyin*, and Peking in the Post Office System.

Gloria Bien

FOR FURTHER READING

Primary Works

Allen, Joseph Roe. *Forbidden Games and Video Poems: The Poetry of Yang Mu and Lo Ch'ing.* Translated and commentary by Joseph Roe Allen. Seattle: University of Washington Press, 1993.

Bei Dao. *The August Sleepwalker.* New York: New Directions, 1990.

———. *Old Snow: Poems.* New York: New Directions, 1991.

———. *Waves: Stories.* New York: New Directions, 1990.

Cheng Naishan. *The Banker.* San Francisco: China Books, 1992.

———. *The Piano Tuner.* San Francisco: China Books & Periodicals, 1989.

Enchi Fumiko. *The Waiting Years.* Tokyo: Kodansha International, 1971.

Finkel, Donald, ed. *A Splintered Mirror: Chinese Poetry from the Democracy Movement.* Translated by Donald Finkel. Berkeley: North Point Press, 1991.

Gu Cheng. *Gu Cheng: Selected Poems.* Hong Kong: Renditions, 1990.

Hwang Sunwŏn. *The Book of Masks: Stories.* London: Readers International, 1989.

———. *The Moving Castle.* Arch Cape, Or.: Pace International Research, 1985.

———. *Shadows of a Sound: Short Stories.* San Francisco: Mercury House, 1990.

Hwang Tonggyu. *Wind Burial: Selected Poems of Hwang Tong-gyu.* Laurinburg, N.C.: St. Andrews Press, 1990.

Inoue Yasushi. *Shirobamba: A Childhood in Old Japan.* Chester Spring, Penn.: Dufour Editions, 1991.

———. *Tun Huang.* Tokyo: Kodansha, 1993.

Kaneko Tōta. See Ueda.

Kawabata Yasunari. *Beauty and Sadness.* New York: Knopf, 1975.

———. *Palm-of-the-Hand Stories.* San Francisco: North Point Press, 1988.

———. *Snow Country.* New York: Knopf, 1957.

———. *The Sound of the Mountain.* New York: Knopf, 1970.

———. *Thousand Cranes.* New York: Knopf, 1959.

Kim Namjo. *Selected Poems of Kim Namjo*. Ithaca: Cornell University East Asia Program, 1993.

Lo Ch'ing. See Allen.

Mishima Yukiō. *Confessions of a Mask*. New York: New Directions, 1968.

———. *Death in Midsummer and Other Stories*. New York: New Directions, 1966.

———. *Five Modern No Plays*. New York: Knopf, 1957.

Pai Hsien-yung. *Crystal Boys*. San Francisco: Gay Sunshine Press, 1990.

Pak Mogwol. *Selected Poems of Pak Mogwol*. Berkeley: Asian Humanities Press, 1990.

Shu Ting. See Finkel.

Tanikawa Shuntarō, *Coca-Cola Lessons*. Portland, Or.: Prescott Street Press, 1986.

———. *With Silence My Companion*. Portland, Or.: Prescott Street Press, 1991.

Ueda, Makoto. *Modern Japanese Haiku: An Anthology*. Toronto: University of Toronto Press, 1976.

Yang Mu. See Allen.

Yu Kwang-chung. *Acres of Barbed Wire*. Taipei: Meiya, 1971.

Secondary Works

Hibbett, Howard. *Contemporary Japanese Literature: An Anthology of Fiction, Film, and Other Writing since 1945*. New York: Knopf, 1977.

Keene, Donald. *Japanese Literature: An Introduction for Western Readers*. New York: Grove Press, 1955.

Lee, Peter H. *Modern Korean Literature: An Anthology*. Honolulu: University of Hawaii Press, 1990.

Liu, James J. Y. *Essentials of Chinese Literary Art*. Flushing, N.Y.: Asia Book Corp., 1979.

CHINA

CHENG NAISHAN

Cheng Naishan (1946–) is a native of Shanghai, China's most cosmopolitan city. Born to a westernized business-class family, she learned English and Western music at home. Her stories often reflect her own experiences of urban life; she has published prolifically since 1979 and has won many literary prizes.

"Why Parents Worry," which first appeared in a collection of Cheng's stories in 1986, follows the experiences of an urban family living through the tumultuous years of recent Chinese history. Like many ordinary Chinese, they tried to escape notice and play the game. In struggling to send his son to study in the West, the father is trying to share with his son an experience he had before mainland China became communist and isolated from the rest of the world. Through the character of the family maid, Cheng shows the failure of the Cultural Revolution of 1966–1976 to create equality between urban and rural life and between educated and illiterate people. The story also demonstrates the failure of the Cultural Revolution to substitute service to state and society for family loyalty and individual advancement.

Why Parents Worry

"Isn't dinner ready yet, Mrs. Zhang? We're going out tonight."

Mr. Zhou, master of the house, sat comfortably at the head of the table, issuing instructions to the family amah,° Mrs. Zhang, relishing the privilege of being the boss. For eight hours a day at the office he played the role of compliant underling, but when he closed the door of his own home, he became resident despot.

"Not ready yet? Well, no hurry, no hurry!" He pronounced a reprieve.

Zhou wielded real power at home. Just look at the way his casual reprieve succeeded in upsetting Mrs. Zhang, who had served in his house for twenty-two years. Experience told her that the real meaning of this pronouncement was "What the hell's keeping you? Hurry up!" Mrs. Zhang was, after all, a competent worker, otherwise the Zhous would not

---

amah: a nanny or wet nurse

have kept her on all these years. She never had a moment's rest, always a full complement of two dishes and a soup to be prepared, and in the midst of all the commotion she never forgot to set aside a portion from each dish before adding the sugar — Mr. Zhou's precious Ah Ping didn't like his food sweet.

As she was bringing the food to the table, Mr. Zhou drew a letter from his pocket. Even though she couldn't read, Mrs. Zhang could tell from the writing on the envelope that it was from her son Fusheng who lived in the countryside. She watched with signs of impatience as the master, with exasperating deliberation, cleaned his glasses and methodically opened the envelope.

"'Dear Ma, Cuilian insists we get a sewing machine and it's got to be a Butterfly brand from Shanghai or nothing. She says she won't join the family otherwise!" Heavens, these country girls really have a lot of nerve" (This from Zhou, not the letter.) "And that son of yours too, as if his mother's living a life of ease in Shanghai. You mustn't spoil children too much, Mrs. Zhang. You should buy some nourishing food for yourself with the little you manage to put aside. 'Cows eat grass, ducks eat grain, and children, too are provided for' . . . 'Ma, you have no idea how well Cuilian and I get on; she, she even let me touch her hand' . . . ha ha ha . . ." The master laughed so hard he had to take off his glasses and wipe his eyes, even the missus was doubled over with laughter. Mrs. Zhang hurriedly set out the food and fled red-faced into the kitchen.

"There's no taking the country out of countryfolk; a daughter-in-law can be had for the price of a sewing machine. It would break my heart if our Ah Ping had been born into a family like that," the wife said pityingly, looking at Mrs. Zhang's prematurely aged figure. But the husband blew her feeling of superiority clean away with a soft nasal "hunh."

"Our Ah Ping *was* born into the wrong family, just a few steps more and he would have made it into my second brother's downstairs. Even if he'd been born into my sister's over in Hongkou he'd have been better off. Look, in just the last six months their son and daughter have gone off, one to Chicago, the other to Los Angeles. Who knows, they might be guzzling Coke and congratulating themselves right now saying, 'If I'd been born into a family like Ah Ping's it'd break my heart.' And my eldest brother, his own nephew same as the others, what would it cost him to put up the money for one more to go overseas? No wonder they say Americans are the biggest skinflints around, with the least family feeling. Three letters and not one answer."

His wife interrupted: "Whose bright idea was it to break with him so completely? In the beginning he wrote four or five times, and not a word from you; you, straight as an arrow, handed the letters over to the leadership. Your second brother wasn't such a die-hard."

Zhou cut her off impatiently: "That's enough, what's done is done." What was it today? He only wanted to shut out the world and lord it over the household, but even here there was no peace. His wife was less and less obedient and there were fewer and fewer times when "his word was law." But the most frightening thing was that he himself felt that he was often too clever for his own good. In this case, for instance, he had definitely been too inflexible toward his eldest brother.

But had it all been so simple? Who would have dared to be tarred with the "American" brush during the fifties? And as for his second brother, it was precisely because Zhou *wasn't* similarly guileless that he'd escaped having a Rightist's cap slapped on his head. That in itself had been no mean accomplishment. People with shaky class backgrounds° like his ought to tuck their tails between their legs and tread lightly. What's more, his persistent circumspection, his — in his wife's terms — "hidebound attitude", was all for the sake of Ah Ping, that only child of twenty-two years of wedlock! Holding that little red body to his bosom twenty-two years ago, he had uttered a silent prayer to heaven: he would do right by the boy — this life he had created, his own flesh and blood, his son! In fact, long before his son had been born, even before Zhou had got married, he had made personal sacrifices for him. There was the girl he'd almost married, his first girlfriend. She was too delicate and it had worried him — perhaps he would never know the joys of fatherhood — so he had grit his teeth and broken off that fairy-tale romance. Never in his wildest imaginings had he thought that, having settled on a wife who was a sound sleeper with a healthy appetite, twelve uneventful years would pass before finally (thank God) his son, in his own good time, arrived.

It was inconceivable to him that his son should be so like himself. An exact replica, as if life could be duplicated after all. Was there really such a thing as "reincarnation"? If he could be reborn, there were so many unfulfilled dreams: first of all, he would plan a carefree childhood for himself. His own childhood had been a vista of unbroken gray; looking back was excruciating.

He came third in a family of four. A third child is doomed to receive very little affection from its parents, who generally dote on either the eldest or the youngest. His father began as a fitter and later opened his own ironworks employing about a hundred workers in the Zhabei section of Shanghai. He made a lot of money but spent all his days managing the business; moreover he was both stingy and harsh with his wife and family. How Zhou had envied the little American boy his own age who lived next door — Peck, the son of a minister. He had such a great pile of toys and picture books and such loving parents. Little Peck often skipped along holding onto his parents' hands as they went on outings. Zhou had never known such pleasure himself. What he envied Peck most was his

---

shaky class backgrounds: those not from a family poor or moderately poor peasants, workers, or soldiers, or those with relatives in the West, risked being persecuted as Rightists

metal construction set; the box even held a little screwdriver and a little wrench; with these you could build a little house, a tank, a crane . . . he used to dream all the time what it would be like to have a construction set like that. It would make him the luckiest boy in the world!

If there *were* such a thing as reincarnation, he would choose a new profession as well. In the beginning, perhaps inspired by that construction set, he had wanted very badly to study architecture, but his father was adamantly against it. In those days, the most useful thing to learn was how to make money. He'd had to go against his own inclinations and study business. Yes, he'd had many disappointments in his life. . . . Of course, reincarnation was impossible; he could only make up for it all the second time around, through his son.

When his son turned four, Zhou could hardly wait; he bought him a construction set. It had cost three *yuan.*° He had never imagined how cheaply his childhood dream could have been realized! The disappointment was that his son took no interest in the toy. In less than three days, the little metal pieces had been scattered about and some were missing. His son had too many toys already; the new one didn't mean that much to him!

Ah Ping had been born during the famine years of the early sixties and though later (thank God) such things as milk powder, honey, orange juice, cod liver oil — the lot — were available in the shops, the prices were frightfully high. Zhou's monthly salary of 100 *yuan* plus his wife's 65 *yuan* was fairly good but it wouldn't stretch to buying such expensive goods. Luckily, however, he was the sole beneficiary of the fixed interest payments on his deceased father's assets amounting to 400 a quarter. His eldest brother had gone abroad to make his way long ago, his second brother had been dubbed a Rightist and the Zhous naturally refused to have anything to do with this "traitor"; his younger sister had married, and married daughters are like spilt water — it was only right and proper that the money should revert entirely to him. But came 1964, a time of political turmoil, the preliminary "four clean-ups" campaign° was underway, and for the sake of his son, he grit his teeth and let the money go. His son was glittering crystal to him; he could not bring himself to sully the boy. And Zhou did all he could to ensure that Ah Ping had no contact with his uncle downstairs, that their family had nothing to do with that Rightist. How could he have done otherwise? He even put up a swinging door on the landing, a blatant indication that one half didn't know how the other half lived. For his son's sake, he could even go the whole eight hours at work without speaking a word. After all, popular wisdom says: misfortune issues from between the lips! He had no friends in his work-

---

yuan: basic monetary unit of the People's Republic of China
four clean-ups campaign: part of the 1964 Socialist Education Movement aimed at purging capitalist influences in politics, economics, organization, and ideology

place, no bosom buddies, his son was all he needed. Even today he was still perfectly happy to be one of the obedient masses, despite the fact that the leadership had undergone more changes than the revolving figures on an old-fashioned paper lantern: from "rebel factions" to "workers' propaganda teams" to "military representatives," right back to the original leaders from before the Cultural Revolution. He had been a law-abiding citizen all along, whether in the very beginning during the mass criticism of "capitalist roaders" or later in the attack on the Gang of Four.° He had always made his views known to the Party branch in writing, in his regular, straight up and down characters. Of course, from time to time he found it very hard to live with his own behavior. But what else could he do? He was doing it for his son. . . .

The door opened with a bang. His son was home, a package held aloft in one hand.

"Dad, Ma, my friend Li got a pair of blue jeans for me, from the smugglers in Wenzhou,° forty *yuan.*"

Forty *yuan* for a pair of cotton trousers! Zhou's heart did an involuntary flip-flop.

But his son turned the pants over with an air of importance and patted the copper label riveted to the back pocket: "Look, genuine Bull Dog brand from the US." He couldn't have known that the old man would be more familiar with the brand than he was. Zhou knew that brand from the late forties, but in those days most people thought skin-tight blue jeans undignified, and only foreign sailors and dandies wore them.

"Times have changed. In those days even Klim milk powder° was being peddled on the street, nowadays you have to have foreign exchange notes to get it." His wife was shaking his absolute authority again.

"Pants like this are pretty expensive in the US — it's synthetic fibers that are cheap over there. Since I can get these for *renminbi*° now, I don't mind paying a little more. Then when I go to the States, to some party, I won't look like such a hick . . ."

From his son's tone of voice one would have thought his father had an endless supply of money.

"How many times have I told you, I'm sending you to the States to study, not so you can go to parties."

"Don't be so strait-laced, Dad, you enjoyed these things once yourself, you've done them all, so why take the official line with me?"

What was this? When had he "enjoyed" them, "done" them?

Gang of Four: Madame Mao Zedong and three of her associates who were blamed for the Cultural Revolution
Wenzhou: a port city in southern Zhejiang province
Klim milk powder: such products were available mainly to the wealthy and those with connections to westerners
renminbi: "the people's currency," of which *yuan* is the basic unit

"Stop pulling my leg. Grandpa was the boss, and you were just like the rich son in the movie 'Midnight,' weren't you? Drinking, dancing . . ."

Kids today, all they know is what they see in the movies, what do they know about life? In spite of the dangers, when Zhou was young he had squeezed onto a third-class train compartment and traveled all the way to Chongqing in order to get into a free, government-supported university. With the Sino-Japanese War raging, all communication with his family had been cut off, even food had become a problem. Like his classmates, he had to work-study, relying entirely on his own efforts to finish. But that period of his life had done a great deal for him. Now people were always impressed with his capabilities, weren't they? But in his heart he knew it wasn't because he had been born clever; he owed it all to that difficult, solitary life in Chongqing!

"Enough, what's the point of trotting out all these old chestnuts? Compared to those kids who do nothing but smoke cigarettes all day and don't study, our Ah Ping is pretty good."

There was something in what his wife said. Though Ah Ping was an only child, he was obedient and had never dared to go his own way. This pair of forty-*yuan* pants now; if his father said a simple "no," he wouldn't dare buy them. But once his father nodded grudgingly, the son bolted down a few mouthfuls of rice and went to his room to try them on.

His son was twenty-two years old, he wanted to look good! Twenty-two years, gone in the blink of an eye. Before Zhou had been able to make careful arrangements for the boy's future, he had grown up. If the truth be told, he'd had his son's future planned out the moment he was born — he would be an architect and realize the unfulfilled dream of Zhou's own youth. But the child had been born during hard times and the Cultural Revolution came along before he'd had even a basic education. Thanks to Zhou's own years of watching his step, the family had slipped miraculously through a breach in that devastating "Great Revolution." But one worry plagued him day and night from then on: that his son might be sent down to the countryside.° Like most people, Zhou made his preparations for this eventuality early. In those days, because of the "Great Standard-Bearer,"° work in the theater troupes was particularly sought after. One could avoid a great deal of back-breaking labor that way, so Zhou bought a violin for his son, even broke his habit of not getting involved with other people and asked someone from the "Taking Tiger Mountain by Strategy" symphony orchestra to find a private teacher for him . . . but his son had no interest in the violin and though he studied for some time, his playing assaulted the ears like the squawk-

---

sent . . . countryside: the practice of sending educated urban youth to the countryside to learn from the peasants by participating in manual labor

Great Standard-Bearer: epithet for Jiang Qing, who as Madame Mao Zedong controlled the arts during the Cultural Revolution

ing of chickens being slaughtered. By then, however, Zhou had seen the light: he had discovered that the key to a child's future lay not in proficiency in a particular skill, but in whether or not he had connections. He began to make friends widely, and because Mrs. Zhang was an excellent Wuxi° cook, his table was soon graced by several illustrious guests wearing red badges and military uniforms. Unfortunately, after all this scheming, as he was waiting for the right moment to ask that his son be put on the list for Jiaotong University or Tongji University, everything changed again and the examination system was reinstated.

It wasn't bad to base acceptance to university on an exam grade, and at least he didn't have to curry favor anymore. Luckily his son was only in Form Three,° there was still time to start over. And the boy tried to make a good showing. At first he had the silly idea of wanting to study Chinese; his father had to give him a good talking to. What future was there in pushing a pencil these days? Naturally science and technology were better bets. If Zhou hadn't allowed himself to be ordered about by his own father, would he be spending his days totting up profits on an abacus now? And though his son had failed the university entrance exam three years running, each year he came a little closer; in last year's exam he scored only three points below the passing grade. Soon Zhou's greatest desire would be realized. But nowadays things could change entirely from one week to the next. Before he knew it, sending one's children abroad to study had become *the* thing to do and Zhou was plunged into remorse once more. Why had he been so inflexible, why had he cut himself off so completely from his elder brother? Now there was no going back. In no time, second brother's two kids had gone abroad with elder brother acting as guarantor. At that point, he just had to brazen it out and write elder brother a "humble pie" letter. His elder brother had readily accepted his apologies, writing back happily about brotherly affection, but when he got to the main point — the matter of Ah Ping's going to the US as a self-supporting student — he began pleading excuses. He was already paying for two, he couldn't manage to support another. After that, he simply stopped writing. What a blow that had been! The letter Zhou had sent three months ago was still unanswered. It seemed as if his brother was purposely trying to provoke him.

To add insult to injury, his younger sister's daughter had flown off to the US with her fraternal uncle's support. In the depths of his despair, Zhou had decided to seek help from his younger sister's in-laws. The ties between them were somewhat remote, but at least they *were* related and it was the only device left him. That man, brother of his brother-in-law, happened to be in Shanghai just now. He was anxious for Mrs. Zhang to

---

Wuxi: (also spelled Wusih or Wuhsi) a city in south China. Chinese cuisine differs not only from region to region but often from city to city.
Form Three: British English for third grade

serve dinner so that afterwards he could go to the hotel for a little visit with this distant relative, and strike up an acquaintance. In desperation, he had even spent 120 *yuan* on a piece of rare wild ginseng!°

"Actually that 70-*yuan* piece they had in the shop didn't look bad either." His wife was thinking of the ginseng, too. Women never see beyond a few pennies.

"These people are experts, they can spot the difference at a glance. Besides, we have to act quickly for Ah Ping's sake. The policy could change at any time. In a few years it might not be possible to send him."

"Where is it you're sending Ah Ping?" Mrs. Zhang had been clearing away the bowls and chopsticks, head bowed. Hearing the worlds "not possible to send him," her heart suddenly sank, but she was instantly aware of the fact that she was exceeding her bounds, so she quickly bowed her head again and busied herself with clearing the table.

"To America." Zhou didn't begrudge her concern; it was obvious that Mrs. Zhang would hate to see Ah Ping go. Her affection for Ah Ping was a source of great satisfaction to him. "The child has grown up, we have to let him see the world, broaden his horizons!"

"America." Mrs. Zhang racked her brains. To her, America meant American imperialism. Her whole notion of America stemmed from skits performed by land reform teams just after Liberation:° long noses smeared with white powder beneath top hats. "Is it very far away?"

"Of course, hundreds of thousands of *li*."° Zhou was growing impatient. Pushing back his chair, he rose to get ready to go out.

With the whole family out of the house, the rooms were wondrously quiet. This time belonged completely to Mrs. Zhang. Having finished the washing up, she lay down on the plank bed in her small room and stretched out her aching legs. These few moments of freedom were so precious she hated to let them slip away in sleep.

"Ma, Cuilian says we've got to have a sewing machine . . ." Her son's words sounded again in her ear. She propped up her tired body and fished a handkerchief-wrapped bundle from under her pillow. Inside were twelve ten-*yuan* notes. Still a bit short. Besides, you needed a coupon to buy a sewing machine. Where would she get the coupon? Right, she'd go to Mrs. Hu, the one she went to the market for every day, she thought her son had some kind of official position in the Commerce Bureau. She pulled herself out of bed. If not for that spend-thrift son . . . !

Fusheng had also been born in 1961, during the hard years. Another mouth to feed. It had seemed that soon none of them would be able to make it. But providentially, that same Zhou family which had once em-

---

ginseng: a plant root believed to have restorative medicinal powers
Liberation: a communist term for the 1949 communist victory
li: measure of distance roughly equalling one-half kilometer

ployed her mother-in-law sent a letter saying they were looking for a wet-nurse, thirty *yuan* a month plus room and board, and she could leave her ration tickets at home. The job was a windfall, a gift from heaven. With many regrets, she dragged herself away from her piteously screaming infant son. She realized then the heavy price this "heaven-sent" job would exact.

Only someone who's done it can know what it's like to be a house-maid. The food is too cold or too hot, too salty or too bland. You're at the mercy of someone else's fussiness and can't answer back. And you have to keep your wits about you. You'd better get things straight the first time; the more you have to be told, the worse it gets. She went home for her first visit after three years. All the girls in the village envied her city complexion and were only too anxious to follow her to Shanghai. But her mother-in-law, who had been a servant herself, patted her shoulder in sympathy. When she picked up that skinny, sallow, undernourished-looking son of hers, her heart contracted with grief, and she didn't want to leave. But her son was still small, if she wanted to raise him to man-hood, she'd need a lot of money! To make up for the wrong she'd done her child by selling her milk as a wet-nurse, she came home every time laden down like an ox with packages big and small. As the years passed, her son did in fact grow up, from a sallow and skinny boy into a strong, sturdy youth, a typical able-bodied worker. But Mrs. Zhang was begin-ning to realize that the possibility of retirement was becoming more and more remote. The older her son got, the more money he needed. There was no lack of people eager to make a match for the boy, for her reputa-tion in the village, though unfounded, was hard to shake: everyone thought she had pots of money stashed away in Shanghai.

Money — whether you had it or not, you had to worry about your son. It was the same for her boss, Zhou, wasn't it? Night and day he grappled with the problem of sending his son overseas. The ways of the world cer-tainly were unfathomable. *She* wanted nothing more than to be near her son each day. America must be so far away. Ah Ping a) couldn't cook, and b) couldn't do his laundry. Could he survive, separated from his parents all of a sudden in a foreign country, living among those blue-eyed big-noses? If he caught a cold or had a fever, who would he go to? Mrs. Zhang knew only too well what it was like to be far away from home! Though the Zhous' house was bigger and brighter than her place in the country-side, though the bathroom was fresher and cleaner than even the public clinic there, though you didn't have to fetch water or gather firewood, and though it was a thousand, ten thousand times better than her place, it was still not home. In the same way a foreign country was somebody else's home, wasn't it? Even if it was the best place in the world, it be-longed to those blue-eyed big-noses and Ah Ping would have to put up with a lot. He suffered from heartburn, too, and he had to have a hot water bottle tucked up in his quilt in the winter, but he always forgot to fill it before going to bed. He needed his amah to do it for him. Who would look after him over there? They wouldn't bother unless it was their own flesh and blood! At that, Mrs. Zhang's nose began to twitch as if she were about to cry. Enough, enough, you can't even take care of your own child, what business do you have worrying about someone else's? If his parents can bear to see him go, what more do you have to say about it? Right now your son's sewing machine was what mattered. You work until you drop, no peace of mind till you're dead and gone! She fixed her hair and tapped timidly on Mrs. Hu's door.

Zhou's wife snapped on the light indignantly, without interrupting her stream of rebuke, "Might as well have thrown that 120-*yuan* ginseng root into the sea. Your sister's brother-in-law is good at faking poverty. Did you see the fur coat his wife was wearing? Our Ah Ping could study several years on what that cost! He just didn't want to help."

Zhou slumped on the sofa, utterly exhausted. To comfort himself he said: "You can't blame him, they worked hard for their money. Besides, coming back to China to visit is a matter of prestige for these people — fur coats, diamond rings — overseas they probably wear themselves out for it, same as our Mrs. Zhang. The people in the village think she's struck it rich in Shanghai, otherwise why does her prospective daughter-in-law keep asking for things; yarn, sewing machines . . . forget it!" He sounded discouraged. "Asking someone for a favor is the same as asking to be humiliated." Now it looked as though his son wouldn't be lucky enough to go abroad. With this thought Zhou found himself caught once again on the horns of his dilemma: if only in the beginning he had . . . This was his very greatest regret. In 1948 when his elder brother was leaving China he had wanted Zhou to go with him; they'd make their fortunes together. But Zhou had been knocking about Chongqing for eight years already, he really didn't want to do more of the same in some foreign country. If only he had made up his mind to go with his brother then, he wouldn't have to worry over his son now!

"Hey, a letter for us!" His wife bent to retrieve the letter that had been pushed under the door. It was the one they'd been waiting for. In the upper right-hand corner of the snow-white envelope, two red and blue lines spelled out the letters U.S.A. But . . . hang on . . . it wasn't elder brother's handwriting, and the street name on the envelope was out of date; still the old one from before Liberation. No wonder the postman had written "trial delivery" on it. The return address read: Peck, Massachusetts, USA. Who was Peck? The addressee, character for character, was clearly Zhou himself. Never mind, these days it was always a good thing to have an overseas relative or friend fall into one's lap. A yellowed photograph slid out of the envelope: a little foreign boy in a sailor suit and a little Chinese boy in his long gown. He remembered now, it was Peck, the minister's boy! The letter said Peck was coming to Shanghai with a big tour group to have a look at his former home, and wondered whether his old friend Zhou was still living in the same place . . . Could this be a dream? Zhou tugged fiercely at his hair, painfully straightened his shoulders and called urgently to his wife. Over and over he impressed upon her that she was not to let the news out, particularly not to second brother's family downstairs. This foreign good will was his alone to enjoy. As his wife assented to his every instruction, Zhou sensed that his tottering authority had been shored up once more. It never occurred to him that the letter had been slipped under his door by his second brother to begin with, that the postman had left it in the mailbox downstairs first.

"Get him to bring us a color TV. Foreigners don't have to pay duty."

A color TV — women couldn't see any further than the tips of their noses, but Zhou had excellent vision. Here was Ah Ping's salvation. Peck was a minister now, with a Ph.D. in theology. For ministers as for Buddhist monks, virtue was the foundation of everything. What's more, the church had always praised and encouraged education — there was hope. "Is that English Bible we turned up in our last housecleaning still around?" he asked his wife.

"Are you planning to pray?"

"Idiot! Peck is a minister! As the saying goes, you have to speak to people as a human and to monsters as a monster."

Everything went more smoothly than Zhou had ever imagined it would. Owing to the Lord's Prayer and the Twenty-third Psalm which Zhou had down pat, Rev. Peck was already well-disposed towards him. During the three days the man was in Shanghai, Zhou hosted two banquets for him: one an imperial-style banquet at the Dahua Guest House, the other a meal at home. He spent over 200 *yuan* on the two, a true instance of "a thousand gold cash for a single smile." Zhou's calculations had included the expectation that Rev. Peck would bring some gifts with him. But wouldn't you know it, Peck turned out to be terribly stingy. The first time he came to Zhou's house he brought a bunch of fresh flowers — those wouldn't last long. The second time, he was empty-handed. Enough, all these were trifles after all, the crux was whether he was willing to shoulder Ah Ping's expenses. So, choosing his moment, just as Rev. Peck was savoring a succulent slice of sea cucumber, Zhou raised the matter with him. But foreigners are really "wet behind the ears," as they say in Shanghai, you could tell from the Reverend's next remark:

". . . your universities are state-supported, why spend your money to send the boy overseas to study?"

How could he explain? In any case, if other people's sons get their share of a good thing, mine isn't going to be left out. Besides, if his son went to the States to study, he might be able to get a green card° and stay there; that was the best way to do it and the real reason why so many went overseas to study at their own expense. People look at such things

green card: a card identifying the bearer as a permanent resident of the United States

differently now; your son might be a war hero or a model worker, okay, but that can't compare with a son who did you proud overseas. The worst-case scenario, of course, was that by some chance your son might not do well in the U.S. But he could always come back and talk about how rotten and corrupt the capitalist system was, how he had abandoned a life of affluence to return to the Motherland, and his future would be assured all the same. In any case, he would have acquired a patina of gold. No matter how you put it, you couldn't go wrong. But of course one couldn't say such things to an American.

"Rev. Peck, we grew up together, you ought to understand that my childhood was extremely unhappy. My father didn't do all he could for me; he didn't fulfill his responsibilities as a father. And now my son . . ." Zhou weighed his words carefully and his fluent English lent them even greater impact. He wasn't just pulling words out of the air on the spur of the moment; he was speaking from his heart. Perhaps he really did love his son too well. Such sincere love elicited an involuntary sigh from Peck.

"All right then. Let me go home and talk it over with my wife. But, Mr. Zhou, don't you feel you're doing too much for your son? For 'Earthly fathers discipline us for a short time at their pleasure, but He disciplines us forever.' We mustn't try to do every single thing for our children, rather we should seek the Lord's will in all things . . ."

Disagreeable cleric! How could he start preaching at this critical juncture? Never mind, strike while the iron is hot. They had to close the deal now.

"With a servant of the all-loving God as his guardian, my Ah Ping will certainly be even more blessed." Zhou hurriedly cut off Rev. Peck's sermonizing and instructed Mrs. Zhang to bring the dessert. But the ever-efficient Mrs. Zhang wasn't paying attention this time. She could be seen standing off to one side, serving tray in hand, lost in thought.

"Mrs. Zhang!" Zhou was a bit put out, maybe she was getting old.

"Mr. Zhou, you ask that foreigner how cold it gets over there in the winter. Ah Ping suffers from heartburn every winter, doesn't he? He's like that here in Shanghai and this is the south; well, does it count as north or south over there?"

Oh, these country people — Ah Ping's future hasn't been settled yet and here she is talking about north and south as if he already had his air ticket in hand! This was the one disadvantage of having an amah: it was like introducing a spy into your midst. He waved an impatient hand at Mrs. Zhang: "This doesn't concern you, hurry up and get the dessert, and whatever you do, don't talk about this all over the place, especially downstairs."

"Rev. Peck, what songs are popular in the States now? Who's number one now that Elvis is dead? Have you been to Disneyland? I want to go there as soon as I get to America. And I want to learn to disco, real American-style disco . . ." His son was babbling away, racking his brain for things to say to Rev. Peck. He was doing quite well. After all, Zhou had hired a private tutor for him at three *yuan* an hour. If not for his foresight, his son's English wouldn't have been up to snuff, and all his efforts would have been in vain.

"But, young fellow," Peck was patting Ah Ping on his frail shoulder, "America is more than Disney and disco; it's a battlefield. And with your physique, I'd say you're too weak to go to war. You'll need to learn to wash cars, mow lawns, paint houses — you'd better prepare yourself for a hard life."

"A hard life." The common expression in Chinese was "eat bitterness." "Eat bitterness, work hard," the phrase seemed so familiar to Zhou, he'd heard it all the time during the "down to the countryside" period, and now it had an inauspicious ring to it. As if Ah Ping wasn't going to America to study, but was being shipped there like the black slaves. Maybe it was just an impression created by Peck's begrudging the few dollars needed. If he thinks he can scare me off so easily, well, he doesn't know who he's dealing with!

Before Rev. Peck departed from Shanghai, Zhou made a special trip to a handicraft shop and spent 460 *yuan* on a pair of exquisite jade carvings as a present for him. The foreigner had been there three days and Zhou had spent altogether 800 *yuan,* the entire sum he had saved for his old age. But he comforted himself with the thought that 800 *yuan* was equivalent to 400 US dollars. That meant he had already paid back 400 dollars. The man couldn't ignore that.

Rev. Peck was as good as his word, entirely worthy of his calling. All the formalities had been carried out within two weeks and he had produced thirty thousand dollars to guarantee Ah Ping, but his letter said that in reality he could only put up twelve thousand dollars for tuition and expenses. Furthermore, Ah Ping would have to pay the money back within two years after graduation. Peck enclosed a lawyer's contract which Zhou was to sign and send back for the record. These Americans did nothing merely for the sake of friendship. The jade carvings, the banquet, not a word about any of it. But anyway, everything was set.

Due to the large sum of money guaranteed and the fact that Rev. Peck was a prominent seminary professor, the American Consulate in Shanghai processed the visa quickly. As Zhou cautiously examined the passport with its visa stamp, he felt there was nothing more in this world to strive for.

"The weather over there . . . ," Mrs. Zhang interjected timidly.

That's right. These last few days he'd been so busy shopping, buying gifts and finding a tailor that he had forgotten whether the climate over there was northern or southern, so he got out a map and looked up the coordinates of Massachusetts.

"Send this along with Ah Ping. His old hot-water bottle cover is worn out, and it seems there won't be anyone overseas to mend it for him. They don't care, if it's not for one of their own. Better take two and be prepared." Mrs. Zhang handed him two hot-water bottle covers sewn of flannel. In the lower right hand corner was an exquisitely embroidered ox head. Ah Ping had been born in the year of the ox. Mrs. Zhang's eyes were red in the lamplight; she had been crying again.

Wasn't taking such countrified things to the US ridiculous? But Zhou was moved by Mrs. Zhang's sincerity. "Don't feel bad, Mrs. Zhang, once Ah Ping finds a good job over there, he'll send you a hundred *yuan* every month for your old age."

"All I want is for him to remember to write to me," Mrs. Zhang squeezed out a smile and as her tears began to flow again, she fled into the kitchen. Send a hundred *yuan* a month? Ridiculous. As if the streets were paved with gold in America, waiting for Ah Ping to come and take it. The villagers thought of her the same way. All they knew was that once in a while she sent forty or fifty *yuan* home. Only heaven knew how she scrimped for that money! A few years ago her son had seemed to be such a good boy. He would see her off at the bus station as if he couldn't bear to part with her. "Ma, I promise I'll get more work points in the future so you won't have to leave home anymore. I'll support you." Those few words had sounded so sweet to Mrs. Zhang. She really couldn't wait for her son to grow up. She'd find him a wife, then she could retire and enjoy her old age. But her son became less sensible the older he got. He wanted this, he wanted that, making a laughing stock of them both. When it came time to choose a wife he paid no attention to his mother's wishes. Now Ah Ping was leaving. Did life have a purpose any longer? Whether Ah Ping did well out of going away or not, Mrs. Zhang would never take a cent from him. What a sin!

In the other room, Zhou was fiddling with the hot-water bottle covers Mrs. Zhang had made while going over in his mind the things that remained to be done, when it struck him that the two intricately-done covers looked extremely attractive in the pale lamplight, unique, like handicrafts. They were after all genuine handmade articles. He had a sudden inspiration: why shouldn't his son take several more along to give as gifts to cement friendships? Foreigners were sure to like that kind of thing.

"Mrs. Zhang, if you have time, make a few more hot water bottle covers to last Ah Ping awhile."

"All right!" Mrs. Zhang agreed readily and immediately donned the apron she had just taken off. She was about to go to see Mrs. Hu to settle the matter of the sewing machine, but no matter how pressing her son's needs, Ah Ping's were much more urgent. His days at home were numbered, and before long he would be alone in a foreign country with no one to answer when he called. Poor Ah Ping! She was glad to have a chance to do a little something for him. She'd wanted to help all along, but hadn't known how and had felt badly about it. Her own milk had nurtured Ah

Ping and she would have no peace of mind until she had done something special for him before he left.

A tailor had been found, gifts bought, guests feted — money had trickled away like water. In less than a month, the savings Zhou had toiled half a lifetime for were all used up. In the end even the money for the air ticket had to be scraped together.

But Ah Ping finally did get off.

"What day will Ah Ping get to America?" Mrs. Zhang anxiously asked red-eyed Mr. and Mrs. Zhou just back from seeing their son off.

"At 8:00 a.m. on the 19th."

"You mean the 20th, don't you? Today is the 19th." Mrs. Zhang corrected him cautiously.

"No, the 19th, you wouldn't understand." Zhou contentedly stuck his feet into the felt slippers his wife brought him. As his son's going abroad had proceeded more and more smoothly, Zhou had recouped his authority at home with increasing rapidity. "It's called a time difference." He wasn't going to explain it to her; country people know nothing. But such simplicity is good: nothing to worry about, no extravagant hopes, no more problems once your son is of marriageable age; at worst you have to worry about buying a sewing machine. "Say, how's that prospective daughter-in-law of yours? Still not willing to make do? Now that she's let your son fondle her hand, who knows what she'll do next? That girl's too greedy."

"You can't blame the child." Mrs. Zhang didn't feel it was right to criticize the daughter-in-law she hadn't even laid eyes on yet, and besides it was hard for young women. If one didn't get a good husband and a few clothes and things for oneself at marriage, there would be no second chance.

"Umm, Mrs. Zhang," Zhou cleared his throat, and steered the subject back to a matter he'd been considering for some time, "With Ah Ping gone, the two of us don't make much housework. We're ready to do it ourselves. You can probably go home and enjoy your old age, can't you? You'll be a grandmother soon!" He had spent all his money on his son. From now on, they would have to live like the woman in Maupassant's "The Necklace," hanging on to every copper.

Mrs. Zhang was dumbstruck. Her mouth worked, but nothing came out and she went back into the kitchen. She had a letter from her son in her apron pocket right now. Mrs. Hu had read it and told her that her son wanted her to buy a watch for his intended.

Zhou plumped up his pillow. His son would be in Japan by now. He was finally a success as a father. From this night on he could sleep soundly. When in the past twenty-two years had he *not* tossed and turned at night worrying about his son? He closed his eyes, but he didn't feel in the least like sleeping. He kept trying the figures over in his mind: five times six equals thirty. His son needed thirty thousand dollars for five years of study. Rev. Peck had lent him twelve thousand. He still didn't know where the other eighteen thousand was coming from. His son was up to his ears in debt and he hadn't even got to America yet! How would he ever pay it all back? Oh Ah Ping, Ah Ping, you're thirty thousand dollars in debt . . . !

He sighed deeply and to avoid thinking about it, groped on the night-stand for a sleeping pill.

In the kitchen Mrs. Zhang went garrulously on, "I beg of you, (this to Mrs. Hu) find me a new employer! I'll baby-sit or take care of someone who's paralysed — it doesn't matter. For my son's sake, and while my old bones can still manage, I have to spend a few more years as a beast of bur-den! If I get a letter from Ah Ping, please forward it to my new job. . . ."

Into the night the neighbors lights still burned and there was an un-usual amount of activity. It was said that their daughter-in-law (new last year) had just given birth to a son and they were celebrating!

Translated from the Chinese
by Janice Wickeri

BEI DAO

Bei Dao is the pen name of Zhao Zhenkai (1949–). Born in Beijing to educated parents, Bei Dao's own education was interrupted by the Cultural Revolution. Once a political activist, he later lost enthusiasm for the movement; in 1969 he was assigned work in a construction company in Beijing. He began publishing poetry in 1972. A cofounder of the underground literary magazine Today, *Bei Dao is a leading writer of what has come to be known as Misty poetry. His work contin-ues to develop, revealing a multifaceted sensitivity. His pen name, which means "north island," was given by friends because he is from the north and something of a loner.*

Bei Dao's story "13 Happiness Street" reveals the dangers of inquir-ing into secrets in a society with a very thin line between political and psychological imprisonment. It is an oblique but daring criticism of the government. Those who have read his fiction and his poetry have said that Bei Dao seems to be two different people when he is writing in poetry and in prose.

It was Bei Dao's poem "Answer," with its defiant tone and striking imagery, that first brought Misty poetry into national prominence when it was published in the official poetry journal Shi Kan *(Poetry Monthly) in 1980. That poem, and the last lines from "Notes on the City of the Sun," are often quoted as representing the disillusionment of Bei Dao's generation.*

13 Happiness Street

I

A late autumn morning. The street was bleak and desolate. A gust of wind rustled the withered yellow leaves on the pavement. The dreary, monotonous cry of an old woman selling ices could be heard in the distance. Fang Cheng pulled his old black woolen coat tightly around himself and kicked a stone on the ground. It wedged itself in the iron grate in the gutter with a clunk. The call from his sister just now had been really too fantastic: young Jun had been flying his kite in this street yesterday afternoon, yes, this same bloody street, when all of a sudden, he had disappeared without a trace; in broad daylight! His sister's sobs, followed by the beep signaling the line was disconnected, had upset him so much that his head was still ringing. Sun, the section head, was sitting opposite him at the time, and had given him an inquisitive glance, so he had put down the receiver and done his utmost to look normal.

Across the road, a row of locust-trees had been sawn down to the roots, the trunks lying across the pavement. A yellow Japanese fork-lift was parked by the side of the road. Four or five men were busy attaching hooks to the sawn-off trees and loading them onto a large truck to the tooting of a whistle.

Fang Cheng approached the old woman selling ices. "Such fine locust-trees, how come . . ."

"Ices, three cents and five cents." The shriveled mouth snapped shut.

"Comrade . . ."

The old woman's strident voice robbed him of the courage to repeat his question. He crossed the road to the truck. A young fellow who looked like the driver was leaning against the front mudguard smoking.

"Excuse me, what's going on here?"

"Don't you have eyes in your head?"

"I mean, what are you sawing the trees down for?"

"Who do you think you are, going round poking your nose into everything? Are you building a house, and you want us to leave you a log for the roof beam? I'll tell you straight, I can't even get one for myself." Flicking away his cigarette butt, the driver turned round and climbed into the driver's cab, slamming the door behind him.

Fang Cheng bit his lip. A middle-aged woman carrying a string bag was walking past. He caught up with her. "Excuse me, where did you get those turnips?"

"At the greengrocer's over the way."

"Oh." He smiled politely and walked with her for a few steps. "How come these trees have been cut down? Such a shame."

"Who knows? I heard that yesterday a kite got caught in the trees, and some young rascal climbed up to get it . . ." She suddenly fell silent and hurried off nervously.

A long shadow slipped across the ground.

Fang Cheng swung around. A man wearing a leather jacket pulled a green army cap over his eyes, gave him a swift glance and walked past.

It was only then that Fang Cheng noticed the high outside wall exposed behind the stumps of the felled locust-trees. The plaster was so old that it had peeled off in places, showing the large solid bricks underneath. He took a deep breath, inhaling petrol fumes mixed with the sweet scent of locust-wood, and walked back along the wall. Before long he came upon a recess in the wall enclosing a gateway guarded by two stone lions. The red paint on the door had faded and was covered with a layer of dust, as if it hadn't been opened for a long time. On it was a very ordinary plaque with the words "13 Happiness Street," and beneath it a cream-colored buzzer. Fang Cheng went to press it, but it wouldn't budge. On closer inspection he realized it was molded from a single piece of plastic and was purely decorative. He stood there bewildered.

As he drew back a few paces, trying to get a clearer view of the whole gate, he bumped into an old man who happened to be passing by.

"Sorry. Excuse me, who lives here?"

He stopped short. The terror that welled up from the depths of the old man's eyes made Fang Cheng's legs go weak. The old man stumbled away, his walking stick beating an urgent and irregular rhythm as he disappeared into the distance.

A young boy walked by, absorbed in whittling a branch from one of the locust-trees with a pen-knife.

"Hey, where's the neighborhood committee office, young man?"

"Turn at the lane over there," the boy sniffled, pointing with the branch.

The narrow lane twisted its way through the shoddy makeshift houses. From time to time Fang Cheng had to walk sideways in order to prevent the boards and exposed nails from catching and tearing his overcoat. At the entrance to what looked like a rather spacious courtyard at the far end of the lane two sign boards were hanging side by side: Neighborhood Committee° and Red Medical Station. Both were covered with the muddy finger-prints of children.

He pushed open the door of the room on the north side of the courtyard and stuck his head inside.

"Did you bring the certificate?" asked a girl busy knitting a jumper.

"What certificate?"

"The death certificate!" she said impatiently.

Neighborhood committee: also called a residents' committee, it helps the government in social surveillance and control

Everything in the room was white: the sheet, the folding screen, the table, the chairs, and also the girl's lab-coat and pallid face. Fang Cheng shivered. "No, no, I've . . ."

"Listen, if we don't sign it nobody's going to let you hold the funeral service!"

"I'm looking for someone."

"Looking for someone?" She looked up in surprise, lifting her hair back with one of her knitting needles. "Don't you know what's proper?"

"But this is . . ."

"The Red Medical Station."

Retreating into the yard, Fang Cheng noticed a dense crowd of people in the room to the south. He walked over and knocked on the door.

"Come in," a voice said.

Inside about a dozen people were seated around a long wooden table, all staring at him in silence. The light inside the room was so dim that he couldn't make out their faces, but judging from their heavy bronchial wheezing, most of them were old women.

"Has it been signed?" The question came from a woman at the far end of the table. From her voice she seemed pretty young; she'd be the chairwoman or something.

"No, I . . ."

"Then they're still alive and breathing," she broke in sharply.

A howl of laughter. One fat old woman laughed so much she started gagging, and someone thumped her on the back.

"I'm a reporter," Fang Cheng explained hastily.

Instantly the room fell deathly silent. They gazed stupidly at each other, as if they were not too sure what he meant.

The chairwoman was the first to break the silence. "Your papers."

Fang Cheng had barely taken out his press card when it was snatched away by the person nearest the door. The card in its red plastic cover was handed round the table for everyone to look at and comment on. As it passed from hand to hand, some of them shook their heads while others spat on their fingers and rubbed it. Finally it reached the chairwoman. Gripping the card, she studied it carefully, then got the old man in glasses beside her to read it aloud. At last she gave a nod.

"Hm. Have you come to take photos?"

A buzz of excited confusion filled the room. Dull eyes flashed, people nudged and tugged at each other, and one old woman who had fallen asleep propped against the table actually woke up. It was as if something that they had been waiting a lifetime for was finally about to happen.

"You can take our picture now, we're in the middle of our political study," the chairwoman said haughtily. "Sit up everyone, and don't look into the camera!"

They all sat up straight, and there was a loud rustle as they picked up the newspapers on the table.

"Hold on, I haven't brought my camera . . . I'm here on another matter. I'm trying to find out who lives at Number 13 Happiness Street."

"How come you never breathed a word of this earlier?" said the chairwoman, obviously quite put out.

"You didn't give me a chance . . ."

"All right then, what do you want to know?"

"It's about Number 13 Happiness Street . . ."

"Someone alive and kicking? That's none of our business. On your way then, and next time don't start gabbling away at us again, these old bones can't take all the excitement."

"Whose business is it?"

"Quite! Let's get on with our meeting. Now, where were we? Oh yes, this case involving Dumb Chen from over in the Fourth Xiangyang Courtyard. He'll live on in our hearts forever and all that, but people have started asking why he's still being issued with a face mask every winter . . ."

"Maybe his corpse is still breathing."

"We'll issue you with a cauldron to lie in when it's your turn to go to heaven, so you won't have to straighten that hunched back of yours . . ." A strange rasping sound came from the corner.

They started to quarrel, their voices getting louder and louder. Fang Cheng took advantage of the confusion to slip out. When he reached the gate he breathed a long sigh of relief, feeling that he had actually almost died himself.

He took a wrong turn. The buildings inside another compound were being pulled down, and clouds of dust filled the air. A crowd of children pressed around the entrance, peering inside. In the yard the workmen were chanting as they swung a wooden pole against the gable of the house to the east. A structure like a well was under construction in the middle of a stretch of rubble.

"What is this place?" Fang Cheng asked the children.

"The local housing authority," a young girl replied timidly.

Stepping over a pile of lime, Fang Cheng ran into a young fellow carrying a bucket of cement. "I'm a reporter, where is your foreman?"

"Hey, Wang . . ."

A head popped out from a scaffold. "What is it?"

"The newspapers again."

Wang leapt down nimbly and put down his trowel, wiping his forehead and muscular neck with his sleeve. "Well, you lot are on the ball all right, it's our first go at this particular innovation . . ."

"Innovation?"

"Sounds as if you're here about cadres doing manual labor again. Your paper's carried that news a good half dozen times already, and the only thing they ever change is my name. If you fellas keep it up it won't be long before I'll have trouble figuring out what I'm called. Take a look at this job. What d'you reckon?"

"What exactly is it?"

"A house, of course. The latest style."

"Actually, it looks like a . . ." he bit the word "tomb."

"A blockhouse, right? But it doesn't have peep holes in the sides."

"What about windows?"

"They'll all be on the roof." Wang rubbed his hands in glee, flicking off small pellets of mud. "Ideal in case of war, keeps out robbers, protects you against both wind and the cold, it's got lots of advantages. It's something we learned about from our ancestors."

Our cave-dwelling ancestors, Fang Cheng smiled wryly.

"The thing is that houses like these are cheap, you can build 'em by the dozen with pre-mixed concrete. They're easier to make than chicken coops, and they're more solid than a blockhouse. If this catches on, you and me'll both be famous. For starters I'll get a new house, and sit in an armchair at the bureau office. But don't put any of that in your story. Here, take a look at the blueprints. We're in the middle of a demolition job, so the air's not too clean. Hey, Li, are you taking that shovel's pulse or what? Look lively now and bring a stool over here . . ."

Fang Cheng felt a bit dizzy. "It's all right, I'll look these over back at the office. By the way, do you happen to know who lives at Number 13 Happiness Street?"

"Dunno, that's not our business."

"Whose is it then? Whose business *is* it to know?"

"Don't blow your top, let me think about it for a second . . . you could try asking around at the bureau, they've got a big map there, it shows everything down to the last detail."

"Good, I'll try them."

"Do us a favor while you're at it, take this blueprint with you and give it to the director. We'll get a pedicab° to take you."

"No need, but thanks all the same."

"This time be sure you don't get my name wrong," Wang shouted after him.

Fang Cheng staggered out and stood in the middle of the road, staring at the sky.

2

The secretary darted out from behind the door, her heels clicking. "Director Ding will be very happy to see you, Comrade Reporter. The other sev-

---

pedicab: a tricycle with a large seat mounted over the back wheels for passengers

enteen directors would also like to talk to you, at your convenience of course. Director Ma would like to give you his view on the question of the revolutionary succession; Director Tian wants to give you a run down on his war record; Director Wang would like to discuss the simplification of Chinese characters . . ."

"Which one of them is the real director of the bureau?"

"Here we make no distinction between the director and assistant directors, we simply list them all in alphabetical order."

"I'm sorry, but I'm a bit pressed for time. I'm here on another matter. Anyway, how do all the directors know I'm here?"

"They were at a board meeting together just now."

"Am I breaking it up?"

"Don't give it another thought. They've been at it for nine days already. They're only too glad to take a break."

The director's office was thick with smoke. A pudgy old man with a healthy-looking complexion standing beside the conference table extended his hand to Fang Cheng with a broad smile. "Welcome, have a seat. Look at all this smoke, it's a form of collective murder . . ."

"What?"

He waved his arms around in the air in an attempt to disperse the clouds of smoke. "The fact that I'm an optimist has been my salvation, let me tell you. Have you heard of a medicine called 'Anliben'?"

"No."

"It's a miracle drug used overseas for people with heart trouble. Does your paper ever send you abroad?"

"The chances are pretty slim."

"Then could you ask someone to help me get some?"

"I'll see what I can do. Do you have heart trouble?"

The director immediately looked glum. "I'm an old man, getting past it. Who knows, maybe the next time you come it'll be Director Wang sitting in this seat . . ." He cleared his throat. "But let's get back to the matter in hand. Major political campaigns bring about major changes, and major changes promote further political campaigns. In the current quarter we've completed 158% of our work plan; compared with the same period last year . . ."

"Excuse me, Director Ding, I haven't come here on a story."

"Oh?"

"I want to make some enquiries about a house. Who lives at Number 13 Happiness Street?"

Beads of sweat appeared on Ding's shiny red face. He pulled out a handkerchief and wiped his face. "You're not trying to trick me with some difficult question, are you? A big city like this, how could I know every house on every street by heart, like a production chart?"

"I heard that you've got a big map here . . ."

"Yes, yes, I almost forgot." Groping for a small bottle in his pocket, he poured out a few pills and popped them into his mouth. "What do you think of the chicken-blood cure?"

"I haven't tried it."

He pressed a button on his desk and the red curtains on the wall parted slowly. He picked up a pointer, whipped the air with it energetically, and went up to the map. "How about the arm-swinging cure?"

"I'm sure it helps."

"Yes, it's very effective. Happiness Street . . . Number 30 . . . ah, a coal depot."

I'm after Number 13."

"13 . . . 13 . . . come and see for yourself, my friend."

It was a blank space.

"How come it's not marked?" Fang Cheng asked in surprise.

Director Ding patted him on the shoulder. "Look carefully, there are quite a lot of blank spots on this map. No one knows what these places are."

"No one knows?"

"Nothing to be surprised about. It's just like all the blank spots in our knowledge of medicine."

"Not even the Public Security Bureau people?"

"Why don't you go and see for yourself, we open out onto their back door; it's very handy. What do you think of gadgets like pacemakers, are they reliable?"

"Pacemakers? I don't know much about them." Fang Cheng felt around in his pockets and fished out the blueprint. "This morning I went to the local housing authority and Wang, the foreman, asked me to give this to you. It's the innovation they've been working on."

"That fellow's too active for his own good. He's like a bloody magician, always coming up with some new gimmick. There's still a lot of major business here we haven't had time to get round to yet." Ding frowned, rolled up the blueprint and threw it into a wastepaper basket in the corner. "It's thanks to people like him that there's never a moment's peace and quiet anywhere."

The secretary appeared at the door.

"A message for all directors. The meeting is about to resume."

Fang Cheng showed his press card to the guard standing at the opening in the iron fence which surrounded the Public Security Bureau. "I want to see the director of the bureau."

"Interrogation Room I."

"Uh?"

"Up the stairs, first door on the right."

"I'm a reporter."

The guard looked at him blankly, not bothering to reply.

Fang Cheng went up the stairs, and with the help of the faint light in the corridor found a door with a brass plaque nailed to it: Interrogation Room I. He knocked. No one answered so he pushed the door open and went in. It was sumptuously furnished, with a red carpet on the floor and some leather chairs set around a tea table. It was not in the least like an interrogation room. He heaved a sigh of relief and sat down.

Suddenly three or four policemen came in through a small side door escorting a man in a grey Mao suit. The man was of medium height, and his swarthy face was like an iron mask, cold and stern. A policeman wearing spectacles moved to his side and whispered something in his ear. He nodded.

"This is Director Liu," Spectacles said by way of introduction.

"Please be seated." The director's voice was deep and harsh. He and Spectacles moved to the chairs opposite and sat down. The other policemen stood at either side of them.

"Director Liu, there's something I would like to ask you," said Fang Cheng.

"Just a moment, first I've got a question for you." After a moment's pause, Liu proceeded. "If I gave you five matches to make a square, how would you do it?"

Fang Cheng stared at him in astonishment.

"Now, don't be nervous."

"I'm not nervous." He thought hard, but his mind was a complete blank.

Suddenly, Liu gave a harsh laugh, and turned smugly towards Spectacles. "This is typical of ideological criminals, they always try and find a way to use the extra match. Ordinary criminals are another case altogether . . ."

"You have a thorough grasp of the psychology of the criminal mind," offered Spectacles obsequiously.

"This is an outrage!" Fang Cheng protested.

"Don't get excited, young man, and don't interrupt me when I'm talking." Liu turned to Spectacles again. "The important thing to note here is that by using psychological tactics you can force the criminal's thinking into a very small space, or shall we say a surface, where he can't possibly conceal himself, and then he's easily overwhelmed. Do you see what I am saying?"

Spectacles nodded. "But . . . but how can you tell he's a criminal? From the look in his eyes?"

"No, no, that's all out-of-date. Ideological criminals can easily disguise their expressions. Listen, everyone you confront is a criminal, and don't you ever forget it."

"Everyone?"

"Yes. That's what class struggle is all about."

"But . . . then . . . that's . . . ," Spectacles spluttered.

"All right, you ask too many questions, I have no alternative but to put you down as ideologically suspect." Rudely cutting Spectacles short, Liu turned and looked sternly at Fang Cheng. "State your business, young man."

"I . . . I want to make an enquiry about a house."

"Good, go on."

"Who lives at Number 13 Happiness Street?"

Director Liu froze, but in an instant a barely perceptible smile appeared on his lips. Spectacles, still looking crest-fallen, opened his briefcase and took out some paper, ready to take notes. The two policemen stood next to Fang Cheng. The atmosphere in the room became tense.

"Your name?" Liu asked sharply.

"Fang Cheng."

"Age?"

"What do you take me for? I'm a reporter."

"Hand over your papers."

Fang Cheng drew out his press card and passed it to one of the policemen at his side.

"Examine it and take his fingerprints. Also, find his file and check his ideological status," ordered the director.

"What am I being accused of?"

"Prying into state secrets."

"Is Number 13 Happiness Street a state secret?"

"Whatever no one knows is a secret."

"Including you? You mean, you don't know either?"

"Me? There's a certain continuity to your case, you won't even cooperate during interrogation."

Fang Cheng sighed.

"Next question. . . ."

Towards evening, Fang Cheng was released.

3

The municipal library was empty except for the faint but pervasive odor of mold. Fang Cheng leafed through the catalogue, finally located the book: *A Study of Grave-Robbing Techniques Through the Ages.* He noted down the call number and rushed upstairs to the reading room.

A middle-aged woman with prominent cheekbones standing behind the desk looked at the slip and then studied him. "Are you an archaeologist?"

"No, I'm a reporter."

"Are you planning to visit some tombs for a story?" she said half-jokingly.

"I want to uncover some secrets."

"What secrets can you possibly find in this book?"

"A place where life has ended can still contain all kinds of secrets."

"Doesn't anyone know what they are?"

"No, because even the living have become part of the secret."

"What?"

"No one knows anyone; no one understands anyone."

The woman with high cheekbones stared at him. "Good heavens, you must be mad."

"It's not me who's mad, it's heaven."

She turned away and ignored him after that. Nearly an hour later he head the clickety-clack of the book trolley, and the book landed on the desk, raising a cloud of dust. Putting it under his arm, Fang Cheng went into the reading room and sat down at an empty desk in a corner. He leafed through the book, taking notes from time to time.

A pale square of sunlight moved slowly across the table. Fang Cheng stretched and looked at his watch. It was getting late. Before long he found himself surrounded by other readers. Strange, they were all concealing their faces behind thick books. Looking more carefully, Fang Cheng shuddered. They were all reading the same book: *A Study of Grave-Robbing Techniques Through the Ages.* He broke into a sweat, and stirred uneasily in his seat.

As he slipped out of the library he was aware of a shadowy figure following closely behind. He went into a small lane and then suddenly turned back. The man didn't have time to conceal himself and they met head-on: it was the fellow in the leather jacket he had bumped into the previous morning in Happiness Street. As soon as he emerged from the lane, Fang Cheng made a dash for a trolley bus at a nearby stop. He jumped on board, and the doors closed behind him with a squeal.

When he got off the bus he looked around anxiously and only relaxed when he felt sure he had not been followed. He thrust his hands into his overcoat pockets and did his best to regain his self-confidence and courage.

At a crossing a boy ran past flying a kite. The string in his hand was taut and the kite danced in the air. A high place, of course! Jun had disappeared while he was flying a kite. It must have been because he had seen something from a high place. What an idiot I've been, he thought, why didn't I think of that earlier? How awful, he'd almost let himself be suffocated like a rat trapped in a hole.

He bought a pair of high-power binoculars at a second-hand store and set off in the direction of Happiness Street, working his way towards his target through a maze of lanes and alleyways. Finally he saw a tall chimney towering alone in a stretch of vacant ground, surrounded on all sides by broken bricks and rubbish.

He made for the boiler-room at the foot of the chimney. A wizened old man was stoking the boiler as an airblower droned in the background. His tattered sweat-stained work clothes were held together at the waist and swung back and forth in time with his monotonous movements.

"Can I interrupt you for a minute!" Fang Cheng called out.

The old man slowly straightened himself, turned his long, skinny body and walked over to the doorway. His face was covered with coal dust and ashes.

"Who're you looking for?" he asked.

"I wonder if you could tell me where this leads to?"

"Heaven."

"No, what I mean is who's the fire for?"

"How should I know. They pay me, I do the work, that's the way it is."

"If they pay you, there must be some evidence for it."

"Ah, yes. Now where's my pay slip got to?" he said, patting himself up and down. "Must've used it to roll a cigarette."

"What was written on it?"

"Let me think . . . seems it might have run something like this: 'Burn enough to make a thousand black clouds.' Hah!" The old man grinned, baring his teeth. Against his grimy face his broken and uneven teeth seemed extremely white.

Fang Cheng took off his black woolen overcoat. "Can I trouble you to keep an eye on this for me. I'm going up to take a look."

"You don't want to leave a note for your family?"

"What?"

"You're the twelfth so far. Just yesterday a girl jumped . . ."

The old man went back to stoking the boiler. Tongues of flames shot forth.

Fang Cheng gazed up at the chimney, which seemed to lean slightly. He went to the foot of the iron ladder and started climbing. The houses grew smaller and smaller and it got so windy that his clothes flapped around him. When he reached the last rung, he steadied himself. Hooking one arm through the ladder, he turned around and began to survey the scene with his binoculars. Rooftops, date trees, courtyard walls . . . all came clearly into view. Suddenly he stiffened, and the hand holding the binoculars began shaking. He couldn't believe his eyes. Finally he managed to collect his thoughts and refocus the binoculars. He searched carefully in every corner, but didn't see even a single blade of grass.

"Oh bloody hell . . . ," he muttered to himself.

As his feet touched ground he heard someone calling out sharply behind him, "Don't move. Where do you think you're going now?" Not at all surprised, he brushed the dust off his clothes and turned around. The man in the leather jacket gave him a shove, and they walked towards a jeep parked some distance away.

Twisting his head, Fang Cheng saw the old man stoking the boiler while thick smoke continued to billow out of the tall chimney.

"Black clouds," he said.

4

Fang Cheng was sent to the lunatic asylum.

When he looked at the people running in circles around the desolate grounds and the outside all covered with weeds, he finally understood: so now he too was inside the wall.

Translated from the Chinese
by Bonnie S. McDougall

Notes on the City of the Sun

Life

It rises, like the sun.

Love

A flock of geese floats quietly
across the desolate virgin land.
An old tree crashes.
A salty rain falls in the silence.   5

Freedom

Tiny scraps of paper
drift on the wind.

Child

Inside, a picture of the ocean folds
into a snowy dove.

Girl

A rainbow gathers   10
trembling feathers from the sky.

Youth

Red waves drown
a lonely oar.

Art

In a splintered mirror blaze
a thousand suns.   15

People

Scattered into grains of shining wheat,
the moon's broadcast across
the open sky, the innocent land.

Labor

One hand encircles
the whole round earth.   20

Fate

A small boy rattles a stick along a railing.
An unlatched gate bangs in the windy night.

Faith

Legions of sheep pour from the grassy pasture
while the shepherd pipes a dismal tune on his flute.

Peace

At the emperor's tomb   25
a rusting musket sprouts a fresh green twig
to make a crutch for some crippled veteran.

Motherland

Wrought on an old bronze shield, she leans
in a dusty corner of the museum.

Life

A net.   30

Translated from the Chinese by
Donald Finkel with Chen Xueliang

Answer

The scoundrel carries his baseness around like an ID card.
The honest man bears his honor like an epitaph.
Look — the gilded sky is swimming
with undulant reflections of the dead.

They say the ice age ended years ago.   5
Why are there icicles everywhere?
The Cape of Good Hope° has already been found.
Why should all those sails contend on the Dead Sea?°

I came into this world with nothing
but paper, rope, and shadow.   10
Now I come to be judged,
and I've nothing to say but this:

Listen. *I don't believe!*
OK. You've trampled
a thousand enemies underfoot. Call me   15
a thousand and one.

I don't believe the sky is blue.
I don't believe what the thunder says.
I don't believe dreams aren't real,
that beyond death there is no reprisal.   20

If the sea should break through the sea-wall,
let its brackish water fill my heart.
If the land should rise from the sea again,
we'll choose again to live in the heights.

The earth revolves. A glittering constellation   25
pricks the vast defenseless sky.
Can you see it there? that ancient ideogram —
the eye of the future, gazing back.

Translated from the Chinese by
Donald Finkel with Chen Xueliang

the Cape of Good Hope: located at the tip of South Africa; its discovery enabled the Europeans to reach Asia by sea
the Dead Sea: a large lake located between present-day Israel and Jordon, whose water is so salty it supports no life

All

All is fated,
all cloudy,

all an endless beginning,
all a search for what vanishes,

all joys grave,   5
all griefs tearless,

every speech a repetition,
every meeting a first encounter,

all love buried in the heart,
all history prisoned in a dream,   10

all hope hedged with doubt,
all faith drowned in lamentation.

Every explosion heralds an instant of stillness,
every death reverberates forever.

Translated from the Chinese by
Donald Finkel with Chen Xueliang

SHU TING

Shu Ting (1952–) is the pen name of Gong Peiyu. Like Bei Dao, a na-
tive of Beijing who was sent to the countryside during the Cultural
Revolution, she is one of the original members of the Misty poets who
published in the underground magazine Today. *Although "Assembly*
Line" seems to despair at industrialized modern life, her poem "Also
All," written in response to Bei Dao, refuses pessimism. Unlike Bei
Dao and Gu Cheng, Shu Ting has remained in China, where she is a
member of the Chinese Writers' Association. She won the National Po-
etry Award in 1981 and 1983.

Also All

In answer to Bei Dao's "All"

Not all trees are felled by storms.
Not every seed finds barren soil.
Not all the wings of dream are broken,
nor is all affection doomed
to wither in a desolate heart.   5

No, not all is as you say.

Not all flames consume themselves,
shedding no light on other lives.
Not all stars announce the night
and never dawn. Not every song   10
will drift past every ear and heart.

No, not all is as you say.

Not every cry for help is silenced,
nor every loss beyond recall.
Not every chasm spells disaster.   15
Not only the weak will be brought to their knees,
nor every soul be trodden under.

It won't all end in tears and blood.
Today is heavy with tomorrow —
the future was planted yesterday.   20
Hope is a burden all of us shoulder
though we might stumble under the load.

Translated from the Chinese by
Donald Finkel with Yi Jinsheng

Assembly Line

In time's assembly line
Night presses against night.
We come off the factory night-shift
In line as we march towards home.
Over our heads in a row   5
The assembly line of stars
Stretches across the sky.
Beside us, little trees
Stand numb in assembly lines.

The stars must be exhausted   10
After thousands of years
Of journeys which never change.
The little trees are all sick,
Choked on smog and monotony,
Stripped of their color and shape.   15
It's not hard to feel for them;
We share the same tempo and rhythm.

Yes, I'm numb to my own existence
As if, like the trees and stars
— perhaps just out of habit   20
— perhaps just out of sorrow,
I'm unable to show concern
For my own manufactured fate.

Translated from the Chinese by
Carolyn Kizer with Y. H. Zhao.

GU CHENG

Gu Cheng (1956–1993), born in Beijing, was sent in 1969 with his fam-
ily to the countryside, which his father, the poet Gu Gong, has de-
scribed as a "cultural wasteland." Returning to Beijing in 1974, Gu
Cheng worked as a carpenter and published his first poem in 1979. He
left China for Stockholm in 1979 and in 1991 was living in New
Zealand. His suicide was reported in the Chinese press in 1993.

Gu Cheng once described Misty poetry as expression of the shared
experience, reality, and ideals of the younger generation, in contrast to
the "competitive versification of editorials" during the Cultural Revo-
lution. Gu Cheng was also an artist; his drawings often appeared in
Renditions, *the translation magazine published in Hong Kong.*

Capital "I"

I stare into the sun, at the bright dawn.
Whirling toward me like a dagger,
like a prismatic intangible vision,
like a fantastic sea, it dazzles me.
Who says metal doesn't dream?   5

Who says blood doesn't yearn?
I want to run, to cry out,
to stand gazing at this sea,
which covers half a continent.

A cold gleaming joy, a rising shimmer of heat,   10
sends me galloping across mountains
as if across a keyboard,
each step raising sudden echoes.
Bright sunflower petals fall like random notes,
the melody dispersing like some imperial family   15
at the end of a long grey corridor of space and time.
Gaping, I inhale the sun. It leaves on the sky
one pale thumbprint called the moon.

This boundless energy sends me
down the winding green yarn of a riverbank,   20
tracing a formless orbit.
The heat of my passion dissipates in the four directions,
riffling the radiant purple curtain of the sky.

Matter's dissolving now,
it's drifting toward me — not like a wave,   25
like an enormous cloud of kisses and embraces.
This buoyant joy dissolves me into a thousand
shapes and colors, molecules, sugars, acids, proteins.
In the tangled seaweed, floating like a soft appalling cloud,
swim frogs and fishes, as life turns slowly vertebrate.   30
Then , from the curves of avoidance and pursuit,
the manifold strategies of camouflage
evolve hot blood, cold blood.

Oh, I laugh at death, that ragged curtain
which will never come down on my miracle play.   35
I'm all humanity, stalking the long corridors of time,
climbing the multicolored cliffs of every continent.
Rivers carry my songs,
earthquakes scatter my bones,
rainclouds rinse my hair.   40
I'm a black boy, wearing a stolen anklet of iron.
I'm a brown girl, polishing the slim throat of an urn.
I'm a snowman, snared in a net of speculation.

No! I'm golden as a harvest,
as a ripe tangerine among green leaves.   45
I'm fresh-mown hay, a shore of exploding sand.

I'm golden. Every golden evening,
gilding the inscriptions on crude monuments,
my dreams engender history.

Perhaps, as the time approaches, I'll grow silent.   50
I'll rise again and again,
like the sun from the fathomless sea,
announcing to the world, in the voice of the spectrum,
rearranging all the characters and the words:
The East is merely a myth no longer!   55

Translated from the Chinese by
Donald Finkel with Yi Jinsheng

Parting

Now, as we cross this ancient threshold,
let's have no farewells,
no valedictions.

They seem so hollow —
silence is best.   5
Reticence is no pretense.

Let's bequeath our memory to the future,
our dreams to the night,
our tears to the sea,
and our windy sighs to its sails.   10

Translated from the Chinese by
Donald Finkel with Yi Jinsheng

A Headstrong Boy

I guess my mother spoiled me —
I'm a headstrong boy. I want every instant
to be lovely as crayons.

I'd like to draw — on chaste white paper —
a clumsy freedom, eyes that never wept,   5
a piece of sky, a feather, a leaf,
a pale green evening, and an apple.

I'd like to draw dawn, the smile dew sees,
the earliest, tenderest love — an imaginary love
who's never seen a mournful cloud,   10
whose eyes the color of sky will gaze at me
forever, and never turn away.
I'd like to draw distance, a bright horizon,
carefree, rippling rivers, hills sheathed in green furze.
I want the lovers to stand together in silence,   15
I want each breathless moment to beget a flower.

I want to draw a future I've never seen —
nor ever can — though I'm sure she'll be beautiful.
I'll draw her an autumn coat the color of candle flame,
and maple leaves, and all the hearts that ever loved her.   20
I'll draw her a wedding, an early morning garden party,
swathed in candy-wrappers decked with winter scenes.

I'm a headstrong boy. I want to paint out every sorrow,
to cover the world with colored windows,
let all the eyes accustomed to darkness   25
be accustomed to light. I want to draw wind,
mountains, each one bigger than the last.
I want to draw the dream of the East,
a fathomless sea, a joyful voice.

Finally, I'd like to draw myself in one corner —   30
a panda, huddled in a dark Victorian forest,
hunkering in the quiet branches, homeless, lost,
not even a heart left behind me, far away,
only teeming dreams of berries
and great, wide eyes.   35

This pining's pointless.
I haven't any crayons,
any breathless moments.
All I have are fingers and pain.

I think I'll tear the paper to bits   40
and let them drift away,
hunting for butterflies.

Translated from the Chinese by
Donald Finkel and Yi Jinsheng

HONG KONG AND TAIWAN

YU KWANG-CHUNG

Yu Kwang-chung (1928–) was born in Nanjing, moved with his family to Hong Kong in 1949, then entered college in Taiwan the next year. He attended the Iowa Writer's Workshop, earned an M.F.A. from the University of Iowa, and taught in the United States as a Fulbright Scholar. Conversant with both English and traditional Chinese litera-ture, Yu travels widely as lecturer and visiting poet, and has edited nu-merous journals as well as compendia of modern Chinese literature and English and American literature in Chinese translation. Yu has translated his own poems into English. Well known in Taiwan, Hong Kong, and on the mainland, Yu has been called the "doyen of modern Chinese poetry."

Yu's first poem was published in 1948. He writes on a great number of themes, revealing a sophisticated view of life and literature. The subtitle of his 1971 collection Acres of Barbed Wire, *"to China, in day-dreams and nightmares," reveals the pain of those exiled from their old homes in the mainland. "The Kowloon–Canton Railway" was for years the only link between the mainland, Hong Kong, and Taiwan.*

If There's a War Rages Afar

If there's a war rages afar, shall I stop my ear
Or shall I sit up and listen in shame?
Shall I stop my nose or breathe and breathe
The smothering smoke of a troubled air? Shall I hear
You gasp lust and love or shall I hear the howitzers°   5
Howl their sermons of truth? Mottoes, medals, widows,
Can these glut the greedy palate of Death?
If far away there's a war fries a nation,
And fleets of tanks are ploughing plots in spring,
A child is crying at its mother's corpse   10
Of a dumb and blind and deaf tomorrow;
If a nun is squatting on her fiery bier°

howitzers: cannons
fiery bier: a coffin on a stand set on fire for cremation; here refers to a form of suicide

With famished flesh singeing a despair
And black limbs ecstatic round Nirvana°
As a hopeless gesture of hope. If   15
We are in bed, and they're in the field
Sowing peace in acres of barbed wire,
Shall I feel guilty or shall I feel glad,
Glad I'm making, not war, but love,
And in my arms writhes your nakedness, not the foe's?   20
If afar there rages a war, and there we are —
You a merciful angel, clad all in white
And bent over the bed, with me in bed —
Without hand or foot or eye or without sex
In a field hospital that smells of blood.   25
If a war O such a war is raging afar,
My love, if right there we are.

Translated from the Chinese
by Yu Kwang-Chung

The Kowloon–Canton Railway

"How does it feel to be in Hong Kong?" you ask.
Holding your aerogram, I smile sadly.
Hong Kong beats with a metallic rhythm, my friend,
Of a thousand steel wheels playing on the steel tracks
To and from the border, from sunrise to sundown   5
Going north, coming south, playing the Border Blues again
      and again,
Like an umbilical cord that cannot be severed, nor crushed
      asunder
Reaching to the vast endless Northland,
The parent body so familiar yet so strange,
Mother Earth joined yet long disconnected.   10
An old cradle rocking far far away
Rocking back your memory and mine, my friend.
And like all raw nerve ends
This railway is specially sensitive,
For right now, on the platform of a small station   15
Holding your aerogram, leaning against the lamp-post
Closing my eyes, just by listening, I can tell

Nirvana: Buddhist term for the state of absolute freedom from pain and care when one
   is released from the cycle of reincarnation

The light knocking of the inbound passenger train,
The heavy hammering, heaven-and-earth shaking, outbound
    freight train,
And the stinking, engulfing, suffocating   20
Hurry, hold your breath, pig train.

Translated from the Chinese
by Stephen C. Soong

PAI HSIEN-YUNG

*Pai Hsien-yung (1937–) was born in Guilin (also spelled Kweilin) in
southwest China. The son of a famous Nationalist general, he grew up
in Taiwan and graduated from Taiwan University before coming to the
United States for the Iowa Writer's Workshop. He holds an M.F.A.
from the University of Iowa and is currently teaching Chinese at the
University of California at Santa Barbara. He has edited literary journals and published stories since 1958 and has collaborated in the
translation into English of some of his own work.*

    *Pai writes in Chinese about Chinese society, especially the society
of Nationalists in Taiwan. Well versed in traditional literature, Pai
writes in a style that is rich and supple, laden with subtle allusion and
symbolism.*

    *"Glory's by Blossom Bridge" is one of the stories first published sep-
arately, then collected in a volume ironically entitled* Taipei People —
*ironic because although the characters have lived in Taipei for nearly a
lifetime, they still regard various places on the mainland as their real
home. This story seems doubly poignant because the proprietress of
Glory's does not belong to the wealthy and once-powerful class that
people many of Pai's other stories.*

Glory's by Blossom Bridge

Talk about our Glory's by Blossom Bridge — now *there* was a shop with a
name to conjure with. Of course I'm talking about the rice-noodle shop
Grandpa owned at the head of Blossom Bridge just outside River East
Gate back in Kweilin. I tell you, there was nobody in all of Kweilin City
who didn't know about Grandpa Huang T'ien-jung° and his noodles.

T'ien-jung: the name literally means "Heaven-Glory"

Grandpa made his start in life selling horse-meat and rice-noodles. He sold them at two coppers a dish, and he was always sure to sell a hundred or more orders a day. If you got there a little late you wouldn't get to eat any, because they'd be all sold out. I can still remember Grandma with her red woolen strings threading those little copper coins, string after string, laughing so she could hardly keep her mouth closed. She used to point at me and say, "Sissy, when the time comes, you sure won't have to worry about your dowry." Even when they had parties in the grandest homes in the city, they'd sent out for our noodles. I used to go with Grandma to make the deliveries. When those swell ladies in the fancy homes saw how cute I was and how I always said the right things, they'd stuff handfuls of tips in my pockets and call me "Rice-noodle maid."

But this place called Glory's by Blossom Bridge that I run now hasn't got the old glamour. I never would have dreamed I'd end up opening a restaurant after fleeing to Taipei.° My husband wasn't a businessman in the first place; he was in the service back on the mainland. As a matter of fact, I was even a battalion commander's missus for a few years back then. Who would have expected that in the battle of Northern Kiangsu my husband would be missing in action, swept off to God knows where. In the panic that followed, we military dependents were evacuated to Taiwan. The first few years, I asked around for news of my husband wherever I went. But later on when he appeared time after time in my dreams, and always covered with blood, I knew he must have gone. Here I was, a lone woman stranded in Taipei. Had to find *some* way to make a living. I scraped together a few dollars here and there and finally had enough to open this little restaurant here on Changchun Road. Before I knew it I'd already been a "Boss-Lady" for over ten years. Why, I can tell you the name of every last person who lives along this section of the road, even with my eyes closed.

Mostly, the people who eat at my place are government workers living from hand to mouth — you know, city clerks, elementary-school teachers, district staff workers, what have you — every one of them with their pockets as flat as dried-out bedbugs. They order a little bit of this and a little bit of that — never anything fancy, just plain run-of-the-mill fare. You have to work harder than an old ox turning a millstone to squeeze any extra fat out of a bunch like that. But I have to say it's been these poor old customers of mine who've supported me all these years; without them, my restaurant would have folded a long time ago.

Quite a few of my customers are from Kwangsi, my home province; it's the taste of real down-home cooking keeps them coming back to my place year after year. I've got a group of them on monthly meal tickets, and every last one of that crew is a good old Kwangsi boy. Whenever we got to chewing the fat, seems like it always turns out we're kinfolk, one

---

Taipei (also spelled Taibei): the capital city of Taiwan

way or another. These old live-alones, some of them have taken their meals at my place three to five years at a stretch; a few made it for as long as seven or eight years and swallowed their last mouthful right here. Like old man Li. He was big in the lumber business way back when in Liuchou. Everybody called him "Half-the-Town Li"; talk was he owned half the houses in town. His son runs a general store down in Taichung; he just took and dumped the old fellow in Taipei, leaving him all by himself and sending him a check every six months. He ate at my place for eight long years — must have broken two dozen of my rice bowls. Had the palsy, and his hands would shake every time he picked up a bowl. The old bird loved to sing the opera *Retribution by Thunderbolt*. The minute he started singing, his nose began to run and two streams of tears flowed down his face. And then one night he ordered himself a whole big spread, cleaned it all up, said it was a grand occasion, his seventieth birthday. Who would have guessed he'd hang himself the next day! We all ran over to see. There he was, the old fellow, hanging from a big old withered tree, his grayed cotton shoes fallen to the ground and his black felt hat rolled away off to one side. As for the food money he still owed me, I tried asking his son for it, but all I got out of that gallows-bird was a big helping of mean back-talk.

We people in the restaurant business can't afford to carry a bunch of free-loaders. After all, we're in it to make a living, not run a poorhouse. It's just my luck that I should have let Crazy Chin eat at my place for over half a year without paying a single cent. He'd been doing fine at his job with the city, and then he had to go and try to get fresh with a female employee and got himself sacked. That's when he went crazy — woman-crazy if you ask me. He said he used to be a magistrate in Junghsien back in Kwangsi; even had two concubines! One day he was a little too free with his hands with a lady customer in my restaurant, and I had to show him the door. Well, then he marched along the street, head cocked to one side and eyes all askew, waving his arms wildly in the air, foaming at the mouth and yellowing, "Clear the road! Clear the road! His Honor the Magistrate is coming!" Another time he went to the market and felt up a vegetable hawker's neenies. She grabbed her basket pole and hit him one right on the head, cracked it open just like a melon. Last August when we had that big typhoon, this area around Changchun Road was completely flooded. Even the tables and chairs in my place floated away. When the water finally went down, heaps of dead chickens and cats came popping out of the ditch along the street, some so cruddy they were covered with maggots, and with the sun beating down on them the whole street stank to high heaven. When the Board of Health came by to decontaminate the area, they drained the ditch and fished up Crazy Chin. He was covered from head to toe in a coat of mud and stiff as a board. Looked like a big tortoise on its back with all four legs in the air. Nobody knew when he had fallen in.

To tell the truth — and I'm not just sticking up for us folks from Kweilin — in a place like our Kweilin, with its heavenly scenery, you'd expect the people to be a bit extraordinary, too. You look at people from little holes like Junghsien and Wuning, those bucktoothed clods with their jawbreaking native jabber — if you ask me, they've all got a wild Miao° tribesman in their family tree somewhere, how could the likes of them compare with us Kweilin folk? You take any of us, man or woman, some of the natural beauty of our mountains and waters is sure to have rubbed off on us. I used to tell that crew of bachelors that came in here: Don't you sell your fairy godmother short. In my day back in Kweilin I was the belle of River East Gate, I'll have you know! When I worked for Grandpa, the soldiers from Headquarters would gather round the door of our noodle shop like flies after blood, you couldn't shoo them away. That was how my husband and me got together. And it was no wonder. Back home there were green hills everywhere — your eyes'll grow brighter just looking at them — and blue waters — you wash in them and your complexion turns smooth and fair. Those days I never dreamed I'd ever live in a dump like Taipei — a typhoon one year, an earthquake the next. It doesn't matter what kind of beauty you are, this weather is enough to ruin *anybody's* looks.

Of all my customers, Mr. Lu was the only one from my home town, Kweilin. You didn't even have to ask; you knew it the minute you saw him. He was polite, thoughtful, an educated gentleman; taught Chinese at the Changchun Elementary School for years. As I remember, he must have been thirty-five or so when he first started eating at my place. He had such refined manners, always quiet and unassuming. Every time he came in for a meal he'd just sit down, bend over his bowl, and mind his own business. When I'd go over to his table to serve him another helping of rice or something, he'd always get up a bit from his seat and say to me with a gentle smile, "Thank you very much, Boss-Lady."

Mr. Lu was a thin fellow, kind of tall, and a little stooped. Had a pale face and a nose straight as a scallion. He looked old for his age, and a bit run-down. His hair had turned gray early, and whenever he smiled you could spot a whole bunch of crow's feet at the corners of his eyes, but underneath it all you could still see the outlines of what must have been a handsome face at one time. I often bumped into him on the street. He'd always have a long string of school kinds hopping and skipping along after him. Every time they crossed the street, he'd stand in the middle of the intersection and spread out his arms to stop the traffic, shouting "Careful, now! Careful!" until the little ones were all safely on the other side. I don't know why, but whenever I saw the patient way he had with his pupils, it always made me think of a gentle rooster I used to have. Why, that rooster would actually mother those chicks. Many a time I saw

Miao: one of the largest ethnic minorities in southern China

him spread his wings way out and shelter a whole flock of them underneath.

It was only after I started chewing the fat with him that I discovered his grandfather was none other than Old Mr. Lu, the well-known philanthropist in Kweilin, Lu Hsing-chang. Old Mr. Lu had been a high official in Hunan Province, an Inspector General. He was the one who set up the Foster Virtue Middle School just outside River East Gate. Old Mrs. Lu used to be very fond of Glory's rice-noodles in thick soup, and I had even been to the Lu residence with Grandma to deliver his orders.

"Mr. Lu," I said to him, "I used to go over to your home in the old days. That was some grand mansion you had there!"

He smiled a bit; after a while he answered, "When we retreated from the mainland our own troops put the torch to it. Burned it down to the ground."

"What a shame!" I sighed. I could still remember that garden of theirs, all red and white with peonies.

Now I ask you, can anybody blame me for playing favorites with a gentleman like Mr. Lu? Think what a good family he came from, and fallen on evil times, too, just like all of us here. You could tell he was a man of real culture, the way he went about his own business and never said anything that would cause the least trouble. He wasn't at all like some of those Miao types from Kwangsi who came in here smashing bowls and breaking chopsticks, yelling and hollering, always bitching about something or other like sand in their rice or flies in their food. I couldn't help getting mad at them. In times like these we're lucky to be alive. But instead of making the best of things they had to be picky about the food. I didn't care what they thought or how envious they were, I always put something extra in Mr. Lu's order — beef, I'd give him the shank cut; pork, all lean meat. At least once a week I'd go into the kitchen and make him a piping-hot bowl of noodles with my own hands: braised beef liver and hundred-leaf tripe, sprinkled with parsley and sesame oil, and topped off with a handful of deep-fried peanuts. I'd serve it to him steaming hot. I'll bet you couldn't find another restaurant in all of Taipei where you could get a meal like that — and don't talk to me about your extra-fine Yunnan noodles either! Well, I gave Mr. Lu that dish as a special treat. To tell the truth, the reason I was trying so hard to get in good with him was on account of Hsiu-hua.

Hsiu-hua was my husband's niece. She was married to a soldier, too, a platoon leader. He was lost in the fighting on the mainland, the way my husband was, but in all this time she hadn't given up hope. She waited and waited; got herself a job in a plant here, weaving hemp sacks. She worked so hard her hands were all calluses, but still she was one of our Kweilin girls, neat, fresh-faced, very decent-looking. Well, I finally got hold of her and tried to make her see the light.

"Hsiu-hua, dear child," I said, "you and Ah Wei loved each other very much. I can understand your wanting to wait for him for the rest of your life; that's a beautiful thing. But take me, your aunt, for an example. Don't you think your uncle and I felt the same way about each other? Yes, I waited, too. Waited till I am what you see today. I'm not complaining, but if I'd known I was going to end up like this, I'd have done things a good deal differently ten or more years ago. Let' suppose your Ah Wei *is* alive. You still can't be sure you'll ever see him again. And what if he's already gone? Then, my dear, I'm afraid all your suffering will have been for nothing."

In the end my words must have found some echo in Hsiu-hua's heart; she covered her face and broke down and cried. If it were anyone else, I'd have thought about it a bit before butting in. But Hsiu-hua and Mr. Lu were both from Kweilin. If I could get them together, it would be a wonderful match. As for Mr. Lu, I even found out how he was situated in a financial way. You see, Mrs. Ku, his landlady, was a mah-jong° crony of mine. That old Hupei bag had a tongue as sharp as a knife; when *she* started jawing about anyone he'd be lucky to escape with his skin! Still, she always stuck up for Mr. Lu, said she'd never in all her born days seen such a well-behaved man. He didn't eat much, didn't spend much, and except for playing his *Hu-ch'in*° and singing a little opera, he didn't have any vices at all. You could always find half a dozen or so school kids at his place at night. He raised chickens with the money he earned from this extra tutoring.

"And those chickens! Why, they're like Mr. Lu's great-grandpa and great-grandma, that's how well he takes care of them!" says Mrs. Ku, laughing. "You've never seen anything like it — the way he tends those chickens! Such patience!"

Every New Year's Mr. Lu would bring two big basketfuls of his black-and-whites to sell in the market. Every last one of the birds had a bright red comb and shiny white feathers. They must have weighed a good seven or eight pounds each. One time, I bought a couple of them myself; cut a big bowl of chicken fat just off the rumps alone. The way Mrs. Ku had it totaled up, counting all the compound interest on his small loans and betting-pool money over the years, Mr. Lu had at least forty or fifty thousand Taiwan dollars stashed away; he could easily afford to take himself a wife.

And so, one New Year's Eve I invited Mr. Lu and Hsiu-hua to come over. I cooked a whole tableful of Kweilin dishes and heated up a steaming pot of Shaohsing wine. I tried my darndest, with a little tug here and a little push there, to get the two of them together. Hsiu-hua did seem interested and kept smiling coyly, but Mr. Lu, big grown man that he was,

---

mah-jong: a game using tiles that resemble dominoes, usually played by four persons, with rules like those for bridge and gin-rummy
Hu-ch'in: a two-stringed fiddle without a bridge

started acting shy. When I egged him on to drink a toast with Hsiu-hua, he actually blushed.

I collared him on the street the next day and asked, "Well, Mr. Lu, what do you think of our Hsiu-hua?" He was so flustered he couldn't say a thing. I gave him the eye and smiled.

"Our Hsiu-hua's been saying such nice things about you."

"Please don't kid me — " he stammered.

"Who's kidding?" I cut him short. "You'd better give me a treat right away, and I'll be your go-between. Why, I can taste the wine at your wedding feast already!"

"Boss-Lady." All of a sudden Mr. Lu pulled a long face and said to me seriously, "No more of this joking, please. I was engaged back on the mainland a long time ago."

He gave me the back of his head and walked off. That made me so mad I shook all over and couldn't say a word for hours. Well! Find me another miserable man like that under the sun! So he thought he was going to eat my hot noodle soup, did he! So who else wasn't paying me three hundred and fifty a month for meals? From now on, just like everybody else — it's fat pork for you, Mister Lu! After that, several times, he tried to strike up a conversation with me, but I gave him the cold shoulder. Not until Hsiu-hua was married, and to a solid businessman at that, did I let some of my anger at Mr. Lu blow away. After all, he was still one of us Kweilin folks. If he'd been from any other place . . . !

One mid-September day, when the heat of early autumn came in fierce as a tiger I was at the restaurant all day and dripping with sweat. By five or six in the afternoon I simply couldn't take it any longer, I turned things over to my cook, grabbed my rushleaf fan and went down to that little park at the end of the street to get some fresh air. There were some stone benches under the big elm tree where you could sit and cool off. I caught sight of Mr. Lu in a T-shirt and a pair of wooden clogs, sitting there by himself. His head was bowed; he was completely wrapped up in his *Hu-ch'in*. I listened to it. Why! He was playing one of our Kweilin operas! It made me tingle all over. Back in the old days in Kweilin I used to be a great opera fan; when stars like Little Gold Phoenix and Seven-Year-Old Prodigy sang, I'd go to the theater every day.

I went right up to him and said, "My, Mister Lu, so you know Kweilin opera!"

He stood up in a hurry and greeted me. "Oh, not really, I just play and sing to myself for the fun of it."

"Wouldn't it be wonderful if I could hear Little Gold Phoenix sing again someday."

"She used to be my most favorite opera singer, too," said Mr. Lu.

"Oh yes! When she sang 'Homecoming to the Cave' it was enough to wring your heart!"

I had to coax him quite a while before I got him to tune up his instrument and sing a passage from "Hsueh Ping-kuei's Homecoming to the Cave." I had never dreamed Mr. Lu could sing a female role, but his voice was pleasant and clear. In fact, his style rather reminded me of Little Gold Phoenix. *"Eighteen long years have taken their toll on Lady Precious Bracelet"* — my heart gave a little twinge when I heard those words.

Mr. Lu stopped playing. "You see?" I said to him with a sigh. "That young wife Precious Bracelet waited eighteen long years, she waited for Hsueh Ping-kuei and got him back after all — " He just smiled and didn't say anything.

"Mr. Lu," I asked him, "what family is your fiancée from?"

"She's one of the Los. Lo Chin-shan is her father."

"Oh, she's one of the Lo girls." I told Mr. Lu about how I often used to go to the Lo store, the Woven Jade Pavilion, to buy silks and satins. Back then in Kweilin their family was making money hand over fist. He listened to me in silence. After a long time he started to talk, thoughtfully and in a low voice.

"She and I grew up together, from the time we were little. We were schoolmates at Foster Virtue." He smiled and clusters of wrinkles appeared at the corners of his eyes. As he spoke, he lowered his head, picked up his bow and absentmindedly played snatches of whatever came to mind. The sun began to set and darkened to a dull red. A breeze blew up. It was warm against the body and blew hard enough to ruffle Mr. Lu's gray hair. I leaned back against the stone bench and closed my eyes, listening to the plaintive note of his bow as it went gently back and forth across the strings. My eyes grew heavy and I dozed off. One moment I saw Little Gold Phoenix and Seven-Year-Old Prodigy on stage in "Homecoming"; the next moment Hsueh Ping-kuei turned into my husband and came galloping toward me on his horse.

"Boss Lady — " I opened my eyes and saw that Mr. Lu had put away his violin and was getting ready to leave. The sky was already filled with stars.

There came a time when Mr. Lu suddenly seemed on top of the world, a rosy glow spread all over his sallow face. Mrs. Ku told me he was actually fixing up his room; he'd even bought a brand new quilt with a red silk cover.°

One day in my place I noticed him sitting alone grinning to himself. "Happy news, Mr. Lu?" I asked. He blushed right away. Then he groped around in his pockets until he finally fished out an envelope of coarse paper, yellowed, but carefully folded.

red silk cover: a quilt with a red silk cover is generally used on the wedding night

"It's a letter from her . . ." he said softly, swallowing hard. He was so choked up he could hardly get the words out. He told me a cousin of his in Hong Kong had finally managed to get in touch with his fiancée She'd already made it to Canton.

"It will take ten gold bars. Comes to exactly fifty-five thousand Taiwan dollars. If this had happened a little while back, I'd never have been able to scrape together that much, but . . ." He blurted out his good news in gasps, pausing for breath in between, and it wasn't until he'd gone on for some time that I figured out he was paying some big operator in Hong Kong to smuggle his fiancée out of the mainland. The going rate was ten gold bars a head. The way he clutched that letter in both hands while he was talking, you'd think it was his very own life he was holding on to.

Mr. Lu waited for a month. The waiting made him so fidgety that just by looking at him I could tell that though his body was still here his soul had flown off someplace else. One day he came in for his meal as usual, took a mouthful, got up again, and walked right out. His face was ashen and his eyes were bloodshot. I ran out and stopped him on the street.

"Is there anything wrong, Mr. Lu?"

His mouth kept opening as though he was about to say something, but he couldn't get it out. And then all of a sudden he shouted with a sob in his voice:

"He's not even human!" He went on talking, and the more he spoke the faster he went, pointing and waving his arms, and out came a whole heap of words. What he said was to garbled you'd have thought he was talking with a mouthful of marbles, but I did manage to make out that he'd sent the money to a cousin of his in Hong Kong; the guy simply pocketed the cash, and when Mr. Lu got someone to look him up the cousin pretended he didn't know a thing about it.

After he'd caught his breath, he mumbled with a bitter laugh, "I'd been saving that money for *fifteen years* — " He nodded his head up and down, up and down, his gray hair sticking our every which way. Somehow or other I was reminded of those black-and-whites he used to raise. Every year at New Year's time he'd be standing in the market holding a rooster with a bright red comb and black and white speckled feathers. How fat he used to get every single one of those birds he fed.

For half a year or so he lost all interest in food and drink. He was a quiet man to begin with, but now you couldn't get a word out of him. When I saw how thin and drawn his face had gotten — it was no bigger than the palm of my hand — I went back to my old habit of feeding him my best piping-hot noodles. I never imagined he'd ever lose his appetite for those noodles of mine, but he did; time after time he'd leave half his bowl untouched. Once he didn't show up for two weeks in a row, and I thought he'd taken sick. I'd just about made up my mind to go pay him a visit when I ran into his landlady Mrs. Ku in the market. As soon as that old Hupei bag set eyes on me she grabbed me by the shoulder, walking beside me, cackling as she went, swearing and spitting.

"These men!" she said.

"My dear Mrs. Ku, what news have you got this time?" My shoulder still hurt where she'd grabbed it. The old snoop, if any married woman in the neighborhood slept with another man, she'd talk about it as though she was keeping watch under her bed.

"What can I say?" She spat hard again. "To think even a man like Mr. Lu would be messing around like that. You'll never guess who he's shacked up with — Spring Maid! The washerwoman."

"Mercy!" I couldn't help letting out a yell.

That female had a pair of boobs on her would be bouncing off your face before she was close enough for you to make out who it was behind them. She wasn't much over twenty and already that rump of hers was puffed out like a drum. When she was scrubbing clothes, there wasn't a single part of her body that didn't jiggle; those big melons of hers would be going up and down like a pair of mallet-heads. Whenever she laid eyes on a man, she'd give him the old come-on smile and bedroom eyes. The thing I remember most about her was that day in the market when a young vegetable hawker did something or other to cross her. Before you knew it, those giant knockers of hers were already rammed into that poor man, all he could do was stumble backwards several steps while she sprayed a volley of spit over him and exploded "Fuck your mother's _____!" What a spitfire! What a tramp!

"Whenever Spring Maid delivered Mr. Lu his laundry in no time flat she'd be worming her way into his room," Mrs. Ku continued. "I knew right off that Taiwanese trollop was up to no good. And then one afternoon when I was passing by Mr. Lu's window I heard all kinds of groaning and moaning. I thought he'd had some kind of accident, so I stood on tiptoe and peeked inside between his curtains. Pew!" Mrs. Ku spat on the ground as hard as she could. "There they were, the pair of them, stark naked in broad daylight! That damn piece was riding on top of Mr. Lu, her hair flying all over the place, she looked just like a lioness. To run into a thing like this, now you tell me, Boss-Lady, isn't that just my luck!"

"Well! No wonder you've been hitting Thirteen Odds at mah-jong all the time these days. You sure stumbled onto a rarity!" I couldn't help laughing; that old nine-headed Hupei bird,° all she did was pry into other people's secrets.

"Aw, you're full of bull!"

"Well," I sighed, "I guess Mr. Lu's got a good thing going there. From

---

nine-headed Hupei bird: a derogatory nickname; such nicknames are often used by people from one province for those from another

now on at least he won't have to worry about finding somebody to do his laundry."

"But that's just the funny part about it!" Mrs. Ku clapped her hands. "Her wait on him? Not on your life! It's Mr. Lu who serves her and treats her like a living treasure. Miss High-and-mighty doesn't even wash clothes any more. Just sits around all day long, her fingernails painted bright red, and listens to Taiwanese opera on the radio. And you'd think Mr. Lu was some old horse or ox, the way he works himself. He's bought a stove so he can cook for her. But the thing that really ticks me off is that now Mr. Lu even washes his own sheets. You can imagine how clean he gets them! When I see them drying out there in the courtyard with all the dirty spots on them, it's enough to make me throw up."

The next day I ran into Mr. Lu and Spring Maid on the street. They were coming right at me, with the woman in the lead. She had her head stuck way up in the air and that big bust of hers sticking out. She was wearing real flashy clothes, had a big splash of bright red rouge on each cheek — even her toenails were painted. She went strutting down the street in full sail, her wooden clogs pounding clippety-clop. Mr. Lu followed along behind her, carrying a shopping basket. When he got close to me I did a double-take. At first I thought he was wearing a black hat, but now I saw he'd dyed his hair jet black. Hadn't done a good job, either; it was coarse and stuck out from his head like wires. His face was so chalky white he must have had cold cream on; his eyes were sunken, the sockets so dark his face was nothing but two black caves in a spooky ground of white. I don't know why, but suddenly I thought of an old actor named White Jade from the days when I used to go to the opera in Kweilin, a man well over fifty who kept on singing young romantic leads. Once I saw him in a piece from *The Dream of the Red Chamber*° called "Pao Yu Wails by Black Jade's Coffin." I was sitting in the front row. He'd absolutely caked himself in white powder for the role, but when he came to the wailing part every wrinkle on his aged face showed through; when he opened his mouth to sing, all you saw was a mouthful of black tobacco-stained teeth. Just to look at him made me feel sick at heart; imagine that part of the young and handsome Pao Yu being played like that! Mr. Lu brushed past me; he turned his head the other way, pretending not to know me, and just walked away behind that Taiwanese wench.

All up and down Changchun Road everybody knew about the incident between Mr. Lu and Spring Maid. I'm talking about the time Mr. Lu got beaten up by Spring Maid and badly hurt. What happened was, she was balling a man in Mr. Lu's room — that young stud from down the street, you know, Little Horse, the shoeshine boy. Mr. Lu ran home so's to catch them in the act. Little Horse flattened Mr. Lu with one kick and took off.

The Dream of the Red Chamber: an opera based on what many consider to be China's greatest novel

Mr. Lu struggled to his feet and slapped Spring Maid's face a couple of times.

"And that's how he brought the whole disaster down on himself!" Mrs. Ku told me the same day. "Could you imagine a more cruel and vicious female in this world? Did you ever see such a thing in your life! She lit into Mr. Lu like a hurricane, climbed all over him, tearing and clawing. And then, with one bite she bit half his ear off! If it hadn't been for me running out into the street and screaming for help, that bitch would have finished Mr. Lu off right then and there!"

Mrs. Ku went on complaining about what bad luck it was to have such an ugly thing happen in her house. She said if she'd had her way she'd have thrown Mr. Lu out that very day. But he'd taken such a beating he just lay there on his bed and couldn't move. When his wound healed, he started boarding at my restaurant again. There was nothing left of him but skin and bones. He still had some bruises on his neck, and his left earlobe was gone; there was a piece of white adhesive on the wound. He'd stopped dyeing his hair, but he hadn't washed out all the old dye; the new hair growing out of his temples was white as could be, but the hair on top of his head was still black, like a pot-cover in; you wouldn't believe how funny it looked. As soon as he came in, all those old Kwangsi duffers who boarded at my place winked at each other and smiled.

One day when I was standing at the bus stop by the Changchun Elementary School, I happened to see Mr. Lu. He was leading a group of kids just out of school; they were all jabbering and horsing around when Mr. Lu suddenly turned and shouted at them.

"Stop fooling around!"

You could tell he was mad as hell; his face turned absolutely purple, his neck was all red, and the veins in his forehead seemed about ready to burst. The kids got really scared and settled down right away, all except one little girl who broke out giggling. Mr. Lu bounded over, stuck a finger in her face, and barked, "How dare you laugh? How dare you laugh at me?"

That made the little moppet shake her pigtails back and forth and laugh even harder. Mr. Lu slapped her face so hard she lost her footing and ended up sitting on the ground. "Wa — " She opened her mouth as wide as she could and started bawling. Mr. Lu hopped up and down screeching at the top of his voice. He pointed down at her.

"You little devil, you've got the gall to push me around, too? I'll beat you, I'll beat you, I'll beat the living daylights out of you, so help me!" and he reached out to grab her by the pigtails.

The other kids were so scared they started crying and yelling for help. People on the street began to crowd around, some of them trying to comfort the kids; then two male teachers from Changchun Elementary grabbed him and hauled him off. His arms waving wildly as he went, Mr. Lu was foaming at the mouth and screeching, "I'll kill her! I'll kill her!"

That was the last time I saw him. He died the next day. When Mrs. Ku went into his room, she found him slumped over his desk. At first she thought he'd fallen asleep; his head was resting on the desk; his fingers were still gripping his writing brush; a stack of composition books was piled up next to his head. Mrs. Ku said the coroner had examined his body for hours without being able to find anything wrong. Finally he filled in the blank under *Cause of Death:* "Heart failure."

Mrs. Ku warned me never to let on to anyone who might come around looking for a room that Mr. Lu had died at her place. She paid some Buddhist and Taoist monks to come over and chant the scriptures so's to help Mr. Lu's soul along on its journey to the next world. I bought some candles and paper money myself and burned them outside the front door of my restaurant. After all, Mr. Lu must have taken his meals at my place for five or six years all told. For that matter, when old man Li and Crazy Chin died, I'd burned quite a bit of spirit money for them to use in the next world, too.

I got out Mr. Lu's bill and totaled it up; he still owed me two hundred and fifty dollars. First I went to the police station and obtained a permit, then I came over to Mrs. Ku's to try to get some of Mr. Lu's belongings so I could sell them and get my money back. A woman like myself in a small business just doesn't have any spare cash — I can't afford bad debts. Mrs. Ku greeted me with a broad smile, probably thought I'd come to ask her to a mah-jong game. When she found out what I was there for, she sneered:

"Think there's anything left for you? Where'd you expect I'd go to recover my back rent?"

She shoved his room key into my hand and stomped back to her kitchen. I went to his room; sure enough, it was empty. There were a few old books stacked on his desk, and a raggedy old writing-brush still stood in its holder. That old Hupei bag must have taken everything that was worth anything and stashed it away somewhere. I opened the closet and found a couple of white shirts with grayed collars hanging inside; in one corner of the closet were a few pairs of yellowed panties. When I gave the room another once-over, I noticed that *Hu-ch'in* of his hanging on the wall, all covered with dust. There were a few photographs hanging next to it. What was this? Wasn't that bridge in the large framed photograph in the middle Blossom Bridge? Our own Blossom Bridge, just outside River East Gate, back in Kweilin? I grabbed a chair and climbed up in a hurry and took the picture down. I carried it over to the window and wiped off the glass with the corner of my jacket, held it to the light, squinted my eyes and took a good look. Oh, yes, there it was, our Blossom Bridge, with the River Li flowing underneath, and there were the two stone pillars with carved dragons on them at the head of the bridge. Two youngsters were standing next to the pillars, a boy and a girl. The boy was Mr. Lu, and the girl must be the Miss Lo he was engaged to. Mr. Lu was in student uniform and duck-billed cap, looking very handsome and clean-cut. I took another look at that girl and couldn't help a silent "Bravo!" Now *there* was a Kweilin girl for you! Her whole body had the grace of the flowing waters of the river, and her eyes, bright and innocent, had the classic upward tilt. Just to look at her was enough to melt your heart. The two of them were standing close together, shoulders touching, leaning against each other, smiling happily. They couldn't have been more than eighteen or so at the time.

No matter how hard I tried I couldn't scare up a thing worth any money in Mr. Lu's room, so I took the photograph. I planned to hang it in my restaurant. Someday if anybody from Kwangsi comes along I'll point to it and tell them that's the Glory Noodle Shop by Blossom Bridge my Grandpa used to run back in Kweilin — right there at the crossroads by the head of the bridge, on the bank of the River Li.

Translated from the Chinese
by William A. Lyell

YANG MU

Yang Mu (1940–) is the pen name that Wang Ching-hsien adopted in 1972, confounding all his friends who had known his work under his previous pen name, Yeh Shan. Born in Hualien in central Taiwan to a family that had lived there for several generations, Yang graduated from Tunghai University, then earned a Ph.D. in comparative literature at the University of California, Berkeley. He is currently a professor of Chinese and comparative literature at the University of Washington, Seattle. He publishes essays and criticism in English under his original name, and poetry in Chinese under the pen name.

Yang Mu's poetry displays his intimate knowledge of traditional Chinese literature. His style combines the compression and suggestiveness of traditional Chinese poetry with contemporary topics, images, and original metaphors. The title "Nine Arguments" alludes to the Songs of Ch'u attributed to the poet Ch'ü Yüan (340?–278 B.C.), but includes references to the flora of the Pacific Northwest (Douglas Fir) and to the tradition of English literature (Decadent School). "Songs to the Tune 'Partridge Skies'" are written in tz'u song patterns dating to the Sung dynasty (906–1279 A.D.). The references to myth and dream carry the poem beyond the images of lotuses and loquats. The association of wine drinking and solitude in "Loneliness" is reminiscent of a poem in which the Tang poet Li Po (701–762) drinks with only the moon and his shadow as companions.

Six Songs to the Tune "Partridge Skies"

1. Douglas Fir

The lawn is not really very damp
Stars fill the small pool
And we have not yet lost our way
As if the flower's fragrance rose not from the ground
But delicately   5
From your shoulders —

Where my two hands interlace
A cloud moves into the evening
Warm air seeps over
The gloomy firs   10

2. Sleeves

We begin to drink
When the dark night is full upon us
Our four sleeves cuddle together for warmth:
We are hesitating catalpa trees

Starting to complain of the noise and silence   15
Of wind-blown snow. In the winter we are always listening
To the same record, I forget the title
The withered branches lift up
A chilling dream past the window
"I know about love"   20
(We begin to drink)
"And I am always waiting for it to come"

3. Swan

Like a boat adrift in the middle of a windless lake
We float on this white cloud between the gunwales
No wind, but with your light breathing   25
We rock like a boat adrift in the middle of a windless lake

The ages have slipped by, ages of
Love — the bottom of the boat is covered
With moss and barnacles
In the middle of that windless lake   30
You have not yet lost your bloom
You are still delicate and pink
Like a swan in the sunset

4. My Loving Vine

Letting down your hair, taking off your clothes
You face the ruins abloom with chrysanthemums   35
And I gaze up at the host of gods
Joyfully perishing
Swirling, intertwining
Becoming my satellite
My loving vine   40

Then you understood
How desolate and distant
I was and how light and spare
You were
My loving vine   45

5. Chrysanthemums

You should have understood then
That love is in the aroma of mint and
Ripe persimmons mixed with
Books of poetry. There was
No need for you   50
To turn your back and say we should wait

You might as well shed your silk garments
Leaving on your necklace and earrings
When the sound of tires rolling through the flooded alley
Becomes distant and faint   55
When the grandfather clock shakes our
Time, and the chrysanthemums fall on the pillow
Petals spreading out across the bed
You might as well do the same

6. Riverbank

Speading out like that is so nice   60
Lute music drifting in
Your eyes are the lamps of the
Decadent School, your hair the grassy plains
Where crusaders stay the night

Scattered clouds surround your limbs   65
Stars rise to shine on your forehead
The moon slides into the river
Below your belly is a blossom spreading
The sound of rain falling off the eaves

And its image, fluttering veins 70
And scattered skeletons

And an even warmer riverbank
Watches us sit anxiously
Clinging to each other

Translated from the Chinese
by Joseph Roe Allen

From "Nine Arguments"

2. Meandering

In spring I go meandering through
The forest of low cooing doves
Seeking the promised
Grasslands with their many lakes, many fish
And many breezes, the reproductive dreams 5
The many myths. I am seeking

The wind in my embrace
Soft as the South in all its sorrow
In its brief moment in history
Quivering by the water's edge, the lotus 10

In summer, the summer
Lingers, matures, and grows full-bodied
In the garden of my making. She wears the clothes
Of orange blossoms easily shed, slippers
Of cherries, and on her head 15
A loquat hat wide-brimmed against the sun
Knowing this, I prepare
For her a bed of laken green
A pillow of snowy carp, and bedding lightly
Woven out of evening stars 20
I know I have kept her here
Dreams are the conversation of doves
Wind, the posture of lakes
And fish, the source of myths
At the water's edge the lotus quivers 25
Green and blue are its reflections

Translated from the Chinese
by Joseph Roe Allen

Loneliness

Loneliness is an elderly beast
Hiding among the rocks in my mind,
His back, a chameleon design,
I know, protectively colors his race.
Dreary are his eyes, forever after   5
The floating clouds far away,
Longing, too, to stretch and wander
In the sky;
Contemplating, he lowers his head,
Lets the storm freely lash   10
The missing violence of his shed skins,
The petrified passion given him with time.

Loneliness is an elderly beast
Hiding among the rocks in my mind;
At thunder strike, he moves slowly,   15
Clumsily walks into my wine glass;
His infatuated eyes
Sadly gaze at an evening drinker,
This time, I know, he regrets
His rash departure from familiar storms   20
For the chill of this wine.
My glass at my lips,
I kindly accept him.

Translated from the Chinese
by Dominic Cheung

LO CH'ING

Lo Ch'ing is the pen name used by Lo Ch'ing-che (1948–). Only age three when his family moved from the mainland, Lo makes his home in Taiwan, where he is known for his painting as well as poetry. After graduating from Fu-Jen University of Taiwan, Lo earned an M.A. in comparative literature at the University of Washington in Seattle, where he was studying when his first collection, Ways of Eating a Watermelon *(1972), won a national prize in Taiwan. Lo has subsequently published many more volumes of poems and has exhibited his paintings in galleries in Tokyo, Honolulu, Brussels, and various cities in Taiwan.*

Lo's poetry is often playful, but underneath the playfulness is a serious search for meaning. Like the followers of Taoism and Zen alluded to in his poem, Lo strips away layers of philosophizing and reasoning to reach for the truth with a childlike mind. "Protest Posters" illustrates a different aspect of his work: it is dedicated to the activists who were jailed for posting demands for democracy in Beijing in 1978.

Six Ways of Eating Watermelons

The 5th Way: The Consanguinity of Watermelons

No one would mistake a watermelon for a meteorite.
Star and melon, they are totally unconnected;
But earth is undeniably a heavenly body,
Watermelons and stars
Are undeniably consanguineous.   5

Not only are watermelons and the earth related
Like parent and child,
They also possess brotherly, sisterly feelings,
Like the moon and the sun,
The sun and us,   10
Us and the moon.

The 4th Way: The Origins of Watermelons

Evidently, we live on the face of the earth;
And they, evidently, live in their watermelon interior.
We rush to and fro, thick-skinned,
Trying to stay outside, digesting light   15
Into darkness with which to wrap ourselves,
Cold and craving warmth.

They meditate on Zen,° motionless, concentrated.
Shaping inward darkness into
Substantial, calm passions;   20
Forever seeking self-fulfillment and growth.
Someday, inevitably, we'll be pushed to the earth's interior,
And eventually they'll burst through the watermelon face.

Zen: a sect of Buddhism that seeks enlightenment through meditation and intuition rather than through study of scriptures

The 3rd Way: The Philosophy of Watermelons

The history of watermelon philosophy
Is shorter than the earth's, but longer than ours;   25
They practice the Three Don'ts:
See no evil, hear no evil, speak no evil.
They are Taoistically *wu-wei*,°
And keep themselves to themselves.

They don't envy ova,   30
Nor do they despise chicken's eggs.
Watermelons are neither oviparous, nor viviparous,
And comprehend the principle
Of attaining life through death.
Consequently, watermelons are not threatened by invasion,   35
Nor do they fear
Death.

The 2nd Way: The Territory of Watermelons

If we crushed a watermelon,
It would be sheer
    jealousy.   40
Crushing a melon is equivalent to crushing a rounded night,
Knocking down all the
    stars,
Crumbling a perfect
    universe.   45

And the outcome would only make us more jealous,
Would only clarify the relationship
Between meteorites and watermelon seeds,
The friendship between watermelon seeds and the universe.
They would only penetrate once again, more deeply,   50
    into our
    territory

The 1st Way:

E AT IT FIR S T.

Translated from the Chinese
by Dominic Cheung

wu-wei: the Taoist idea that by not striving for anything one can achieve everything

Protest Posters

For Wei Ching-sheng and his companions

They issue the rules continuously:
Nail the white clouds onto the wide blue sky
Paint the frozen rivers onto the parched earth

But stealthily we
Stick the posters onto   5
The vacant, hopeless eyes
Solidifying our strength in each
Hand with its pulsating veins

If they are white clouds, then let them flow and flap
Flapping as posters of incomparable purity flap   10
Caught in the hungry, eye-straining gaze of the world

Each word of protest
Becoming a drop of sweet summer rain
Melting a million frozen rivers and streams
Overflowing into hands interlaced with veins like subway maps   15
Seeping through the paper dikes that their rules have glued
          together

> January 1979

> *Translated from the Chinese*
> *by Joseph Roe Allen*

Don't Read This

— an experiment

. . . please don't read this piece! The contents are thin, without rhyme or reason, full of

empty promises, clumsy and absurd: You should heed my warnings. Put it down right now, you've got more important things to do. Truthfully all truth in this world is truly already in front of you, there is already nothing to say about it all. What I discuss someone else has already actually done: what I don't discuss someone else has thought of, this is the reality of the situation, heed my warning, don't read any further; there are only black graphite squiggles below, and empty white space. Do not under any circumstances read any further. If you do go on, you will hate yourself for it, you will be shortchanged, you will certainly get nothing in return. But, my God, look at you, you still won't listen, what a pain you are, you self-righteous son of a bitch, you arrogant slob, you jerk, you idiot, you don't understand how things are, you won't change your pigheaded ways, you . . . should know, should know that you have utterly misused your time here, just as you and I, and all the people in the past have mis

used their lives, utterly misused them, utterly . . .

Translated from the Chinese
by Joseph Roe Allen

JAPAN

KAWABATA YASUNARI

Kawabata Yasunari (1899–1972) was the first East Asian to be awarded the Nobel Prize in literature, which he received in 1968. Born in Osaka, he lost his parents and most of his relatives at an early age. He earned a degree in Japanese literature from Tokyo University in 1924 and published his first important work, The Izu Dancer, *in 1925. He was associated with a group called the Neo-Sensationalists, who opposed the realism then in vogue.*

Kawabata writes in a lyrical, impressionistic style tinged with deep melancholy. He is best known in the West for his novels. Over the course of his life, Kawabata wrote more than a hundred of the very short pieces represented here, which he named "palm of-the-hand" stories and which he believed to express the essence of his art. These stories, two or three pages long, address themes such as the passage of time, the evanescence of beauty, and the mystery of human relationships, familiar to readers of his longer works.

Up in the Tree

Keisuke's house was on the shore where the great river began to enter the sea. Although the river ran alongside the garden, because of the somewhat elevated embankment it could not be seen from the house. The old shore, lined with pines and slightly lower than the embankment, seemed part of the garden, its pines the garden pines. This side of the pines, there was a hedge of Chinese black pine.

Michiko, forcing her way through the hedge, came to play with Keisuke. No, she came just to be with him. Both Michiko and Keisuke were fourth graders. This ducking through the hedge, instead of coming in by the front gate or by the garden gate in back, was a secret between them. For a girl, it wasn't easy. Shielding her head and face with both arms, bent over from the waist, she would plunge into the hedge. Tumbling out into the garden, she would often be caught up in Keisuke's arms.

Shy about letting the people in the house know that Michiko came every day, Keisuke had taught her this way through the hedge.

"I like it. My heart pounds and pounds like anything," Michiko said.

One day, Keisuke climbed up into a pine tree. While he was up there, along came Michiko. Looking neither right nor left, she hurried along by the shore. Stopping at the hedge where she always went through, she looked all around her. Bringing her long, triple-braided pigtails in front of her face, she put them into her mouth halfway along their length. Bracing herself, she threw herself at the hedge. Up in the tree, Keisuke held his breath. When she'd popped out of the hedge into the garden, Michiko did not see Keisuke, whom she had thought would be there. Frightened, she shrank back into the shadow of the hedge, where Keisuke could not see her.

"Mitchan,° Mitchan," Keisuke called. Michiko, coming away from the hedge, looked around the garden.

"Mitchan, I'm in the pine tree. I'm up in the pine tree." Looking up toward Keisuke's voice, Michiko did not say a word. Keisuke said, "Come out. Come out of the garden."

When Michiko had come back out through the hedge, she looked up at Keisuke.

"You come down."

"Mitchan, climb up here. It's nice up here in the tree."

"I can't climb it. You're making fun of me, just like a boy. Come down."

"Come up here. The branches are big like this, so even a girl can do it."

Michiko studied the branches. Then she said, "If I fall, it's your fault. If I die, I won't know anything about it."

First dangling from a lower branch, she began to climb.

By the time she'd gotten up to Keisuke's branch, Michiko was gasping for breath. "I climbed it, I climbed it." Her eyes sparkled. "It's scary. Hold me."

"Hmm." Keisuke firmly drew Michiko to him.

Michiko, her arms around Keisuke's neck, said, "You can see the ocean."

"You can see everything. Across the river, and even up the river . . . It's good you climbed up here."

"It *is* good. Keichan, let's climb up here tomorrow."

"Hmm." Keisuke was silent a while. "Mitchan, it's a secret. Climbing up the tree and being up here in the tree — it's a secret. I read books and do homework up here. It's no good if you tell anyone."

"I won't tell." Michiko bowed her head in assent. "Why have you become like a bird?

"Since it's you, Mitchan, I'll tell you. My father and mother had an

---

Mitchan: "chan" is an affectionate diminutive suffix for names, for example, Mitchan for Michiko, Keichan for Keisuke awful quarrel. My mother said she was going to take me and go back to her parents' house. I didn't want to look at them, so I climbed a tree in the garden and hid at the top. Saying, 'Where's Keisuke gone to?' they looked all over for me. But they couldn't find me. From the tree, I saw my father go all the way to the ocean to look. This was last spring."

"What were they quarreling about?"

"Don't you know? My father has a woman."

Michiko said nothing.

"Since then, I've been up in this tree a lot. My father and mother still don't know. It's a secret," Keisuke said again, just to make sure. "Mitchan, starting tomorrow, bring your schoolbooks. We'll do our homework up here. We'll get good grades. The trees in the garden are all those big camellia trees with lots of leaves, so nobody can see us from the ground or anywhere."

The "secret" of their being up in the tree had continued for almost two years now. Where the thick trunk branched out near the top, the two could sit comfortably. Michiko, straddling one branch, leaned back against another. There were days when little birds came and days when the wind sang through the pine needles. Although they weren't that high off the ground, these two little lovers felt as if they were in a completely different world, far away from the earth.

Translated from the Japanese by Lane Dunlop

Immortality

An old man and a young girl were walking together.

There were a number of curious things about them. They nestled close together like lovers, as if they did not feel the sixty years' difference in their ages. The old man was hard of hearing. He could not understand most of what the girl said. The girl wore maroon *hakama°* with a purple-and-white kimono in a fine arrow pattern. The sleeves were rather long. The old man was wearing clothes like those a girl would wear to pull weeds from a rice field, except that he wore no leggings. His tight sleeves and trousers gathered at the ankles looked like a woman's. His clothes hung loose at his thin waist.

They walked across a lawn. A tall wire net stood in front of them. The lovers did not seem to notice that they would run into it if they kept walking. They did not stop, but walked right through the net as a spring breeze might blow through it.

---

hakama: loose trousers tied at the waist with a cord and worn over a kimono

After they passed through, the girl noticed the net. "Oh." She looked at the man. "Shintarō, did you pass through the net, too?"

The old man did not hear, but he grabbed the wire net. "You bastard. You bastard," he said as he shook it. He pulled too hard, and in a moment, the huge net moved away from him. The old man staggered and fell holding onto it.

"Watch out, Shintarō! What happened?" The girl put her arms around him and propped him up.

"Let go of the net . . . Oh, you've lost so much weight," the girl said.

The old man finally stood up. He heaved as he spoke. "Thank you." He grasped the net again, but this time lightly, with only one hand. Then in the loud voice of a deaf person he said, "I used to have to pick up balls from behind a net day after day. For seventeen long years."

"Seventeen years is a long time? . . . It's short."

"They just hit the balls as they pleased. They made an awful sound when they struck the wire net. Before I got used to it, I'd flinch. It's because of the sound of those balls that I became deaf."

It was a metal net to protect the ball boys at a golf driving range. There were wheels on the bottom so they could move forward and back and right and left. The driving range and golf course next to it were separated by some trees. Originally it had been a grove of all kinds of trees, but they had been cut until only an irregular row remained.

The two walked on, the net behind them.

"What pleasant memories it brings back to hear the sound of the ocean." Wanting the old man to hear these words, the girl put her mouth to his ear. "I can hear the sound of the ocean."

"What?" The old man closed his eyes. "Ah, Misako. It's your sweet breath. Just as it was long ago."

"Can't you hear the sound of the ocean? Doesn't it bring back fond memories?"

"The ocean . . . Did you say the ocean? Fond memories? How could the ocean, where you drowned yourself, bring back fond memories?"

"Well, it does. This is the first time I've been back to my hometown in fifty-five years. And you've come back here, too. This brings back memories." The old man could not hear, but she went on. "I'm glad I drowned myself. That way I can think about you forever, just as I was doing at the moment I drowned myself. Besides, the only memories and reminiscences I have are those up to the time I was eighteen. You are eternally young to me. And it's the same for you. If I hadn't drowned myself and you came to the village now to see me, I'd be an old woman. How disgusting. I wouldn't want you to see me like that."

The old man spoke. It was a deaf man's monologue. "I went to Tokyo and failed. And now, decrepit with age, I've returned to the village. There was a girl who grieved that we were forced to part. She had drowned herself in the ocean, so I asked for a job at a driving range overlooking the ocean. I begged them to give me the job . . . if only out of pity."

"This area where we are walking is the woods that belonged to your family."

"I couldn't do anything but pick up balls. I hurt my back from bending over all the time . . . But there was a girl who had killed herself for me. The rock cliffs were right beside me, so I could jump even if I were tottering. That's what I thought."

"No. You must keep living. If you were to die, there wouldn't be anyone on earth who would remember me. I would die completely." The girl clung to him. The old man could not hear, but he embraced her.

"That's it. Let's die together. This time . . . You came for me, didn't you."

"Together? But you must live. Live for my sake, Shintarō." She gasped as she looked over his shoulder. "Oh, those big trees are still there. All three . . . just like long ago." The girl pointed, so the old man turned his eyes toward the trees.

"The golfers are afraid of those trees. They keep telling us to cut them down. When they hit a ball, they say it curves to the right as though sucked in by the magic of those trees."

"Those golfers will die in due time — long before those trees. Those trees are already hundreds of years old. Those golfers talk that way, but they don't understand the life span of a man," the girl said.

"Those are trees my ancestors have looked after for hundreds of years, so I had the buyer promise not to cut the trees when I sold the land to him."

"Let's go." The girl tugged at the old man's hand. They tottered toward the great trees.

The girl passed easily through the tree trunk. The old man did the same.

"What?" The girl stared at the old man and marveled. "Are you dead too, Shintarō? Are you? When did you die?"

He did not answer.

"You *have* died . . . Haven't you? How strange I didn't meet you in the world of the dead. Well, try walking through the tree trunk once more to test whether you're dead or alive. If you are dead we can go inside the tree and stay."

They disappeared inside the tree. Neither the old man nor the young girl appeared again.

The color of evening began to drift onto the small saplings behind the great trees. The sky beyond turned a faint red where the ocean sounded.

Translated from the Japanese
by J. Martin Holman

The Cereus

For three summers now, Komiya had invited several of his wife's school friends to look at the night-blooming cereus.

"Beautiful," said Mrs. Murayama, the first to arrive, as she stepped into the parlor. "See how many there are. More than last year." She gazed at the cereus. "There were seven last year? How many are there tonight?"

It was an old-fashioned Western frame house with a larger parlor. The table had been pushed aside and the cereus was at the center on a circular stand. The stand was slightly below knee level, but Mrs. Murayama was looking up at the blossoms.

"Like a white fantasy." She had said the same thing last year. Two years before when she had first seen the cereus, she had said the same thing, with rather more enthusiasm.

She went nearer and looked up at it for a few moments and then turned to thank Komiya.

"Good evening, Toshiko," she said to the girl beside him. "Thank you for letting me come. You're bigger and prettier. The cereus is blooming twice as well as last year and so are you."

The girl looked up at her but did not answer. She did not seem shy but she did not smile.

"You must have worked very hard on it," said Mrs. Murayama to Komiya, "to have it blooming so nicely."

"I think this will be the best evening this year." Hence the sudden invitation, he no doubt meant to say, though somehow his voice did not say it.

Mrs. Murayama lived nearby, at Kugenuma. He had called her and told her that this was the evening, and she had called her friends in Tokyo. She told him the results: two of the five women invited had other engagements and a third would have to wait for her husband to come home, and Mrs. Imasato and Mrs. Omori would definitely come.

"Mrs. Omori said that since there would only be three of us she wondered if she might ask Shimaki Sumiko to come along. She's not been here before. She's about the only one in the class left unmarried."

Toshiko got up and started out through the door beyond the cereus.

"Let's look at it together, Toshiko," said Mrs. Omori.

"I saw it bloom."

"You actually saw it come into bloom? With your father? You must tell me what it was like."

The girl went out without looking back.

Two years before, Mrs. Murayama remembered, Komiya had told her that it came into bloom like a lotus, waving as if in a gentle breeze.

"Does she dislike seeing her mother's friends? Is it that she doesn't want to hear about her mother? I wish Sachiko were with us. Though if she were here I suppose you wouldn't be troubling yourself."

Mrs. Murayama had first seen the cereus when she had come one summer evening two years before to tell him that his estranged wife wanted a reconciliation. She had come again with several friends and asked him to forgive his wife.

They heard an automobile, and Mrs. Imasato had arrived. It was nearly ten. The cereus opened in the evening and the blossoms faded at two or three in the morning. It was a flower of a single night. About twenty minutes later Mrs. Omori arrived with Shimaki Sumiko. Mrs. Murayama introduced Sumiko to Komiya.

"She's too young and pretty. That's why she's still single."

"It's because I've been ill so much." Sumiko's eyes were shining as she looked at the cereus. She was the only one who had not seen it before. She walked slowly around it and brought her face near.

The blossoms came from thick stems at the end of longish leaves. The great white flowers were swaying gently in the breeze through the window. It was a strange flower, the petals somehow different from those of a long-petaled chrysanthemum or a white dahlia. It was like a flower in a dream. A profusion of deep-green leaves stretched upward from the bamboo that supported the three stalks. There too were the most flowers. As with other varieties of cactus, the pistils were long and leaves grew from other leaves.

Sumiko did not notice that Komiya, struck by her intentness, had come up beside her.

"There are considerable numbers of them here and there in Japan, but it is unusual to have thirteen blossoms in one night. It blooms six or seven nights a year. Tonight seems likely to be the best."

He told her that what looked like a large lily bud would be blooming tomorrow. Of the little bean-like protuberances on the leaves some would be leaves and some would be buds. It would take a month for the smaller buds to bloom.

Sumiko was enveloped in the sweet perfume, sweeter than a lily but not as insistent.

Not taking her eyes from the cereus, Sumiko sat down. "A violin. Who is playing?"

"My daughter."

"What a pretty piece. What is it?"

"I'm afraid I don't know."

"A good accompaniment to the cereus," said Mrs. Omori.

After looking at the ceiling for a time, Sumiko went out on the lawn. The sea was immediately below.

She said when she came back inside: "She was on the balcony upstairs. She wasn't facing the sea but standing with her back to it. I wonder if that is better."

Translated from the Japanese
by Edward Seidensticker

ENCHI FUMIKO

Enchi Fumiko (1905–1986) was born in Tokyo and at age seventeen withdrew from school to study with a private tutor. Her father was a famous scholar of Japanese literature, and her grandmother took her often to the Kabuki theater. She married in 1927 and had a child. In her early career she wrote many plays before turning to fiction. She published a first volume of fiction in 1939, and began to publish prolifically after 1953.

Enchi combines her knowledge of classical Japanese literature with a modern sensibility in her work. Her novel The Waiting Years *(1957) depicts the life of an intelligent woman who awaits revenge on a profligate husband. Her "Love in Two Lives: The Remnant," also translated as "A Bond for Two Lifetimes — Gleanings" (1958) is an eerie story about a sexually repressed woman. She wrote essays and literary criticism as well as fiction, and published in 1972 a translation of the eleventh-century* Tale of Genji *into modern Japanese.*

"Boxcar of Chrysanthemums" presents the gentle, self-sacrificing ideal Japanese woman through the eyes of a professional woman who sees her from a distance and hears about her indirectly over the course of twenty years. The former has chosen life with a retarded husband and raises chrysanthemums to give him pleasure. Traditionally, the chrysanthemum, which blooms in autumn, and spreads its fragrance when more fragile flowers have passed with the summer, symbolizes strength and endurance.

Boxcar of Chrysanthemums

It must have been seven or eight years ago, since the highway wasn't as good as it is now, and traveling by car wasn't easy.

I was still staying in my summer house in Karuizawa° even though it was mid-September. One day a women's group in the nearby town of Ueda asked me to give a talk. I've forgotten what kind of group they were, but I left my house in the late afternoon and spoke to the audience right after dinner, for less than an hour. If my memory is correct, it was a little after nine when I got on a train to go home.

It was too late for the express train that ran during the summer, but I heard there was a local that went as far as Karuizawa, and I decided to take it since I wanted very much to return home that night. There was no second class (in those days seats were divided into second and third

---

Karuizawa: a summer retreat in the mountains northwest of Tokyo

class); the third-class cars were old and looked to be of prewar vintage. There were only a few passengers.

Although I said, "How nice, it's not crowded," to the people who came to see me off, I realized after the train started to move how uncomfortable it is to ride on an old train that makes squeaky noises every time it sways, and that has dirty, frayed, green velveteen upholstery.

Well, even if this is a local I'll be in Karuizawa in two hours or so for sure, I said to myself as I turned to look out the window. The moon was nearly full and boldly silhouetted in dark blue the low mountains beyond the fields beside the tracks. The plants in the rice paddies were ripe, so of course I couldn't see the moon reflecting on the water in the fields. Plastic bird rattles here and there glittered strangely as they reflected the moonlight. The clear dark blue of the sky and the coolness of the evening air stealing into the deserted car made me realize keenly that I was in the mountain region of Shinshu, where fall comes early.

I was thinking that I wanted to get home quickly when the train shuddered to a stop at a small station. We had been moving for no more than ten minutes. I couldn't complain about the stop since the train wasn't an express, but it didn't start up for a long time even though no one was getting on or off. It finally moved but then stopped again at the next station, took its time and wouldn't start again, as it had done before.

The four or five passengers in my car were all middle-aged men who looked as though they could be farmers from the area. There was no one sitting near me, and I didn't feel like standing up to go and ask about the delay. I looked out the window and saw several freight cars attached to the rear of the car I was in. It seemed that the cars were being loaded with something.

I realized then that this was a freight train for transporting cargo to Karuizawa that also happened to carry a few passengers. If I had known this earlier, I would have taken the local-express that left an hour before, even if I had had to rush to catch it. But it was too late for regrets; I told myself it would do no good to get off at an unfamiliar station late at night and resigned myself to the situation. The train would get me to Karuizawa sometime that night, no matter what; with that thought in mind, I felt calmer.

I took a paperback book from my bag and tried to read, but the squeaking noise of the car made it difficult to concentrate. I was tired, but I couldn't sleep because of the chilly air that crept up my legs and also because of my exasperation with a train that stopped so often.

When the train stopped for the fourth time at a fairly large station, I got off to ease my irritation. It would probably stop for ten minutes or so, and even if it started suddenly I thought I could easily jump on such a slow-moving train.

A few passengers got off. Some long packages wrapped in straw matting were piled up near one of the back cars, and the station attendants were loading them into the car as if they were in no big hurry. The packages were all about the same size, bulging at the center like fish wrapped in reed mats, but the station attendants were lifting them carefully in both hands, as if they were handling something valuable, and loading them into the soot-covered car.

I was watching the scene and wondering what the packages were when I suddenly noticed a moist, plant-like smell floating in from somewhere. Then I heard a woman's voice ask hesitantly, "Have you already loaded ours?"

I turned toward the voice. A middle-aged woman with her hair pulled into a bun was standing behind me. She wasn't alone; beside her was an old man with white hair and sunken cheeks. The moment I saw the pupils of his eyes with their strangely shifting gaze, and his slightly gaping mouth with its two long buck teeth and fine white froth at the corners, I was so startled that I stepped back a few paces.

"The Ichiges," one of the station attendants said to another, motioning with his eyes, and then he turned to the old man. "Yes, I loaded them. I put them in the best spot. They'll be in Tokyo tomorrow and will be the best flowers at the flower market," he said, speaking to the man as if he were a child.

The old man nodded with a dignified air.

"Oh, that's nice, isn't it? Now you don't have to worry. Well, let's go home and go to bed," the woman said, also as if she were humoring a child, and patted the old man's shoulder, which looked as stiff as a scarecrow's.

The old man stood there and said nothing. Meanwhile the packages were being loaded one after another, and by then I realized that the fragrance in the air was coming from them.

"Oh, that one over there! Those are our mums!" the old man yelled suddenly, extending his arms as if he were swimming toward the package the station attendant was about to load on the train. The old man's little nose was twitching like a dog's. "That smell . . . It's the Shiratama mum."

"Is it? Well, then, we'll ask them to let you smell them. The train's leaving soon, so you only smell once, all right?" the woman said and gave the station attendant a meaningful look. He put down the package the old man was trying to press his nose against and loaded another one first.

"That's enough now. You said good-bye to Shiratama, didn't you?" The woman spoke as if she were talking to a small child and put her arm around the stooping old man. She then took his hand and placed it gently on her lips. The old man let go of the package as if he were under a spell and stood up with his wife.

The door of the freight car finally closed, and the starting signal sounded. I got on the train in a hurry but didn't know quite what to make of the strange scene I had just witnessed. I couldn't believe that what I'd seen wasn't an illusion, like a scene from a movie.

"I feel sorry for them. Living on into old age like that."

I turned around. A middle-aged man in a gray jacket was sitting across the aisle from me. His face was dark and wrinkled from the sun, but he didn't look unpleasant. I realized that he hadn't been on the train before we stopped at the last station.

"That man — is he mentally ill?" I asked, unable to suppress my curiosity.

"Not mentally ill, more like an idiot. I think the term they use nowadays is 'mentally retarded.'" The man spoke without using any dialect. "The old man himself doesn't understand a thing, so he's okay, but I feel sorry for his wife. She's been married to that man for over twenty years now. If he'd been born into a poor family, marriage would have been out of the question, but simply because his family was wealthy, all kinds of cruel things happened."

Not only did the man speak without an accent, but his manner of speaking was smooth and pleasant. The name Ichige that the station attendant had mentioned turned my consciousness to some troublesome, submerged memory, but instead of mentioning this, I said, "Were those chrysanthemums they were loading in that boxcar? That old man was smelling them, wasn't he?"

"Yes, those were the chrysanthemums they grow in their garden. Mums are the only thing the old man cares much about. When they send some off he comes with his wife to watch, whether it's late at night or early in the morning."

"Then all of the packages are chrysanthemums?"

"That's right. Most of the flowers that go to Tokyo at this time of year are. Lots of farmers around here grow flowers, but they're all sold in Tokyo, so it's a big deal. Not only flowers, either. The people who work in the mountains around here collect tree roots, branches and other stuff, put prices on them and send them to Tokyo. Once they get them to market they can sell them, I guess, because money is always sent back. Tokyo's a good customer that lets the landowners around here earn money that way."

"I see. I was wondering why we were stopping so often to load things. It's a mistake for people to take this train," I said, smiling.

"You're right. It takes a good three hours to get to Karuizawa on this train."

"Oh, that's awful! No one told me that at Ueda when I got on."

"I don't think the people around here know that there's a train running at this hour that carries mums. Well, you might as well just get used to it and consider it an elegant way to travel."

My family would worry if I got to Karuizawa after midnight, but as the saying goes, there's nothing you can do once you're on board; even if no one had told me that I'd have to resign myself to the situation, I had no choice but to do so.

And so our conversation returned to the couple who grew chrysanthemums. The man across from me, whose name was Kurokawa, said he used to teach at an agricultural institute in Tokyo, but after he was evacuated to this region during the war he bought an orchard and settled down. He made extra income by collecting alpine plants, something he liked very much. He was taking this train because he had decided on an impulse to go to the town of Komoro and then climb Mt. Asama° early the next morning.

It was the year after the end of the war when Kurokawa learned about Ichige Masutoshi and Rie.

Luckily Kurokawa didn't have to leave the country to do his military service, so as soon as the war was over he went to a village where his family had been evacuated. The village wasn't far from where he was born, and since he had never been particularly fond of city life and had also been hit hard by the war, he decided to settle there. At first he taught at a middle school in a nearby town. It was quite a while later that he bought an orchard and began to grow grapes and apples for a livelihood.

Food was scarce for most people in those days. No one grew fruit or flowers; everyone was busy growing potatoes and corn on the plots of land that weren't suitable for rice paddies. Kurokawa's father was still alive and healthy then and worked hard with his wife and daughter-in-law to grow vegetables. After living there for a while, Kurokawa noticed a new Tokyo-style house on a fairly large piece of land not far from his house. On his way back from school he often saw a woman in her thirties busily working in the garden behind the house. She wore a kerchief over her head and work pants, but her fair, unburned complexion and fine features had a calm sadness that reminded him of classic Korean beauties.

"That house is built in a different style from the others around here. Was it built during the war?" Kurokawa asked his father one evening during supper.

"That one? That's the house Ichige from Tokyo built during the war." His father, born and raised in that region, said this as if his son would know who Mr. Ichige was even if he didn't explain.

"Who's Ichige?"

"Ichige? He's the owner of a big paper company in Tokyo. I heard that he went bankrupt after the war. His father was the famous Ichige Tokuichi."

"Oh, I see." Kurokawa finally remembered the name. "But he's been dead for a long time, hasn't he?" Kurokawa had heard of Ichige Tokuichi of the Shinshu region, one of the success stories of the Meiji era.°

Mt. Asama: the highest active volcano in Japan
Meiji era: 1867–1912; a period when Japan modernized rapidly

"Right. Tokuichi was the father of Hanshiro, who was also known as a fine man. Hanshiro built the house, but his only son, Masatoshi, and his wife live there now."

With this as a beginning, Kurokawa's father then continued: Masatoshi was Ichige's legitimate heir, but he had contracted meningitis as a child, and although he was not actually an idiot, he was capable of only a few simple words. When he reached adulthood, however, it was decided that he should have a wife. Rie, who had come from the city of Iida to work as one of the Ichige's servants, was chosen as the human sacrifice.

"That's ridiculous, like a feudal lord and his serf. There's something wrong with any woman who would go along with it, too," Kurokawa snapped, but secretly he couldn't comprehend how the ladylike woman he saw when he passed the back of Ichige's house each morning and evening could be so lacking in expression and yet also give an impression of innocence and purity.

"That's what everyone says at first. When I heard the story, I despised the woman for agreeing to marry a man like that, no matter how much money was involved. But you know, after we came here that house was built nearby, and so I've seen a lot of Rie. She always showed up for volunteer work days and air raid drills, and ever since I was head of the volunteer guards I've known her well. Your dead mother and your wife Matsuko would agree that there's nothing wrong with Rie. She works harder than anyone else and doesn't put on the airs of a rich person. The catty local women used to sit around and drink tea and make fun of the Tokyo women who were evacuated here, but they stopped at Rie. They agreed that she took good care of that idiot husband of hers and only pitied her.

"It was like that for two or three years, and then before the war ended Hanshiro died of a stroke. His mother and son-in-law were careless and used up what money there was. They say only that house is left. In these times when there isn't much food, Rie has a hard time finding enough potatoes and flour to feed that glutton of a husband. She knits things for the farmers and sews clothes for their kids. You can't do that much for others if you're a fake and just trying to make a good impression. Sometimes I even wonder if she's a reincarnation of Kannon° . . ."

Kurokawa's father spoke earnestly. He seemed to believe what he was saying. He was the kind of old-fashioned man who would want to believe that a person like Rie was a Kannon, or at least her reincarnation; at the war's end and in the years that followed he had seen whatever trappings human beings find to wrap themselves up in cruelly pulled off to reveal their naked, shameful parts.

Kurokawa certainly understood his father's feeling. He realized that he too wanted to purify his image of Rie and think of her as a reincarnated Kannon. Rie had lived up to the expectations of Kurokawa's father and

Kannon: the Buddhist goddess of mercy

had continued to be a devoted wife for more than ten years. She had converted most of Ichige's land into apple orchards and supported her husband and herself with this income. Growing chrysanthemums was partially for income but partially because Masatoshi enjoyed looking at flowers. Kurokawa said there didn't seem to be much money in it.

"It was two years ago, I think. Rie won some kind of prize. Hmm, what was it called? It was to commend her for having devoted herself to her mentally retarded husband for so many years; you might say for being the model of the faithful wife. In any case, it's a rare thing these days, and I think she deserved the praise."

While I listened to Kurokawa's long story, the train kept stopping at every station, and it looked as though chrysanthemums wrapped in straw mats were being loaded into the freight cars.

Between Komoro and Oiwake the train picked up speed. The moon seemed to be high in the middle of the sky; I couldn't see it from the train window, but the rays of moonlight had become brighter, and they shone upon the scene along the tracks with the coppery glow of an old mirror. This copper color changed to the smoky silver of mica when we reached a plateau and a mist settled onto the ground. After Kurokawa got off at Komoro, the only passengers left were a pair of men sitting near the far entrance to the car. Since it was late at night when we reached the high land, a chill that was enough to shrivel me crept up from the tips of my socks as I sat there and quickly permeated my lower body.

I didn't actually mind the chill, even though I shrugged my shoulders now and then and pressed my knees together tightly, shivering. I was too absorbed in adding some facts from my own memory to the story that Kurokawa had told me about Ichige Masatoshi and his wife.

When I heard the names Ichige Tokuichi and Hanshiro, I was reminded of the story I had almost forgotten about the retarded son of the Ichiges. I had barely stopped myself from saying to Kurokawa, "Yes, of course, I've heard about him too."

I happened to have heard about the marriage between Masatoshi and Rie just about the time it took place. It was a year or so after the outbreak of the China Incident,° when the image of the red draft notice calling soldiers to the army burned like fire in young men's minds. I had a friend whose husband was a psychiatrist, and although he practiced primarily in one of the private hospitals, he spent a few days a week at the Brain Research Institute of S Medical School. Interns and volunteer assistants who worked at this Institute often gathered at my friend Nagase's house to talk. I became acquainted with this group in the course of writing a play that dealt with a mental patient; I visited the hospital to ask the doctors questions about their experiences. One day when I met with

the China Incident: the Japanese reference to the Sino-Japanese war, part of World
    War II

three or four of these young doctors at Nagase's house, I noticed that Kashimura, who had always been with the group, was missing.

"Where is Dr. Kashimura? Is he on duty tonight?" I asked. The young doctors looked at each other and laughed before saying things like, "I guess you could call it 'duty,'" or "He sure is on duty," or "It's some duty."

I thought he might have gone to see a lover, and so I kept quiet, but then Nagase interrupted and said, "It's all right to tell her. It might be helpful to her."

"It's not a very respectable story, though."

"But a job's a job. Maybe she'll write a story about how we have to do this kind of work to support ourselves."

One of them sat up straight and said, "Kashimura is on night duty tonight at the home of one of the patients."

"I see. Does the patient get violent?" I asked without hesitation, since such cases are common among psychiatric patients.

"Yes, you couldn't say he *doesn't* get violent, but it's a tricky point." The young man who spoke, Tomoda, looked at another and said, "How was it when you were there?"

"Nothing happened, fortunately. You always had bad luck, didn't you?"

Tomoda nodded. "Yeah, my luck is bad. I'll probably die first if I go to war."

"I don't agree. You got a chance to see things you can't usually see. A voyeur would even pay for the chance."

"Idiot! Who said I'm a voyeur?"

"If everybody talked like that, no one would understand. I'll tell the true story in a scientific way without any interpretation," Nagase said, and he then told me the story of Ichige Masatoshi's marriage. Of course he didn't mention the name, but I learned of it quite a while later.

When Masatoshi reached physical maturity, his father consulted with a professor of psychiatry because he was troubled about how to find a partner to meet his son's sexual needs.

"The best way would be to provide him with one woman who would be kind to him. You should disregard her family background and her appearance and find someone who would take care of him like a mother," the professor told the father.

Masatoshi was particularly pitiful because his mother, Shino, had always disliked her retarded eldest child and had barely tolerated living in the same house with him. When she was young, Shino had been a hostess at Koyo-kan, a famous restaurant of the Meiji period, and had been popular among aristocrats and wealthy merchants because of her beauty.

Ichige Hanshiro had won her and made her his wife. For Shino the marriage meant an elevation in her own status, but her own background made her unyielding and vain, and she was determined not to be outdone by anyone. Her daughter was normal and married a man who was adopted into the family, but Shino was ashamed because she couldn't show off her only son in public. This shame turned into a hatred that she vented on Hanshiro.

Since Hanshiro had a sense of responsibility as a father, Masatoshi was raised at least to give the impression of being a son of the Ichige family. If the matter had been left to Shino's discretion, he probably would have been confined to one room and treated like a true moron.

When Masatoshi reached puberty he would sometimes become excited like a dog in heat and chase the maids and his sister. When Shino saw this happen, far from feeling sad, she would grow so livid that the veins would stand out at her temples.

"It's your responsibility! You let him wander around the house like an animal! Let's hurry and put him in a hospital. If we don't, all of our maids will leave us, I assure you," she shrieked at her husband.

"You don't have to shout for me to understand. I have my own thoughts about this," Hanshiro said calmly. Shino, who had given birth to Masatoshi, had no comprehension of the pain and unseverable strength of the parental bond Hanshiro felt in his very bones.

The next day Hanshiro went to see the psychiatry professor again and asked him to arrange for his son to be sterilized before he was married.

"I know a woman who might become my son's wife, but I can't imagine bringing the subject up to her whenever I think of the possibility of a child being born. Once the operation is finished, though, I think I can hope for a marriage. I feel sorry for the woman who'll be my son's wife, but from a father's viewpoint, I would at least like to give him the experience of living with a woman."

The professor agreed to Hanshiro's request, and the operation for sterilizing Masatoshi was performed in the surgery department of the hospital where he worked. It was a very simple procedure and was guaranteed not to interfere with the performance of the sex act.

It was said that after this Hanshiro talked to Rie about marriage. No one knew how Rie had reacted, or how long it had taken her to accept the proposal, or what sort of conditions Hanshiro had promised. It was clear only that Rie was not promised a bright future. The young couple began their married life in a small house that was fixed up for them in a corner of the grounds. It was originally built as a retreat. Rie took care of Masatoshi by herself, without any help from the household maids.

On formal occasions like weddings and funerals, Hanshiro and his wife attended with their daughter and her husband — their adopted son and an executive at Hanshiro's company — and their second daughter, who was also married. Of course Masatoshi didn't go along and neither did Rie.

"When they were married, he gave Rie a lot of stock in the company," one of Hanshiro's employees said, as if he had been there and seen this happen.

What I had heard at Nagase's house, that several young psychiatrists were hired to oversee the married relations of Masatoshi and Rie, was true; they were dispatched because it was assumed that there would be some times when Rie would be subjected to some violence. Hanshiro had heard from the psychiatrists that retarded men like his son sometimes perform the sexual act interminably, beyond a normal limit, since they are unable to control themselves, and that in some cases women had been killed as a result. To assure Rie's safety, Hanshiro had arranged for young doctors from S Medical School to take turns standing by every night in a room next to the couple's.

In teaching hospitals before the war, many young doctors worked for nearly nothing after receiving their degrees before they found a position somewhere. Of course not all of them had fathers who owned private clinics, so even if they were single it wasn't easy for them to support themselves unless they did some moonlighting.

The job at the Ichiges' was unusual even for psychiatrists, and the pay was much more than the average. There were many applicants. The professor chose several whom he felt could keep a secret; three of them were among the five or six young doctors who came to Nagase's.

"Rich people do such awful things. In fact, that woman was bought, but to have a doctor waiting on them like that . . . It's like some kind of show. Even if the father did want his son to enjoy sex, it's too big a sacrifice. Why didn't he have them castrate his son instead of sterilizing him? I think that father is perverted." I spoke forcefully. I couldn't control my anger while listening to the story. Looking back on it now, I realize that at age thirty or so I knew little of life's unavoidable bitterness. I feel ashamed that I was so naive, but at that time I detested not only Hanshiro — though I didn't know his name then — but also Rie, the woman bought to be Masatoshi's wife, for her cowardice.

"Hey, don't get upset so fast. All of that made life a little easier for these guys," Nagase said, trying to act the mediator.

"That's true," I said, but I still felt revulsion, even toward Tomoda and Kashimura, who had worked for the Ichiges.

They say that when the wind blows, the cooper prospers; applying this logic, I could find no reason to criticize a man like Ichige Masatoshi, who had in fact helped the poor young doctors. Leftist ideology would probably explain this as the contradiction inherent in capitalistic society. Still, I simply could not feel comfortable with a situation where young, single doctors watched a young couple in bed from beginning to end, paying diligent attention until the two fell asleep. If one does not make a fool of himself when doing such things, then he is making a fool of his charges. The doctors were too young and well educated to see themselves as fools, and if they were making fun of someone else, it was of the woman who was the victim of this marriage. Obviously I didn't like their making fun of her or their seeing her as an object of erotic stimulation. At the same time that they were ridiculing her, they were acting like fools who couldn't see the spittle on their own faces. Someone had used the word "voyeur," but I had thought at the time that there was a basic difference between a voyeur and someone who kept such a nightly vigil.

After that I heard nothing more about the Ichiges from the young doctors, but through Nagase I learned there were in fact times when what had once seemed an absurd possibility had come to pass; Rie had fainted once, and there was a big row when Kashimura went to take care of her. It turned out that Masatoshi had forced himself on Rie when she was menstruating, and as a result she had lost a great deal of blood.

The interns from S Hospital must have stood duty at the Ichiges' for about a year when they decided there was no longer any danger and so stopped going there. A few years later, in the spring after the outbreak of the Pacific War,° Kashimura was drafted as a military doctor and left to go to the South Seas. At the party to see him off, he came to me with a sake° cup in his hand.

"I've been wanting to talk with you, but it seems like time is running out. If I return safely I'll tell you. It's about the family where I did night duty," he said.

"Oh yes, that family," I said, nodding. It was better not to mention the Ichiges' name in a place where there were so many people.

"The wife — Rie, I mean — I fell in love with her. To tell the truth, I wanted to marry her and talked to her about it." Kashimura spoke loudly, without concern for the people around him. Going to the battlefield seemed to have made him free from the petty restraints of normal times.

"Did you really?" I was intrigued and looked into Kashimura's eyes. I remembered that I had once secretly scorned the trio who had done that night duty for the Ichiges, including Kashimura. Now that I heard from Kashimura himself words that seemed to prove he had not been making a fool of either himself or Rie, I couldn't help reacting with a tense curiosity.

"What did she say?"

"She said no. She really loves her husband. But she said she was grateful for my having asked. She said it was more than she could have expected, after I had seen her in such unsightly circumstances. Masatoshi couldn't go on living, and probably wouldn't live for very long if she left, she said, and when she thought of this she felt sorry for him and couldn't possibly leave. Then she cried and cried. I thought there was nothing else I could do, and so I gave up," he said. Kashimura's face was flushed with sake, and tears welled up in his bloodshot eyes.

"I got married after that and have children now, but I haven't forgotten

the Pacific War: part of World War II, in which Japan conquered large parts of Southeast Asia

sake (also spelled saki): Japanese rice wine

her. For a while I thought I had to rescue her from that place, but now it seems natural that she stays with that husband," he said.

"Why were you attracted to her in the first place?" I asked Kashimura impatiently, trying to make sense of a situation I could not comprehend in many ways.

"Well . . ." After thinking for a moment, Kashimura said, "I felt the same as I would if my mother were in an animal cage. It was like a bad dream."

"Does she look like your mother?"

"No, not at all." Kashimura shook his head vigorously.

"What are you two talking so seriously about?" said a colleague of Kashimura's, patting his shoulder. Seeing this as a chance to excuse himself, Kashimura stood up to leave. He didn't seem particularly interested in talking with me anymore.

I thought about my brief conversation with Kashimura more than once after I returned home that night, and I tried to imagine what this woman Rie, whom I had never met, looked like. His words about his mother being in a cage excited my imagination, but in truth I couldn't picture Rie herself.

She was the daughter of a quilt merchant in the city of Iida. Her father had not been very well off, and although she only finished grammar school, like many children in those days, she was smart, wrote neatly, learned to sew and knit after arriving at the Ichiges', and acquired the knowledge of a high school graduate. Nagase said he had not heard any rumors about her family receiving a large sum of money when she married.

I suspected that she might have had something physically wrong with her as a woman, but when I learned that Kashimura had proposed to her after doing that strange nightwatch, I decided Rie must be normal.

It was extraordinary that a man who had witnessed a most private part of her life would ask her to divorce Masatoshi and marry him. Kashimura was a quiet, scholarly type — tall, well-built, and handsome. He was popular among the nurses and patients at the hospital, and I wondered how Rie felt when she was proposed to by a man who was beyond comparison with her husband. It puzzled me that she could calmly refuse such a proposal, since she was only twenty-four or twenty-five.

Four or five years after the end of the war, I learned from Tomoda, an old friend of Kashimura's, that Kashimura had died of malaria in the South Seas.° Since my friends the Nagases had moved to the Kansai region after the destruction of the war, I heard almost nothing about that group of friends.

I myself went to Karuizawa to live after I lost my house in the bomb-

---

died . . . in the South Seas: many Japanese soldiers fighting in Southeast Asia during World War II had no way of knowing when the war ended, and remained "missing in action" for many years

ings. A year after the end of the war when I returned to Tokyo, I became very ill, and for a year or two after having surgery I struggled to keep going during the hard times, even though I was still not completely well. In those days of rapid change after the war, I might have heard about the death of Ichige Hanshiro and the subsequent collapse of his family business, but it was not until I heard the news of Kashimura's death that I remembered Rie and her husband, whom I had forgotten; I thought at the time that I might write a story with Rie as the central character.

By then I had gained firsthand experience with the extreme situations of life, having gone through a war and a serious illness that had been a matter of life and death. I had lost the naiveté that had made me feel indignant about Hanshiro for having married his retarded son to a girl like Rie, as if it were a privilege of the bourgeois class. Nevertheless, Rie still remained a mystery to me.

When I thought about the story I would write about Rie, I imagined Masatoshi as the young kleptomaniac owner of an old established shop. His wife, ashamed of her husband, had an abortion, but unable to get a divorce, she continued to live with him as the lady of the household. She then fell in love with a young employee and in the end poisoned her husband.

This was all my own fabrication, but since it had been Kashimura's death that prompted me to start writing it, the metamorphosis of the main female character into a malicious women left a bad taste in my mouth, for this would surely have made Kashimura sad.

Later I thought off and on of writing down just what Kashimura had told me that night, a more lucid account that would convince even me, but the limits of my own imagination simply did not include a woman like Rie. I felt that if I forced myself to write, the character of Rie would end up being like a listless, white cat. Meanwhile the months and days passed, and once again I almost forgot the name Ichige.

Only one or two other passengers, shrugging their shoulders as if they were cold, got off the train with me. The chrysanthemums were still shut in the freight cars, so their penetrating fragrance didn't reach the platform.

I didn't see a taxi in front of the station, so after I called home from a public phone and asked someone to meet me with a flashlight at the corner of a dark field, I started walking alone through the town.

The moon was at its zenith, and the night mist was hanging low under the cloudless sky, spreading its thin gauze net over the pine trees and the firs. I could see the swirling motion of the mist underneath the street lamps, where the light made a circle. As I walked along, treading on the dark shadows that seemed to permeate the street, my footsteps sounded clear and distinct. Between the stores with their faded shutters I could hear the thin, weak chirping of some insects. It felt like autumn in the mountains.

Now I recalled fondly that I had been riding on a freight train full of chrysanthemums. In those dark, soot-covered cars hundreds and thousands of beautiful flowers were sleeping, in different shades of white, yellow, red, and purple, and in different shapes. Their fragrance was sealed in the cars. Tomorrow they would be in the Tokyo flower market and sold to florists who would display them in front of their shops.

"She's a white chrysanthemum, that's what she is," I said, and wondered the next moment to whom I was speaking. I realized immediately, however, that I was addressing the dead Kashimura. The words had come out so effortlessly that I felt vaguely moved.

That evening at O Station I had seen Rie with her husband for the first time, though only for a few minutes. Then by chance I had heard from Kurokawa about her recent life. Twenty years had passed since I had heard about Rie at Nagase's house. After that I had heard Kashimura's brief confession at his farewell party, and after the war I learned of his death. Did Rie know that he had died in the war? It didn't really matter now. I felt that Kashimura wouldn't mind if she was uninterested in his life and death.

Seeing Rie that night and hearing Kurokawa's story didn't add anything new to my image of her. Rie was the same as she had been; I was the skeptical one who hadn't believed she was like that.

Rie's devotion to Masatoshi had seemed absurd to me. I had no reason to say she was a fake, but I simply couldn't accept a way of thinking that was so different from my own. What I mean is that I couldn't accept what she did without imagining that some handicap was part of her devotion — she must have been jilted or raped or experienced something to make her unhappy. I even wondered if religion had motivated her, an inclination to follow an authority higher than that of human beings. That was why, when I had intended to write about Rie, I had explored the psychology of a woman who would kill her husband, and who was not at all like Rie. Even though Kashimura had said he had had no difficulty accepting Rie's refusal, I couldn't.

But now I was humbly reaching out to Rie. I wanted to accept the Rie who had lived with Masatoshi as she was and to disregard her background, any misfortunes she had had before her marriage, or any religious inclinations. I wanted to take her hand and say "I understand."

Did this mean that I had grown old? Should I be grateful that I had reached an age when I could accept without explanation the fact that human beings have thoughts and behavior that seem beyond rational comprehension? I felt a sense of joy in thinking of the flat features of Rie's melancholy, middle-aged face as being somehow like the short, dense petals of a modest white chrysanthemum.

Translated from the Japanese by
Yukio Tanaka and Elizabeth Hanson

INOUE YASUSHI

Inoue Yasushi (1907–) was born in Hokkaido, the eldest son of an army doctor. He began writing poems while in junior high school, then became obsessed with judo in high school. In 1930 he entered Kyushu University to study law, but soon left to spend time in Tokyo before transferring to Kyoto University to study philosophy. He graduated in 1936, a year after his marriage. He worked at a newspaper in Osaka until his enlistment in 1937, when he was sent to northern China, became ill, and returned home the following year. At the end of the war Inoue began to write poems, novellas, and the genre by which he is best known, "middlebrow" novels.

In both his historical novels and those that depict modern man, human loneliness is a constant theme. Some critics have described his novels as "too lyrical," with the explanation that Inoue had written poetry before he wrote fiction.

The Boy

The boy got off the train at a town in the north, well known for its great fires in the quick hot weather. It was the season when large pomegranates are lined up on greengrocer's stalls. The boy stayed there for two days, hoping to see the sky burn red with flame; but nothing happened.

The boy took the night train farther north; moved to a town where mirages occurred. The town was thronged with people for the festival; the sea glimpsed at the end of streets was rough. The boy stayed there for two days more; small driftwood floating on a sea where nothing strange seemed likely to occur.

Three days later the boy got down at an unknown station on the peninsula. He walked the narrow, walled, fish-smelling streets; came out upon a cliff. The sea was spread before him; the sunset sky of a breathtaking beauty. And so he threw himself down from the cliff there. He did not know it, but in that region this spot was famous for the number of its suicides.

Translated from the Japanese
by Dennis Keene

River Light

The stone steps went steep down to the water's surface. At high tide they were covered halfway up, but when the tide was out the lowest cleared the water, covered with seaweed and small shells.

When I was there washing my hands one early evening, the soap suddenly slipped from me. As if alive it tailed and flipped in the water, and then was gone, sunken in those depths. Later I felt an enormous sense of loss, because no matter what I did it would not come back twice into my hands.

This happened when I was a boy, and since then I have never had a loss quite so complete as that. For I had understood that river light, that light still held in water when the rest is dark, is different from all other forms of light; a light preceding tragedy's last curtain.

Translated from the Japanese by Dennis Keene

The Beginning of Autumn

That morning, as I quit my bed, something like a bird's shadow crossed my mind, flashed over me for a moment, then was gone. I do not know if it was light or dark; I do not know if it was warm or cold. That day, all day, I thought only of something like a bird's shadow.

That evening, as I took my walk, I found a tiny puddle hidden in thick grass. As I gazed down at it I faintly heard the dripping sound of water. I tried to listen closely, but I did not hear the sound again.

That night I slept among things like bird shadows, like sounds of dripping water. I spent the night enclosed in these uncertainties. And so I could find rest, protected as I slept by vague, uncertain things.

Translated from the Japanese by Dennis Keene

Elegy

Five days after you died a wind blew and brought down the last leaves on the oak. One month after you died there was a small earthquake. And thirty-nine days after you died it snowed. On the night of that next day snow fell again. And then all day the next day after that, a peaceful winter sun shone down, bringing a rare red sunset in the evening. The trees were black beyond remaining patches of white snow, and the red sky combed all those trees together, scattering flecks of fire about them. I sat on a chair on the porch and watched it; and then for the very first time I could believe that you were now no longer in the world. And then I heard it for the first time too; in that funereal, mourning landscape, the sound of a bell which kept on tolling for you.

Translated from the Japanese
by Dennis Keene

Old Man in a Turban

He sat on the expanse of grass, crosslegged in contemplation, an old man in a turban. When he opened his eyes I asked him what he prayed for. He said he prayed for freedom from all mind, all thought. I asked him then how one might enter these mindless regions. He said you hold the tongue in the center of the mouth, making quite sure its sides touch against nothing.

In foreign countries, in hotels at dawn, I have at times tried squatting on my bed, straight-backed, doing the way he said. And then sometimes the flames flicker about me; or a bleak north wind is blowing through the room; or a winter shower falls and passes by. I am the guardian deity, god of fire; I am the great Zen poet on Cold Mountain; I am the Foundling, his companion.°

Opening my eyes I feel myself in exile. I get down from the bed and open the window. The desert I have traveled for over a month now, sleeps in the dark before dawn. The bazaar which must, once again today, barter off all its last remaining jewels, is sleeping too. Then I recall the old man in the turban, seeing the face of a man who is alone. The face of a man in exile for scores of years now.

Translated from the Japanese
by Dennis Keene

the great Zen poet . . . his companion: Cold Mountain is the name of both the well-known Chinese Zen poet and where he lived with his companion, the Foundling. Having achieved the Buddhist goal of freedom from attachment to worldliness, they had no need for names, titles, or family relationships.

KANEKO TŌTA

Kaneko Tōta (1919–) began to write haiku as a young boy, under the influence of his father, who was a regular contributor to one of the best-known haiku magazines. Tōta graduated from Tokyo University in 1943 with a degree in economics and pursued a successful career in banking while continuing to write haiku, of which he has published several volumes. In his early work he wrote on political and sociological themes but later returned to an interest in nature.

Tōta accepts the traditional 5–7–5 syllable pattern as a poetic framework, once remarking that the fixed verse form yields the beauty of finality in this life where nothing is final. He questions the traditional requirement of a season word, however, arguing that in today's urban environment, with central heating, air conditioning, and florist shops, the seasons no longer play an essential role in Japanese life. Still, many of Tōta's poems use the season word to great effect.

Tōta once noted that many modern haiku have about them "a smell of raw humanity," but that too few have achieved the crystallization formed by the compression of words within the haiku's peculiarly stringent form, which produces an interior tension and expansiveness and "a feeling of potential (even imminent) explosion." For him, the best haiku produce a feeling of intensely hard substance comparable to a diamond cut to a precise pattern, maximizing the transmission of white light.

Haiku

Above the crumbled bricks
a butterfly, its heart attached
here to the slums.

On the hill, a withered farm;
in the valley, no cogitation.   5
Clear water is all.

Like something totally
alien, a fresh pine cone
sits upright on the grass.

Ephemerae swarming   10
at a bridge lamp — I arrive
and gain a shadow.

At many street corners
streetwalkers fight with each other —
tangerines are dry.   15

Factory dismissing the workers —
it vomits cloudy autumn water
into the canal.

A white human figure
far, far away, walks on the farm   20
in order not to fade.

After a heated argument
I go out to the street
and become a motorcycle.

Like an arm overstretched   25
and tired, reddish brown smoke
rising from a steel mill.

Like squids
bank clerks are fluorescent
from the morning.   30

Translated from the Japanese
by Makoto Ueda

MISHIMA YUKIŌ

Mishima Yukiō (1925–1970) is the pen name of Hiraoka Kimitake.
Born in Tokyo to a samurai family, Mishima graduated from the Uni-
versity of Tokyo and worked in the ministry of finance before he be-
came a writer full time. He pursued the ancient ideals and arts of the
samurai, including physical fitness, swordsmanship, and karate. Versa-
tile and dramatic, Mishima adapted the traditional Noh drama to the
modern stage, wrote Kabuki plays, and even acted in his own plays. He
wrote numerous essays, short stories, and novels. Many of Mishima's
works are available in English.

Mishima's Yoroboshi: The Blind Young Man *(1965) is an adaptation*
of a well-known Noh drama. Like the traditional Noh, it is nonrepre-

sentational, elusive in meaning, and concentrated in emotion. It centers on a single character (the shite*), with a secondary character (the* waki*) serving as foil, and with two attendants each. Unlike the traditional Noh, there is no chorus, music, dance, or mime; the characters appear in modern clothes, without masks. Women do not appear in the traditional Noh, but here the* waki*, instead of being a priest, is a female judge. Toshinori's adoptive parents have already learned the Buddhist lesson that all human attachment can only lead to suffering; his birth parents labor under the futile hope of finding filial love after years of separation.*

Yoroboshi: The Blind Young Man

CHARACTERS

SAKURAMA SHINAKO   a member of the Board of Arbitration
KAWASHIMA   Toshinori's stepfather
MRS. KAWASHIMA   Toshinori's stepmother
MRS. TAKAYASU   Toshinori's real mother
TAKAYASU   Toshinori's real father
TOSHINORI   a blind young man

Time: Late summer — from afternoon to sunset.
Place: A room in a domestic relations court.

[As the curtain rises, SHINAKO *sits at stage center while the* KAWASHIMAS *and the* TAKAYASUS *are seated, respectively, at stage left and stage right. After a short pause.]*

SHINAKO *(an attractive woman past forty dressed in a kimono)*: It's terribly humid, isn't it? As you can see, we don't even have a fan . . .
    [Everyone remains silent. With no other recourse, she laughs.] The domestic relations court has such a tiny budget. And though we are members of the Board of Arbitration, which sounds rather impressive . . .
    [Everyone remains silent. After a short pause.]
    Please. Speak up. This isn't a place for a quarrel.
KAWASHIMA: It was such a surprise . . . We never dreamed that we'd ever meet Toshinori's real parents . . . It's been fifteen years since we first found him . . . Fifteen long years . . .
MRS. KAWASHIMA: *[wiping away her tears with a handkerchief]*: And after fifteen years, he's just like our own child . . .

SHINAKO (looking at papers): Toshinori is twenty now?

[The TAKAYASUS remain silent as their attention is constantly drawn toward the door.]

KAWASHIMA Yes . . . That's right.

MRS. KAWASHIMA: I can recall it so clearly. We had no children, but my husband and I discussed the possibility of adopting a child. And if we did, we wanted to personally save a child who was at the utmost depth of misfortune and to give him all earthly pleasures.

KAWASHIMA: Soon after the war in autumn when we began to feel the chill in the evening breeze . . .

SHINAKO (leafing through papers): You found Toshinori in an underground passageway in Ueno.

MRS. KAWASHIMA: Even today I can remember it clearly. We saw a helpless, blind child in rags, begging. He was sitting on a dirty straw mat, next to his grimy boss . . . After one glance, I knew this child had to be ours . . . Although he was blind, he had serene eyebrows and a fair, noble face. In that dark and sour-smelling underground passageway, there was a special glow around this child. He looked like a prince.

KAWASHIMA: I offered his boss a satisfactory sum, and we promptly took charge of him. His natural refinement became apparent when we brought him back to our house and bathed him. First, we provided him with a warm bed and hot meals. He accepted them so naturally. Next, we tried to restore his sight. This is one thing we have been unable to accomplish, so far. His eyes were burned by the flames as he ran about in confusion during an air raid.

MRS. TAKAYASU (as if obsessed, she begs SHINAKO): Please let us see that child, immediately.

TAKAYASU: Now, shouldn't we do that after we hear their story, dear?

MRS. KAWASHIMA (to SHINAKO): He was just an innocent child, then. So we couldn't find out exactly what happened. He said that after his home was destroyed in an air raid — and probably after he lost his parents — he had lived by depending on others. We felt such compassion for him. Though things were scarce those days, we tried our best to raise him with utmost care and affection.

SHINAKO: It's fifteen years now . . . Toshinori is quite attached to both of you?

MRS. KAWASHIMA: Absolutely.

SHINAKO: And he was never fearful or aloof?

MRS. KAWASHIMA: No. As a matter of fact, he was totally spoiled.

KAWASHIMA: You'd better tell her the truth, dear. Frankly, Toshinori's personality has a strange aspect. It's like a hard shell that we simply can't penetrate.

MRS. TAKAYASU (getting angry): He's not like that!

KAWASHIMA: How would you know! You only had him for five years when he could still see. Unfortunately, that child's strange personality developed after he became blind.

MRS. TAKAYASU *(crying):* Poor darling! Poor darling!

TAKAYASU: And what do you mean exactly by saying you can't understand him?

KAWASHIMA: There's no simple explanation. Well, for example . . . That child shows no emotion. When he heard that his real parents were found, he didn't react at all. And on our way here, he looked extremely bored. But, at other times, he would suddenly get excited over something trivial and become unruly . . .

MRS. TAKAYASU: Toshinori isn't like that! Once he sees our faces . . .

KAWASHIMA: May I remind you that he's blind.

MRS. TAKAYASU: That doesn't matter . . . Once he hears our voices, the shell around his heart will melt away instantly, and he'll be his old, gentle self. Ahh, within the past fifteen years, there hasn't been a day that I didn't think of him. You've been living with his body for the past fifteen years, but I've been living with his spirit . . . We resigned ourselves to his death. We held his funeral and put up a tombstone. But even then, we still couldn't give up completely. And when my husband and I started to search among the waifs in Ueno . . . Ahh . . . By then Toshinori was already with you. We spent fifteen years living with two dreams about that child — about his being alive and his being dead. When we visited his grave covered with the red blossoms of crape myrtle, we felt as if he was alive somewhere. But when we saw the soiled faces of the homeless children, we felt as if he was already dead. We were haunted by feelings of both hope and despair. It was like not knowing exactly whether we belonged — out in the sun or in the shade. In other words, in the shade, we were distracted by the sunlight, and once in the sun, we could not forget the dreaded shade. When we saw a cloud at the seashore, we thought it looked just like our child. And when we heard the voice of the neighbor's child coming from across the fence, we were startled, thinking it was our own Toshinori's. When we saw the flowers blooming in the garden, we could not decide whether we should take them to his grave or arrange them in his empty study . . . and . . . Can you imagine our surprise when we found out quite by chance that we was being cared for by the Kawashimas!

KAWASHIMA: "Being cared for" is hardly appropriate, Mrs. Takayasu. Even legally, he's already our child.

MRS. TAKAYASU: But actually, you must be anxious to get rid of such a blind and twisted eccentric?

MRS. KAWASHIMA: How can you say that!

KAWASHIMA *(to his wife):* Let her have her say, dear. In any case, they can't do anything about it. That child has no desire to go back to his real parents.

TAKAYASU: You have such confidence!

KAWASHIMA: And why not! To be honest, that child is a kind of maniac. Since we've patiently endured his madness, we have the right to scoff at your naive sentimentality. We've stubbornly endured his madness and have even become as one with him in body and spirit. You'll never understand the horror of this bond. We've brooded over killing that child a number of times . . .

MRS. TAKAYASU: So they were treating him cruelly, after all!

KAWASHIMA: Toshinori's blindness saved his life and also saved us from committing a crime. You simply have no idea.

MRS. TAKAYASU: You call that adorable Toshinori a maniac!

TAKAYASU: They're trying their best to find fault with him.

MRS. KAWASHIMA: Well, just wait and see whether both of you can manage him.

MRS. TAKAYASU: What great educators you are!

TAKAYASU: You're the ones who drove him to madness.

MRS. KAWASHIMA: No. You who abandoned him to the flames are to blame. You were only thinking of yourselves . . .

MRS. TAKAYASU: We abandoned him? You say we abandoned him?

SHINAKO: Please restrain yourselves. You mustn't get emotional. In any case, this is a place of peace where all disputes should end with smiles. I hold an invisible balance in my hand and mete impartially to both parties their appropriate satisfactions and also dissatisfactions. In my eyes, the flames of anger are like a sculpture of agate . . . And the churning water of the rapids is like a crystal relief. For some reason, the tangled-up knitting yarn and the tightly clinging ivy are, to me, mere illusions — just deliberate tricks played by a strange, evil spirit. And all complicated situations are also illusions. The world is actually simple and eternally silent. At least, I believe that. So, I have the courage of a white dove that descends on the sand of a bull ring during a savage fight and waddles about awkwardly. Why should I mind if my white wings are spattered with blood? Blood and fighting are both illusions. And I can walk calmly among you . . . Just like a dove strolling on a beautiful temple roof next to the sea . . . Are you ready? It's now time for all of you to meet the individual in question. I'll bring Toshinori here. *(She exits.)*
[A moment of anticipation. Off stage.]
Toshinori, please come here.
[Leading TOSHINORI *by the hand,* SHINAKO *enters. He wears a well-tailored suit. He has on a pair of dark glasses and uses a stick.]*

TAKAYASUS: Toshinori! *(They try to embrace him.)*

SHINAKO: Please sit here. *(Leading* TOSHINORI *to a chair next to hers.)*

The people sitting to your right are your real parents.

[TOSHINORI *is aloof.*]

MRS. TAKAYASU *(crying):* My, how he's grown! You can't see Mother? Poor darling. Dear, that child is so overwhelmed he's speechless. Touch my hands. Touch my face. Then you'll know I'm your real mother.

[MRS. TAKAYASU *draws near* TOSHINORI *and tries to take his hands. He abruptly brushes aside her hands. With reluctance she returns to her seat, crying.*]

TAKAYASU: Stop crying, dear. His behavior shows they've filled him full of bad opinions about us. We must be very patient and wait until his heart softens.

MRS. KAWASHIMA: You can imagine whatever you please. Hasn't it turned out exactly the way we imagined, dear?

KAWASHIMA: Well . . . It looks that way.

SHINAKO: What happened, Toshinori? Your mother's crying.

TOSHINORI: So what? I can't see anyway.

SHINAKO: But surely you can hear her voice.

TOSHINORI: It's a dear voice.

TAKAYASU: Toshinori! You're beginning to recognize us!

TOSHINORI: Recognize what? I only meant that I missed the sound of someone crying. I hadn't heard that for a long time. It's a typically human sound. When this world comes to an end, man will lose his power of speech and only cry out. I'm sure I've heard that crying once before.

MRS. TAKAYASU: You're gradually beginning to remember, Toshinori. Isn't it a voice you've definitely heard before?

TOSHINORI: There you go chattering again. You ruin everything through words. The humanness of the sound has faded away again . . . It's terribly hot. Like being in a furnace. The flames are blazing furiously on all sides. The flames are dancing around me in a circle. Isn't that so, Miss Sakurama?

SHINAKO *(smiling faintly):* No, it's summer now. Besides, you're wearing a suit like a proper gentleman.

TOSHINORI *(feeling himself):* This is what they call a necktie . . . A white shirt . . . A jacket. They're the clothes I wear just as I'm told. I don't exactly know how they look on me. This is what they call a pocket. It holds matches spilled out from matchboxes, loose change, transfers, safety pins, losing lottery tickets, dead flies, and pieces of an eraser . . . It's a worthless bag where you always find such things mixed in with lint. And this entire outfit is a perfectly safe uniform called a suit. It's proof that the wearer is faithful to the routine, daily existence.

MRS. TAKAYASU: He's grown up all twisted! Just listen to the way he talks.

TOSHINORI: You know, Miss Sakurama, I don't give a damn about appearances. What I understand is this feeling of being strangled and this feeling of the sweat-soaked underwear sticking to my skin. I've been forced to wear a silk collar and a cotton straitjacket. Isn't that so? I'm a naked prisoner.

MRS. KAWASHIMA: Of course, you are. You're a naked prisoner. You're forced to wear a collar and a cotton prison uniform.

TOSHINORI: Exactly. Mother is always so understanding.

MRS. TAKAYASU: How can I bear this, dear? He still hasn't called me "Mother."

TOSHINORI: You want me to call you "Mother"? Then you'll have to agree with what I say. Am I a naked prisoner with a collar?

MRS. TAKAYASU: That's absurd! You have on a fine suit.

TOSHINORI: You see? She's totally unfit to be my mother. Father, am I a naked prisoner?

KAWASHIMA: Of course, you are. You're a naked prisoner.

TOSHINORI: Uncle Takayasu?

TAKAYASU (*after a slight hesitation*): Of course. You're a naked prisoner.

MRS. TAKAYASU (*excitedly, following suit*): You're a naked prisoner! A naked prisoner! There's no doubt about it.

TOSHINORI (*laughing until tears roll out of his eyes*): Ha, ha, ha. Now I've got two sets of parents.
[*Strange silence.*]

SHINAKO: Then let's get down to the main issue. First, we'll hear from the Kawashimas.

TOSHINORI: Miss Sakurama. Why do you speak? Why do you speak words? You should either be quiet or cry. You have such a beautiful voice. It's wasted when you speak.

SHINAKO: However . . .

TOSHINORI: "However," you say? I won't listen to excuses . . . Do you think mere words will sway me? They're like fog or mist. Do you think something visible will do that? I'm blind, you know. Something I can touch with my hands? I only feel unevenness. A human face? That's just unevenness, too.

MRS. KAWASHIMA (*with customary obsequiousness*): That's very true. The human face is just unevenness.

TOSHINORI: A light shines in all directions from the center of my body. Can you see this?

MRS. KAWASHIMA: Of course, I can.

MRS. TAKAYASU (*eagerly*): Of course, I can.

TOSHINORI: Good. You've got eyes solely for this purpose. To see this light. Otherwise, it's better you should lose your eyes somewhere.

MRS. TAKAYASU (*to* TAKAYASU, *in a whisper*): Poor darling. He's always worried about his eyes. What a pity.

TOSHINORI (*rising, highly excited):* What are you chattering about? Shut up!

[*As if dealt a blow, all become silent.* TOSHINORI *again sits down.*]

. . . Now listen to me. You all have eyes just to see what I tell you to see. In other words, your eyes are a form of responsibility. Your eyes are responsible for looking at whatever I want you to see. And only then, your eyes become a noble organ taking the place of my own eyes. Suppose I want to see a large, golden elephant wending its way through the blue sky? You must see it instantly. A large yellow rose casts itself out of a window on the twelfth story of a building. When I open the refrigerator door late at night, there's a white, winged horse crouching inside. A cuneiform typewriter . . . A dark green, deserted island inside an incense burner . . . You must all instantly see that kind of miracle — any kind of miracle. You're better off blind if you can't . . . By the way, can you see the light shining in all directions from the center of my body?

KAWASHIMA: Of course, I can.

TAKAYASU: Ahh . . . Ahh . . . I can see.

TOSHINORI (*covering his face, sadly):* Ah, I have no form. When I touch my face and body like this, it's simply unevenness, everywhere. This can't be my form. It's only the extension of unevenness found everywhere on the face of the earth.

MRS. TAKAYASU: Toshinori!

TOSHINORI: I don't have a form, but I'm light. I'm a light inside a transparent body.

KAWASHIMA: Of course, you're a light.

TOSHINORI (*spreading open his jacket):* Look carefully. This light is my spirit.

MRS. TAKAYASU: Your spirit?

TOSHINORI: Unlike the rest of you, my spirit wanders naked around this world. Can you see my light shining in all directions? This light can burn another body, but it also relentlessly produces burns on my spirit. Ahh, it's such a struggle to live naked — like this. It's such a struggle . . . Since I'm a hundred million times more naked than the rest of you . . . You know, Miss Sakurama, maybe I'm already a star.

KAWASHIMAS, TAKAYASUS: Of course, you're a star!

TOSHINORI: That's right. A distant star, many light years away. Otherwise, unless the source of my light was so far away, how could I be living here, so serenely? Because this world is already gone.

MRS. TAKAYASU: What are you saying?

TOSHINORI: This world is already gone. Can you understand? If you're not a ghost, then this world must be. And if this world isn't a ghost . . . (*He points directly at* MRS. TAKAYASU.) You are!

MRS. TAKAYASU: Ahh! (*As she starts falling,* TAKAYASU *grabs her.*) That child has finally gone mad!

TAKAYASU: Get hold of yourself. If you lose your mind, too, it's the end of everything!

KAWASHIMA: Didn't I say he was a maniac? Nevertheless, he does say highly clever things. And rather than be his parents, we've become his good friends.

MRS. KAWASHIMA: Anyway, we knew you couldn't manage him.

TOSHINORI: Give me a cigarette. My tongue is coated since I've spoken so eloquently.

KAWASHIMA *(approaching him, opens a cigarette case):* Well, choose whichever you like.

TOSHINORI: You've kept an assortment of cigarettes in stock for me as usual. Watch me, Miss Sakurama. I can tell them apart by simply feeling them. *(Holds one between his fingers.)* This one? It's a Camel?

KAWASHIMA: Yes.

TOSHINORI: And this is a . . . Navy Cut. I'll take one.

[KAWASHIMA *offers him a light.*]

TAKAYASU *(to his wife):* You see. When he's like that, he's a completely normal individual. He acts exactly like a proper gentleman. *(To* TOSHINORI.*)* You like English cigarettes?

TOSHINORI: Yes.

TAKAYASU: I'll bring you some next time.

TOSHINORI: Oh, thank you. While I'm puffing on a cigarette, that time is for smoking.

KAWASHIMA: You can accept it with composure.

TOSHINORI: Exactly. I don't mind riding the subway or shopping at a department store. And there's no need to criticize the daily lives of others. Unfortunately, to those who can see, the picture of their daily lives is clearly visible. Fortunately for me, I can't. That's the only difference. And it's better not to see, for things are bound to have a frightening appearance . . . I don't mind watering the plants and flowers in the garden or using the lawn mower. And I can do frightening things without seeing! After all, isn't it frightening that flowers bloom in a world already ended? And to water the ground of a world already ended!

MRS. KAWASHIMA: Of course. Its frightening.

KAWASHIMA: We're all living in terror.

TOSHINORI: Even so, the rest of you don't recognize that terror. You're living like corpses.

KAWASHIMA: That's right. We're corpses.

MRS. KAWASHIMA: I'm a corpse, too.

MRS. TAKAYASU: It's bad luck to talk about corpses.

TAKAYASU: Now, now. You don't understand, dear.

TOSHINORI: What's more, you're all cowards. You're insects.

MRS. KAWASHIMA: Cowards!

KAWASHIMA: Insects!

MRS. TAKAYASU: That's how they spoil the child. Parents aren't insects.

TAKAYASU But if you want Toshinori back, there's no other way except to agree with him.

MRS. TAKAYASU: *(with extraordinary determination):* Then I'm an insect, too. But call me "Mother."

TOSHINORI *(without emotion):* Mother . . . insect . . .

MRS. TAKAYASU: He's finally called me "Mother"!

TAKAYASU: And I heard "insect," too.

TOSHINORI: You're all stupid morons.

(Momentary hesitation.)

KAWASHIMAS, TAKAYASUS: We're all stupid morons.

[Short silence. The big window at upstage center gradually catches the colors of the sunset. TOSHINORI *puffs on a cigarette as if thoroughly enjoying its taste.]*

SHINAKO: It may be partly my fault, but we're getting nowhere. I can clearly see that the Kawashimas and the Takayasus have the same splendid qualifications to be parents. Since both parties have such deeply sincere parental feelings, even I can't help being moved to tears. Unfortunately, at this point, the contest is a draw. The balance with Toshinori at the fulcrum doesn't seem to swing in either direction. As a member of the Board of Arbitration, I believe I should ask both parties to retire to another room. Then I'll have a long, heart-to-heart talk with Toshinori. How does that sound to all of you?

[Both parties nod approval.]

Then let's proceed accordingly . . .

[As the KAWASHIMAS *and the* TAKAYASUS *retire offstage,* SHINAKO *sees them to the door.* MRS. KAWASHIMA *reenters and then leads* SHINAKO *to a wing of the stage.]*

MRS. KAWASHIMA: Though I think you already know, that child is dangerous. Very dangerous. And you must be careful of the venom he carries.

SHINAKO: What do you mean by that?

MRS. KAWASHIMA *(smiling sweetly):* What do I mean? . . . I can't tell you that. I'm only speaking from my own experience.

*[*MRS. KAWASHIMA *leaves.* SHINAKO *walks to the window upstage center.]*

TOSHINORI: Have they all gone?

SHINAKO: Yes.

TOSHINORI *(with a cold smile):* . . . Hee, hee. I've cleverly driven them away!

SHINAKO: You mustn't talk that way about your parents who are so kind to you. They both love you from the bottom of their hearts.

TOSHINORI: The parents who adopted me are already my slaves. And my real parents are unredeemable fools.

SHINAKO: I don't want you to talk that way.

TOSHINORI: What does everyone want with me? I have no form at all.

SHINAKO: Form is important. After all, your form isn't your own. It belongs to society.

TOSHINORI: Then you're concerned about my form, too?

SHINAKO: Of course, I am. As long as I have eyes, there's no other way for me to make a judgment.

TOSHINORI: But I can't see your form. It's unfair. Stepmother says you're beautiful.

SHINAKO: That's silly. Besides, I'm already an old woman.

TOSHINORI (rising, very angrily): What is age? Age! Age is a single path in total darkness. And you can't see where you've been or where you're going. So distance doesn't exist. It's all the same whether you're walking or standing still. Or whether you're going forward or backward. On this dark path, the seeing become the blind, and the living, the dead. And like me, everybody uses a cane and wanders about, groping his way with his feet. In other words, the infant, the youth, and the aged all are huddled together quietly in the same spot — like insects swarming noiselessly on top of a withered branch in the evening.

SHINAKO: When you say that, it gives me courage. Society only judges people by age, especially women.

TOSHINORI: The seeing eye sees only form.

SHINAKO (gazing through the window): What a fantastic sunset!

TOSHINORI: The sun is setting, isn't it?

SHINAKO: The rays of the setting sun seem to be dancing all over the window.

TOSHINORI: The window you're looking through faces east, doesn't it? Isn't the sun about to set in the east?

SHINAKO: What are you saying? The sun sets in the west. The back gate below the window faces directly west. And beyond it across the wide road I can see the sun sinking into the tops of the trees in the park. Thanks to the park, the sky is open, and I can look across at a full sunset.

TOSHINORI: That's why the sun is setting in the east. You just said the western gate, but that rundown western gate directly faces the eastern gate of Hell.° And that invisible eastern gate of Hell faces this direction from beyond the sunset — with its dark mouth wide open. And before this gate, the black sand, always swept and purified, lies waiting for the footprints of the newly arriving guests.

eastern gate of Hell: refers to traditional Japanese ideas of where the gates to Buddhist Paradise are located

SHINAKO: Your manner of teasing frightens people. Oh, now all the lights in the park have been turned on. The sky is like a blazing furnace, and the green of the forest is especially bright. So the row of park lights shines faintly like unpolished, blue gems . . . The windows of the moving cars are flaming red, reflecting the sunset.

TOSHINORI *(facing the window for the first time):* I can see it, too.

SHINAKO: What? . . . You can see?

TOSHINORI: Of course, I can see that flaming red sky.

SHINAKO: Toshinori! Can you really? Then why didn't you tell us that . . .

TOSHINORI: I can only see this flaming red sky. So clearly and in such detail . . .

SHINAKO: My!

TOSHINORI: You think that's the setting sun. And you think it's a sunset. You're wrong! That's the scene of the end of this world. *(Rising, he walks over to* SHINAKO *and places his hands on her shoulders.)* Now listen! That's not the setting sun!

[Fearfully, SHINAKO *withdraws herself beyond his reach and looks up at* TOSHINORI'S *face. Standing by the window and facing the audience,* TOSHINORI *speaks. Eventually,* SHINAKO *turns her back to the audience and motionless gazes at the window. The deep red outside the window mysteriously intensifies.]*

I'm certain I've seen the end of this world. I've even seen that final flame which burned out my eyes during the last year of the war when I was five. Ever since then, the flames at the end of this world have been burning furiously in front of my eyes. Like you, I tried a number of times to convince myself that it was just a quiet scene at sunset. But that was no use. What I saw was definitely this world enveloped in flames. See! The countless flames rain down from the sky. Every house starts to burn. Every window of every building spews out flames. I can see it clearly. The sky is full of sparks. The low-hanging clouds are dyed in poisonous purple, and these same clouds are mirrored on a river which is already flaming red. The sharp silhouette of a large steel trestle . . . The pitiful sight of a big tree enshrouded in flames with its top completely sprinkled with sparks, swaying in the wind . . . The small trees and the thickets of bamboo grass all wear emblems of fire. In every corner, the emblems and border decorations of fire vigorously move on. The world is strangely quiet. And in this stillness, a single sound resounds and echoes from all directions like inside a temple bell. It's a curious sound like a groan, as if everybody is reciting the Buddhist scripture. What do you think it is? Can you tell me, Miss Sakurama? It's neither speech nor singing. It's the agonized cry of humanity. I've never heard such dear voices. And I've never heard such sincere voices. Humanity will never raise such sincere voices except at the end of this world. Can you see? Surely you can . . . the people burning here and there? Under the fallen beams, under building blocks, within imprisoned rooms — men burning everywhere. And naked, rose-colored corpses, lying here and there. The rose-colored ones — as if they had died of shame. And poppy-colored ones . . . And pure black ones — as if they had died of remorse . . . Naked corpses of every color . . . Oh, yes, the river is full of the dead, too. I can see it now. Its surface no longer reflects anything. And the closely packed, floating corpses slowly move toward the sea. Toward the sea where the purple-colored clouds overhang. The flames press forward everywhere, one after another. Aren't the flames pressing forward? Can't you see? You can't see that, Miss Sakurama? *(Running to the center of the room.)* The flames are everywhere. To the east, to the west, and to the south and north. A wall of flame looms quietly in the distance. A small flame rises from there. It flies directly for me waving its soft hair. It circles around me as if teasing. Then it stops in front of my eyes and seems as if it were peering into them. It's hopeless! The flame! It leaped into my eyes!

[*Covering both of his eyes,* TOSHINORI *collapses.* SHINAKO *looks back, but remains in a daze for a moment. Then she quickly runs over to him, kneels down, and grabs hold of him. At that moment, the sunset outside the window begins to fade rapidly.*]

SHINAKO: Get hold of yourself, Toshinori! Get hold of yourself!

TOSHINORI *(finally regaining consciousness):* Did you see the end of this world? You did, didn't you, Miss Sakurama?

[*Long pause.*]

SHINAKO *(after some hesitation comes to a decision):* No, I didn't.

TOSHINORI: You're lying. You're hiding it from me.

SHINAKO *(gently):* No. I didn't see it. I only saw the sunset.

TOSHINORI: You're lying!

SHINAKO: I don't lie!

TOSHINORI *(violently brushing her aside):* Go away! I hate women like you. They're always lying. Go away instantly!

SHINAKO *(rising quietly):* I'm staying here.

TOSHINORI: Didn't I tell you to go? You're disgusting!

SHINAKO: No, I won't.

TOSHINORI: Didn't you hear me say you were disgusting?

SHINAKO: Yes, but I'm still staying.

TOSHINORI: Why?

SHINAKO: . . . Because I'm starting to like you a little.

[*Pause.*]

TOSHINORI: You're trying to take the scene of the end of this world away from me.

SHINAKO: That's right. And that's my job.

TOSHINORI: I can't live without it. And you're going to take it away from me though you realize it?

SHINAKO: Yes.

TOSHINORI: You don't care if I die!

SHINAKO *(smiling):* You're already dead.

TOSHINORI: You're a disgusting woman! You really are!

SHINAKO: But I'm staying here. You want to make me leave? . . . Yes, I'll tell you how. Just ask me to do you a small favor. Something trivial having nothing to do with the end of this world or a sea of flames.

TOSHINORI: Do you want to go?

SHINAKO: No, I always want to stay with you.

TOSHINORI: I just have to ask you a small favor, Miss Sakurama?

SHINAKO: Yes.

TOSHINORI: Give me your hands.

SHINAKO *(extending her hands):* Like this?

TOSHINORI: You've got soft hands. I thought you'd suffered much more.

SHINAKO: No, compared to you, I don't know suffering.

TOSHINORI *(proud smile):* I only have to ask as if I were speaking to a servant?

SHINAKO: You should rather say, "Speaking to an older sister."

TOSHINORI: Hee, hee. I'm hungry.

SHINAKO: Yes, it's already supper time.

TOSHINORI: Can you give me something to eat?

SHINAKO: Shall I go out and get you something?

TOSHINORI: Just anything. As long as you can do it right away.

SHINAKO: Fine, leave it to me. *(Taking* TOSHINORI *by the hand, she makes him sit in his chair. The room is already dark.)* You wait here quietly for me.

TOSHINORI: Uh-huh.

[As SHINAKO *begins to leave through another door than the one used by the others, she presses the light switch. The room suddenly brightens up.]*

SHINAKO: I'll be right back.

TOSHINORI: Uh-huh.

[Smiling, SHINAKO *starts to leave.]*

Miss Sakurama . . .

SHINAKO: What is it?

TOSHINORI: You know . . . I don't know why, but everyone loves me.

*[*SHINAKO *leaves, smiling. In the brightly lit room,* TOSHINORI *remains, all alone.]*

Curtain

Translated from the Japanese
by Ted T. Takaya

TANIKAWA SHUNTARŌ

Tanikawa Shuntarō (1931–) was born in Tokyo, began to write poetry at age eighteen, and published his first book in 1952. His father, a philosopher and educator, supported his decision not to attend university and encouraged his writing; the father's interest in Zen may have influenced some elements of the son's poetry. Tanikawa has published in many artistic forms, including drama, film scripts, essays, and children's books. His work in English translation by William I. Elliott and Kawamura Kazuo won the American Book Award.

Although Tanikawa's poetry is innovative and experimental, he is one of Japan's most popular poets. Although some elements in his work such as the uses of indirection, asymmetry, surprise, and love of paradox have been associated with Zen and can be associated with Taoism, Tanikawa is not a Zen poet.

The selections are from his book of prose poems, Definitions, *(1975).*

The Sanctity of Trivial Things

Trivial things which vaguely lie in trivial forms and ways connected in no way to other things of no account. How to account then for their trivial being in the world, when there's no way of finding out that can be found? Trivia lying idly in indifferent poses pose no threat to our own being the time being, although the no-accountedness of things of no account accounts perhaps for our continuing confusions over them.

These things can unaccountably brush hairily against our hands, or flash and dazzle to confront our eyes. They make a noise that deafens sometimes, or they can shock the tongue with bitterness. And so distinguishing trivia from one another is to forgo definitively that in which true triviality lies. And so to grasp the trivial in one exclusive yet illimitable shape would not then contradict with seizing trivia as these countless finicky bits of no account, and yet such triv . . . (this part has been blotted out).

The writer cannot speak of trivial things in trivial ways. He speaks of things of no account as if indeed they always were of some. And so to measure them, to argue for their use or uselessness, to stress the fact that they are there, accounting for the feel and taste of them, is only to breed more illusions over things of no importance. The reason that they are beyond our definition lies maybe in the structure of our language, or in the fact of language wrought as style, or simply in perhaps some intellectual failing of the author? The reader is free to judge this as he will.

Translated from the Japanese
by Dennis Keene

Obsession with an Apple

You can't say it's red. It's an apple — not a color. You can't say its round. It's not a shape but an apple. You can't say it's sour. It's not a taste but an apple. You can't say it's expensive. It's not a price — it's an apple. You can't say it's pretty. It isn't beauty — it's an apple. You can't classify it, because it's not a fruit but an apple.

It's a flowering apple, a fruit-bearing apple, an apple that trembles on a branch in the wind. It's a rain-beaten apple, a peckable apple, a pickable apple. It's an apple that falls to earth, an apple that rots. It's a seed-bearing apple, a budding apple, an apple that need not be called an apple. An apple that need not be an apple; an apple that may be an apple. Apple or not, one apple is all apples.

Jonathan, crab, golden, winesap, Fuji, Tsugaru apples. One apple. Three, five, a dozen apples. Fifteen pounds, twelve tons, two million tons of apples. Apples to be produced, apples to be transported. Apples to be weighed and packed and sold. Apples to be sprayed, digested, consumed. Apples to be annihilated. Apples! Apples? That one, that one there, that one over there.

That one there, there in the basket. That one falling off the table, that one transposed to canvas, that one to be baked in the oven. A child holds it and bites it. That one, there. However much it rots, however many are eaten, apples go on growing on trees and endlessly filling the stores, shining. Of what is an apple a replica? Of what time a replica?

We can't answer. It's just an apple. We can't ask. It's just an apple. We can't discuss it. Finally, it's nothing but an apple, even now . . .

Translated from the Japanese by
William I. Elliot and Kawamura Kazuo.

A Personal Opinion about Gray

There has never been a perfectly white white. Even in a perfect white an imperceptible trace of black is present and that is invariably the very nature of whiteness itself. White does not regard black as hostile; instead, white produces black because of its whiteness; white promotes black. From the very onset of whiteness, white points toward blackness.

Whatever tones of gray it may undergo in its long journey toward black, white never ceases being white until the instant it turns into complete black. Even if white is violated by such non-white elements as shadow, dullness or absorption of light, white keeps shining behind a mask of gray. White dies in an instant. In that instant, white vanishes without a trace and complete black is born. But —

There has never been a perfectly black black. In a black that completely lacks radiance, an imperceptible trace of white is present, like a gene, and that is invariably the nature of blackness itself. From the very onset of blackness, black points toward whiteness . . .

Translated from the Japanese
by William I. Elliot and Kawamura Kazuo

Impossible Approach to a Glass

In most cases it has a bottom but no top and is cylindrical. It is a cavity standing upright, an enclosed space closed towards the center of gravity. It can contain a given amount of liquid, without permitting it to spread, within the field of gravity. When it contains only air, we say it is empty, but even then its outline is clearly revealed by light, and the existence of its mass can be ascertained, without instrumentation, at a clear-headed glance.

When we flick our nails against it it vibrates and produces sound. It is sometimes used as a signal, and rarely as a unit of music. Its sound has a sort of stubborn self-sufficiency with no outside application and it threatens our ears. It is set on a table. Over and over again a hand grasps it. Often it slips from our hands. We can indeed deliberately fragment it, easily, and so it contains potential as a weapon. Even shattered, however, it still exists. If at this very moment all the glasses on earth were suddenly broken, we could still not escape its existence. Though its name varies from one culture to another because of various systems of transcription, it already exists for us as one common fixed idea, and even if its actual manufacture (from glass, wood, iron, clay) were to be forbidden under pain of death, we should nonetheless still be unable to escape the nightmare of its existence.

It is an instrument whose chief purpose is the satisfaction of our thirst, and under extreme circumstances it has no more use than a hollow formed by two cupped palms, but in the context of multiple forms of contemporary life it doubtless maintains silence as a form of beauty, now in the morning sunlight, now under artificial light.

Our intelligence, our experience and our skill have produced it on this earth and named it, and we refer to it by a single series of sounds as though it were completely natural, but as to what it truly is no one can claim to have an exact answer.

Translated from the Japanese
by William I. Elliot and Kawamura Kazuo

HAYASHI MARIKO

Hayashi Mariko (1954–) was born after the American occupation of Japan to a family that ran a bookstore. An avid reader from an early age, she eventually received a degree in literature from Nihon University. She began her career by writing advertising copy but has devoted herself full time to literary writing since 1984. She has published several volumes of fiction and essays, among which If I Can Make the Last Train *and* To Kyoto *won national prizes. Her work has been both praised and censored for revealing much of herself. Some carry westernized titles like* Starry Stella *and* Tennessee Waltz.

"Wine" shows a young woman caught between East and West, old and new. Traveling abroad, she tries on the role of wine connoisseur as a badge of sophistication and brings home a very expensive bottle of French wine. Not really liking wine, she decides to present it as a gift — but to whom? She finds herself caught in a web of traditional Japanese etiquette, which she rejects but cannot fully escape.

Wine

Our tour guide, Nicole, shrugged her shoulders slightly as she descended the stairs leading to the cellar. I knew that this was something she habitually did when she was feeling self-satisfied. Although it was only our second day in Quebec, I wondered how many times we had already seen her do this. She was a plump, good-natured woman of middle age. Similarly, whenever she was bored by the chateau or neighborhood through which she was guiding us, she showed it plainly on her face. At such times, we felt obligated to keep up a running volley of *très bien's.*

Suddenly she began to speak in rapid French. Our interpreter, Mrs. Endo, translated it into Japanese that had a slightly odd intonation.

"I'm going to show you Canada's best wine cellar. You rarely see a cellar this fine — even in France."

Oh, wine. Just hearing the word makes me feel tense. Being a free-lance journalist, I think that I have a wider smattering of miscellaneous knowledge than the average woman. But wine is my one weak area. Two years ago I wrote an article about wine for a certain women's magazine. The sommeliers and oenophiles I met at that time thoroughly annoyed me. They were able to recite from memory tediously long names of wines that I wouldn't remember even if I heard them a hundred times, and they spoke in the secret language of vintages. And they had a strange look in their eyes to begin with. After seeing the way they appeared to lick their lips when discussing the better specimens, I vowed never to set foot in the territory of wine again.

But I also hate to be seen as an ignorant child. So I sometimes skim articles about wine before going to restaurants and bars. Naturally, though, I tend to forget everything I've read by the time I reach my destination.

"This is a famous wine cellar," Mrs. Endo said, pushing the wooden door open. "People come from as far away as Montreal to buy wine here. Because the province of Quebec has a direct link with France, this cellar has an extensive collection of wines that you can't get elsewhere."

The moment I set foot in the wine cellar, I was at a loss for words. I had never been in a place so authentic, and I was overwhelmed by the sight. The low brick ceiling extended as far as the eye could see. Small lamps burned here and there in the dim, chilly room. When my eyes became accustomed to the dimness, I could see dull light reflecting from the round bottoms of thousands of bottles. It reminded me of a study lined with foreign books.

Apparently the wine cellar was part of Nicole's standard tour. She guided us into the interior of the cellar with a practiced air.

She suddenly turned around to face me in front of the racks and asked me in English if I liked wine. Her English pronunciation was as poor as that of most Quebecois.

"I like to drink it, but I don't know that much about it," I replied, in equally halting English. As if he had overheard, a man appeared before us. Tall and bearded, he looked like a scholar. Or at least like someone who worked in a bookstore. Just as I was wondering why it is that men involved with wine so often have a scholarly air, I surprised myself by murmuring, "Maybe I should buy a bottle to take home as a souvenir."

Nicole snapped her fingers happily. She said something in French that I couldn't really understand, but I took it to mean "Just as I expected." The bearded man was called over.

"This lady says she would like you to select a good bottle of wine for her," Mrs. Endo murmured. Holding up one finger, as if to say, "Leave it to me," the man began selecting bottles of wine from a nearby rack.

"He says that he knows Japanese people like white wine and that he would suggest something like this."

Mrs. Endo's finger, the nail painted pink, pointed to the price tag. "Ten dollars: a little over two thousand yen. Is this what you had in mind?"

"No," I answered decisively. At that moment, I was afflicted with a sudden urge to confound these foreigners. They were mocking me with their talk of a two-thousand-yen bottle of wine. Even in Japan I drink wine a bit more expensive than that. I wondered if I looked that young and impoverished.

"Since this is such a good opportunity to do so, I want to try a good wine. I'd like to splurge and spend about ten thousand yen and drink it at the hotel."

"Ten thousand yen? Well." Mrs. Endo, eyes widened, was clearly not being sarcastic. "I live here, and I've never had wine that expensive. You must be rich, Ms. Sone."

"Not at all. But a wine of that price would cost five or six times that much in Japan, so experiencing one here would give me something to remember back in Japan."

Mrs. Endo communicated that to Nicole and the man, who were looking at me dubiously.

"He wants to know what kind of wine you like." I may have imagined it, but I felt that his attitude toward me had become a bit more polite. It was truly regrettable that I couldn't think of the name of any particular wine at that moment.

"Ten thousand yen. A wine of around that price." As I said that I was sure that the man was laughing at me inside. His expression didn't change, however, and he began jingling the keys attached to his belt.

"He says the expensive wines are over here." The racks were in an enclosure shaped like a cask. He unlocked it and beckoned to me. The area inside, which measured about six feet by nine feet, seemed to be walled in with bottles of wine. You could tell at a glance that they were old, because the labels had faded or peeled off altogether. To mask the confusion that had engulfed me, I picked up one of the bottles.

"Oh, you have this one. . . . "

Naturally I had no idea what wine it was. But under the circumstances I felt that I had to say something like that.

Holding a bottle in each hand, he seemed to be asking my opinion. Rather than the labels, I looked at the price tags below them, but I couldn't make them out.

"Forty-five dollars. That's just about right, isn't it?"

At the sound of Mrs. Endo's voice I said, "Yes, yes," over and over.

"This is a great wine. It would cost you the equivalent of . . . ah, let's see . . . eighty thousand yen, even to drink it in a Canadian restaurant."

"Is that right — would it cost that much? Let's all drink a toast with it tonight."

"Great. I'd like to join you," Omura, the photographer, said loudly. He hadn't spoken up to that point.

The man was smiling at us and putting the wine into a box. He was trying to stuff packing in around it, so awkwardly that I couldn't bear to watch.

"Oh, never mind. Will you please tell him that we're going to be drinking it soon, so he can just put it in a paper bag." Before I finished speaking, Mrs. Endo exclaimed "Oh, dear," in a soft but piercing voice. "Ms. Sone, look. What should I do?" She was pointing at the cash register, which was displaying the figure 145. "I mistook the price. I thought something was strange. He kept saying that this wine would cost several hundred thousand yen in Japan, and I kept wondering how something that cost only ten thousand yen could be worth that much. What should I do?"

Mrs. Endo, the wife of a businessman, was only called upon as an interpreter during the busy season. She was showing a surprising lack of sophistication by acting as flustered as if this were her own problem. "It's my fault. I didn't see the number one in front of the price. What should I do? It seems absurd to pay a hundred and forty-five dollars for a bottle of wine."

That scarcely needed to be said. Because I was on a trip, I had decided to buy a bottle of wine in the ten-thousand-yen class, more than I would usually spend. But I had had no intention of spending more than three times that amount.

"What shall I do? Shall I have him exchange it for that two-thousand-yen bottle we were looking at earlier?"

Apparently noticing something odd about the way we were acting, the man stopped wrapping up the wine. He looked at me with his blue-green eyes. At that moment I decided to bear the heavy expense rather than submit to the humiliation of explaining what had happened.

"I can't say I made a mistake about the price. It seems like I'm being given a punishment for showing off, but that's all right. I'll take it."

Two days later I was on a plane heading back to Tokyo. The box holding the wine was bulkier than I expected; with it and my carry-on bag, my hands were full. I couldn't get it all the way under the seat so it stuck out into the aisle a bit.

"Miss?" A Japanese flight attendant approached me with a smile that was rendered utterly insincere by the cold look in her eyes."Let me take that paper bag for you."

"No." I shook my head. "This is a very expensive wine. I'm worried about turbulence, so I want to keep it close by." I was trying to put into practice the smattering of knowledge I had: "Hold wine when riding on a plane."

"But it will be in the way of the other passengers, so I'll take it for you," she said, still smiling.

"All right. It won't be a problem if I hold it in my lap, will it?"

With her lips resuming their normal position, she left without saying anything further. I held it like that for a while, but it was tiring. I pulled my bag in front of me with my feet and put the wine on top.

Walking around carrying a bottle of wine was like walking around carrying china. At each hotel and airport along the way, I said in English: "This is a very expensive wine. Be careful, please." I ended up carrying it myself rather than entrust it to a porter. I realized that I had become more neurotic than I would have thought possible. I couldn't bear it — each time the plane shook, I felt as though the wine were emitting a little cry. "I'm being ridiculous," I smiled wryly to myself. I was acting just like those crazy oenophiles — the ones who treat wine as though it were a baby, saying that it breathes. Wasn't I the one who was supposed to have scorned them? Then, the moment I happened to buy some expensive wine, I had gotten all flustered and could think of nothing else.

"Hey, what are you going to do with that wine?" Omura asked from the seat next to mine. I felt guilty that the part of the package I couldn't let go into the aisle was infringing on his leg room, but I didn't mention it. I had asked him to hold the paper bag for me countless times, and each time I had begged his pardon most humbly.

"I just wanted to try a thirty-thousand-yen wine." Naturally I had cancelled the promised wine party at the hotel. I had decided to take the wine back home with me, murmuring over and over to myself. "When I get back to Tokyo I'm going to sell it to someone for a really outrageous price."

"I'll call you if I open it."

"It's also nice to give a party to pay homage to a bottle of wine. You know, with some cheese to go with it."

"I didn't realize. . . . Do you know a lot about wine, Omura?"

"No, just what the average person knows. As it happens, before we went to Canada I was working on a project involving wine."

"I suspected as much." I laughed softly with him.

"The best thing would probably be for you and your boyfriend to drink it together, wouldn't it?" Omura yawned as he spoke, as if he were sleepy.

"That would definitely be a waste. How could a child like him possibly understand wine?"

"What do you mean, a child? He's the same age as I am, isn't he?"

"Is that right? I thought you were older than he is."

I thought of Kunihiko's face, which looks like a child's when he gets angry. Four years my junior, he was a photographer like Omura.

"You're terrible — just because you're attached to him you treat the rest of us as if we were your uncles." Closing his eyes, Omura laughed.

Kunihiko was there to meet me at the airport. Because I had ordered him to be. I had contributed half the money for our used Honda on the condition that he would be the driver. We dropped Omura off along the way and headed to Yoyogi, where I was renting a two-bedroom apartment.

"What did you bring me?" As soon as we were alone together, Kunihiko's tone became flirtatious. He had a mustache, but it had the unintended effect of emphasizing the childishness of his face.

"I got you a book of photographs."

"That's kind of austere. Don't you have anything more exciting?"

"When it was time to leave I didn't have many dollars left, and I ended up buying something boring. I wasn't able to get much of anything for myself, either."

"What do you mean, something boring?"

"A thirty-thousand-yen bottle of wine."

"I've drunk wine worth that much before. Last year when we finished that special edition, the chief editor treated us to some in Roppongi."

"Let me explain something to you. When you buy wine at a restaurant, it costs three times the original price. Furthermore, when it's imported there are other added costs. So how much do you think a thirty-thousand-yen bottle of wine would cost in Japan?"

"I see." Kunihiko gave a whoop of joy. "Let's drink that expensive wine together! To celebrate your homecoming."

"You've got to be kidding." I sniffed. "That would be casting pearls before swine. I'm sure you have no idea of the trouble I went through to bring this wine back here. I'm going to let someone who can really appreciate it drink it."

"You scare me."

I was in a bad mood. Kunihiko was acting as though he wanted to stay over, but I chased him off early, saying I was tired.

"What do you mean? I was looking forward to seeing you." It couldn't quite be taken as a parting shot, but with those words he left, clutching the book and T-shirt I had brought him. Hearing the Honda's engine in the distance, I collapsed on the sofa. I had heard the gossip. A twenty-year-old layout artist had fallen madly in love with Kunihiko. They had probably seen each other constantly while I was away. I hadn't failed to notice the new decoration on the car window. Kunihiko may have put it there deliberately for me to see. Maybe it was just my fatigue and the sentimentality that accompanies coming home from a trip, but I was beginning to think that our relationship might be ending.

Still lying down, I looked at the paper bag that was next to the suitcase and wondered where I should keep the wine. I had heard that you're supposed to keep it in a cool place where the temperature is stable, but there was no such place in my apartment. The rainy season had ended while I was in Canada, and now I could see the midsummer sun through the curtains. I knew the apartment was probably like a steam bath when I wasn't there. I had to hurry up and give the wine to someone.

But who? Among my acquaintances, Kishima, an illustrator, knew the most about wine. More of an artist than an illustrator of late, Kishima was actually famous. He was also widely reputed to be a snob. I had heard that he had pet snakes in his huge Japanese-style mansion in the Hongo section of the city and that he played with them amid his art nouveau furniture. He had a weakness for good food and fine wine and often wrote essays on those subjects. In fact, I had become acquainted with him after I had been to pick up a manuscript from him. Kishima would understand the value of this wine and appreciate it more than anyone else, but I didn't know him well enough to give it to him as a gift. Besides, a thirty-thousand-yen item that represented the height of extravagance to me might well seem commonplace to him. The thought of this rankled me, somehow.

I wanted to use this wine on someone who would really appreciate it. In that sense, Morita seemed to be my only possibility. He was the assistant editor of a women's magazine that gave me a lot of work. In fact, this Canadian assignment was the type of thing that could have easily gone to someone else if it hadn't been for his strong backing of me. We were fairly close, too, perhaps because we were close in age. A rugby player in his college days, Morita had a slightly rough way of dealing with people that I found refreshing. If anything, I prefer men who are a little thick-skinned.

"Hi, it's me."

"So, you're back safely."

"I'll come in to the office tomorrow."

"There's no hurry. You can wait until the photos have been developed."

"I brought back some wine."

"Oh, yeah? Is Canadian wine supposed to be good?"

"It's not Canadian. I hadn't known it, but a lot of good French wine is shipped to Quebec."

"That's great."

Morita had a loud voice. And as often seems to be the case with loud-voiced men, he liked to drink. He also loved to teach women things. I had gone with him to countless bars and listened to his lectures.

"Red should be chilled for just thirty minutes. Exactly thirty." So he would order the bartender, tapping on his watch. His greatest happiness was to put on an act of this sort, first becoming a regular customer and then a valued patron who received special treatment.

"Is it Bordeaux or Burgundy?" I could picture his face as his voice came over the receiver. He was probably talking loud deliberately, so the entire editorial department would be able to hear him.

"How should I know? I think it was Chateau something."

"You don't even know that 'Chateau' is part of the name of the really good Bordeaux wines?"

"I'm not the connoisseur you are, Mr. Morita."

"You don't have to be a connoisseur to know that much. Spell the name for me."

"Right now?"

"Yes. Go on."

I put my hand in the paper bag reluctantly. For some reason I felt really angry. Every woman hates to tear open a package that has been wrapped so carefully.

"Let me see. S, A. . . ."

"Wait a minute. I can't understand it like that. Read it correctly, in French."

"I can't. I forgot all my French after college. I studied it as my second foreign language."

"Never mind, then."

The sound of Morita clicking his tongue came clearly over the receiver. He was known for his impatience.

"Okay, then, be sure to bring it tomorrow. Without fail."

He hung up without waiting to hear my response. He had said he could wait for the manuscript, but when it came to something he wanted, it had to be tomorrow.

"What are you talking about? The truth is, you don't know anything," I said aloud. Everyone knew that. Every person with any sense soon realized that although Morita put on a brave front he was actually timid. As a native of rural Kyushu° who had come to work at a publishing company, he concentrated all his energy on not being made a fool of. He really did know a lot about music, fashion, new shops, and food. But because he tried to show off his knowledge, the lengths to which he had gone to obtain it soon became obvious to people. The same was true of wine. I had seen this once. Morita had a small card with a table of vintages printed on it. He carried it around with him and was always trying to memorize it.

"Thirty minutes. Chill it for exactly thirty minutes." Those words must have appeared in some magazine as well.

I seemed to have become malicious ever since I had bought the wine. I no longer wanted to give it to Morita. If possible, I thought, I wanted this wine to be drunk by a man who was close to perfect. But was there such a person in my life?

When I woke up it was dark. It was three o'clock in the morning. Unbelievably, I had been asleep on the sofa for more than twelve hours. This was no way to get rid of my jet lag. As I feared, when I started to get up I felt slightly nauseated. It wasn't good that I had had to miss going to the doctor for a while.

About this time last year, I had lost consciousness and been taken to the hospital. They couldn't determine the cause, and I went around to a number of hospitals to have tests. Then the editor of a health magazine told me about the Okamura Clinic on the Ginza.° The Okamura Clinic is

Kyushu: one of the four islands forming Japan
Ginza: the major commercial district of Tokyo

for rich people, and when I heard the name I knew it wasn't my kind of place. But the editor kindly wrote me a letter of introduction, and I was able to get an appointment with Dr. Okamura himself. When he determined that my blackout had been the result of autonomic ataxia caused by fatigue, I felt admiration for him and understood why he had the reputation he did. I didn't have to become an in-patient; instead I started going to the clinic every ten days. Normally people treated by the head doctor at a clinic slip him tens of thousands of yen in addition to the usual fee as a token of their appreciation, but Dr. Okamura understood that I was a single woman. I had never given him so much as a bottle of whiskey.

I should give the wine to the doctor, I thought. Morita will probably complain a lot, but he's a simple man, so I'll be able to get out of it somehow. Dr. Okamura is a far more appropriate recipient for my wine than Morita.

Not only was he a famous doctor, he was also reputed to be a man of refined tastes. He wrote haiku that were sometimes published in magazines. He was also reputed to be the president of a sumo° fan club.

I prettied up the wine. I didn't think the paper bag from Quebec would be appropriate, so I went to a specialty shop and bought some high-quality rice paper. I thought that a ribbon would be overdoing it, so I attached a light green seal.

Wrapping it up in a kerchief, I headed over to the Okamura Clinic on the appointed day. In the three days I had spent taking it easy at home, my jet lag and fatigue had completely disappeared. I had worn jeans the entire time I was in Canada, but today I wore a white linen dress.

My heart raced when I imagined the expression on the doctor's face when he received the wine. He would appreciate its value more than anyone. A lot of his patients were the owners of the Ginza's oldest shops. Surely there would be someone to appreciate it with him.

But I couldn't decide when to give the doctor the wine. There were many other doctors and nurses in the examining room, and I usually wasn't even with him for five minutes.

"You're not having the headaches anymore. Let me check on you again in ten days." With those words, the doctor swiveled around in his chair to face his desk, and the beautiful gray hair on the back of his head faced me. I hadn't had a chance to give him the package that I had left by the door.

I had no choice but to leave it at the reception desk. Naturally, that wasn't the way I would have liked to present it. I had imagined the ripping of the paper and his exclaiming, "Oh, Chateau. . . ." He would certainly have pronounced it correctly. But apparently the doctor and I would not be playing out that scene after all.

___

sumo: a form of wrestling that many consider to be the national sport of Japan. The average sumo wrestler weighs over 300 lbs.

"Uh, this is for Dr. Okamura. . . ." As I uttered the words, I realized that I had forgotten something important. My name wasn't on the package. As an emergency measure I decided to tape a piece of paper with my name on it to the package.

"Could you please lend me some tape?"

The receptionist seemed to understand what I was trying to do. Nodding pleasantly, she opened a drawer. But the tape wasn't there.

"It was over there." She got up, and, following her with my eyes, I got a clear view of the area she was referring to. There was a huge pile of packages on the floor. Attached to each was a piece of white paper with bold black letters indicating that it was a midyear present. Absent-mindedly, I, who hadn't engaged in the practice for many years, had completely forgotten about the custom of giving midyear gifts to one's social superiors, and even when the season for such giving was.

"Oh, no," I thought immediately. My wine was definitely not a midyear gift. It was not something that could be reduced to that sort of formality. Besides, who knew what would happen to it once it got mixed up in that huge pile. It would end up sharing a fate with the other, boring gifts, like golf balls, white shirts labeled with the name of the tailor who made them, and imported whiskey. My wine had to be something special that existed only for its own sake. It couldn't possibly be left amid this crowd of other things.

Carrying my package, I started walking briskly.

"Here's the tape!" the woman shouted.

"That's all right. I forgot the card."

The moment the automatic door opened, hot air seemed to come up from the ground and envelop me.

"Now what am I going to do?" In my arms, the wine was gasping for breath too. I could hear it saying that it didn't want to go back to that hot apartment.

"What am I going to do? What am I going to do?"

At almost exactly noon, the Ginza around me seemed to flatten into the background, the way things do in old films. Walking along in my white clothes, I felt ludicrous, as if I myself were a present wandering around in search of a recipient.

Translated from the Japanese
by Dawn Lawson

KOREA

HWANG SUNWŎN

Hwang Sunwŏn (1915–) was born near Pyongyang in what is now North Korea and received his university degree in English literature at Waseda University in Japan in 1939. On his return to Korea that year, he went into hiding to avoid conscription into the Japanese occupation forces. When Korea was liberated from Japanese rule in 1945 and divided at the 38th Parallel, like a great number of Koreans, his family fled the Soviet-occupied north for the U.S.-occupied south. Hwang taught at a high school, then, from 1957 to 1993, taught Korean literature at the University of Seoul.

Hwang's literary career spans six decades. His early work comprises two volumes of poetry published while he was in college. He has published several novels and numerous short stories. "Cranes" (1953) tells the story of two young men from the same village near the border between North Korea and South Korea who now find themselves on different sides of the Korean war. "Masks," the title story of a collection called The Book of Masks, *written between 1965 and 1975, tells the story of a soldier killed in the same war and follows him through a cycle of reincarnation. The stories are "masks" in that each shows a visage of broader human experience.*

Cranes

The northern village lay snug beneath the high, bright autumn sky, near the border at the Thirty-eighth Parallel.° White gourds lay one against the other on the first floor of an empty farmhouse. Any village elders who passed by extinguished their bamboo pipes first, and the children, too, turned back some distance off. Their faces were marked with fear.

As a whole, the village showed little damage from the war, but it still did not seem like the same village Sŏngsam had known as a boy.

At the foot of a chestnut grove on the hill behind the village he stopped and climbed a chestnut tree. Somewhere far back in his mind he heard

---

Thirty-eighth Parallel: the border between North and South Korea

the old man with a wen° shout, "You bad boy, climbing up my chestnut tree again!"

The old man must have passed away, for he was not among the few village elders Sŏngsam had met. Holding onto the trunk of the tree, Sŏngsam gazed up at the blue sky for a time. Some chestnuts fell to the ground as the dry clusters opened of their own accord.

A young man stood, his hands bound, before a farmhouse that had been converted into a Public Peace Police office. He seemed to be a stranger, so Sŏngsam went up for a closer look. He was stunned: this young man was none other than his boyhood playmate, Tŏkchae.

Sŏngsam asked the police officer who had come with him from Ch'ŏnt'ae for an explanation. The prisoner was the vice-chairman of the Farmers' Communist League and had just been flushed out of hiding in his own house, Sŏngsam learned.

Sŏngsam sat down on the dirt floor and lit a cigarette.

Tŏkchae was to be escorted to Ch'ŏngdan by one of the peace police.

After a time, Sŏngsam lit a new cigarette from the first and stood up.

"I'll take him with me."

Tŏkchae averted his face and refused to look at Sŏngsam. The two left the village.

Sŏngsam went on smoking, but the tobacco had no flavor. He just kept drawing the smoke in and blowing it out. Then suddenly he thought that Tŏkchae, too, must want a puff. He thought of the days when they had shared dried gourd leaves behind sheltering walls, hidden from the adults' view. But today, how could he offer a cigarette to a fellow like this?

Once, when they were small, he went with Tŏkchae to steal some chestnuts from the old man with the wen. It was Sŏngsam's turn to climb the tree. Suddenly the old man began shouting. Sŏngsam slipped and fell to the ground. He got chestnut burrs all over his bottom, but he kept on running. Only when the two had reached a safe place where the old man could not overtake them did Sŏngsam turn his bottom to Tŏkchae. The burrs hurt so much as they were plucked out that Sŏngsam could not keep tears from welling up in his eyes. Tŏkchae produced a fistful of chestnuts from his pocket and thrust them into Sŏngsam's. . . . Sŏngsam threw away the cigarette he had just lit, and then made up his mind not to light another while he was escorting Tŏkchae.

They reached the pass at the hill where he and Tŏkchae had cut fodder for the cows until Sŏngsam had to move to a spot near Ch'ŏnt'ae, south of the Thirty-eighth Parallel, two years before the liberation.°

wen: cyst or skin blemish
liberation. the communist term for the communist victory

Sŏngsam felt a sudden surge of anger in spite of himself and shouted, "So how many have you killed?"

For the first time, Tŏkchae cast a quick glance at him and then looked away.

"You! How many have you killed?" he asked again.

Tŏkchae looked at him again and glared. The glare grew intense, and his mouth twitched.

"So you managed to kill quite a few, eh?" Sŏngsam felt his mind clearing itself, as if some obstruction had been removed. "If you were vice-chairman of the Communist League, why didn't you run? You must have been lying low with a secret mission."

Tŏkchae did not reply.

"Speak up. What was your mission?"

Tŏkchae kept walking. Tŏkchae was hiding something, Sŏngsam thought. He wanted to take a good look at him, but Tŏkchae kept his face averted.

Fingering the revolver at his side, Sŏngsam went on: "There's no need to make excuses. You're going to be shot anyway. Why don't you tell the truth here and now?"

"I'm not going to make any excuses. They made me vice-chairman of the League because I was a hardworking farmer, and one of the poorest. If that's a capital offense, so be it. I'm still what I used to be — the only thing I'm good at is tilling the soil." After a short pause, he added, "My old man is bedridden at home. He's been ill almost half a year." Tŏkchae's father was a widower, a poor, hardworking farmer who lived only for his son. Seven years ago his back had given out, and he had contracted a skin disease.

"Are you married?"

"Yes," Tŏkchae replied after a time.

"To whom?"

"Shorty."

"To Shorty?" How interesting! A woman so small and plump that she knew the earth's vastness, but not the sky's height. Such a cold fish! He and Tŏkchae had teased her and made her cry. And Tŏkchae had married her!

"How many kids?"

"The first is arriving this fall, she says."

Sŏngsam had difficulty swallowing a laugh that he was about to let burst forth in spite of himself. Although he had asked how many children Tŏkchae had, he could not help wanting to break out laughing at the thought of the wife sitting there with her huge stomach, one span around. But he realized that this was no time for joking.

"Anyway, it's strange you didn't run away."

"I tried to escape. They said that once the South invaded, not a man would be spared. So all of us between seventeen and forty were taken to the North. I thought of evacuating, even if I had to carry my father on my back. But Father said no. How could we farmers leave the land behind when the crops were ready for harvesting? He grew old on that farm depending on me as the prop and mainstay of the family. I wanted to be with him in his last moments so I could close his eyes with my own hand. Besides, where can farmers like us go, when all we know how to do is live on the land?"

Sŏngsam had had to flee the previous June. At night he had broken the news privately to his father. But his father had said the same thing: Where could a farmer go, leaving all the chores behind? So Sŏngsam had left alone. Roaming about the strange streets and villages in the South, Sŏngsam had been haunted by thoughts of his old parents and the young children, who had been left with all the chores. Fortunately, his family had been safe then, as it was now.

They had crossed over a hill. This time Sŏngsam walked with his face averted. The autumn sun was hot on his forehead. This was an ideal day for the harvest, he thought.

When they reached the foot of the hill, Sŏngsam gradually came to a halt. In the middle of a field he spied a group of cranes that resembled men in white, all bent over. This had been the demilitarized zone along the Thirty-eighth Parallel. The cranes were still living here, as before, though all the people were gone.

Once, when Sŏngsam and Tŏkchae were about twelve, they had set a trap here, without anybody else knowing, and caught a crane, a Tanjŏng crane. They had tied the crane up, even binding its wings, and paid it daily visits, patting its neck and riding on its back. Then one day they overheard the neighbors whispering: someone had come from Seoul with a permit from the governor-general's office to catch cranes as some kind of specimens. Then and there the two boys had dashed off to the field. That they would be found out and punished had no longer mattered; all they cared about was the fate of their crane. Without a moment's delay, still out of breath from running, they untied the crane's feet and wings, but the bird could hardly walk. It must have been weak from having been bound.

The two held the crane up. Then, suddenly, they heard a gunshot. The crane fluttered its wings once or twice and then sank back to the ground.

The boys thought their crane had been shot. But the next moment, as another crane from a nearby bush fluttered its wings, the boys' crane stretched its long neck, gave out a whoop, and disappeared into the sky. For a long while the two boys could not tear their eyes away from the blue sky into which their crane had soared.

"Hey, why don't we stop here for a crane hunt?" Sŏngsam said suddenly.

Tŏkchae was dumbfounded.

"I'll make a trap with this rope; you flush a crane over here."

Sŏngsam had untied Tŏkchae's hands and was already crawling through the weeds.

Tŏkchae's face whitened. "You're sure to be shot anyway" — these words flashed through his mind. Any instant a bullet would come flying from Sŏngsam's direction, Tŏkchae thought.

Some paces away, Sŏngsam quickly turned toward him.

"Hey, how come you're standing there like a dummy? Go flush a crane!"

Only then did Tŏkchae understand. He began crawling through the weeds.

A pair of Tanjŏng cranes soared high into the clear blue autumn sky, flapping their huge wings.

Translated from the Korean by Peter H. Lee

Masks

Wounded by a bullet in the leg, the soldier fell. As he tried to lift himself, a bayonet pierced his chest. In the instant he lost consciousness, the face of his attacker was imprinted on his eyes as though burned there. The blood from the soldier's chest flowed into the yellow earth of this desolate battlefield. It was at the foot of a hill far from his home, yet it resembled the land around his own village.

His blood soaked into the earth and became earth. The dead soldier had been a farmer, and for him soil was life itself. At first this soil was a deeper shade than the rest, but gradually it became all one color.

The roots of a purple eulalia reed furtively sipped the soldier's life, and he became reed.

A jumble of combat boots trampled the reed and moved on. In winter, boots heavier than before trod upon the snow-covered reed. Time after time they trampled it and left, but the plant did not die. After the boots had moved on, the reed was blown by the breezes in spring, bathed in sunbeams, washed by rain and dew, covered with snow, and blown once again by the spring breezes. In the late spring the reed was cut down by a farmer's scythe and carried to a stable.

Here the reed became a bull. Just as the dead man had done when he was a farmer, the bull's owner cared for it as if it were the most important member of his family. Now the soldier worked hard alongside the farmer. He worked until his skin was bruised and swollen, but keeping the farm alive from year to year was not easy. Then a flood swept away the fields, and one night that autumn the farmer stifled the sound of his own crying as he stroked the scruff of the soldier's neck. The soldier passed through the market, then went by train to the slaughterhouse. He was hung up in a butcher's in the city, where meat was cut and sold from his carcass. There he saw someone he knew — the one who had pierced his chest with a bayonet at the foot of the hill. He was begging for food. He ate a piece of the meat from scraps he had begged at a restaurant, and the soldier entered this man.

The man tossed away his empty begging tin and hoisted himself up, one sleeve of his worn-out work clothes dangling where he had no arm. He went toward the iron foundry where he had worked as a lathe operator before the war took his arm. He strode inside and approached his former boss.

"Good day."

The foundry master's face showed his displeasure. He crushed out his cigarette with the toe of his shoe.

"Don't worry, I haven't come here to badger you, sir. I've come here to work as I did before."

The master cast an uncomfortable glance at the armless sleeve.

"What are you looking at?" The man eyed the master squarely and continued, "I was wounded in the leg by a bullet, but does that mean I can't operate a lathe?"

The man shifted his body as he spoke, his empty sleeve dangling at his side.

Translated from the Korean
by Martin Holman

PAK MOGWŎL

Pak Mogwŏl (1916–1978) was born in South Korea and established himself as a major poet in his youth. He continued throughout his life to write poetry, publishing five volumes. He is also known for his essays, translations, and children's poems.

Pak's early poems, set in the landscape of South Korea, are described as "romantic-pastoral." When he turned to writing of the hardships of urban life in Seoul, nature continued to be a source of solace. By the time he was in his forties, aging had already become an obsessive theme. His later work is philosophical, reflecting Taoist ideas. The language of his poems is plain, natural, and often powerful. These selections are from Unordered *(1979).*

An Empty Glass

Empty is
      a glass
          clear with emptiness,
this winter morning when
the world is transfixed in icicles,   5
this winter morning when
the world burns in dry sticks.
But there cannot be in this world
things that are empty and void.
One fills   10
      with cool resignation
or the water of faith.
This morning, my hand, creative,
fixes roses,
      Josephine Bleuneuse,   15
the most seductive of roses,
in the center of
        the clear glass.

Translated from the Korean by Uchang Kim

Burial

Thought of things
that are being buried under snow
within the iron fence of the curfew.
The ease of burial
and soft forgetfulness   5
makes the world cleaner.
The iron fence goes under the snow
and falls into sleep.
The white lines of rules come loose
dimly over the veil,   10
and the morning comes
in which no footsteps echo.

Translated from the Korean by Uchang Kim

Footprints

Evening comes in the color of grapes
to the snow-covered frontline.

Within the truce zone
foxes wander with frozen noses,

weaving their way among trees,   5
and disappear over the head of the stream.

A pheasant flutters up in surprised flight
from a tangled thornbrush.

Footprints come alive
as dawn brings light.   10

Within the tightening dragnet
of the search party, mountain berries

peep out in the snow
like drops of blood, a stifled cry.

Translated from the Korean by Uchang Kim

A Trip to Yongin°

We made a short trip by bus,
as directed by the minister,
my wife and I.
Fifteen hundred won°
per square meter, a reasonable price,   5
said the real estate agent.
My eyes groped around the sunny side
and looked at my wife,
and she looked at me
with eyes of the western sky.   10
Darkness descended on the peaks;
lights came on one-by-one
in the far villages, making
the land all the bleaker.

Yongin: an area in the outskirts of Seoul. In this poem, the poet goes with his wife to
find a grave site for himself.
won: basic monetary unit in South Korea

Let us go back, my wife said,   15
with a sob in her voice, sending a chill to my heart.
We took the same express bus for return,
looking at the image of man and wife
on the bus window, while the hand
of the wind and sand caressed my heart.   20
The land we seek is no longer here.
The window reflected like a screen
two grave mounds and a stone slab.
What was crying was
neither the sound of wind   25
nor beast.

Translated from the Korean by Uchang Kim

Winter Living

Snow has fallen on snow,
the truly light, the bright
falling in the backyard,
on the wall.
I passed this winter,   5
chewing crumbs of barley bread,
catching snow like crushed grains.
This snow must be
the last snow of winter.
There is nothing one could do   10
except to find reconciliation
in something like this
on an occasion like this,
in this place under clouds —
My winter living   15
sustained by chewing crumbs
and catching snow grains in two hands.
In this land under clouds,
there is nothing one could do
except to find reconciliation   20
in such a way as this.
Chewing crumbs of barley bread,
I catch in my two hands
the truly light, the bright.

Translated from the Korean by Uchang Kim

KIM NAMJO

Kim Namjo (1927–) was born in Taegu in South Korea. She received a degree in Korean literature from Seoul National University in 1951 and taught at Sungmyong Women's University beginning in 1955. She has served as president of the Catholic Writers' Association, is married to a sculptor, and has four children.

Kim is known as the poet of love and of the candle. A long sequence of poems entitled "Candlelight" combines the two themes with that of poetry itself. Two shorter selections here treat the same themes. "Winter Christ" is an example of her many poems which express religious feeling.

Love Song

From deepest root
to topmost crown
my loneliness
is what I must give
to you.   5
This heart
circling the seamless ring
of heaven from origin in the east
past the end of the western horizon
returns once again.   10

Translated from the Korean by
David R. McCann and Hyunjae Yee Sallee

Gift

I

I am earth,
yet you light me
like a candle.
All of my life
I have been a stone,   5
and yet you pattern me

like a jade.
For the first time,
I experience
such a miracle in my life. 10

2

Loving more, the more I can love,
and praying, the more I can pray . . .
Such a strange swelling;
a strange power, not at all
my own. 15

3

What you gave,
the leaves
and flowers,
yield to fruit
as time passes. 20
Today,
I receive
a golden seed
that passed through the scorching heat
of the sun. 25

Translated from the Korean by
David R. McCann and Hyunjae Yee Sallee

Winter Christ

Today
as he walks the snow-covered hills and fields
his clothes are white as the snow,
and his bare feet are whiter still.

Where long ago he crossed over the waters, 5
the river now is frozen,
a vast crystal of ice.
He crosses over
the piercing, needle-sharp cold.
His bare feet, whiter than white. 10

I would weep.
Lord of the snowy day
ceaselessly, ceaselessly
drawing the blood of the new spring
mixed with his precious blood   15
from all the depths of earth
and sea in this fathomless,
hair-raising cold.

Translated from the Korean by
David R. McCann and Hyunjae Yee Sallee

HWANG TONGGYU

Hwang Tonggyu (1938–) has published several volumes of poetry, a
collection of critical essays, and has co-edited a poetry magazine. The
eldest son of the novelist Hwang Sunwŏn, he was educated at Seoul
National University and Edinburgh University, and took part in the
International Writing Program at the University of Iowa. He is a pro-
fessor of English at Seoul National University, has translated the
poems of T. S. Eliot and Robert Lowell into Korean, is an admirer of
Yeats and Baudelaire, and admits to Western influence in his work.

In an article prepared for a forum on modern literature in Korea in
1984, Hwang declares the Western-inspired, experimental Korean po-
etry to be the work of bad poets, and the tradition-inspired poetry too
repetitious and mediocre; instead he seeks a middle ground between
them, just as he seeks the middle ground between pure poetry and a
poetry of commitment. Others have described Hwang's style as com-
passionate, honest, and at times dense and elliptical.

Four Twilights

I

Glad omen.
The Chunghŭng monastery° is burnt down,
The Taehwa Palace° is in ruins.

Chunghŭng monastery: a temple in Seoul, which crumbled in 1915 leaving only the
foundation
Taehwa Palace: a temporary royal palace built in 1129; only the ruins remain

I balanced a boulder on the cliff
And, looking up day and night,   5
Trained my eyes.
I can see it.
In June a continuous rain,
In December came long snow.
It's easiest to take life easy;   10
So easy
I had nights of insomnia.
Glad omen.

2

Irrelevance,
Alternating seasons,   15
Winds over the spring hills,
The clanking of bells in late autumn.
Inconvenienced,
My ancestors
Fled to the island of Kanghwa.°   20
When winter covered the hills with snow,
Shivering in the cold, I saw sunbeams
In the mouse holes on palace walls.
As I grew older, I made friends
In the dark alleys.   25
Irrelevance.

3

The wine brewed from yam
Was not sweet on my tongue.
When I grew thin, I had my clothes taken in
And went out, unperturbed, to see a woman   30
To tell her a long story.
Nothing was easier than deliverance —
Every night I cast off my desire, my skin,
Every morning I found myself
Where I had been the night before.   35
Every night a dream of shipwreck
Shook me awake at midnight. I drank
Young wine and went back to sleep.
Every morning I remembered the blinding sunlight.

Kanghwa: a mountainous island on the west coast off Seoul, a place of refuge for the
  royal court during the Yi dynasty

4

Fear assaults me when I walk by the deserted shore.   40
The girls at South Bank swear
That I'm not yet an old man.
But I'm afraid I may want to die.
My debts being small, my death
Won't make anybody sad.   45
Hands in pockets,
I watch the drunken sailors scuffle
Under blossoming clouds. I sit
On a deserted boat and smoke.
I'm afraid of the sea at dusk,   50
Though I know nothing about hell.
Darkness seeps into me before swallowing the sea.

Translated from the Korean
by Peter H. Lee

Port of Call

I reached the port on foot.
A long wind from cold places
Shook the houses by the sea;
The lights crept lower and lower,
The sky threatened a long snow.   5
I crumpled the paper bills with ugly pictures
Into my pocket.
I stubbed out the half-burned cigarette like my shadow
And went down to the shore,
My mind at peace.   10
The dark hulls creaked in the winds,
Craning their necks to see the port.
Two or three gulls went chasing
Snowflakes in the darkening sky.

Translated from the Korean
by Peter H. Lee

Wild Geese

At the upper reaches of the northern Han°
I was not just sad
Seeing all the field cannons march
Down the snow-drifted valleys.

Wild geese came flying low.   5
I slept and awoke to find myself
Looking through field glasses instead of dreams.

It was a winter of five months
With a few geese here and there.
I saw them strut with their breasts high;   10
No, they were making love.
A frightening view with a cartridge-belt at my waist.
I wept, laughed, and was reprimanded.

But a new dream came, a dream
Of uncharted land,   15
The guns made love with their barrels jumping high.
I dreamed in spite of all
And waited and waited fearlessly,
Forgetting dog-tags, frost-bite, even my life.

Translated from the Korean by Peter H. Lee

Song of Peace

I'm told
We are a puny race.
Doors locked even in daytime,
Bathing our eyes with Trust Drops,°
We read essays, hugging the stove.   5

Dragging the anguish of no place to hide
Like a common soldier,
Travel the country from Kimhae to Hwach'ŏn,°
Winter fatigues hanging on you,
A canteen flapping at your side,   10

northern Han: a river in South Korea
Trust Drops: a brand name of an eye lotion
Kimhae to Hwach'ŏn: from a district in Kyonsang province to a district in Kangwon

Wherever you turn, barbed wire;
Wherever you turn, checkpoints.
I do not understand this love,
This smothering jealous love.

I spread my gloved hands, palms up.　　　　　15
Snow falling for some time now,
A snow colder than snow.

Translated from the Korean by Peter H. Lee

ABOUT THE EDITORS

Arthur W. Biddle (General Editor) is a professor of English at the University of Vermont, where he teaches courses in non-Western literature, American literature, and composition. As a Fulbright Fellow he lectured on American literature at Utkal and Patna Universities in India and the University of Hong Kong. He likes to engage other cultures through travel as well as reading and has visited or lived in Eastern and Western Europe, North Africa and the Middle East, South Asia, and East Asia.

Biddle has published eleven books, including *The Literature of Vermont; Reading, Writing, and the Study of Literature;* and *Angles of Vision,* an introduction to literature anthology. His interest in writing across the curriculum is reflected in his *Writer's Guide* series of books for students of biology, political science, history, and psychology and in *A Community of Voices: Reading and Writing in the Disciplines.* Currently he is at work on a volume of letters between the Trappist monk Thomas Merton and the poet Robert Lax.

Angelita Reyes (The Caribbean) is an associate professor of Women's Studies and the Center for Advanced Feminist Studies at the University of Minnesota. She has been a Rockefeller Humanities Scholar in the Women's Studies Program at the University of Iowa since 1989. Her research and pedagogy focus on postcolonial women's literary criticism and writings. Her archival research of the 1856 Margaret Garner fugitive slave incident, which inspired Toni Morrison's *Beloved,* has received much attention. She recently completed a book entitled *Crossing More Bridges: Representations of the Mother-Woman in Postcolonial Women's Writing.*

Mbulelo Mzamane (Sub-Saharan Africa) is an associate professor of English and director of African Studies at the University of Vermont. Born in South Africa, he was exiled for thirty years by the *apartheid* government. He returned to his homeland in 1993 to serve first as chair of the English department and then as Rector and Vice Chancellor (president) of the University of Fort Hare. Mzamane's writing includes critical studies of Athol Fugard, Sembene Ousmane, and Ngugi wa Thiong'o, as well as original poetry, fiction, and drama. His latest works are the forthcoming *Oxford Book of South African Short Stories* and *Isimame: Women Writers in South Africa.*

Miriam Cooke (The Middle East) is a professor of Arabic literature at Duke University, where she has also taught courses in Asian and African literatures. Born in the United States and educated in Great Britain, Cooke has spent long periods in the Arab world, particularly Lebanon, Egypt, and Morocco. Her books include *The Anatomy of an Egyptian Intellectual: Yaḥyā Ḥaqqī* (1984) and *War's Other Voices: Women Writers on the Lebanese Civil War* (1988) She has coedited *Opening the Gates: A Century of Feminist Writing* (1990), *Gendering War Talk* (1993), and *Blood into Ink: South Asian and Middle Eastern Women Write War* (1994). Her current research interests revolve around issues of war and gender in Arabic literature.

Roberto González Echevarría (Latin America) is the Bass Professor of Hispanic and Comparative Literatures at Yale University, where he has chaired the Department of Spanish and Portuguese and the Council on Latin American Studies. González Echevarría's *Myth and Archive: A Theory of Latin American Narrative* (1990) received awards from the Modern Language Association of America and the Latin American Studies Association. Among his other books are *Relecturas* (1976), *Calderón and la critica* (1976), *Alejo Carpentier: The Pilgrim at Home* (1977), *Isla a su veulo fugitiva: cusayos críticos sobre literatura hispanoamericana* (1983), *The Voice of the Masters: Writing and Authority in Modern Latin American Literature* (1985), *La ruta de Severo Sarduy* (1986), and *Celestina's Brood: Continuities of the Baroque in Spanish and Latin American Literatures* (1993). González Echevarría is coeditor of the forthcoming three-volume *Cambridge History of Latin American Literature,* and is a frequent contributor to *The New York Times Review of Books.*

Vinay Dharwadker (South Asia) is an assistant professor at the University of Oklahoma, where he teaches modern literatures, literary theory, and Indian and non-Western literatures. He recently published *Sunday at the Lodi Gardens* (1994), his first book of poems, and *The Oxford Anthology of Modern Indian Poetry* (1994), which he coedited with A. K. Ramanujan. He is currently editing *The Columbia Book of Indian Poetry* and completing translations of modern Hindi and Marathi poetry. Dharwadker is a native of Pune, India.

Gloria Bien (East Asia) was born in Lanzhou, China, and came to the United States as a child. She received her Ph.D. in comparative literature from the University of Washington. She is currently an associate professor of Chinese at Colgate University, where she teaches the Chinese language, literature in translation, and a course entitled Women in China. Bien has published articles on French and Chinese literary relations in such journals as *Comparative Literature Studies, Studies on Voltaire and the Eighteenth Century,* and *Tamkang Review.* Recently she has begun to explore multimedia computer-assisted language teaching.

ACKNOWLEDGMENTS

Chinua Achebe. "The Madman" from *Girls at War and Other Stories.* Copyright © 1972, 1973 by Chinua Achebe. Used by permission of Doubleday, a division of Bantam Doubleday Dell Publishing Group, Inc.

M. Gopalakrishna Adiga. "Do Something, Brother" from *Sixteen Modern Indian Poems,* edited by A. K. Ramanujan and Vinay Dharwadker. Copyright © 1989. Reprinted by permission of *Daedalus,* Journal of the American Academy of Arts and Sciences, from the issue entitled "Another India," Fall 1989, Volume 118, Number 4.

Shmuel Yosef Agnon. "At the Outset of the Day" from *Twenty-One Stories,* edited by Nahum Glatz and translated by Segal. Copyright © 1970 by Schocken Books, Inc. Reprinted by permission of Schocken Books, published by Pantheon Books, a division of Random House, Inc.

Zamiruddin Ahmad. "Purvai — The Easterly Wind" from *The Tale of the Old Fisherman: Contemporary Urdu Short Stories,* edited and translated by Muhammad Umar Memon. Copyright © 1991 by the author; translation copyright by the translator. Used by permission of the translator.

Ama Ata Aidoo. "Something to Talk About on the Way to the Funeral" from *No Sweetness Here.* Copyright © 1988. Used by permission of the author.

Suad al-Mubarak al-Sabah. "A New Definition of the Third World," "A Thousand Times More Beautiful," "A Covenant," "Sojourn Forever," "Free Harbor," and "You Alone" from *The Literature of Modern Arabia.* Copyright © 1989. Reprinted by permission of Routledge and Kegan Paul, Ltd.

Badr Shakir al-Sayyab. "Rain Song" and "Song in August" from *Modern Arabic Poetry,* edited by Salma Khadra Jayyusi. Copyright © 1987. Reprinted by permission of Columbia University Press.

Reinaldo Arenas. "The Wounded" copyright © 1980. Reprinted by permission of the publisher, *Latin American Literary Review,* vol. VIII, no. 16, 1980, Pittsburgh, Pennsylvania.

Khalida Asghar. "The Wagon" from *The Tale of the Old Fisherman: Contemporary Urdu Short Stories,* edited and translated by Muhammad Umar Memon. Copyright © 1991 by the author; translation copyright by the translator. Used by permission of the translator.

Miguel Angel Asturias. "Angel Face." Reprinted with the permission of Atheneum Publishers, an imprint of Macmillan Publishing Company, from *El señor presidente* by Miguel Angel Asturias, translated from the Spanish by Frances Partridge. Copyright © 1963 by Victor Gollancz, Ltd., under the title *The President.* Originally published in Spanish under the title *El señor presi-*

dente in Mexico in 1946. Republished in Spanish under the title *El señor presidente* by Editorial Losada, Buenos Aires in 1952.

Layla Baalbaki. "A Space Ship of Tenderness to the Moon" from *Modern Arabic Short Stories*, edited and translated by Denys Johnson-Davies. Copyright © 1981. Used by permission of Denys Johnson-Davies.

Bei Dao. "Notes on the City of the Sun," "Answer," and "All" from *A Splintered Mirror: Chinese Poetry from the Democracy Movement*, translated by Donald Finkel and Chen Xueliang. Copyright © 1991 by Donald Finkel. Reprinted by permission of North Point Press, a division of Farrar, Straus & Giroux, Inc. "13 Happiness Street," translated by Bonnie S. McDougall, from *Renditions Magazine*, Autumn 1985. Copyright © 1985 by the Chinese University of Hong Kong. Reprinted by permission of the Research Centre for Translation of the Chinese University of Hong Kong.

Jorge Luis Borges. "The Circular Ruins" from *The Aleph and Other Stories*, translated by Norman Thomas di Giovanni. Translation copyright © 1968, 1969, 1970 by Emece Editores, S. A. and Norman Thomas di Giovanni. Used by permission of Dutton Signet, a division of Penguin Books USA Inc.

Edward Kamau Brathwaite. "Red Rising" from *Sun Poem*. Copyright © 1982. Reprinted by permission of Oxford University Press (UK). "Xango" from *X/Self*. Copyright © 1987. Reprinted by permission of Oxford University Press (UK).

Haroldo de Campos. "Two Concrete Poems." Copyright © 1968 by Haroldo de Campos.

Alejo Carpentier. "Like the Night" from *The War of Time*, translated by Frances Partridge. Copyright © 1970. Reprinted by permission of Andrea Estelman Carpentier c/o Warren Cook Literary Agency.

Aimé Césaire. Excerpt from *Return to My Native Land*. Copyright © by Aimé Césaire. Permission requested.

Cheng Naishan. "Why Parents Worry," translated by Janice Wickeri, from *Renditions Magazine*, Spring 1987. Copyright © 1986 by the Chinese University of Hong Kong. Reprinted by permission of the Research Centre for Translation of the Chinese University of Hong Kong.

Michelle Cliff. "If I Could Write This in Fire, I Would Write This in Fire" from *The Land of Look Behind: Prose and Poetry*. Copyright © 1985 by Michelle Cliff. Used by permission of Firebrand Books.

Julio Cortázar. "Continuity of Parks" from *End of the Game and Other Stories*. Copyright © 1963, 1967 by Random House, Inc. Reprinted by permission of Pantheon Books, a division of Random House, Inc.

Anita Desai. "The Farewell Party" from *Games at Twilight and Other Stories.* Copyright © 1978 by Anita Desai. Reprinted by permission of HarperCollins Publishers, Inc.

Dhoomil. "The City, Evening, and an Old Man: Me," translated by Vinay Dharwadker. Copyright © 1989. Reprinted by permission of the translator.

Assia Djebar. "There Is No Exile," from *Women of Algiers in Their Apartment*, translated by Marjolijn de Jager. Copyright © 1992 by the Rector and Visitors of the University of Virginia. Reprinted by permission of the University Press of Virginia.

Enchi Fumiko. "Boxcar of Chrysanthemums" from *This Kind of Woman: Women Writers 1960–1976*, edited by Yukiko Tanaka and translated by Elizabeth Hanson. Copyright © 1982. Reprinted by permission of Stanford University Press.

Nissim Ezekiel. "Minority Poem" and "In India" from *Collected Poems, 1952–1988, of Nissim Ezekiel*; copyright © 1989 by Nissim Ezekiel. Used by permission of Oxford University Press (India).

Forugh Farrokhzad. "Window" and "Friday" from *New Writing from the Middle East*, edited by Leo Hamalian and John D. Johannan. Copyright © 1978 by Leo Hamalian and John D. Johannan. Used by permission of the Balkin Agency, Inc.

Rosario Ferré. "The Youngest Doll," from *The Youngest Doll*, reprinted by permission of the University of Nebraska Press. Copyright © 1991 by the University of Nebraska Press.

Carlos Fuentes. "The Doll Queen" from *Burnt Water*, translated by Margaret Sayers Peden. Translation copyright © 1969, 1980 by Farrar, Straus & Giroux, Inc. Reprinted by permission of Farrar, Straus & Giroux, Inc.

Gabriel García Márquez. "Balthazar's Marvelous Afternoon" from *No One Writes to the Colonel*. Copyright © 1968 in the English translation by Harper-Collins Publishers, Inc. Reprinted by permission of HarperCollins Publishers, Inc.

Gagan Gill. "A Desire in Her Bangles," translated by Vinay Dharwadker. Permission requested.

Lorna Goodison. "The Mulatta and the Minotaur," "Lullaby for Jean Rhys," "Nanny," and "For My Mother" from *I Am Becoming My Mother*. Copyright © 1986 by Lorna Goodison. Used by permission of New Beacon Press.

Yasmine Gooneratne. "Menika" from *An Anthology of Modern Writing from Sri Lanka*, edited by Ranjini Obeyesekere and Chitra Fernando. Copyright © 1981. Reprinted by permission of the Association for Asian Studies, Inc.

Nadine Gordimer. "Comrades" from *Jump*. Copyright © 1991 by Felix Licensing, B.V. Reprinted by permission of Farrar, Straus & Giroux, Inc.

Gu Cheng. "Capital 'I,'" "Parting," and "A Headstrong Boy" from *A Splintered Mirror: Chinese Poetry from the Democracy Movement*, translated by Donald Finkel and Yi Jinsheng. Copyright © 1991 by Donald Finkel. Reprinted by permission of North Point Press, a division of Farrar, Straus & Giroux, Inc.

Nicolás Guillén. "Ballad of the Two Grandfathers" and "The Grandfather" from *Callaloo Magazine*, vol. 10, no. 2, 1987. Copyright © 1987. Translated by Jill Nethchinsky. Reprinted by permission of the Johns Hopkins University Press.

Emile Habibi. "The Gipsy" from *Edebiyat* Magazine, 1989. Translated by Hilary Kilpatrick. Copyright © 1989. Reprinted by permission of the Middle East Center of the University of Pennsylvania.

Hayashi Mariko. "Wine," translated by Dawn Larson, from *New Japanese Voices*, edited by Helen Mitsios. Copyright © 1991 by Helen Mitsios. Used by permission of Grove/Atlantic, Inc.

Bessie Head. "The Collector of Treasures" from *The Collector of Treasures*. Copyright © 1977 by the Bessie Head Estate. Used by permission of John Johnson, Ltd., London, and Heinemann Publishers (Oxford), Ltd.

Sadeq Hedayat. "The Stray Dog" from *New Writing from the Middle East*, edited by Leo Hamalian and John D. Johannan. Copyright © 1978 by Leo

Hamalian and John D. Johannan. Used by permission of The Balkin Agency, Inc.

Nazim Hikmet Ran. "On Living," "The Strangest Creature on Earth," "Some Advice to Those Who Will Serve Time in Prison," "Awakening," and "Evening Walk" from *New Writing from the Middle East,* edited by Leo Hamalian and John D. Johannan. Copyright © 1978 by Leo Hamalian and John D. Hamalian. Used by permission of the Balkin Agency, Inc.

Hwang Sunwŏn. "Cranes" from *Modern Korean Literature: An Anthology,* edited and translated by Peter H. Lee. Copyright © 1990. Used by permission of the University of Hawaii Press. "Masks" from *The Book of Masks: Stories* by Hwang Sunwŏn, edited and translated by Martin Holman. Copyright © 1976 by Hwang Sunwŏn; English translation copyright © 1989 by Readers International, Inc. Used by permission of Readers International, Inc.

Hwang Tonggyu. "Four Twilights," "Port of Call," "Wild Geese," and "Song of Peace" from *The Silence of Love: Twentieth Century Korean Poetry,* edited by Peter H. Lee. Copyright © 1980. Used by permission of the University of Hawaii Press.

Inoue Yasushi. "The Boy," "River Light," "The Beginning of Autumn," "Elegy," and "Old Man in a Turban" from *The Modern Japanese Prose Poem,* edited and translated by Dennis Keene. Copyright © 1980 by Princeton University Press. Reprinted by permission of Princeton University Press.

Ghassan Kanafani. "The Death of Bed Number 12" from *Modern Arabic Short Stories,* edited and translated by Denys Johnson-Davies. Copyright © 1981. Used by permission of Denys Johnson-Davies.

Kaneko Tōta. Haiku poems from *Modern Japanese Haiku: An Anthology,* edited and translated by Makoto Ueda. Copyright © 1976 by the University of Toronto Press. Used by permission of the University of Toronto Press.

Vinda Karandikar. "Traitor," translated by Vinay Dharwadker, from *Public Culture,* vol. 2, no. 2 (1990). Copyright © 1990. Reprinted by permission of the University of Chicago Press. "The Knot," translated by Vinay Dharwadker Copyright © 1990 by Vinay Dharwadker. Reprinted by permission of the translator.

Kawabata Yasunari. "Up in the Tree" and "Immortality" from *Palm-of-the-Hand Stories,* translated by Lane Dunlop and J. Martin Holman. Translation copyright © 1988 by Lane Dunlop and J. Martin Holman. Reprinted by permission of North Point Press, a division of Farrar, Straus & Giroux, Inc. "The Cereus" from *Contemporary Japanese Literature* by Howard Hibbet, editor. Copyright © 1977 by Alfred A. Knopf, Inc. Reprinted by permission of the publisher.

Kim Namjo. "Love Song," "Gift," and "Winter Christ" from *Selected Poems of Kim Namjo,* translated by David R. McCann and Hyunjae Yee Sallee, Cornell East Asia Series, no. 63 (Cornell East Asia Program, 1993). Copyright © 1993 by David R. McCann.

Jamaica Kincaid. "Girl" from *At the Bottom of the River.* Copyright © 1978, 1983 by Jamaica Kincaid. Reprinted by permission of Farrar, Straus & Giroux, Inc.

C. S. Lakshmi. "A Rat and a Sparrow," translated by A. K. Ramanujan. Copyright © 1992. Used by permission of *Chicago Review.*

Shankar Lamichhane. "The Half-Closed Eyes of the Buddha and the Slowly Setting Sun" from *Himalayan Voices: An Introduction to Modern Nepali Literature*, edited and translated by Michael Hutt. Copyright © 1991 the Regents of the University of California. Used by permission of the University of California Press.

George Lamming. "A Wedding in Spring." Copyright by George Lamming. Permission requested.

P. Lankesh. "Bread" from *New Writing in India*, edited by Adil Jussawalla; translated by A. K. Ramanujan. Copyright © 1974.

José Lezama Lima. Excerpts from *Paradiso*, translated by Gregory Rabassa. Translation copyright © 1974 by Farrar, Straus & Giroux, Inc. Reprinted by permission of Farrar, Straus & Giroux, Inc.

Clarice Lispector. "The Crime of the Mathematics Professor" from *Modern Brazilian Short Stories*, edited and translated by William Grossman. Copyright © 1967 The Regents of the University of California. Used by permission of the University of California Press.

Lo Ch'ing. "Protest Posters" and "Don't Read This" from *Forbidden Games and Video Poems: The Poetry of Yang Mu and Lo Ch'ing*, translated by Joseph R. Allen. Copyright © 1993 by the University of Washington Press. Reprinted by permission of the University of Washington Press. "Six Ways of Eating Watermelons" from *The Isle Full of Noises: Modern Chinese Poetry from Taiwan*, edited and translated by Dominic Cheung. Copyright © 1987. Reprinted by permission of Columbia University Press.

Earl Lovelace. Excerpts from *The Dragon Can't Dance* by Earl Lovelace. Copyright © 1979. Reprinted by permission of Andre Deutsch Ltd.

Mahasweta Devi. "Breast-Giver," translated by Gayatri Spivak, from *In Other Worlds: Essays in Cultural Politics*. Copyright © 1987. Used by permission of the publisher, Routledge, New York.

Naguib Mahfouz. "Zaabalawi" from *Modern Arabic Short Stories*, edited and translated by Denys Johnson-Davies. Copyright © 1981. Used by permission of Denys Johnson-Davies.

Jack Mapanje. "Messages," "On His Royal Blindness Paramount Chief Kwangala," and "When This Carnival Finally Closes" from *Of Chameleons and Gods*. Copyright © 1991 by Heinemann Publishers (Oxford) Ltd. Reprinted by permission of Heinemann Publishers (Oxford) Ltd.

Paule Marshall. Excerpt from *The Chosen Place, The Timeless People*. Copyright © 1969 by Paule Marshall. Reprinted by permission of the author.

Naiyer Masud. "The Color of Nothingness" from *The Color of Nothingness: Modern Urdu Short Stories*, edited and translated by Muhammad Umar Memon. Copyright © 1991 by the author; translation © 1991 by the translator. Used by permission of the translator.

Mishima Yukiō. "Yoroboshi" from *Modern Japanese Drama*, edited and translated by Ted T. Takaya. Copyright © 1979. Reprinted by permission of Columbia University Press.

V. S. Naipaul. Excerpt from *The Mystic Masseur*. Copyright © 1957 by V. S. Naipaul. Reprinted by permission of Viking Penguin, a division of Penguin Books USA Inc, and Wylie Aitken & Sons, Inc.

Kunwar Narayan. "Preparations of War," translated by Vinay Dharwadker. Copyright © 1992. Used by permission of *Chicago Review*. "Archaeological Find," translated by Vinay Dharwadker, from *Public Culture*, vol. 2, no. 2 (1990). Copyright © 1990. Reprinted by permission of the University of Chicago Press.

Emily Nasrallah. "Our Daily Bread" from *A House Not Her Own*. Copyright © 1992 by Emily Nasrallah. Used by permission of the author and gynergy books, Canada.

Njabulo Simakahle Ndebele. "Death of a Son." Copyright © 1987 by Njabulo S. Ndebele. First published by *Tri-Quarterly Review* in 1987. Reprinted by kind permission of the author and Shelley Power Literary Agency, Inc.

Pablo Neruda. "The Heights of Macchu Picchu" from *Canto General*, translated and edited by Jack Schmitt. Copyright © 1991 Fundacion Pablo Neruda, Regents of the University of California. Used by permission of the University of California Press.

Agostinho Neto. "Night," "Kinaxixi," "African Poetry," and "Western Civilizations." Copyright by Agostinho Neto.

Ngugi wa Thiong'o. "Minutes of Glory" from *Secret Lives*. Copyright © 1975. Reprinted by Heinemann, a division of Reed Elsevier Inc., Portsmouth, NH.

Grace Nichols. "Tropical Death" from *The Fat Black Women's Poems*. Copyright © 1984. Reprinted by permission of Virago Press Limited "Wherever I Hang" from *Lazy Thoughts of a Lazy Woman*. Copyright © 1989. Reprinted by permission of Virago Press Limited.

Gabriel Okara. "Piano and Drums," "You Laughed and Laughed and Laughed," and "Once upon a Time," from *The Fisherman's Invocation*. Copyright by Gabriel Okara.

Sembene Ousmane. "Tribal Scars or the Voltaique" from *Tribal Scars and Other Stories*. Copyright © 1974 by the author. Reprinted by permission of Heinemann, a division of Reed Elsevier Inc., Portsmouth, NH

Okot p' Bitek. "My Husband's Tongue Is Bitter" and "What Is Africa to Me?" from *Song of Lawino and Song of Ocol*. Copyright © 1984. Used by permission of Hayanga & Company.

Pai Hsien-yung. "Glory's by Blossom Bridge" from *Wandering in the Garden, Waking in a Dream*; copyright © 1982 by Pai Hsien-yung. Used by permission of the author.

Pak Mogwŏl. "An Empty Glass," "Burial," "Footprints," "A Trip to Yongin," and "Winter Living," from *Selected Prose of Pak Mogwol*. Copyright © 1980. Used by permission of Asian Humanities Press, a division of Jain Publishing Company.

Nicanor Parra. "Litany of the Little Bourgeois," "Mummies," "Test," and "I Take Back Everything I've Said" from *Poems and Anti-Poems*. Copyright © 1967 by Nicanor Parra. Reprinted by permissions of New Directions Publishing Corp.

Octavio Paz. "San Ildefonso Nocturne" from *The Collected Poems of Octavio Paz 1957–1987*. Copyright © 1986 by Octavio Paz and Eliot Weinberger. Reprinted by permission of New Directions Publishing Corp.

Amrita Pritam. "Process of Creation," translated by Vinay Dharwadker. Copyright © 1994 by *World Literature Today*. Reprinted by permission of the editor. "The Weed" from *The Penguin Book of Modern Indian Short Stories*. Copyright © 1980 by Anita Pritam. Used by permission of the author.

Dahlia Rabikovich. "The Dress," "The Sound of Birds at Noon," "Pride," "From Day to Night," and "Distant Land" from *New Writings from the Middle East*, edited by Leo Hamalian and John D. Johannan. Copyright © 1978 by Leo Hamalian and John D. Johannan. Used by permission of the Richard Balkin Agency, Inc.

A. K. Ramanujan. "Love Poem for a Wife 1" and "Small-Scale Reflections on a Great House" from *Relations*. Copyright © 1971. Reprinted by permission of Oxford University Press (UK).

Jean Rhys. "The Day They Burned the Books" from *The Collected Short Stories of Jean Rhys*. Copyright © 1968 by Jean Rhys. Used by permission of the Wallace Agency, Inc.

João Guimarães Rosa. "The Third Bank of the River" from *The Third Bank of the River and Other Stories*, translated by B. Shelby. Copyright © 1968 by Alfred A. Knopf, Inc. Reprinted by permission of the publisher.

Juan Rulfo. "Tell Them Not to Kill Me!" from *The Burning Plain and Other Stories*, translated by George D. Schade. Copyright © 1967. Reprinted by permission of the University of Texas Press.

Nawal Saadawi. "She Has No Place in Paradise" from *She Has No Place in Paradise*, translated by Shirley Eber. Copyright © 1987. Reprinted by permission of Reed Consumer Books Ltd.

Enver Sajjad. "The Bird" from *The Color of Nothingness: Modern Urdu Short Stories*, edited and translated by Muhammad Umar Memon. Copyright © 1991 by the author; translation copyright by the translator. Used by permission of the translator.

Tayeb Salih. "The Doum Tree of Wad Hamid" from *The Wedding of Zein*. Translated by Denys Johnson-Davies. Copyright © 1967. Used by permission of Denys Johnson-Davies.

Indira Sant. "Her Dream," translated by Vinay Dharwadker. Copyright © 1990 by Vinay Dharwadker. Reprinted by permission of the translator. "Household Fires" from *Sixteen Modern Indian Poems*, edited by A. K. Ramanujan and Vinay Dharwadker. Copyright © 1989. Reprinted by permission of *Daedalus*, Journal of the American Academy of Arts and Sciences, from the issue entitled, "Another India," Fall 1989, Volume 118, Number 4.

Simone Schwarz-Bart. Excerpt from *The Bridge Beyond*. Copyright © 1980 by Editions du Seuil. Used by permission of Georges Borchardt, Inc.

Leopold Sedar Senghor. "Black Woman," "Prayer to the Masks," "Totem," "Luxembourg 1939," "New York," "Be Not Amazed," "In What Tempestuous Night," "Senegal," and "Visit" from *The Collected Poetry*. Copyright © 1974 by Leopold Sedar Senghor. Used by permission of the University Press of Virginia.

G. Shankara Kurup. "The Master Carpenter" from *Sixteen Modern Indian Poems*, edited by A. K. Ramanujan and Vinay Dharwader. Copyright © 1989. Reprinted by permission of *Daedalus*, Journal of the American Academy of Arts and Sciences, from the issue entitled, "Another India," Fall 1989, Volume 118, Number 4.

Shu Ting. "Also All" and "Assembly Line" from *A Splintered Mirror: Chinese Poetry from the Democracy Movement*, translated by Donald Finkel and

Yi Jinsheng. Copyright © 1991 by Donald Finkel. Reprinted by permission of North Point Press, a division of Farrar, Straus & Giroux, Inc.

Kedarnath Singh. "On Reading a Love Poem" from *Sixteen Modern Indian Poems*, edited by A. K. Ramanujan and Vinay Dharwadker. Copyright © 1989. Reprinted by permission of *Daedalus*, Journal of the American Academy of Arts and Sciences from the issue entitled, "Another India," Fall 1989, Volume 118, Number 4.

Wole Soyinka. "The Strong Breed" from *Collected Plays 1*. Copyright © 1973. Reprinted by permission of Oxford University Press (UK).

Tanikawa Shuntarō. "The Sanctity of Trivial Things" from *The Modern Japanese Prose Poem*, edited and translated by Dennis Keene. Copyright © 1980 by Princeton University Press. Reprinted by permission of Princeton University Press. "Obsession with an Apple," "A Personal Opinion about Gray," and "Impossible Approach to a Glass" from *62 Sonnets and Definitions: Poems and Prosepoems*, translated by William T. Elliott and Kawamura Kazuo. Copyright © 1992. Reprinted by permission of Katydid Books and William T. Elliott.

Luisa Valenzuela. "The Censors," translated by David Unger. Translation copyright © 1982 by David Unger. Used by permission of Harold Ober Associates, Inc., and Susan Bergholz Literary Services.

Mario Vargas Llosa. Excerpt from *The War of the End of the World*, translated by Helen R. Lane. Translation copyright © 1984 by Farrar, Straus & Giroux, Inc. Reprinted by permission of Farrar, Straus & Giroux, Inc.

Shrikant Verma. "Process of Change," translated by Vinay Dharwadker. Copyright © 1990 by Vinay Dharwadker. Reprinted by permission of the translator. "Half-an-Hour's Argument," translated and copyright © 1990 by Vinay Dharwadker and Aparna Dharwadker. Used by permission of the translators.

Derek Walcott. "Sea Grapes," "The Swamp," and "The Castaway" from *Collected Poems 1948–1984*. Copyright © 1986 by Derek Wolcott. Reprinted by permission of Farrar, Straus and Giroux, Inc.

Yang Mu. "Six Songs to the Tune 'Partridge Skies'" and "From 'Nine Arguments'" from *Forbidden Games and Video Poems: The Poetry of Yang Mu and Lo Ch'ing*, translated by Joseph R. Allen. Copyright © 1993 the University of Washington Press. Reprinted with permission of the University of Washington Press. "Loneliness" from *The Isle Full of Noises: Modern Chinese Poetry from Taiwan*, edited and translated by Dominic Cheung. Copyright © 1987. Reprinted by permission of Columbia University Press.

Yu Kwang-chung. "If There's a War Rages Afar" from *Acres of Barbed Wire*, translated by Yu Kwang-chung. Copyright © 1977 by Yu Kwang-chung. "The Kowloon-Canton Railway," translated by Stephen C. Soong, from *Renditions Magazine*, Autumn 1975. Copyright © 1975 by the Chinese University of Hong Kong. Reprinted by permission of the Research Centre for Translation of the Chinese University of Hong Kong.

Joseph Zobel. "The Gift," reprinted from *From the Green Antilles: Writings of the Caribbean*. Copyright © 1966. Used by permission of the author.

INDEX